Foreword

Welcome to the sixth edition of *Live and Work in France*. If you're familiar with the older editions you'll find that the book has been significantly overhauled. We hope to give you a more personal take on life in the country of Marion Cotillard and Nicolas Sarkozy, Simone de Beauvoir and Zindine Zidane. We have retained the wealth of practical and helpful detail that is such a feature of previous editions (indeed we've added to it and updated it, recognising the shift to online culture). However, the personal dimension has also been expanded. Not only have I, as an author, mined my own experiences of living and working in Paris and Amiens, Avranches, Bourges and Montpellier but I've spent a lot of time hunting down individuals whose stories contribute to a better understanding of the issues that newcomers have to contend with.

You could do worse than turn directly to the *Personal case histories* at the end of the first chapter. We feature Karalyn Montiel's warts-and-all account of the struggle that many Americans in Paris go through today to find a foothold in French society. You can also read Charles and Kath Dunstan's success story of the gîte they own and run in Brittany, having planned their retirement to the region many years in advance, bought a property and done it up with the help of local artisans and tourist development grants.

Rajaneesh Dwivedi, born in Benares, India, selected Montpellier as his destination more or less at random 10 years ago and has made a life there as a musician and an IT programmer. We also get the professional views of Sarah Bright Thomas, a member of the Toulouse bar, and Philippe Certain an estate agent in Leucate, a village on the Mediterranean a few kilometres up the coast from Perpignan.

I myself, until very recently, lived and worked as a translator and English-language teacher in and around Paris. I've been able to bring the benefit of my firsthand knowledge of French culture to bear on the material in this new edition. I've chosen to cover subject matter such as the recent resurgence of women in top jobs in French politics but also, just as importantly, the practical side of daily life. Some sections, like the *Choosing where to live section* in the chapter, *Setting Up Home*, are entirely new. In this section, we give a unique outline of each district of Paris and useful information on what it is like to live in that particular part of town.

An editorial decision was made with the 2008 *Live and Work in* editions, to emphasise the 'how to' aspects of the practicalities of foreign living. We aim not simply to describe what's going on but rather to provide the reader with the tools 'to do it themselves'.

We want the pages of your copy to become as smudged with thumbprints as any of the other DIY manuals on your shelf. Each section, although complimenting the others, stands alone and can be consulted individually.

The French experience can be a great adventure. This book aims to be your companion in that adventure. Our hope is that your French project be achieved as smoothly as possible so that you can make the most of what this truly great country has to offer. The French dream is no mirage. Quality of life surveys regularly put France at the top of world rankings and, at least for EU citizens, it is a dream that is more and more easily accessible all the time. The countryside, the food and the wine, the history and the artistic heritage are second to none. Nevertheless the culture is distinct and unique and handling the potential difficulties requires an insider's touch. *Live and Work in France* can serve as a door onto aspects of French culture that might otherwise take much longer to apprehend. We wish you all the best in your venture.

Jack Sims
Paris
March 2008

Contents

Contents

Live&Workin

France

Live&Workin

France

Victoria Pybus &
Jack Sims

Sixth Edition 2008

crimson

Published by Crimson Publishing
www.crimsonpublishing.com

4501 Forbes Blvd., Suite 200, Lanham MD 20706

Westminster House, Kew Road, Richmond, Surrey TW9 2ND

Distributed in North America by National Book Network
www.nbnbooks.com

Distributed in the UK by Portfolio Books
www.portfoliobooks.com

Sixth edition

A catalogue record for this book is available from the British library.

ISBN 978 1 85458 419 9

Printed and bound by Colorprint Offset Ltd, Hong Kong

Acknowledgments

Thanks are due to the following in no particular order for their invaluable help in compiling this book: Marc Vervel, Sarah Bright Thomas of Bright Jones Avocats, Dawn Alderson of Russell-Cooke Solicitors, Gordon Eaton of Agence Eaton Assurances, Philippe Certain of Agence du Midi, the French Chamber of Commerce in Great Britain, the Franco-British Chamber in Paris, Claire Oldmeadow and The Language Network, Libération, Grayia Piras, Teresa Scotto di Veneto, Jean Charles Pham. Thanks also to Fabienne Rangeard, Rajaneesh Dwivedi, Jean Ramm, Karlayn Monteil, Tamsin Williams, Laurie Baird, Sophie Le Corre, Robert Hoehn, Keith Sprague, Adam Zanders, Jeff Gross, Charles and Kath Dunstan, Abraham Paris, Emma Corney, Susan Hodge, Sara Wilson, Magalie Morel, Tim Swannie, Islay Currie, Peter Stone and Richard Coman for talking to us about their experiences of living and working in France.

Special thanks go to Carly Robinson for her invaluable research assistance, ensuring that the new edition is bang up-to-date.

How to use this book

Telephone numbers:

Please note that the telephone numbers in this book are written as needed to call that number from inside the country you will probably be calling from. For example, a British removals company to France will be given as a UK number; a French removals company from the UK will have its international prefix.

To call another country from France dial 00 before the number for the country concerned, then the subscriber's area code minus the first zero, then the subscriber's number.
To call France from another country dial 00 33 followed by the number minus the first zero.

France is divided into five broad geographical zones numbered one to five:
01 for Paris and Ile de France
02 for the north-west
03 for the north-east
04 for the south-east and Corsica
05 for the south-west

Note that The 01/02/03 etc is used for all regions regardless of whether you are making a local or a long distance call.

Exchange rates:

Euro €	British pound £	US dollar $	Australian dollar A$
€1	£0.79	$1.55	A$1.63
€10	£7.90	$15.50	A$16.25
€20	£15.80	$31	A$32.50
€50	£39.50	$77.60	A$81.30
€100	£79	$155.30	A$162.50
€1,000	£790	$1,553	A$1,625

At time of press

Why Live & Work in France?

■ ABOUT FRANCE

More tourists visit France each year than any other country and it's easy to see why: a proud history and heritage, a beautiful capital, 28 of UNESCO's World Heritage Sites, wonderful landscape, winter sports (*la montagne*), beach holidays (*la mer*), large expanses of forest and an infrastructure second to none, as well as the great tradition in food and wine. The British have been doing the sums on the housing market, weighing things up and moving over in droves for the past two decades. For Americans and other nationalities who want to come and settle or even just try out a life in Paris without the benefit of EU immigration papers, things can be a lot more complicated. Henry Miller has a lot to answer for!

■ REASONS TO LIVE IN FRANCE

As many readers will have done, I started my French adventure with a holiday visit, walking the narrow medieval streets in the centre of Montpellier, enjoying a glass of St Christol on a terrace, cooling off at the beach in Palavas and tasting oysters at a restaurant in the harbour. When I did decide to move, I was surprised at the extent of the culture shock I felt. Having studied French at university, I already spoke the language well and thought I'd be able to integrate easily. But studying and holidaying in France hadn't prepared me for actually living in the country. And it isn't just that I had to get used to new ways of doing things, new ways of working, new ways of interacting. I had to get used to the French way! France remains unique in terms of customs and outlook. Whether you move to a region with a high concentration of British homeowners such as Provence or Poitou-Charentes (according to the most recent statistics there are now 12,000 British residents there) or take up a post in Paris, the much-discussed cultural difference is something you'll have to come to terms with.

And come to terms is what you'll have to do if you stay! The French are a people with strong opinions and you can't help but feel this the moment you set foot in the country. They are also a people of profound contradictions. One in four French have a grandparent from elsewhere and yet France can be intensely intolerant of those who don't conform to French ideals. European and internationalist too, the French are nevertheless a people that often seems impervious to outside influences. They are

FACT

According to French, British and American government statistics on English-speaking residents in France, there are:

■ 125,000 British residents, most of them en province, in the provinces

■ 100,000 to 200,000 Americans, mostly in and around Paris

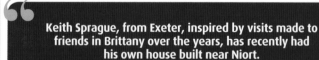

Keith Sprague, from Exeter, inspired by visits made to friends in Brittany over the years, has recently had his own house built near Niort.

I have a part share in a light aircraft and I can be down at the house in three hours door to door. One hour to Brittany! One evening I left my office in Exeter at quarter to six and I was sitting having a beer on the terrace of my friend's place in Brittany by 7:10.

glorious in their incapacity to learn English and naturally protectionist of their own language. The national religion is not Catholicism but rather Republicanism and its precepts are widely confused with the laws of nature. These precepts are zealously protected and the intellectual apparatus needed to do so is cultivated as a necessity. In French life what appears to be the shortest route is almost certainly not and common sense most definitely does not prevail. As a pragmatist and an Anglophone you'll find it impossible to feel neutral about this culture.

Nevertheless, the French way works! You may not understand how or why, but it does. With productivity levels the envy of the industrialised West, in spite of (or perhaps because of) such long holidays, the French economy is the sixth largest in the world. The highly interventionist state (it employs more than a quarter of the active population) works as a buffer between its people and globalisation, *la mondialisation*, and in no other country is the word so often heard. The political consciousness of the ordinary Frenchman or woman is extreme.

According to the French themselves, their country is currently in crisis. Deep down, however, they almost certainly don't believe their own rhetoric. Where would they be without their famous introspection? It's very much this national self-regard that provides such a shield against, for example, American cultural imperialism and, while it can be infuriating, it may well be what protects what those who choose to move to France so love about it.

Until recently I lived and worked in Paris as a translator and an English language teacher. So my French experiences are much closer to those described in *A Year in the Merde* (Stephen Clarke's comic best-seller about a young Englishman who has been commissioned to set up a chain of teashops in Paris) than those in *A Year in Provence*. Of course, Peter Mayle's book sparked a great wave of British house buying in the French countryside in the 1990s. A decade and a half later, something like over 500,000 Brits own properties in France. *A Year in the Merde* is unlikely to do the same for Paris.

Although at 20,000, Ile de France (Paris and around) has more British residents than any other French region, this total is dwarfed by the number of French in London.

A linguistic viewpoint

The French ear is conditioned not to pick up on other languages. A comparatively exceptional (in terms of other languages) lack of variation in the tone of French vowels not only means that the nuances of the sounds of French make small pronunciation differences important (and difficult for the foreigner). It also means that those who have been brought up there find the larger variations in sounds of other languages difficult to key into. It's as if the wide valleys of the Loire, the richness and fertility of the soil and the pleasant climate have conspired to create a stable and contented linguistic self-sufficiency.

> **Fabienne Rangeard, originally from near Challans in the Vendée, has lived and worked in London for the past 15 years**
>
> *One thing I can't stand about France is that you can't have a family meal without talking about politics. But I have to say that living in London, I've gained a new perspective on French life. It's true, the middle-class view of France, all the markets and so on... we bring it on ourselves. The French are slow in catching up with modern attitudes, but when I go back I think, 'it's not a bad way to live'.*

Paradoxically, it could be said that if you want to get a flavour of today's France, come to London! This is exactly what Nicolas Sarkozy did during the French presidential campaign in 2007. In a reference to the 250,000 French nationals currently living and working there, he called the British capital 'the seventh French city'. With an increasingly high proportion of retirees in the French population, the French political elite cannot ignore this exodus of the highly-qualified young and not-so-young. President Sarkozy has begun his term of office noisily and energetically and is heralded by some as the Thatcherite answer to French vested interests. Others fear he will further inflame the large immigrant community (five million Muslims currently live in France) and undermine social services, traditionally so highly valued by the French. Whatever the result, it is unlikely that France will allow herself to be led off quietly. The new President will need all his energy to achieve his goals.

Although to some extent the old adage holds true that the English go to France for pleasure and the French to England for business, this does need to be qualified by the fact that many of the British now living in rural France have also set up their own businesses there. Small business owners will probably benefit from the new regime. Sarkozy has, for example, talked about reforming the notorious *taxe professionelle* (tax on businesses) but setting up there is still much more complicated than in places such as the UK. Living out the dream of a rural existence isn't necessarily easy economically, but if you're willing to take on board the French way of doing things, you might just make a success of it.

FACT

■ Most estimates of the American population in France put the figure somewhere around 100,000, not including government staff and the army, with most of this in and around Paris.

■ PROS AND CONS OF LIVING IN FRANCE

In the past century as a whole, the destinations most often considered for emigration tended to be the countries of the 'New World' (i.e. the USA and Canada), and Australia and New Zealand. In the past two decades this has changed, mainly because these countries now have much more restrictive immigration policies and fewer work opportunities than they used to. At the same time, settling in another EU country is becoming easier. If you are British, France is a logical choice. The Channel Tunnel and low-cost flights have brought France even closer. It's likely that many UK citizens, who had previously never thought of it, will become aware of the new opportunities being offered by the EU for work and business, or a holiday home or retirement, and will seriously consider moving abroad.

Of course France is home to many major national and international companies, which offer a full range of career opportunities with good pay, conditions and opportunities for development. The quaint old France of vineyards, village cafés and rickety 2CVs, or *deuches* (pronounced 'dersh' – from *deux chevaux*) as they are known in France still exists to some extent, but French industries are generally acknowledged to be as dynamic as in the USA and more so than in the UK; this includes the scientific and hi-tech sectors. However, other industries (financial services) fare less well and whether you stand to gain or lose will depend on your area of work.

Overall, French wages and salaries tend to be slightly higher than in Britain but lower than in North America. Overall taxation is much higher (45.3% of the national wealth) than most other European countries. The largest difference with Britain is the extensive social security payments that have to be paid by employers. The complex taxation system in the USA makes it harder to give comparisons but the National Bureau of Economic Research estimates that combined federal, state and local government taxes mean that most workers pay out about 40% of income in tax.

Although living costs differ between France and other countries, property is still cheaper in France than in either the UK or the USA. As a result the French resident can usually enjoy a higher disposable income; this can benefit retirement and

Pros and cons of living in France

Pros
■ France is famed for its quality of life
■ Rates of pay are good
■ Land and property are relatively cheaper
■ Hi-tech industries are advanced and successful
■ Dining out costs much less
■ Most regions have a pleasant climate
■ An unspoiled countryside with a rich culture
■ Excellent public transport and high-speed train network

Cons
■ Necessary to speak French
■ Some jobs in France do not have same prestige or pay as in other countries
■ The French are not always receptive to foreign employees
■ The particularities of the French system can be bureaucratic

holiday home-buyers as well as working residents. However other living costs, particularly food and some utilities, are more expensive than in Britain or in the USA.

French income tax for average earners tends to be lower than in many countries, with the tax rate for the lowest earners starting at 7.5%. However, taxes in France absorb up to 60% of an individual's income and France has a top income tax rate of 40% for higher earners. Social security contributions are high, and total deductions from an average French salary may be greater than at home. There are many high-profile tax exiles. Those most likely to benefit from moving to France include families with several children: paid maternity leave,

Key features of life in France

- Renting in France usually requires a lot of paperwork. See *Setting up home*
- Any EU citizen has the right to settle in France. Non-EU citizens usually need to be employed by a company in France before they arrive
- Living costs are not cheaper in France; many things including utilities, meat and books are more expensive than in the USA or in the UK
- Quality not quantity. French households typically spend 25% of their disposable income on food, often shopping in small specialist shops
- As of November 2007, expat residents no longer have automatic access to the health system. See *Daily life* for details
- *La vie associative*. There are 800,000 government-sponsored associations in France. Activities range from politics to sport, the arts and pretty much anything else you can think of
- The French are, on the whole, not a religious people, although there is a strong value system based on Republican ideals (there is also a large Muslim population)
- Inheritance laws favour children over spouses. Be sure to look into this *before* you buy
- The *commune* is the smallest administrative unit and has significant powers over local community affairs
- Culture and the arts are highly valued by the community at large and artists receive significant government funding

healthcare, education and child benefits up to the age of 22, are all strong incentives to move to France.

France has always been seen as offering a stylish way of living. Most parts of the country have beautiful scenery and some, such as the volcanic Auvergne and the majestic Alps, are outstanding. There is probably more scenic variation in France than almost any other country in Europe. Rural France has an unhurried pace of life: food, drink and social life are regarded as priorities. Some of the big cities and industrial belts surrounding them can be congested and polluted and suffer from chronic youth unemployment and all the social problems associated with similar deprived areas elsewhere.

Moving to Europe from across the Channel or the Atlantic involves an obvious language hurdle and it's certainly a challenge if you don't speak French. That said, many people do go without speaking the language and there's no better way to learn but the process of integration will of course take time and effort.

■ PERSONAL CASE HISTORIES

Karalyn Monteil

Originally from Chicago, Karalyn Monteil has lived in Paris for the past 10 years. She works for UNESCO and is married to a French architect, Philippe. They have one daughter and live in the 15th *arrondissement* (district). Karalyn came to France without work papers or any knowledge of the language and without knowing anyone.

How did you go about trying to establish a life in Paris?

I quickly realised I didn't have many options. I was 27 and already had a career but I ended up taking a job as an au pair because that way I could get free accommodation and thought I'd be able to learn French. I had a really negative experience, first with a family who would only speak to me in English and who imprisoned me in a house down in St Tropez. With the second family I had in Paris I had time to do some freelance writing with *Paris Voice*. I wasn't paid (no papers) but they let me put free classifieds in for jobs I could earn money from. The problem was I couldn't get a bank account or a cell phone (at that time you had to show a *carte de séjour* before you could get a phone) so I got a pager and I used to get people to phone me at the phone booth down in the street. I did a lot of phone classes from phone booths in the street. I also used to do power walking classes, walking executives home from work and speaking English on the way or intensive business English lunches where I could eat for free!

I did a lot of that and slept on a lot of French couches. Finally I met an American who let me a small studio in the 20th without asking for papers. I was still doing a lot of freelance writing for guide books but I was struggling to pay the rent. I was living on lentils and rice and cycling everywhere to save money. I used to have to go and queue up at the EDF office and pay my electricity in cash because I didn't have any other way of paying.

How did you find work in the international sector?

I was really tempted to go home several times. After a year and a half my old company back in Chicago called me to offer me my old job back but then I met someone at a barbecue who worked for the OECD [Organisation for Economic Co-operation and Development). I hadn't thought about international organisations as an option but they can employ Americans. I interviewed with the OECD and they offered me a secretarial job right away but when I got home after the interview I balled my eyes out. I hadn't come to France to work as a secretary. At that point I'd decided to go home. I called the OECD back and left a long rambling message about how I was a writer and although I appreciated the offer it wasn't what I wanted. They actually called me back and offered me a two-month writing position with the education section. That was the first time I had official papers. Up till then I'd been going to Switzerland or London every few months to get my visa renewed.

You've written a film script on how it really is to live as an American in Paris.

Yes. It's called *Bienvenue à Paris*. The OECD job was part-time and I was still doing freelance writing for Elle.com and working on the script. The job was secure but I ended up taking a job with Elle because that was more the sort of work I wanted to be doing. Then they decided to move the English writing team to New York! At that point I realised my only option was in the international sector if I wanted to stay in France. I borrowed some money for rent and decided to give myself three or four months to finish the script (which I haven't had time to promote yet) and get a job. After that, if I still didn't have anything I was going to go home.

Someone I knew knew someone working at UNESCO and they photocopied me the page of the contact numbers of people in the culture sector. I started calling at random and telling my story and how I really wanted to stay and work in Paris. Eventually I got some leads. Every Monday for two months I called the director of the World Heritage Centre. I'd get through to the secretary and the director would always be busy but eventually I spoke to him and went in for an interview. I thought I'd just get an unpaid internship but they gave me a one-month contract as editorial assistant on the World Heritage Review which kept getting renewed for two years until I got offered a temporary post co-ordinating the museum programme in post-conflict countries. I then did a master's in museum studies by correspondence at the University of Leicester to help me get qualified for the post and now there's a permanent position coming up that I'm applying for. UNESCO was never able to get me my *carte de séjour* for some reason and I finally only got one when I had a French baby last year.

What about family life and friends?

In general, if you have a baby and you're in another country you miss your family more. Thank god for Skype and webcams so that my parents can speak to my daughter and read her a bed-time story.

There are definitely cultural issues. The French have a tendency not to want to bother other people. Americans are more open. That sometimes can be embarrassing for my husband at the bakery or the café or whatever. With his family it's nice because you get an insight into the French way. Philippe was shocked when he came to Chicago at how we all help ourselves to food individually whenever we want. But sometimes here, it's just too much eating. Even lunch is a three course meal. It's nice though that the French take the time to eat, sit down and have a picnic by the Seine or whatever. I see things changing though. I see the French going to Auchan or Franprix or whatever and getting more interested in prepared foods, which lead people to eat faster and get fatter.

I'd say I'm more integrated into the international community than the French community. It's true I do know a lot of Americans but it's only recently I've started to value their friendship. The French have their friends from childhood and it's not always easy to break into those circles. I have French friends but they're more international French if you know what I mean.

Any advice for any Americans coming over?

Respect the culture you're trying to integrate into, the language, and cultural things like saying hello before you ask a question. Little things so we don't come over as ugly Americans, such as not speaking too loudly at the table in the restaurant. Ask people if they speak English before you launch into whatever you have to say.

Charles and Kath Dunstan

Charles and Kath Dunstan have been living near the village of Neuillac in central Brittany for the past eight years. Back in the 1980s, they were running their own business in the UK, doing very long hours, when they made the decision to retire to France. They both speak good French (Kath used to be a French teacher) and are well integrated into the local community. They own and run the St Samson Gîtes (www.st-samson.co.uk), three handsome-looking buildings that they renovated partly themselves and partly with the help of the local and national tourist boards.

How did you go about the renovations?

We did it gradually. We bought the property in 1991. It was totally in need of renovation. We did the cottage ourselves with the help of an English carpenter who came over for a few weeks. Then we rented the cottage out and moved into a caravan on site. For the stables and the dairy, we had both national and regional development grants. We had to put up 50% of the cash ourselves and guaranteed to use local artisans. There are no general builders over here. We employed a plumber, roofer and mason, and they all worked well together. There's a 10-year guarantee on all the work done. We sourced the artisans through the *mairie* at Neuillac, got some *devis*, some quotes, and went ahead with the work.

How's the business going?

Brittany is becoming over *gîted* and you need to make sure your place stands out. That's why we put in the swimming pool that meets all the French regulations and is heated and last year we put in wireless internet throughout the property, which attracted clients immediately. We keep the place to a high standard with nice furniture and *objets d'art* and we advertise with Brittany Ferries, which gives us a cushion. We get bombarded by people who build tourist sites on the net. They always give you a free trial and if we pick up clients through their site then we subscribe the following year. We get a complete mix of nationalities: French, Brits, Americans, Italians, Dutch.

What's life in the village like?

We're very impressed with the *maire*. He has a high level of decision making for such a small village. If he wants something to be done, he'll allocate the budget and go ahead and do it. There're two village halls and a massive sports hall. It's a lively village. We're well accepted and are members of the Comité des fêtes and the local Club des retraités. We play *boules* there on Thursday afternoon and do a walk with them once a week. Afterwards we usually go back to the clubhouse for cake and wine. The farm next to us is not a working farm and, something that we're quite proud of, whenever there's a death in the village we get called and it's our responsibility to go to the chapel next door to ring the bell for five minutes every day before the funeral. We mix with both French and English out here. Sometimes we have a dinner party and it'll be all French, sometimes all English and sometimes a mixture.

Are there a lot of other English in the area?

Well yes. The small builder's merchant I use, two-thirds of his clients are English. Both he and his wife speak English. And property prices have trebled since we bought. We got our place for 12,000. A similar place now would be more like 45. A lot of the English who come here have difficulties. If I see someone in the Bricomarché trying to explain themselves in French I help them out. A lot of them don't have any idea. They aren't really here for the culture, the way of life, the open spaces. It's escapism. I was walking round the *Troc et pousses*, the fleamarket, on Saturday and I said to Kath that I was ashamed to be English. A lot of people come over and claim French social security. I don't blame Sarkozy for changing the law. People think they'll be able to start a business and they haven't thought it through and then they end up having to sell up and go back.

Sarah Bright Thomas

Sarah Bright Thomas is a partner in Bright Jones, a cabinet d'avocats in Toulouse. Both she and the other partner, Julia Jones, are British but went to university in France and trained in French law. Both then joined the Toulouse bar. Sarah has been working as a lawyer in Toulouse for 10 years and Julia for nine.

What advice would you give to prospective buyers?

The first thing I would say is, you wouldn't go ahead and buy a house in England if you didn't understand what your solicitor was telling you, so why do that here? We get involved in a lot of litigation for people with swimming pool problems or rights of way because people have signed things they don't understand. Also, you need to know what the best purchase vehicle is for you because of French inheritance laws.

Inheritance and tax

I give a lot of advice on inheritance and tax. What I would say to people is, make sure you get advice before you start, whether you're going to buy *en tontine* or what because these things are a lot cheaper to sort out at the beginning. Make sure you've got a professional who understands the French system and can explain it to you. It's a very different system over here and Sarkozy's just gone and changed things again.

What's the difference between an avocat and a notaire?

An avocat is like a barrister. A notaire does conveyancing. Avocats are not allowed to do conveyancing, which is quite confusing for clients. But we take clients through the purchasing process, not just in terms of the legal side but we also explain what's going on. We can't actually draw up the deeds and publish them in the land registry (*publicité foncière*). That's the preserve of the notaries, but they don't litigate so they often can't see the drawbacks of the deeds they draw up.

Are there any other things buyers should bear in mind?

Once you've signed the *compromis de vente* you can't go back. There's a clause in the code civil, and this applies to any purchase in France, which says that once you've agreed on the purchase and the price, the sale is perfect, *la vente est parfaite*. Once the suspensive conditions are realised you must go ahead and buy. So you shouldn't go into a *compromis* unless you're sure.

You should always make sure you check the deed for rights of way too. There are rights of way you couldn't imagine. If any work has been done over the last 10 years, make sure you obtain the certificate of guarantee from the seller as that goes with the house not the person. Sewage problems too. You're supposed to have a mains in France. Maybe the *fosse sceptique* is not *conforme*.

Also people should make sure they have their project worked out before they come. They can't just set up here as an estate agent for example. There are regulations. People get themselves into illegal situations because they don't register, not because they mean to do anything wrong but because they don't know what they're doing.

Rajaneesh Dwivedi

A couple of years after graduating from Keele University in Music and IT, Rajaneesh Dwivedi decided to move to Montpellier. He'd been working for an IT company in Clapham and living in Forest Hill. He was looking for something different and not knowing France well, more or less picked Montpellier at random. He went down to try it out and was quickly taken with the town.

What were your first impressions on arriving?

There is an initial feeling of being pleasantly blinded by the newness of everything, as if in a toy shop. Since I didn't really speak or understand any French I ended up following round the few acquaintances I'd made, in a bit of a bubble, not really understanding where I was going or what I was doing, which was quite fun actually. Once things got a bit more familiar, I ended up addressing more practical issues like where to stay and eat and how to make money.

There comes a phase after a few months, though, where I ended up missing 'home' and found myself comparing the bureaucratic efficiency of the two countries and generally finding fault. I found myself seeking out comfort foods and other familiar rituals. Thankfully this didn't last long as I realised that it was just a need to feel more integrated and take the plunge to make things work. It was then that I started to get a deeper appreciation of the subtleties of the place and the warmth, honesty and heartiness that the French are so good at. Interestingly, it was also around this time that things suddenly clicked into place with the language, at around six months, when I also dreamt for the first time in French. Avoid the trap of seeking out other English speakers too early in the game.

How did you go about looking for work?

As I say, initially, learning French was the big challenge for me. I had some savings so I'd budgeted for a few months. I play the bass and I was able to pick up some casual work as a musician. This was also a great way of meeting people and making contacts. Montpellier is quite a young town with a large student population and it wasn't difficult to get to know people, though, as I say, this was on a fairly superficial level at first. Later I was able to use my IT skills to get work, though it did take time and a few *mauvais plans* [dodgy situations] to get something satisfactory. It's not easy to find work in Montpellier as there's a fairly high unemployment rate, though I'm lucky in that there are a number of high-tech businesses that have established themselves here. I started out as a programmer on a team of software designers a few years ago but as the company I work for has a lot of international clients, I have now taken on the role of product trainer.

What's the music scene like down there?

Plenty of *mauvais plans* but as you get to know people and what's happening, there's some pretty exciting stuff going on. I played a lot of jazz when I first came down. Now I'm doing afrobeat with a group called Fanga and we tour all over the country.

Have you any regrets?

I did try and move back to England at one point. I stayed for about a month. I can't see myself going back now.

Laurie Baird

Laurie Baird is an electronics engineer from Dunfermline and has lived and worked in Grenoble for the past 20 years. He is married to a French woman and has two daughters.

How is it that you came to move here?

I was recruited by a headhunter. I wasn't specifically looking for a job in France. They were looking for people for a new development centre in Grenoble. Workwise it wasn't too difficult at the beginning because I was with a company run by British management and IT stuff is generally English oriented. At first I used to stick with British co-workers outside work too. It was a big step getting out of that environment into French companies. I forced myself to socialise with the French, watch TV in French and read in French. My first independent job here was with a *société de service*, doing contracts in various companies. Then one of those companies took me on permanently.

What comments do you have about the French working environment?

There are a lot of things you can criticise here. They're disorganised and explosive but you find yourself becoming the same way. SD, the company I work for now, is a Franco-Italian company and we actually have an induction course there where one of the things they say is that unless you keep reminding a French person or an Italian that you want something done, they won't do it because they'll think it isn't necessary.

The working laws in France protect production industry. I left the UK just after the miners' strike. French governments can't get any reforms through. People will go on strike for anything. I mean they block the ports if diesel goes up. There's lots of job protection. People don't get fired easily. They tend to get put in the cupboard and you wait till they leave of their own accord. In France people stay in the same company for a longer period. People are worried about retirement. You have to give Sarko credit. He can be a bit extreme but he's trying to bring through what he said he would.

One thing I should say is that I appreciate the 35-hour week. It gives you extra holidays, up to eight days holiday extra a year. People appreciate that. The thing they've brought in about instead of taking the days off, you get paid, it's alright but I like the long weekends. They're talking about getting rid of the 35-hour week but people like it.

What's it like bringing up a French family?

In terms of identity you get more and more attached to your roots and you don't want to lose them. When my kids were born I wanted to speak to them in English so I started socialising with the English again. I got satellite TV and now I try to watch films in English. My youngest daughter (11) is very attached to her English heritage but the older one (14) isn't so keen. I haven't taken French nationality. The kids have dual nationality.

The French, language wise, you can't have a good conversation with them unless you speak French. At the beginning, it's quite frustrating because everyone speaks so slowly to you. You feel on your own in a foreign country. Sometimes you want to throw it all in.

What about the education system?

There's a lot of stress on the kids at school. Work, work, work it is. It's horrific. I don't know what it's like in Britain now, but when I was at school, it definitely wasn't like that.

The electronics industry needs young blood. There are lots of partnerships with universities and engineering schools, people studying for doctorates also working in the company.

What do you like about the Grenoble area?

I love the area. I'm always happy to get back from Paris when I go there. Great weather. The countryside. We're based in the country, just 20 minutes from the ski stations.

Fabienne Rangeard

Originally from the Vendée, Fabienne Rangeard has been living and working in the 'seventh French city', that's to say London, for the past 15 years. Here she shares some of her impressions on London and how living there has changed her perspective on her own country.

An island mentality?

With Britain there's definitely an island mentality. In Primrose Hill last year, the organic shop started doing a market on the street in front of the shop and one resident complained about the smell of the cheese. Probably the same people who go over to France in the summer and rave about the markets. I would say that the Londoners are more relaxed than the Parisians though. That struck me last time I was in Paris, how suspicious people are.

I would say that the Londoners are more relaxed than the Parisians though.

Elections?

I make a point of voting in the EU elections and for the mayor of London, partly I think because I can't vote in general elections here. I would never give up my French passport. Somehow, I wouldn't want to vote in the general election here. I feel that that's British politics and although it has an impact, it's not something for me to say anything about.

Work?

There are more opportunities in London in my field, in localisation and translation. At the beginning, I did apply for an editorial assistant's job. At the time I felt like I was being discriminated against because I was French. The thing is there are so many applicants for those positions. They were just cherry picking the Oxbridge graduates.

The English on the French and the French on the English.

I would say the standard of English has improved among young French. There was general mistrust before but there's less antagonism from the younger generation. But for me to move back to France now, I don't know. One thing that really irritates me when I go back home is when people say, 'Voila l'anglaise.' Just because I live here doesn't mean I reject France. It's not necessarily a choice, just the way things have worked out. My job doesn't allow me to go back much. But I do think I'm completely assimilated. I am French and I'll always be French. I'm here on an observing mission. But it does scare me to think of going back. It's not a decision I would take lightly. I've definitely taken on British traits, but also the fact that I live in a city... people would think I'm a hippy or a feminist.

I would say the standard of English has improved among young French. There was general mistrust before but there's less antagonism from the younger generation.

Over the years I've come to appreciate more what France stands for, the whole concept of a democracy based on the revolution. One thing I can't stand about it though is you can't have family meals there without talking about politics. Last time I was over, my brother said, 'I don't understand you being a lefty but living in a country with a monarch.' The middle class view of France, the markets etc, we [the French] bring it on ourselves. We're slow in catching up with modern attitudes. When I was over last time, I watched a 90-minute programme about cheeses! There's nothing wrong with maintaining rituals. I've come to understand how the French system works and why. The inter-racial problems in France – attitudes are still very old fashioned. It's not as bad in Britain.

Before You Go

◼ VISAS, WORK PERMITS AND CITIZENSHIP

Red tape – C'est qui le responsable?

The French are notorious for their red tape and it can be frustrating for a foreigner trying to navigate the administrative system. Even if you speak French well you can feel quite disenfranchised with the bureaucratic language and the French state employee's highly developed sense of the limits of their area of professional responsibility. Half the battle is speaking to the right person. You will need to be patient and put up with the odd brush off, but when you do finally reach *le responsable* they will often be only too happy to demonstrate extensive knowledge of their area of expertise. The situation may even turn out to be far less rigid than you had originally been led to believe, and you may find yourself filling with a warm sense of relief and congratulating the French on their wonderful contradictions.

If you've tried all possible avenues with the local authorities and still haven't got the response you think you should have, it might be worth contacting SOLVIT.

 SOLVIT: (http://ec.europa.eu/solvit) SOLVIT is a European Commission sponsored online problem-solving network in which EU Member States work together to solve – without legal proceedings – problems caused by the misapplication of Internal Market law by public authorities. Americans may also get help from SOLVIT.

The current position

Europe has been a union for just over 15 years (the Maastricht treaty was signed in 1993) and in accordance with the 2004 EU directive on residence permits, there are no restrictions on citizens from one of the 'older' 15 EU member countries to live and work in any of these 15 countries. The situation is slightly different for the so-called accession countries, the 10 eastern European countries that joined the union in 2004, but permits are gradually being phased out for them. This and a few other formalities you should bear in mind, whichever part of the EU you are from, are covered below (see EU nationals).

If you are from another part of the world you will be need to obtain a specific visa, known as a *visa de long séjour*. You must get this visa in your home country before you come to France (this is different from the three-month tourist visa that is issued on arrival). Then once you are in France, you must also apply for a residence permit, the *carte de séjour*. The procedures for obtaining these documents and the circumstances under which they are granted are discussed below in the section on Non-EU nationals.

 TIP

◼ Keep a sense of humour and don't take personally what may appear to be off-hand behaviour! And remember how hard it can be to obtain the equivalent documentation for those wishing to stay in your country.

EU nationals

Nationals of the original 15 EU countries, namely Austria, Belgium, Denmark, Germany, Greece, Finland, Ireland, Italy, Luxembourg, the Netherlands, Portugal, Spain, Sweden and the UK, and the accession countries, Cyprus, Malta, the Czech Republic, Estonia, Hungary, Latvia, Lithuania, Poland, Slovakia and Slovenia have a right to settle permanently in France. Citizens of Norway, Iceland and Lichtenstein, which are part of the European Economic Area (EEA) and Switzerland have similar entitlements.

The *Loi Sarkozy II* states that EEA and Swiss nationals, with the exception of nationals of the 10 Eastern European accession countries, are not required to hold a short-term residence permit (*carte de séjour*). But, in a change from the *Loi Sarkozy* of 2003, you should register with your local *mairie*/préfecture if you intend to stay longer than 90 days. Nationals of the 10 accession countries need residence permits for stays of longer than 90 days and when they intend to work or carry out a professional activity in France (see *Getting a carte de séjour*). All family members accompanying EEA/Swiss nationals who are not EEA/Swiss nationals themselves must obtain a residence permit if they plan to stay longer than 90 days.

In a departure from the *Loi Sarkozy* of 2003, which waived registration altogether, *Loi Sarkozy II* requires EEA/Swiss nationals who move to France to register their intention to stay at their local *mairie*. Although the administrative framework for registration, *la declaration d'enregistrement*, is not in place at the time of writing, it is imminent. As part of the declaration, you will need to state whether you are coming to France as a professionally active person, or as a student, or as a retiree with the means to support yourself, or whether you are without a professional activity but with the means to support yourself. This measure is, in part, a response to the large numbers of EU nationals coming to France to benefit from the particularly well-funded welfare system, including so-called health tourists. Health reforms introduced in autumn 2007 indicated that the French government was not going to allow EU retirees of active age to access the French healthcare system. Pressure from the British and other EU national governments, however, led to the announcement that those who were resident before 23 November 2007 would still qualify for healthcare. For more on this see the Health section in the chapter *Daily life*.

To sum up:

- EEA/Swiss nationals don't need permission or a visa before leaving for France or at the point of entering France. In other words, there is no difference whether you are entering France as a tourist or as a potential resident.

- Equally, those who have taken up a job in France, or who intend to look for one on arrival can enter the country without any formalities and documents except a valid passport of another EU country. But there are some restrictions on work permits for nationals from accession countries (unlike in the UK, Sweden, Ireland, Spain, Portugal, Greece and Finland where accession country nationals have complete freedom to work). France has announced a progressive and controlled lifting of these restrictions and will do so after consultations with labour unions as to which occupations have recruitment pressures.

Non-EU nationals

It isn't easy to get permission to live and work in France if you aren't an EU national, unless you have family there or you can persuade a French national to marry you! With high unemployment and concerns about the impact of immigrants on social services, France is keen to discourage immigration and in any case must observe EU rules.

Non-EU citizens require a Schengen visa to enter France, which allows a stay of up to three months (*visa de court séjour*/short-stay visa). Citizens from some countries, notably Canada, the USA, Australia and New Zealand, do not need to apply for the visa in advance as it can be given at the port of entry. You should, of course, check on the current situation before departure.

Officially, non-EU nationals aren't allowed to travel to France as tourists to look for work. So it's usually necessary to have found a job and obtained a long-stay visa (*visa de long séjour*) from outside France – and to have been granted a work permit, an *autorisation de travail* for the position (NB A *visa de long séjour* is the document that is required for any long stay and is a separate document from the *autorisation de travail* or work permit that is only required if you intend to work while in France). For anyone who isn't an EEA/Swiss national, finding a job in France is difficult. Priority in terms of employment goes to EEA/Swiss nationals. If you are American, you will have to prove that you are more qualified than anyone in the EU. The people with the best odds therefore tend to be those in highly specialised fields. Theoretically, if you are hired by a French company, the company will do the paperwork for you. In reality, it's a bit of a catch-22 with companies saying you need a permit before they will hire you, but of course, the French government won't give you a permit unless you already have a job. One solution is to get a job with a company that has branches in France and then get transferred. You may also apply for a long-stay visa, stating that you don't intend to work while in France.

Once you have the *visa de long séjour*, you can travel to France to take up residence. You then need to apply for a *carte de séjour*.

Students

If you are accepted on a course in France and meet the financial requirements (a monthly financial guarantee of around $600–$800 or €500 – you will need a bank statement or a notarised declaration from a sponsor) you can apply for a visa for the length of the course. You will need a *préinscription*, a document from the school where you intend to study stating that you have been accepted. The school must be recognised by the French Education Ministry. *La fac*, a French state university (usually around €300 per year) is cheaper than a private school (perhaps €400 a month) but you can usually only enrol at *la fac* (short for *faculté*) at the beginning of the year. Students can apply for a work permit once they are in France to work a limited number of hours each week (60%).

There are various schemes for Americans and other non-EU nationals wanting to come to France, such as au pair work and internships. For details contact a French consulate or check the Useful contacts section. Americans wishing to study in France must now process an application through Campus France before they apply for their visa.

Students from outside the EU can work for six months in France after graduating. Go to www.vosdroits.service-public.fr and click on 'Particuliers' then 'Etrangers en France' then 'Séjour des étrangers' and 'Etudiants étrangers'.

Useful contacts

CEI (Centre d'Echanges Internationaux): www.cei-frenchcentre.com. Runs a work placements in France programme. This organisation is recognised by the French Ministry of Employment and can validate work placements found by students themselves

French Embassy: *French Cultural Services Internships/Stages* ☎202 944 6011; www. ambafrance-us.org/intheus/embassy.asp. Offers internships in French businesses, public institutions and non-governmental organisations for one to nine months for undergraduate or graduate students. Help with applications given

Association for International Practical Training (AIPT): 410 997 2200; email aipt@aipt.org; www.aipt.org. Considers applications from graduates and professionals and students who want to pursue a paid business internship in France for up to 18 months

French-American Chamber of Commerce (FACC): ☎212 867 0123; www. ccife.org/use/new_york. Has a similar scheme to AIPT (see above). FACC in New York has an international career development programme for Americans to work as trainees and interns in France. These programmes also help Americans obtain

Working holiday

France currently has working holiday agreements with Canada, New Zealand and Australia. This allows young people aged between 18 and 30 years (inclusive) at the time the visa application is made, to live and work in France for up to one year. You will need to have proof of a return ticket, or enough funds to purchase a ticket, proof of sufficient funds to cover your initial expenses, and also proof you have insurance. Applications are processed at your local French embassy or consulate – contact them directly for more information and application forms.

permission from the French government to live and work in France once they have received an offer of a full-time paid training position. Applicants should be American citizens aged 18–35 and available for up to 18 months (three months minimum)

French-American Center: ☎212 343 2675 email jhr2001@aol.com; www.frenchamericancenter.com/English/internship.asp. Offers unpaid internships, basically in and around the Montpellier area and coordinated by the French-American Center of Montpellier for one to three months. Accommodation is provided with a French family or private residence. All kinds of businesses sponsor these internships. The registration fee of $125 does not include living or food costs

Visa application procedure for US citizens

American citizens should apply for a French *visa de long séjour* before leaving the USA if they are planning to stay for longer than three months. The visa must be applied for at the French Embassy or a French consulate in the USA (www.consulfrance-washington.org). Applications for a visa from other countries or after arrival in France aren't usually permitted.

The requirements for the long-stay visa application as listed on the website are:

- Current passport
- Four copies of the long-stay visa application form
- Five passport photos
- Proof of residency in the USA
- Bank statements and other proof of financial assets sufficient to support you while living in France
- Copy of expatriate health insurance document (note: most US providers don't cover for overseas)
- Certificate of good conduct from your state police
- Letter certifying that you will not have any paid activity in France, signed and dated
- Proof of French residence (lease, utilities bill or a *certificat d'hébergement*)
- Non-refundable visa fee of around $130

You may also be asked for a birth certificate or a marriage certificate. The above list is only indicative. You are strongly advised to consult the consulate website fully as requirements depend on your circumstances. You need to make an appointment with the appropriate consulate for your state and present the visa application documentation in person. The visa process is lengthy as your application and documents have to be sent to France. It will usually take two to three months to complete.

Le Certificat d'Hébergement/proof of residence

One difficult criteria to fulfil can be the proof of French residence. If you are going to France to look for property to rent or buy you might not have arranged

TIP

If you have friends or contacts living in France they can obtain a *certificat d'hebergement* from the local *mairie*. This says that you will be staying at their address in France. As there is no checking when you get to France, you don't actually have to stay with them at all.

accommodation. Again, check exactly what is needed with the consulate before making the visa application appointment.

Procedure for getting a carte de séjour

Contact the nearest appropriate authority once in France – they will supply the necessary forms. You should go either to the local *préfecture de police* (police station) or the town hall (*mairie*). In Paris only, you must go to the police station of the *arrondissement* (district) in which you are living.

The *carte de séjour* carries a small stamp duty for issuing and renewing it – the same amount that a French national pays for a *carte d'identité*. The response to applications varies a great deal. The time between application and receipt of a *carte de séjour* can vary from a few weeks to several months (up to seven months has been reported).

In general the ritual and the documents required vary greatly from office to office and from official to official. People who have been through this procedure report different versions of the process, so you need to be flexible. You should have all the possible documents required before you start your application. Also, remember that not one, but several copies of each are likely to be required.

All applications for a *carte de séjour* have to be accompanied by a valid passport, four passport photographs, a full birth certificate and marriage certificate (if applicable). You may also be asked for your birth certificate (both parents' names need to be on this) or marriage certificate officially translated (though this is becoming less and less of a requirement). Circumstances for which this might be necessary include getting married in France, which requires a legalised translation of your birth certificate.

> ## Adam Zanders, an American living in Paris, gives some advice to those applying for a *carte de séjour*.
>
> Catastrophe! C'est une catastrophe! That's what you'll hear a French person saying when there's a long queue at the supermarket and only one cash desk on. But they don't have to wait in line at the prefecture! I mean, psychologically, you have to be prepared for these people. If you only want to have to line up there two or three times rather than four or five then listen carefully. I mean, these people are not there to help you! If it's your first trip to France and you don't speak good French, make sure you go along with a French friend. Otherwise you won't even get beyond the acceuil. They'll shoot something off at you very fast in French and then look over your shoulder at the next person. You can stand there and try and talk to them but you won't get anywhere after that. It's a test of patience. They'll tell you no for so many reasons. You'll think you have everything in your packet but they'll find something that doesn't fit. Every single document has to be copied. And another thing, try to get there early otherwise you could end up waiting in line and have to come back the next day. And bring headphones and a magazine.

TIP

◼ If you are having documents translated and legalised make sure you get extra copies of each at the same time, in case you need them in the future.

FACT

TRANSLATING DOCUMENTS

■ The French consulate will give you a list of translators. In order to produce a legal translation, the translators must be sworn in *(assermenté)* which adds to the cost. Some mairies, basically the ones who have a lot of English-speakers coming to them, will accept documents in English.

Employees

Employees also need to present proof of their employment and having found accommodation (bought or rented) in France. If you have bought property, you should ask the notary *(notaire)* who handled the sale for a *certificat* for this purpose. For rented accommodation, a receipt for the rent is usually enough. If it is a friend's flat, then they can provide an *attestation d'hébergement* (proof of lodging) and their *carte d'identité*. You will also need a contract of employment, and your employer should give you several copies of a *Certificat d'Emploi* on headed paper confirming your passport number, the date from which you are employed and the gross salary. Alternatively, bring along a pay slip *(bulletin de salaire)*. If you are self-employed you should provide some proof of being in business or of being self-employed. If you are setting up as self-employed you need evidence of your status, such as a membership of a professional or trade body, a VAT number, or registration on a trade register. If you don't intend to work you will need proof of income.

If you are looking for work in France, some job centres and employers, sparked by France's recent clampdown on illegal workers, will ask for a *fiche d'état civil* (a French administrative document confirming your civil status), which you can get from the town hall and which requires the same documents as the *carte de séjour*.

Other documents that could be requested

■ a medical certificate from a local doctor
■ affidavit that you don't have a criminal record

It may take some time and several visits to satisfy the officials that they have the information they require. You should eventually be granted *carte de séjour* if all is in order. Initially this may be a temporary carte/receipt, which is valid for three months and can be renewed until the residence permit is issued.

Velib, the municipal bike service

Students

Anyone studying in France will have to prove they are enrolled in an educational establishment (*inscription*), recognised by the Education Ministry, for the main purpose of following a course there and that they are covered by health insurance (as are members of their family accompanying them to France). You will also have to give an assurance in the form of a declaration or proof of adequate resources for support.

Entering to start a business

EU nationals who wish to enter France to start up a business are free to do so and no prior authorisation is required (further information is given on this in the chapter Starting a Business).

Non-EU nationals wishing to do the same thing require *une carte d'identité de commerçant étranger*, for which they should consult the French Consulate.

Entering France to take up a trade

EU nationals are free to enter France to ply any trade. However, tradesmen should check that their qualifications are recognised in France. If this is the case, simply register with the *Chambre des Métiers* and retain documentation to this effect. Details of setting up a business in France are given in the section on Starting a business in the chapter Working in France.

Entering France with retirement/ non-working status

EU nationals may retire to France or live there without having any means of gainful employment as long as they can support themselves financially. For further information see the section on Retirement in the chapter Working in France.

Consular registration

Once you have taken up residence in France (i.e. you have been there for over three months), you should register with your embassy or nearest consulate. This can also be done on arrival.

British consulates in France

For UK citizens, there are British consulates in all areas of France. This registration allows UK authorities to keep emigrants up to date with any information they need to be aware of as British citizens resident overseas, and enables them to trace individuals in the event of an emergency.

The consulate can also help with any information regarding an emigrant's status overseas, diplomatic or passport problems, emergencies, e.g. the death of a relative overseas, and your right to vote in elections back home once resident overseas. However, they don't function as a source of general help and advice, nor as an employment bureau.

Remember that passports need to be renewed periodically: your consulate can advise on this.

Nationality and citizenship once in France

As a passport holder of a foreign country permanently resident in France, an emigrant remains a national of their own country, not a French citizen. However, if you are an EU national you will have most of the rights and obligations of a French national but you can't vote in national elections.

France is aiming to crack down on *les clandestins/les sans papiers* (illegal immigrants). Most come from north Africa, but there is a steady traffic from Albania, Turkey (some fleeing the right wing backlash in Germany), the Balkans, Afghanistan, former Russian republics, and even Pakistan, Angola, China and India. The main entry points are France's Mediterranean borders with Spain and Italy. Previous governments naturalised some of the *clandestins* who could show they wanted to settle in France and satisfied qualifying criteria, such as showing themselves already well-integrated into French life/having children born in France/students/political refugees in danger if they returned to their home country.

President Sarkozy set up a new ministry, the Ministry of Immigration, Integration, National Identity and Codevelopment, which recently announced that illegal immigration was down, immigration of those coming to join their families was down and that immigration of those coming to France to work was up. If these figures are accurate, they would indicate that immigration is now putting less of a burden on French social services than before. The announcement was greeted with a great deal of scepticism however.

Children born in France

Anyone born in France is automatically entitled to choose French nationality at age 18 provided that they are resident in France and living there permanently, or for lengthy periods and have spent at least five years there since the age of 11. They also have the right to refuse French nationality.

Summary ℹ

As an EU national, as long as you have a job or business or can prove independent means, and have a home (whether bought or rented) you basically have a right to live and work in France. If you aren't from the EU, you have to have formal permission in advance, which is subject to the French authorities' discretion.

For further information, see the section on embassies in the appendix.

FACT

■ Foreign nationals can apply for French citizenship after five years' residence in France. Citizenship is awarded at the discretion of the French authorities but the only basic requirements are that the applicant is of 'good character' and is fluent in French. You can get details from the local *préfecture*.

FACT

HOW MANY *CLANDESTINS* ARE THERE IN FRANCE?

■ Estimates vary wildly, from three to five million. As many as 200,000 are probably entering the country each year. The cost of repatriating one illegal immigrant is thought to be €13,000.

■ THE LANGUAGE

Ecoutez! Repetez! Ecoutez! Repetez!

English speakers know more French than they think: some of the many French words used in English and English words used French are listed below.

French used in English		
à la carte	*de rigueur*	*je ne sais quoi*
à la mode	*double entendre*	*laisser faire*
au contrraire	*en route*	*ménage à trois*
avant garde	*en suite*	*prêt-à-porter*
cause célèbre	*esprit de corps*	*pot-pourri*
c'est la vie	*fait accompli*	*raison d'être*
cordon bleu	*faux pas*	*sang froid*
coup d'état	*femme fatale*	*tête-à-tête*
coup de grâce	*force majeure*	*tour de force*
crème de la crème	*haute cuisine*	

English used in French	
je suis un peu busy	*tres looké* (with a particular look)
un coup de blues (a bit depressed)	*Elle est vachement love de lui*
un type clean (respectable looking guy)	*un mailing*
Il était completment destroy (wasted)	*un manager*
C'est un embarrassement (with English pronunciation)	*limite nervous breakdown*
Il était très fair play	*Je suis overbooké*
C'est fashion	*une soirée people* (show biz soirée)
le feedback	*Le shopping*
un feeling	*elle est shooté* (high)
faire un footing (go for a jog)	*il a fait son show* (perform, informal or formal)
C'est vraiment fun comme truc	*tu nous fait un sketch là* (over dramatisation)
un gentleman	*C'était un peu speed* (a bit of a rush)
C'était hard (hardcore)	*le stop* (hitchhiking)
C'est hype (hot, fashionable)	*talkie walkie*
Il est parti en live (he lost it)	
une soirée VIP (letters spoken individually with English pronunciation	

Rajaneesh Dwivedi, who moved to France from the UK 10 years ago, talks about his experiences with learning the language.

There is an initial feeling of being pleasantly blinded by the newness of everything, as if in a toyshop. Since I didn't really speak or understand any French I ended up following round the few acquaintances I'd made, in a bit of a bubble, not really understanding where I was going or what I was doing, which was quite fun actually. Once things got a bit more familiar, I ended up addressing more practical issues like where to stay and eat and how to make money.

There comes a phase after a few months, though, where I ended up missing 'home' and found myself comparing the bureaucratic efficiency of the two countries and generally finding fault. I found myself seeking out comfort foods and other familiar rituals. Thankfully this didn't last long as I realised that it was just a need to feel more integrated and take the plunge to make things work. It was then that I started to get a deeper appreciation of the subtleties of the place and the warmth, honesty and heartiness that the French are so good at. Interestingly, it was also around this time that things suddenly clicked into place with the language, at around six months, when I also dreamt for the first time in French.

We've included specialised glossaries in their relevant sections: banking, building renovations, business, insurance, internet, labelling, mortgages, motor insurance, post, property ads, road signs and telephone.

The English language influence on French is much more recent than French on English. So much so that anglophones (a term used far more in France than anywhere else) are often unaware of the English words that have a French origin. Nevertheless, thanks to William the Conqueror (*Guillaume le Bâtard*) many French words are familiar. After the arrival of the Normans in Britain, this is what happened to the food on our plates:

- Cow became beef (*bœuf*)
- Calf became veal (*veau*)
- Sheep became mutton (*mouton*) and
- Pig became pork (*porc*)

In the vocabulary table above, the examples of English used in French are taken from spoken French, slang French, perhaps ironic and mostly recent usage. The French examples from English have long been part of the language and are used differently, to add a bit of sophistication to a phrase, a bit of *je ne sais quoi*. Like English, French is a great literary language, but unlike English, French has struggled to shed the weight of this literary heritage and invent new forms. English speakers take for granted that their mother tongue is the lingua franca the world over and, as such, isn't the property of any particular nation.

TIP

■ Avoid the trap of seeking out other English speakers too early in the game.

The French haven't embraced the dominant English-speaking world culture and the French take on life is heavily influenced by the natural protectionism their language gives them. In many ways *l'exception française* (an argument that allows the authorities to subsidise and protect French-language culture with measures such as reserving 40% of play time on all radio stations for French music) boils down to a difference in temperament.

Those from English-speaking cultures who come to France to work are struck by the hierarchical nature of French companies, a way of working that tends to impose a structure before examining what can be achieved rather than looking first at what needs to be done. This is in marked contrast to the goal-driven British and American work ethic. No wonder then that the French have a solid reputation in long-term planning! And so it goes with the language. Sentences are long and adjectives are placed after a noun, rather than before. This isn't simply a matter of form but represents the French preference for going from the general to the particular, rather than the other way round. The rhythms of the two languages are also in stark contrast, French more modulated and fluid, English bouncing between highly stressed and unstressed syllables. Paradoxically in English, subject matter determines speech patterns and makes coverage of emotionally intense content more risky. French allows you to get much closer to the core of what you are talking about without ever losing your *sang froid*.

Is it essential to learn French?

Of course, for anything more than a very basic job you will need to speak, or to be prepared to learn how to speak French accurately and fluently. Not knowing the language may well leave you feeling quite isolated whereas learning it will open up an entire culture.

> **TIP**
>
> ■ The key to becoming integrated in daily life is to learn the language.

> **Laurie Baird is an electronics engineer from Dunfermline and has lived and worked in Grenoble for the past 20 years. He is married to a French woman and has two daughters.**
>
> I was recruited by a headhunter. I wasn't specifically looking for a job in France. Work-wise it wasn't too difficult at the beginning because I was with a company run by British management and IT stuff is generally English oriented. At first I used to stick with British co-workers outside work too. It was a big step getting out of that environment into French companies. I forced myself to socialise with the French, watch TV in French and read in French. At the company I'm with now, the working environment is in French but there's a lot of communication in English because it's a multinational.
>
> When my kids were born I wanted to speak to them in English so I started socialising with the English again. I got satellite TV and now I try to watch films in English. My youngest daughter (11) is very attached to her English heritage but the older one (14) isn't so keen.

Many Europeans are adept at speaking foreign languages, and will often willingly speak English, or put up with English speakers' laborious attempts in their own language. But the French aren't generally strong in languages. Although the situation is changing, as more and more young French travel, you will find that plenty of even younger French people don't have much knowledge of English.

Regional accents

The southern accent is the strongest, so that even foreigners can hear it. It is characterised by a nasal twang and adding a 'g' sound to many words so that *vin* is pronounced 'ving', *maison* becomes 'maisang', and the emphasis on the final 'e' which makes 'France' sound like 'France-er.'

France's professional classes have traditionally favoured a Parisian accent, or no accent, but as nationality is becoming more difficult to cling on to in an increasingly federated Europe, regionality is enjoying resurgence. French mobile phone companies have introduced regional accents to their voice-mail message services, and regional accents can be heard on the news on TV and radio.

Learning French

Of course, many people already have some familiarity with French, say from what they learned at school. But it maybe a good idea to study it again in a more systematic way. Some approaches to learning the language are dealt with below.

Self-study courses

Self-study courses are a good way of getting a handle on the basics, but ideally they should be complemented by a language course/evening class, or conversation exchange. The traditional self-study courses consist of course books and audio or video tapes, but there are an increasing number of courses online. Some of these are interactive, with the possibility of contact with a native speaker by email and phone. Generally the first lesson is provided on a trial basis (try www.learningfrench.co.uk) The BBC has a large range of self-teaching courses and many of these involve online

TIP

◼ The advantage of self-study courses is that they allow you to absorb material at your own convenience and learning pace. Possible disadvantages are that you need to be self-motivated and can't practise one-to-one conversation.

What about slang?

Le verlan, the French word *l'envers* (which means the other way round) written backwards, is slang that was developed in the *banlieues*, the suburbs. In *le verlan*, *arabe* becomes *beur* and *flic* (police) becomes *ceuf*. *Le verlan* is fully integrated into the French language. President Sarkozy has famously referred to his Justice Minister, a woman with dual French/Moroccan citizenship, as *ma beurette* (my Arab girl).

The London foreign language bookseller Grant & Cutler
(☎020 7734 2012; contactus@grantandcutler.com; www.grantandcutler.com)
has a comprehensive range of course books and dictionaries.

learning (see www.bbc.co.uk/languages/french). These courses are for beginners, improvers and French for work. One good American course is French in Action, based on 52 videos of 30 minutes each which provide a good grounding of everyday French supported by workbooks and accompanying texts. There is also a range of learn French software which you can buy for your computer.

Some courses on the market are aimed at holidaymakers so check the contents of the course carefully to find the most appropriate. Linguaphone (www.linguaphone. co.uk) has courses which range from beginner to very advanced level but these aren't cheap.

Language course providers

Alliance Française: www.alliancefr.org. Created in 1883 in Paris by the French government, AF is a worldwide French teaching organisation with 770 schools in 135 countries. It offers courses and cultural activities with opportunities to meet and mix with native speakers. Courses aren't cheap. For information on lessons and activities run by the Alliance Française in different parts of the world, call 0033 (0)1 42 84 90 00 or email info@alliancefr.org.

The Berlitz School of Languages: www.berlitz.com. This is an international organisation with 400 centres in 60 countries. It offers language tuition specifically tailored to the individual's requirements. The cost of the courses available can vary enormously depending on the standard of the student and the intensiveness of

 If you live in the UK, you can contact Learn Direct, a government-funded agency (☎0800 101 901; www.learndirect.co.uk) for details of the nearest French courses in your area.

Private tutors/conversation exchanges

It is always worth checking the personals on internet forums or in the national and regional press for the possibility of finding a private tutor. Alternatively post a 'French Tutor Wanted' advertisement yourself. The aim should be to find a native French speaker who can provide individual tuition in the specific areas in which you require help. Alternatively, if you are already following a course, either self-study or evening classes and you just want to practise speaking, you can try to fix up a private conversation exchange with a native speaker who will speak French with you in return for similar practice in English.

the course. One advantage of the Berlitz schools is that courses begun in one place can be completed in another. So you could start learning in your own country and continue with the same course structure in France.

Part-time courses

The advantage of evening classes is their low cost compared with commercial intensive courses run by private schools. The disadvantage is that most classes only have one two to three hour session per week so you need to supplement the classes with a conversation exchange (see below) or an Anglo-French social/cultural group so you can consolidate through practice, what you have learned in class. Most local colleges of further education run language courses.

Language courses in France

Various French language courses are available in France for foreigners. These courses are aimed at a range of abilities and needs, and are sometimes arranged as learning holidays, possibly including accommodation with French families. Many French universities offer such courses and can be approached for details:

■ Souffle (www.souffle.asso.fr) is an association of schools and universities around France offering quality French language programmes. You can request a brochure or contact your local school through its website.

■ L'Office Nationale de Garantie des Séjours et Stages Linguistiques (www.loffice. org) has its own quality label supported by the French government on selected courses.

A booklet listing all of the universities in France which offer these courses can be obtained, free of charge, from the Ministry of Foreign Affairs in France. The non-profit making cultural organisation, Alliance Française (www.aliancefr.org) also runs courses. Private schools throughout France also organise courses.

CESA Languages Abroad has been organising language courses for nearly 25 years. The minimum course is two weeks but private tuition programmes can be arranged in France for a week in a choice of locations including Paris, the Loire Valley,

 CESA Languages Abroad: ☎ +44 (0)1209 211800; www.cesalanguages.com

the Côte d'Azur, the Atlantic seaboard and Brittany. CESA provides comprehensive advice on the colleges, the local area and the programmes offered to clients of all ages (14–60+) and caters for a wide range of linguistic abilities from non-existent to degree level.

Useful contacts

EF International Language School: (☎+44 (0)207 341 8500; fax +44 (0)☎207 341 8788; eflanguages@ef.com; www.ef.com) is part of EF Education, the world's largest private educational organisation. EF provides highly intensive personalised language training for the business world as well as courses for adults of 16 years and over in small groups. EF students learn on location in France (schools in Nice and Paris), studying in an international environment while living among native speakers to maximise exposure to the language and culture. The experience and expertise of

EF's instructors, the flexibility of weekly course start dates as well as the pleasant and professional course centres in France all translate into convenient and effective language learning for students of all levels and abilities.

The Eurolingua Institute SARL: +33 (0)☎4 67 58 20 17; www.eurolingua.com; info@eurolingua.com. This is the largest organisation of its kind, currently teaching 12 languages in 40 countries, and providing unique and affordable opportunities for people from 16 to 75 years, and from all walks of life, to learn languages in the countries where they are spoken. In France, individual and group programmes take place all year round at the Eurolingua Institute at Montpellier in the South of France. Accommodation is arranged with a local and inspected host family. Special summer programmes are run from June to August. Also unique one-to-one homestay, living as the only student in the teacher's own home, is available in most French regions. One-to-one and group homestay programmes take place at Eurolingua's French language institute, Eurolingua Espace Langues in Montpellier and a wide range of regional centres

Find out if there are any Anglo-French clubs or societies in your area, as these may organise social events or discussion groups. Also worth contacting is the Franco-British Society (www.francobritishsociety.org.uk), which arranges various discussion groups and social events concerned with Anglo-French culture and relations.

◼ BANKING AND FINANCE

Banking requirements

You should think of opening a French bank account at an early stage in planning a move to France. Even before you move to France, you will need funds for buying or renting a property, legal fees and deposits etc., so this doesn't just apply to those who are moving to France permanently.

In the short term it is possible to manage without a French account. Credit cards and travellers cheques are widely accepted. However, the fees, which are charged for these services can make a long-term stay in France without a French bank account very expensive. Visa Delta debit cards are widely used for withdrawals or payment for goods, while cards with the Cirrus logo can be used to withdraw money from cash points displaying the same logo.

Credit cards

French credit cards have long contained a microchip. But it's been noted that France is the worst country for recorded credit card theft, and Paris and Nice are the worst areas.

Money transfers

In July 2003 a new system of transferring funds in euros was introduced for intra-EU credit transfers. It uses an account holder's unique International Bank Account Number (IBAN) and a Bank Identifier Code (BIC) – also known as the 'SWIFT' code – which is a unique code allocated to every bank. Banks are obliged to provide bank statements with the IBAN and BIC printed on them. Firms issuing invoices within the EU now have to print their IBAN and BIC numbers on their invoices.

Other ways of transferring money are just as simple but may be more expensive than using the IBAN and BIC. To transfer money from a UK or US bank account to a French one, or vice versa, you simply provide your bank with the name, address and account number of your French bank account. The procedure is known as a bank transfer in the UK and, in France, as *un virement*. Some banks, e.g. the Royal Bank of Scotland in the UK and Credit Commercial de France (CCF) belong to the IBOS instant money transfer system (as do JP Morgan, Silicon Valley Bank, Wachovia Bank NA, US Bank, Nordea, Banco Santander and HSBC). CCF has 180 branches in France and you can transfer money on the same day to any one of them from other banks in the IBOS system.

Another fast way of transferring funds is through an international computer system called 'Society of Worldwide Interbank Financial Telecommunications' (SWIFT). Members include the HSBC bank and in the UK the Alliance and Leicester building society. Enquire at your bank for further details. Transfers usually take 24 (sometimes 48) hours.

Another possibility is European-wide Girobank Eurogiro. This takes three working days to transfer funds between post offices and there is a fixed charge, no matter what the amount, and it is considerably cheaper than the SWIFT inter-bank system. Even cheaper is the 10-day service. New customers simply open an account at the

TIP

Even if you only have a holiday home in France it can be useful to have a French bank account as regular bills, such as those for local taxes and utilities can be paid by direct debit from your account when you aren't in residence.

Keeping a UK or US account

Many expatriates decide to keep a bank account in their country of origin even after moving permanently to France and opening a French account. This account may then be drawn on if you return for a holiday at some point, or if you need to order any home comforts not available in France from mail order.

post office solely for international transfers. This system is adequate for holiday homeowners and those who want their pensions sent to them at minimal cost.

Of the UK retail banks, Barclays offers the Priority International Payment service, which takes one to two working days and for which there is a flat fee charged. Lloyds TSB has a similar system in place called TSB Offshore or Worldwide.

Exchange control

Although France has no exchange controls – meaning that French residents can open an account in any country and take an unlimited amount of money out of France – there is protocol for larger sums of money. It is obligatory to inform the French inland revenue of any new account on your annual tax return. In addition, international transfers in excess of €10,000 or a foreign currency equivalent other than bank transfers must be declared to the authorities, who will provide a certificate confirming customs approval. The limit for declarations on cash entering or leaving France was raised to €10,000 in June 2007 in line with EU-wide regulations.

Choosing a bank

Many international banks have branches in France so it's worth asking your current bank if they have branches or associated companies there. It may be useful to stay with them if they do, as they should be able to give advice on problems you may experience.

Government holdings in all kinds of companies in France, including banks, were sold off through the international markets in the 1990s. The major clearing banks are Banque National de Paris (BNP Paribas), Crédit and Société Générale. The Société Générale, the BNP and Crédit Lyonnais were all privatised and in 2003 Crédit Lyonnais was taken over by Crédit Agricole. These can be found in the boulevards and market places of cities and towns, large and small, throughout France.

Minitel/internet banking/phone banking

French banks are the subject of many complaints from the French themselves. They have archaic opening hours: some close for lunch and, owing to regulations dating

Fastest way to transfer money

The fastest way (and the most expensive) of sending money is the Telegraphic Transfer (TT). Western Union, MoneyGram and American Express are the best known companies as they operate worldwide. The transfer is simple. A person pays the money at the sending office, and within 15 minutes it can be collected at the receiving office – literally while you wait. Western Union can be reached in Paris on ☎01 60 45 72 73. Also available is MoneyGram (in Paris ☎01 53 27 95 56) which has agents in 170 countries.

back to 1937, all have to be closed for two days a week. Some banks close on Mondays and are open on Saturday. There are usually long queues and service can be mind-numbingly slow. For those willing to use the Minitel (still widely used for banking services and apparently happily co-existing alongside the internet) or the internet for banking, life can be a lot easier using an online service. With Minitel or the internet you can transfer money between your accounts, buy and sell shares, read your statements and get instant readings of the Paris stock exchange. This means you need only go to the bank in person to make deposits and collect chequebooks or cards.

Cooperative banks/mutual credit organisations

There are many cooperative banks/mutual credit organisations in France. They began as regional community assistance organisations working for the mutual benefit of client and organisation. Although these operate exactly like mainstream banks and offer most banking services, each office is an independent organisation, rather than a branch of a clearing bank. Credit Agricole is the largest organisation of this type, and with almost 10,000 offices worldwide you can find branches in almost every town of any size. The mutual credit organisations are cooperatives and it is possible to become a member and invest in their shares. You usually need to become a member if a loan or mortgage is needed but this is optional if you merely wish to deposit money or to have a cheque account with them.

Many corporate banks and finance companies in France, such as Banque Paribas, provide business banking facilities but not personal accounts. Savings banks (*caisses d'épargne*) are also to be found although these can only offer a limited range of services such as savings accounts and loans for property.

Opening an account

As most regional branches of French banks probably won't have staff who speak English, try to brush up on your French or find some other method of making financial transactions in France that doesn't involve French banks. An exception is the Crédit Agricole in Calvados (☎+33 (0)2 31 55 67 89; britline@ca-calvados.fr; www.britline. com) which has now become a dedicated direct banking branch with English staff offering all the French banking services including bank accounts, mortgages, savings accounts, direct debits (e.g. for utility bills on your French property), share brokering etc. by telephone, fax, email, website and online banking. This means you can open

The Post Office

When looking at banking in France it's worth considering the Post Office, which offers cheque accounts and savings and investment schemes and has more branches in France than any bank. Many people find a Post Office account is useful for paying bills by direct debit. The French equivalent of Girobank is CCP (Compte Cheques Postaux)

FACT

■ Mobile phone banking (ie managing your account from your phone) is taking off in France and is offered by most of the main banks including BNP Paribas, Banco Popular France and Société Générale. Get in touch with your bank for further details.

FACT

■ If you have taken a mortgage with a French bank this branch may also be the logical choice for your bank account; in any case, the bank may insist on this.

an account at Crédit Agricole of Calvados from anywhere in France without visiting the bank in person. HSBC also offer services managed by English-speaking staff. For Americans, there is the Banque Transatlantique, which specialises in expatriate banking services. The main office is in Paris but you can open an account in the USA at Banque Transatlantique (☎202 429 1909; www.transat.tm.fr) and then have it transferred to a local branch in France.

Alternatively, you can open an account in France in person. French banks have improved their image and consequently bank managers and manageresses (*gérant(e)* or *responsable de l'agence*) tend to be more accessible than they used to be, and to make an effort to meet new clients personally. When opening a French bank account be prepared, if requested, to show all your identification documents, including passport, *carte de séjour*, property deeds or rent documents, birth certificate, etc. and in addition, proof of income such as pay slips or a tax return is also required. The banks must satisfy themselves that you aren't banned from operating a bank account, as frequently happens to those who misuse them in France (see below). You will also require a reference from your UK or US bank, preferably in French. However, all this bureaucracy can be avoided by opening an account from a UK or US branch of a French bank. Cheque books and monthly statements will be posted to your home address.

If you want to manage your current account online from home you can use Minitel's *Banque a Domicile* (home banking) service. It gives you 24-hour access to your account so you can pay bills, make transfers, etc. when it suits you. There is a charge for this service.

Bank accounts

Various types of account are available which broadly compare with those elsewhere in that there are current accounts, deposit accounts and also various types of savings plans.

A current account is known as a *compte de chèque*. Until recently it was illegal in France for banks to pay interest on credit balances. There are often maintenance charges and also transaction charges, e.g. on direct debits and most current accounts, even if your account remains in credit.

There are many different types of deposit accounts (*comptes sur livret*) in France: the interest rates and minimum deposit periods vary from bank to bank. In France individuals are allowed a deposit savings account on which the interest paid is free of tax. The limit to these accounts is about €15,000, although the interest rates paid are modest. Most banks offer these schemes under varying brand names.

Cheques

The information on cheques may not be positioned in the way you are used to: the banks will supply a specimen if asked. In France cheques aren't negotiable to a third person.

Cheque guarantee cards as such aren't used, and so when using a cheque you may be asked for some other form of identification. However, when opening an account you should request a debit card, the *Carte Bleu*. As well as being preferred by traders to personal identification for large amounts of money, the *Carte Bleu* also enables you to draw out money, and to obtain a current statement of account, from cash machines throughout the country.

Clearing cheques

Cheques usually take longer than three days to clear from, or be credited to, an account in France. This is especially the case if they are from, or destined for, a bank account in a different branch in another part of France, or if they have come from abroad. In most cases, deposits of foreign cheques made out in euros or other currencies will be credited only on actual receipt of the funds from the payer (known as *crédit après encaissement* or CAE). The other kind of cheque clearing is *sauf bon fin* (SBF), when you are credited for the cheque within six days, but the credit can be withdrawn if the cheque is returned unpaid.

In some cases it can take as long as 12 days to clear a cheque, so it can be hard to keep track of your finances. There is no such thing as a post-dated cheque in France; it will be considered valid from when the bank receives it, regardless of the date on it. However, if the date is more than a year old, it will not be cleared.

Bouncing cheques

One of the main differences between the French and British banking systems is that in France it is a serious offence to write a cheque with insufficient funds to meet it. A period of 30 days is allowed for the account to be put in order. Should this prove impossible the bank automatically blocks the account for a period of one year, during which time the offender is banned from writing any further cheques. This is known as an *interdiction bancaire*. Offenders' details are kept on a central list by the Banque de France for a period of three years. If he or she tries to open another account, the police are informed.

Stopping cheques

In France it isn't possible to stop cheques for reasons such as buying faulty goods. To do this will result in legal repercussions that will keep the lawyers happy for months at your expense.

Bankers cheques (*chèques de banque*) cannot be treated as cash. Bankers drafts have to be paid into your account and cleared in the usual way.

Charge cards and other banking services

Credit cards don't exist as such in France. Instead, charge cards (*carte bancaire de paiement*) are issued. Each month, the total accrued to the charge card is automatically debited from your account. A good many banks and stores provide charge cards, for which there is an annual fee. Probably the best known is the *Carte Bleu*, which is widely accepted in France. There is also an international version, the *Carte Bleu*/Visa, but this still has to paid off at the end of each month.

Charge cards are quite widely accepted in France, although not to the same extent as in the UK or USA. These cards can also be used to withdraw cash from cash dispensers and most large shops, hypermarkets, restaurants, hotels and even autoroute tolls accept charge cards. There are also card-operated petrol stations and the minimum service, 24-hour 'pit-stop' hotels where access is by credit card. However, don't take this for granted in remote rural establishments.

Direct debits (les prélèvements automatiques)

Direct debits are a convenient way of paying regular bills for utilities, especially if you are only based in France for a few months of the year or are making only periodic visits there. Services such as electricity and telephones will be cut off if payment is late. A similar service can be arranged through the Post Office.

Domestic (i.e. internal) money transfers are known as *virements*, while international ones are *transferts*.

Main commercial clearing banks

- *Banque Paribas*: www.banqueparibas.net.
- *Barclays Bank SA*: www.barclays.fr
- *Banques Populaires*: www.banquepopulaire.fr.
- *Crédit Agricole*: ☎01 41 89 00 00; www.credit-agricole.fr
- *Crédit Commercial de France (CCF)*: www.hsbc.fr
- *Crédit Mutuel*: www.creditmutuel.com.
- *Crédit du Nord*: www.credit-du-nord.fr
- *Société Générale*: www.socgen.com

Useful contacts

Girobank plc: ☎0121 454 8000; www.girobank.net.

Banking glossary	
English	French
annual percentage rate (APR)	*TEG*
annuity	*l'annuité*
automated banking lobby	*libre service bancaire*
automated teller machine (ATM)	*guichet automatique*
balance	*le solde*
bank acccount	*un compte en banque*
bank charges/interest	*l'agio*
bank code	*code banque*
bank identity record	*relevé d'identité bancaire*
bank statement	*un relevé de compte/extrait*
bankers draft	*un chèque de banque*
beneficiary	*bénéficiaire*
bounced cheque	*un chèque sans provision*

Banking glossary

English	French
branch	agence/guichet
branch code	code guichet
bridging loan/finance	crédit relais
cash	argent liquide
in cash	en espèces
cash dispenser	Distributeur automatique des billets
cash withdrawal	un retrait d'espèces
cheque	un chèque
cheque book	un chèquier/carnet de chèques
cheque deposit	remise de chèque
coins/change	la monnaie
commission charged on receipt of an international currency transfer	un commission de repatriement
counter (bank counter)	guichet
credit your account	approvisionner
current account	compte de dépôts
debit	un débit
deposit	un dépôt
to deposit money in an account	déposer de l'argent
deposit account (for savings with a passbook)	compte sur livret
direct debit	un avis de prélèvement
endorse (ie sign the back of a cheque)	endosser
exchange rate	le taux de change
expiry date	date d'expiration
fees	les frais
foreign currency	la devise
insurance cover for accidental death	parrainage/compte parrainé
a savings account	compte de dépôt
a joint current account	joint/commun
a mortgage	crédit hypothécaire
mutual fund	société [d'Investissement à capital variable (SICAV)/fonds commun de placement (FCP)
investment	un placement
overdraft	un découvert
overdraft charge	agio

Banking glossary

English	French
overdrawn account	*un compte débiteur*
payslip	*une fiche de salaire*
personal loan	*un prêt personnel*
PIN	*la code confidentiel*
power of attorney	*un procuration*
previous balance	*ancien solde*
profitability	*la rentabilité*
proof of address document	*un justicatif de domicile*
repayment schedule	*le tableau d'amortissement*
remittance	*remise*
secured loan	*un prêt garanti*
seizure of funds	*saisie attribution*
share	*l'action*
share in a cooperative	*un part sociale*
standing order	*ordre permanent/virement automatique*
to stop a cheque	*faire opposition*
tax	*l'impôt*
transfer	*un virement*
valid	*valable*
value date (when a transaction is actually credited/debited to/from an account)	*jour de valeur*
to withdraw money (from an account)	*retirer (de l'argent)*

The euro (€)

The euro as the European monetary unit was legal tender for paper transactions for over three years (and for a while the euro and French franc were run in tandem) before the euro became the single currency in 12 countries including France in January 2002. The franc ceased to be legal tender on 17 February 2002.

The UK isn't part of the euro zone and the rate of the euro fluctuates against sterling. At the time of press it was £1 = 1.34 euros and €1 = £0.75 (US$1 = €0.69 and €1 = $1.45).

Euro notes (billets): there are seven denominations of values: 5, 10, 20, 50, 100, 200 and 500. Banknotes are the same for all the eurozone countries

Euro coins (*monnaie*): come in eight values from one cent to €2. There are 12 stars to represent the Community countries of Europe on the heads side; on the reverse is Marianne, symbol of the French republic with the French motto: *liberté,* *fraternité, egalité* (liberty, brotherhood, equality). You can view the coins and notes on the website of the *Financial Times* (www.ft.com)

■ COST OF LIVING

- Newspaper   €1.10
- Roundtrip train fare between Paris
  and Marseille   €135
- Pack of cigarettes   €5
- Domestic postage   €0.50
- One night in a two-star hotel   €70
- Baguette   €0.90
- Litre of unleaded petrol   €1.18
- 6 organic eggs   €1.56
- 2.5 litres of emulsion   €47.30
- A meal in a restaurant   €15

According to the National Institute for Statistics and Economic Studies (l'INSEE, www.insee.fr), the consumer price index in France is up around 18% over the past 10 years. The cost of living has certainly risen significantly. As in many countries in Europe the prices of a whole range of goods rose significantly after the adoption of the euro. Add to the euro effect the rises in the price of housing (doubled since 1998) and the recent worldwide petrol and food price increases and you will begin to see that France is no longer a cheap destination. Most overall comparisons with the UK do still tend to indicate that the cost of living is around 25%–35% lower in France but these figures usually include things such as mortgage costs and tobacco, alcohol and car expenses (all lower in France), which may or may not affect you. Anyone intending to set up house there needs to look at the individual factors that will have an impact on their way of living.

Your perception of costs will vary depending on where you are from. With the euro currently quite strong against the pound and the dollar significantly weaker, prices are have generally risen comparatively in France for people whose income isn't in euros. Americans will find food, petrol, books and clothes more expensive (high VAT in France) but health and education

In search of the most expensive cup of coffee in Paris

much cheaper (government subsidised). Brits will find certain items on their food bill falling, especially fresh vegetables (which can often be sourced locally) and alcohol, but wherever you are from you may actually find yourself spending more in the large number of small, high-quality, specialist food shops France is so famous for, than you did back home at the supermarket. The French themselves don't skimp on food, dedicating around 25% of their disposable income to it. This is just one example of why it is difficult to compare like with like.

Brits will also have the additional cost of health insurance. Healthcare isn't free in France and recent changes in the law for EU expats mean that some expats will no longer qualify for the *Couverture Maladie Universelle* (CMU) that until recently covered 70%–85% of health costs for all EU expats. Health insurance may now become a significant additional cost for those moving there from the UK. Of course, the cost of a policy varies a great deal depending on your circumstances and extent of cover but to give a general idea, for a typical policy available to a 55-year old you can expect to pay from €1600 to €5000 annually (for details see the Health section in the chapter *Daily life*).

Of course, lower house prices are the main reason for the influx of many foreigners to France over the past ten years and in spite of recent rises, properties there are still a good deal. Here is a breakdown of what you can expect to pay for a 120sq m property in various regions in France:

- Brittany   €220,000
- Lower Normandy   €202,000
- Provence/Alps Cote d'Azur   €374.,000
- Ile de France   €346,000
- Paris (city)   €713,000

In general, older houses in the countryside tend to be better value for money and as the size of the house increases, so the price per square metre falls. For

Typical rents

Property	Area	Rent per month (unfurnished)
3 bed flat	Paris suburbs (80sq m)	€1,000–1,400
1 bed flat	Paris suburbs (35sq m)	€400-700
3 bed flat	Within Paris (80sq m)	€1,200-2,000
1 bed flat	Within Paris (35sq m)	€750–1200
2 bed town house	Normandy	€500
1 bed apartment	Montpellier	€500

more information on house prices and rents visit the French Federation of Estate Agents website (www.fnaim.fr). If you buy a property that needs renovating, remember that artisan costs (and some say do-it-yourself (DIY) costs, although there is disagreement on this) tend to be higher in France (see 'Buying property' in the chapter *About France*). And if you are living in rural France, you will almost certainly find that you have high petrol/diesel costs as you will be doing higher mileage.

Again, the cost of utilities varies depending on whether you are based in the town or the country. Property-based taxes are generally lower than in the UK. Electricity is cheap. Water is metered but it can be a significant cost in the south of France. Outside of major towns there is little mains gas. This means you will have to use diesel, wood, electricity or bottled gas, all of may be more expensive than you are used to. Diesel for heating and hot water in a family-sized house may cost around €1,500 annually. You may also need to factor in air-conditioning and, especially for Americans who are used to low phone tariffs, phone costs – calling mobiles back home is likely to push up the phone bill quite some!

Finally let's take a look at salaries. Across the board, salaries are slightly lower (see the Robert Walters website www.robertwalters.com/salarysurvey), and your income tax bill is likely to be lower too. However once you have added mandatory social security payments, the burden will almost certainly be higher. It is important to consider your change in circumstances too.

Unemployment is high and varies significantly from region to region, (according to the EU website (www.europa.eu.int/eures) the figures for Ile de France are low, as is Limousin at 6.8% but Languedoc-Roussillon has figures of well over 12%) with young people finding it hard to get a foothold in the job market. Many expats

Eurostar terminal

set up their own businesses but you should remember that although in the long run charges may not be higher than elsewhere, start-up costs can be because you have to start paying contributions before you start earning. For more on starting a business and working in France see the chapter *Working in France*.

■ GETTING THERE

From the UK

Travel agents can, of course, offer advice on travel to France by air, train or ferry, but they are fast becoming obsolete as a way of booking flights, ferries, etc. now that it has become easy to book online. There are still several flight discounters, airlines, etc. that specialise in offering discount fares, many of which are supported by websites and advertising campaigns and/or they feature in the main or travel sections of newspapers.

Train via the Channel Tunnel

Eurostar runs 17 trains daily to Paris from London. Travel times were cut by 20 minutes at the end of 2007 with the introduction of the new route from St Pancras

 Eurostar ☎08705 186 186; www.eurostar.com; a passenger only service

A Eurostar breakfast

station and you can now travel from London to Paris in two and a quarter hours. A new station has also opened at Ebbsfleet in Kent. The train arrives at the Gare du Nord and passengers have to travel by the *métro* to either the Gare du Lyon or Montparnasse to connect with TGV and other French rail services. Tickets bought some time in advance start at £59 return. A return is usually cheaper than buying a one-way ticket. Services also run to Lille.

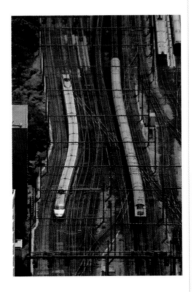

For details of the TGV services in France see the 'Transport' section of the chapter *Daily life*. You can book tickets for all SNCF (French railways) services via their website (www.raileurope. co.uk). You can also book by calling 0 8448 484 064 for all tickets including Eurostar. There is a separate number for Motorail (☎0 8448 484 050) or Snow Train (☎0 8448 484 088). It is also possible to book through trains to various French destinations with Eurostar.

The service for passengers and their vehicles is Eurotunnel/Le Shuttle which leaves from the Terminal in Folkestone (☎0 8705 353 535; www.eurotunnel.com) and arrives at Calais. The short but boring journey takes 35 minutes and unlike the ferries and hovercraft the tunnel service is immune to bad weather conditions. Tickets can be bought through travel agents, the above websites, or at the station on departure.

If you are in the USA but will go to France from UK, you can book Eurostar and TGV tickets, French rail passes and packages, and point-to-point tickets in France through www.raileurope.com.

Under-26 discount rail tickets can be obtained from Rail Europe (☎08705 848848; www.raileurope.co.uk), and the Trainline (www.internationaltrainline.com) offers Eurostar tickets to France and tickets and reservations for rail across Europe, and rail passes.

UK to France by train – find out more

An excellent website 'How to travel by train from London to France' (www.seat61.com/France.htm) gives information on travel between London and all the main destinations in France including Lille, Strasbourg, Biarritz, Lourdes, Bordeaux, Marseille and the Alps, including sample fares and booking details. It also gives timetables of the journeys from London to these destinations.

Ferries below can be booked direct with their operators or online through all-ferries websites such as www.aferry.to (also does Euro Tunnel), www.directferries.com (☎0870 222 3312), www.ferrybooker.com and www.ferrycrossings-uk.co.uk.

By sea

Rather than abandon ship in the face of Le Shuttle and Ryanair, the ferry companies have increased their fleets, and in some cases revamped them to provide swish onboard facilities. Of course this is a more expensive solution than the low airfares available with budget airlines (see below) but a good solution if you want to take your car.

◤ Ferry companies

Brittany Ferries: UK booking office ☎0870 9 076103; France booking office +33 (0) 82 5828 828; www.brittany-ferries.com/. As its name suggests Brittany Ferries has the monopoly on the sailings to the Breton ports: from Portsmouth to Caen, Cherbourg and St Malo; Plymouth to Cherbourg and Roscoff, and Poole to Cherbourg. Brittany ferries runs a club for owners of properties in France. Payment of an annual membership fee entitles members to up to 33% discount. For more details click on Property Owners Travel Club on the website.

Condor Ferries: ☎01202 207216; reservations ☎0845 609 1024; www.condorferries. co.uk. Small company sails from Portsmouth, Poole and Weymouth to St Malo via the Channel Islands.

Norfolkline: ☎0870 870 10 20; www.norfolkline.com Ferry Dover/Dunkerque. Comparative newcomer (2001) with special offers out of season. Pet travel scheme booking service.

P&O European Ferries: ☎08716 645645; email help@poferries.com www. poferries.com. P&O does the Dover/Calais route with departures approximately every hour and a journey time of 75 minutes. It also operates daily sailings from Hull

to the Belgian port of Zeebrugge, which can make a useful alternative to the French ports during the busiest periods; it is only 19 miles further from Paris than Calais.

Sea France: ☎0871 663 2546; in Calais: 33 (0) 825 0825 05; www.seafrance.com. Dover to Calais.

SpeedFerries: ☎0871 222 7456 (from within the UK), 0044 (0) 8702 200 570 (from outside the UK); www.speedferries.com. High-speed ferry service introduced 2004. State of the art catamaran races between Dover and Boulogne in 50 minutes. Capacity 200 cars and 800 passengers. Fares from £36 return. Budget airline style ticketing system with earliest booking securing the cheapest fares.

Transmanche Ferries: ☎0800 917 1201; www.transmancheferries.co.uk. Operates a service from Newhaven to Dieppe/Le Havre and from Portsmouth to Le Havre.

LD Lines: ☎0844 576 8836; www.ldlines.co.uk. Operates the same routes as Transmanche.

By air

There is a great choice of flights and airlines to choose from from Heathrow, Gatwick, Stanstead and London City to Paris-Charles de Gaulle (also called Roissy-Charles de Gaulle) and Paris-Orly. Most international flights go to Charles de Gaulle where you can walk from the arrivals area into the TGV station (i.e. without leaving the airport). From Charles de Gaulle there are train connections to Lyon, Rennes and Brussels (90 minutes), without going into central Paris. To get into Paris you take an RER (the urban train network) into the Gare du Nord. Orly Airport makes more sense if you are (a) going to south Paris or (b) if you are connecting with an a domestic flight, as Orly is the hub for the domestic network.

Of course there are low cost options to most large French cities from the UK with Ryanair and Easyjet, amongst others. There are flights from London's Heathrow and

 Air France (UK ☎0870 142 4343; France ☎01 58 68 68 68; www.airfrance.co.uk)
British Airways (☎0870 850 9850; www.british-airways.com)
British Midland (☎0870 6070 555; www.flybmi.com)

Gatwick airports to most large provincial French cities and from UK regional airports including Stanstead, Luton, East Midlands, Glasgow, Manchester, Bristol and Liverpool.

◼ Useful contacts

Air France: UK ☎0870 142 4343; France ☎01 58 68 68 68; www.airfrance.co.uk. Air France has flights from 19 UK airports including London's City Airport (to Paris-CDG and Paris-Orly). Some good value special offers are available. Flies to most large towns in France from the UK.

Direct from USA, Air France flies direct from a number of cities in the USA. Check their website for details; www.airfrance.us

British Airways: ☎0870 850 9850; www.british-airways.com

British Midland Airways: ☎0870 6070 555; www.flybmi.com

Easyjet: ☎0871 244 2366. www.easyjet.com

European Executive Ltd.: www.euroexec.com. Flies from Brighton (Shoreham Airport) to Le Touquet. Fast check-in, avoid larger airport congestion

Flybe: ☎0871 700 2000 or from outside the UK +44 (0)1392 268500; www.flybe.com. Flights mainly from south and south-west of England

Flyglobespan.com: ☎08712 710 415; www.flyglobespan. Scottish budget airline with flights from Edinburgh to Nice

Jet2.com: ☎0871 226 1737; flights to France from Leeds Bradford, Manchester, Belfast, Newcastle and Edinburgh

Ryanair.com: ☎0871 246 0000 or from France ☎0892 232 375; www.ryanair.com

Thomsonfly: UK ☎0871 231 4691; www.thomson.co.uk

By coach

There are regular coach services from London to France. Other routes from UK cities may also be available. The biggest operator is Eurolines which is part of the National Express group.

Also check out *Busabout* (www.busabout.com) which has a range of European destinations. Online booking tells you which routes and times are busy and which have plenty of spaces.

 National Express: +44 (0)087 1781 8181; www.nationalexpress.com/eurolines. London to Paris (incl. Euro Disney), Montpellier, Perpignan, Bordeaux, Nice, Chamonix, Grenoble, Strasbourg, etc; over 75 destinations in France served.

From the USA and Canada

Most flights from the USA and Canada go via Paris from where connecting flights or trains can be arranged to other parts of France in advance if required. As stated above, you can book Eurostar and TGV tickets, French rail passes and packages, and point-to-point tickets in France while in USA through www.raileurope.com.

By air

◼ Useful contacts

Air Canada: www.aircanada.ca

Air France in the USA: ☎1 800 237 2747; Canada: ☎1 800 667 2747; www.airfrance.com

American Airlines: ☎1 800 433 7300; www.aa.com. Flies to both Paris Orly and Paris CDG

British Airways: ☎1 800 247 9297; www.british-airways.com

Continental Airlines: ☎1 800 231 0856; www.flycontinental.com

Delta Airlines: ☎1 800 241 4141 (US); www.delta-air.com

United Airlines: ☎1 800 538 2929; www.ual.com

US Airways: ☎1 800 622 4322;www.usairways.com

Virgin Atlantic: ☎1 800 821 5438; www.virgin-atlantic.com

◼ Discount travel

Air Brokers International: ☎1 800 883 3273; www.airbrokers.com

Nouvelles Frontières: www.nouvelles-frontieres.fr. French discount firm to USA and Canada

By rail

Check the following websites for schedules and fares for travel on French railways (SNCF) and the TGV highspeed network:

- www.raileurope.com
- www.sncf.fr

French Government tourist offices

Canada: Maison de la France Canada: ☎514 288 2026; canada@franceguide.com; ca.franceguide.com

Ireland: Maison de la France Ireland: ☎15 60 235 235; infoie@ie.franceguide.com

U K: Maison de la France Great Britain: ☎09068 244123 (calls charged at 60p per minute); info.uk@franceguide.com; uk.franceguide.com

USA: Maison de la France United States: 1(514)288 1904; Los Angeles ☎310 271 6665; Chicago; ☎312 327 0290; info-us@franceguide.com; us.franceguide.com

■ PLANNING AN INTERNATIONAL MOVE

When planning your move, it's worth bearing in mind that there may be difficulties with electrical repairs and ordering new parts. If you intend to take only a small quantity of items, it may be more economical to transport them yourself. The alternative is to use a removals company. The British Association of Removers (BAR) will provide a list of firms and general information on moving possessions overseas. BAR also has an International Movers Mutual Assurance fund set up by the overseas group of the BAR. This means that clients' interests are protected if a member company goes bust.

Useful addresses in the UK

Allied Pickfords: freephone ☎0800 289 229 or from outside UK ☎+44 (0)208 219 8000; www.alliedpickfords.co.uk

Anglo French Euro Removals: UK 01233 660963; France ☎+33 (0)5 45 30 71 88; www.anglofrench.co.uk

Bishop's Move: www.bishopsmove.com. Regular departures to all parts of France. All aspects of removal and storage

Ede Brothers: sales@edebros.co.uk, www.edebros.co.uk. Family-run firm established in 1926. All areas of France

Farrer & Fenwick Removals: ☎+44 (0) 1932 253737; www.farrerandfenwick. co.uk. Offices in Surrey and the Pas-de-Calais

French Moves: based in the UK and France. French office ☎05 53 01 46 92; UK office: ☎01932 881634; enquiries@frenchmoves.co.uk; www.frenchmoves.co.uk

Kidds of Yorkshire: 0800 252220; www.kidds.co.uk

 British Association of Removers ☎ 01923 699 480; www.bar.co.uk

The Old House (Associated Moving Services): London office: ☎0208 947 1817; www.amsmoving.co.uk. Moving to France over 45 years. Fully bonded members of BAR. Overseas. Full and part loads; free quotations and advice

Robinsons International Removals: ☎0800 833 638; www.robinsons-intl.com

US international removers

Allied International Moving Services: www.alliedintl.com

United Van Lines Inc.: www.unitedvanlines.com

Vanpac International: www.vanpac.com

Customs regulations

There are no restrictions to moving your household goods to your French residence. The removal company will simply fill in a form declaring what they are carrying. There is a restriction on bringing large quantities of one item, which would give rise to the supposition that you are intending to trade in that item. The limit on bringing in cash was raised to €10,000 in June 2007 in line with EU-wide regulations. In theory you could be asked to produce receipts for the goods that you are carrying with you. If you have already bought property in France then you should carry a copy of your *acte de vente* (deed of purchase) with you, and other proof that you are resident in France.

Reports vary considerably as to the attitude of French customs officials. Some who have been through the procedure found French customs ignored them, while others have undergone a very thorough check. As long as a sincere attempt is made to cooperate with French customs they can be quite helpful. Special regulations apply to the import of motor vehicles (see below).

Taking your car

Some take the view that it isn't worth importing a car with a right-hand drive to France. It will be inconvenient to drive and worth very little when you come to sell it. It also attracts the attention of burglars.

If you do want to import a car to France then the regulations are as follows:

- You can import into France one vehicle acquired in another EU country, duty free (*en franchise*). If it's a new vehicle you should be able to prove that you have paid VAT in the EU and can produce the original bill of purchase as well as

General conditions of import

- EU nationals may take any household goods and effects into France, tax and duty free, whether they are new or not
- It is advisable to carry a certificate of ownership of French property in case you are stopped in a random customs check
- There are special regulations regarding the import of a car (see below)

the vehicle registration document issued in the EU country where the car was purchased. Also you should be able to convince the French authorities that you are taking up residence in France

◼ Commercial vehicles don't qualify for duty-free entry, but motorcycles, caravans and mobile homes do – and on the same terms as cars

◼ Be sure to take the registration document (V5), tax disc, MOT (if applicable) and insurance papers. Under EU regulations, insurance taken out in the UK is now valid in France. You should check with your insurance company about this

◼ Make sure customs officials are told that the car is for permanent import. There will be additional form filling at the border, and forms will be provided which are required to register the car in France. Note that cars which are to be based permanently at a secondary or holiday home will normally be admitted free of tax

◼ It is necessary to register the car in France within one year of taking up residence and obtain a *carte grise* (French registration document). See the 'Getting around' section in the chapter *Daily life* for more on registration and other regulations once your car is in France

Taking your pets in and out of France

Many people moving to France would like to have their four-legged friends – *animaux de compagnie* – with them abroad, and in some ways this has become a routine procedure. France declared itself rabies-free in 2002, but there are still occasional cases of rabid animals being brought into the country (usually from Africa), so there is always a risk that the disease will return.

EC regulation No. 998/2003, which came into force on 3 July 2003 and was applied on 3 July 2004, introduced the EU pet passport, which is recognised by all Member States and certain non-EU listed countries such as Gibraltar, Norway, San Marino and Switzerland. The pet passport replaces the PETS 1 certificate and the PETS 5 certificate previously required to enter other EU countries. The previous requirements for a microchip, vaccination, satisfactory blood test at an EU-approved laboratory, and the six calendar month wait from the date the blood sample is taken haven't changed for EU and other listed countries. The pet passport is also valid if you are planning to bring the pet back to the UK.

Check out the UK Department of Food, Environment and Rural Affairs (DEFRA) site (www.defra.gov.uk) for information about domestic rabbits and pet rodents, birds (except certain poultry), ornamental tropical fish, invertebrates and amphibians and reptiles, which are also covered by the regulation. If you want to bring in a parrot or similar bird you will have to swear that you aren't going to resell it in France, and agree to a veterinary inspection. The local French consulate will advise you on other types of animals. If you are in the UK, DEFRA can provide forms for France or if you are thinking of exporting animals other than cats and dogs the PETS Helpline will give you the number of the section you need to call.

Non-EU pets

The situation for dogs coming from outside the EU is different. A blood sample taken from your pet has to be sent in advance to a laboratory in Nancy for testing. The animal also has to fulfil the conditions given above for UK animals. Regulations do change and the best people to ask for up-do-date information are specialised pet-carriers (see below) or your nearest French embassy. The French government hasn't publicised the rules on the internet.

Pet travel insurance

See the websites:

- www.mrigroup.com
- lwww.petplan.co.uk
- www.pinnacle.co.uk

If you are returning to the UK

You can bring your pet back into the UK as long as you follow the rules laid down by the DEFRA in the Pets Travel Scheme (PETS). This includes all the same requirements you need to obtain the EU passport to take a pet to France. Remember six months have to elapse after a successful blood test following vaccination against rabies before you can get your vet to fill in the appropriate sections of the passport, so you need to plan ahead. When in France, the cat or dog must first be microchipped and then vaccinated and blood tested.

The requirement for animals to be treated for ticks and tapeworms 24–48 hours before being checked-in with an approved transport company to travel to the UK also remains. Pets must not have been outside any of the qualifying countries in the six calendar months immediately before travelling to the UK and must enter the UK using an approved transport company on an authorised route. Call the PETS Helpline on 0870 241 1710 or visit the website for further information.

Useful contacts

Airpets Oceanic: ☎0800 371554; from outside the UK ☎+44 1753 685571; info@airpets.com; www.airpets.com

Dogs Away: ☎ 08450 17 10 73; from outside the UK ☎+44 (0)1322 529 767; email contact@dogsaway.co.uk; www.dogsaway.co.uk

Independent Pet and Animal Transport Association: ☎+1 903 769 2267; inquiries@ipata.com; www.ipata.com

Par Air Services: 01206 330332; parair@btconnect.com; www.parair.co.uk

Pets Travel Scheme: ☎0870 241 1710; www.defra.gov.uk

If you buy a dog or cat in France, there is no legal requirement to have a microchip implanted unless you are taking it abroad. There is, however, a tradition in France (and other EU countries) that pedigree dogs are given a name beginning with the same letter depending on the year. A similar tradition applies to horses.

Providing a European door to door removal and relocation service, including a Unique DIY European removal service. Rent a Truck or rent a lorry with driver to reduce your costs and increase your flexibility.

TEL: +33 (0) 494 43 02 39 EML: enquiry@theroadahead.co.uk

www.theroadahead.co.uk

Looking for a removal company?

I would not hesitate in recommending The Road Ahead for a move to France. Quite apart from offering the best-priced removal service I could find, the whole process was easy, convenient and reliable. From the first contact with the office to the drop-off, I can't fault them – professional, experienced, good-humoured, unflappable, bilingual.... I could go on. The move was a very stressful time for us, as anyone attempting the same uprooting will know, and I found them reassuring and supportive all the way. – *Kathryn*

Our move went exactly according to plan and we had the most helpful driver anyone could want. Not only was your service the most competitive we could find in practise it could not be faulted well done and many thanks for a first class job. – *Colin*

What will you say?

Setting Up Home

■ HOW DO THE FRENCH LIVE?

The housing crisis of the post Second World War years lasted much longer in France than in Britain or even Germany. Finally the country embarked on a massive building programme in the 1960s and 1970s of which the HLM (*habitation à loyer modéré*) is the most prolific result. This type of state housing brought about a substantial improvement in France's accommodation situation, but did little to enhance the appearance of the peripheries of most of the big cities where they were built. Many of the developments are characterless and many of the satellite towns created, especially around Paris, are bleak places, but at least they are built to a reasonably good standard and include all modern services.

Buying an apartment is still the norm and even an ideal for many. Semi-detached houses are quite rare, which is a good thing, as the French tend to be noisy neighbours. In a country with as much space as France, it would be perverse to force people to share a party wall and the absence of one is a positive selling point. There are also housing estates in France, or *lotissements*. The main downside is that the houses will be uniform and unimaginatively designed. Most rentals are private, long-term contracts. France has concentrated its social problems in low-rental housing blocks of flats or HLMs in the worst-off urban areas, but in many towns HLMs are good places to live, and not sink estates.

First-time buyers are often forced to buy in unfashionable suburbs as city centres become too expensive. There is also now talk of the *désertification* of some city centres, meaning that they are more and more inhabited by under-30s and immigrants, groups who can only afford to rent, with a consequent decline in shopping facilities. As in other western European countries, many middle-class French are leaving the city centres and moving to the suburbs. This has become possible with better train services and roads; with the TGV one can commute huge distances. It also means that there are more houses with large gardens

Paris v province

'What I don't like about the provinces,' the writer Christine Angot tells us provocatively in an interview with French daily, *Libération* (31 August 2006), 'is that everyone puts the accent on quality of life. How many square metres, price, proximity, whether there are traffic jams or not, whether it's noisy or not, whether the shops are busy. I can't stand it. It drives me crazy. Whether it's sunny... In the south it's sunny. Great! You can go out in a t-shirt in January! I lived in Nice for ten years and in Montpellier for ten years. Everyone's proud of living in the south because they can eat outside in their shirtsleeves in January. It's not that I mind, it's just that I don't find it interesting.'

being built and a greater interest in gardening and DIY is also evident. There is also a growing trend for more professionals to work from home in the countryside, as well as for internet-based businesses to move out of town. The depopulation of the countryside has stopped in most areas outside the centre, as more and more town-dwellers look for ways to move into the countryside. Even so, there are two million abandoned houses, which accounts for the large numbers of country properties available at very low prices in less popular areas.

◼ CHOOSING WHERE TO LIVE

Christine Angot's comments should be read as part of the sort of verbal tennis French writers and indeed the French as a whole so delight in. She is of course balking at what Christine sees as provincial intellectual laziness. The debate within France on Paris versus *la province*, or the provinces, is economic as well as cultural and artistic. As in every European capital except Berlin, life in Paris is more expensive than in the rest of the country. Many of the young and not so young are nevertheless prepared to put up with cramped Parisian living conditions in return for the benefits of what they see as a more culturally enriching lifestyle. The popular mayor of Paris, Bertrand Delanoé, does a lot to focus the cultural life of the city, instituting events such as the now famous *Paris Plage*. In a nation with such traditional great differences between town and country, the anonymity of a big city is still what attracts many people to the capital. The French move house far less than the British or Americans and regional identity is still strong. It's not unusual for a French person who has lived in Paris for a number of years to tell you that they still live (*j'habite dans le...*) in whatever *pays* their family is from, rather

> ❝ **Rajaneesh Dwivedi is a musician and a trainer for a French software manufacturer. Fed up with an overly hectic London lifestyle he moved to Montpellier 10 years ago and has been living there ever since.**
>
> I didn't know anything about the town or even much about France before coming down here. I just saw it on the map, noticed it was beside the Med and decided to give it a try. I didn't even speak any French. I don't see myself moving back to the UK now. I've got too used to the sun. I'm lucky enough to be able to combine my IT skills with my knowledge of English and French. I started out as a programmer on a team of software designers a few years ago but as the company I work for has a lot of international clients, I have now taken on the role of product trainer. ❞

than telling you they are from there (*je suis de...*).

Like the Brits, the French list climate as a significant factor in choosing where to live. Montpellier and other towns in the south have grown significantly over the past few years. House prices in the Hérault, the *département* most favoured by the French, bear this out. Significant decentralisation of power to the regions means that regional towns have become more self-promoting and economically proactive. Well-paid skilled work is available throughout the towns and cities of France.

How many English speakers live in France and where?

While the French have gradually gravitated away from the countryside, the British and other nationalities have begun filling the gap created by what is known in France as *désertification*. In spite of complaints about rising house prices there is a recognition that *les étrangers* do contribute to rural life, restoring properties that would otherwise have been abandoned and providing work for local artisans. Rural municipalities and *départements* continue to make efforts to keep rural communities alive, providing incentives to French residents wishing to return to the countryside.

Statistics on the number of English speakers living in France vary a great deal depending on sources and definition. There are no official statistics from the French authorities but some estimates put the figure as high as 500,000.

A breakdown of British and Americans thought to be resident indicates, however, that the real total may be significantly lower.

Statistics: Brits and Americans living in France

Under European Union (EU) rules British nationals are no longer required to apply for a residence permit (a *carte de séjour*) and this makes it hard to be certain of the actual numbers of residents from the UK. Going on the most recent figures released by INSEE (the National Institute for Statistics and Economic Studies), we can say that there are currently around 125,000 British residents spread throughout France. Most estimates of the American population in France put the figure somewhere around 100,000, not including government staff and the army, with most of this in and around Paris. Although INSEE's figures for Americans are much lower they do confirm the concentration of Americans around the capital. Brits with French properties number approximately 550,000 with the majority of these being holiday or second homeowners.

Moving to France from the UK

For Brits buying property in France, choosing where to do so may well be dictated by transport links to the UK. France is the number one cheap flight destination from UK airports and most areas of the country are within easy reach for short breaks. Cheap flights have had a dramatic impact on the price of properties in some areas. Of course, this makes prices vulnerable to route changes by flight companies but with projected figures on air travel showing a doubling of numbers of British passengers over the next 25 years, it seems unlikely that this will be a significant worry. Properties close to the Channel ports in Normandy and Brittany are of course immune to such risks. The Pas de Calais is not popular with second homebuyers, as the climate is too similar to that of the UK. The area is, however, increasingly being seen as a good choice for commuters, known in France as *frontaliers*, or those wishing to enjoy the French way of life while remaining within easy reach of the south-east of England. As of November 2007, however, 20 minutes travel time were taken off the Eurostar link to London. Estate agents in the Pas de Calais are reporting a significant increase in interest from UK buyers. Although house prices have increased in France in recent years, the cost of property has risen even faster on the other side of the Channel. For those who can't afford to buy in the UK, the commute to France is becoming a very real alternative. Provence and the Côte d'Azur (or French Riviera) remain popular with certain buyers, even if the coast is overdeveloped. Properties with a good view of the sea command a 50% premium over those without one. To get away from tourists and live in the 'real France', it's becoming more and more necessary to head inland.

France has seen unusually rapid rises in property prices in popular areas. As already mentioned, prices have been rising fast in the Hérault. Corsica has also been seeing high annual rises. In 2003 and 2004 prices nationally went up by 14.2% and 15.3% respectively. They have continued to increase but are now doing so at a slower rate, down to 7.1% in 2006 and 3.8% in 2007. The huge influx of Brits has certainly affected prices, but by the same token the slowdown in the UK market is leading to a drop in the number of those going to France to look for property. Tougher lending conditions as a result of the subprime crisis and an economic slowdown both in Britain and France mean that the current property climate is uncertain, with stagnation even possible. Rather than simply buying a second home, the trend is now for Britons to move to France and start a business. There are fewer real bargains available in the previously very popular areas. The stagnation of property prices in the Netherlands and Germany has also affected the level of home-buying activity by foreigners.

The traditional bastion of British homeowners, the Dordogne, has become very expensive, and many are now buying in Charente instead. The Lot and Tarn have already become almost as expensive as the Dordogne. The Ariège and Aude are no longer all that cheap. The British still perceive the Pyrénées Orientales as 'too far away'. Attention has shifted to the previously unfashionable central regions of Limousin and Auvergne, but these areas are more attractive to those who would like to remain in France for the longer term.

FACT

UK OFFICE OF NATIONAL STATISTICS

■ Of the 400,000 long-term emigrants from the UK last year, 24% moved to France and Spain.

FACT

■ A survey on house prices in areas near cheap flight destinations found that between 2001 and 2006 prices of homes in south-west France near Bergerac airport rose by 157%.

A 'For Sale' sign in Bergerac en Dordogne

■ CHOOSING WHERE TO LIVE

The neighbourhoods of Paris

Most of the Paris we see today is a result of a 19th century urban remodelling, the so-called Haussmannisation (named after the Baron Haussman who was commissioned by Napoleon III to restructure city). The works (1852 and 1870) encompassed all aspects of urban planning (streets and boulevards, regulations imposed on facades of buildings, public parks, sewers and water works, city facilities and public monuments) and transformed the old Paris, a dense labyrinth of medieval narrow streets and half-timber houses. Haussman levelled entire quarters to make way for wide tree-lined boulevards and expansive gardens with their cafés and shops.

Unchanging borders, strict building codes and lack of developable land have kept the capital relatively small so that it takes less than three hours to walk across the city from north to south. The Paris Métro system has 16 lines and distances between stations are generally quite short. Cycling is becoming more and more popular since the setting up of more cycling paths and the introduction of the *Vélib* service (2007), a network of docking stations around Paris for more than 10,600 bicycles available at modest rental prices to the public. Life is getting harder for cars as the town becomes deliberately less car friendly. The closer to the centre you are, the tougher the restrictions. If you want to run a car in Paris, the best idea is to rent a *box* (a garage space).

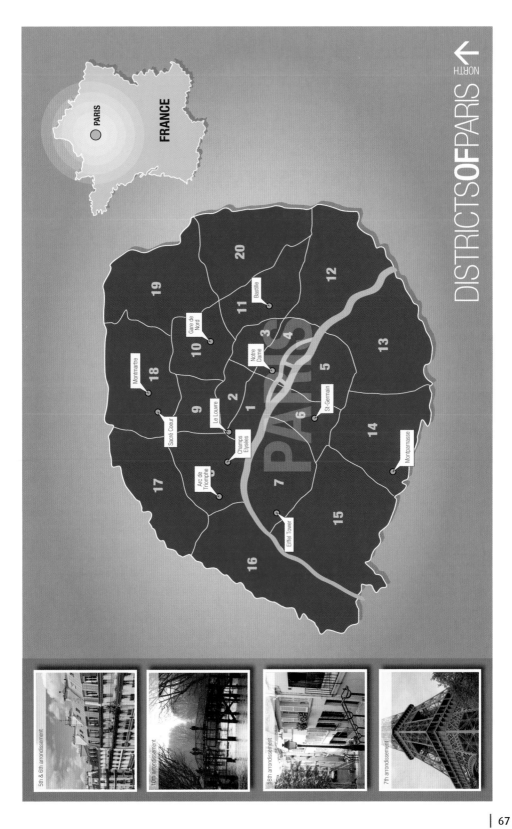

DISTRICTS**OF**PARIS

NORTH

FRANCE
PARIS

20
19
12
11   Bastille
10   Gare de Nord
18   Montmartre
3   Notre Dame
4
13
9   Le Louvre
2
5
1
Sacré Coeur
St-Germain
6
17   Arc de Triomphe
Champs Elysées
14   Montparnasse
7
15   Eiffel Tower
16

5th & 6th arrondissement

10th arrondissement

18th arrondissement

7th arrondissement

The city is divided into 20 *arrondissements* (municipal boroughs) arranged in the form of a clockwise spiral. It is divided in two by the River Seine: *Rive Droite* (the Right Bank, north) and *Rive Gauche* (the Left Bank, south). Rather than deal with the *arrondissements* in numerical order here, we have chosen a more geographical approach, beginning with the Left Bank.

Finding an apartment in Paris can be a excruciating experience. If you do it by yourself (i.e. without an agency, using only classified advertising), you will have to see it as a full time job for two or three weeks. For further information on the formal minutiae of renting, see the later sections in this chapter. Below we provide average rental prices for unfurnished apartments without charges (an extra €100–€400 a month). Note, the prices given are the prices you can expect to pay as a well-informed foreigner (you may pay much more). You will meet locals paying far less but they will be in social housing or government apartments, or in residences with protected rents, which you will not have access to.

The Left Bank or Rive Gauche

The Left Bank bears traces of the roman origins of the city: the Roman amphitheatre and baths are in the heart of the Quartier Latin, which is also one of the city's most romantic districts. This is the Paris of artists, writers, and philosophers, of Sartre, Hemingway and other famous members of the artistic community in Montparnasse.

■ 5th and 6th

The Quartier Latin (5th and 6th) is known for its village-like atmosphere of bistros, cinemas and jazz cafés. Housing la Sorbonne, the Ecole Normale Superieure and Jussieu, it's a major educational centre but also the fashionable quarter for anyone who wants to live in the heart of things. Drink in the various cafés, visit the Institut du Monde Arabe, stroll in Jardin de Luxembourg or wander the fashionable shops on Boulevard Saint Germain.

The area is popular with students, teachers and single expats on short-term contracts. Families could find living here a bit stressful.

■ The 7th

Here you will find the National Assembly and numerous government ministries as well as major tourist attractions such as the Eiffel Tower, the Hôtel des Invalides (Napoleon's burial site), the Champ de Mars, Ecole Militaire and the Musée Rodin.

This is a sophisticated urban quarter with handsome buildings overlooking small gardens. Apartments here are expensive but generally come with attractive features such as marble fireplaces, high ceilings and wooden floors. The 7th attracts executives and international officials because of its closeness to Unesco and the Organisation for Economic Co-operation and Development (OECD). Residents enjoy the leafy boulevards, gardens and the quiet atmosphere. Parking is usually easy.

■ The 15th

This is mainly a residential neighbourhood with little tourism, but two lovely parks (Parc André Citroen and Parc Georges Brassens). The main streets (the rue de Commerce, Cambronne and La Motte Picquet) are busy with shops. The 15th also shares the lively Montparnasse district with the 14th. There is a community feel, chic on its border with the 7th, but mostly affordable. With modern and traditional

---

TIP

■ Ask your employer about the 1% scheme, as you may qualify for cheaper rent through this scheme, which is supported by any large employer in and around the capital. Go to www. pap.fr to get a more detailed idea of prices of different-sized apartments in different areas of the city.

QUARTIER LATIN: THE FACTS

■ Rents are high: (1,000/month for a studio to €2,500 for a three-bedroom apartment.
■ Good for students
■ Buzzing night life
■ Great cultural offer
■ Parking is difficult

Apartments in the Quartier Latin, 5th and 6th

architecture, most streets are calm and relaxed. On the Seine, a number of high-rise apartment blocks give great views of the city. The parks, shops and range of apartments make the 15th a favourite with families. Good access to Versailles and La Défense business district.

■ The 14th

The area around Boulevard Montparnasse used to be very popular among American expats. There's a great café-restaurant culture and night life with brasseries such as La Coupole or La Closerie des Lilasí, famous for famous clients (Picasso, Hemingway, Lenin and Trotsky). Many Breton *crêperies* can be found off the boulevard (Gare Montparnasse is the terminus for trains from Normandy and Brittany) and there's a great choice of cinemas and a shopping complex at the foot of Tour Montparnasse.

Further into the 14th the neighbourhoods are more residential with good access to the *péripherique* (the ring road) and Orly airport. Rents are reasonable to high. The 13th, 14th and the 15th have changed less over recent years, in terms of population make-up and feel, than the residential areas of the Rive Droite. Strange to say for one of Europe's busy capitals, certain quarters can feel tyrannically calm at times.

■ The 13th

Another residential *arrondissement*, it has the largest Chinatown in Paris. Near the river is the new Bibliothèque François Mitterand and there is a busy night scene in music bar-boats (Batofar) moored on the Seine.

The north-west has some of the charm of the Latin quarter, but the outer areas are dominated by high-rise and industry. On the whole, the 13th is calm, has plenty

A row of town houses in Butte aux Cailles

of green areas, good local shops and reasonable rents. There are both traditional (north) and modern (south) apartments and there is good access to suburbs in the south and east. La Butte aux Cailles is a quaint little hamlet, with charming gardens and restaurants.

The Right Bank or Rive Droite

The Rive Droite includes 14 of the 20 *arrondissements*, ranging from some of the richest parts of the city in the 16th *arrondissement* round to the more working class north and east (18th round to the 12th). All of these less central *arrondissements* are where the main residential areas are while the 2nd, 8th and 9th have active business areas. The 1st and the 4th have extensive shopping and administrative activity. The centres of night life are in the redlight district around Pigalle, the trendy Oberkampf and Bastille, as well as Le Marais and some more upmarket clubs and restaurants off the Champs Elysées.

■ The 16th

Rents in the 16th are some of the highest in Paris, with the minimum for a one-bedroom apartment starting at €1,200 and €2,600 for a three-bedroom pad. The large and light properties make for an upmarket, conservative, residential area including Auteuil and Passy (with an almost village ambiance), many embassies and the widest boulevard in Paris, the Avenue Foch. The Bois de Boulogne borders its western side, increasing the already attractive aspects of the 16th for families. Some of the top sporting venues in France are here: Roland-Garros, and the Parc des Princes among others. Business activity is considerable (especially in the area around Kléber) with the number of jobs almost equalling the number of inhabitants. Culturally, places of note are the Trocadéro, just across the Seine from the Eiffel Tower, and the Palais de Tokyo, a centre for contemporary art and the Radio France building.

The 17th

The 17th is split between a more working class northern area around Place de Clichy and Pigalle and exclusive quarters to the south, with important business activity, especially in the financial sector near Parc Monceau. Along the Boulevard de Clichy, there are some good-value residential streets (especially on the south side where you will find plenty of small boutiques and nicely kept cafés and restaurants). Here, you're within walking distance of Montmartre and the night life of Pigalle. Les Batignolles is another oasis of greenery, a park very much in the French style around which a popular organic food market is held once a week. The Palais des Congrès will be well-known to many, perhaps as a premier conference centre but also because buses leave from here for the low-cost airport in Beauvais.

The 18th

The 18th is made up of three main areas, the touristy Montmartre (with the Basilica Sacré-Cœur and its view over the city), the redlight district around the Moulin Rouge (shared with the 9th) and the African and North African area to the east. Dropping down from Montmartre, the scenery changes suddenly after crossing the Boulevard de Barbès. Known as the Quartier de La Goutte d'Or there is a colourful market but also problems with drugs and prostitution, and this was the only area within Paris itself to feature in the riots at the end of 2005 (otherwise confined to the *banlieues* (suburbs)). Rents here are some of the lowest in Paris but much more expensive in Montmartre and Abbesses, which are both pleasantly residential but can become over-run with tourists. The bars and restaurants on rue des Abbesses are popular with locals and many of the café-terraces are busy right through the winter, the clientele clustering under overhead gas heating. There are also many artists/creators/designers' shops in the small side streets.

The 19th

Situated next to the *péripherique*, La Villette is one of the cultural centres of the city, with the Cité des Sciences and Cité de la Musique and open grassy areas near the Canal Saint Martin. *La Pétanque* (boules) is played along the banks of the canal and people come to picnic there or go to the nicely situated cinemas by the water. Populous residential areas stretch up from the Avenue Jean Jaurès and the Buttes Chaumont (a large, popular park for both joggers and sunbathers). This is one of the few *arrondissements* in Paris with a growing population. Rents are reasonable and there is more open space than in any other *arrondissement*.

The 20th

Belleville and Ménilmontant are two more of the city's most cosmopolitan areas and Belleville has the second largest Chinatown. These are traditionally more working class districts but are subject to the general gentrification that has taken place in all the more working class areas of the city over the past 20 years. Rents are low but rising and properties here include more houses (rather than apartments) than you will find in the other districts of the city.

Monmartre, 18th

The 20th also houses some of the city's most famous dead: Jim Morrison, Oscar Wilde, Chopin, Edith Piaf and Proust (to name but a few) are buried in the Père Lachaise cemetery.

The 12th

A thriving business district has grown up around the new Ministry of Finance at Bercy and other new developments include the renovation of the Cours St Emillion (old storage area for the wine industry) which now houses bars, restaurants and a large cinema. The Parc de Bercy and the Promenade Plantée (a raised garden walkway) make this district ideal for families looking for a bit of space. Rents are comparable to the 20th or the 19th. Easy access to the busier shopping and cultural districts in the centre of the city.

To the east of the 12th are some of the more affordable residential areas around Bois de Vincennes (Vincennes is the large green area to the east of the city and contains a large lake and zoo), including Montreuil and Fontenay-sous-Bois.

The Cité de Science, 19th

The 11th

The 11th stretches down from the Place de la République to the Bastille and includes a picturesque food and craft market, with

Pere la chaise cemetery, 20th

THE 18TH: THE FACTS

- Rents: €550–€1,000 for a one-bedroom flat and upwards of €1,500 for a three-bedroom apartment
- Tourists throng Montmartre
- Barbès is colourful but edgy
- Parking difficult
- Artists' and designers' boutiques near Abbesses

children's play areas along the continuation of the Canal Saint-Martin (underground at this point). The rue Oberkampf and the surrounding streets have a lively night life with bars and small clubs popular amongst young Parisians. As a result, many single adults live in this district but there are also more family-oriented parts and the 11th is not so central as to be too busy and over-run. The long Boulevard Voltaire leads down to Place de la Nation.

■ The 10th

Two of the busiest stations in Europe are found in the 10th: the Gare du Nord, for the Eurostar to London and the Gare de l'Est for trains to Strasbourg, Geneva and Germany. The Boulevard Magenta, with its controversial tree-lined cycle lanes stretches down the west side of the *arrondissement*. The Canal Saint-Martin also goes north to south and has become a popular hang-out for young Parisian Bobos (*Bourgeois-Bohèmes*) and families. Property prices have consequently risen and what used to be a very working class district, popularised in the classic movie, *L'hotel du Nord* - "*Atmosphere! Atmosphere! Est-ce que j'ai une gueule d'atmosphère?*", has seen old workshops gradually being renovated into trendy apartments.

The 10th also has a thriving Indian/Sri Lankan area, with shops and low-priced restaurants near the Gare du Nord and the Passage Brady.

■ The 9th

The 9th and the 10th are far less populous than the *arrondissements* that border them to the north

THE 19TH: THE FACTS

- Rents: €700 for a one-bedroom apartment or €1,700 for a three-bedroom family-sized place
- Open spaces and cultural areas
- Ideal for families
- Parking available
- Cosmopolitan, residential feel

and east. The 9th stretches down from the redlight district at Pigalle to the Grands Boulevards and the shopping areas on Boulevard Haussman (the Galéries Lafayette are the Parisian equivalent of London's Harrods with designer labels having their own sections and a large food hall downstairs). The area south of Pigalle contains some lively clubs and bars in its small streets but also has family-friendly pockets. The 9th shares a thriving business area around Opéra with the 8th and the 2nd.

■ The 8th

The Champs Elysées is no longer as classy as it once was but is still Paris' premier shopping street, leading from the Place de la Concorde (at the top of the Tuileries) up to the Arc de Triomphe. There are many other places of interest in the 8th, including the presidential compound around the Elysée Palace as well as several ministries and museums. Due to administrative, business and commercial activities the working population far outweighs the residential one and rents here are on the high side.

■ The 4th

The 4th is less of a residential area and rather a great mix of lively bars, restaurants, boutiques, art galleries, beautiful squares and the Pompidou Centre. The narrow medieval streets of one of the oldest Parisian districts known as the Marais are now one of the

THE 20TH: THE FACTS

- Rents: €700–800 for a one-bedroom apartment
- Parc de Belleville
- Cosmopolitan cuisine: Chinese and North African
- Variety of properties including some houses
- Jim Morrison's grave

Living near a forest

There are also wonderful forests all over Ile de France and you could do far worse than choose to live in a dormitory town near one of these. Property will generally be considerably cheaper and excellent transport links mean commuting is not too arduous – one barometer of this is the fact that translations of chapters of Mills & Boon novels (les romans à l'eau-de-rose) are cut down to two-thirds the length in French, so as to fit in with reduced commuting times. The best-known forest is, no doubt, Fontainebleau, but perhaps even more beautiful is the forest in Vallée de la Chevreuse (St-Rémy-les-Chevreuse on RER B to the southeast of Paris). L'Ile Adam to the north also has some pleasant areas, though parts of neuf-trois, as this département is known to its residents, are rundown high-unemployment districts with all the associated social problems. To the east of Paris you will find the reasonably priced districts of Fontenay and Nogent, still close to Paris and bordering the Parc de Vincennes.

most bustling areas of the city and the diverse Jewish, artistic and gay communities give the area a cosmopolitan soul.

To the south is the Hotel de Ville, the central city hall, and the shops of the rue de Rivoli. The bank of the Seine then overlooks the two islands of St Louis and La Cité, which are also included within the fourth *arrondissement*. The islands are now one of the most sought after and expensive residential areas of Paris.

The 4th Arrondissement

The 3rd

The 3rd makes up a relatively small area, with a small but rapidly expanding Chinatown. It becomes more trendy towards the south with a labyrinth of narrower southern streets leading to the Marais, the Picasso museum, the National Archives and renaissance Place des Vosges. Mostly however, the pace is more pedestrian with the tiny parks, restaurants, cafés and bars. Apartments are less grandiose than in other areas but charming nevertheless.

The 2nd

Three main areas: the trendy Montorgueil is lively both day and night with local commerce, cafés, restaurants and bars, and is a favourite for the young and young at heart. The business district near Bourse, the old stock exchange, is busy during the day but relatively peaceful once the traffic dies down. Opéra offers a livelier evening scene and remains busy day and night. Apartments near Opéra are chic and popular with tourists but it's rather soulless as a residential community.

The boulevards, which form the border of the second, such as the Grands Boulevards and Etienne Marcel are popular shopping districts and also offer typical but unremarkable cafés and brasseries.

The 1st

A large part of the surface area of the 1st is taken up by the Tuileries gardens and the Louvre. The Banque de France is also headquartered here and the rue de Rivoli houses many luxury goods and fashion boutiques. The 1st is, not surprisingly, the least populated of all the Parisian *arrondissements* and it's extremely difficult to find rented accommodation here even if you can afford it. There is a significant working population centred on business, retail and administrative activities. Les Halles, the largest shopping centre within Paris, is here.

Living outside 'La Périph'

In spite of the reputation of the *banlieues* as dangerous places to be, this by no means covers all outlying districts, some of which are as chic and well-to-do as the centre of town and certainly offer a better quality of life in terms of space and closeness to nature.

La Défense, to the west of Paris is one of Europe's busiest business districts. La Grande Arche is at the western-most end of a 10km axis that leads from the Obelisk at Place de la Concorde, through the Arc de Triomphe and Neuilly-sur-Seine. Other impressive modern architecture towers above the surrounding residential areas of Puteaux, Courbevoie, Suresnes and St Cloud. These areas tend to be upmarket and popular with executives with jobs in La Défense. To the south and the terminus of the tram that goes round the west side of Paris to La Défense is the booming commune of Issy-les-Moulineaux. The proactive mayor has attracted a great deal of business to the commune over the past 20 years.

■ RENTING

Accommodation available to rent

It's quite possible to search for properties to rent over the internet (see Finding accommodation for some useful sites). You will almost certainly need to be on the spot to finalise any arrangements but at least a web search can give you an idea of what's available before you go. It may take some ingenuity to stay for a few months in your chosen area because French property rental laws are notoriously rigid. It doesn't help if you simply turn up with the cash in your hand either! There is a dearth of short-term rented property at a reasonable price and it's in the owner's interest to have a formal contract drawn up whatever length of time you may wish to stay. Tenants are heavily protected by the law, and it's almost impossible to evict them unless they do something extremely serious. Paradoxically, this has created enormous problems for those who don't have the necessary documentation (including foreigners!). If you are a tenant then you will most likely be asked to sign a contract. Even for short-term rentals, a contract is required. Informal arrangements are possible with some foreign owners; these are advertised in local cafés and other expatriate hangouts as well as in magazines and on websites.

The law makes a clear distinction between furnished and unfurnished property. Anything that has the basics you need for daily life can be rented out as furnished, or *meublé*. Furnished accommodation is governed by the *Location Libre* rules, which favour owners over tenants. If anything is missing from the furnishings then the premises are considered unfurnished. There is plenty of furnished accommodation available in large French towns but it's harder to find elsewhere, except for holiday lets. Equally, smaller apartments tend to be furnished but larger apartments or houses usually come unfurnished. Furnished rentals are covered by a minimal number of regulations in the Code Civil. If the rental qualifies as furnished, then the period of the lease can be set at 6, 12 or 24 months. The contract will specifically state that the rules of the 1989 law on rentals (updated in 2007) don't apply to: *location saisonnière* (seasonal rental), *résidence secondaire* (not the principal residence) or *logement de fonction* (rental linked to the exercise of a job).

About leasing

Most long-term lets come under the 1989 law, with a minimum three-year lease where the lessor is a private person or a family business, or six years where the lessor is a company. The lease is automatically renewable for another three years, unless the owner can give compelling reasons for ending it, e.g. they intend to sell the property, they need it for their family, or the tenant has broken the terms of the lease. The owner has to give six months' notice before ending the lease, otherwise it continues automatically for another three years. The tenant can give three months' notice to leave, or possibly one month if he or she can prove that they are forced to leave by circumstances beyond their control, e.g. because of loss of employment, being posted by their employer to another area, health reasons if they are over 60, etc. The contract can be for less than three years, but not less than one year, as long as the lessor informs the lessee before the contract is signed that the property is to be sold or used by a family member. The reason for having a shorter lease must be put in the contract, and the lessor has to inform the lessee that the event that requires the lease to end has actually happened, two months before the end of the lease.

Renting costs

For the most recent statistics visit www.fnaim.fr. Statistics for rentals are published as per square metre. Larger apartments/houses are relatively cheaper as they comprise more square metres. Rentals are subject to state controls. Rentals can be increased at the start of a new contract, or when an existing contract comes to an end. Price rises have not been extreme. Between 1997 and 2008 they rose at an average 3.5% per year, the largest rise being in the Côte d'Azur, and increasingly popular cities such as Paris, Montpellier, La Rochelle and Tours. Brittany and Alsace-Lorraine have had the lowest rises. Rental values don't vary by a great deal around France; it's only in Paris and the centre of some big cities that prices are very high.

Letting contracts under the 1989 law don't permit rent rises higher than the rate of inflation. If the rent is obviously too low, then the owner can make a case for raising it. In Paris, the rules are more flexible, and owners can raise rents in relation to the going rate for the particular type of building in the area. Rent can also be raised if the owner has spent money on doing up the property, so that it has increased in value.

In addition to the rent there may well be compulsory insurance cover (*multirisques habitation*) and service charges (*les charges locatives*, which cover things such as

Typical Rents		
Property	Area	Rent per month € (unfurnished)
3 bed flat	Paris suburbs (80 sq m)	€1,000–1,400
1 bed flat	Paris suburbs (35 sq m)	€400–700
3 bed flat	Within Paris (80 sq m)	€1,200–2,000
1 bed flat	Within Paris (35 sq m)	€750–1,200
2 bed town house	Normandy	€500
1 bed apartment	Montpellier	€550

lift costs, cleaning and maintenance of shared areas, gardening and the *concierge*), in the case of an apartment block. Apartments are usually in a *copropriété*, jointly owned and run by its co-owners. Some of the residents in the *copropriété* are owner-occupiers, and others will be tenants.

Finding accommodation to rent

You can find advertisements for rented accommodation in many of the same publications and websites as those advertising property for sale. Local newspapers also often carry rental ads. Look under *locations*. French estate agents or *immobiliers* deal with rental accommodation as well as property for sale; some of them specialise in this area. Otherwise it's a matter of looking on notice boards, or in shop windows, or in the windows of properties, where there will be signs saying '*A louer*' (for rent).

For foreign house-hunters the situation can be a difficult one. Short-term rented accommodation in tourist areas is expensive, and you may have to resort to house-sitting, or to renting *gîtes* which are sometimes uncomfortable out of season. If you are looking for a *gîte* you could start by consulting the following websites:

FUSAC (France USA Contacts) and Craig's List

FUSAC is a free magazine containing classified ads for the English-speaking community of Paris and the surrounding area but rentals or house sitting opportunities for the rest of France are also sometimes advertised. It comes out every two weeks and you can find it in Parisian cafés, bookstores, internet cafés and so on. You can also check out offers online at www.fusac.fr.

Another useful site is www.craigslist.org, which has local classifieds and a wealth of other information on forums for jobs, housing, for sale, personals and other services.

- www.rentals.com
- www.locations-vacances-en-france.com
- www.appart-in-france.com
- www.toutpartout.com

The following websites have extensive information on short-let accommodation and a wide choice of rentals:

- www.only-apartments.com
- www.marie-a-tout-prix.com
- www.perfectplaces.com

Otherwise you can try to come to some arrangement with a foreign property-owner, by advertising in the usual French property magazines such as the *Particulier à Particulier* which has an excellent site in English and French at www.pap.fr.

The rental agreement

Documentation
If you find property to rent while you are on the spot, you should have certain documents with you to present to the agent/landlord:
- Photocopy of your passport (pages with name, date, and place of birth, dates of issue and expiry).
- Employer's attestation, stating salary.
- References from previous leases.

Problems you may face without local references or a credit history
If you don't have a French bank account and if you don't have references from previous leases you must at least provide the agent/landlord with bank statements from your account back home, although this will normally not be sufficient. Usually you will need to open a French bank account as soon as you begin renting. This will also be useful in establishing connection with basic utilities.

The extensive legislation designed to protect tenants has in many ways backfired as it means that landlords/ladies are reluctant to sign a contract with anyone who can't back up their signature with further proof of being able to service rental payments. In many French towns where there is a shortage of rental accommodation, young people often struggle with this issue, having to fall back on help from family and friends or sometimes resorting to desperate measures such as forging pay slips!

If you decide to rent direct from the owner of a property, make sure you understand the rental agreement fully before you sign or hand over any money. If you are renting in France for the first time, it's advisable to get help from a French friend or another neutral third party.

Les enfants de Don Quichotte

Les enfants de Don Quichotte, an association set up to show solidarity with the homeless, or *sans abris*, organised a flamboyant demonstration in December 2006. They set up a line of red tents on both sides of the Canal Saint-Martin in the 10th *arrondissement* in Paris to highlight the problems certain sections of the population have in finding housing. The movement spread throughout the country and red tents appeared in Strasbourg, Bordeaux, Dax, Toulouse, Lille, Marseille, Nice, Aix-en-Provence, Avignon and Lyon. They succeeded in gaining a great deal of media attention and promises from the authorities that new housing would be provided.

Issues covered in the rental agreement

A lease is generally simply known as a *bail* (plural *baux*), but it can be called a *bail de location,* a *bail locatif* or a *bail d'habitation.* The contract is a *contrat de bail.* Lessees have certain basic rights that can't be infringed, one of them being the right to keep a pet (although this could be challenged in a court if you have an exotic animal such as a monkey or a boa constrictor). You have a right to register a company at your rented address for a period of five years. If there is nothing to prevent you in the lease, you can work from home as a self-employed person, but you will not be able to receive customers at home or take deliveries of goods. If you intend to work from home, then you will most likely have to take out a *bail mixte,* i.e. a mixed lease, permitting professional activities. An ordinary lease will usually have a clause preventing you from carrying out professional activities using your rented accommodation. The lessor can't compel you to pay the rent by standing order. You can, if you wish, pay in cash.

Basic rental agreement

■ A rent review clause in the lease can only be exercised once a year; until now rent increases have been limited to a statutory amount linked to the Cost of Construction Index. President Sarkozy has asked for increases to be linked to the Consumer Price Index. In practice, increases have been higher in large towns over recent years.

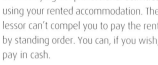

■ Giving notice, making complaints, etc, must always be done by registered letter (*lettre recommandée*), otherwise the notification has no legal force.

A landlord/lady will usually ask for *le dépôt de garantie* (bond and deposit), but the latter may not exceed the equivalent sum of two months rent and this must be returned to the tenant within two months of the end of the lease, less any outstanding rent. At the time of writing, discussions are under way to reduce this to one month's rent but no legislation is yet in place. In addition you will need to pay one month's rent in advance, plus other costs such as building charges.

■ The tenant is obliged to pay certain service charges and to insure with a suitable company (see Insurance below) of his or her choice. Typically, electricity is metered and paid for by the tenant, although water charges may be part of the service charges. There will be clauses about the use to which the property can be put. You can't run a business from a property which involves customers coming to the property, or deliveries of goods, unless you have the permission of the owners.

■ It's advisable to have an inventory (*état des lieux*) of the contents of the property and their condition prepared at the start and the end of the lease in order to prevent disputes when it comes to the deposit being returned. Tenants are strongly advised to take dated photographs of any existing damage to the property, with a conventional rather than digital camera. You may find that landlord/lady will try to keep back some of the deposit unless you can show when you leave that the condition of the property is the same as when you arrived.

Insurance for tenants

A tenant (*locataire*) should always arrange appropriate insurance for the property. Apart from being sensible and prudent, it's a legal requirement that one has third-party insurance for property. It's usual to extend this basic insurance to cover all risks, including theft and damage by fire, with a comprehensive policy known as an *assurance multirisques*. Obtaining this cover may be compulsory in the case of a rented property, but you can open a policy with whichever insurance company you choose; the landlord/lady can't dictate this. Check that the previous policy has actually been cancelled. If your rented home is part of a *copropriété* then, in most cases, the *copropriété* will provide and charge you part of the cost of the *multirisques* insurance to cover the building as a whole.

Insurance rates are on a scale of charges according to square metres and the location. There are some areas, including Paris, Marseille and parts of the Côte d'Azur where high crime levels make it difficult to obtain more than a very limited theft insurance at anything like a reasonable price. For documents in English on French insurance, see the website www.ffsa.fr. Insurance firms are listed under Insurance.

TIP

■ You shouldn't underestimate the need for documentation when looking for rental accommodation in France as this can prove a very real obstacle to moving in.

Useful contacts

At Home in France: ☎+1 541 488 9467; info@athomeinfrance.com; www.athomeinfrance.com. Properties all over France

Just France: ☎+1 610 407 9633; info@justfrance.com; www.justfrance.com. Superior and luxury vacation and holiday rental properties all over France

Chez Nous: ☎0870 336 7679 (from the UK); www.cheznous.com. Search for properties online. Prospective tenants deal with owners direct

Cosmopolitan Services Unlimited: ☎+33 (0)1 44 90 10 10; email see website; www.cosmopolitanservices.com. Relocation assistance for both companies and their executives

Paris Appartements Services: ☎+33 (0)1 40 28 01 28; info@paris-apts.com; www.paris-apts.com. Short-term fully furnished Parisian flats available from a minimum of five nights in the best locations in the heart of the city. Take advantage of rates at €100 per day, including tax, weekly cleaning and linen changes for stays of seven days and more

Quality Villas: ☎+44 (0)1442 870055; www.quality-villas.co.uk. An established family business that lets out privately owned French properties; additional services including maids, chef/cook or babysitter can be arranged if required. Properties publicised on their site are personally checked out

Apartrental: ☎ in France: +33 (0)6 27 79 40 44; in Australia +61 (0) 419 511 861; in USA +1 267 761 8662; email see website; www.apartrental.com. For Paris and the south of France

Caretaking/house-sitting

For those -wanting to live in France economically, there is an alternative to renting.
There is definitely scope for caretaking foreign-owned properties and this can be

TIP

■ A rental agency will charge a commission, which is usually split between the lessor and the lessee. But if the accommodation is furnished the lessee usually pays all of the commission, which can be as much as two months' rent. It's therefore to your advantage to locate rental accommodation by word of mouth or through newspaper adverts placed by individuals.

> *Geoff Halstead and partner Judith Lee left for France intending to stay for several years*
>
> We didn't want to buy because we wanted some degree of freedom to move. At first we considered buying a mobile home, but on a logistical basis it seemed daunting. We then thought the only real alternative would be to rent a series of properties in different regions, but this would have been expensive. Finances have, however, been eased because we have now arranged to be winter caretakers for a group of cottages in Brittany on a nil rent/nil salary basis. In effect this means that we live rent free for seven months out of 12.
>
> To get this offer we placed an advert in French Property News (www.french-property.com) offering our services as no cost 'guardians' (caretakers) to anyone with property anywhere in France. Judging by the response, there is potential for this kind of arrangement.

i Visit www.mindmyhouse.com or www.sabaticalhomes.com for ideas about living as a caretaker.

Home exchange *i*

An alternative way to explore a region before looking for a property is to swap your home with a French family. There are several agencies based in Britain and the USA that facilitate this. As France and Italy are much in demand you need to plan in advance to set up a swap. They generally work on the basis that you pay a subscription to have your details entered in an exchange directory. Most of those participating are either professional people, with or without children, or retired.

TIP

■ The specifics of the rental arrangement should be carefully checked in each case, as the *copropriété* insurance may not cover damage and/or theft, which is limited exclusively to your private areas of the building.

an excellent way of getting to know a particular region before committing yourself to a huge outlay. In recent years several websites promoting house-sitting opportunities have appeared. Some charge a small fee to the house-sitter while others are free.

Useful addresses

Dial An Exchange: various contact numbers worldwide at www.dialanexchange. com. A worldwide holiday homeowners' club which enables owners to swap empty weeks in their property for weeks in other holiday homes worldwide. Also recruits local agents willing to work flexible hours

Green Theme International: admin@gti-home-exchange.com; www.gti-home-exchange.com

Home Base Holidays: www.homebase-hols.com. Member of the First Home Exchange Alliance, along with one US and two French agencies: The Invented City, Troc'Adhero and Green Theme

HomeExchange Inc: www.homeexchange.com. US-based agency

Intervac International: www.intervac.com and www.intervac.co.uk; started in 1953 as a home swap club for teachers, who still make up 30% of its members

The Invented City: info@invented-city.com; www.invented-city.com

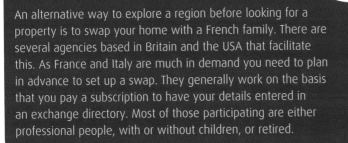

■ LOCAL TAXES

There are two types of property tax in France, *taxe foncière* and *taxe d'habitation*, both of which are calculated on the basis of an assumed rental value (*valeur locative*). These taxes are payable annually on 1 January and it's the person owning or occupying the property on that date who has to pay the full amount. It's a tenant's duty to notify the local authorities when he or she takes up residence in an area. If you buy property, then the *notaire* (notary) who handled the sale will inform the local authorities that you are now resident.

Taxe foncière

Taxe foncière is a land tax which is levied on the owner of any plot of land, except where the buildings are used exclusively for agricultural or religious purposes. For more details see 'Buying property'. In the case of rented property, it's the owner of the property who pays. They can put a clause in the rental contract requiring the tenant to reimburse them.

Taxe d'habitation

This is an occupancy tax levied on all property residents in France, regardless of whether they are the tenant or the owner of the property in which they live. The principle is that the person who has the property at their permanent and exclusive disposal on 1 January of a given year is the one who pays the *taxe d'habitation*. If the owner can prove that the property is uninhabitable, i.e. has no furniture in it, or is being renovated, they can qualify for a temporary exemption. This should be negotiated with the *Trésor Public*. A person who rents a property for a short term shouldn't pay the *taxe d'habitation*. Otherwise, the tenant pays the *taxe d'habitation*. Unoccupied, but habitable, holiday homes are liable for *taxe d'habitation*. There are however, various reductions which can be claimed from this tax if the applicant is either retired or has an elderly, dependant relative living with them: further details can be obtained from the local *mairie*. The *taxe d'habitation* is also calculated on the basis of a nominal rental value by the municipality and is adjusted annually to take account of inflation.

Taxe professionnelle

Anyone who makes a living from renting out property is liable to pay the *taxe professionnelle*. Owners of *gîtes* may or may not have to pay it, depending on the local municipality. Otherwise this is a tax paid by individuals and companies carrying on non-salaried business, i.e. the self-employed. The *taxe professionnelle* is very lucrative for municipalities and gives them half their source of income. As a tax on the self-employed, it's unpopular and seen as a disincentive to setting up your own business. One example of the incongruities of the *taxe professionelle* is that you aren't liable to pay the tax if you are an artisan without any employees. As such it's also a disincentive to taking anyone on. President Sarkozy has spoken out against the tax on several occasions and it may well be reformed as part of his programme for encouraging small businesses. At the time of writing however, no legislation had been passed.

Taxe balayage

Taxe balayage is the local road-cleaning tax; it can be charged to tenants. The rubbish collection tax, *taxe d'enlèvement des ordures ménagères,* can only be charged to tenants if it forms a separate item on the local tax bill.

█ UTILITIES, PHONE AND INTERNET

The image many outsiders have of France as resistant to globalisation and clinging to a stagnant social market model does not tally with the way in which successive French governments have privatised state-owned companies over the past two decades. Included are banks such as the BNP or Crédit Lyonais, the oil group Elf that has now been absorbed into Total and more recently autoroutes and airports.

The drive for privatisation in France

In 2005, after ceding France Telecom, the government carried through initial public offerings (IPOs) on the two giant utilities, Gaz de France (GDF) and Electricté de France (EDF). In spite of strong resistance from unions, over half the employees from each utility bought shares, giving them an enhanced stake in their employer's success. Long before President Sarkozy's flamboyant measures to reform labour laws, the French government had identified privatisation as a means of quietly removing itself from the cycle of industrial action that has plagued it for years.

What though does this mean for the consumer in terms of the supply of basic utilities? At the time of writing, liberalisation in the energy sector was only starting to make itself felt but will certainly do so more over the next few years. In contrast with energy, the telephone, internet and mobile phone market is already very competitive.

Deregulation of the energy market

In July 2007 the supply of electricity and gas to French households was deregulated. This means that EDF and Gaz de France no longer have a monopoly. France is one of the last countries in the EU to respond to the European-wide liberalisation of energy markets. As such it has learnt from the experience of countries such as the UK, Sweden and the Netherlands. In these countries, in broad terms, deregulation led to three types of offer being provided by different suppliers, and French suppliers have more or less adopted the same model: offers with guarantees on prices for one, two or three years; dual fuel offers (gas and electricity from the same supplier); and green energy offers. In the Netherlands, government subsidies made green energy a particularly attractive option and a high proportion of consumers made the switch, most often subscribing to the green offer provided by their old supplier. In the UK many users were induced to change supplier, attracted by price reductions in what became a very competitive market. The impact was not entirely positive as shown by the high number of complaints to the consumer body Energy Watch. Many

complaints centred on overly aggressive sales tactics, mistakes in billing and poor levels of customer service. Eight years on from the opening of energy markets in the UK, more than 50% of households have changed supplier. Recent price rises in deregulated markets are to a large extent due to rises in oil prices and the need for investment in infrastructure.

Traditionally electricity prices in France have been very competitive, due largely to the fact that around 85% of energy generated by EDF is nuclear energy. French households are likely to continue to have some of the lowest energy bills in Europe. Consumer surveys also show a high level of satisfaction with service.

The options now open to French consumers are whether to stay with their old supplier on a regulated tariff, subscribe to an open market offer with their old supplier or subscribe to an open market offer with a new supplier. There are currently

The deregulated market: what options for the individual consumer?

When markets were opened in 2007 one strong disincentive to changing suppliers was that once you moved away from EDF or Gaz de France you forfeited your right to their state-regulated tariffs. EDF (for electricity) and Gaz de France (for gas) still supply energy on a tariff structure regulated by the state, the *Commission de Régulation de l'Energie* (CRE), which are based on the old tariffs. Some new suppliers have been offering slightly lower prices, but because there is no guarantee that open market prices will remain low in the long term consumers have been reluctant to opt for what was an irreversible switch. Consumer associations such as the *Que Choisir* (www.quechoisir.org – a French language site) advised against changing supplier largely for this reason. A new law has changed this and may lead to more interest in alternative suppliers. It's only the generation and supply of energy that is now open to competition, not distribution. Distribution is managed by the *gestionnaire de réseau*, still EDF or Gaz de France in 95% of cases. If you are constructing or renovating a property you will probably need to contact your local *genstionnaire de réseau* to organise connection to these utilities.

FACT

■ In a recent survey by Eurobarometre on the advantages of opening the energy market to competition, 'Changing to a cleaner supplier' was the response most frequently cited by French households, far more times than 'Getting a better price' or 'Getting a better service'.

10 electricity suppliers and four gas suppliers operating nationally. EDF and Gaz de France supply both electricity and gas, but the regulated tariff for electricity is only available from EDF and the regulated tariff for gas only from Gaz de France.

It's important to know that meter readings are managed by the *gestionnaire de réseau*, not the supplier and that the choice of supplier is up to the occupier (the tenant rather than the owner). Make sure you get the *gestionnaire de réseau* to read the meter (*relevé spécial*) when you move in to new accommodation and remember you will need a bank statement and some other form of identification to set up your account. Electricity meters are read every six months, bills are sent every two months and the intervening readings are estimated. If you are never in when the meter reader calls you can arrange to send readings yourself, at a stipulated time.

The power supply in France is pretty much the universal standard (220–240V). Most appliances will work once you have the right adapters or plugs connected.

 The French language consumer information website, www.energie info.fr, explains the deregulated market and is an essential resource for information on energy supply in France.

Electricity tariffs

What makes life more interesting in France is that you can choose your level of power supply! You can upgrade or downgrade between 3kW and 36kW and various levels in between according to the size of your house, the type of heating you use, the number of electrical devices you use, your peak times of consumption and so

3kW	lighting, fridge, TV, computer, vacuum cleaner
6kW	washing machine, dishwasher, electric cooker, water heater
9kW	allows you to run two of the above simultaneously, along with the lighter appliances
12kW–36kW	makes it possible to run heavy equipment simultaneously, and electric heating as well.

on. Electricity is supplied at different kVA or kilovolt amperes (colloquially kilowatts or kW) depending on customer requirements. The following will give you an idea of how many kilowatts you might require:

The above are charged at different monthly rates. If you use very little electricity and only require 3kW then you can get a very low monthly standing charge. If you can remember not to run more than one heavy amperage appliance at a time then you may manage with 6kW; 9kW will give you more of a margin for error. If you increase the kilowattage higher than 12kW you may have to install heavier wiring to the electricity meter.

The higher your kW rating, the higher your standing charge. If you find your power keeps tripping off it's quite likely to be at a time when certain appliances are in use and your supply is insufficient to cope with the demand. Some people are quite happy with this arrangement and content to keep the lower rating supply, switching off the offending appliance and switching the power back on each time it happens. Otherwise you can upgrade.

There are three different tariffs for electricity consumption: the *Tarif de Base,* the *Tarif Heures Creuses,* and the *Tarif Tempo.* Which one is suitable for you depends on how much electricity you use:

■ *Base*: basic tariff for 3–18 kW use

■ *Heures Creuses/Heures Pleines*: allows you to benefit from cheaper electricity at periods of low demand. For 6–36 kW

■ *Tempo*: for heavy users, above 9 kW. The price varies according to three tariffs, with 300 white days, 43 blue days, and 22 red days, when the price is very high. This requires installation of a system to let you know what tariff is in force at any particular time

Gas

In urban areas you may have access to *gaz de ville,* mains gas. There is a similar payment system in place to electricity, with different tariffs depending on how much gas you use. Bills are sent every two months. Elsewhere it's usual to rely on bottled gas; it's easy to have it delivered to your home, or you can fetch it yourself. There is a choice between propane and butane. Propane is reckoned to be more suitable for properties where the temperature goes below freezing in winter. You may find you can't cook in the winter if you rely on butane. Alternatively you can have a *citerne* or metal container of about 2cu m installed on your property, which is periodically filled by a tanker with liquefied gas. The *citerne* should have a meter to show how much gas is left.

Water

Mains water is supplied by Générale des Eaux, now Véolia, and other local companies around France. Lyonnaise des Eaux is well known. There have been water shortages in central and southern France in recent years during hot weather. The water supply is metered and can cost twice as much as in some other countries such as the UK. There will be a meter outside the property. For more information on supply and connection when buying a property see the chapter *About France.*

FACT

■ The mains water supply is safe to drink, if not always that tasty. The French consume a lot of bottled mineral water, on average 100 litres per person per year.

> To find out the local price of water, and the nearest supplier visit
> www.generale-des-eaux.com

On average, mains water costs €2.8/cu m. The average person in the north of France uses 43cu m a year, while on the Côte d'Azur the figure is 74cu m. In Paris it's 66cu m. Evidently, it's worth investing in water-saving measures if possible.

Heating

Gas central heating is not common outside the cities; in much of France there is no mains gas supply. You are then left with a choice between cheap rate electricity, oil-filled radiators and wood-burning stoves. There are further implications for those buying property.

Water heaters

Besides the usual kinds of water heaters you will find the *chauffe-eau* (short for *chauffe-eau à accumulation*), a tank with a double skin that heats water using cheap tariff electricity or gas. A *chauffe-eau direct/à faible capacité* heats water at the point of delivery, i.e. by gas.

Whatever kind of heating system you use, be aware of the dangers of carbon monoxide poisoning. Every year 300 people are killed by this odourless gas in France and thousands injured by the careless use of gas or oil heaters in confined spaces without sufficient ventilation.

Telephone and internet services

As mentioned above the French telephone system has been deregulated and you can choose from different operators that offer competitive packages (prices are comparable with the UK but higher than in the USA) that often include television and internet connection. Among these are France Telecom, Neuf Cégetel, Talk Talk, Alice and Tele2. Price comparisons and other information can be found on the website www.comparatel.fr, which also gives information on mobiles. ADSL is the term the French use for broadband (actually an English acronym for asynchronous digital subscriber line!). ADSL is increasingly being extended to more rural areas.

It used to be said that France was some years behind in terms of internet use and availability. This was to some extent because of the pioneering system known as Minitel, which started in France in 1983 and provided a service similar to the internet many years before the internet was widely available elsewhere. Minitel consists of a keyboard and screen that sit alongside your telephone. Although Minitel has largely been superseded by the internet it's still popular and is likely to continue being used until at least 2010.

If you are travelling around in France it can be difficult to find cybercafés outside tourist towns. Internet terminals can be limited. Minitel can be used free in post offices.

British handsets need an adapter to work in France; the British variety have three wires, while the French have only two. Keys on French telephones are much the same as on British or American ones. The only point to note is that the hash symbol is

■ The ComparaTel website has a useful webpage where you can find out which operators supply which areas. You enter your phone number and the site tells you which operators supply that line and whether broadband and TV are available as part of the package, known as *dégroupage*.

■ As a precursor to the internet, Minitel is a source of national pride! You can access Minitel by logging on to www.minitel.fr. In 2007 €130 million worth of business was done on Minitel; €16 billion worth of business was done on the internet, however, up 35% on 2006.

Leaving a message on an answer phone

A typical French answer message goes something like this: *'Bonjour! Vous etes bien sur le 09 98 77 23 79. Je ne suis pas disponible actuellement. Veuillez laisser un message ou rappeler ultérieurement.'* Remember that in France, when quoting telephone numbers, people always group the numbers in pairs. The above number would therefore read: zéro neuf, quatre-vingt dix huit, soixante dix-sept, vingt trios, soixante dix-neuf.

called *dièse* – the same as a 'sharp' in music – needed for cheap-rate telephone cards. Both business and private numbers are on the Yellow Pages site, www.pagesjaunes. fr. A telephone directory is an *annuaire*. France Telecom's monopoly on directory enquiries, *les renseignements*, has been replaced with a series of expensive (mostly costing well over €1 per call) six-figure numbers beginning with 118 and operated by various operators. For a full list, see www.appel118.fr. Telephone boxes mostly work with cards; those that work with coins are inside cafés or other private buildings, so it's useful to have a card with you. However you're probably best getting a cheap mobile with a pre-paid card, *carte prépayée,* on arrival, as not only are public phones expensive but it can also be difficult to find one when you need it.

Mobile phones

Bouygues, SFR, Orange, Carrefour Mobile, Fnac Mobile Neuf Mobile, and Virgin Mobile are some of the main mobile network operators. Of course it's possible to use international roaming and there has been talk in Brussels of reducing the cost of using your phone when you travel, but this remains a pricey option. If you spend any amount of time in France you will probably want to buy a mobile phone there. You can try replacing the SIM card in your phone with a French one, so you can carry on using the same phone. You could use a multi-country operator that offers short-term contracts. One such is Transatel which offers a two-month contract under the name LeFrenchMobile (www. lefrenchmobile.com). These are 50% cheaper than pre-paid for national calls and 75% cheaper for international calls. In addition you get a local French number and you can keep your number for €5. You can order by filling in the form on the website or you can call ☎+33 170 752 400. Another provider of discount mobile services is www. teleconnectfrance.com The company provides SIM cards that enable foreign clients arriving in France to get cheap calls. You can also purchase foreign pay-as-you-go SIM cards from a website such as www.0044.co.uk, which enables you to make calls at local rates and get incoming calls and text messages free. If your phone is 'SIM-locked', i.e. the card can't be changed, then you will have to get a French mobile.

Unless you are officially resident in France, a French mobile phone company will only let you use a phone with a pre-paid card, on production of your passport. To take out a contract package, *un contrat* (i.e. not a pre-paid card) for a mobile phone you need proof of identity and proof of address. You also have to produce a RIB – a bank account number – which is in any case unavoidable if you pay by direct debit. You may be asked to show you have a French credit card. Coverage: as of December 2007, mobile phone companies are required to publish detailed coverage maps. For further discussion in English and French on this and other telecoms issues go to www.arcep.fr. L'ARCEP, *l'Autorité de Régulation des Communications Electroniques et des Postes*, is the state regulator for telecoms and postal services.

The mobile phone market is competitive and rapidly changing. As mentioned above you can find a reasonably clear overview of the different deals on offer at the website www.comparatel.fr.

◼ WHERE TO GET FURNITURE

Good-quality furniture can be picked up very cheaply from second-hand dealers (*les brocantes*) and salesrooms (*dépôt ventes*); there is always IKEA, of course. Also keep an eye on expat forums. Those moving back home will probably be looking to get rid of their furniture. Some foreigners travel round looking for cheap furniture to sell on. If you are looking to buy crockery, cutlery and other goods cheaply, then

Telephone/internet connections glossary	
abonnement	contract/phone plan
ADSL	broadband
audiotel/numéros a coût partagé	premium rate numbers
carte prépayée	pre-paid card (used for mobiles not on a contract)
contrat à 12 mois	12-month contract
dégroupage	bundle
un fixe (ligne fixe)	landline
forfait (forfait illimité)	your number of minutes
GPRS (3G)	GPRS
GSM	GSM
Illimité soir et weekend	unlimited calls at night and at the weekend
mains libres	hands free
offre sans abonnement	not on a contract
portable or *telephone portable/mobile*	mobile (the word portable can also refer to a laptop)
rappel automatique	callback
SMS	text message (short message service system!)
sonnerie	ring tone
télécharger	download

La brocante: a family pastime

In the summer months brocantes are held in towns and villages throughout France (including Paris) and are often a place for people to meet, eat some local produce cooked on the spot and share a glass of rosé. You can find out where the nearest brocante is being held by consulting the local paper.

there is another invaluable publication, *Factory Shop Guide for Northern France* by Gillian Cutress and Rolf Stricker (this was out of print for several years but a new edition was recently published in paperback); the French equivalent, *Guide des Magasins d'Usine* by Marie-Paule Dousset, is more expensive but a good substitute. If you are looking for something extremely cheap, then watch out for *braderies* – northern French markets selling off new goods at rock-bottom prices.

There are not very many places you can rent furniture in France. Two sites where you can find furniture to rent are: www.in-lease.com and www.thenewparentsguide.com (furniture for young children).

Most foreign electrical goods will work in France with suitable adapters; the only exception is goods with an internal timer, which it would be best to buy in France. DVDs do have compatibility problems if they come from the USA. Generally, unless you buy an all-region DVD player you have the option of selecting the zone you want to watch your DVD with, and then you have to stick with it.

Useful websites

- www.annuairedelabrocante.free.fr
- www.bradcante.com
- www.euroantic.com
- www.la-brocante.com
- www.pagesbrocante.com
- www.officielle-presse.com. Official listings of all fairs, markets and junk shops

Buying Property

For many people owning a property in France is the culmination of a dream they have been planning for many years. Perhaps they have been visiting France as tourists throughout their life and have decided to buy a house there to spend holiday time in and perhaps eventually move to. Time and again you hear French property experts say: 'Rent first before you buy'. This gives you a chance to get to know the region you are investing in and find out about potential pitfalls at a more leisurely pace. More information on renting can be found in the chapter *Setting up home*.

Nevertheless, renting first is not the only way to go about buying and there are many professionals who specialise in helping foreigners in their search for a house in France. You will find many useful contact details listed in this chapter.

French property magazines and estate agents naturally like to make out that the sun always shines in France, and nothing can ever sour your dream. Buying property in France is an adventure, and even for someone with experience of the British or American property market, something of a leap into the unknown. Not all of the 'property advisers' who advertise their services in magazines and on the internet necessarily know what they are talking about. The fact that somebody has a website doesn't mean that they are reliable. It's essential to take advice from qualified people. There are those who would like to take you for a ride, or as they say on the Riviera, '*vous prendre pour un Anglais*'.

There is, however, little room for negotiation in the very popular areas of western France – everything depends on how long the property has been on the market, and the general trend in prices at the time (which at the time of writing is levelling off and even beginning to fall). Patience is a key to not rushing into an expensive mistake.

Where foreigners often go wrong is in underestimating the cost of renovating a broken down property. Artisans' costs are relatively high in France, and there are risks in engaging the services of uninsured and unregistered foreign builders. The possibilities of beautifying your property are as endless as your imagination, but the chances of regaining your investment are limited, unless you pick up something in a very popular holiday location. It's entirely fanciful to buy something in the hope of selling it at a profit a few years later – French capital gains tax will take a lot of your profit away, unless you are selling your principal residence. Foreign buyers do sometimes go bankrupt, or more often, sell at a loss, so it pays to think twice.

A further main consideration are the very high purchase costs. You should expect to pay up to 10% of the purchase price on fees. These include the so-called '*notaire*'s fees' which are mainly taxes that go to the state rather than into the *notaire*'s pockets, as many people mistakenly imagine. Fees for arranging mortgaging are also steep. All in all, the system discourages people from speculating in property. The French system is a good one, but the assurance of a trouble-free buying process does come at a price.

Sarah Bright Thomas, an avocat in Toulouse, has some advice for foreign buyers:

The first thing I would say is, you wouldn't go ahead and buy a house in England if you didn't understand what your solicitor was telling you, so why do that here? We get involved in a lot of litigation for people with swimming pool problems or rights of way because people have signed things they don't understand. Also, you need to know what the best purchase vehicle is for you because of French inheritance laws. Inheritance and tax. I give a lot of advice on inheritance and tax [see 'Inheritance Law and wills' below]. What I would say to people is, make sure you get advice before you start, whether you're going to buy en tontine or what because these things are a lot cheaper to sort out at the beginning.

Once you've signed the compromis de vente (preliminary sales agreement) you can't go back. There's a clause in the code civil, and this applies to any purchase in France, which says that once you've agreed on the purchase and the price, the sale is perfect, la vente est parfaite. Once the suspensive conditions are realised you must go ahead and buy. So you shouldn't go into a compromis unless you're sure.

Also people should make sure they have their project worked out before they come. They can't just set up here as an estate agent for example. There are regulations. People get themselves into illegal situations because they don't register, not because they mean to do anything wrong but because they don't know what they're doing.

At the end of the day, it cannot be stressed enough that you should take suitable professional advice, even if this costs you more in the short term. This applies most of all to making the right arrangements for your heirs. It's expensive and sometimes even impossible to undo mistakes that are made at the time of purchase.

■ THE PROPERTY MARKET

The right property for you

Buying your French property should be the experience of a lifetime, if it's approached in the right way. It would be disingenuous to say that no one has ever regretted buying property in France. The main causes of disappointment are buying in the wrong location, and not setting a realistic limit on the budget.

If the property needs renovating, ask for some quotations beforehand. You should have outline planning permission – a *certificat d'urbanisme* – before buying if you are planning a change of use or large-scale renovations. Your *notaire* will advise you on whether you need this.

TIP

■ It's wise to decide on your budget and stick to it, no matter how tempted you might be to spend an extra €20,000 or whatever.

Is the property right for you?

Going through this list of simple questions will help you to see whether a property is the right one for you.

- What is my budget?
- Do I need to rent it out to make it affordable?
- How much work does it need, and what will it cost?
- How easy is the property to get to?
- Are there any airports nearby?
- Do I want to live there all the year round?
- Is the climate bearable in the winter?
- How close is it to tourist attractions?
- Will I or my partner be able to pursue our hobbies there?
- Will we or our family still want to use it in 20 years' time?

It's risky to buy a property if you can only finance it by renting it out or running *gîtes* (self-catering accommodation). More and more foreigners are buying in France with the same idea, while the tourist market is actually contracting. It's far more realistic to have a profession that you can carry on in France which leaves you financially secure, rather than struggling.

Old versus new

It's an oddity of the French property scene that the French consistently prefer new-build or completely renovated property, leaving the decrepit character farmhouses to the foreigners. The French have seen what the British and other foreigners can do with old properties, but not that many are interested in imitating them. Old barns are of no interest whatever to the local people, who are amazed that foreigners are willing to take them on. Incomers look for a beautiful location, and authenticity, while what the French really want is elegance and convenience. The most telling statistic is that an average new property is worth 40% more than an old one. It's therefore important to understand that it may be very difficult to recoup the investment that you make in renovating an old property in a remote area, unless you are lucky enough to find another foreigner who happens to like it.

Advantages of the old:

- The property has an authentic feel and rustic charm
- There will probably be more land attached to it
- The garden will be well established
- You know from the outset what you are buying
- The view will probably be better than with new property
- There will be more craftsmanship in the construction
- You are more likely to be able to rent it out to holidaymakers

Advantages of the new:

- There will be a garage or parking spaces already built
- The kitchen will be more modern
- The wiring and plumbing won't need replacing
- The building is guaranteed for 10 years from construction
- You can design the property yourself
- The heating will be more efficient
- There should be insulation
- On some developments, there are shared sports facilities

TIP

Even though you may know what you are looking for, it's useful to consider a checklist of the pros and cons of old versus new.

The great majority of foreigners would prefer to buy an old property, even if it has some defects, and needs more maintenance than the new. The average first-time buyer in France will buy an apartment in a *copropriété*. The crucial point for foreign buyers is: Do I want to rent it out? If you plan to make a living from bed-and-breakfast, the property will have to be substantial, and even more so for *gîtes*. If you only intend to live there for part of the year, and rent it out the rest of the time, there is more leeway. Holidaymakers will be quite satisfied with an apartment or a standard French holiday bungalow, as long as it's near the sea or the ski slopes.

Buying uncompleted property

It's common in France to buy property on the basis of plans – *achat sur plan* – or which has not yet been completed – *vente en l'état futur d'achèvement* (VEFA). A developer – *promoteur constructeur* – buys a piece of land, arranges for planning permission, and then looks for potential buyers before the property is built, or when it's partially built. The dwelling can be an apartment, or an individual house, as in the case of a *lotissement* or estate. The first step in the process is to sign a preliminary contract, or *contrat de réservation*, with a developer. The contract must contain certain information, as well as any get-out clauses in the sale:

> **Charles and Kath Dunstan run a *gîte* in Britanny that they renovated themselves. Charles says:**
>
> Brittany is becoming over gîted and you need to make sure your place stands out. That's why we put in the swimming pool that meets all the French regulations and is heated and last year we put in wireless internet throughout the property, which attracted clients immediately. We keep the place to a high standard with nice furniture and objets d'art and we advertise with Brittany Ferries, which gives us a cushion. We get bombarded by people who build tourist sites on the net. They always give you a free trial and if we pick up clients through their site then we subscribe the following year. We get a complete mix of nationalities: French, Brits, Americans, Italians, Dutch.

- The habitable surface area
- The number of main rooms
- A list of any attached rooms, or spaces
- The location of the building in the estate
- The technical quality of the construction, with a list of the materials to be used
- The provisional price of the building, and any conditions that allow for the price to change
- The date by which the final contract can be signed
- Where relevant, any loans that the developer intends to obtain for the buyer
- The conditions for paying the deposit

The buyer has the right to ask for changes to the contract. Once the contract has been received by registered post, there is a seven-day cooling-off period during which the buyer can change their mind.

The deposit – *dépôt de garantie* – depends on the length of time before the completion of the project: 5% if within one year, under 2% if between one and two years, and no deposit if beyond two years. The deposit will be returned if:

- The sale doesn't go through
- The sale price exceeds the provisional price by 5%
- The buyer fails to obtain a mortgage
- Equipment that has been promised is not installed
- The property falls 10% in value

The developer is legally required to present a guarantee that the project will be finished, or a guarantee of full reimbursement if it's not completed. In most cases the developer will have their own guarantor, a bank or cooperative society, as a backer. The second, final, contract is signed once the building programme has been decided on, and construction can commence. A draft of the *contrat définitif de*

Faults in new constructions

There are two categories of faults that can appear in new constructions: the *défaut de conformité* and the *vice de construction*. The first is where an incorrect piece of equipment has been installed, e.g. a shower instead of a bath. Payment for the item can be withheld until the fault has been rectified. *Vice de construction* covers bad workmanship or mistakes in installing equipment. A new building comes with a guarantee that the construction is satisfactory. The guarantee covers any faults that the buyer may find within the first year of occupation, and ensures that all faults are corrected. The builder must have an insurance policy, the *assurance dommage ouvrage* to cover against claims.

vente (final sales agreement) is sent to the buyer at least a month before the signing date.

Payment
Under normal circumstances, the buyer pays in four instalments, which include the deposit:

- 35% when the foundations are completed
- 70% when the roof has been built and the terraces are no longer exposed to water
- 95% when the building has been completed
- the final 5% is payable at the handing-over stage, unless there is a dispute.

When the property is ready to be handed over, there has to be a formal *réception des travaux* between you (or your representative) and the developer – the *maître dourage*. The *réception des travaux* (acceptance of the works), can take place with or without

reservations. The final 5% of the payment is known as the *retenue de garantie* and this can be withheld until any defects have been put right, or to cover your own expenses in putting them right if the builder fails to do the work. If the 5% is withheld, it should be deposited in an escrow account held by a *notaire*.

Before the handing over the buyer should inspect the building, with the help of an expert if necessary, to determine if there are any faults that need correcting. Electrics and heating should be tested. At the *réception des travaux* you will sign a document – a *procès-verbal* – accepting the handover. You can only refuse to take over the building if there are serious defects or equipment is missing. At the handing over the developer has to show that they have the necessary insurance policy to cover their *responsabilité décennale* – the compulsory 10-year guarantee against major construction errors. There is also a two-year guarantee – *garantie biennale* – against faults in the equipment, such as the fitted kitchen, heating and double glazing.

Taxation
As far as taxes go, there are both advantages and disadvantages to buying a new property. The downside is that 19.6% TVA (value added tax; VAT) is payable, although this can be avoided in some circumstances. The costs associated with the purchase, to be paid to the *notaire*, are reduced to about 2–3% of the price, before TVA. There is a 20% reduction if you buy a unit in a development of more than 10 units. In addition there is the *taxe de publicité foncière* (tax for legal obligation to post publicly the information on a sale) – at 0.615% of the price before TVA, and approximately €1000 in charges.

TVA is also payable if you buy a property within five years of its completion. TVA is only payable the first time the property changes hands within the first five years after construction, unless this was through a *marchand de biens* (property developer). Professional advice is essential if you are looking for ways of avoiding TVA.

Leaseback
Leaseback, or *le leaseback*, is a useful scheme, somewhat like 'buy-to-let', but within a formal structure that guarantees your investment is safe. It was originally started by

**TVA CAN BE
AVOIDED IF:**

- You buy property under a leaseback scheme
- You run a hotel or similar TVA-registered business from the property
- You let the property to someone running a hotel
- You sell the property at a loss within five years of purchase
- You are a *marchand de biens* (property developer)

the French government as a way of encouraging private investors to fund new tourist accommodation. The idea is quite ingenious: you agree to buy a new or completely rebuilt property in a tourist complex, and then lease it back to the developer for a period of between nine and 20 years. The developer's management company runs it for you, and guarantees a rental income, which goes towards paying off any loan that you have taken out to buy the property. The property must only be let to tourists. You can have the use of the property during the off-season the less you use the property the more you benefit financially, however. At the end of the fixed leaseback period, you are the owner of the property, and you can do with it what you wish; hopefully you will be sitting on a substantial profit.

You benefit right at the start because the French government repays the 19.6% TVA that is normally charged on new buildings, thus reducing the purchase price. For the rest you can take out a mortgage in the usual way. You should also consider the Capital Gains Tax situation at the end of the leaseback period, in case you want to sell on. Leaseback schemes will mainly be found in tourist areas on the coast, in Paris, and in the Alps, although other rural leaseback schemes are becoming more popular.

Because the term 'leaseback' is now such a buzz-word, it's sometimes used for ordinary buy-to-let, and there have been cases of mis-selling; make sure that there is a guaranteed annual return on the property to pay off your mortgage, and that the developer takes on the task of finding holiday tenants. Some companies that deal in leaseback properties are listed below. Others can be found through the organisation NAEA (recently Fopdac joined with the NAEA; see www.naea.co.uk).

Useful addresses

French Buy 2 Let.com: ☎+33 954 81 95 68; www.frenchbuy2let.com.

Pierre et Vacances: www.pierreetvacances-immobilier.com. Large French holiday company which pioneered leaseback. Properties available to rent or own around France including ski resorts.

Selectis Estate Agency: ☎04 94 565 565; selectis@wanadoo.fr; www.selectis.fr.

Villas Abroad (Properties) Ltd: ☎020 8785 6188;villasabroad@keme.co.uk; www.villasabroadproperties.co.uk.

Vivre en France: ☎020 7515 8660; www.vefuk.com.

Buying land for building

It's not unusual for the French to buy a piece of land with the intention of building a property on it themselves. There are, naturally, a lot of formalities involved; this is not something you could do while sitting at home in another country. In many ways, it could be an ideal solution. Building land is cheap in the countryside, and you will have complete control over the design of your property.

A lot of land cannot be built on, especially on the coast. Agricultural land is also protected. Many *communes* have a PLU – *Plan Local d'Urbanisme* – which states which pieces of land may be built on. Linked to this is the COS – *Coéfficient d'Occupation des Sols* – a figure giving the maximum amount of square metres of surface area that can be built on each square metre of land. The implication is that if you want to build a property with a greater surface area, you will have to pay a penalty, if permission is granted at all. If the *commune* has no PLU, then the use of the land is decided by central government. The required outline planning permission

– the *certificat d'urbanisme* – will only be granted where there are adequate access roads, drains, water and electricity supplies, and so on.

A usual way to buy land for building is to buy a plot in a *lotissement* or new estate; otherwise you may find a single plot or *parcelle* by looking in the usual property magazines.

Look in the local *Plan Cadastral* or Land Registry, to see what the precise measurements of your piece of land should be. If the boundaries are not clearly defined then you will need the services of a *géomètre-expert* – see www.pagesjaunes.fr – to carry out the *bornage*, that is to put in markers to show the boundaries. For companies selling land visit the following websites:

- www.allobat.fr
- www.terrain.fr
- www.terrain-a-batir.com
- www.terrains.com
- www.villesetvillages.fr

TIP

If you are thinking of buying land for building, it's vital to be aware of any plans on the part of the local authorities to construct new roads, industrial parks, etc.

Pre-emptive rights/droit de préemption

In many areas, the state, or state organisations can have pre-emptive rights on land purchase. Even after you buy a piece of land, the state can make a compulsory purchase order; you will receive 10% compensation. It's also conceivable that a private person has a pre-emptive right, or some other right, such as the use of the land for a fixed period, or rights of way. In order to avoid pointlessly acquiring land, it's essential to conduct a search of all the possible *servitudes* or obligations attaching to a piece of land.

In agricultural areas, the main organisation to watch for is the SAFER – *Société d'Aménagement Foncier et d'établissement Rural* (www.safer.fr) – which exists to ensure that agricultural land, forests and fields are put to appropriate use, and in particular to try to bring small parcels of land under one ownership. The *notaire* handling the sale is legally obliged to inform SAFER of the impending transfer. Where it appears that there is going to be a change in the use of land, the SAFER can intervene and negotiate with the seller to find a more suitable use for the land, or SAFER can buy the land and sell it on.

Where the land is being sold to family members, or co-heirs, the SAFER will not intervene.

Building your own property

There are several ways you can go about building your own property. You can either hire an architect to design the building, or design it yourself, if it's fairly small, or go to a builder and ask them to supply you with a ready-made plan. If you choose to take a ready-made plan, then the contract you sign is a *contrat de construction d'une maison individuelle avec fourniture de plan*. The terms of the contract are strictly regulated by law. The builder must have financial guarantees and insurance.

> **Keith Sprague is nearing the end of the process of having his own house built on a plot of land bought in the village of St Genard, near Melle, 20km from Niort.**
>
> We went to a French property exhibition in Edgbaston, looking for French sites. There was a stand set up by a French builder accompanied by a lawyer and an agent to help search for pieces of land. The builder had a selection of houses they could build. We went over and found the land with the help of the agent. He'd taken us to see another place but unfortunately it had already gone and when we were driving back to the airport we just saw a piece of paper in the hedge advertising a 'parcelle'.
>
> It's good to have people who can do the whole package for you. We know somebody who didn't do proper searches and went in and bought somewhere. When they went down the next year, a bungalow had been built on the plot of land next to them, blocking their view.
>
> We bought a plot that already had planning permission allocated in the village as a possibility to be built on. We went to see the mayor and told him what we wanted to do. The builder drew up the plans, with some modifications we wanted (an extension) and it was accepted. With our lawyer and the farmer who was selling the plot we went to the notaire and bought the land. We ended up buying an extra strip, four acres altogether. It took 12 months from finding the site to when we got the planning permission for our house. We set up an SCI, which is a French family company, to build houses on the plot for ourselves and our children. That was 12 months ago and the roof is just going on now. We decided to build a new house because we think it'll be easier to sell to the French if we ever do want to sell it.
>
> The build cost is quite reasonable once you have the land. Build quality is excellent and all work is guaranteed. You know from day one what it's going to cost – no hidden costs of anything they might find if you were trying to renovate. There was an 18-month process guarantee from the builders.

Payments are made according to a well-defined schedule:

- 15% on starting the work
- 25% on completion of foundations
- 40% on completion of walls
- 60% when the roof is put on (*mise hors d'eau*)
- 75% on completion of walls (*mise hors d'air*)
- 95% when the heating, plumbing and carpentry are completed
- 100% at the hand-over

The more usual procedure is to hire an architect to draw the plans. The contract evidently needs to include details of estimates of the cost and stage payments. The actual building work is usually handled by a *maître d'œuvre* or master builder, who oversees the whole process, and engages the various specialist tradesmen. A *maître d'œuvre* will not be as highly qualified as an architect, but will have more time to spend on-site. Note that the person who engages a *maître d'œuvre* is called the *maître d'ouvrage*. The contract you sign with them is the *contrat de maîtrise d'œuvre* which is again not regulated by law. The *maître d'œuvre* will normally hire tradespeople who they have worked with in the past, or they may give the job to a local cooperative. In other respects, many of the details of having your house constructed are similar to those described in the section on buying property which has not yet been completed – see *vente en l'état futur d'achèvement* or VEFA above.

Buying at auction

The idea of buying at auction may not occur to many foreigners, but there are real bargains to be found if you are prepared to take a risk, and the process itself holds some excitement. Fewer than 1% of property transactions in France take place through auctions; in an average year only 500 properties are sold in Paris by this method, and perhaps only 250 in the rest of the country. About 25 buyers attend an auction on average; the prices realised depend very much on the current climate of the property market. Auctions (*ventes aux enchères*) can be divided into three types: *vente judiciaire*, *vente de notaires*, and *vente de domaines*.

> **Charles and Kath Dunstan run a *gîte* in Britanny that they renovated themselves. Charles says:**
>
> Brittany is becoming over gîted and you need to make sure your place stands out. That's why we put in the swimming pool that meets all the French regulations and is heated and last year we put in wireless internet throughout the property, which attracted clients immediately. We keep the place to a high standard with nice furniture and objets d'art and we advertise with Brittany Ferries, which gives us a cushion. We get bombarded by people who build tourist sites on the net. They always give you a free trial and if we pick up clients through their site then we subscribe the following year. We get a complete mix of nationalities: French, Brits, Americans, Italians, Dutch.

Ventes judiciaires

This type of sale occurs when the owner of a property has gone bankrupt or defaulted on their mortgage payments. It's a forced sale by the creditors, i.e. mortgage lender. They take place less and less and are really a last resort for creditors. Sales are advertised in the local press, in *Le Journal des Enchères* (every two months), *Les Affiches Parisiennes* (www.affiches-parisiennes.com), and in the *Programme des Ventes* given out by the clerk of the lower court (*greffier du tribunal*). To bid at the sale, you hire a lawyer (*avocat*) registered at the court where the sale is going to take place. You give them a *mandat* (authorisation) to bid up to a certain limit, and a certified cheque for 20% of the maximum sum you are prepared to bid. Your lawyer will not exceed the amount you have stated unless you are standing next to them at the sale and give permission to bid higher.

If your bid is successful, you have 30 days to pay in full in the event that a property has been seized by the creditor (*saisie immobilière*) and three months in the case of bankruptcy proceedings (*mise en liquidation*). Properties with sitting tenants or squatters are best avoided, otherwise you will be involved in a long legal fight to evict them.

Ventes de notaires

In this case properties and goods are voluntarily submitted for auction by their owners at a *séance d'adjudication* or auction. Sales are publicised in a national bulletin (*Les Ventes aux Enchères des Notaires*). Again, you can't bid directly yourself, rather you are represented by your *notaire*. Owners use this type of auction in the hope of gaining a higher price than through the usual channels. If you are looking for prestigious older properties you may get a good deal here.

Ventes des domaines

The state sometimes sells properties at auction: these are announced in the *Bulletin Officiel d'Annonces des Domaines*. You are required to deposit a certified cheque for 5% of the estimated price in order to bid.

Vente à la chandelle

The 'auction by candle' is a relic going back to the 15th century. The idea is that three tapers are placed on a board: the first two are lit simultaneously, and burn down within tens of seconds, while bids are made. The third taper is then lit, and if no higher bid is made then the property is sold. Nowadays, the tapers are being replaced with electric lights. This is not the end of the matter: if a bid of 10% more than the successful bid is made then the property has to be auctioned all over again, but this rarely happens. The latter condition doesn't apply to the *ventes des domaines*.

Anyone interested in auctions should look at the magazine *Journal des Enchères* which covers every kind of auction, including furniture, antiques, etc. Useful websites are:

■ www.licitor.com

■ www.ventes-judiciaires.com

■ www.encheres-paris.com

Other ways of buying

Rent-to-buy/location accession

It's possible to enter into an agreement with an owner whereby you rent the property for a number of years before buying it. The seller incorporates a clause in the contract promising to sell you the property. The clause is only activated when the prospective buyer pays a 5% deposit into a blocked account. From then on, the tenant/buyer makes further payments towards the eventual purchase price, on top of their rent. After an agreed time – usually two or three years – the buyer then has the option of paying the remainder of the purchase price. If the potential buyer changes their mind there is a small penalty to be paid to the seller. If the seller breaks the contract there is a heavier penalty up to 3% of the value of the property.

▥ Rente viagère

This system may be unfamiliar to you, although it does have something in common with an annuity taken out on the value of your house. The idea of the *rente viagère* (literally meaning 'income for life') is that you come to an agreement with the owner of a property that you will pay them a certain monthly sum and in exchange the property will revert to you on the owner's death. The buyer also pays out an initial sum known as a *bouquet* equivalent to 20%–30% of the total price. The person who pays out the money is the *débirentier* and the one who receives money is the *crédirentier*. There are two types of *viager*: one where the *crédirentier* continues to live in the house, and the other where they live elsewhere.

Properties are sometimes sold with the elderly person included, so to speak. Thus one may see ads giving the cost of the property, the age and sex of the occupant, and how much you have to go on paying them. If you want to sell your property *en viager*, visit www.viager.fr.

▥ Timeshare/co-ownership

Timeshare has as bad a reputation in France as anywhere else. Unfortunately, the paranoia about timeshare is entirely justified, but the French legal system leaves less scope for timeshare crooks than other countries, however, and there is far less timeshare property available than in Spain or Portugal. You can see the type of properties available at www.redweek.com. You can also buy timeshare through private advertisements in magazines such as *Particulier à Particulier*.

The idea behind timeshare seems sensible enough at first sight. Instead of renting a room in an expensive hotel on the French Riviera, or a chalet in the Alps, you buy a share in a timeshare company that gives you the right to use a property for a certain number of weeks for the rest of your life, and to pass it on to your heirs. The catch is that you never actually own any part of the property: you just have a right to use it for a fixed period each year. The French often call timeshare '*multipropriété*', which is entirely misleading: you never own the property. It should really be called *multilocation* (i.e. multiple rental) or *multi-jouissance* or *jouissance en temps partagé*. Under the French system, you are buying shares in a timeshare company, which you can then sell on if you want or leave to your heirs. If the timeshare company goes out of business you will lose the right to use the property, and you may even be held liable for some of the company's debts. You can take out a loan to buy the timeshare (if you can find a lender), and there can be a get-out clause in the timeshare contract if you fail to get a loan. You are allowed to rent out the property for the weeks that you have bought, which could make you a profit. The contract doesn't have to be signed in the presence of a notary; usually it's done *sous seing privé*, or 'under hand'.

Under French law the timeshare contract must include a 10-day cooling-off period after you have sent off the signed contract, during which you can change your mind. The seller is not allowed to ask for or receive any money until the end of the 10-day cooling-off period. The contract should give the identity and address of the sellers, and all the costs involved, the location and description of the property, and the weeks you can use it for.

Dealers who resell timeshares should be members of the OTE – Organisation for Timeshare in Europe (www.ote-info.com). The French also have their own timeshare consumers' organisation – www.apaf-vtp.com – with all the same tales of woe as elsewhere, and a useful list of companies to avoid.

■ French-style co-ownership: multipropriété

Instead of getting involved with timeshare, it's more sensible to buy a property jointly with some other like-minded people, and agree on who will use it at what time of the year. This is not a cheap option, but you will at least be the owner of part of the property. The important thing is to draw up the deed of sale correctly, and this can only be done with a lawyer who is familiar with French property law. The most suitable form is a *Société Civile Immobilière*, as long as it's constituted correctly.

An SCI is particularly useful where several unrelated people own shares in a property, and wish to be free to pass their share on to others. The SCI is a company, but is not subject to corporation tax. It's treated as 'fiscally transparent'; the directors are taxed as individuals. If you are from the UK and hold property through a company you could also be liable to UK tax on directors' benefits in kind, and the tax bill would have to be shared out between the owners. Owners pay for the running costs of the property in proportion to the number of weeks they use the place.

■ Copropriété

This is also a type of co-ownership that is usually applicable to apartments, although it can be used for any kind of building split into several units. As there is no such thing as leasehold in France, *copropriétés*, in which a group of owners run a building themselves, are extremely common and many foreigners find themselves involved with one. It should be said that, while there is no leasehold, the land on which a

Co-ownership – getting it right

Selling your French property to a group of owners, while keeping a part for yourself, is an ideal way to retain the use of your property for some weeks of the year, while at the same time regaining the money you invested in it. An agency in the UK – OwnerGroups Company (☎01628 486350; www.ownergroups.com) – specialises in finding and handling the purchase of property for the purpose of co-ownership. Its fee is 6.5% of the value of the property.

building stands could be owned by someone else. A property company can buy parts of a *copropriété* and has the right to be represented at meetings.

Any building or buildings divided between several owners with private and common areas automatically comes under the 1965 law on *copropriétés*. The group of owners, or *copropriétaires*, automatically constitutes a *syndicat de copropriété*. The owners are legally obliged to appoint a *syndic* or manager responsible for the day-to-day running of the building; they are also required to elect a *conseil syndical* (council of the syndicate) for a three-year term and to hold annual general meetings (AGMs).

There is a basic text that defines the conditions under which a *copropriété* functions, known as the *règlement de copropriété*. This includes:

- ◗ A list of the common and private areas
- ◗ The uses to which the property may be put, e.g. whether you can run a business from it
- ◗ The administration of the common areas
- ◗ The division of the charges

The *syndic*

The *syndic* – the manager of the property – deals with the day-to-day running of the property. A part of their job is to keep a logbook of all the maintenance of the building, and to give advice to the owners. They are expected to present a provisional budget for the year at the AGM, and to keep accounts of the running of the property. The *syndic* maintains a bank account in the name of the syndicate. As a rule, the *syndic* doesn't need to go to the *conseil syndical* to carry out urgent repairs. There is generally an agreed figure which the *syndic* may spend for necessary repairs without calling a general meeting.

A general assembly of the *copropriétaires* can be called at any time by the *conseil syndical*, or by the *copropriétaires* holding at least 25% of the votes. There has to be at least one assembly per year. If you rent out your part of the *copropriété*, your tenant can take part in an assembly, but they can't vote on the same motions as you. The *syndic* will notify you at least 15 days before the meeting that it's happening. Any of the *copropriétaires* can ask for an amendment to the order of the meeting. You can appoint a representative to attend the meeting in your place.

Motions concerning the day-to-day running of the *copropriété* are passed by simple majority. Matters affecting the basic running of the *copropriété* must be approved by two-thirds majority. Some other matters, such as changing the division of the charges, can only be approved by unanimous vote. All the *copropriétaires* should receive a notification within two months of the decisions taken at the meeting. Decisions can be challenged in a court of law, unless you have already voted in favour of them.

The general assembly is required to elect a management board – *conseil syndical* – whose term of office runs for three years. *Copropriétaires*, their partners, and their representatives are all allowed to sit on the board. The board chooses a president who stays in contact with the manager of the property.

The *syndic* can be appointed by the general assembly of the *copropriété*, by the board of management, or they may be named in the constitution of the *copropriété*. Since their task requires specialised knowledge in accounting and law, the *syndic* usually holds a professional qualification, the *carte professionnelle de gestion immobilière*. It's virtually a requirement to have a professional *syndic* if there are more than five or so *copropriétaires*.

The terms of the *syndic's* remuneration are negotiable. There is no legal obligation to pay the *syndic*; the job could, in theory, be done on a voluntary basis. Their term of office is for three years. If it can be proved that they have made a serious mistake, the *syndic* can be dismissed by a simple majority vote at a general meeting. The *copropriétaires* are entitled to look at the accounts of the *copropriété* in between notification of a general meeting and the meeting itself. The accounts of the *copropriété* are separate from the *syndic*'s own personal accounts. If the *syndic* is suspected of taking bribes from suppliers you would need a court order to look at their accounts. The *copropriétaires* have a right to instruct the *syndic* to use, or not to use, the services of a particular company.

> **Peter Stone owned a two-bedroom apartment in St Malo, Brittany, for 10 years in a *copropriété* in an old building which required some renovation:**
>
> I rarely went to the meetings of the copropriété. The syndic was generally very slow to do repairs; at one point I did some work on the plaster myself and all the other people thanked me effusively. Another time a woman who had water running into her flat had already waited four months to have something done; when I went to the manager and told him firmly that I wanted it fixed before I left he did it within a week. Straight talking is generally the best way to get things done in this kind of situation.

There are strict rules about what you can change in your part of the *copropriété*, since any changes to the property affect all the owners. You need the permission of the *syndic* for any redecoration, new shutters, plastering and so on. Anything that alters the external appearance of the *copropriété* is of concern to all the members. Needless to say, any work that is to be done to the common areas is the responsibility of the *syndic*.

You will receive a regular bill for insurance, cleaning, maintenance and so on in the communal area. The cost of heating the common areas is also shared. There may also be a charge for the television aerial. The *syndic*'s remuneration is paid by all the owners.

The percentage of the charges that you are due to pay depends on the value of your part of the *copropriété*. You will have to pay for your share of a service, even if you do not make use of it, unless there is some good reason. For example, if you live on the ground floor, you do not pay for the lift. The list of charges and their distribution is included in the regulations of the *copropriété*. There is a time limit if you want to object to the amount you have to pay: either five years from the publication of the regulations, or within two years if you buy a share in a *copropriété*, but only if this is the first time it has been sold. Since the beginning of 2003, the percentages of charges and the way these are calculated have to be included in the regulations of the *copropriété*.

If you are thinking of buying into a *copropriété* be sure to look at the minutes of the last three years' AGMs at the very least.

Farms and vineyards

The French government is keen to encourage foreigners to take over farms since so many French farmers are giving up and moving to the cities. Local governments in central France are particularly interested in attracting new farmers, but newcomers may not get a very friendly welcome from the long-established locals. There are grants available for setting up farms. The first port of call is the departmental ADASEA or Agence Départementale pour l'Aménagement des Structures des Exploitations Agricoles. See www.adasea.net, www.cnasea.fr and www.safer-fr.com.

Buying a vineyard

It's also possible to buy a vineyard; there are several successful British and other foreign vineyard owners. It's really a matter of doing your homework, and watching out for potentially useless vineyards – for example, when the vines need to be replanted and you can't harvest grapes for the next seven years.

Range of prices for a 120sq m property in 2007	
Area	**Price**
Brittany	€220,000
Lower Normandy	€202,000
PACA	€374,000
Ile de France	€346,000
Paris city	€713,000

■ PRICES

Thanks to the internet, and the flood of French property magazines, it has become much easier than before to stay up to date with French property prices. Remember to add on 10% to cover *notaire*'s fees and other costs. One also needs to consider whether the estate agent's commission is included in the price. These days it's usually already added in to the price.

The range of prices is immense. The extraordinary bargains that were available until 2002 are becoming rare. Aquitaine and Languedoc-Roussillon are catching up with Provence. Paris is not that expensive unless you want to be in one of the super-chic *arrondissements* (see below). The Côte d'Azur still has affordable apartments if you feel this is the place to be. The determining factors are climate, the proximity of a TGV station (prices shoot up close to one), views of the sea, proximity to ski slopes, and whether a place is perceived to be 'remote'. As regards flying time, and distance from airports, most of central and eastern France is remote for the British; the second home market is overwhelmingly concentrated on the western side of the country (as it is for Americans, Belgians and Dutch). The Germans have in the past bought heavily along the eastern border, but they have withdrawn in recent years. There is also a well-established Swiss presence in the south-east.

Some parts of France will never be fashionable and prices will never rise very much. Economically prosperous areas such as Alsace-Lorraine and the Lyon-Grenoble-Annecy triangle will remain relatively expensive, but these don't attract second homebuyers, rather it's those who come to France to work who look for property here. If population movements are anything to go by, the South of France, the west coast south of Brittany, and the south-west quadrant are the areas where prices will stay firm, and those are the areas safest to invest in.

Paris

Most people live in apartments; there are few houses on the market within the Boulevard Périphérique which delimits the city. Property prices are, roughly speaking, 30–60% of those in London, but there are vast differences between the 20 *arrondissements* (administrative areas). The *arrondissements* are arranged like a snail shell, going clockwise from the centre. The 1st and 2nd are the historical centre, with world-famous landmarks. The Marais (the 3rd and 4th *arrondissements*) was formerly the aristocratic area, as well as the Jewish quarter, and is very trendy with a lot of bars and discos and is also the gay area. The 5th includes the Sorbonne and the

Quartier Latin, and the well-known Left Bank (Rive Gauche), haunt of intellectuals. The 6th and 7th are expensive and exclusive, with many government buildings and large open spaces. The 8th, or Right Bank, includes the shopping centre of the Champs Elysées, and is highly sought after and expensive. The 9th is an area of theatres, cinemas and department stores and is not highly regarded as far as accommodation goes. The 10th has the Gare du Nord and Gare de l'Est, has become more fashionable, especially with young professionals and couples. The 11th, the Bastille area, is trendy, as is the 12th which has been revitalised by large building projects. The 13th, 14th, 15th, 16th and 17th are residential. The Bois de Boulogne alongside the 16th adds to its attractions. The 18th was very attractive in the past but has gone downhill with the spread of the redlight area around Montmartre and Pigalle. The 19th and 20th, in the north of the city, are more downmarket areas.

Outside Paris is a large area of suburbs as well as countryside. Central Ile de France is known as *la petite couronne*, and includes Hauts-de-Seine, Seine-Saint-Denis and Val-de-Marne. Paris is also a *département*. The rest of Ile de France is *la grande couronne*, comprising Seine-et-Marne, Yvelines, Essonne and Val-d'Oise.

FACT

■ For more information on the Paris area, see the 'Neighbourhoods' section in the chapter *Setting up home*.

Property

Almost all residential property in central Paris dates back to the 19th century, when the city was completely rebuilt under the direction of Baron Haussmann. There are plenty of modern villas and mansions outside the inner city. As far as Paris goes, the only property you could expect to afford would be an apartment. Houses rarely come on the market, and are worth millions in the upmarket *arrondissements*. A three-bedroom house in a good area can be had for €300,000. There are very expensive suburbs: wealthy Americans live in a ghetto in St Cloud. Versailles, Fontainebleau and St-Germain-en-Laye are as upmarket as they sound. Sèvres, and Meudon are somewhat less expensive suburbs on the western side. Meaux is the cheapest suburb.

There is now a marked tendency for the better-off to leave the centre of the city for the suburbs, while the city is more and more packed with immigrants and young people. Paris is by far the most expensive place to live in France. Prices of basic commodities in shops are roughly comparable with those in London, i.e. far more expensive than the rest of France. Property prices in Paris proper are not likely to go up that substantially, given that the average income of the residents is going down. A one-room flat in central Paris will cost upwards of €130,000. As in other European cities, prices are worked out based on the square metres occupied and currently the average is around €5,700 with a great range between the different *arrondissments*.

■ ESTATE AGENTS

The estate agency profession is not as highly developed in France. Until recently property sales were handled by *notaires*; the profession is still quite new. On the positive side, French estate agents are more relaxed and less cut-throat than elsewhere, but they can also seem amateurish by UK and US standards.

The need for agents arises because many foreign buyers only have time to search for properties during their holidays. Agencies in France and in the UK can help you to overcome the inconveniences of dealing directly with French estate agents or *immobiliers*. Most UK-based agents don't deal directly with properties themselves,

FACT

■ In certain areas – especially the Côte d'Azur – there are professional estate agents who specialise in dealing with foreigners.

> **Philippe Certain runs an estate agency in Leucate, up the coast from Perpignan (☎04 68 40 04 06; http://agencedumidileucate. free.fr). Here is his advice to prospective English-speaking buyers:**
>
> The first piece of advice to anyone wanting to buy a house in France is to learn the basics of our language before coming to the land of the froggies! Having lived in Hong Kong, I speak English (and Chinese!) and it's always amusing to see the relief on the faces of those who come to the office when they realise they have finally found an agent who can understand them. Even if it means I end the day with a bit of a headache! Last Saturday, an English client informed me that they had just come from 'Kill' which I understood to mean Kiehl in Germany. In fact, they'd just been in Quillan, a small French town 80 miles from Leucate. In order to go unnoticed it is advisable to drive on the right side of the road and best to find a car with the steering wheel on the usual side so as not to give away your provenance too easily. If England has beaten France in the Six Nations that year, it is best to avoid the subject. Beer is banished in all seasons, as here Le Fitou is what we drink. Don't get angry if we call you English instead of Irish or Scottish or even American. It's hard for us to tell the difference!

but rather put you in touch with *immobiliers* in the area you are interested in, and generally organise your house-hunt for you. The advantage is that you don't have to deal directly with French *immobiliers*, and your language abilities are not going to be tested. Some – but not that many – French estate agents speak good English, and there are more and more foreign estate agents in France, so whether you feel you need another intermediary is up to you.

The English-speaking agent receives shares the commission with the *immobilier*, which can be as much as 50% of the total commission where there is a long-established partnership. The agent may add on his own fees, which could amount to 1% or 1.5% of the value of the property. There is usually a signing-on fee, which is refunded in the event that you buy the property.

Apart from agents, there are property consultants who do research for potential buyers, and offer every kind of hand-holding service, which can include arranging flights and stays in France, and advice on dealing with the buying process. A consultant will be paid by the customer directly for their services.

French *immobiliers'* commissions vary from region to region, and are on a graduated scale depending on the value of the property. The minimum is around €2,000. With very cheap properties the commission can be up to 20%; above about €250,000 the commission will not exceed 2.5%. Up-market properties in Paris or in tourist areas also attract high commissions; the total commission is unlikely to be less than 3%; the average amount is 5%, but it can go a lot higher. There are no legal limits on an *immobilier's* commission.

It's vitally important to find out at the start who is going to pay the *immobilier's* commission. It's now usual for the seller to pay, meaning that it's included in the advertised price. Indeed it's no longer even mentioned in advertisements who is to pay the commission. But there is nothing to prevent the seller asking the buyer to pay the commission, or for the buyer and seller to split the commission, but whatever is decided on, it must be stated in the *compromis de vente* (preliminary sales agreement). You should ask about the commission, because there is always a chance that the price quoted is *net vendeur*, i.e. the price the seller will receive. Foreigners are also sometimes quoted prices 'with all costs included', which allows the agency to slip in a few more thousand pounds unnoticed.

French estate agents' qualifications

A French-based estate agent must have professional qualifications and a licence from a Chambre de Commerce. According to the 1970 Loi Huguet, estate agents must have:

- A diploma in law, e.g. DEUG
- *or* a baccalaureate or other degree, and one year's work experience in an estate agency
- *or* 10 years' experience in an estate agency

Anyone who acts as an *immobilier* without a *carte professionnelle* is liable to a heavy fine and a jail sentence, and this has happened to some foreigners who, perhaps in ignorance of the law, have worked with *notaires* selling properties in France. They may have done a good job for their customers, but they still broke the law. The *carte professionnelle* has to be renewed every year. For an inside view of the estate agency business it's worth reading Alan Biggins' *Selling French Dreams* and *A Normandy Tapestry*.

You can ask to see any of the documents mentioned above. They should be on display in the agent's office. Estate agents must have a guarantee fund or bond to protect the interests of their clients. They don't need to be members of a national organisation of estate agents such as the FNAIM (Fédération Nationale des Agents Immobiliers et Mandataires) or SNPI (Syndicat National des Professionnels Immobiliers). All estate agents must have professional indemnity insurance as well.

Estate agents have negotiators working in their offices, but each main office must have a holder of a *carte professionnelle*. Some branch offices have an *agent*

Notices estate agents are required to display in their office

- The number of their *carte professionnelle*
- The amount of their financial guarantee
- The name and address of their guarantee fund
- The name of their bank and the number of the account into which funds have to be paid
- The amount and percentages of commission

TIP

As a general rule of thumb, if a property is advertised with several agents for a long time, you can assume that it's difficult to sell, and you can offer a lot less than the asking price. You may see the same property photographed from different angles.

de commerce or a *fondé de pouvoir*, someone who is mandated by an *immobilier* to negotiate contracts on their behalf. The *immobilier* has a time-limited *mandat* or mandate from the seller to negotiate on their behalf. It's common practice for a seller to give several agents a so-called *mandat simple* to sell property on their behalf. Where the agent has the exclusive right to sell the property you will see *en exclusivité* on the advertisement; the agent has a *mandat exclusif* which may give him or her the right to carry out the sale themselves, or to allow the seller to deal directly with the client.

Only half of properties in France are sold through *immobiliers*. The rest are sold privately, through *notaires* or at auctions (see below). Going round villages asking if there are any properties coming on the market, or if anyone has died recently, can pay dividends. Even paying a local to act as a spy for you could save you a great deal of money.

Property viewing

You may begin the process by looking on the internet at some adverts, or in some French property magazines, and contacting an *immobilier* who will, if you are lucky, send you some details of the properties they have available. French *immobiliers* don't go for hard-sell techniques and their publicity materials are not of high quality (except for higher priced properties). The role of the *immobilier* is to show people round the property. They stand to make a considerable sum of money if the property is sold through them. They will, not, however, put *A Vendre* (For Sale) on the property, for fear that potential buyers will trace the owner and deal directly with them. The For Sale sign will only be put up by private sellers, or if the owner is not easily traceable. You won't be given the keys to the property and sent to go and look for it, first because you will probably not be able to find it, and second, because you may find the owner and negotiate a private deal. For this reason you are accompanied on your house-viewing visits by an agent or the *immobilier*. They don't give out precise addresses of properties, but rather put 15 km from such-and-such a village. Since several properties in a village can have the same name, it could take a long time to find the one you are looking for. If you are taken around by an agent, you will be asked to sign a *bon de visite* at the start to prove that the agent has taken you to see the property, and that he or she is entitled to the commission if it's sold.

The main thing to watch out for is that you are actually shown the properties you are interested in. It happens all too often that buyers go out to France to look at a cottage and then find that they are being shown châteaux and barns, and everything but what they wanted, because that is all the agent has on their books. Part of the problem is that prospective buyers may not be talking to the right agent to start with. A local country

> Jean Ramm and her husband are the owners of a house in the village of Bosville in Normandy. This is Jean's account of buying the property and their subsequent experiences there.
>
> In May 2002 we were in our early sixties and retired from full-time work. We used an English solicitor in moving towards the compromis de vente after which we decided to trust the notaire presiding over the sale for both sides. The final acte de vente was signed in September. Our two-bedroom house with potential for loft renovation is in the centre of a small village with a school, church and shop. Every Monday at nearby Cany Barville, there is a market and the place is buzzing. Our property came with a field and apple orchard. What do we do with the spare land? The locals knew. One summer a man grazed his horses in our field and brought us organic vegetables in return. The elderly widow across the road used our apples to make cider, giving us many bottles.
>
> We like Normandy. It's an enormous region. We're in a hardworking agricultural area, Seine Maritime. Crops are the familiar sugar beet, potatoes, wheat, barley, beans. Working farmers are in abundance. Tractors, often pulling gigantic implements, trundle along the side roads (and not-so-side roads!). We have easy access by Dieppe or Boulogne. Any traffic problems tend to be on the UK side. Our village is 7 miles from the nearest beach, Veulettes-sur-Mer. Nearby resorts are full of character. History resonates. Many small art exhibitions are held in season, even in supermarket foyers. Randonnées pass through our village and there are off-road cycle tracks a short drive away. We haven't renovated the loft. We've used a local roof tiler, a plumber, a chimney sweep and a man to cut our roadside hedge. Generally people have been friendly and the bureaucracy manageable.
>
> Gradually our French has improved, although the Normandy accent is tricky. Similarly they find our own standard-English type French a bit confusing. Language-wise we fair better in Paris. C'est la vie.

estate agent won't carry large villas and châteaux, because no one in the village would be able to afford one. The other pitfall is to make sure that the property you specifically want to see has not already been sold to someone else. An attractive-looking property on the internet may not be available any more by the time you get to France. Agencies outside France may be slow to find out whether a property has been sold.

Customers should also observe certain formalities in relation to agents. It isn't possible to pack in several viewings a day when properties are so remote that it could take half a day to see just one. For this reason French estate agents will be reluctant to arrange viewings unless they have already met you in person. They generally make a point of finding out if you are serious or not; they may well ask you straight off. It's sensible to let agents know if you can't make it to a viewing. A mobile telephone is essential so you can keep in touch.

Simply going to see the property once is of course not enough. Ideally you should go there several times without the agent, talk to local people, and see the place at different times of day and on different days of the week. Would the property still appeal to you on a dark rainy day in the middle of winter? Are there any smelly farmyards or noisy neighbours in the vicinity? Most importantly, try to find out if there are any major developments planned in the area. The *immobilier* may forget to mention that a wind farm is going to be built on your doorstep in two years' time or that a motorway will soon pass your front door. The local *mairie* (town hall) can tell you if someone is planning to build a housing estate next door to you. This is particularly important if you want to run *gîtes* or *chambres d'hôtes* from your property. Better road or rail connections can be to your advantage as well, and increase the value of your property. The locals will know about these things, so try to spend time talking to them.

Marchands de Biens

As well as *agents immobilier* there are also *marchands de biens* (dealers in property or property developers), the main difference being that a *marchand de biens* buys and sells properties in their own name to make a profit, while an *immobilier* is legally not allowed to buy or sell in their own name. Anyone who makes a living from regularly buying and selling property or land has to register with the chamber of commerce; they are taxed according to a special regime, not on the basis of capital gains, and they pay TVA on the profit they make on selling a property. They are only subject to very low registration charges on the purchase of property as long as they resell the property within four years. It's common practice for a *marchand de biens* to make a down payment on a property while looking around for a potential buyer, but they do have to own the property for three months before they resell it. They take the risk of having to pay hefty tax penalties if they don't find someone to buy the property within four years, or if, in the case of land, they don't start building something, which means that they can be pressured to sell at a cheap price. Their general method is to buy cheap run-down properties, especially where the owner has recently died, to do it up, and sell it on.

UK estate agents

Many UK-based estate agents deal in French property. The large organisations dealing at the top end of the market will have offices in both countries. British-owned estate agents in France operate under French law, and are not essentially different from French *immobiliers*, except insofar as their staff speak English and understand the needs of foreign buyers. When dealing with UK-based agents it's necessary to find out first whether they are actually estate agents or simply intermediaries between customers and French *immobiliers*. Those given below will offer a full service to buyers.

UK and US-based estate agents

A Home in France: ☎0870 748 6161; info@ahomeinfrance.com; www.ahomeinfrance.com.

A House in France Ltd: www.french-property-news.com.

Alpine Apartments Agency: ☎01544 388234; www.alpineapartmentsagency.com.

Beaches International Property Ltd: ☎01562 885181; www.beachesint.com.

Capital Mover Ltd: ☎020 8746 0857 (UK); www.capitalmover.com. Individually designed new-build throughout France.

Currie French Properties: ☎01223 576084; www.french-property.com/currie.

David King Associates: ☎020 8671 1111; www.dkassociates.co.uk.

> ## Tim Swannie originates from Harrogate, North Yorkshire. Tim relocated to Mougins where he set up the property search company Home Hunts.
>
> Buying property abroad can be a daunting task. What do you want? Where do you want to be? Who should you contact? What steps should you take? That is where we come in. Home Hunts specialises in finding property in the South of France for local and international clients. We have a team of consultants situated throughout Provence and the Côte d'Azur.
>
> We receive enquiries from all over the world as well as a large number of requests from local property seekers who simply don't have the time or energy to find property themselves. We are completely independent and work with a wide range of estate agents throughout the south of France, so we have access to a great selection of homes. The service we offer is free. The selling agent pays us a commission for introducing the buyer, enabling us to provide this all-encompassing service for no cost to the buyer. We work on a no sale, no fee basis so clients have no obligation to purchase. By offering an in-depth and open service we have found our clients are usually happy to deal exclusively with us.
>
> We work closely with our clients, providing advice on areas, offering local knowledge as well as conducting the search for properties. We arrange viewing visits, book flights and accommodation if required and meet customers at the airport. We take our customers around relevant areas and show them a selection of properties to match their needs. We negotiate with the selling agents on our clients' behalf, help to arrange surveys if required and basically take the hard work out of the house buying process. We also offer financial and legal help as well as assistance with removals, renovations and even letting of the home if requested.
>
> In my experience, our clients have found our service useful because they know they can leave things in our hands without having to worry. We are in constant contact with the selling agents, notaries, lenders, surveyors and so on to ensure everything runs as smoothly as possible. We have an excellent reputation for our professionalism and honesty and plan to keep building on this for years to come.

The National Association of Estate Agents (NAEA) (☎+44 (0)19266 496800; www.naea.co.uk) represents a group of estate agents dealing in foreign property.

Domus Abroad: ☎020 9455 0015; www.Domusabroad.com. Services for both buyers and sellers.

Dordogne & Lot Properties: ☎01865 558659; www.dorlotproperties.net.

Eclipse Overseas: ☎01425 277137; www.french-property.com/eclipse. Normandy, Charente, Loire, Vendée, Brittany, Dordogne.

European Property Search: www.europeanpropertysearch.com.

Fourways French Properties: ☎01297 489366.

The French Property Shop: ☎01233 666902; www.frenchpropertyshop.com.

Francophiles Ltd: ☎01622 688165.

Gascony Property: ☎01702 390382; info@gascony-property.com; www.gascony-property.com.

Hamptons International: ☎020 7758 8488; info@hamptons-int.com; www.hamptons-int.com.

Hexagone France Ltd: ☎01303 221077; info@hexagonefrance.com; www.hexagonefrance.com.

La Résidence: ☎01491 838485; www.laresidence.co.uk.

Latitudes: ☎020 8951 5155; fax 020 8951 5156; www.latitudes.co.uk.

Leisure & Land: ☎020 8952 5152; www.leisureandland.com. Specialises in income-producing properties.

Mistral Estate Services: www.real-estate-in-france.com. US-based agent with a French network of real estate agents and property owners and able to provide a listing of all kinds of real estate including vineyards, villas, châteaux, farmhouses for leisure, work, retirement, business, etc.

Propriétés Roussillon: ☎0121 459 9058; fsales@proprietes-roussillon.com; www.proprietes-roussillon.com. All areas.

Sifex Ltd: ☎020 7384 1200; www.sifex.co.uk. Exclusive properties in Southern France. Châteaux in all regions of France.

VEF (Vivre en France) UK: ☎020 7515 8660; www.vefuk.com.

Villas Abroad Ltd: ☎020 8785 6188; www.villasabroadproperties.com.

Waterside Properties International: ☎01903 850017; www.watersideproperties-int.co.uk.

World Class Homes Ltd: ☎01582 832001; info@worldclasshomes.co.uk; www.worldclasshomes.co.uk.

France-based estate agents

ABC Immobilier: 41 ave Clémenceau, 34500 Béziers; ☎04 67 49 20 10; www.abc-immo.fr.

Agence Arago: ☎01 53 10 25 50; www.agence-arago.fr. Founded 1935.

Agence Christol: B.P.50, 25 blvd Gambetta 34800, Clermont-L'Hérault; ☎04 67 96 00 60; www.openmedia.fr/christol. Specialises in the Languedoc mostly less than half an hour's drive from Montpellier.

Agence Hamilton: 30 rue Armagnac, 11000 Carcassonne; ☎04 68 72 48 38; info@agence-hamilton.com; www.agence-hamilton.com. Languedoc, Midi-Pyrénées.

Agence Hermann de Graaf: Le Bourg, 24800 St Jean de Côle; ☎05 53 62 38 03; www.immobilier-dordogne.com. Dordogne.

Agence L'Union: Charles Smallwood, Place de la Halle, 82140 St Antonin-Noble-Val; ☎05 63 30 60 24; www.agencelunion.com. Tarn, Tarn-et-Garonne, Lot, Aveyron.

Agence Tredinnick: ☎05 45 32 41 33; props@charente-properties.com; www.charente-properties.com.

Agence Vallée des Rois Sarl: 23 rue de L'Hotel de Ville, 49250 Beaufort-en-Vallee, France; ☎02 41 45 22 22; www.loireproperty.com. French agency with British staff. Loire Valley between Angers and Saumur.

Charles Loftie Immobilier: Les Places, Les Arques, 46250 Cazals; ☎ 05 65 22 83 50; www.charles-loftie-immo.com.

Coast & Country: 'La Palombière', 71 ave de Tournamy, 06250 Mougins; ☎04 92 92 47 50; info@coast-country.com; www.coastandcountryfrance.com.

Jon Coshall, Eymet Immobilier: 7 rue du Temple, 24500 Eymet, Dordogne, France; ☎05 53 22 50 25; www.eymet-immobilier.com.

Janssens Immobilier: Cours Elzear PIN, Bonnieux; ☎04 90 75 96 98; www.janssensimmobilier.com. Luberon.

L'Affaire Française: 25 Grand Rue, Jarnac 16200; ☎05 45 81 76 79; www.French-Property-Net.com. Charente, Dordogne, Limousin.

La Foncière Charentaise: www.french-property.com/lafc. Poitou-Charentes region.

Langlois Gordon Hay: ☎05 45 95 08 51; www.lghfrance.com. La Rochefoucauld, Montbron, Nontron, Angoulême.

Properties in France Sarl PIF: ☎02 41 52 02 18; www.propertiesinfrance.com.

Nowak Immobilier: 20 rue de Pont des Barres, 86400 Civray; ☎05 49 87 03 82; www.nowakimmobilier.fr.

Papillon Properties: ☎01799 527809; www.papillon-properties.com. Offers properties in the Poitou-Charentes.

Purslows Gascony: Chateau de St. Maur, Mirande, 32300 France; ☎05 62 67 61 50; www.purslows-gascony.com. Sells farmhouses, small châteaux and manoirs, many already restored.

Roussillon Properties Int. Ltd: www.roussillonproperties.com.

Vialex International: Carl Scholfield, rue Messager, 47470 Beauville, France; ☎ 05 53 95 46 24; www.vialex.com. French/English partnership specialising in south-west France (Lot, Lot et Garonne, Lot, Tarn and Atlantic and Andorra).

Property consultants

Although it is sometimes difficult to separate them from property agents, there are some consultants who offer wide-ranging services covering all aspects of property purchase.

A Home in France: ☎0870 748 6161; info@ahomeinfrance.com; www.ahomeinfrance.com.

Homehunts: ☎0870 44 66 43; www.home-hunts.com. PACA (Provence-Alpes-Côte-d'Azur).

PWT NormandyLife; ☎02 33 79 08 68 (France) or 01273 422 143 (UK); info@normandylife.com; www.normandylife.com.

Sam Crabb: ☎01935 851155; www.samcrabb.com. Independent consultant since 1993.

◼ HOW TO FIND A HOUSE

In the UK, the first place one might consider looking would be British newspapers: the *Daily Telegraph* has regular adverts for French property, and *The Times* also carries some adverts (these are generally in a high price bracket; some are from private advertisers). There are generally few adverts for property in French newspapers; the national newspapers advertise very little. *Le Figaro* has a section for Paris.

French *immobiliers* are not that keen to send lists of properties to anyone based outside France; they prefer to deal with people who are on the spot. If you are travelling around France, it's easy to pick up lists of property that are left outside *immobiliers* all the year round.

There is a wealth of French websites with property adverts, and there are numerous French magazines with adverts sorted by department (see websites below). The main national magazine for second homes is *Résidences Sécondaires* which also has interesting articles about the property market. The main publisher for holiday properties and rentals is *Indicateur Bertrand*, and it has specialised magazines for Paris, Rhône-Alpes and the south. For more downmarket properties, it's best to try to get hold of local estate agents' lists. The cheapest properties are

Charente maritime

often in the hands of *notaires*, who will advertise on the internet. There are separate
magazines for new property developments, mainly apartments, e.g. *Immobilier
Neuf*. Magazines and websites that advertise private sellers' property will generally
have the word *particulier* in them, meaning 'private person'.

Internet

Thousands of properties are advertised on the internet in French and English. The
estate agents' websites given below, and above under 'Estate agents', are one
starting point. *Notaires*' websites (see below) often have a section on property
and carry some very general information about legal issues. General websites on
property carry a wealth of useful information, and offer the possibility of advertising
your own requests. Newspapers have *immobilier* sections on their websites (given
below).

Useful websites
- www.alps-property-finder.com
- www.everythingFrance.co.uk
- www.findyourproperty.com
- www.frenchconnections.co.uk
- www.french-property.com
- www.frenchpropertylinks.com
- www.french-property-news.com
- www.frenchways.com
- www.green-acre.com
- www.homesoverseas.co.uk
- www.houseweb.com

- www.livingfrance.com
- www.skiproperty.com

Private advertisers

- www.appelimmo.fr
- www.entreparticuliers.fr
- www.explorimmo.com
- www.journaldesparticuliers.com
- www.kitrouve.com
- www.lacentrale.fr
- www.lesiteimmobilier.com
- www.pap.fr
- www.paruvendu.fr

National property websites

- www.123immo.fr
- www.abonim.com
- www.century21.fr
- www.fnaim.fr. National estate agents organisation
- www.immoneuf.com. New property
- www.lesiteimmobilier.com
- www.letuc.com
- www.logic-immo.com
- www.nexdom.com
- www.orpi.com
- www.partenaire-europeen.fr
- www.proprietesdefrance.com. Upmarket properties
- www.seloger.com
- www.snpi.com. National estate agents organisation

Golf websites

- www.europegolftravel.com
- www.golfagora.com
- www.doucefrance.com/golf

French property magazines

- www.appelimmo.fr
- www.immobilierenfrance.com
- www.immoneuf.com
- www.indicateurbertrand.com
- www.residencessecondaires.com

General information websites

- www.ademe.fr. Agency promoting environmentally friendly building

- www.anah.fr. National association for housing improvement
- www.anil.org. State agency for housing information
- www.fnaim.fr. Estate agents' organisation
- www.ideesmaison.com. Information on building new property
- www.immoprix.com. Prices of property and land by areas
- www.immostreet.com. General information
- www.infologement.fr. Mortgage advice
- www.juri-logement.org. Legal information
- www.logement.org. General information
- www.panoranet.com. Information on mortgages and insurance
- www.seloger.com. General information
- www.service-public.gouv.fr. Government information site
- www.snpi.fr. Estate agents' organisation
- www.uncmi.org. National union of residential property builders
- www.unpi.org. Proprietors' union

Notaires' websites

- www.notaire.fr
- www.immonot.com
- www.min-immo.com

Many *départements* have their own *notaire* websites: try chambre+des+ *notaires*+(name of *département*).

Newspapers

Alsace: *L'Alsace* (www.lalsace.fr); *Dernières Nouvelles d'Alsace* (www.dna.fr/dna)

Aquitaine: *Sud Ouest* (www.sudouest.com); *Nouvelle République des Pyrénées* (www.nrpyrenees.com)

Auvergne: *Centre France-La Montagne* (www.centrefrance.com)

Brittany: *Ouest France* (www.ouestfrance-immobilier.com); *Télégramme de Brest* (www.letelegramme.com)

Burgundy: *Bien Public* (www.bienpublic.com); *Journal du Saône-et-Loire* (www.lejsl.com)

Centre: *Berry Républicain* (www.centrefrance.com); *La Nouvelle République* (www.lanouvellerepublique.fr); *La République du Centre* (www.larep.com)

Champagne-Ardennes: *Journal de la Haute Marne* (www.journaldelahautemarne. com); *Libération Champagne*

Corsica: *Corse Matin* (www.corse.info); *Journal de Corse* (www.jdcorse.com)

Franche-Comté: *Progrès de Lyon* (www.leprogres.fr); *Voix du Jura* (www.voixdujura.fr); *L'Est*

Languedoc-Roussillon: *Midi Libre* (www.midilibre.fr); *Dépêche du Midi* (www.ladepeche.com); *L'Indépendant* (www.lindependant.com); *Lozère Nouvelle* (www.lozere-nouvelle.com)

Limousin: *Centre France-Le Populaire du Centre* (www.centrefrance.com)

Lorraine: *Est Républicain* (www.estrepublicain.fr); *Liberté de l'Est*

TIP

Reading the local newspaper can help you to know more about an area.

(www.lalibertedelest.fr)

Midi-Pyrénées: *Nouvelle République des Pyrénées* (www.nrpyrenees.com); *La Dépêche* (www.ladepeche.fr)

Nord-Pas de Calais: *La Voix du Nord* (www.lavoixdunord.fr)

Normandy: *Ouest France* (www.ouestfrance-immobilier.com); *Informations Dieppoises* (http://infos-dieppoises.fr); *La Manche Libre* (www.lamanchelibre.fr)

Paris-Ile-de-France: *Le Parisien* (www.leparisien.fr); *Nouvel Observateur Paris-Ile-de-France* (www.parisobs.com)

Pays de la Loire: *Ouest France* (www.ouest-france.fr); *Presse Océan*

Picardie: *Courrier Picard* (www.courrier-picard.fr); *Voix de l'Aisne* (www.nordnet.fr/voixdelaisne)

Poitou-Charente: *Charente Libre* (www.charente.com); *Sud Ouest* (www.sudouest.com)

Provence-Alpes-Côte d'Azur: *La Provence* (www.laprovence-presse.fr); *Nice Matin* (www.nicematin.fr); *Var Matin* (www.varmatin.com); *La Marseillaise* (www.journal-lamarseillaise.com)

Rhône-Alpes: *Progrès de Lyon* (www.leprogres.fr); *Le Dauphiné Libéré* (www.ledauphine.com)

Understanding property advertisements

Property advertisements in French can be hard to interpret. Estate agents don't give detailed measurements of rooms. By law, the advertised price must include the estate agent's commission. Some agents still advertise *net vendeur* (i.e. the price the seller gets), which will be indicated by the abbreviation *HNC* or *n.c.*

Some aspects of property terms are baffling: the terms T1, F1, Formule 1, and Type 1 all mean exactly the same thing: one room + a kitchen and bathroom (which may be very small). The word English people take to mean a room – *une chambre* – actually means a bedroom; a room is *une pièce*. Some words can give rise to odd misunderstandings. If the advert says there is a *verger* included, you shouldn't imagine that you are taking over a vicarage; it means an orchard. Ads also use the English word *standing* meaning quality. The term *haut standing* implies a high-quality development, while *moyen standing* might be a warning that this isn't such a good area. Houses on *lotissements* are modern and uniform in style, but not necessarily in a bad area.

The term *maison de bourg* is used for a town centre house; the original meaning was a house within a fortified hilltop village. Nowadays, *bourg* implies that there are some shops in the vicinity. The term *bourgade* means much the same. The term *bungalow* implies a holiday home, which may not be suitable for year-round occupation. A *plain-pied* is on one storey. A *pavillon* is another ambiguous term, which could mean any detached house, but generally refers to a small holiday villa.

It's normal, but not obligatory, to give the habitable surface area of the property in the advert. There is a law (Loi Carrez) that requires the surface area of an apartment

Glossary of property advertisements

à débattre	negotiable
à rénover	to be renovated
aménageable	can be put to use
appentis	lean-to
attenant	adjoining
bastide	Provençal country house
bergerie	sheep farm
bien(s)	goods, property, estate, assets
bornage	boundary marking
bornes	boundary markers
buanderie	washhouse
carrelage	tiling
carrelé	tiled
cave	cellar
cellier	storeroom, pantry
chai	wine/spirit storehouse
chauffage fuel	oil heating
chaumière	thatched cottage
clôture	fencing, paling, hedge or other enclosure
colombage	half-timbering typical of Normandy
combles aménageables	loft conversion possible
CC/commission comprise	estate agent's commission included
débarras	junk-room
dépendances	outhouses
double séjour	large living room
écurie	stables
en exclusivité	only one estate agent is handling the sale
F1/Formule 1	one room + kitchen/bathroom
FAC/frais agence compris	agency's commission included
fermette	converted farmhouse
gentilhommière	country seat
grange	barn
grenier	attic
HNC/honoraires agence non compris	agent's commission not included
hors frais de notaire	notary costs not included

Glossary of property advertisements

HT/hors taxes	not including taxes
immeuble	apartment block, or commercial property
locataire	tenant
longère	Breton stone farmhouse
lotissement	housing estate
maison d'amis	weekend house
maison de caractère	dilapidated or unusual
maison de maître	substantial old townhouse
maison mitoyenne	semi-detached/terrace house
mas	traditional Provençal L-shaped villa
n.c./non compris	not included
piscine	swimming pool
plain pied	one storey
pressoir	cider-pressing building
prestations	features
ravalement	rendering
refait à neuf	completely renovated
rez/rez de chaussée/ RDC	ground floor
rez de jardin/RDJ	garden level
salle	living room
sans mitoyenneté	no commonly owned boundary walls or structures
sans vis à vis	no houses opposite
SdB/salle de bain	bathroom
SdE/salle d'eau	washroom
séj/séjour	living room
séjour cathédrale	open-plan living room on two floors
sous-sol	below ground-level
T1	Type 1; same as F1
TBE/très bon état	very good condition
TTC/toutes taxes comprises	all taxes included
terrain à bâtir	building land
tomettes	floor tiles
verger	orchard
vue imprenable	unrestricted view

in a *copropriété* to be given in the contract. Ads for newly built houses will always give the habitable surface area. The glossary above should guide you through the idiosyncrasies of property ads.

◤ FINANCE

Once you agree the purchase price, the next step is to sign a preliminary, legally binding contract, *le compromis de vente* (or a *promesse de vente*), and to open a French bank account ready to pay the deposit (which may be 5%–10% of the purchase price). If you have not already opened an account your mortgage lender may suggest a suitable bank. It's always preferable to have your offer of a mortgage before you sign any legally binding contract. For many buyers this may mean remortgaging their property in their home country, particularly if the interest rates in Euroland are lower than in your country.

As regards opening a bank account in France from the UK, see the section on 'Banking and finance' in the *Moving to France* chapter.

French mortgages

French mortgages – *hypothèques* – may work in a rather different way to what you are used to, even if they appear similar at first sight. The repayment mortgage is the only type available. Fixed-rate mortgages are by far the most common; it's also possible to mix fixed and variable rates, or to adjust the number of years you need to pay off your mortgage. The variable rate mortgage is the most flexible. Lump sums can be paid off and the mortgage redeemed early without any financial penalties. You can also move to a fixed rate without any charge. There can be hefty financial penalties for early redemption of a fixed rate mortgage.

The basic type of mortgage is the *hypothèque conventionelle*, the only type available if you intend to use the loan to carry out renovation or to build a new house. There are non-refundable costs of 2%–3% payable on taking out the loan. Where you are buying existing property, whether new or old, you can apply for another type of mortgage loan, the *privilège de prêteur de deniers* (PPD), which isn't subject to the registration tax and is thus less costly. Some loans are guaranteed by a mixture of PPD and *hypothèque*; the PPD can't be used to borrow money for construction or renovation costs. The third type of loan is the *caution* or *fonds de garantie* where another person or organisation stands surety for the repayment of the loan.

There is also a basic difference in concept: the mortgage lender doesn't hold the deeds to your property as security; these remain with the *notaire*. All property and land is registered with the *cadastre* – the French land registry – and given its own unique number. This is stated in the *acte de vente* (sale agreement), which remains with the *notaire*, while you have a copy. Your mortgage is registered with the local *bureau des hypothèques*, and there is a fee to have the mortgage removed once you have paid it off. When you take out a loan (*prêt*) you give the lender a *hypothèque* or charge on the property, which allows them to auction it off if you default on the loan.

The market is highly competitive: lenders advertise all sorts of attractive rates. One trick is to forget to mention the cost of death insurance – *assurance décès*. What you need to look at is the final rate – the *taux effectif global* or *TEG* – including insurance and charges. Lenders are required to furnish detailed information on the monthly repayments, the rate of repayment, and total amount repaid. You shouldn't sign a mortgage contract until the small print has been explained to you clearly.

French mortgage lenders

French banks and French mortgage providers are very different. Banks, such as BNP and Crédit Agricole, will usually only lend in their own particular area local to the branch and will usually insist that you visit them in person to open your bank account with them and complete and provide all the mortgage paperwork. Mortgage providers will lend in any region of France regardless of which office you go to. The mortgage providers don't have any banking facilities of their own, but many have arrangements with other banks to allow them to open an account for a mortgage applicant without the need to visit a bank.

French lenders don't like to pre-approve mortgages. All mortgages are full status, meaning full proof of identity, income and loans, up-to-date bank statements, etc. have to be provided. To underwrite a file completely for mortgage approval is as much work as underwriting a mortgage application. There is no guarantee that the client will return to the lender for their mortgage. This doesn't prevent you

New mortgage v remortgage

There are two possibilities: one is to remortgage your present property, the other is to take out a mortgage with a French bank using a French property as security. Remortgaging in your own country may be easier in some ways, but you could end up putting your present home at risk for the sake of buying property in France. For example, if interest rates are less stable in your country than in France, and likely to remain higher. In the case of the UK, the European Base Rate was 4% at the end of 2007 compared with 5.75% for the Bank of England Base Rate. On the other hand, the charges involved with setting up a French mortgage (*frais d'hypothèque*) are high and have to be paid up-front. French banks and mortgage providers have very strict rules about how much they will lend (see below). Lower interest rates, however, make the French mortgage more attractive at the end of the day. One solution is to go through a broker in your own country which will smooth the process, usually at a fairly minimal cost.

from sounding the lender out about a mortgage, but it's up to you to find out whether you are going to qualify.

The Loi Scrivener and protection for borrowers

Borrowers are generally well protected, but in spite of the strict rules defaults among foreigners are common, mainly because the borrower has spent too much doing up a dilapidated property, or hasn't worked out a proper business plan. In the case of default, the property is compulsorily sold at auction and will fetch considerably less than if you had sold it yourself. The law generally favours owners, and it takes a long time before a forced sale can take place.

The *Loi Scrivener* – passed in 1979 and named after Madame Scrivener who promoted it – provides for transparency in the mortgage application process, and some protection for borrowers. The main provisions include:

■ The lending organisation must first state in writing: the lender's name and address, the type of loan, the property that is to be acquired, the rate of interest, total repayment and the time period of the loan, and the fact that the property purchase is dependent on obtaining the loan. There is a *délai de réflexion* (cooling-off period) of 10 days before the offer of the loan (*offre de crédit*) can be accepted and any funds transferred

■ The initial offer of credit (*offre préalable de crédit*) will state in writing: the identity of the lender and borrower; the type of loan; the amount of the loan; and the date from which funds will be available; and the repayment terms. In the case of variable rate mortgages, the interest rate taken as a reference point, and the actual repayment rate, are stated. The offer also includes the insurance required by the bank, namely death/invalidity insurance; the guarantees and guarantors (if any) in case of default; and the costs of early repayment, or transfer of the loan

■ Once the offer has been received by registered post by the borrower and guarantors (if any), the borrower has 10 days to reflect before they can accept it. The acceptance can be sent by ordinary post. The offer of credit remains open for 30 days

The actual loan contract (contrat de prêt)

The lender can't change the conditions of the loan offer for 30 days; during this time the borrower can look at other offers. Personal guarantors (*cautions personnes physiques*) may guarantee all or part of a loan. No money will be paid to the borrower or any third parties until the offer has been accepted.

It will be stated in the *compromis de vente* that the purchase of the property will only take place on condition that the purchaser obtains a mortgage: the so-called *condition suspensive de prêt* (loan get-out clause), also known as the *clause suspensive de prêt*. Once the prospective buyer has obtained an offer of a mortgage, they are obliged to go through with the purchase of the property, even if they turn down the mortgage. The buyer will be in breach of contract if they haven't made efforts to obtain a mortgage within a reasonable time, or if they have made misleading statements about their income or assets. The *condition suspensive* cannot be used as a way of evading one's obligations.

The offer is accepted with the proviso that if the actual mortgage contract isn't concluded within four months of acceptance, then the borrower is no longer bound by the contract. If for reasons beyond the borrower's control the sale of the house doesn't go through within four months of acceptance of the mortgage, then they are freed from the mortgage contract. The borrower will, however, have to return any moneys, and pay a small compensation to the lender.

If the borrower becomes involved in litigation in connection with building work related to the house purchase, he or she may not stop repayments. This is only allowed with the authorisation of a magistrate. Once the case has been settled repayments recommence.

If the buyer has stated in the *compromis de vente* that they don't intend to seek a loan, and then decide to ask for one anyway, they are no longer protected in the same way by the *Loi Scrivener*.

To understand the likely amount of your monthly repayments, check out the following table, which gives monthly payments per €1,000. Pound sterling or dollars can be substituted for the euros.

The amount you can borrow

French regulations mean that your monthly repayments can't exceed 33% of your gross income less social charges (which are far higher than income tax). The 33%

FACT

■ In the case of early repayment, the penalty can't exceed the equivalent of six months' interest, and never more than 3% of the total of the principal sum remaining. The amount can also be less.

Monthly loan repayments

Interest rate p.a.	Repayment mortgage with a term of n years: amount in euros*				
	5	10	15	20	25
1%	17.08	8.75	5.98	4.60	3.77
2%	17.51	9.19	6.42	5.05	4.23
3%	17.93	9.63	6.88	5.52	4.72
4%	18.36	10.07	7.35	6.01	5.23
5%	18.78	10.53	7.83	6.53	5.77
6%	19.21	11.00	8.33	7.06	6.33
7%	19.65	11.47	8.84	7.60	6.91
8%	20.08	11.95	9.37	8.17	7.51
9%	20.52	12.44	9.90	8.74	8.12
10%	20.95	12.93	10.44	9.33	8.75

*Interest calculated daily.

has to include the monthly cost of existing mortgage/rent, other loans, credit card repayments, maintenance payments and the repayments of the proposed mortgage itself. At the same time, the costs and taxes associated with the property purchase, between 10% and 15% of the purchase price will also be taken into account. Mortgage lenders' websites will give you a rough idea of how much you can afford to pay (see www.adomos.com; www.guideducredit.fr; www.patrimoine.com). If you have a partner their income will be taken into account. It is less certain whether projected rental income will be taken into account; it's usually taken into account if you are purchasing a property through a leaseback scheme.

French lenders will lend rather less for a second home purchase than for a principal residence. The amount may be only 50% of the purchase price. The greater the proportion that you can pay in cash (*l'apport personnel*) the more likely they are to go to the 33% ceiling on your personal income. They are not keen to lend if you are still paying off a mortgage in your home country, depending on how much there is to pay and your income. On the other hand, they tend to ignore things such as UK National Insurance contributions (which are relatively small compared with French social charges) and take your gross monthly income as a basis for calculation.

▦ Calculating how much you can afford to borrow (capacité d'endettement)

Your net (joint) monthly earnings including investment income
Take 33% of this amount
Deduct rent, loan repayments, alimony payments, etc.
The result is the amount that you can repay per month on a French mortgage

Charges and procedures involved with French mortgages

The amount, interest rate and payment terms of the mortgage must be the same in the *acte de vente* as in the mortgage contract. Any discrepancies should be rectified. The charges are:

- ▦ The *frais de dossier* (lender's fees): approximately 1% of the loan
- ▦ Fee for opening the dossier (*ouverture de dossier*): €200–€1,000
- ▦ Fee for arranging insurance: 0.4%–0.5% of the loan
- ▦ *Notaire*'s emolument: €3,400 for a property more than five years old costing €300,000
- ▦ Fee for registering the mortgage with the Bureau des Hypothèques
- ▦ Other small charges and taxes

The maximum fees come to about 5.9% for a loan of €50,000, or 3.5% on €200,000. Some of the above fees are negotiable. French mortgage lenders generally

Documents required to apply for a French mortgage

- Copies of all the usual identification documents of all applicants: i.e. passport, birth/marriage/divorce certificates, and *carte de séjour* (residence permit) if you have one
- Notarised letter from your partner agreeing to a mortgage being taken out on the property, if they are not an applicant
- Your salary slips from the last three months
- Letter from your employer stating that you are employed
- Tax returns/statements from previous year
- Full accounts for three previous years, and current accounts, if you are self-employed
- Proof of current outgoings, such as rent, loan repayments, alimony, child support payments, etc.
- Business plan, or projected rental income, if you plan to make money from your property
- Application form and fee
- Copy of the *compromis de vente* (preliminary contract)
- Results of a medical examination (sometimes required)

only cast a rapid eye over the property to satisfy themselves that it isn't about to collapse; they are well-informed about the property market and know better than foreign buyers how much money it is safe for them to lend. You need to have money available in your French bank account to pay the fees given above when the *acte de vente* is signed, otherwise the deal cannot go through. Lenders require payments to be made by direct debit from a French bank account, which you will have to open before you apply for a mortgage in any case.

If your mortgage is in sterling or other non-euro currency, a revaluation clause (*clause de réévaluation*) may be inserted in the contract. The clause can work in favour of the lender or the borrower. If the euro has fallen in value against your home currency during the repayment period, you will be required to make up the difference to the original value in euros. The borrower may ask for a clause protecting them against a rise in the euro.

Only once the *acte de vente* has been signed, and the mortgage registered, will the *notaire* arrange for the release of the loan funds. A different situation exists if you are having a new house built. Funds are released in stages (stage payments), depending on how far construction has advanced. You only pay interest on the amounts released, not on the whole.

Mortgage glossary	
apport personnel	buyer's percentage payment
assurance décès/invalidité	death/invalidity insurance
assurance perte d'emploi	unemployment insurance
échéance modulable	variable redemption date
échéance fixe	fixed redemption date
échéancier	repayment schedule
frais de mainlevée d'hypothèque	fee for removing mortgage charge from Registry
indemnité de résiliation	early repayment penalty
mensualités	monthly repayments
prêt à taux capé	capped-rate loan
prêt à taux fixe	fixed-rate loan
prêt à taux révisable/variable	variable-rate loan
prêt relais	bridging loan
remboursement	repayment; reimbursement
remboursement anticipé sans frais	penalty-free early repayment
résiliation	cancellation
TEG (taux effectif global)	annual percentage rate (APR); effective interest rate

FACT

A property cannot be sold with a mortgage charge attached to it, unless the loan is about to be paid off.

Once the mortgage has run its course, there is a further two years to wait before it's automatically erased from the mortgage register. If you sell your property before this time, you will have to pay to have the mortgage cancelled.

Mortgage insurance

Mortgage lenders insist that you take out death/disability insurance – *assurance décès/invalidité* – even if it's not compulsory by law. The type of insurance is *assurance décès temporaire*, running for the lifetime of the mortgage contract. The premiums are lost; there is no payout at the end. Another type of death insurance – *assurance décès vie entière* – which runs until the time you actually die, does have a payout. French life insurance – *assurance vie* – is another type of savings product, unrelated to mortgages. About 2% of applicants for death insurance are turned down because of serious health problems; another 8% are only offered limited insurance; 90% are accepted. Insurance against unemployment – *assurance perte d'emploi* – is not compulsory, but is used quite a lot, since France has very high unemployment. You cannot be considered for unemployment insurance until you have been working for an employer for six to 12 months.

FACT

You can insure yourself against being forced to sell your house at a loss – *protection revente* – because of circumstances outside your control, such as divorce. The amount covered is only 10% of the purchase price or €15,000 at the most. House and contents insurance is compulsory for all owners and tenants.

Renegotiating a mortgage

Under certain circumstances it's possible to renegotiate the terms of a loan. If you are struck by a serious illness, or other circumstances beyond your control arise that make it impossible to meet your repayment schedule, you have a right to ask for a reduction in the interest rate of the loan. If the loan was taken out at a high rate of interest and rates have since gone down, you can try to negotiate with the lender for a reduction, but you will probably be turned down. You can then cancel the loan and find another lender at a lower rate of interest. At the time of writing, interest rates are low, and there isn't much reason to expect them to go much lower. Moving from a fixed to a variable rate mortgage incurs fees.

How the French buy property

The French state has various schemes in place to encourage people to save up to buy a property. The most popular is the PEL (*Prêt d'épargne Logement*); you are required to save up to a certain limit for four years, after which you are guaranteed a mortgage and you receive a premium from the state. The LEL (*Livret d'épargne Logement*) is a similar scheme but you only save for 18 months.

Then there is the so-called 1% loan, subsidised by businesses with more than 10 employees. A 0% loan is available to those who renovate properties over 20 years old, where the renovation costs exceed 35% of the price, but the loan only covers 20% of the purchase price. The state underwrites loans for properties over 20 years old, with certain conditions attached, the so-called *prêts conventionnés*. State functionaries are guaranteed loans at competitive rates. Anyone who is permanently resident in France could qualify for one of these loans.

There is also the possibility of avoiding mortgage costs completely by using a specialised co-operative organisation (*mutuelle*) to act as guarantor for the loan (for which there is a charge). Equally, if you work for the railways, post office, Air France, the education ministry, etc., these bodies act as guarantors for your mortgage loan. None of this is of much comfort to foreigners, perhaps, but gives one some idea of the advantages that the French enjoy when it comes to borrowing money.

Loi Robien-Borloo

Designed to encourage investors to invest in buy-to-let (as part of government measures to provide a solution for the lack of rental property) this law enables you to receive certain tax advantages when you become the owner of a new property that is rented for a period of nine to 15 years.

Loans for main residence

The loi Robien-Borloo gives a tax credit to French residents who take out a loan to buy or build their main residence. This tax credit of 20% or the loan interest paid each year, up to a maximum of €3,750 for a single person and €7,500 for a couple can be set against income tax. It's aimed at people from modest incomes to help them get on the property ladder.

Mortgage brokers/advisers

Banque Transatlantique: www.transat.tm.fr. A French bank for newcomers to France. Bank accounts, mortgages (up-market properties in Paris and selected provincial areas), legal and tax information

Barclays France: ☎0810 090909; www.barclays.fr. A list of branches is available on their website

Charles Hamer: ☎+44 (0)1844 218956; www.charleshamer.co.uk

Conti Financial Services: ☎01273 772811; enquiries@mortgagesoverseas.com; www.mortgagesoverseas.com. Well-established independent mortgage brokers

Credit Agricole: The Credit Agricole has an excellent network of branches throughout France, many of which have English speaking staff offering a global banking service including property finance and insurance. However, the website is difficult to navigate. We recommend you enter 'credit agricole' + 'mortgages' + 'France' into your search engine (Google) to get the coordinates of a number of regional sites in English

Finance Immo: ☎04 93 629 639; www.financeimmo.com. They will negotiate a loan with a partner bank

Mortgage France: ☎05 62 09 38 41; www.mortgagefrance.com. Arranges mortgages all over France at no cost to applicant. Useful website

Templeton Associates: UK ☎01225 422282; info@templeton-france.com; www.templeton-france.com. French mortgage and finance experts

UCB International Buyers: ☎02 51 86 68 29; customerservice@ucb.fr; ucb-french-mortgage.com. Part of BNP Paribas. This is a subsidiary dedicated to working with international buyers. See the website for their branches in France

The amount which can be borrowed on a property over five years old is usually up to 85% of the purchase price, not including the *notaire* or estate agent's fees. New properties are treated differently, in that if they are under five years old, the purchase price will include TVA of 19.6% the first time it changes hands. It is possible to borrow up to 95% of the purchase price ex-TVA. In practice 100% mortgages are available but special terms would have to be negotiated. Note that as in the UK, mortgages on a property cannot be transferred from owner to owner as is possible in the USA.

■ INHERITANCE LAW AND WILLS

The subject of succession tax (*droits de succession*) and gift tax (*droits de donation*) needs to be carefully considered before you buy a property in France. Failure to take the right steps before signing an *acte de vente* can have serious consequences for your heirs; it's difficult to make changes to the *acte de vente* once it has been registered. If your family situation is at all complicated – many foreign property-buyers have been married more than once – then legal advice is a necessity, and highly desirable even in straightforward situations. Several names are given below.

The first issue to consider is that of domicile, which rests on legal precedent. Domicile is something like nationality, but harder to lose. Loosely speaking, your country of domicile is the one where you have had the longest-lasting ties during your lifetime, or the country you intend to return to after living abroad. If you were resident in France on your decease, the French tax authorities will claim that your heirs should pay French succession taxes on your worldwide assets, or at the very least on your assets in France. In the case of the UK, the tax authorities are very reluctant to concede that a British citizen is no longer domiciled in the UK. Foreign domicile can only be established after 'exhaustive enquiries'.

There are potential advantages to being taxed in France if the inheritance exceeds the UK inheritance tax threshold. The top rate in France of 40% only kicks in on inheritances over €1.7 million (£1.3 million). Important changes were introduced to inheritance law in France in 2007. The *Loi TEPA* (Law no. 2007 1223, dated 21 August 2007) abolished inheritance tax for the surviving spouse. This only applies to inheritance not lifetime gifts. Lifetime gifts between spouses are still subject to the €76,000 threshold (see below).

If you are relatively wealthy, you will want to disperse your assets in good time, leaving as little as possible for the taxman. The good news for Brits is that there is a double taxation agreement between France and the UK concerning inheritances, so as long as you are open and honest about matters you won't have to pay inheritance taxes twice. There is also a general principle, however, that you pay inheritance tax in the country which has the higher rate.

Inheritance explained

According to the French system of inheritance tax – strictly speaking 'succession rights' or 'succession taxes' (*droits de succession*) – you are not free to leave your assets to anyone you please. Blood relatives come before your spouse or partner, who may be treated almost as though they were strangers, unless you take appropriate measures. The logic behind this is simple. Napoleon saw that too many men were leaving their properties to their mistresses, or their wives, so he instituted a system that would ensure that property remained with the blood family.

French succession taxes

Under French law, one part of your assets has to be left to specified members of your family (*la réserve légale*), while the rest is yours to do with as you please (*la quotité disponible*). Blood relatives are entitled to inherit in descending order.

Grandchildren become reserved heirs if the children are no longer living. Brothers and sisters can be disinherited. They only inherit automatically if there are no descendants, ascendants or spouse. If deceased, nephews and nieces can inherit in their place. Children of the current marriage are treated equally with children of previous marriages, and children born outside marriage, including half-siblings of the deceased's children. The principle that children born out of 'adultery' have equal rights with their half-siblings has only recently been accepted in France. In the absence of the above, relatives take precedence over non-relatives, depending on their relationship to the deceased, up to the fourth degree. Relatives beyond the fourth degree are considered to be unrelated for the purpose of inheritance tax.

The *Loi TEPA* changed the rules of the 2005 French Finance Act, raising succession tax threshold rates to further favour the children of the deceased. The previous system provided that a personal allowance of €50,000 was given to each child when one parent died or had made a gift. In addition, an estate allowance of €50,000 was to be divided between all beneficiaries. Under the new regime, the personal allowance has been increased to €150,000, but the global estate allowance no longer applies. The €150,000 exemption applies for each child. Inheritance and gift taxes between parents and children are levied at the following rates.

Between siblings, the allowance has been raised to €15,000 which applies to gifts and inheritances. In addition, if the siblings are living together and are older than 50 or are disabled, the estate of the deceased passes to the sibling without inheritance tax. Brothers, sisters and grandchildren pay at rates of 35% (€15,195–€23,299) and 45% on the excess. More distant relatives up to the fourth degree pay at 55%. Anyone else pays at 60%.

Matrimonial regimes and succession

The law distinguishes between three types of partner: a marriage partner; a *concubin* with whom you live without entering into a legally recognised partnership,

FACT

RESERVED HEIRS

◼ Children: 50% for the first child; 66.6% between two children; 75% between three and above. No distinction is made between children from a first and subsequent marriage

◼ Parents: Where there are no children, parents receive 25% each. A single surviving parent can only receive 25%

◼ Spouses: Only become reserved heirs if there are no direct ascendants or descendants

Tax percentage	Children/parents
0	The first 151,950
5	The next 7,600
10	7,699–11,548
15	11,548–15,195
20	15,195–526,762
30	526,762–861,053
35	861,053–1,722,105
40	1,722,105 and over

known as a *union libre* (roughly equivalent to a 'common-law partner'); and a partner with whom you have entered into an official notarised civil contract, the PACS (*Pacte Civil de Solidarité*). The latter was instituted in 1999 to improve the lot of gay couples; the contractants make themselves liable for each other's debts and agree to support each other; they can file joint tax returns from the time that they enter into their civil contract in the same way as married partners. Any two people who are not closely related can enter into a civil contract, whether they are couples or just live together. The PACS can be dissolved as well. If you simply live with another person in *union libre* then your partner is treated as unrelated, and pays the full 60% rate.

If you become resident in France, you can change to a more suitable marriage regime specifying how assets are divided on the death of one partner. In all there are five different marriage regimes, making the system very complex. Changing marriage regime is costly, at least €1,500. Evidently, you need to take professional advice if you want to change your marriage regime. You can only change your marriage regime if you are actually resident in France, and it needs to be done before you buy a property. Note that many couples moving to France go for the *communauté universelle avec clause d'attribution intégrale* as until the *TEPA* law this was the simplest way of allowing your partner to acquire all your assets on your death without any succession tax being paid; only 1% registration duty is payable. Although this change is no longer needed for avoidance of inheritance tax, it is necessary to avoid the French inheritance rules of forced heirship. You must still go for the *communauté universelle* if you want all your estate to go to your spouse on your death. Your children and other heirs then have to wait for the

If you have a partner

French law is far less favourable to partners; to improve the partner's situation the law was changed in 2002, the main change being that the surviving partner has the option of remaining in the marital home for the rest of their life. The partner can also choose to move out of the property, and receive their part of the assets of the deceased. This is often the best solution where several children jointly inherit a property and want to dispose of it. It can be too much of a headache staying on in a property which is owned by children of your partner's previous marriage whom you don't get on with.

second partner's decease before they can inherit their rightful share. This solution can't be used to disinherit children from the deceased's previous marriages. This regime does mean that each partner is liable for the debts of the other and that the surviving partner can do what they want with the assets, and may use them to benefit his or her new partner.

Another possibility is the *communauté légale réduite aux acquêts* – where only the assets acquired during the course of the marriage are common property. A simpler solution is the *régime de séparation des biens* – separation of estates – where the marriage partners' assets before and during the marriage remain completely separate. The French authorities assume that you are married under the *régime de séparation des biens* if your marriage was contracted in the UK, and for most marriages in the USA (a few states influenced by French law have a different system).

For *donation entre époux* (gift between spouses), an act which can be registered with a notary for a minimal cost, see below.

Buying en tontine

The *tontine* was thought up by an Italian banker, Lorenzo Tonti, in the 18th century. In France it's more correctly called a *clause d'accroissement*. This is where two or more people, whether married or not, acquire assets, on the understanding that the one who lives the longest acquires the whole, thus entirely cutting out the inheritors of the other members of the *tontine*. For legal purposes deceased members of a *tontine* – and, by extension, their inheritors – are treated as though they never had any share in the assets. The survivor is treated as though they owned the property from the day that it was bought. Where the partners are unrelated, or *concubins*, the 'winner' of the *tontine* is subject to succession tax at 60% on half the value of the property, unless the property is worth less than €76,000 and it is their principal residence, in which case the survivor only pays much lower transfer taxes.

Partners can enter into a *tontine* if they have roughly the same life expectancy and can therefore profit equally from the *tontine*. They should also contribute equal amounts to the purchase. You can't buy *en tontine* with your children as partners, or with someone who is likely to die soon. A disadvantage of a *tontine* is that it's impossible to sell your part of the *tontine* since the buyer will lose everything if the person they bought their share from dies before the other members. If your partner in the *tontine* is also your spouse, then any dispute becomes very unpleasant. All the members have to agree to dissolve a *tontine* and it's still a costly and slow process.

Spouses married under the separate estates regime – for instance, which means everyone married in the UK, and most couples married in the USA – can enter a *tontine* and could benefit from this arrangement. The main advantage is that it allows you to decide who will inherit your property. It is effective in cutting the family of the partner who dies first out of the will. It is not actually tax-efficient (except for very cheap properties), since there is only one heir in this situation, and no flexibility as to who inherits.

Setting up a Société Civile Immobilière (SCI)

A potentially useful way of minimising succession taxes is to buy your property through an SCI which you have set up yourself. You are then the owner of the shares which you can give to your children during your lifetime. This is best done at the start, otherwise you will have to pay transfer taxes if you sell the property to the SCI later. There are considerable costs involved; setting up the SCI costs on average €2,500. There will also be Capital Gains Tax (*l'impôt sur les plus values immobilières*) to pay when the property is sold (see below).

If you already own a property and want to set up an SCI, the most effective method is to transfer only the *nue propriété* (ownership without lifetime interest or *usufruit*) of the property to the SCI, which has a far lower value than the *pleine propriéte*, while retaining the *usufruit* for your lifetime. You would then give your child(ren) the shares in the company that correspond to the *nue propriété*, and pay a small amount of gift tax on the amount.

The main requirement of the SCI is the holding of an annual general meeting. Decisions about the running of the company can be made by majority shareholder voting, thus avoiding the problems of the *indivision* where unanimity is required between all the partners.

The SCI isn't ideal if you are planning to run *gîtes*, or *chambres d'hôtes*. The solution is to rent the property out to another business structure, a SARL. There are also certain implications from the point of view of UK tax authorities which concern directors' benefits-in-kind. If the tax authorities are aware that as a director you have the free use of a property in France for holidays then you can become liable for income tax on the assessed benefits-in-kind. The way around this is to ensure that shareholders are not managers – *gérants* – of the company.

You should seek expert legal advice if you are thinking of setting up an SCI. While it's not that difficult to set one up, the terms under which it is set up must be carefully considered. The SCI is useful for expensive properties. It is also very useful where unrelated people wish to buy a property together, such as in the case of co-ownership.

Buying en indivision

The concept of *indivision* is fundamental in French law. Where two or more persons buy a property jointly they automatically enter into an *indivision*, unless they opt for another regime, such as the *tontine* or the SCI. The term *indivision* came about because, while the members of the *indivision* have separate shares, the assets themselves are not divided up. Members of the *indivision* can leave if they wish, or ask to have the *indivision* dissolved through a court of law. Couples married under the regime of common property – *communauté des biens* – automatically have equal shares in a property, given that their names are on the *acte de vente*. There is also the possibility that only property that is acquired during the marriage is commonly owned. Under the regime of separate estates – *séparation des biens* – the property can be divided up unequally, or only one partner may own it.

Where two or more heirs inherit a property, they automatically enter an *indivision* and become *indivisaires*, until such time as the members decide to end the *indivision*. If you go to a *notaire* and ask to see their portfolio of properties, you may see a file of 'problem' properties, where the owners are *indivisaires* or several people have some claim to a property. Often it is more convenient to rent the property out and leave matters alone. The *indivisaires* can decide to prolong the *indivision* for a certain length of time, and make up a *convention d'indivision*, a written contract. Once the members fall out with each other the only solution is to break up the *indivision*. Serious problems can arise if one member dies. The positive side of the *indivision* is that it's easy to enter into; no written agreement is required. Each member retains their share of the property and benefits proportionally from the income generated.

Using gifts to favour your heirs

Depending on your age, you can lighten the tax burden by giving away assets in good time. Gift tax – *droits de donation* – is payable at the same rates as inheritance tax (i.e. the personal allowance between parents and children is €150,000 but this isn't the case between spouses who must still pay gift tax for gifts within the lifetime of the donor on gifts over €76,000). It has to be paid immediately, but the donor can pay the tax on behalf of the donee. Tax is reduced if the donor dies more than six years after the gift is made. In France an additional tax-free amount of €20,000 was allowed for gifts to children and grandchildren over 18 between 25 September 2003 and 30 June 2005. This measure was extended to gifts made to great-grand children or nieces/nephews, with the allowance increased to €30,000. The donor must be under 65 when the gift takes place and the donee over 18.

Donation entre époux/donation au dernier vivant

These are two names for one type of gift. The gift can be written into the marriage contract in which case it's irrevocable; otherwise it can be revoked without informing the partner. The *donation au dernier vivant* means 'gift to the survivor'. The survivor only receives the assets on the death of their partner.

The *donation entre époux* is of benefit to the spouse when the deceased leaves family members who are reserved heirs. Without the *donation entre époux*

The six years' rule

In France the estate allowance is renewed every six years. This means that if a gift is made between parents and children of, say, €100,000 then no gift tax is paid because it is under the threshold of €150,000. If the parent then dies within six years, the child will be taxed on the money received from the estate less an allowance of €50,000 (€150,000-€100,000). If the parent dies after the period of six years, the child's estate allowance will still be €150,000. The gift allowance of €30,000 described above isn't part of the six years' rule. The estate allowance won't include the gift of €30,000.

the surviving partner will receive less than they would have if their partner had made the *donation*. On the death of the partner the survivor can opt to continue to have the *usufruit* or benefits of the spouse's entire assets for the rest of their lives, while the children have the *nue propriété*, i.e. they own the assets without having the use or profit of them. The surviving partner can manage the deceased's portfolio of investments, but they can be challenged by the deceased's blood relatives if they appear to be mismanaging the assets. The survivor can also opt to receive the part of the inheritance that they are allowed as *pleine propriété* (see *Reserved Heirs* above), without the *usufruit*, or to have 25% *pleine propriété* and 75% *usufruit*. This regime is particularly useful where there are children from previous marriages.

The *donation entre époux* may not be the best method of reducing succession taxes; it's simpler and cheaper to put the provisions you want in your will. You should take legal advice before making a gift to ensure that this is best for you. This type of gift must be registered with a *notaire*. It's doubtful whether non-residents can enter into a *donation entre époux*.

Disinheriting a partner

Since 2002, it has become much more difficult to disinherit a partner entirely. As a minimum, the surviving partner should receive either 25% of the full property or the *usufruit* of the property for their lifetime. Tax on the *usufruit* has been increased to reflect the increased life span of surviving spouses. The surviving partner has an absolute right to remain in the marital home for one year from the decease, even when the home is rented. Although various provisions can be put into a *testament authentique* to try to prevent the surviving partner from continuing to occupy the conjugal home, these are not likely to stand up in a French court. A great deal depends on how many reserved heirs there are.

Disinheriting other family

If you want to favour your partner and provide them with an income for life, the simplest thing to do is to sell your property for a *rente viagère*, a pension annuity. The buyer often pays an initial 20%–30% of the price, and then an agreed annual sum to you and your partner, until your death. The contract includes a clause that your partner then receives the annuity until they die. The property then passes to the buyer. Your family can't make any objections.

Wills

It's possible for a Brit to pay inheritance tax on a second home in France to the UK taxman. But such an arrangement may not be in your interest and could get you into trouble with the French authorities. If you are from the UK, one procedure is to make a UK will, after taking advice from someone familiar with French inheritance law, and have it translated into French and notarised, but having a will translated by an official translator can be very expensive, and the results may not even be that accurate. The other possibility is to make up a UK will with no mention of your French property. The French will only relates to your French assets. Before you make a will in France, you should take professional advice to make sure that it doesn't conflict with, or invalidate your other will. Provisions in your other will can be taken

FACT

■ Fewer and fewer buyers are willing to enter a *rente viagère*, given the increasing life expectancy of sellers.

Houses along the river in Strasbourg

The three types of will

- Holographic (*testament olographe*): entirely in the person's handwriting, it is best done in French, and is generally not witnessed. If you choose, you can register it with the central register of testaments, the Fichier de Dernières Volontés. Most wills in France are in this form
- Authentic (*testament authentique*): can be printed or written and has to be witnessed by two notaries or one notary and two other persons. Automatically registered with the Fichier de Dernières Volontés
- Secret (*testament mystique*): a will made or dictated by a person who then hands it over in a sealed and signed envelope to a notary in the presence of two witnesses. The notary writes on it 'sealed document' or other comments. The testator either leaves it with the notary or keeps it themselves

TIP

- Leave copies of your will with a notary in France. If your heirs don't know where your will is or you lock it away in a safe deposit box in a French bank, this can make life difficult. You will help your heirs immeasurably by making sure that they have easy access to documents.

into account by the French authorities, as long as they are not in conflict with French law. Care needs to be taken if you make up another will at a later date: clauses such as 'this will invalidates all previous wills' can be disastrous if you have two wills.

The holographic testament is generally the best, with the proviso that someone needs to know where it's kept. The secret testament has virtually fallen out of use.

Inheritance procedures

Once someone has passed away, the family and/or partner need to visit the notary who dealt with the deceased's will as soon as is practically possible after registering the death at the town hall. The surviving partner, potential inheritors, the executor or creditors can request a *greffier en chef* (chief clerk) from the local civil court to put seals on the deceased's property (*pose de scellés*) if they believe there is a risk of theft or fraud. The *greffier* can make up a list of the goods and conduct a search for a will.

The names of the heirs are listed on the *acte de notoriété*, a legal document made up by the *notaire* or by a chief clerk of the court. This doesn't mean that heirs can immediately take their part of the inheritance, or that they are bound to accept an inheritance encumbered with debts. An heir can register the deceased's car in their name, with the right documents, and the agreement of the other heirs, before the estate is finally divided up.

The documents required to start the inheritance process include:

■ The death certificate

■ A copy of the French will

■ A copy of the British will, translated into French

■ The names of all the potential inheritors

■ Marriage/divorce certificates

■ Death certificates of deceased former inheritors still mentioned in the will, if any

In the course of time, you will need to produce documents relating to all of the deceased's bank accounts, investments and properties. The inheritors, and anyone who has received gifts from the deceased subject to gift tax, are required to file a *déclaration de succession* within a year. Interest is payable on the succession tax after six months if the deceased died in France, or 12 months if abroad. The *déclaration* is a form obtained from the French tax office. Foreigners will find it convenient to mandate a notary to make the *déclaration*. The succession tax has to be worked out by the person filling in the *déclaration*. The tax authorities can challenge the value you place on a property, by comparing it with similar properties in the area.

The tax doesn't come out of the inheritance; the inheritors are required to pay it together before they can receive the inheritance. It is possible to ask for a delay in payment of up to 10 years; you can also ask to pay in instalments.

It's possible to use an executor (*exécuteur testamentaire*) named in your will in France, but this is probably best avoided, unless you have reason to believe that your next of kin are untrustworthy or incompetent. Unless the executor is a notary, the French authorities may assume that the executor is actually an heir and charge them the maximum rate of tax: 60%. The executor is charged with filing the *déclaration de succession* correctly. They are entitled to payment for the work they do, which can come to a substantial sum, another reason to avoid using them.

For a detailed overview of French succession law, see Henry Dyson's *French Property and Inheritance Law* (Oxford University Press). This is a technical work written for lawyers, but still comprehensible to laypeople. For a general overview of inheritance in the UK and France, see Bill Blevins and David Franks' *Living in France*, published by Blevins Franks Ltd. If you read French, then you can find the latest information on www.lesechos.fr or the government website, www.service-public.gouv.fr.

◼ IMPORTING CURRENCY

When buying property in France you will, under normal circumstances, have to pay in euros, the local currency. In the days of foreign exchange controls before 1974, it was usual to take a suitcase full of bank notes over to France to pay for property. Thanks to the EU, you can take as much cash as you like with you if you're from the UK, but there is no advantage in doing so, and it's certainly risky. If you take more than €10,000 in cash in or out of France you are required to declare it.

Currency is nowadays usually sent using electronic transfer; the SWIFT system is the most well known. There are charges involved at both ends so you need to know who is paying for them, and how much the receiving bank in France is likely

TIP

◼ For those who prefer to know exactly how much money they have available for their property purchase, forward buying is the best solution.

An imposing property in the Loire Valley

to charge. The receiving bank should charge very little (see the section on 'Banking and finance' in the chapter *Before You Go*).

A specialised company such as Currencies Direct (☎0845 389 3000, http://currenciesdirect.com) can help in several ways, by offering better exchange rates than banks, without charging commission, and giving you the possibility of 'forward buying' – agreeing on the rate that you will pay at a fixed date in the future – or with a limit order – waiting until the rate you want is reached. Payments can be made in one lump sum or on a regular basis. It's usual when building new property to pay in four instalments, so-called 'stage payments'.

There is a further possibility, which is to use the services of a law firm to transfer the money. They can hold the money for you until the exact time that you need it; they will use the services of a currency dealer themselves.

■ INSURANCE (ASSURANCES)

The French insurance market is very competitive and high profile. You could add your French property to your current home insurance, as long as it fulfils French legal requirements. However, the received wisdom is that it's better to insure with a local company in France who are able to handle claims in English, so that you get a quick response in case of problems. Having your claim translated into French is expensive and time-consuming. There are English-speaking agents in many parts of France who can arrange insurance for you. Some agents sell policies for only one company (*agents généraux*), and others deal with several (*courtier d'assurances*).

House and contents insurance

The basic house and contents insurance is the *assurance multirisques habitation*, also often called *assurance multirisques vie privée* or *la multirisque*. This will include cover against natural disasters as a matter of course. Civil liability insurance – *responsabilité civile propriétaire* – is essential, in case an event on your property affects your neighbours. Your possessions also need to be insured. This kind of policy doesn't insure you against personal accidents, unless you ask for it. There are numerous formulas for the *assurance multirisques*, depending on your requirements.

It's possible to take over the existing insurance from the previous owner of the property you are buying; if you say nothing then that is assumed. If you don't wish to continue the same insurance policy – generally the wisest course of action for foreign buyers – you are required to present another policy to the *notaire* before you can sign the final *acte de vente*.

It's normal to insure the contents of your property as well. The current market value or *valeur vénale* of the items is used to work out the amount of cover; depreciation is taken into account. The insurers can insist on shutters being fitted to windows and bars on doors, and other security measures. You need to keep receipts, guarantees, photographs, etc. of your possessions in a safe place for any claims.

If there is nothing of value in your property you can take out a basic insurance against damage from natural causes, vandalism, terrorist acts, etc., known as an *assurance multirisques d'immeuble*. This is used by *copropriétés* (a building's joint management committee) and some owners of blocks of flats. This will be calculated

TIP

■ Read the small print in the policy, and watch out that you are not underinsured.

by the square metre. There should be a clause in which the insurer agrees to rebuild or restore the property to its original state within two years in the same style.

Insurance copropriétés

In the case of a *copropriété*, the building insurance will be taken care of by the manager of the property, and your share of the premiums will appear on the monthly charges. You are responsible for insuring your own possessions, and for third party insurance for anyone visiting your premises.

Holiday homes

Burglaries of holiday homes are common, especially on the Riviera, or any isolated area. An insurance policy for a principal residence isn't suitable for a holiday home; there are usually clauses making the policy void if the house is left empty for more than 30 days. To get insurance cover, you will be expected to put in additional locks, shutters, burglar alarms and grills. Some owners go so far as to install webcams so they can watch their property being broken into. The longer you are away from the property, the higher your premiums will be, and the less likely the insurers are to cover valuables. Premiums vary widely around the country; they are highest in the south-east where there are more fires than in the rest of France.

Terms and conditions

Thefts

It is a condition of insurance policies that you report thefts within 24 hours to the police, or as soon as possible, if you want your claim to be taken seriously. The police will give you a form – *déclaration de vol* – with the details of what you have lost. You need to inform the insurers within two working days of the theft and send the receipt of the *déclaration* by registered post (*recommandée*), with an *avis de réception* (AR) or confirmation of receipt. It's advisable to telephone the insurer immediately and they will send you a confirmation. You then draw up a list of the stolen goods and send it by registered post.

Natural disasters

There is a whole raft of regulations about which natural events count as disasters or *catastrophes naturelles*. The amount of time you have to report a disaster ranges from four days for hail to 10 days after a storm, if this has been declared a *catastrophe naturelle* in the official journal. Your house insurance should cover not only *catastrophes naturelles* but also all kinds of other natural risks. You don't have to pay for cover against snow, unless you think it's necessary. Check that the policy covers damage to electrical items as well.

Checking the small print

Look carefully at the small print in the policy to see what conditions are set for reporting damage, thefts, etc., and any exclusions. Check for the *franchise* or excess,

Insurance glossary	
assurance multirisques habitation	house and contents insurance
bris de glaces	window breakage
cambriolage	burglary/housebreaking
certificat de perte	police statement listing your losses
effraction	breaking and entering
franchise	excess (GB); deductible (US)
grêle	hail
incendie	fire
police	policy
protection juridique	legal protection
résiliation	cancellation
responsabilité civile	civil liability
risques locatifs	tenant's liability
store	heavy shutters
vol	theft
volet	shutters

i.e. the first part of the claim that isn't paid. Taking videos and photos of property is an eminently sensible precaution to make sure you are paid in full. You can use a court bailiff – *huissier* – or an insurance expert, to prepare a report on damage to your property (for a fee). The insurance company will usually send their own expert to draw up a report on your loss.

Policies are renewed automatically (*tacite reconduction*); you are given a period of time before the renewal date when you can cancel the policy. Once the date has passed it's too late to cancel. Premiums should be paid by standing order, within 10 days of the set date. You will receive a warning (*mise en demeure*) from the insurer. If you haven't paid within 30 days your policy will be cancelled, but you will still be liable for the outstanding amount and the insurer's costs.

Insurance of schoolchildren

The state school system obliges parents to insure their children when they undertake voluntary activities. Private schools set their own rules. If one of your children goes to a state school and another to a private school you may be able to put them both on one policy. The *assurance scolarité* should cover not only harm that a child could occasion to third parties, but also any harm that could come to him or her (*garantie individuelle accidents*) which isn't included in your usual house insurance. Without this insurance, your child won't be allowed to go on excursions. You can go further and insure your child's belongings, or against all sorts of disease; the sky is the limit.

Where to find insurance

Insurance companies are listed in the French yellow pages under *assurances;* some agents advertise in the French property magazines such as *French Property News.*

Below are some insurance companies specialising in foreign homes, as well as other types of insurance.

Agence Eaton: ☎02 97 40 80 20; sales@french-insurance.com; www.french-insurance.com. Bilingual insurance bureau

AXA Courtage: www.axa.fr. List of agencies on site. Large French insurer with branches in UK

Barlow Redford & Co: ☎+44 (0)1582 761129;

Cabinet FX Bordes: ☎05 53 61 03 50. General agents for French insurance company; based in Perigord. Household insurance

Copeland Insurance: ☎+44 (0)20 8656 2544; info@acopeland.com; www.andrewcopeland.co.uk. Buildings and contents insurance for France and special scheme for UK-registered cars in France

MMA: www.mma.fr. Agencies all over France

O'Halloran & Co: ☎+44 (0)1522 537491; www.ohalloran.org.uk. Will arrange cover for holiday homes in Europe

Towergate Holiday Homes Underwriting: ☎0844 736 8261; www.towergateholidayhomes.co.uk. Specialists in providing cover for holiday homes, chalets and caravans in Europe, with policy wording to meet local requirements, including the payment of insurance taxes. Premiums and claims in sterling. Policy wording in English with French translation available. Extension to pay for emergency travel to your home in the event of a claim. In-house claims service

Useful publications

Buying a House in France, by André de Vries. Published by Vacation Work Publications; www.crimsonpublishing.co.uk

Taxation in France and Letting French Property Successfully, Published by PKF Guernsey, these are regularly updated and give detailed information on the current tax scene. See www.pkfguernsey.com

French Property and Inheritance Law, by Henry Dyson, Published by Oxford University Press

Living in France, by Bill Blevins and David Franks. Published by Blevins Franks, www.blevinsfranks.com. Extensive guide to taxation, social security and other legal aspects.

Starting a Business in France, by André de Vries. Published by Vacation Work Publications. The only detailed guide in English to starting a business in France currently available

■ INSPECTIONS AND SURVEYS

Having a property surveyed before you buy it is more or less a matter of course in some countries such as the UK, but not so in France. Fewer than 3% of buyers have a survey done in France against 95% in the UK.

The reasons for the lack of interest in surveys are cultural. In the countryside people assume that if a house looks solid it isn't likely to fall down within their lifetime. French property sellers may not accept a clause such as 'subject to survey' in the preliminary contract. Any general survey should be done before signing the preliminary contract. If you want to secure the property by signing a preliminary contract, but you have a concern about a specific aspect of the property, it may be possible to insert a clause requiring further checks to be done.

There is no such profession as 'chartered surveyor' in France. There is the *géomètre-expert*, whose job is to calculate the surface area of buildings and land, and then there are architects who do some surveying as well. Specialised firms of surveyors are hard to find, and their services are expensive since they have to keep a whole group of different professionals working together under one roof. Information can be found on www.geometre-expert.fr.

Compulsory surveys

In some respects, there is protection for buyers from *'vices cachés'* – latent faults – in that an inspection has to be done everywhere in France for the presence of asbestos. Surveys for termites and lead paint are not required in every case. The inspection is done at the expense of the seller of the property, who has to present the expert's report when the pre-sale agreement is signed. The expert who carries

Savoie-Tignes, a great skiing destination

out the work isn't allowed to have any links with firms who carry out treatment for termites, asbestos or lead paint. One can look under *expert* in the yellow pages. Note that the term *expertise immobilière* refers to valuations; people who carry them out are often *notaires*, not surveyors. Technical surveys come under *expertises techniques*. Some *notaires* have surveyors working for them.

Termites

The original law intended to protect house-buyers from insect infestations dates from 1999; it was originally intended to cover not only *termites* but also other kinds of insect infestations, such as death watch beetle (*grosse vrillette*) and woodworm (*petite vrillette*), as well as dry rot, wet rot and other fungi. The subsequent decree from 2000 only mentions termites. Other wood-eating insects are not covered, nor are dry rot and wet rot. Inspections only have to be done where a prefectural decree has been issued requiring one; much of the south-western quarter of France comes under this category. The expert will draw up an *état parasitaire*. If the expert notices other signs of wood-eating insects apart from termites, they will mention them, but the search is basically only for termites. The report is valid for three months and must be presented at the signing of the *acte de vente*.

The worst infestations of termites are in the Landes, followed by Gironde, Charente Maritime, and Lot-et-Garonne, where over half the *communes* are affected. The Dordogne is also quite badly affected, as are parts of the Loire Valley. The only way to be entirely certain whether there is a termite infestation in your *commune* is to ask the *préfecture* or *mairie* (local government offices).

Asbestos/amiante

The requirement to carry out inspections for the presence of asbestos was extended to all properties for sale starting from the beginning of 2003. The *compromis de vente* cannot be finalised without the survey report, which is carried out at the expense of the seller. Out of the three types of asbestos, blue and brown asbestos are known to be dangerous; white asbestos is apparently harmless. Asbestos can be found mixed with cement, plaster and paint, and has been used for pipes, wall panels, floor tiles, corrugated sheeting and slates. It has also been used a lot in industrial and commercial buildings. In itself, asbestos doesn't present a risk unless it starts to flake and release dust. The technical expert who prepares the report will tell you what action needs to be taken. You shouldn't try to remove or cut through asbestos-containing materials yourself.

Lead/plomb

Paint containing lead was widely used until recently. It presents a danger to human health where it flakes off or turns to dust. This can cause the syndrome known as *saturnisme* in French, a retarding of the brain functions, hence one will see notices about *la lutte contre le saturnisme*, 'the struggle against saturnism'. The main victims are immigrants living in damp old houses in big cities.

The seller of a property is required to call in an expert to prepare a report – a *diagnostic plomb* – in areas where there is a prefectural decree in force. This only concerns properties built before 1 January 1949. The report is valid for one year and is to be presented before signing the pre-sale agreement. Where there is no prefectural decree in force requiring an inspection, you need to be on your guard

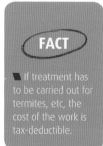

that there is no lead paint in the basement of the property you want to buy, or elsewhere. Once you sign the contract accepting the property in the condition in which it is sold, there is no way to obtain compensation if you find lead paint later on, unless you can prove that the seller deliberately misled you.

Radon gas

This is a colourless, odourless gas, released by the breakdown of uranium. About 9% of all lung cancers are caused by radon gas. Unhealthy concentrations can be found in houses built on granite, such as one might find in some parts of Brittany.

Boundaries

When buying a property, you need to know where the boundaries lie, otherwise you may find that you have less land than you expected. It's quite common for there to be no precise boundaries between properties. The *géomètre-expert* establishes *bornes* or boundary markers. See www.geometre-expert.fr.

UK surveyors

Since there is a gap in the market not filled by French surveyors, a number of British chartered surveyors have started business in France, mainly in the south-west where there is a lot of old property to be bought for renovation. Some are based in the UK and France, and will travel out to France for you. There are also British architects who carry out surveys, prepare applications for building permits, etc. French surveyors should belong to the Ordre des Architectes. Names and co-ordinates are given in property magazines and English-language newspapers.

The following are all qualified surveyors.

Nick Adams: ☎05 49 75 37 70; info@adamsgautier.com; www.adamsgautier.com. Mid south-west France

James Latter: ☎02 31 90 17 70; www.surveyors-en-france.com. Normandy, Pays de Loire, Ile de France

Ian Morris: ☎01684 576775 (UK); tel 04 67 89 43 46 (FR); www.surveyors-en-france.com. Languedoc-Roussillon, Midi-Pyrénées, Aquitaine

Nick Norrie: ☎07979 771166/01869 346973; office@subject2survey.fsnet.co.uk; www.subject2survey.com

Pierre Weingaertner: ☎06 60 55 29 74; www.surveyors-en-france.com. PACA

Surveyfrance: ☎01394 610227; www.surveyfrance.co.uk

■ PURCHASE AND CONVEYANCING PROCEDURE

Notaires

Notaires have the monopoly on conveyancing in France. Access to their profession is very restricted. In order to become a *notaire* you have to train for seven years, and then buy a licence (*charge de notaire*) from someone who is giving up the profession. Often the licence is passed down through a family. It's not possible to have all the French legal processes dealt with by British-based lawyers, but many British firms have formed partnerships with their counterparts on the other side of the Channel with whom they can liaise. There are lawyers in the UK who are also qualified to practise in France.

It's normal for the *notaire* appointed by the seller to handle the transaction. They may have handled the sale of the property in the past. The buyer is entitled to appoint their own *notaire* without paying any additional costs; the two *notaires* share the fees between them. Although a *notaire* may know a great deal about the property being sold, they are not likely to tell you anything more than they have to. The most important thing to understand is that the *notaire* doesn't look out for your interests. One of the biggest mistakes that Britons make in France is to imagine that a *notaire* is the equivalent of a solicitor. If you want impartial legal advice it's best to approach a bilingual lawyer or *avocat*; some are listed below. Few *notaires* speak good English, and they will be doubly cautious about giving advice in a foreign language.

The *notaire*'s main concern is to ensure that they don't make an error and leave themselves open to being sued. The chances of a foreigner successfully suing a French *notaire* are slim. Since *notaires* also act as tax collectors, you should be on your guard about what you tell them. *Notaires* are supervised by the departmental *chambre des notaires* and have professional liability insurance. The websites of *chambres de notaires* can be found using the suggested searches given above.

Functions of a notaire

You may be told that 'We don't use *notaires* in property transactions in France.' There is some truth in this. A property transaction can be carried out through private treaty – *sous seeing privé* – but such an agreement is only binding on the parties who have entered into it: it's legally inferior to an *acte authentique* signed by a *notaire*. A foreign buyer should never enter into an *acte sous seeing privé*. If you want a deed of sale that is binding on third parties, then the intervention of a *notaire* is legally necessary at the signing of the *acte de vente*. The *notaire* will deposit a copy of the *acte* with the deed and mortgage registry (*bureau des hypothèques*) and that is it. As a foreigner buying property in France, it would be foolish not to use a *notaire*, otherwise you leave yourself at risk of all sorts of unpleasant surprises later on after you have taken possession of your property.

Among other things the *notaire* will:

- Conduct a search in the land registry to see whether any third parties have any claim on the property, or the right to use the land for any purpose
- Transfer your money via an escrow or blocked account to the seller, while ensuring that all fees and taxes have been paid in full
- Ensure that any pre-emptive rights on the property are 'purged'
- Witness the *acte de vente* or other agreement to sell the property to you

Pre-contracts

Once you find a property that you like, the next step is to make an offer. Private sellers will ask for rather more than the property is worth, and you can reasonably offer 5%–10% less than the asking price. In the areas where there is a lot of foreign interest and prices are rising, there is rather less scope for bargaining. Knowing how long a property has been on the market is a useful guide to bidding. The offer is made to the estate agent, or the vendor if it is a private sale. You can make a formal written offer, an *offre d'achat*, or *promesse d'achat* – promise to buy – which the seller can consider. It only becomes legally binding on the seller if he or she accepts it. You are not allowed to make any deposits accompanying an *offre d'achat*. On the whole, it's simpler to make a verbal offer, and then ask for a preliminary contract to be drawn up.

If your offer is accepted, a preliminary contract – an *avant-contrat* – will be drawn up. Although there is no legal obligation to use a preliminary contract, it is universally used. There are two main types of contract in use in France: the *compromis de vente* which is binding on both parties, and the *promesse de vente* (promise to sell), which is binding on the seller, and which gives the buyer the chance to renege on the contract (while forfeiting their deposit). The latter is used north of the River Loire, including in Paris.

The promesse de vente

With the 'promise to sell' the seller commits him or herself to selling within at least one month, or more usually within two to three months. In return the potential buyer will pay an *indemnité d'immobilisation*, a sum that compensates the seller for temporarily taking their property off the market. The usual amount is 10% of the

Before signing the pre-sale contract

Because of the binding nature of pre-contracts, you must go through the following points before you sign anything:
- Are you sure that you can use the property for your intended purpose?
- Have you obtained preliminary planning permission for any work you want to do?
- Does the sale include all the outbuildings and attached land, without reservation?
- Are the boundaries of the property clearly marked out?
- Are there any rights of way over the land?
- Do any third parties have any rights relating to the property?
- Will you share property rights over boundary walls with neighbours?
- If the property is recent, have you seen the handing-over report: the *procès verbal réception des travaux*?
- Has planning permission been obtained in the past for any work?
- Has the contract been checked by a qualified person?

You have the right to obtain an extract from the land registry (*extrait de matrice cadastrale*) from the *mairie* to verify the above points.

sale price. The *promesse de vente* can be signed in the presence of a *notaire*, or can be signed privately. The seller pays a charge of several hundred euros to the *notaire*. If the *promesse* is signed privately, it is signed in triplicate, and one copy is deposited with the *recette des impôts* (tax office).

It's strongly recommended that the *indemnité d'immobilisation* be paid into a blocked account held by a *notaire*, and not directly to the seller. If you exercise your option to purchase – *lever l'option* – the *indemnité* will be deducted from the sale price. If the deal falls through, the *indemnité* will be returned to you if one of the get-out clauses can be invoked within the allotted time; otherwise you will lose it outright.

The *compromis de vente*

The more common type of pre-contract, or *avant-contrat*, also goes under the name of *promesse synallagmatique*, since it binds both seller and buyer. It is usual to pay 5%–10% of the sale price as a deposit or *indemnité*; this isn't the same as the *indemnité d'immobilisation* mentioned above. The deposit should be paid into a blocked account – *compte séquestre* – held by a *notaire* or by the estate agent.

The nature of the deposit is vitally important. If it is an *arrhes*, then the buyer can withdraw from the agreement but will forfeit the deposit. If the seller decides not to sell, then they are required to pay the buyer twice the amount of the *arrhes* as compensation. A variation on this type of deposit is a *dédit*, a specified sum that is forfeited if the buyer pulls out of the deal.

The more usual type of deposit, the *acompte* – which can be translated as 'down payment' or 'instalment' – has more serious implications. In this case the sale is

FACT

▪ It is in the buyer's interests to sign the *promesse* in front of a *notaire*. The *notaire* won't witness a contract unless they are satisfied that it is free of flaws.

TIP

■ Getting out of a *compromis de vente* will be expensive and difficult, so you must be entirely satisfied that the contract is worded the way that you want.

legally enforceable on both the buyer and the seller. There is no way to prevent the sale from going ahead. The nature of the deposit will be stated explicitly on your *compromis*.

The *compromis de vente* can be signed in front of a *notaire*, for which there is a charge. You have a week's cooling-off period after receiving the draft *compromis de vente* by registered post, during which you can decide not to go ahead with the deal. All payments should be made by cheque or bank transfer through the estate agent or *notaire*'s blocked account. It is no longer allowed to pay deposits in cash, and you shouldn't agree to any request to make such a payment.

The contents of the compromis de vente

It's important to understand that signing the *compromis de vente* virtually makes you the owner of the property you are promising to buy. If you sign a *promesse de vente* the seller remains the owner of the property.

You may be asked to sign a standard printed contract by the estate agent, which won't contain the get-out clauses that you need. While there are no standardised requirements as to the content, the contract should at least contain, or be accompanied by the following:

- The *état civil* (entry in the population register) of the buyer(s) if they are already resident in France
- Details of passports, birth certificates, marriage certificates, divorce certificates
- Official declaration as to the marriage regime, or civil partnership contract (PACS)
- A description of the property, including outbuildings
- The address
- The surface area of the land
- The habitable surface area of the property (compulsory in the case of *copropriétés* (joint ownership committee for the building))
- Proof that the seller is the rightful owner of the property, i.e. an authentic copy of the previous *acte de vente*
- The agreed selling price of the property
- Name of the *notaire* handling the sale
- Who is to pay the notary's fees and other costs
- Who is to pay the estate agent's commission
- The property's unique number in the *Plan Cadastral* – land registry
- Any equipment or fixtures included in the sale: e.g. fitted kitchens, burglar alarms
- Results of reports on termites, lead and asbestos
- Details of guarantees with newer properties
- Date by which the *acte de vente* is to be signed
- Receipt for any deposit
- Date on which you will have the use of the property
- Penalties if one of the parties withdraws from the deal
- Get-out clauses: *conditions suspensives*
- Who will be responsible for dealing with *vices cachés* or 'latent defects'

The last point is very important. Generally there is a clause stating that the property is sold as seen, on the assumption that the buyer has had enough time to check the condition of the property. If the vendor hides a defect in such a way that a reasonably attentive buyer could not be expected to see it then the vendor can be pursued through the courts. If the vendor is a property professional then he or she has to be completely open, and cannot hide behind any clauses about *vices cachés*. It's up to the buyer to have a survey done to be entirely certain about the condition of the property.

Property can't be sold without the compulsory survey for asbestos, and for termites and lead, if required. The *notaire* will not allow the sale to go through if these surveys haven't been done. If the property is less than 10 years old, it will be covered by a *garantie décennale* – a 10-year insurance policy against major construction defects. Minor repairs and building work will be covered by a two-year guarantee against faulty workmanship. Once a buyer agrees to take responsibility for hidden defects, then there is no further room for negotiation if any are found. Another solution is for either the seller or the buyer to take out an insurance policy against the discovery or appearance of major faults in the building. The policy will cover you against faults in the walls and foundations for five years, in the secondary construction (e.g. roof) for three years, and in the heavy equipment (e.g. lifts and heating) for one year.

Get-out clauses

The negotiation of *conditions suspensives* (popularly called *clauses suspensives*) is an area where expert legal help can be very useful. The most usual one is that the signature of the final deed is dependent on obtaining mortgage finance, the *condition suspensive de prêt*. This get-out clause shouldn't be treated lightly. If you don't make reasonable efforts to obtain mortgage finance, and you are shown to be acting in bad faith, then you could lose your deposit. If you require a loan to complete the purchase, you can benefit from the provisions of the *Loi Scrivener* as regards get-out clauses – see 'French mortgage lenders', above.

Other clauses can be inserted, e.g. you can make the purchase dependent on being able to sell your existing property. For example, you can put in get-out clauses such as:

- The owner has to carry out necessary repairs
- There are no works planned by the local government that would interfere with your use of the property
- Building permits can be obtained
- A report on the presence of 'termites' has to be produced
- No one is going to exercise pre-emptive rights on the property
- The property will have no sitting tenants
- There are no legal constraints on the owner selling the property
- The dimensions of the property correspond to what is in the contract

A variation on the term *condition suspensive* is a *condition résolutoire*: a clause that nullifies the contract automatically if its conditions are met.

Rights and obligations/servitudes

In between the signing of the *compromis de vente* and the *acte de vente*, the *notaire* has some time in which to make enquiries about the status of the property. Between

TIP

■ It's easy enough to find out if the local municipality is planning to construct a main road or do some other works near your property in the near future, by asking the local *Division Départementale de l'Equipement*, the town-planning office.

one and three months can elapse between the preliminary and final contract signings; two months is a normal interval. During this time he or she will be able to obtain clearance from any bodies – such as SAFER – that might have pre-emptive rights over the property that they don't intend to exercise them. SAFER has the right to match the highest offer made for your land/farm so that it can sell it on to another farmer. The *notaire* should establish that there are no mortgages still applying to the property. In the case of property that has been completed recently the seller will have to supply a *certificat de conformité* from the *mairie* certifying that all the necessary building permits were obtained when the property was constructed, and no regulations regarding urban planning have been broken. Properties have been known to be modified or even built without planning permission, so it pays to be on your guard.

The matter of *servitudes*, that is rights and obligations, is particularly important. The most common type of *servitude* is where a farmer has the right to use part of your land, or allow animals to roam on it, or to draw water from your well. Your neighbour may have obtained the right to make windows in a wall overlooking your property, a *servitude de vue*. The biggest headache can be rights of way – *droits de passage* – which allow hunters to walk over your grounds on their way to a designated hunting area. If you see notices saying *chasse gardée* or *chasse privée* you know that there will be hunters in the vicinity. It's quite likely that your *notaire* will ask neighbours to sign a document agreeing that they have no right of way over your land.

If you are worried about *servitudes* and other claims by third parties, it's possible to take out an insurance policy guaranteeing good title to the property for a small sum. The French insurers, Axa Courtage, offer title insurance, known as Assur'Titre; this can be obtained via London & European Title Insurance Services, see www.europeantitle.com.

The acte final

After a period stated in the preliminary contract the parties will proceed to signing the final deed of sale, known as the *acte authentique de vente*. Only *actes* witnessed by a *notaire* are considered *actes authentiques*, legally binding on third parties. The *acte de vente* is signed by the buyer, the seller and one *notaire*. If there are two *notaires*, one acting for the buyer and one for the seller, only one of them will witness the *acte de vente*. Which one depends on local custom.

You will be sent a *projet de l'acte* – a draft of the *acte de vente* – well in advance; a month is normal. This will contain much the same information as the original *compromis de vente*. You will be asked to produce originals of your birth/marriage/divorce certificates, and they may have to be translated and notarised; ask well in advance. At this point you should have made arrangements for payment of all the sums involved in the purchase, including the taxes and notary's fees. The *notaire* will in any case require advance payments to cover his or her expenses. If a mortgage is involved, the *notaire* will draw down the money from your bank account.

Power of attorney

A date will be fixed for the signing. Very often there are last-minute hitches and the date may be put off. For this reason it's highly desirable to arrange to give a trusted person a power of attorney – a *mandat* – to act on your behalf if you can't attend the actual signing. The signing must take place on French soil. For practical reasons, the power of attorney is best made up in the French form. It should be witnessed by a notary, or at a French consulate. If it's witnessed by a British notary public, it will have to be legalised by the Foreign and Commonwealth Office (www.fco.gov.uk) to make it valid in France. The document should state what powers you are giving to your representative.

Translating the *acte*

An interpreter must present if the person signing the *acte de vente* isn't of French nationality. There is no legal requirement to supply an English translation; many *immobiliers* (estate agents) have a translation of the *compromis de vente* available, if not the *acte* itself. An English translation has no legal force in any case. The presence of an interpreter makes it impossible for the buyer to claim that they did not understand what they were signing, and thus protects the *notaire* from being sued. The cost of an interpreter is steep – as much as €350 – because they need to be approved by the *préfecture*. The *notaire* will most likely say nothing in English during the signing, for fear of misleading the English buyer, even though he or she will speak in English before and after.

The actual signing

Assuming that all the loose ends are tied up, you will be invited to the signing of the *acte de vente*. This will be an interesting experience, or perhaps nerve-racking if there are last-minute hitches. Apart from yourself, the seller and the *notaire*, and their clerk, there may be other interested parties present. By this point, all the necessary funds should have been transferred to your *notaire*'s blocked bank account. There are various taxes and fees to be paid at the last minute, and you should be prepared for this. It is highly embarrassing to find that the sale can't go ahead because you haven't left any money in your French bank account. You should also have paid the first insurance premium on the property, *before* signing the *acte de vente*. Subsequent payment dates are based on the date of the signing.

Certain items will often be mentioned in or attached to the *acte de vente* that won't have appeared in the *compromis de vente*, such as:

- Details of mortgage loans
- Full description of the property, with details of previous sales
- Details of the insurance policy on the property
- The amount of Capital Gains Tax payable by the seller; or exemption
- Reports on the presence of termites/lead/asbestos
- Statement that the buyer accepts the property in the condition it's sold

You will be asked to confirm that all the information you have given is truthful: the *affirmation de sincerité*.

Costs associated with property purchase

The high level of costs involved with property purchase is one of the main reasons that property prices don't go up very fast in France. The fees and taxes that have to be paid to the *notaire* and to the state are inaccurately referred to as *frais de notaire*, when only a part of them go to the *notaire*. The *notaire*'s own emoluments are based on a sliding scale between 5% and 0.825% + TVA at 19.6%, depending on the value of the property. Some properties, so-called Group 2 and Group 3, attract smaller *notaire* fees, but most fall into Group 1. The *notaire*'s fees are fixed by the state, and are not negotiable. It's normal practice for the *notaire* to ask in advance for more than the final bill, to cover for all eventualities, so you will probably receive a small repayment.

It follows from the above that the *notaire*'s fees will come to about 1% of the sale price, except for very cheap properties, where they will be slightly higher. In addition there are the *droits de mutation* – transfer taxes – adding up to 4.89% on old property, made up of:

Taxe départementale	3.60%
Frais de recouvrement	0.09% (2.5% of the above)
Taxe communale	1.20%
Total	4.89%

The *frais de recouvrement* are the expenses involved in collecting the *taxe départementale*. TVA is levied at 19.6% on new properties. The same rate is applied to extensions, garages and outbuildings added on by the seller in the past 10 years, which could come to a substantial amount.

Notary's fees	
up to €3,049	5%
€3,049–€6,098	3.3%
€6,098–€16,769	1.65%
€16,769 and above	0.825%

There are some other fees to be paid, namely:
- The salary of the keeper of the land registry: 0.10% of the sale price
- Costs of registering a mortgage, at about 2%
- Costs of paper, official forms, stamps, extracts from the land register, etc. paid by the *notaire*

Finally, there is the commission payable to the estate agent or *immobilier*, which can range from 3% to 10% or even more with very cheap properties.

Before signing the *acte de vente*, it's advisable for you or your representative to check again on what is included in the sale price. The contract will state whether you will have vacant possession – *possession libre* – or if there are any tenants present. In some countries such as the UK it is assumed that once the final contract is signed the property is available to move into, but this doesn't always happen in France. If the sellers wish to remain for a few weeks, you can expect them to pay you something as compensation.

After the sale

Once the *acte de vente* has been signed, the *notaire* has to pay all the taxes and commissions (unless you are paying the *immobilier* directly) out of the sums that you have passed over to them. The title is registered with the *bureau des hypothèques*, the register of deeds and mortgages, as well as the mortgage, if any. Eventually you will receive a certificate informing you that the title has been registered. The whole process will take some months. The original title deed remains with the *notaire*. They are authorised to make authentic copies if necessary.

Under-declaring the sale price

It was once common practice to under-declare the sale price so as to save on taxes and fees, while paying a part 'under the table', or *sous la table*. There is no advantage in the long run to the buyer, since they will be penalised with higher Capital Gains Tax in the future when they resell. The penalties for under-declaring are serious. The one way around this is for the seller to leave some furniture or other moveable goods in the property, which can be given a slightly inflated value, thus reducing the taxes payable.

Special procedures in relation to copropriétés

Apart from the asbestos report, there is also a requirement for the *copropriété* to draw up a report on the solidity of the structure, and many other aspects – the

diagnostic technique – at the time of setting-up the *copropriété* where the property is more than 15 years old. This is a measure to prevent unsound blocks of flats being turned into *copropriétés* without proper repairs. You should also ask to see the *carnet d'entretien*, or log-book of the building, to see what kind of repairs have been carried out in recent years.

The manager of the *copropriété* will most likely be present at the signing of the *acte de vente*. This should contain details of what percentage of the communal areas belong to you – your *quote part* – and what percentage of the communal charges you will be required to pay.

Notaires as estate agents

It might come as a surprise to you that a *notaire* can also act as an estate agent, especially in western France and in country areas. Many French wouldn't dream of using an *agent immobilier* to find property. *Notaires* keep lists of properties; they often have the best deals around. They make very good estate agents: they have the best database on property prices, they are keen to make a quick sale to get their clients out of difficulty, and they are more likely to give an honest description of the property, compared with an *immobilier*, who will try to embellish on its merits. The *notaire* will require a commission on the sale, but not as much as an *immobilier;* you can reckon on paying 3% of the sale price including TVA.

Some properties held by *notaires* have 'problems' associated with them. This mainly happens when legatees find themselves in a situation known as *indivision* after someone has died, when two or more people have rights to the proceeds of a sale, and neither can sell without the other's agreement. There are also properties which have *servitudes* or obligations attached to them, e.g. someone has the right to live in the property for the rest of their life, or someone has a right to use the land or rights of way.

Law firms dealing with French property

Ideally, you will want to use the services of a UK law firm, with lawyers qualified in both UK and French law, or if you are resident in the USA or elsewhere, get advice from a lawyer in your home country as well. Some firms have French lawyers working for them in the UK, or have offices in France. Such lawyers can advise on whose name to put the property in, and what measures to take to minimise inheritance taxes. The *acte de vente* still has to be signed in front of a French notary and registered in France.

Useful addresses

A Home in France: ☎0870 748 6161; www.ahomeinfrance.com. Run by Danielle Seabrook, this company offers complete bilingual legal assistance to British residents to manage their risk in buying in a foreign jurisdiction. Also has an office in Chinon, Indre-et-Loire

Bennett & Co Solicitors: ☎0870 428 6177; www.bennett-and-co.com

Blake Lapthorn Linnell: www.bllaw.co.uk; various offices in the south of England. Has an in-house team of three French lawyers. Offices in Oxford, Fareham, Southampton and Portsmouth

Bright Jones: ☎+33 (0)5 61 57 90 86. Firm of two British lawyers who are trained avocats in France. Provide a range of legal advice on property buying throughout France

Fox Hayes Solicitors: ☎01132 496 496; www.foxhayes.co.uk. Contact Graham Platt: qualified both in Britain as a solicitor, and admitted to practise as an Avocat in France. Deals with property, company, litigation and probate

French Lawyer: Isabelle Cès; ☎0845 644 3061; info@french-lawyer.com; www.french-lawyer.com

Howard Kennedy Solicitors: ☎020 7636 1616; www.howard-kennedy.com. Large London firm dealing with the top end of the market

The International Law Partnership; ☎020 7061 6700; info@lawoverseas.com; www.lawoverseas.com. Specialising in foreign property purchase

Kingsfords Solicitors: ☎01233 624544; www.kingsfords-solicitors.com. British lawyers with expertise in French conveyancing. Fixed-price property buyer's package and other services

The International Property Law Centre: ☎0870 800 4565; www. internationalpropertylaw.com. Contact senior partner and solicitor Stefano Lucatello, an expert in the purchase and sale of French, Italian, Portuguese, Spanish, Cyprus, Bulgaria and Dubai property and businesses, and the formation of offshore tax vehicles and trusts

Liliane Levasseur-Hills: ☎01483 424303. Fully qualified French *notaire* offering assistance with buying and selling French property, French inheritance law, and French wills

Pannone & Partners: ☎0161 909 4136; www.pannone.com

Prettys Solicitors: ☎01473 232121; www.prettys.co.uk. Prettys' French Property Group are multi-lingual and assist clients on the whole process of buying a property in France including advising on obtaining finance and insurance, French Income and Capital Gains Tax, and issues with wills and future considerations

Russell-Cooke: ☎020 8789 9111; www.russell-cooke.co.uk. Large firm with French law and property department, headed by Dawn Alderson, qualified in both English and French law and member of the Bordeaux bar

Stephen Smith (France) Ltd: ☎01473 437186; www.stephensmithfranceltd.com. Stephen Smith is the author of *Letting Your French Property Successfully*, published by PKF Guernsey

Taylors Solicitors and Notaries Public: www.taylorssolicitors.co.uk; various UK offices

Turner and Co Solicitors: ☎0121 200 1612; turneranco@aol.com; www.french-property-news.com/turnerandco.htm

Thrings and Townsend Solicitors: ☎01225 340000; www.ttuk.com. French property purchase, setting up a French business. Offices in Bath, Bristol, Swindon and London

◼ RENOVATING PROPERTY

Most foreign property owners will tell you that, while French builders are good at their job, they are also in great demand and booked up for months in advance. For

> **Charles and Kath Dunstan run a _gîte_ in Brittany that they renovated themselves. They used an English carpenter at first but later found using local tradesmen no problem at all.**
>
> We did it gradually. We bought the property in 1991. It was totally in need of renovation. We did the cottage ourselves with the help of an English carpenter who came over for a few weeks. Then we rented the cottage out and moved into a caravan on site. For the stables and the dairy, we had both national and regional development grants. We had to put up 50% of the cash ourselves and guaranteed to use local artisans. There are no general builders over here. We employed a plumber, roofer and mason and they all worked well together. There's a 10-year guarantee on all the work done. We sourced the artisans through the mairie at Neuillac, got some devis, some quotes, and went ahead with the work.

EU nationals there is naturally a great temptation to bring over your own builders who are ready and willing to get on with the job. Not using the local tradesmen, however, may create resentment and put you on bad terms with the village. You also need to consider that non-French builders may be quite unqualified to make repairs to traditional French buildings, and will probably only have rudimentary French. Work done by builders registered in France has to be insured for 10 years – the _garantie décennale_. You should be wary of using unregistered foreign builders, unless you know them well, because of the insurance implications. You are 100% liable if the builder is injured, and you won't have the usual guarantee against bad workmanship. In addition you will not qualify for grants towards doing the work, and the cost won't be taken into account in reducing your Capital Gains Tax liability if you sell within 15 years.

All tradesmen in France should be registered with the local _chambre des métiers_ and have an official business number: the SIRET. This is shown on advertisements. One will find numerous English-speaking tradesmen advertising in French property magazines, many with a SIRET number, the others in the process of applying for one: SIRET _en cours_. The normal procedure is to ask for an estimate – a _devis_ – from several tradesmen; the _devis_

A crumbling house in Marseilles

is then binding. TVA is levied at only 5.5% on work done to restore or maintain properties more than two years old.

If you are having a substantial job done, involving several tradesmen, you may wish to appoint a *maître d'œuvre* to supervise the whole operation. You will need to draw up a written contract with the *maître d'œuvre*.

Before building work begins, you can draw up an *état des lieux*, a description of the property, in the presence of the builder so that you have some evidence if they damage trees or verges. They may, of course, not agree to this. There are plenty of English and other foreign builders (especially Polish builders), carpenters, etc. English-speaking tradesmen advertise in the French property magazines, such as *French Property News*, *France* and *Living France*. The local English-language press also carries adverts: see *Riviera Times*, *Riviera News*, and *The News*. Their websites have some classified adverts: see above.

Grants

It is worth enquiring about grants – *subventions* – for restoration. The best person to ask is always the local *maire*. The ANAH – *Association Nationale pour l'Amélioration de l'Habitat* – has offices in every DDE – *Division Départementale de l'équipement*. See the website: www.anah.fr. There are more generous grants available for listed buildings and buildings considered to be noteworthy because some famous person lived there; the disadvantage is that you will be obliged to use authentic materials, and you won't be free to use the colour of paint that you might want. The bureaucracy involved tends to discourage people from applying for grants. If you start work before receiving permission, then you will lose the grant. There are more possibilities if you are planning to start a business or run *gîtes*. Some *communes* may offer grants towards the cost of being connected up to the electricity or water supply. The *mairie* will let you know what is available.

Building/renovation glossary

French	English
abri	shelter
accès	access
accotement	roadside verge
adossé	backing onto
affaissement	subsidence, collapse, sinking
affaisser	subside
aggloméré	agglomerate, chipboard
sgrafe	staple, wall tie, retaining clip
aiguisoir	sharpener, whetstone
alimentation en eau	water supply
aménagement	conversion, fitting out
aménagement du grenier	attic conversion
antigel	frost protection, anti-freeze
appui	abutment, support, window sill
ardoise	slate tile
are	100sq m
argile	clay
armature à toit	roof support
arpent	4221sq m.; 1.043 acres
arrhes	non-returnable deposit (pronounced 'aarr')
âtre	fireplace, hearth
badigeon blanc (de chaux)	(lime) whitewash
badigeonner	to whitewash
bande de calfeutrement	draught excluder strip
bauge	clay and straw daub
béton armé	reinforced concrete
béton prepare	ready-mixed concrete
bloc à poncer	sandpaper block
boiserie	woodwork
boulon	threaded bolt, pin
branchement	connection, electrical lead, junction
cailloutage	pebbledash
canalisation	ducting, pipework
caniveau	road drain
carie	rot
chauffage central	central heating

Building/renovation glossary

French	English
chaux hydratée/éteinte	slaked lime
chaux vive	quicklime
cintré/cinglé	arched, vaulted (also slang for crazy)
cloison	partition wall
cloqué	blistered (paint)
cloquer	to set (e.g. of glue), to blister
coffrage	casing, formwork, shuttering
couvreur	roofer
crépi	roughcast rendering
cuvette	toilet basin, bowl
debit	discharge, yield, debit
déblayage	excavation
devis	estimate
disjoncteur	circuit-breaker
double vitrage	double glazing
écrou	nut
écrou à oreilles	wing nut
encastré	embedded, flush, built-in (e.g. cupboard)
enduit	rendering, coating
entretien	maintenance
entretien et réparations du toit	roof check & repairs
équerre	set-square, angle-bracket
espagnolette	shutter bar; shutter bolt
essente	wooden shingle used in alps, vosges
étagère	shelving
évacuation des eaux usées	drainage
éverit	everite; white asbestos
facture	invoice
fibre de verre	fibreglass
flotteur	ballcock
foreuse	electric drill
fosse	ditch
galet	pebble, cobble
gazon	turf
gond	hinge

Building/renovation glossary

French	English
gouttière	gutter
gravier concassé	gravel
haie	hedge
hectare	2.471 acres; 10,000sq m
installateur	fitter
isolation	insulation
lambrissage	wainscoting, panelling
latte	batten, lath
lauze/lave/platin	thick stone slate
lavabo	wash basin
lime	file
lucarne	dormer window
maçon	builder
madrier	massive beam
marchand de matériaux	builder's merchant
mastic	mastic
mazout	heating oil
menuisier	joiner, carpenter
menuisier	carpenter
moellon	quarried stone
moellon brut	rough stone
moquette	fitted carpet
moulure	moulding
nappe phréatique	water table
nivelle	spirit level
nivellement	levelling
norme française	French standard
ossature	framework
panne	pantile; also breakdown
panneau de plâtre	plasterboard
parpaing	breeze block; block exposed at both faces of a wall
pignon	gable
pignon á gradins	flemish-style stepped gable
placoplâtre	plasterboard
plafond suspendu	suspended ceiling
plafonneur	plasterer

Building/renovation glossary

French	English
planches	floorboards
paltrier	plasterer
plomberie	plumbing
plombier	plumber
ponceuse	sander
poteau	post
poutre	roof beam
poutre apparente	exposed beam
poutrelle	smaller roof beam
prise	electrical socket
rabot	plane
ramoner	to sweep a chimney
ravalé	resurfaced, newly rendered
ravalement	resurfacing, rendering
remblai	embankment, hardcore
remise	storeroom
rive	edge of roof or panel, riverbank
sable	sand
scie	saw
serrure	lock
souche	chimney stack (visible part)
stère	1cu m
tamis	sieve
tapisser	to wallpaper, upholster
tapisserie	wallpaper, wall-covering, tapestry, upholstery
tôle ondulée	corrugated steel sheet
tôle zinguée	galvanised steel sheet
tondeuse	lawnmower
torchis	cob, wattle and daub
tournevis	screwdriver
tout-à-l'égout	mains sewerage
trappe de visite	inspection hatch
trop-plein	overflow pipe
Tuile	flat tile of baked clay
tuile canal	Spanish-style pipe tile
tuile faîtière	ridge tile

Building/renovation glossary

French	English
tuile flamande (*panne du nord*)	s-shaped flemish pantile
tuyau	pipe, tube
vane	valve
vernis	varnish
vers de bois	woodworm
vilebrequin	brace and bit
voyant	inspection window
zingué(e)	galvanised

The details of property renovation are beyond the scope of this book. There are more and more books on the market that deal with renovation; the best is David Everett's *Buying and Restoring Old Property in France* (2005), which is mainly concerned with restoring rather than buying. If you read French, it's worth getting *Architecture Rurale et Bourgeoise en France*, by Georges Doyon and Robert Hubrecht, a fascinating survey of traditional building techniques and terminology covering the whole of France, which can be bought through www.amazon. fr. This gives advice on how to restore properties in an authentic style.

Glossaries of French building terms

Building has its own terminology, which is generally ignored in the big French-English dictionaries. The more basic terminology is explained in the Canadian *Grande Dictionnaire de Terminologie*, available free on www.granddictionnaire.com. Jean-Paul Kurtz's *Dictionary of Civil Engineering*, both French-English and English-French is available on Amazon. Hadley Pager Info (www.hadleypager.com) publish a range of French/English technical glossaries, including *Glossary of House Purchase and Renovation Terms* (56 pages), and *Concise Dictionary of House Building, Arranged by Trades* (256 pages).

Which kind of swimming pool?

Deciding on what kind of swimming pool to install isn't an easy decision. The three main possibilities are the pre-fabricated fibre-glass pool, a galvanised steel construction with a vinyl liner, or reinforced concrete. The first crucial point is to determine the water table of the land. If the pool bottom is below the water table then you will first have to install pumps to drain the land before you can install the pool. Should it rain heavily you will need to pump out again, otherwise your pool could literally float away, or, if it is made of concrete, it could break up. In any case, it would be unwise to empty your pool in this kind of situation without expert assistance, since the weight of the water could be keeping it anchored to the ground.

■ *Bakewell Pools*: ☎01865 735205; www.bakewellpools.co.uk

■ *Christal Pools*: ☎01384 440990; www.christalpools.com

Swimming pools

A swimming pool (*piscine*) isn't just a luxury in France: if you are buying a property of a substantial size to rent out to an up-market clientele then it is virtually a necessity, whether you are on the French Riviera or in Normandy. The presence of a swimming pool is the most crucial factor in determining the pulling power of your property, and installing one is an investment well worth making. It's important to bear in mind that a swimming pool entails substantial running costs.

A concrete construction consists of a double layer of blocks with steel reinforced concrete inside. Another possibility is a prefabricated fibre-glass pool which is then back-filled with pea-shingle. The UK (Oxford) company, Bakewell Pools (www.bakewellpools.co.uk), can arrange for the pools to be delivered anywhere in France (they are manufactured in Dijon), for a uniform price; you can install it yourself (DIY) or with the help of local contractors. Another possibility is to bring over a pool from the UK, in the form of metal sheets with a vinyl liner. The pool can be flat-packed and loaded onto a trailer. The advantage in this case is that the pool can be erected above ground, or even on top of a building, avoiding the water table problem. This is less desirable if you plan to rent out your property, as holiday-makers tend to dislike above-ground pools. There is also the possibility of a smaller plastic pool of which there are plenty available in France.

France has numerous swimming pool manufacturers. If you want to know more about French pools, there is a dedicated magazine: *Techniques Piscines* (www.techniques-piscines.fr).

Construction of swimming pools up to 20sq m doesn't require a *permis de construire* but you must apply for an exemption using form PC156. The local mayor or town planning authority may raise objections, so it is essential to find out first what you can do. In principle, the authorities are not allowed to stop you from building your pool. An experienced swimming pool contractor will be able to advise you on the procedures. You can't build a swimming pool within view of a road, as the sight of scantily clad swimmers could cause a traffic accident or build anything closer than 3m to someone else's property or boundary, or half the height of the adjoining wall if this exceeds 6m.

Strict new regulations came into force in May 2004, making it compulsory for safety devices to be installed to prevent young children from drowning. Owners of rental properties had to install safety devices immediately, from 1 May 2004; owners of private pools now also have to comply. There are several means of childproofing pools. One is to install fencing, which has to be at least 110cm high. Another is to install a cover, either electrically or manually operated, which can't be removed by a child under 5. You could also make a shelter to cover the pool completely; this has the advantage of also keeping the water temperature higher. Most owners, however, go for an alarm that is set off if someone falls into the water. This is the cheapest and least intrusive option, but it may not be the most effective. There is a €45,000 fine for failing to install safety devices. Insurers will make it obligatory for you to comply with the law.

Planning permission

Planning permission – the *permis de construire* – is needed for most alterations to property; even if you don't require a PC (permis de construire), you will need to enter a declaration that you are exempt. To be on the safe side you may wish to obtain outline planning permission first, a *certificat d'urbanisme*, which is treated below.

- The first rule to remember is that if your restorations or building work cover more than 170sq m – this is the total floor area, whether one or more storeys – you have to have architect's plans drawn up.
- The second rule, as given in the last section, is that you can't build anything within 3m (10ft) of a neighbouring property, or half the height of a neighbouring wall if it exceeds 6m.

It is not necessary to enter the application for the PC yourself; your architect or *maître d'œuvre* or your representative (*mandataire*) can do this for you, but you are ultimately responsible if the right PC has not been acquired first. The forms you need are held by the *mairie*; they are exactly the same throughout France.

Calculating the surface area of the works is a complicated process. A distinction is made between the *surface hors œuvre brute* or *SHOB* (the total surface area including cellars and roof spaces and the thickness of the walls, but not including inaccessible flat roofs or terraces at ground level), and *surface hors œuvre nette* or *SHON*, the surface area used for deciding whether you need a PC or not, which allows you to subtract some surfaces according to complicated formulae. If you are unsure about the surface area concerned you can consult an *architecte conseiller* working for the municipality or other state body, free of charge.

It is not always necessary to get a PC for minor work to the house, nor for some smaller external constructions, but it's necessary to enter a *déclaration de travaux exemptés de permis* for any building work that is exempt from a PC. The request for the PC is sent to the *mairie* by registered letter (*recommandée avec demande d'avis de réception* (or *accusé de réception*), or it can be delivered by hand; you will be given a receipt (*décharge*). The authorities have 15 days to send you a *lettre de notification* with the number of your PC registration, and the length of time it will take them to deal with your PC, which is usually

> ## Richard Coman on troubles with the *tout à l'égout*
>
> For about 10 years we were fine with our *fosse septique* (septic tank) but then we were told by the commune that we had to be on the main drainage system, the *tout à l'égout*. The contractors had to use dynamite because the ground was solid granite under 3 inches of soil. Then the next-door neighbour found cracks in his walls and accused us of having planted trees too close to his house. I had got a *pépiniériste* [nurseryman] to plant some trees along our boundary 14 years earlier, but he had failed to observe the regulation that says you can't plant trees within 3m of an adjoining property, so I had to ask him to come and dig the trees up. On top of that the contractors who dug the sewage trenches left a huge mound of granite chippings on my land. I went to see the *maire* and got a London firm of translators to write a business letter in French, at great expense, but to no effect. Finally I had the *notaire* threaten legal action, which did the trick, but of course I had to pay the legal fees.

two or three months from the date on your *avis de réception* or *décharge*, a period known as the *delai d'instruction*, unless the authorities get a court order giving them more time. If the authorities fail to give a decision within the stated time then it's assumed that the PC has been granted automatically, a PC *tacite*. The *mairie* will handle the application in urban areas, or pass it on to the relevant intercommunal authority. A printed version of your application will be posted on the wall in the *mairie* with your name and address, so that anyone can raise objections if they wish. A PC is valid for two years.

If the *mairie* turns you down, you have two months to apply again. If you are refused again, you can go to a *tribunal administratif* to contest the decision or to claim damages. You can ask for an *attestation* that no negative decision has been given if you want to be on the safe side. Any work involving a change of use or which increases the number of rooms in the house (e.g. making a workshop or converting a loft into a bedroom), affecting the taxable value of the property, will require a PC. Changing windows or installing double-glazing requires a PC. Knocking out walls always requires one; putting in new internal walls doesn't.

Items that are exempt from the PC include terraces and walls under 2m, or any structure with a surface area (SHOB) of less than 20sq m added on to an existing construction. A completely new construction with a surface area of more than 2sq m and taller than 1.5sq m does require a PC; walls between 2m and 12m high require a PC. Some work requires another form, the *déclaration de travaux*, a statement that you intend to carry out work, colloquially shortened to '*travaux*'. This includes greenhouses (of normal size), uncovered swimming pools, rendering, and minor alterations to your house. Your *déclaration de travaux* must be displayed on the wall of the *mairie* within eight days of receipt. The administration has one month (sometimes two months) to respond; once this time has passed it's assumed that your *déclaration de travaux* has been accepted.

Planning permission rules are complex, and you should ask the *mairie* before

FACT

■ The opinion of a local builder isn't always reliable: the owner of the building is liable, not the builder.

Snow stops construction in Samur

carrying out any building work, however minor. It's important to understand that a *permis de construire* never allows you to demolish an existing building. For this you need a *permis de démolir*.

It is easy enough to go to the local office or *Sub-Division de la Direction d'équipement* (there are several in every *département*) to get an opinion about what type of PC you need. The authorities are tougher about PCs in some *communes* than in others; on the whole they are being applied more and more strictly everywhere in France as time goes by.

Several bodies are involved in granting the PC. Apart from the *mairie*, the *conseil municipal* and the *Direction Départementale de l'Equipement* have to give their approval. If you are carrying out work in an area subject to flooding, namely the Loire Valley or near the Rhine, a state-appointed engineer has to assess the application. If you are building within 100m of a cemetery the *mairie* has to be consulted.

The *Direction Départementale des Affaires Sanitaires et Sociales* and the *Sous-Commission Départementale d'Accessibilité des Personnes Handicapées* also have to give their approval if you are building or converting property for holiday complexes. The number of bodies that have to give their approval depends on the nature of the work.

Special rules apply if you are carrying out work on or next to or within view of a listed building or site. The authorities have four months after acknowledging receipt of your application to consider the case. You should never assume that you have tacit approval where listed buildings are concerned, even if you hear nothing from the authorities. If the application is passed to the national ministry of public works they are not necessarily required to give you any response. If you are working within 500m of a listed site, you may be told to use only certain kinds of building material, which can make the work far more expensive.

Types of building permits

demande de permis de construire	request for a general-purpose PC
demande de permis de construire une maison individuelle	request to construct or modify a private dwelling, where works are not exempted from PC
demande de permis de construire modificatif	request for minor modification to an existing PC; for major modifications an entirely new request for a PC must be entered.
demande de permis de démolir	request for permission to demolish.
demande d'autorisation de coupe	request to cut back or cut down trees

Documentation for PCs

The documents and plans that are required are listed on the PC application form. These will include:

■ A plan of the piece of land

■ A site plan with the proposed work, between 1/100 and 1/500 with the orientation, and the property

■ The *volet paysager*, two photographs of the property, from close up and distance

■ Plans of different floors of the property

■ Decisions regarding rights and obligations (*servitudes*)

■ Documents concerning grants

It's possible to begin your building work before obtaining a PC, on the understanding that a PC is generally granted for the type of work you are undertaking, but as an outsider it pays to be doubly careful about following the rules, even if you risk making life more difficult for yourself. All PCs are granted *sous réserve du droit des tiers* – with the reservation that third parties' rights are not affected. Having a *certificat d'urbanisme* (CU) or PC doesn't mean that your neighbours cannot raise objections if you are building something that overlooks their property, or if you infringe on some 'easement' or *servitude* that affects their property. These are matters of private civil law where the *mairie* has no say. The *mairie* won't necessarily be aware of all the easements affecting your property, unless they are mentioned in the land registry, i.e. the *conservation des hypothèques*.

You can still be taken to court after construction work has been completed if the alteration to the property has a real effect on your neighbours' rights to the peaceful enjoyment of their property. The best advice is to talk to your neighbours at the planning stage and get their agreement before you start any actual work. If they don't give their agreement then you will need to engage the services of an *avocat*. Your lawyer can go as far as to ask all the neighbours to sign a document that they renounce any rights of way over your land, etc.

When the work starts you enter a *déclaration d'ouverture de chantier* (declaration the work has begun). The authorities have the right to inspect the building site to ensure that you are respecting the terms of the PC. The PC has to be displayed on a *panonceau* or panel at the entrance to the building site for two months so that third parties can enter objections if you have failed to take their interests into account when you applied for the PC. After building work is completed you have 30 days to enter a declaration that you have done the work according to the terms of the PC *(déclaration d'achèvement des travaux)*. The authorities can inspect the work; they will then send a *certificat de conformité* within three months. No *certificat* needs to be issued if the work has not created any new surface outside the *surface hors œuvre brute* or SHOB (see above).

Certificat d'urbanisme

Prior to applying for a PC, you may want to obtain outline planning permission, or a *certificat d'urbanisme* (CU). Anyone can apply for a CU, even before they have bought a property or piece of land. The application for the CU – *demande de certificat d'urbanisme* – requires plans and maps of the property, in four copies, and a description and drawings or photos of the work you propose to do. You can expect a decision within two months. It is compulsory for the seller to obtain a CU where land is being sold to build on, except where this comes under the law governing housing estates or *lotissements* (see below). This includes selling a part of the land that your property is sitting on. In other respects the CU is an opinion on whether a piece of land can be built on or not in relation to the town planning laws. Or it can be an opinion on an actual building project.

Most *communes* have a *Plan Locale d'Urbanisme (PLU)*, or a *Plan d'Occupations des Sols (POS)*, which states how many buildings with how much floor area can be put up on a certain piece of land. Each area of the *commune* has a coefficient – the *Coefficient d'Occupation du Sol (COS)*, a number used to calculate the maximum SHON or floor area (defined above) that can be constructed. If the COS is 0.40, then it allows you to build 200 sq m of SHON on a 500 sq m piece of land. In some cases you will be allowed to build more, but you will then have to pay financial penalties.

A CU will only be granted for land that is *viabilisé* – namely, where there are adequate roads and utilities, a pre-condition for it becoming *constructible*. Agricultural land is generally not *constructible* and is never likely to be. Not surprisingly, land that is *non-constructible* is worth very little, but there are plenty of owners who will hang on to their *non-constructible* land in tourist areas, in the hope that some day in the future it will become *constructible*. The CU is delivered within two months of the application, if it's not turned down. You then have one year during which you are more or less guaranteed a PC, although it can still be denied if you do something illegal.

There is another type of document that one can apply for, the *note de*

■ As a foreign buyer, you need to be especially careful that where land or property is sold with a CU included, the CU is going to be valid for long enough for you to obtain the PC, because CUs will only run for one year. Buyers are sometimes told that a CU has been obtained, when it has already lapsed.

renseignement d'urbanisme – also an opinion on whether something is *constructible* or not. The *note de renseignement* has no legal force, but it is popular with *notaires* because it makes them money, as does the CU. All one can say is that it gives buyers more security. Even then this may not be enough. If you are planning to construct something close to a listed building, then a departmental official, the *Architecte des Bâtiments de France* has to be involved. He or she may add more conditions to the permit, such as the type of building materials you can use, which will make the job far more expensive.

A recent property will have a CU: you couldn't build it without one. Older properties won't have a CU necessarily, unless someone applied for one, but there should have been a PC. There is the outside risk that a property was built without planning permission in the past. Once it has been standing for 30 years then the authorities can't make you demolish it.

◼ LETTING YOUR PROPERTY

Once you have your French property you may want to let all or part of it, either as a business, or just until you assume permanent occupation. Letting property is a commercial activity if the letting income exceeds €23,000 annually. Letting also carries certain legal and taxation implications that shouldn't be overlooked. There are also considerable expenses involved in advertising rental property, unless you are doing it on a very casual basis.

Tax implications of renting out

Renting out your property has important tax implications, particularly for non-residents. For a start, the law requires that non-resident ownership is registered with the *Centre des Impôts des Non-Résidents* (9 rue d'Uzes, 75094 Paris Cedex 02; ☎01 44 76 19 00; www.impts.gouv.fr). Revenue from letting is known as *revenus fonciers*. Non-residents in receipt of any income obtained from sources based in France should obtain forms 2042 and 2044 from the French Embassy or Consulate in their own country, or from the above address. Returns have to be submitted annually to the Centre des Impôts des Non-résidents in Paris, before 30 April. It is usually possible for the property owner to appoint a representative in France to deal with taxation affairs and the *notaire* may well be able to arrange this. Note that a financial penalty may be incurred by registering late.

If you are non-resident and let out furnished property in France then you are subject to a flat rate 25% French income tax, as long as the lettings are under €23,000 and are not your main source of income. In this case you are taxed under the *Micro-BIC* regime, which doesn't allow you to claim any expenses or depreciation, but you benefit from a fixed 72% deduction for your expenses. If you are resident in France and letting property as a business, you will be liable for French income tax as part of your regular income, and you will need to go to the local *centre d'Impôts* to pay your taxes.

The *notaire* and any estate agent will be able to draw up a letting contract for you. An estate agent appointed to supervise the lettings for you, the owner, must be licensed to do this. With more expensive properties, it is usual to ask for a substantial deposit to cover damage. This is the only way of protecting yourself against inconsiderate tenants.

Depending on the type of people you are renting out to, you may also be able to dispense with a contract entirely after the first season. It depends on how trustworthy your tenants appear to you. If you only want to attract more refined clientele, then it would be advisable to advertise in more upmarket magazines. If your advert appears on a general website, then you have no control over who uses your property.

Specialised property management agencies advertise in the usual French property magazines. You will need to pay them anything up to 20% of the rental. There are also potential problems in making sure that all the rental is handed over; you may need to find ways of checking on when there are tenants in the property.

An excellent company which lets out privately owned French properties is the established family business Quality Villas (see below) who also arrange additional services including maids, chef/cook or babysitter, if required by the clients, making your property appeal to a wider type of customer. They also personally check out the properties publicised on their site.

FACT

You will have to remain with GdF for a minimum of 10 years, otherwise you would be required to repay the grant you have received.

Useful contacts

Breakaway Holiday Homes: ☎01903 741010; info@breakawayhomes.com; www.breakawayhomes.com. Offers management services to owners of caravans and park homes

Chez Nous: ☎0870 197 1000; www.cheznous.com. Owners pay to be listed on the website and prospective holidaymakers contact the owners direct

Cottages4you: ☎08700 782 100; www.cottages4you.co.uk

Quality Villas: ☎01442 870055; www.quality-villas.co.uk. See description in section above

Renting Abroad: Prestbury Holdings Ltd; info@renting-abroad.com; www.renting-abroad.com

Villarama: www.villarama.com

Gîtes and chambres d'hôte

Many foreign buyers hope to make a living from running *gîtes* (self-catering accommodation) and *chambres d'hôte* (bed and breakfast). There is now an over-supply of such holiday accommodation, and it would be unwise to rely entirely on income generated in this way. Running *gîtes/chambres d'hôte* is demanding, and not to everyone's taste. In the case of *chambres d'hôte* it is usual to offer dinner, unless you are very close to some decent restaurants. You are in frequent contact with your guests, so this is hardly a job for shy misanthropes. It's easier to run *gîtes* as you are not obliged to have much contact with guests; you just need to be nearby to deal with any difficulties, or appoint someone to do the job for you. If you decide to apply for a grant from the local *Conseil Régional* via the *Gîtes de France* (GdF) organisation then there will be strict conditions attached. The sums available for grants vary considerably, depending on the area and the year. The grant will only be paid if you observe the requirements of GdF to the letter. These include detailed specifications about the fittings, even down to the type of mattresses to be used; regular refurbishment is also stipulated. Rooms have to be of a minimum size, and the building must have a rustic appearance (apart from being in the countryside).

Assuming you are successful, and pass the inspections, you will then be listed

> ## Charles and Kath Dunstan explain how they manage their *gîte*.
>
> Brittany is becoming over gîted and you need to make sure your place stands out. That's why we put in the swimming pool that meets all the French regulations and is heated and last year we put in wireless internet throughout the property, which attracted clients immediately. We keep the place to a high standard with nice furniture and objets d'art and we advertise with Brittany Ferries, which gives us a cushion. We get bombarded by people who build tourist sites on the net. They always give you a free trial and if we pick up clients through their site then we subscribe the following year. We get a complete mix of nationalities: French, Brits, Americans, Italians, Dutch.

in the GdF catalogue, and in exchange you will pay a percentage of your letting income to them, about 15%. Each room is given a separate *épi* (wheat ear) rating, depending on whether it has an en suite bathroom or not, and so on. As long as you pay your subscription to GdF you will be able to put up the GdF signpost outside your property. GdF specifies the minimum period and the months (always including July and August) that your accommodation should be available: three months is a minimum. The rest of the year you can do as you please: deal directly with customers, rent out long-term, etc. Owners who are within the GdF system are required to let GdF handle bookings for them.

It's up to you if you want to make additional efforts to advertise your property; most French owners leave the entire process to GdF. Owners keep GdF informed about availability, so GdF can update its website. GdF will send a contract to the holidaymakers; they are expected to pay in full six weeks before arrival. Because *gîte* holidays are meant to be affordable, there is no obligation to provide bed linen or cleaning. You are entitled to charge extra for such services. It's not customary to provide any meals, however.

GdF isn't the only organisation through which you can advertise your property. There are the websites above. If you want to be included in the Chambre d'Agriculture booking system then there is a weekly fee of 12% of the rent. In the case of websites, you may just pay an annual flat-rate fee. To promote your *gîte* or *chambres d'hôte* it is better to have your own website and to advertise in magazines, all of which costs money. You can only charge high rates if you have something special to offer, which could be a swimming pool, or sports facilities, or by linking courses to your stay. If you are close to major cultural attractions, or to the Normandy battlefields, you stand more chance of making a decent living.

■ SELLING YOUR PROPERTY

It is usual to place the property with an estate agent or a *notaire*, who will add their commission to the selling price. It is now usual for the seller to pay the commission. There are foreign estate agents in many areas who will do a better job of marketing your property than a French one would. The main thing is to have a good photograph of your property; this isn't as easy as it sounds, and you may be best advised to use a professional photographer.

You can try to advertise it privately, or put your house on an English website featuring private sellers. Most British sellers try to sell to other foreigners, on the basis that they can expect to obtain a better price. In the current economic situation, the British are more likely to pay a little over the odds, while the poverty-stricken Germans will pay less. It's normal to emphasise the amount of attic space that could be converted, and to mention the proximity of railway stations and airports.

The regulations governing French estate agents or *immobiliers* are very strict. A prospective seller can choose to give the *immobiliers* a *mandat simple* or a *mandat exclusif*. In the first case, you can place the property with as many estate agents as you like, or find a buyer yourself. The *immobilier* receives the commission if he or she introduces a successful buyer to you. With a *mandat exclusif* only one estate agent will look for buyers. You have to specify whether you wish to retain the right to look for buyers yourself – a *mandat exclusif simple* – or whether you give up that right – the *mandat exclusif absolu*. In the first case, the agent's commission is reduced if you find a buyer yourself; in the second, you would have to pay the agent an indemnity if you found a buyer yourself.

A *mandat* is only valid for a limited period. The seller can withdraw from the *mandat*, subject to certain conditions. After three months, a *mandat exclusif* can, in all cases, be cancelled through a registered letter.

Defects in the property

Owners are required to have reports drawn up on the possible presence of termites where there is a prefectural decree in force, and lead paint for pre-1949 buildings. Drawing up a report on asbestos has been compulsory everywhere in France since the start of 2003, regardless of the age or condition of the property. The seller pays for the report. As a general rule, the seller cannot be held liable for *vices apparents*, or defects that should be obvious to anybody. The issue of *vices cachés*, or latent defects, is more complicated. It is normal to insert a clause into the final contract freeing the seller of responsibility if the buyer subsequently discovers latent defects, but this doesn't protect the seller from claims for compensation if it can be shown that the seller could reasonably have been expected to know about the defect.

Taxation

If you sell your French property within 15 years of having acquired it, then you will be liable to pay French Capital Gains Tax or *Impôts sur les plus values* (IPV) on a graduated scale. If you are selling your principal residence then there is no liability for IPV. A non-resident who owns a second home in France will be liable for IPV. The *plus value* on your property sale is worked out by deducting the original purchase price – *prix d'achat* – from the selling price – *prix de cession*. The costs associated with buying the property are added on to the original purchase price, thus reducing your liability. You can opt for a lump sum of 7.5% to cover such a costs. Also added on is the cost of building work, extensions, renovations, etc. if you have owned the building for more than five years. It is advisable to have all the original receipts and invoices from when the work was done. If this isn't possible, a state-appointed expert may produce a valuation of the work, or you may opt for a flat rate 15%. If you or your family did the work yourselves this can also be taken into account, either using a valuation by an expert, or by multiplying the price of the materials you used by three.

Your capital gain is taxed as income at 16% if you are an EU resident and 33% for non EU residents, with a further 11% in social security taxes also payable if you are resident in France. If you sell the property within five years of acquiring it, or it is repossessed, the gain from the sale of the property is added directly to your income tax liability, and the tax has to be paid immediately. Where there is a long-term gain, the capital gain is payable at the time of signing the final deed of transfer (*acte de vente*). The *notaire* will take the amount of IPV out of the sale proceeds. Sellers are not required to enter a special declaration for IPV. The tax can't be deferred. The gain is reduced by 10% for every full year after five years since the purchase of the property. Thus after 15 years there is no more IPV to pay. There are also deductions for holiday homes that have been owned for more than five years, which you have always had it at your disposal.

Non-residents are taxed at 16% on their capital gains from the sale of property; the EU doesn't permit France to charge the 10% social security taxes to non-residents, on the grounds that non-residents don't benefit from France's social security benefits. If a non-resident is considered to have been trading in property then IPV is payable at 50% on the capital gain. The provisions of France's Double Taxation Agreement with your country may apply.

You should make enquiries about possible ways of avoiding IPV, before you try to sell the property. If you can show that the sale of the property was forced on you by family circumstances or because you had to move to another part of the country, you can claim exemption. No IPV is payable if you receive the property as an inheritance, as a gift, or through a divorce settlement. If you originally received the property free of charge, the fair market value at the time you acquired it is taken as the purchase price; there are no deductions for any taxes paid at the time on the transfer of the property.

Taxe foncière

Taxe foncière is a land tax, which is levied on the owner of any plot of land, except where the buildings are used exclusively for agricultural or religious purposes. The payment of the *taxe foncière* is waived for two years on land

---

Exemptions from IPV

There is a complete exemption from IPV in some situations, for example:

- You are a pensioner or officially incapacitated and not liable for income tax
- The property has been your habitual principal residence since you bought it, or at least five years (even if owned through a SCI)
- You have owned the property for more than 15 years
- The sale price of the property is under €15,000

The Great Hall of Sarzay Chateau, B&B accommodation

where building or restoration work has recently been carried out. In certain cases the period during which the *taxe foncière* isn't payable may be extended, for instance, on areas of land where buildings have been newly constructed. This tax is calculated on the basis of the nominal rental value as decided by the relevant department of the *cadastre* (land registry). Rates vary widely all over France; the rate is generally highest in poor urban *communes*, and lowest in wealthy suburbs. In the case of rented property, it is the owner of the property who pays, but they can put a clause in the rental contract requiring the tenant to reimburse him.

◼ UTILITIES

Electricity

Many foreign property-buyers take little notice of the state of the wiring in the property that they are thinking of buying, something that can prove to be an expensive mistake. While they think nothing of spending thousands of euros on a bathroom suite, they find it hard to bear the prospect of spending €5,000 or more on bringing the wiring of the house up to standard.

Promotelec, the organisation that promotes higher standards of electrical equipment, estimates that there are 7 million dangerous electrical appliances in France. The main problems are lack of, or insufficient earthing, corroded wiring and unsuitable circuit-breakers. In older properties you can still find WWI-style cotton-covered wiring. Old plastic plugs can literally fall to pieces in your hands. Apart from any risk of electrocution, if you are taking over an older property it is essential to find out whether the wiring can handle heavy-amperage equipment such as washing machines and electric cookers. If you need to run electric heating at the same time as other heavy equipment such as an electric cooker, a water heater or a washing machine, then you will require a supply of at least 12kVA (kilovolt amperes or kilowatts), for which heavier wiring is needed to the electricity meter.

The basic system of wiring in French houses is what is known as a 'spur' system. A ring main is a way of connecting a series of power sockets. The cabling starts and ends at the fuse box, having gone through each socket on the circuit so creating a 'ring'. The 'spur' system used in France starts at the fuse box and can either daisy chain on from one socket to the next or can branch out from a junction box. Consequently more fuses can blow if you overload the system. The ring main system is inherently safer because there are fuses in the plugs themselves. In your French house you will find two types of socket: two-pin sockets for low-amperage equipment, and two-pin sockets with an earth pin (*prise de terre*) for heavier appliances. Ordinary light switches are used in bathrooms, something that is illegal in some countries such as the UK. On the other hand, all wiring in the wall has to be enclosed in a plastic tube, or *goulotte*.

If you buy a house without an electricity supply, Electricité de France (EDF), will connect you to the grid. If you can't see an electricity pylon nearby then your connection could cost more than the property itself. If the electricity has been cut off for work to be done, then you will require a *certificat de conformité* or CC from the safety organisation Consuel (www.consuel.fr) to certify that the system is safe before EDF will reconnect your supply. Consuel doesn't inspect an electrician's work unless there is a good reason, neither does it certify that your system conforms to a certain level. They will only test the earths and the consumer unit (*tableau principal*).

If you are intending to buy a property in France, then it's in your interest to ask the seller to allow a *Diagnostic Confiance Sécurité* to be carried out. This is a 40-minute inspection covering a list of 53 points resulting in an objective assessment of the state of the wiring of your house. Once the inspection has been carried out, you can call in an electrician to give an estimate (*devis*) of the cost of any work needed. Needless to say, if your prospective seller refuses to allow a DCS then you should be suspicious. Don't be fobbed off with assurances that everything is fine with the wiring.

Having the house rewired can be disruptive as well as expensive, because of the necessity of taking out at least some of the plaster. There are therefore grounds for asking for a reduction in the price of the property to cover the costs. At the same time you can take the opportunity of installing the most-up-date energy-efficient system.

 A DCS can be arranged through EDF (http://particuliers.edf.fr) or through Promotelec (www.promotelec.com).

Water

It's essential to check the reliability of the supply if you are buying property. Water leaks should be reported quickly.

If there is no water supply to a property, one can either arrange for a connection to be made, or try to sink a well – *puits* – on the land or tap into an underground spring. The quality of the water has to be analysed first before you can use it. Water with a high nitrate content – where there is intensive agriculture – presents a real health risk. In the case of an apartment without a water supply the situation can be even more difficult, since the local water company will only make one connection to a property.

Heating

The subject of heating is often overlooked when looking at a property when the weather is sunny. Northern France is as cold as, for example, southern England in winter. You may get away without central heating – *chauffage central* – in the south of France, but you will still need some kind of heating. Upland areas, such as the Massif Central, can be bitterly cold in winter.

Gas central heating is not common outside the cities; in much of France there is no mains gas supply. Although one can run gas central heating from a *citerne* in one's garden, the experience of foreign property owners has been that this isn't a good solution. You are then left with a choice between using cheap rate electricity or heating oil – *mazout* or *fioul* (which is the English word *fuel*). The downside of oil is that the price can fluctuate a lot. One solution is to combine electricity and oil in a system called Bi-Energie, which you can switch over to oil when electricity is at peak rate.

If the property is to be left unoccupied during the winter then central heating may be unnecessary. Wood-burning stoves are a good solution, with some portable heaters or oil-filled radiators as a back-up. Wood is sold by the *stère* – a measure of 1cu m. If you are interested in using solar panels or heat exchangers, contact the energy efficiency organisation ADEME (www.ademe.fr).

Septic tanks/fosses septiques

The state of one's septic tank is a favourite subject of conversation with foreign residents in France. Septic tanks are common in France, where many properties are far from the local sewage system. There is a trend in France to connect more properties to the main sewage system, known as *tout à l'égout*. There are some costs involved for the owner. Cess pits – *puisards* – where all the waste simply goes into a hole in the ground are being phased out, and it is no longer legal to build one.

The idea of the septic tank is to process the waste from toilets, and other used water, through the natural action of bacteria, so that eventually only fairly harmless water is left. All the waste runs into the first settling tank, or septic tank, where the solid matter sinks to the bottom, while scum forms on the surface. The naturally present bacteria break down the waste matter, releasing methane, so no naked flames! The remainder goes into a second settling tank, which should be half the length of the first tank, and then into a 'drain field' or system of soakaways, with

a series of drain pipes or drain tiles laid on gravel. The drain pipes or tiles are perforated so that the effluent filters away into the ground. Before the effluent reaches the soakaways, there has to be an inspection chamber, or *regard de visite*. The solid matter in the septic tank has to be emptied once in a while, the so-called *vidange*. The interval depends very much on how well the tank is maintained. The local municipality will recommend at what intervals the tank should be emptied. Anywhere between two and 10 years is possible.

If you are looking at country properties, make sure to find out whether there is a *fosse septique*. If there is none you will be required to install one. Since the whole contraption extends at least 70ft from the house, it is essential to have enough land to build one. The larger your *fosse septique* the less trouble it will give you. You can't construct anything over the *fosse septique*, and there should be a minimum of trees around it. You should also look at the slope of the land, and make sure that the water table isn't too close to the surface. Generally, *fosses septiques* work better in hotter climates, which favour the breakdown of the waste. The price of new *fosses septiques* is going up rapidly because of ever more stringent regulations. For suppliers look at French property magazines, or the website www.profosse.com.

Daily Life

■ CULTURE SHOCK

Initially, anyone who goes to live in a foreign country will find that all the daily rituals, previously taken for granted, now pose seemingly insurmountable challenges. The French do have a very distinct approach to many aspects of life. You'll have to accept that there will be a certain amount of culture shock. But many of the things that you can't stand or understand will become the things you actually appreciate about life in this unique country.

Friends and family who go along with someone who has a job in the new place may be particularly prone. Being plunged into an environment where you can't communicate with the people can cause confusion and anxiety. Other

> **Sophie Le Corre is a French woman in her mid-30s working for an international company in Paris. She lived in London for seven years during her 20s. Here she talks about bridging the gap between the two cultures and how this process makes her feel.**
>
> I didn't go back to France very much while I was living in London and before that I'd been travelling a lot. I'd lost track of France quite a bit. I had to readapt. I remember clearly not knowing where to find a letterbox or where to find a taxi. I'd lost my reference points. No black cabs and no red letter boxes. I found the Parisians grumpy. Every time you wanted something, they'd say no. The English are nice to you by and large. I didn't find the French very smiley. Then after a while you don't pay attention to it anymore.
>
> I speak English and write English every day in my job. I like it. I'd miss it. I've never worked in a French working environment. I've never had the experience of looking for a job in France. I don't know what it is to work in a typically French company. If I lost my current job, I'd certainly look for another international environment, whether in Paris or abroad. I could imagine myself going back to London if I had a job opportunity.
>
> The French environment? I don't know. Fear of the unknown. I'm pretty sure there would be a difference in working habits. I can feel that with our French clients. It feels like they're not as reactive and that it's more hierarchical, a bit heavy. It's different...
>
> I always envy people who've lived somewhere for many years and have many connections. Potentially I could be living anywhere. I've now been living in Paris for as long as I was living in England. I feel like I've been much more socially involved here. I've lived two different lives. In London I was in a couple but in Paris I've lived the life of a single person. It's easier to build up a social circle in Paris. London is a harsh town. In Paris it feels much more like a village.

> I always envy people who've lived somewhere for many years and have many connections.

symptoms might be sadness, depression, frustration or anger, preoccupation with health, insomnia, idealising your old country or trying too hard to absorb everything that's new, inability to solve simple problems, feelings of insecurity or inadequacy, developing stereotypes of the new culture, developing obsessions such as over-cleanliness, longing for family, feelings of being overlooked.

The main ways of combating the feeling are to be active but patient and to be easy on yourself. Remember how normal the feeling is. It can help to get things off your chest to people from your own background who are feeling the same way, but remember living solely within an expat community means you may also be feeding off everyone else's neuroses.

The intention of this chapter is to provide as much as possible of the practical information required for coping successfully with various aspects of French life. If you haven't already decided whether living and working in France is for you, the following information could help you make up your mind, or, assuming that you have already made the decision to go, it could act as a day-to-day survival guide. Note, however, that there are bound to be regional and local variations in most of the aspects covered – so it's best to check details with those who are already living in the region, or other appropriate sources. In France there are particularly striking differences between town and country, which may affect the procedure required in doing even the most mundane things.

■ SETTLING IN

Meeting people

The best and easiest way to meet people anywhere is through work. However, this may be more difficult in France than elsewhere because of the sharp dividing

Karalyn Monteil speaks about her social life in Paris.

There are definitely cultural issues. The French have a tendency not to want to bother other people. Americans are more open. That sometimes can be embarrassing for my husband at the bakery or the café or whatever. I'd say I'm more integrated into the international community than the French community. It's true I do know a lot of Americans but it's only recently I've started to value their friendship. The French have their friends from childhood and it's not always easy to break into those circles. I have French friends but they're more international French if you know what I mean.

TIP

■ The French tend to respect other people's space and may appear less forthcoming than, say, Americans.

| 193

line which exists between work and home, business and pleasure: colleagues in France who have worked together for many years may never become anything more than acquaintances. If this is the case, then try to make the first approach, perhaps by inviting colleagues home to meet the family or for a drink or meal: this is unlikely to offend and at worst would be considered some curious foreign practice. Senior business people almost always invite colleagues or contacts for a meal in a restaurant, rather than in their home, and the choice of the right place is crucial.

Like anywhere, people in France are people. Some are more gregarious than others. It might take a bit of time, but there's no reason why you shouldn't be able to develop a social circle. Shared interests are obviously a great way of getting to know others.

In towns and cities there is the usual impression that everybody is too busy to say more than 'hello'. One of the best ways of forming social contacts is to not be afraid to ask for help, or to offer it, to neighbours and people in the local area or at work. Such attempts at integration will stand a much better chance of success if carried off in good French. Those who live in an apartment block should try to form an acquaintance with the *concierge* (often a female or a couple who takes care of the building). The *copropriété* (joint ownership committee) regime which operates in many apartment blocks can also be a good means through which to meet people.

Keeping in touch with family and old friends

Webcams, Skype and the internet mean that it is now relatively simple to keep in touch with anyone anywhere around the world, but carrying on life in a culture so different to your own can sometimes mean that you go through periods when it is hard to make the effort to keep links going. Many people find that periodic trips back home can really recharge their batteries, and help give them perspective on their new life.

For Brits, transport communications with France are now so efficient and cheap that logistically, it's as easy to make trips back and forth as it is to have weekends away within Britain. You'll probably find that you'll be getting visits from those after a holiday in the Languedoc or a weekend in Europe's capital of romance.

One thing worth bearing in mind is that, although the cost of international calls is now negligible in theory, calling mobiles internationally from France can still be quite expensive.

FOOD AND DRINK

Shopping in France is a revelation if you are used to mass retailing, which may have made the whole process very efficient but less interesting. Of course France has its share of hypermarkets around which family shopping increasingly revolves, but for the moment at least, alongside them traditional specialist and family shops still survive. It's therefore possible to enjoy efficient individual service and to appreciate the quality and variety of the goods themselves.

The quality of food produced and the cost of eating out in France are viewed by many expatriates as reasons enough for living there, and few countries can rival the range and appeal of the regional specialities on sale. Some indication of the emphasis on gastronomic merchandise in France is that as much as a quarter of the average French family budget is spent on food and drink although more of this is being spent more on convenience foods than hitherto.

While traditional, independent food shops, which offer individual service and top-quality goods, are still prolific in France there is also the other end of consumerism in the form of the massive hypermarkets (*les hypermarchés*) such as Auchan, Mammouth, Carrefour, Géant and Leclerc, which sell every product imaginable at competitive prices while still paying keen attention to quality. Supermarkets (*les supermarchés*) in France tend to be smaller and more expensive than in the UK or USA, and are more like self-service grocery stores. The ED and Franprix chains are the least expensive.

Most shops keep long and convenient continental hours, typically from 8am to 7pm (allowing for regional variation). Small shops take an afternoon break, which lasts longer the further south you go. In some

If you are from the UK...

To satisfy expatriate cravings for the comfort of 'traditional' British food products including Ambrosia creamed rice, Cadbury's creme eggs and chocolate fingers, Jaffa cakes, English mustard, Monster Munch, Marmite, Marks and Spencer foodstuffs, Heinz beans, Christmas puddings and many more, order them online from www.xpatshop.co.uk; www.expatdirect.co.uk, www.expatshopping.com, www.britishcornershop.co.uk, expatshopping.com and www.expatessentials.co.uk, among other websites

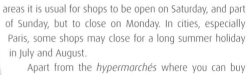

areas it is usual for shops to be open on Saturday, and part of Sunday, but to close on Monday. In cities, especially Paris, some shops may close for a long summer holiday in July and August.

Apart from the *hypermarchés* where you can buy everything, shops in France tend to segregate trades. For example, the *boulangerie* sells bread (and sometimes biscuits) while the *pâtisserie* sells cakes and pastries and may also be a café. Similarly, the general butcher is the *boucherie*, but for pork you have to go to a *charcuterie*. Sometimes the *charcuterie* will also sell a range of cooked meats, not just pork. A *boucherie chevaline* is a butcher who sells horsemeat, while a *traiteur* sells ready made up meat dishes, often for the catering trade. Fresh fruit and vegetables are best bought in open markets held several times a week, but most towns have a greengrocer, usually as part of a shop selling *alimentation* (general provisions). *Primeurs* are early fruit and vegetables but can also mean greengrocers.

Many French consumers have a definite preference for fresh foods wherever possible and they expect to select these individually from the shelves and not to buy them pre-packed. Frozen foods have long been available and now convenience ones are also gaining popularity. Also on the increase are internet grocery shopping services and home delivery (*livraisons à domicile*) if your bill comes to more than a stipulated amount. It's always worth asking a shop if they will do this, especially for bulky items.

Organic food (*le bio* – short for *biologiqe*)

According to the Agence Bio, a government funded public interest agency (www.agencebio.com) 7% of the French population now eat organic food every day and the numbers have been growing over recent years. The amount of land under cultivation for organic produce is also increasing every year. In 2006 there were 11,402 organic farms managing 560,838 hectares, making up 2% of agricultural land. The highest growth rates are in Pays de Loire, Poitou Charentes and Centre and the region with the largest area under organic management is currently Midi-Pyrénées.

There are organic shops (*les magasins bios*) in all towns of any size and in a lot of smaller communities too. You can find organic vegetable stalls in all markets and many farms organise home basket delivery through co-operative organisations. All packaged organic food in France must carry the AB (Agriculture Biologique) label.

Wine and spirits

As one might expect from a major wine-producing country, wines of all types and qualities seem amazingly cheap, and even the most modest French home usually has a cellar to accommodate them. One of the pleasures of being an expatriate in France is being able to enjoy the local wines and to buy direct from the local

Sunday bio marché in Paris

producers. Of course, this applies to other consumables as well, particularly cheeses.

Stronger alcoholic drinks produced in France are about the same price as in many other countries, but you are likely to find better quality and more choice than you do in your own country.

■ SHOPPING

Non-food shopping

As far as non-food shopping is concerned, French consumers tend to have less choice and more expense than in the UK or the USA. Opening hours are shorter for non-food stores, although *hypermarchées* are open late most evenings and sell virtually every general-use line imaginable, from clothes to car body panels and tyres.

A *pharmacie* will only sell drugs and medicines and probably not toiletries, and perfumes are only sold in *parfumeries*. A *quincaillerie* is a hardware shop. Newspapers and magazines are most commonly sold at a tobacconists – *un tabac* – or news-stands.

Domestic appliances

When it comes to buying domestic appliances, such as cookers, fridges, microwaves, televisions and video recorders, the French pay more for these goods than you may be used to. The main reason for this is that in the past cheap Japanese and Far Eastern imports were restricted or highly taxed, and consequently many of the goods available in the shops were of French manufacture only. This situation has now changed due to a relaxation on import restrictions brought in by the European Union (EU), which is also affecting other sections of the retail sector such as textiles. Many companies including Daewoo, Sharp and Philips produce electrical goods in France.

TIP

■ When small-store shopping, it is important to know where to go for different items.

Clothes

As you would expect *haute couture* is generally very expensive. This is obviously due to the reputation France holds for quality and style and you'll probably find some items irresistible all the same. As mentioned above, one recent change in clothes shopping is the quantity of cheap imports, meaning that, like everywhere else, the price of clothing has fallen recently. French people tend to have a small wardrobe of high quality, expensive clothes.

Secondhand shops and flea markets

Since many French clothes are well-made and stylish, it is often worth looking in second-hand (*d'occasion*) clothes shops and for period clothes, the *marchés aux puces* (flea markets) can yield some real gems in vintage designer stuff.

Factory shops

It is possible to hunt out bargains, particularly in factory shops (*les magasins d'usine*). The website www.marquesavenue.com details surplus designer stock available at its outlets: Côte d'Opal, Paris, Metz, Romans and Troyes. The website gives a list of designers stocked. The handy guide *The Factory Shop Guide for Northern France* by Gillian Cutress and Rolf Stricker is now back in print in a new revised version, listing shopping outlets (with maps and travel directions) for bargain designer clothes for adults and children and household name brands for cookware and coordinated household linens from Calais to Boulogne and eastwards into Belgium and southwards as far as Troyes. There is also *Born to Shop in France* by Suzy Gershman and published by Frommer.

Internet shopping

This has taken off in France in recent years. Some sites are listed below:

- *www.alapage.com*: leisure items including books, CDs, DVDs, videos, computer games
- *www.bouticheval*: everything for the horse and rider
- *www.but.fr*: all kinds of stuff for the home (computers, furnishing and furniture, white goods, etc)
- *www.grossbill.com*: online sales of computers and associated peripherals

Shopping for bargains in Paris

The Parisian flea markets are good for clothes and other things and can be a fascinating way to consume hours. Three of the best known are situated on the *Périphérique*. The Puce de St-Ouen at Clignancourt, is in fact many markets from smart to downright shanty, all in the same neighbourhood. For example you can buy antiques at Marchés Vernaison and adjacent Dauphine while Marché Serpette has a more eclectic range of goods and junk and so on until you descend into the ropey areas where there seem to be more shifty looks to the square metre than bargains. You have to go to the other side of Paris to get to Porte de Vanves market, which is the place to look for second-hand clothes and domestic bits and pieces, and where you can find quality items among the junk. In the east of Paris the Marché Porte de Montreuil is the most junky of all the markets thronged with people haggling over discarded items.

- *www.leguide.com*: website that lets you compare prices of online retailers
- *www.topachat.com*: computers for offices and personal computers and information technology bits

TVA

Taxe sur la Valeur Ajoutée is levied on almost everything in France, including food, books and utilities. There are two rates: a standard rate of 19.6% and a reduced rate of 5.5%. The reduced rate applies to food, medicines, travel, most hotels, books, and utilities; standard TVA at 19.6% is levied on most other goods and services. These disparate rates account for the fact that while some things in France seem comparatively cheap, others seem expensive.

Shopping/customs allowances within the EU

There are guidelines (but no precise limits except on credibility) for duty paid items for personal use, bought in one EU state (e.g. in supermarkets and shops) and taken to another. Above all the citizen will have to satisfy the customs that the items are for personal use and not for resale in another country. The guidelines are in the region of 10 litres of spirits, 20 litres of fortified wine, 90 litres of wine of which not more than 60 litres is sparkling and 110 litres of beer. There are also reasonable limits for tobacco products.

Labelling and guarantees/warranties

Typical labelling on goods and food:

- *Date limite de consommation (DLC)*: use before the date marked
- *La date limite d'utilisation optimale (DLUO)*: best before the date marked
- *Demi-écrèmé*: semi-skimmed (on milk)
- *Entier*: whole, for milk and dairy produce
- *La guarantie commerciale*: the guarantee given by a particular maker or producer. It will have limitations for duration and what it covers
- *La guarantie légale*: the guarantee required by law against defective items. It allows the buyer to obtain a replacement from the vendor
- *Ni repris, ni échangé*: no return or exchange
- *Normalisation Française (NF)*: guarantees an item conforms to existing French safety standards
- *CE*: a logo found throughout the European Union certifying conformity to European standards
- *Le label rouge*: red label indicates top quality French standards of food
- *Appelation d'origine contrôlée (AOC)*: certified wine from a particular area. Quality wine
- *AB (agriculture biologique)*: food grown organically or made from organic ingredients
- *La viande bovine française*: guaranteed French beef

◣ PETS

As in other European countries it is usual for dogs to have an identity number tattooed inside one of their ears. This is performed by a vet and costs in the region of €45. The idea is to prevent rabies certificates being used for more than one animal. The numbers are lodged on a central computer controlled by the Société Protectrice des Animaux (SPA), which can be contacted if the dog goes missing. This is also the only sure way of identifying your pet as there is no system of dog licensing.

The French are fond of pets. But there are a few differences in attitude towards dogs in particular which will strike the British and Americans. For instance it is not uncommon in smart restaurants to see women guests (and occasionally men) arrive with underarm pooches which may even be provided with food, and sometimes a plate by the restaurateur. It is compulsory for dogs to be kept on leads in public parks

and gardens and failure to comply can result in an instant fine. In some parks dogs are banned completely.

Dogs

Man's best friend is much in evidence in France, there being eight million of them; more than in any other European country. The French equivalent of Britain's Crufts Dog Show is held outdoors at Longchamps during the summer, but is more relaxed and informal. It's a popular day out with French people who like to bring their own not-so-pedigree canines along. The French have an appealing selection of mongrels, often very shaggy and of indeterminate ancestry. The smaller more endearing ones tend to be family pets. The notorious pit bull is as much in a class of its own in France as in other countries. Defined as a dangerous dog, the pit bull must be muzzled in public and (in Paris at least) be listed on a police register.

French attitudes towards animals

The French are not so squeamish and sentimental about animals generally. Animal rights groups do exist (famously fronted by Brigitte Bardot), but they are not as strongly supported or as zealous as in the UK or the USA. There is a tendency not to neuter dogs and cats, which leaves many feral and strays on the loose. Many thousands annually end up in the dog pounds (*les fourrières*) where they are sometimes put down within a few days. The French animal protection society is the *Société Protectrice des Animaux* (SPA) but it is under-funded and overwhelmed. SPA has its own animal refuges and dog pounds around the country and holds adoption days. For more details, see the SPA website (www.spa.asso.fr).

TIP

■ For details of taking your own pets to France, see 'Planning an international move' in the chapter *Before You Go*.

'Beware the dogs', says Jean Ramm, who, with her husband, has a house in Bosville, not far from Fecamp in Normandy.

I was bitten by a dog in the village. Also, our golden Labrador was contaminated by pesticide and died of poisoning. The lesson here is, if you suspect crop spraying, keep your dog on a lead.'

Bullfighting

There has been a revival of bullfighting (even though 70% of French people say they disapprove of it), centred on Nîmes in the South of France. Nîmes has an ancient tradition of the art, and owing to a revival of regional traditions and a new mayor, there are now three *ferias* (festivals) a year and it has become trendy to attend (i.e. Parisians go). Note that older aficionados say that the revival is a watered-down version of the full-blooded original: the bulls have their horns blunted and are selected from weak specimens.

Birds

There are around 300 birds on the list of protected species in France. Of these about 65 are legal quarry for enthusiasts of *la chasse*. The only useful common bird, which is not protected, is the common or garden pigeon – not to be confused with turtle doves, which are slightly protected. British sensitivities are generally outraged by the French inclination towards hunting small birds and serving them whole, either baked in pies or as bite-sized appetisers. However, hunting is liable to strict controls including a setting aside of 20% of each hunting territory for conservation purposes.

Foreign homeowners' may find birds nesting on or about their properties. If you have protected species such as the *la dame blanche* (barn owl), or *la hirondelle* in buildings you are trying to renovate the best way to lure them away is to build special nesting boxes nearby. This procedure also applies to the bat (*le chauve-souris*). More information can be obtained from the La Ligue pour la Protection des Oiseaux (☎05 46 82 12 34; www.lpo.fr), or the SPA (☎01 43 80 40 66).

Importing pets to the UK

For UK citizens, remember that if a pet you acquired in France, or one which you brought with you and which has been living in France accompanies you back to the UK, you can use the PETS passport. For full details of the necessary procedures see the section on pets in the chapter *Before You Go*.

◼ TELEPHONES AND THE INTERNET

Telephone

Thanks to an annual research and development budget of more than a billion dollars, telecommunications in France have up-to-the-minute technology. Up to 1998 the state operator France Télécom had a monopoly on telecommunications in France. After a gradual process of deregulation the market is now entirely liberalised.

TIP

■ For telephone installation and billing arrangements see the chapter *Setting up home.*

French telephone numbers were all simplified in October 1996 by making them all nine-digit (10 digits if you count the zero in front) numbers wherever you are in France. France is divided into five broad geographical zones numbered one to five: 01 for Paris and Ile de France, 02 for the Northwest, 03 for the North East, 04 for the South East and Corsica, and 05 for the South West so for instance a Paris number will begin with 01, a Toulouse number with 05 and so on. Note that The 01/02/03 etc is used for all regions regardless of whether you are making a local or a long distance call. To call another country from France dial 00 before the number for the country concerned, then the subscriber's area code minus the first zero, then the subscriber's number. To call France from another country dial 00 33 followed by the number minus the first zero. To call mobile phone numbers, dial the subscriber's number minus the zero (also nine digits). Note that telephone numbers are usually given in pairs (separated with full stops when written).

Cheap rates

A large number of different packages are available offering different national and international rates. Usually you'll pay €20 or €30 per month including broadband internet and often free/very cheap international calls. See the chapter *Setting up home* for further information. Calling mobiles internationally can be expensive.

Telephone cards

Des cartes téléphoniques can be bought in post offices, *tabacs* (tobacconist) and newsagents. They come in units of 50 or 120 and can be used in telephone booths displaying the blue bell sign. It is also usually possible to receive incoming calls at public telephones. You can also buy pre-paid telephone cards to make calls to some countries.

Emergency and information numbers

See the section on emergency services.

Telephone prefixes

Some telephone numbers have prefixes. Apart from the numbers listed below be wary of other numbers beginning 08 as they will be premium rate numbers. By law, the charge rate for these numbers has to be displayed in their advertisements.

■ 0800 – (*numéros verts*) are toll-free (if calling from a landline)

■ 0801, 0810 or 0811 – (*numéros azurs*) are numbers charged at the local rate (day and evening rates apply)

■ 082020, 082022 cost €0.09, 0820 costs from €0.12 and 0825 costs €0.15 per minute – (*numéros indigo*) more expensive than a local call.

> **Karalyn Monteil used phone booths a lot when she first moved over from Chicago in 1997.**
>
> I managed to get work giving English language classes by telephone but as I didn't have my own flat and couldn't get a cell phone (at that time you had to show a carte de séjour before you could get a phone) I got a pager and used to get people to call me at the phone booth down in the street. I gave a lot of phone classes from phone booths in the street.

Other telephone services and fax

All the usual telephone services are provided in France, including operator, transfer charge calls and a voice-messaging service (3672 Memophone). Many of these are also available with Minitel (see below).

Fax machines (known as fax, *téléfax* or *télécopieur*) were unknown in France before 1988, but a postal strike acted as a catalyst and enabled fax companies to exploit the panic of businesses and professionals. Since then, the fax has become as indispensable in France as elsewhere.

◼ Payphones and télécartes

There are over 158,000 card-operated payphones in France. Telephone cards (*télécartes*) can be bought in post offices, *tabacs*, etc. There are also 60,000 public telephones in bars, restaurants and other establishments.

In large cities and airports you can find telephones that accept bank cards. A voicemail service lets callers from public telephones leave messages for numbers that do not answer or are engaged.

◼ Mobile phones

See the section 'Utilities, phone and internet' in the chapter *Setting up home*.

◼ Telephone directories and pages jaunes

Les pages info, which form part of each *departement*'s telephone directory (*l'annuaire*) are a useful source of addresses for most aspects of daily life from hospitals and public transport to schools and administrative services; or you can look on the website www.pagesjaunes.fr (online Yellow Pages).

Telephone glossary	
abonné	subscriber
un abonnement	subscription
un appel	a (telephone) call
conversation à trois	conferencing
décrochez	pick up the receiver
une facture détaillé	itemised bill
memo d'appel	alarm call
raccrochez	hang up
le répondeur	answer machine
signal d'appel	call waiting
le téléphone sans-fil	cordless phone
la tonalité	dialing tone
transfert d'appel	call transfer

■ Ex-directory

For a fee, France Telecom will put you on their *liste rouge* (ex-directory list).

For further information on telecoms in France (in English and French) go to www.arcep.fr. L'ARCEP, l'Autorité de Régulation des Communications Electroniques et des Postes, is the state regulator for telecoms and postal services.

Minitel

In 1983, a decade before the World Wide Web, the French had Minitel which was perhaps one of the most exciting developments in French telecommunications and the most successful and widespread system of its kind in the world. Basically, Minitel is a computer terminal, which is linked to the videotext/teletext information system called Télétel through France Telecom, its owner. By using a Minitel terminal any telephone subscriber can access directory enquiries nationwide and as well as public and professional services. There were 6.5 million terminals in use in France at Minitel's peak in 1997 and this was the main reason that the internet was slow to catch on at first.

Use of the service is charged at a basic rate per hour and the terminal is rented from France Télécom for a monthly fee. A whole list of services is available on Minitel from board and video games to directory enquiries services in English, German and Spanish, and it provides a bank of information on weather, road conditions etc. You can book and pay by telepayment for airline, train or theatre tickets and read the pages of a favourite newspaper on the screen. Newer services include instant messaging, news, horoscopes, shopping and classified advertising. The great advantage of Minitel is that it is a two-way system: money can be transferred between bank accounts, bills paid, and shopping ordered and paid for. Subscribers can leave messages for each other in 'electronic mailboxes'.

Internet glossary	
adresse électronique	email address
annexe	attachment
arobase	@ (at)
courriel/mél	email
fureter/naviguer	to browse/navigate
lien/hyperlien	link/hyperlink
mot de passe	password
moteur de recherche	search engine
page d'accueil	home page
rafraîchir	refresh/reload
se loguer	to log on
signet	bookmark
télécharger	to download
tiret	hyphen
trois double-vé	www

Despite the visionary brilliance of Minitel, which preceded commercial use of the internet by years, it has largely been superseded by the internet. France Télécom has made Minitel available to anyone with an internet connection and there are mobile phone services. For further information on these and other services visit the Minitel website (www.minitel.fr).

The internet

France was a relative latecomer to the net but caught up quickly. Users of the net are known as *internautes*. There are a range of internet service providers (*fournisseurs d'accès à internet* (FAIs). For more information see the section 'Utilities, phone and internet' in the chapter *Setting up home*.

■ THE POST

The French postal service is a public service company and with the 2009 EU target for liberalisation of all national postal services fast approaching, has done much in recent years to throw off its old-fashioned image and reputation for inefficiency. New services include free, permanent email accounts, streamlining deliveries and carrying out a modernisation of all post offices. *La Poste* has also been allowed to develop its banking services, gradually offering more and more of the services that conventional banks offer.

There are over 17,000 post offices (known as *la poste* or *bureau de poste*) and they are open 8am–7pm (with a lunch break in some areas) and 8am–12pm on Saturdays. There is a 24-hour main post office in Paris on the rue du Louvre. *La Poste* has its own website at www.laposte.fr and has recently opened an English language site at www.laposte.com in recognition of the large number of English speakers using its services. Most information on its services can be found here. If only *un timbre* (a stamp) or two is needed it is more usual to buy these at a *tabac*. In areas where there has been a rural exodus leaving mostly the elderly and infirm, the post office has adapted its services to take this into account. In other cases, the postmaster may be a part-time job, which can be doubled up with being a shopkeeper, garage-owner and so on.

Significant political opposition to streamlining the number of post offices means that senior management has decided to position its branches as distribution centres, providing additional client services such as swimming pool tickets or SNCF (national railways) tickets. In fact liberalisation has been under way for a while, with heavier letters and parcels already open to competition. However it is very unlikely that *La Poste* will be privatised in the near future and receives significant subsidies from the government. *La Poste* is regulated by ARCEP.

Urgent and business mail

It is not customary to use the regular postal service for urgent letters as this can take a few days to arrive in another part of France. Instead, there is an extra fast delivery service *Chronopost* which assures delivery throughout France by the next morning. There are special services for businesses including mailouts (*téléimpression*) and express, local, national and international parcel delivery.

Addressing post

Always use the postcode on items sent within or to France: this is the five-figure code written before the city or town name. It is the first two numbers of this code that signify the *département* name.

Some addresses contain 'Cedex' which may be followed by a single number. This stands for *Courrier d'Entreprise à Distribution Exceptionnelle* and is for a post box number for bulk or administrative deliveries. It should be included if it is given in an address.

Private post box/poste restante

Those who live in a remote area might have their post delivered to a box (*boîte postale*) rather than to their home and in this case the address may be a B.P. number. A temporary arrangement can also be made to have letters sent c/o *Poste Restante* at the nearest main post office (*Poste Centrale*) and held there until you are ready to collect them. A small fee is charged and proof of identity is necessary when collecting mail.

Registered mail

For official and other important documents you will probably want a proof of postage or receipt:

Post office glossary	
adresse de l'expéditeur	return address
adresse de réexpédition	forwarding address
affranchir	to frank
affranchissement des envois	postage
avis de livraison/de reception	advice of delivery
une boîte à lettres	post box
un code postal	post code
un colis	parcel, package, packet (also *un paquet*)
un colis avec valeur déclarée	insured parcel
une collecte	a mail collection
le courrier	mail
courrier prioritaire	priority mail
envelope prêt-à-poster	pre-paid envelope
le facteur	postman
imprimés	printed matter
port payé	postage paid
pré-timbré	pre-stamped
les rebuts	undeliverable items
réexpédier	re-address
retour à l'envoyeur	return to sender

- *Lettre recommandée simple*: a letter registered at the post office with a sender receipt
- *Lettre recommandée avec accusé de réception*: a registered letter which has to be signed for by the recipient. The sender (*expéditeur*) is given a form to complete with the name and address of the addressee (*destinataire*). The recipient signs a postcard on receipt of the letter and the card is then posted to the sender as proof of receipt

If you are the addressee for registered mail and you are not at home to sign for it, the postman will leave you a postcard (*un avis de passage*) with the times and days when you can collect it from the post office.

Forwarding mail

If you have a friend or neighbour who is willing to forward your mail, they can do this by obtaining a special envelope *une enveloppe de réexpédition* from a post office which can then be posted in a letterbox. This is a free service.

You can also pay the post office to redirect your mail to your new address by completing an *ordre de réexpedition*.

Post office financial services

Since 2006 the Post Office has operated financial services under the name La Banque Postale, set up after a law was passed allowing it to operate banking services along the lines of conventional banks. While continuing its commitment to a democratic service through the 17,000 post offices, it now also provides a wider range of loans and mortgages, manages unit trusts (OPCVM) through its asset management arm as well as other services, such as life assurance.

Junk mail

You should be able to stop a large part of junk mail (*le courrier indésirable*) by communicating in writing to the *Fédération des entreprises de vente a distance* (60 rue de la Boétie, 75008 Paris; ☎01 42 56 38 86).

■ WASTE AND RECYCLING

FACT

■ One of the main problems, like everywhere else, is that the amount of . waste per person is rising and now stands at 360 kg/person/year.

Most studies put France somewhere in the middle of the EU recycling league, recycling about 30% of household waste, ahead of Britain but behind Germany and the Netherlands. Waste collection is organised by local government and is paid for out of local taxes. ADEME, the government agency responsible for the environment aims to encourage recycling by making it a cheaper alternative for communes than other methods of waste disposal.

Companies which sell consumer products have to pay a tax depending on the volume of packaging and types of materials used and this revenue then goes to support what is known as *le tri*, sorting of rubbish. *Communes* receive financial support according to the tonnes of rubbish sorted. Some municipalities are far more advanced than others in terms of implementing *le tri* and whether you are provided with different bins for paper, glass and plastic and cans will depend on your municipality.

■ HEALTH

Health insurance and hospitals

In general the French hospital and healthcare system is very good; so good in fact that the World Health Organization considers it the best in the world. Such high standards come at a price, which includes nearly 10% of French GDP (7.7%

in the UK) and a healthcare budget deficit of €6 billion a year. Successive health ministers have introduced remedial reforms to try to cut costs. In 2003 over 600 medicines (out of over 4,000 prescription drugs) were reclassified as non-essential or 'comfort' medicines and are now only reimbursed by the 'Secu' at 35% (instead of 65%); 84 were dropped from the health service list altogether. The health service is also fuelled by national hypochondria. The French spend over €300 per head a year on pharmaceutical remedies which is close to the UK's €275 but much more than in America (€175), and they take three times as many anti-depressants as other EU countries. This love affair with doctors and pills extends even to children; 4% of children under 9 years are on prescription mood-modifying drugs and pupils are taking their exams in pharmaceutically induced state of composure.

The French healthcare system is a combination of private and public health care services: the national health care service is available but it functions in a particular way. In most cases you cannot obtain free treatment at the point of delivery. You pay for treatment and then reclaim most about 70% (only 60% if you don't first register with a *médecin traitant*, a GP, who then refers you like in the UK – this is a recent change and part of the reforms aimed at cutting costs) and have insurance (*une mutuelle*) for the rest.

One point to bear in mind if you are British is that once you leave the UK you are no longer entitled to use the British National Health Service (NHS) free of charge, unless you return to the UK permanently. Of course, treatment is available in the case of any accident suffered while on a visit, but routine treatment cannot be claimed free of charge. When visiting France, while still resident in the UK, most treatment can be obtained with the European Health Insurance Card (EHIC) and a reciprocal agreement.

Health insurance contributions

French workers are required to contribute to the social security system (*sécurité sociale*). This applies both to the employed and self-employed. The contributions are calculated as a percentage (usually about 20%–25% of your salary) of taxable income: employers must also pay a contribution towards their employees' costs. A foreign individual must begin contributing once in possession of the *carte de séjour* and register at the local *sécurité sociale* or health insurance office (*caisse primaire d'assurance maladie*). The address can be obtained from the local *mairie* (town hall). These contributions provide for a range of health and social security benefits for the contributor and their dependants.

Medical treatment for non-resident foreigners

Foreigners who are non-residents, even though they are from elsewhere in the EU will only receive doctor/hospital treatment if they pay first and then apply for reimbursement.

■ British expatriates

If you are working in France but are continuing to pay UK national insurance contributions you will be covered if you have applied for form E101 or E106 (depending on your length of stay). Those on business trips or short stays or visits who are not covered by an EHIC will have to choose between returning to the UK for free treatment or paying upfront to go to a French hospital. Charges would be in the region of €1,000 per day for an in-patient (non-serious) including treatment and drugs, accommodation and food and up to €3,000 for more intensive treatment (e.g. a heart operation requiring intensive care). Note that anyone requiring unexpected emergency treatment will still be treated without paying first. During visits to the UK, you can also continue to use the British NHS while living and working in France, provided that you are still registered with the Department for Work and Pensions (DWP) in Britain. However, this dispensation is only while you remain a UK resident. Once you have become a French resident you will have to start paying French social security contributions in order to be able to use the French health service. Alternatively, you can take out private medical insurance.

Those who have retired to France and are entitled to a UK state pension should obtain form E121 from the DWP (www.dwp.gov.uk) before they leave the UK. If you retire early without a state benefit you will not be covered by French social security. However, there is a concessionary period of up to two and a half years during which you can still receive UK NHS treatment, provided that your British National Insurance contributions are up to date, and you have obtained form E106 from the DWP before you leave the UK.

Non-working foreigners in France and private health insurance

One recent change in French healthcare cover for EU expats received a lot of coverage in the press because of the large number of early retirees it affected in France. EU expats who are not officially retired, not working and have been living in France for less than five years are no longer covered by the CMU (Couverture Maladie Universelle) but must take out 100% private cover. The outcry came because the French government initially introduced this measure retroactively. This meant that many people who had already moved to France could no longer access healthcare there and were in the position of not being able to take out private insurance because of having serious health problems that insurance companies would not cover. After pressure from the British government, the French health minister announced that anyone who had moved to France before 23 November 2007 would still qualify.

Social security card

A French social security card contains 13 digits which represent your age, sex, date of birth, country of origin and your code. It will appear on your pay slip and you must write it on any *feuille de soins* (see 'Using doctors and dentists').

> ## Sarah Bright Thomas, a lawyer based in Toulouse, comments:
> There is talk amongst local estate agents that the measure has affected the confidence of prospective property buyers from the UK but there really is no reason why it should. Many people will end up paying less with a private health policy than they would previously have done within the social security system for their complementary cover. All it requires is a little forward planning.

French social security and non-EU nationals

Some other countries not in the EU have reciprocal agreements with France regarding social security benefits, and these include the USA and Canada. Their nationals retain an attachment to the social security of their own country that is responsible for providing payment for work absence due to illness, work-related injury or maternity leave. For details of how to receive French benefits contact the Division des Relations International of CPAM (Caisse Primaire d'Assurance Maladie)..

What social security entitles you to

Payment into *sécurité sociale* entitles both you and your dependants to medical treatment, and other expenses, free of charge up to a statutory limit for each type of treatment. Often, *sécurité sociale* pays for only a percentage (usually 70%–90%) of the treatment (40%–70% for medicines) and the patient is liable for the rest. *Sécurité sociale* will only pay the full cost of treatment for more serious illnesses and in specific hospital practices. Hospitals and general practices are basically allowed to charge what they like for their services. However, in each locality a group of doctors from certain hospitals and general practices agree to charge fees within the limits set by *sécurité sociale*. Therefore, if you use the facilities that these hospitals and practices (known as *conventionné*) offer, treatment undertaken should not cost any more than is stipulated by the authorities.

Private versus conventionné treatment

The alternatives are either to opt for totally private treatment or to make up the difference between *conventionné* rates and whatever the hospital or practice which you have chosen charges. Private health treatment is extremely expensive and the vast majority of people choosing this option take private health insurance (see below) to pay for it. The facilities in *conventionné* hospitals tend to be basic but are generally considered good.

French private health insurance

So, an element of personal contribution is involved between the cost of treatment, even in *conventionné* facilities, and the percentage (usually 70%) that *sécurité sociale* pays. In certain cases this difference could amount to quite a lot of money and most people take out an insurance policy specifically to cover this shortfall. The premiums involved are quite low and most industries, occupations and professions have special plans (called *complémentaires* or sometimes *mutuelles*) which employees can join to cover this. Joining such plans can sometimes be a condition of employment. In other cases contributions are paid as part of the employment package.

Choosing a complementaire

Over the past few years, government reforms have shifted some of the burden for paying for healthcare onto complementary insurers, which means premiums have gone up. This trend is likely to continue. Insurers use all sorts of criteria when deciding on the premium but not all use the same criteria. Premiums in Paris are, for example, often much higher. Make sure that the policy recognises the *Loi Levin*, a French law designed to protect the subscriber. You should also give some consideration to

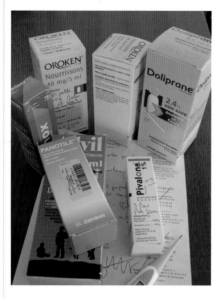

the question of *dépassements*. As mentioned above, there is a *tarif conventionné*, which are set costs for set treatments stipulated by the government. Many healthcare providers will however charge more than this: €40 rather than €20 for a consultation for example. Your complementary cover may state that it covers you for 100% of costs beyond what is paid by the *sécurité sociale* but this doesn't mean 100% of all costs. It means 100% of costs up to the *tarif conventionné*. You would be liable to pay the rest (the *dépassement*) out of your own pocket unless you had taken out cover for that.

The EHIC

In the initial moving period, or on holiday visits, or while on a speculative visit to France to look for work, you will probably not be covered by *sécurité sociale*, and in such cases, you can take out private travel insurance. However, it is also possible to obtain free, or mainly free, treatment under a reciprocal agreement which exists between some EU countries. To qualify for such treatment you need the EHIC (European Health Insurance Card). UK citizens should go to the Department of Health website at www.dh.gov.uk to apply for the EHIC online. Citizens of other countries should check with their national health department for their specific requirements.

Once in France, anyone who requires treatment should go to a *conventionné* doctor, dentist or hospital. Although they will probably have to pay for treatment, up to 75% of this can then be refunded, as long as the procedure detailed on the EHIC is followed. However, you should note that as a percentage of the treatment costs are still not covered by the EHIC you should have travel health insurance cover for the balance.

An EHIC usually expires after a three-month period and is not valid once you have left the your country permanently or are employed in France. It can sometimes be renewed and it is also possible to get an 'open ended' EHIC if you make frequent trips abroad for a longer period than three months. However, after three months in France permanent arrangements should be made. In the UK, details of social security, health care and pension rights within the EU and are obtainable from main post offices and the DWP, Overseas Directorate (www.dwp.gov.uk).

The E101, E121 and E128

In the case of UK, HM Revenue and Customs (www.hmrc.gov.uk) issues an E101 to UK nationals working in another EU country to exempt them from paying social security contributions in that country because they are still paying them in their home country.

The E128 entitles you to medical treatment in another EU country where you are working, or if you are a student. You have to obtain an E101 *before* you can obtain an E128.

If you are retired, you will need to get an E121 from the DWP to receive state healthcare in France.

Private medical insurance

Those who are going to France seeking work, or who spend a few weeks or months a year there, will require private medical insurance to cover the balance of the cost not covered by the EHIC (see above). If you already hold private health insurance you will find that most companies will switch this for European cover once you are in France. With the increase of British and foreign insurance companies offering this kind of cover, it's worth shopping around as cover and costs vary.

Useful contacts

Agence Eaton: Continent Assurances; ☎02 97 40 80 20;
www.french-insurance.com. Bilingual insurance bureau. All types of insurance

Amariz Ltd: ☎0117 974 5770; amariz@lineone.net; www.amariz.co.uk

AXA PPP Healthcare: ☎0870 608 0850; www.axappphealthcare.co.uk

British United Provident Association (BUPA): ☎01273 208181;
info@bupaintl.com; www.bupa-int.com. BUPA International offers a range of worldwide schemes for individuals and companies of three or more employees based outside the UK for six or more months

Centers for Disease Control and Prevention: ☎404 639 3534/800 311 3435;
www.cdc.gov. General travel health advice

Community Insurance Agency Inc.: ☎847 897 5120; info@ciainsagency.com;
☎1 800 344 9540 (toll free). International health coverage agency

Exclusive Healthcare Ltd.: ☎0121 2882 363; in France: +33 (0)870 44 91 75 and +33 (0)4 94 40 31 45; enquiries@exclusivehealthcare.com;
www.exclusivehealthcare.com. Insures expatriates living in France;
offers a free information service

Exeter Friendly Society: ☎01392 353535; sales@exeterfriendly.co.uk;
www.exeterfriendly.co.uk

Expacare: ☎01344 381650; info@expacare.com or visit www.expacare.net.
Specialists in expatriate healthcare offering high-quality health insurance cover for individuals and their families, including group cover for five or more employees.
Cover is available for expatriates of all nationalities worldwide

Goodhealth Worldwide (Europe): ☎0870 442 7376; www.goodhealthworldwide.com; offices in Antibes, Bordeaux, Nice, Paris area, Sellians, St. Raphael and Toulouse

Healthcare International: ☎020 7665 1627; enquiries@healthcareinternational.com;
www.healthcareinternational.com

HIFAC Health Insurance: ☎0871 424 0022; www.insurancewide.com. Provides access to all the top private medical insurance providers

IHI – International Health Insurance Danmark: ☎+33 (0)4 92 17 42 42; ihi@ihi.com; www.ihi.com

Taurus Insurance Services Ltd.: ☎+350 52776; sales@taurusinsuranceservices. com; www.taurusinsuranceservices.com. Health, travel and accident insurance providers to the expatriate community

Tredinnick Insurance: ☎+33 (0)5 45 82 42 93; insure@tredinnick-insurance.com; www.charente-properties.com. Bilingual insurance brokers. Private health and 'top-up' policies to the French social security system and other types of insurance

Using doctors and dentists

It is as well to line up a family doctor/general practitioner (GP) (*médecin généraliste*), and a dentist or optician who can be consulted if necessary, soon after arrival. You need to be registered with a GP (*médecin traitant*), to get maximum reimbursement from the *securité sociale* (see above). You can easily change your *médecin traitant*. Most people will choose a doctor near where they live or work for convenience. Before making an appointment you should check the charges in advance of any medical or dental practitioner because if they are not *conventionné* (part of the French national health system), a very large contribution will have to be made. Most of these services will provide immediate treatment in the case of an emergency. Night and Sunday duty doctors can usually be contacted through the local police station (*commissariat de police*).

La Carte Vitale

Residents of France are issued with a Carte Vitale (*carte d'assurances maladie*), a smart card with a microchip which makes the whole process of reimbursement from the state and *mutuelle* (complementary insurance) faster and simple as information can be transferred directly to the data centre at the *caisses d'assurances maladie* (state health insurance) via a terminal operated by the health professional. Reimbursements can arrive in your nominated bank account within five days. Note that a refund cannot be obtained for medicines bought without a doctor's order.

From 2007 a new version of the Carte Vitale was introduced (Vitale 2) and the new system is supposed to be completely in place by 2011. It has also become obligatory for each patient to have an electronically stored medical dossier (*dossier médicale personnel*/DMP). The personal medical dossier is not stored on the Carte Vitale, but Vitale 2 will be used to access the dossier by a registered health professional who is handling your treatment. The aim of this new system is to prevent the duplication of medical tests, which patients could (and frequently did) demand from several different doctors under the previous unregulated system. It will, however, be possible for individuals to inspect the information on the Vitale and correct any mistakes that may have been made. The Vitale 2 will be sent automatically to current holders of the Vitale card. There are a number of informative French websites which deal (in French) with the issues surrounding the Carte Vitale and the personal medical dossier including www.assurancemaladie.sante.gouv.fr/ and www.ameli.fr (L'Assurance Maladie enligne).

Alternative medicine

Homeopathy and acupuncture are well-respected alternative medical treatments (*les médecins douces*) in France. They are recognised by French social security although homeopathic medicines are not reimbursed to the same level as other medicines. As the charges for *médecines douces* are generally higher, full costs are not usually reimbursed by independent health insurance either (i.e. *les complémentaires*) although this is changing as these treatments become more popular and insurance companies move to satisfy demand. Normally you will find such doctors by word of mouth or ask in the pharmacy, etc. Osteopathy is popular but not as much as in some other countries such as in the UK. However it is not recognised by French social security.

Pharmacies

French doctors have a wide selection of remedies at their disposal and there is a tendency to prescribe elaborate pharmaceutical compositions, when an over-the-counter remedy would be just as beneficial. All medicines in France are expensive so you should ensure you are covered by a combination of the EHIC (for EU nationals) and travel insurance, or by national or private health schemes, if you need prescriptions. When your local pharmacy is closed at the weekend, holiday, etc. there will be a sign on the door of the nearest duty pharmacist (*pharmacie de garde*). These are also usually given in the regional newspaper.

Using hospitals

In an emergency, you can go to any hospital with casualty facilities. The emergency ambulance will select the closest. If less urgent treatment is needed then your doctor or specialist will refer you to an appropriate hospital: this might be a *conventionné* hospital, or a private one if such a preference has been indicated. Outpatient treatment is charged for and the cost must be recovered as for doctors and dentists.

FACT

Currently Europe accounts for 58% of the homeopathic market and France is responsible for a third of this. Only the Netherlands spends more money a year on homeopathic medicine. In France 47% of costs for homeopathic doctors are reimbursed.

In the case of inpatient treatment the system varies. Some hospitals are publicly run and some are private clinics. They may charge the full cost and provide a certificate, which can be used to reclaim a part of the charges as described above. Other hospitals may claim the *sécurité sociale* contribution direct from the Caisse Primaire, and just expect you to pay the balance (e.g. 25% for medical treatment). Note that treatment for serious illnesses is refunded at 100%. Some hospitals make a fixed daily hospital charge (*forfait journalier*) accommodation charge which *sécurité sociale* doesn't cover; this could be up to the equivalent of €120 to €160 per day.

Sometimes it is possible to agree in advance with social security that they will pay your expenses for an operation or treatment in a private clinic under a *prise en charge* (payment of expenses).

Reclaiming medical fees

At the end of a course of treatment any expenses which have been paid out and which are recoverable under *sécurité sociale* need to be reclaimed (see 'La Carte Vitale' above).

It is advisable to be privately insured for the portion of medical expenses that are not covered by *sécurité sociale*. These can then be reclaimed separately from the insurance company. Under this arrangement, if extra insurance has been taken out, the medical treatment will cost nothing except perhaps a small policy excess. The general rule to remember in France is that everyone is entitled to fairly good, cheap medical treatment under an effective national health service. However, most people take additional steps to improve the level of care to which they are entitled and to gain further protection against costs involved.

TIP

Ensure you claim for everything that is covered.

Useful contacts

American Hospital: ☎01 46 41 25 25; www.American-hospital.org

Anglo-American Pharmacy: 6 rue de Castiglione, 1st Arrondissement, Paris; ☎01 42 47 60 72 96

British Pharmacy (SNC): 62 Av. des Champs Elysées, 75008 Paris; (☎01 43 59 22 52)

British and American Pharmacy: 1 rue Auber, 75009 Paris; ☎01 47 42 49 40

Régime Social des Indépendants: ☎01 77 93 00 00; www.le-rsi.fr. Advice on national health insurance for the self-employed

Caisse Primaire d'Assurance-Maladie de Paris: Fonction des Relations Internationales, 173–175 rue de Bercy, 75586 Paris Cedex 12; ☎01 40 19 55 23. Information and refunds

HM Revenue and Customs: ☎0845 3021479. Provides basic information about healthcare for people going outside the UK and supplies healthcare certificates E128 and E106

English Medical Centre: 8 bis rue Quinhault, 78100 St Germain-en-Laye; ☎01 30 61 25 61

Hertford British Hospital: 3 rue Barbès, 92300 Levallois-Perret, Paris; ☎01 46 39 22 22

Hôpital Hôtel Dieu: 1 pl. Parvis, Notre Dame; ☎01 42 34 82 43

SOS Médicins: Paris 01 43 37 77 77 for medical emergencies only. Alternatively, dial 15 for an emergency ambulance

The emergency services

Ambulances

In France, there is no national ambulance service but each area has its own Service d'Aide Médicale Urgence (SAMU). The national telephone number is 15. When you, or the person assisting you, call this number, the operator will take down the name, address and symptoms of the patient and connect you with the doctor on call (*docteur de permanence*). According to the demands of the situation, a doctor or ambulance team will be sent to administer first aid or transport to hospital. Charges are levied correspondingly.

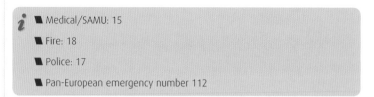

- Medical/SAMU: 15
- Fire: 18
- Police: 17
- Pan-European emergency number 112

Emergency and information numbers

For directory enquiries see the section 'Utilities, phone and internet' in the chapter *Setting up home*.

Dialling emergency numbers from private telephones is free but in payphones you need to insert €1 minimum or a *télécarte* to get the phone to work. Your coin will be refunded and no charge will be made. Alternatively, you can dial the pan-European emergency number 112, which is also the number you should dial from a mobile.

Sarkozy and eduction

Nicolas Sarkozy has announced a change in emphasis in primary education to reorient it towards a return to fundamentals such as the French language and maths. He has also announced a package for the underprivileged *banlieux* (suburbs) as part of a programme to create equality of opportunity and address social problems that have erupted in the form of riots over the past few years. This will include an increase in the number of placements, *stages*, available for those on secondary school vocational courses. These plans are in their early stages at the time of writing however and it remains to be seen what effect changes will have on the ground.

◼ THE EDUCATION SYSTEM

School education in France

The French education system is regarded as one of the most thorough and exacting in the world. But the recent reductions in the number of teachers, the switch to a four-day week and decentralisation of funding making it the responsibility of local government have been heavily criticised within France. Many argue this will produce huge inequalities between the poorest and the richest regions in terms of resources available to education departments.

French education is highly centralised with a national curriculum that ensures national uniformity. At one time school timetables were identical in every school in every part of the country. Now, however, the regions have a certain amount of autonomy in this respect. The system is almost entirely based on state schools (*l'écoles publiques*). Less common are the private schools (*école privée*) which are often religiously based: although fee-paying, most of these are also, in part, state or church subsidised.

State financial assistance can be direct, in the form of allowances given at the beginning of the school year for 6–16-year-olds on the basis of family income. Transport support is also provided. Sometimes municipalities award scholarships to support pupils in their studies.

Education in France is compulsory, by law, from 6 to 16 years, and is free, except for university. Parents may be expected to pay for books and materials which can amount to several hundred euros per pupil per year, although generally, such costs are borne by the municipality (for primary schools) and by the conseils généraux (county councils) for colléges. Most schools are now changing to the four-day week (i.e. no school on Wednesdays or Saturday mornings). To compensate for this about 12 days will be taken from the school holidays. These extension-of-term dates are set by the local authority and vary from region to region so find out what is happening in your local area from the *mairie*. The only thing that is certain at the time of writing is that the hitherto usual French system of having Wednesday

A typical French classroom

afternoon free and working on Saturday mornings is no longer prevalent.

The French approach to education concentrates on training the mind. One of its strengths is that French schools place particular emphasis on the sciences, which accounts for the country's leading position in many scientific and technical industries. French students also spend a lot of time on written French compared with English in English or American schools. Grammar and sentence construction are closely scrutinised.

Here we can see how fundamentally language structures the learning process both in France and Anglophone countries. French is a far more structured and regulated language than English. There is consequently a hierarchy in terms of your mastery of the rules of expression. This fundamentally affects teaching style, not just in French but in all disciplines. Much emphasis is placed on the assimilation of a programme of what is considered vital information from teaching staff, many of whom lecture rather than teach. The approach in France is often thought to be more intellectual but all the learning by rote does shift attention away from independent initiative on the student's part.

In terms of language teaching, the effects of this method have been disastrous. In spite of the many hours spent on language teaching, traditionally foreign languages have been taught in the same systematic and academic way as French itself with not enough emphasis on oral practice, meaning that many students leave school after many years of study without any confidence in terms of expressing themselves in a foreign language. Efforts have been made to address this in recent years, including the introduction of language teaching in primary schools. Of course, language teaching in English speaking countries leaves just as much to be desired, but France does stand out in the non-English speaking world because of the low general level of competence in English.

Sport

Although there is an allowance for sports as part of the secondary education curriculum, sport has never been a high priority in French schooling in terms of creating an ethos in the way it has been in British or American schools. This doesn't mean that sport is not valued in France but it doesn't have the same importance in terms of fostering a feeling of identity as it has traditionally been the case elsewhere.

Grades/classes

Secondary school classes are named like a countdown to take-off, so that your first year is *sixième*, second *cinquième* and so on up to *première*, with the final year, *terminale*, the year you take your *baccalauréat* (or bac for short).

Cycles pédagogiques

The education is divided into *cycles pédagogiques* with target attainment levels for each cycle, rather than for the end of each year of schooling. Nursery school is included in the *cycle d'apprentissages* (introduction to basics) for 5–8-year-olds which also includes the first two years of primary school. The next cycle is the *cycle de consolidation* (8–11 years) then *cycle d'observation* (11–13 years), *cycle d'orientation* (13–15 years) and finally *cycle de determination*.

French school term dates

In general terms, school starts in September and there are five school terms each year, with the summer term a couple of weeks longer than the others. French schoolchildren have a particularly long summer holiday, extending throughout July and August.

The structure of school education

Although not compulsory, nursery schooling (*l'école maternelle*) for 2–6-year-olds is free and widely used. Under the 1989 Education Act a place at nursery school must be available for any 3-year-old whose family wishes it, in a school as near as possible to their home. There is also pre-nursery school (*jardins d'enfants*) for 2–3-year-olds.

FACT

◼ Under EU regulations, any EU citizen must be treated in the same way as national citizens in having access to French education if they so wish.

Zèro de conduite (Zero for conduct) by Jean Vigo

Zèro de conduite is one of the all-time great French films (made in 1933) that covers life in a French boarding school. It is a hugely poetic and entertaining treatise on anarchy, animated by the rebellious school *surveillant* (playground assistant – a post that still exists in French schools, with additional responsibilities of supervising detentions and free periods and providing educational support). Zero is the lowest possible mark obviously. In French education, marks are given out of 20, with a pass being 50% or 10 marks.

■ Detailed information on the education system is available from your French Embassy. See also www.onisep.fr, website of the Office National d'Information sur les Enseignements et les Professions (ONISEP).

Compulsory primary education (*l'école primaire/école élémentaire*) begins at 6 years. Under the French class-grading system pupils begin in the 11th grade and work upwards to the first. Grades 11 to 7 comprise the primary stages. These are followed by the next stage, secondary education (*collège*) which begins at the age of 11 and lasts until age 15. There are different stages of secondary school: the *collège d'enseignement secondaire* (CES), and then *lycée* or technical school (*le lycée technique*) from the age of 15.

In the third grade, depending on their aptitudes and the advice of teachers in consultation with their parents, students will either embark on studies leading to the *baccalauréat* (see below), or take technical or vocational options leading to various qualifications: *Brevet de Techniciens* (BT), *Brevet d'Etudes Professionnelles* (BEP) or *Certificat d'Aptitude Professionnelle* (CAP).

The first grade is the last year of compulsory education. Around 75% of pupils stay on after the first grade in *la classe terminale*. Most of the *terminale* students prepare for the *baccalauréat* examination taken at the age of 18/19. The *bac* is a competitive exam but pass rates have improved dramatically over recent years and now stand at almost 90%. As it is essential for entry into many professions and university its attainment is earnestly pursued and encouraged. Students can choose the emphasis of the *bac* from several options including literature, mathematics and sciences but within each of these categories all the subjects are compulsory. There are seven types of *baccalauréat* divided into two groups.

- *General Baccalaureat*: (L) Literature, (ES) Economics and Social Sciences, (S) Science and (SMS) Medical and Social Sciences
- *Technical Baccalaureat*: (STT) Science and Tertiary Technologies, (STI) Science and Industrial Technologies and (STL) Science and Laboratory Technologies

The different types of baccalaureate are rated in importance: a *baccalauréat* which is arts-based is ranked lowest, while the science-based *baccalauréat* is considered more prestigious. Those who have passed the *baccalauréat* are known as *bacheliers*.

French schools and foreigners

Foreign residents' children living in France will have three main schooling options: to attend boarding school in their native country, to take up the opportunity to go to a

> **Laurie Baird has been living and working in France for over 20 years and is married to a French woman. They have two daughters. Laurie describes the education system as being tough.**
>
> There's a lot of stress on the kids at school. Work, work, work it is. It's horrific. I don't know what it's like in Britain now, but when I was at school, it definitely wasn't like that.

French state or private school, or to go to an international school in France.

Those who decide to send their children to state school in France will be obliged to send them to the one designated for their area. The local *services des écoles* (schools information service) in the *mairie* can supply a list of local schools at all levels. The *mairie* in each municipality is responsible for registering pupils in primary and nursery schools. It can also provide parents with the addresses of the regional and district education offices, which carry all the necessary information on entry to secondary education (first and second cycle). Most children in a French state school adapt comfortably within six months and are fully fluent within a year. Some schools in areas where there are large numbers of foreigners' families offer extra French lessons to help them adapt.

Alternatively, those who are interested in private schools will find both day and boarding schools. If you are able to afford private schooling, one of the advantages is likely to be smaller classes, which would probably prove a less intimidating environment than large state school classes, especially for pupils who are hesitant in French.

Problems parents should consider

It is perfectly possible for expatriates to send their children to French state schools. Their decision to do so may depend on the stage of education reached and whether or not a complete change of system and coping with lessons in a foreign language, would constitute more of a disruption than a benefit. While, for instance, children will learn about *nos ancêtres les Gaules* (our ancestors the Gauls) rather than about say, our ancestors the Anglo-Saxons, etc. (incidentally in the framework of the EU, there have been interesting experiments at co-operation in French and German schools in recent years to come up with a combined history curriculum, with all the re-examination of national identity that this involves), it is generally the case that

TIP

For information on pre-university education, parents should make the town hall of their municipality their first stop.

Observations

Which course of action you take will very much depend on circumstances. Take advice from the schools and advisory bodies involved. Children embarked on school-leaving courses may be best left undisturbed, although there are definite language and other benefits to studying in another country at any age. Younger children may be able to pick up sufficient French depending on their ability. It is generally accepted that toddlers who haven't yet mastered English can probably learn enough French if they are immersed in it, to start in the French system at nursery school so that by the age of 6 they can compete perfectly well with French children at primary school.

Foreign residents whose children have been through the French education system are usually more than satisfied with the pedagogical standards. It is, however, true that French students are put under a lot of academic pressure from an early age.

TIP

Supplementary lessons in the French language could be arranged until fluency has been established.

younger children will find it easier to integrate into the French system as they have less difficulty in becoming bilingual.

The other possible problem that school students may have to consider is that if their parents return to their home country they may have to switch back into that country's system. Since there is as yet no system of equivalents in the EU, except at final year level this contingency would need careful consideration. One possibility is to find a school in your own country that follows the International Baccalaureat (IB) that can be followed in other countries including France, where it is taught. Note that the IB is not the same as the French *baccalauréat*.

School and family exchanges

Provided that children are at least 15 years, school exchanges can be arranged through an international education programme such as that run by AFS International Youth Development. School exchanges for younger children aged 9–11 can be arranged for six months through En Famille International Linguistic and Cultural Exchanges, which provides host families with a child of the same age who then comes to stay with you for six months.

Useful contacts

AFS UK: International Youth Development: ☎0113 242 6136;
info-unitedkingdom@afs.org; www.afsuk.org
En Famille International Linguistic and Cultural Exchanges: ☎05 57 435 248;
www.enfamille.com. Organises study exchanges for six months for younger children aged 9–13 years

Bilingual, English curriculum and international schools

◼ Bilingual schools

Alternatively, there are a number of bilingual schools, including the Lycée International de St Germain en Laye, and the International School of Paris. The former follows the National French curriculum but also provides courses in the history and culture of other countries in the language of that country, which can be incorporated into the international baccalaureate; the US curriculum is also offered. The latter has particular expertise in the IB.

◼ British School of Paris

The only school in France to offer the UK curriculum is the British School of Paris, which takes pupils from 4 to 18 years and caters for English-speaking children of over 30 nationalities. It is a non-profit association of France and is managed by a board of governors under His Excellency the British Ambassador. The British School is located on two different sites in the western suburbs of Paris. The Junior School at Bougival uses a mixture of new and traditional methods based on the National Curriculum with emphasis on instruction in the French language. Both music and drama, together with varied sports and extra curricular activities are available. Computer instruction is also given. All staff are involved in providing pastoral care and arranging extra-curricular activities.

◼ International schools

Most international schools are in Paris but they can also be found elsewhere in

France: the Bordeaux International School started in 1988 and provides a British-style international education for ages 4 to 19 and intensive language courses for teenagers and adults. There is also the International School of Sophia Antipolis near Nice which specialises in International and French baccalaureate education and also the English-speaking European School at Mougins (Cannes).

Places in bilingual and international schools tend to be much in demand and entrance requirements stiff, so plans need to be made well in advance.

◼ International schools in Paris (With language of teaching)

American School of Paris: ☎01 41 12 82 76; www.asparis.org; email: admissions@asparis.org. US curriculum and IB. English

British School of Paris: ☎01 34 80 45 95 senior school; ☎01 39 69 78 21 junior school; www.britishschool.fr. UK curriculum. English

College International de Fontainebleau (Anglophone section): ☎01 64 22 11 77; www.anglophonesectionfontainebleau.com

Ecole Active Bilingue: ☎1 45 00 11 57. British/American/French curricula. French and English

Ecole International de Paris: ☎01 45 75 62 98; infovh@eabjm.com; www.eabjm.com. French national curriculum and IB

L'Ermitage-International School of France: ☎01 39 620402 ermitage@ermitage.fr; www.isbi.com

Eurécole: ☎01 40 70 12 81; 01 40 70 91 07. National and International curricula. French, English, German, Spanish

The International School of Paris: ☎01 42 24 09 54; www.isparis.edu email: info@isparis.edu. UK and US curricula and IB. English

Lycée International de St Germain en Laye: ☎01 34 51 74 85; US and French National curriculum and optional IB

Marymount International: ☎01 46 24 10 51; www.marymount.fr. US curriculum. English

United Nations Nursery School: ☎01 45 27 20 24. US and national curriculum. English

◼ International schools outside Paris

American International School on the Côte d'Azur: Nice; ☎04 93 21 04 00; josephine.fellows@cote-azur.ccifr Instruction in English for ages 4 to 18, international curriculum leading to IGCSE and IB

Bordeaux International School: Bordeaux; ☎05 57 87 02 11; bis@bordeaux-school.com www.bordeaux-school.com; US and UK curricula. English and French. Also has kindergarten and primary sections

Cité Scolaire Internationale: (Section Anglophone) Lyon Cedex 07; ☎478 69 60 06; www2.ac-lyon.fr/etab/lycees/lyc-69/csi/accueil.html. English and Welsh national curriculum (basis for English tuition) and French national programme GCSE/Cambridge/IB

CIV International School of Sophia Antipolis (Nice): Alpes Maritimes; ☎(0)4 92 96 52 24; admissions@civissa.org; www.isbi.com. IB, French national curriculum. English and French

Collège-lycée Cévenol International: Le Chambon-sur-Lignon; ☎04 71 59 72 52;

lecevenol@aol.com; www.members.aol.com/lecevenol. French national curriculum, national curriculum with international option French and English

College et Lycée de Sèvres: Sections Internationales de Sevrès, rue Lecocq, Sèvres 92310; ☎01 46 23 96 35; . English, French and German

L'Ecole des Roches: Verneuil sur Avre; ☎02 32 23 40 00

International School of Nice: Nice; ☎(0)4 93 21 04 40; www.isn-nice.org

Mougins School: (Mougins near Cannes) Mougins Cedex; ☎04 93 90 15 47; www.mougins-school.com; information@mougins-school.com. British curriculum

Strasbourg International School: Strasbourg; ☎388 31 50 77

Further information about education

Centre d'Information et de Documentation Jeunesse (CIDJ): ☎01 44 49 12 00; ommunication@cidj.asso.fr; www.cidj.asso.fr

Centre National de Documentation sur l'Enseignement Privé:☎01 47 05 32 68; www.fabert.com

European Council of International Schools (ECIS): ☎01730 268244; www.ecis. org. Can provide a list of schools abroad offering the British Curriculum

Ministère de l'Education Nationale et de La Culture: ☎01 49 50 10 10; www.education.gouv.fr

Office National d'Information sur les Enseignements et les Professions (ONISEP): Service de vente par correspondence; ☎01 40 77 60 00; www.onisep.fr

Further education

France has over 2 million students and as in many developed countries the number of young French people entering further education is rising. The result of

an ever higher rate of entrants is that the university system is overstretched. In other countries including Britain, students try to go to the best centre for their chosen discipline, or failing that, to wherever they can get in with their results, regardless of location or preferences, whereas in France it remains usual to go to the nearest university. This is not by any means obligatory, and indeed it is perfectly possible for someone from Montpellier to study in Paris, but it is not encouraged – for instance cheap university accommodation is not so readily provided. In order to cope with an increasing number of students the French government has expanded the number of places available, in some cases even renting space to do this. There are around 100 existing institutes of higher education and among them over 70 traditional universities. Largely due to the rapid expansion of higher education, many French universities do not enjoy quite the same reputation as the rest of the education system. Of the top 10 French universities, five are in Paris, and the number one is the *Université Paris-Dauphine* (also called Paris IX), which has close links with industry and commerce and specialises in economics and business studies.

No such patchy reputation exists for the *grandes écoles* which are regarded as the source of industrial and commercial grey matter by France's employers. The *écoles* have their own entrance examinations on top of the *bac*; one, the ENA, takes only graduates. The *grandes écoles* generally offer three-year courses in a variety of subjects and their emphasis is on applied or vocational aspects. Almost all France's engineering and business education and much scientific education and education for the elite in public service has traditionally been the preserve of the *grandes écoles*. The universities on the other hand offer much more academic courses and some major vocational education particularly in law, computer science and all medical studies.

The structure of higher education courses

The systems of the *grandes écoles* and the universities are very different. The *écoles* award *diplômes* which take three years (five, if you include the two years intensive preparation for the entrance exam, *le prépa*).

University studies are divided into cycles. The third cycle is for postgraduate studies. Various diplomas and degrees are awarded by universities and these are known familiarly by their acronyms: DEUG, DEUT, DESS, etc. The more recognisable ones are: *la licence, la maîtrise, le DEA and DESS* and *le doctorat* which roughly correspond to the BA, MA, and PhD. A distinguished additional qualification, the

The Bologna Process (ECTS)

At the Bologna Conference in June 1999, 29 countries signed a common text, with the following aims:

- Implement an easily comprehensible and comparable system to promote legibility and facilitate international recognition of degrees
- Organise training and education for a 1st cycle aimed at the job market and a 2nd requiring achievement of the 1st
- Validate this training/education by a system of accumulation of credits transferable between establishments
- Facilitate mobility of students, teachers, lecturers and researchers
- Co-operate by means of assurance of quality of education
- Give a definite European dimension to university education

Regular conferences since then have gradually implemented the programme.

Habilation à Diriger des Recherches, authorises the holder to direct the studies of research students and is awarded at professorial level.

After two years a university student is awarded either a DEUG (*Diplôme d'Etudes Universitaires Générales*) or a DEUST (*Diplôme d'Etudes Universitaires Scientifiques et Techniques*). The DEUST is more vocationally oriented and includes a compulsory *stage* (practical experience training).

The DEUG or DEUST gives entry to the second cycle of study, which also lasts two years. At the end of the first year a *Licence* is gained and the fourth and final year leads to the *Maîtrise*. Recent changes to this system are due to the ECTS, the European credit transfer system, introduced to unify diverse national systems and make it easier for EU students to gain equivalence in different countries. This means that in France, *le masters* (a new term) is now replacing the old postgraduate qualifications, the DEA and DESS (see below).

Qualification levels are often expressed as *Bac* + x (i.e. the number of years of study). The majority of graduates will be *Bac* + 4 which is roughly the same as a *diplôme* from a *grande école*.

In addition to the *diplôme* or various university qualifications, many graduates are now taking additional qualifications at technician level in an effort to combat graduate unemployment. These qualifications can be obtained at *Instituts Universitaires de Technologie* (IUTs) and also be taken on a part-time study basis at other institutions. The qualifications include: *Brevet de Technicien Supérieur* (BTS) and *Diplôme Universitaire de Technologie* (DUT). At *Instituts Universitaires Professionnalisés* (IUPs) the technical qualifications are a *diplôme d'études universitaires professionnalisées* and a *mâtrise* awarded at the end of the first and second years of study respectively. Both IUTs and IUPs are technically part of the university system, but they offer very specialised qualifications.

Postgraduate study

There are various levels of postgraduate studies at the universities. One year of study known as a *Diplôme d'Etudes Approfondies* (DEA) or the *Diplôme d'Etudes Supérieures Spécialisées* (DESS), now being replaced with *le masters* (pronounced without the s). At the time of going to print, the DEA and DESS are being replaced with *le masters* but it is useful to know the previous terminology as the change will no doubt take a few years to fix in people's minds and, of course, those who have already graduated will hold the old qualification. Generally speaking the DEA or its corresponding masters is regarded as preparation for a doctorate for which thesis preparation is usually one or two years. The DESS (or, again, its corresponding masters) is thought of more as a vocational qualification complete in itself. The doctoral system in France has been overhauled and there is now only a single *doctorat* which has replaced the *doctorat du troisieme cycle* and the *Doctorat d'Etat* which were for advanced academic research.

Continuing/adult education

France has no distance learning facilities for further education. However, anyone can study with the UK's Open University (www.open.ac.uk) while being based in France (you don't have to be British). Nonetheless, France is very keen on continuing education (*education permanente*) and there are various schemes for encouraging

FACT

◼ At doctoral level, much of the research done in French universities is supported by the *Centre National de la Recherche Scientifique* (CNRS). The CNRS publishes a series of *Annuaires* with details of its activities and a *Répertoire des Unités de Recherche du CNRS* which lists the main centres of research.

those in employment and others to keep learning for further study and qualifications. There are also studies aimed at retired people. Universities are very active in this area, and so enquiries at your local university in France are a good place to start.

Some French universities have been offering another qualification, *Les Licences Professionnelles*, which are generally for subjects related to a professional career in the industries for which there are currently insufficient qualified personnel. These include computing, e-commerce, transport and finance, or newer industries such as water management. Such *Licences* are intended to be part of a lifelong learning and experience programme.

MBA courses

Many MBA courses and business schools in France attract French and foreign students. Perhaps the best known is INSEAD, a pure business school, based at Fontainebleau. In addition, five of the *grands écoles* offer two-year MBA courses:

- *L'Ecole des Hautes Etudes Commerciales* (HEC)
- *L'Ecole Supérieure des Sciences Economiques et Commerciales* (ESSEC)
- *L'Ecole Supérieure de Commerce de Paris* (ESCP)
- *L'Ecole Supérieure de Commerce de Lyon* (ESCL)
- *Le Centre d'Enseignement et de Recherche Appliqués en Management de Nice* (CERAM)

In addition the *Ecole des Affaires de Paris* (EAP), also called the European School of Management, has a European Masters in Management programme which includes one year in France and a year each in two of its overseas branches in Germany, the UK and Spain. Also, the Institut Supérieur des Affaires (ISA), HEC School of Management in Paris and Groupe ESC Lyon.

The grandes écoles

Many French students planning their future careers dream of entry into the *grandes écoles*, which occupy much the same place in the higher education system of France as the ancient universities of Oxford and Cambridge do in Britain or the 'Ivy League' universities in the USA, i.e. they represent the highest academic achievement. Most of the dozen or so top establishments which merit the term *grandes écoles* were founded in the 19th century to train academic elites in the new technical and scientific subjects and to provide top-calibre staff for the military, civil service, business, education and research cadres of France. The majority of *grandes écoles* are controlled by the ministry to which their speciality is linked, which means, in effect, that they are outside the university system.

Some of the best known *grandes écoles* are in Paris: the Ecole Polytechnique is one of the oldest, having been founded in 1794 to teach engineering; it later changed to military engineering under Napoleon. To this day it remains closely linked with the military: its director is a general and students wear military uniform on important occasions. Although graduates are awarded a *Diplome d'Ingénieur* and the rank of second lieutenant, many resign their commissions on graduation and head for the fleshpots of industry and commerce. Ex-polytechnicians are known as *Anciens X* after their badge of crossed cannons.

Founded about the same time as the Ecole Polytechnique and equally famous (though less prestigious now) is the Ecole Normale Supérieure, originally founded to train *lycée* (high school) teachers for the whole of France. Its students are divided

Entrance to the *grandes écoles*

Apart from the ENA, prospective entrants for the *grandes écoles* should have the *baccalauréat*, preferably with distinction (*mention*), after which they are required to complete a rigorous preparatory course, the CPGE (*classe préparatoire aux grandes écoles*) lasting two to three years at the end of which they sit a fiercely competitive examination (*un concours*). About 50% of candidates drop out at the preparatory stage and an even greater percentage are weeded out by the entrance examinations. With such high standards it is hardly surprising that the reputation for excellence in the *grandes écoles* persists. There are always rumblings of criticism against such elitism which, it is said, confers life membership of an exclusive club on the already privileged (i.e. those from professional and higher cadres backgrounds). Entrance to the *grandes écoles* from a blue-collar background are still way below those at French universities generally.

into *scientifiques and littéraires*. Public figures including President Pompidou and Jean-Paul Sartre have been among its graduates.

Probably just as famous as the above is the Ecole Nationale d'Administration (ENA), founded in 1945 by de Gaulle as a training establishment for top civil servants (*hauts fonctionnaires*). Unlike other *grandes écoles* only graduates are accepted. From the ENA they pass into the highest echelons of state administration, the Grands Corps d'Etat, including the French equivalent of the Treasury, Inspection Générale des Finances. Posts are also allocated in the diplomatic and other administrative careers including the prefectoral system. Past alumni (known as *énarques*) include a high proportion of recent prime ministers as well as former Presidents Giscard d'Estaing and Jacques Chirac. Many German civil servants are graduates of ENA.

Other *grandes écoles* include *écoles vétérinaires, écoles de commerce,* five *écoles des mines* (formerly for mining, nowadays for general engineering). There are also *grandes écoles* for the sciences and humanities.

Foreigners in French higher education

Foreigners account for about 15% of the total intake enrolled for higher education (*l'enseignement supèrieure*) in France annually. Applicants from other countries should have attained university entrance level exams, which are officially recognised as the equivalent of the *baccalauréat*. Anyone with resident status applying from within France will follow the same system as the French. Applications from abroad, can be made by obtaining an admission request (*une demande d'admission*) from the cultural section of the French Embassy. The same department will also supply detailed information on further education in France, including French government scholarships to study in France.

A new site, Campus France (www.campusfrance.org, in French, English and Spanish) set up by the Ministry of Education, has a wealth of practical information for foreign students wishing to study in France.

Applicants will also require a thorough knowledge of the French language. Special preparatory courses are available and a language test is obligatory before the start of the academic year. Further details are obtainable from the French Embassy.

French student identity cards are obtainable from the Centre Regional des Œuvres Universitaires et Scolaires (CROUS) of which there is one in every university town. The CROUS at 8, rue Jean Clavin has a special bureau, the Service de l'Action Sociale, to deal with students' problems.

Student programmes of the European Union

The SOCRATES-ERASMUS Scheme: www.socrates-uk.net. The EU-inspired ERASMUS (European Action Scheme for the Mobility of University Students) was started in 1987 and enables students from one EU country to study at a university in another EU country for up to one year on a bursary awarded by the EU. The scheme is administered from Brussels at the Erasmus Bureau. Details can be obtained from the website. The deadline for applications is 31 October in the year preceding the proposed academic year of study. Applicants from the UK can contact the UK Socrates-Erasmus Council (www.erasmus.ac.uk).

Leonardo da Vinci: www.leonardo.org.uk. Provides for university students and recent graduates to undertake periods of industrial training with companies in other states. The maximum duration is 12 months. The scheme doesn't supply bursaries, so it is up to individual employers to decide. However the scheme will subsidise language tuition and day-to-day subsistence (food and travel allowance).

Useful publication and contact for students

Higher Education in the European Community – A Student Handbook: European Commission. Contains information on courses on offer and entry qualifications, scholarships, insurance, costs and advice for disabled students. Out of print at the time of press.

The European Choice: www.eurochoice.org.uk. Eurochoice is a guide to higher education in Europe and tells you how to study in France and the rest of Europe. Gives details of all the various EU schemes to promote student mobility and also information about financial support.

Useful contacts

If you are coming from outside F rance, with qualifications from another country, the following organisations can assist with evaluation of your qualifications for France.

Ministère de l'éducation nationale, de l'enseignement supérieur, et de la recherché, Direction des relations internationales et de la cooperation (DRIC): Bureau DRIC B4, 110 rue de Grenelle, 75007 Paris; ☎01 55 55 04 15; www.education.gouv.fr; www.education.gouv.fr

French Embassy Cultural Department: ☎020 7073 1300; www.ambafrance.org. uk. Information on studying in France

French Institute: ☎020 7073 1350; www.institut-francais.org.uk

European Business School: 27 Blvd Murat, 75016 Paris; ☎+33 (0)1 40 71 84 93; www.business-school-paris.com

The European School of Management (ESCP-EAP): 79, avenue de la République, 75543 Paris Cedex 11; ☎01 49 23 20 00; info@escp-eap.net; www.escp.ccip.fr. Branches in Oxford, Madrid and Berlin

INSEAD: Blvd de Constance, 77305 Fontainebleau; ☎01 60 72 40 05; www. insead.edu/MBA. One of the most highly regarded international business schools and offers MBA, executive education and company-specific courses. Teaching is in English. Note that there are many employment opportunities on campus for bilingual (French/English) people, especially in administration

■ SOCIAL SERVICES

Claiming the UK job seeker's allowance in France

One of the advantages of labour mobility within the EU is that it is possible for those who are currently unemployed and claiming benefit, or eligible to claim it, to have it paid in another EU country if planning to go there to look for work. You have to have been claiming UK unemployment benefit for at least four weeks prior to departure and you can arrange to have the benefit paid in France, at UK rates, for up to three months while you are looking for a job. In order to do this, you should inform the UK office through which you are claiming benefit, of your intention to seek work elsewhere in the EU. You will need to do this at least six weeks in advance of your departure.

Your local job centre will inform the Overseas Benefits Directorate of the Department of Work and Pensions who will decide whether to provide you with the form E303, which is the standard EU form authorising another member state to pay your benefit. When you go to France you should present the form to the authorities in the area where you intend to look for work. This will be at the local office of the national employment service ANPE (Agence Nationale pour l'Emploi), or the *mairie* if there is no nearby ANPE. The DWP Overseas Office in the UK will give you advice on where to register abroad. As there may be delays in payments received abroad, even when the procedure is meticulously followed, it is advisable to have some emergency financial resources of your own to fall back on.

Anyone tempted to chuck in their present job to go on the dole for the requisite number of weeks before departing for France should remember that by making yourself voluntarily unemployed you render yourself ineligible for Unemployment Benefit for six months. If you go on holiday to France and then decide to stay on and look for work, you will not be able to arrange UK benefits to be paid in France.

TIP

■ Your local job centre should have a leaflet for people going abroad or coming from abroad plus an application form for transferring benefit.

TIP

■ Check and clarify your position before leaving the UK – contact the International Office of the Overseas Benefits Directorate (☎0191 218 7777; www.dwp.gov.uk), the office that deals with UK benefits being paid overseas.

Social security in the UK

Anyone who has been living and working in the UK will have been paying UK national insurance contributions which entitle the contributor to various social security benefits, including unemployment benefit and a state retirement pension. However, if you are about to go on a job hunt in France you might want to consider that if you are planning to return at a later date and you are not working, then by keeping up national insurance contributions you will make sure you are entitled to all the usual benefits.

If a UK national works in another EU country and then returns to the UK, the fact that contributions have been paid there should keep their UK contributions record up to date. However, if they haven't worked in France that record may lapse, although you are usually given the option to pay off the shortfall within a certain time limit.

Social security in France

France has a highly developed system of social security (*sécurité sociale*) benefits. The important implications of this regarding health benefits are dealt with earlier in this chapter. There are however, other sickness and invalidity benefits, rent allowances and pensions, etc. available.

Social security contributions in France are treated as a fund quite separate from the money raised by the government from income tax. This is one of the reasons

Les intermittents de spectacle

The scheme for *les intermittents*, as they are known, provides a salary for those involved in artistic performance professions when they don't have work. This is not only paid to musicians and actors, and to technical staff involved in, say, lighting or sound, but also, on occasion to administrative staff. No such system of support for artists exists anywhere else in the world. Incredibly (for those not accustomed to the French system) the salary is paid according to earnings while working which means that high profile film stars, such as Fabrice Luchini and others, have been able to make enormous claims based on already high wages. France is split over whether or not the system should remain in place, some suggesting that artists have had it too easy for too long, others standing up for those who chose creative careers. Attacks on schemes such as this by successive French governments are partly the cause of the French people's rejection of the EU constitution in the referendum in 2006. The popular right and left came together to reject the pro-European recommendations of the French political establishment, united, for different reasons, in their belief that Europe is eroding cherished French values.

that rates of income tax don't seem high by European standards but social security contributions are much larger than in many countries. The size of these contributions has been a problem for successive governments. In the run up to the single currency, the French government was pledged to implement radical cuts in public spending in order to reduce taxes and welfare charges. This has resulted in tougher measures for groups such as the *intermittents de spectacle*. These measures are part of wider-ranging attempts to introduce tighter conditions on unemployment pay generally, which is paid according to previous salary levels (see below). President Sarkozy has been very vocal about his plans to reform pensions, unemployment insurance and other aspects of *la sécu* (social security), but has already met with stiff opposition.

Social security contributions *(cotisations)* are payable by both employees and employers as a percentage of the gross salary earned: those who are self-employed must also contribute. The employee's contribution (see below for amount) is deducted at source, so those working legitimately in France will automatically be included in the scheme, even before they have obtained *la sécu*. In this respect the scheme is very much like the National Insurance contributions payable in the UK.

All those who pay into *sécurité sociale*, and their dependants, are entitled to the benefits of the scheme. Those who are not working may join if they wish, although few do, presumably because if they can afford not to work they don't require the benefits, or prefer to use private insurance schemes. Retired people are entitled to the medical benefits free of charge (but not unemployment benefits).

Eligibility for French benefits

As long as you have made the minimum contribution to the *sécurité sociale* (deducted from your salary at source) you will qualify for a whole range of benefits. The benefits available include the following: medical insurance, unemployment benefit, sick pay, retirement pension, death grant, maternity benefit, housing benefit (for low income/ employees or families), family allowance and industrial accident insurance.

If you are living in France and have had a low income for two years before applying, you can claim a substantial part of your rent from the French social security. You should apply for this at the CAF *(Caisse d'Allocations Familiales)*. You will need a signed letter from your landlord stating the amount of your rent, a declaration of income for the calendar year preceding the year of benefit, and various other documents which the CAF will tell you about.

Claiming French benefits

When claiming benefits, an EU national, resident in France claims just like any French national and is entitled to the same treatment. For example, the employment-based benefits can be claimed at the branch of the nationwide employment organisation, Agence Nationale pour l'Emploi (ANPE), or from the local *mairie* if there is no ANPE. Unemployment benefit is claimed from a separate organisation (see below).

Unemployment insurance

Unemployment *(chômage)* insurance is financed by employee/employer contributions underpinned by a state fund. Benefits are paid out by ASSEDIC

(*Associations pour l'emploi dans l'industrie et le commerce*, Associations for employment in industry and commerce)

Benefits are paid as a percentage of the claimant's former salary, subject to a minimum and maximum. Although the system is being gradually tightened up, payments can still be very generous. The industrial accident insurance meets all medical and rehabilitation costs involved with any industrial accident, and provides a pension to the injured and their dependants.

Private top-up schemes

In most cases the levels of benefits paid by *sécurité sociale* are considered adequate but modest. A great many employees take out private insurance schemes to top up the state benefits. This is particularly true in the case of health benefits (see the section on 'Health' earlier in this chapter) and pensions (see 'Retirement' in *Working in France*).

National Insurance contributions

The basic level of employee national insurance contribution in France is currently approximately 19%–24% of the gross salary. These contributions are deducted at source by the employer and typical employee contributions are made up of the following: 5.9% health insurances, 7.6% pension (*la retraite vieillesse*), 2.79%–3.37% unemployment benefits. In addition there is normally a contribution of about 2% for an extra pension fund (*la retraite complémentaire*). The last contribution may vary in amount from one employer to another. Further details of social security payments and benefits and how to make/claim them may be found in the chapter *Working in France*.

Income support

In Britain, anyone coming from a EU country can claim income support in Britain whether they have worked there or not. In France, eligibility for the equivalent, *Revenu Minimum d'Insertion* (RMI), of €447.91 per month for a single person and €671.87 per month for a couple (figures date from January 2008), is limited to those aged over 25 who have lived in France for three years. A government reform of the RMI came into force on 1 January 2004 introducing a new 'minimum employment income', the *revenu minimum d'activité* (RMA). RMI/RMA is now administered at the *département* level where it is decided who is admissible for RMI/RMA and where recipients are monitored to ensure their reintegration into the workforce.

The European Commission can be contacted about individual cases through: European Commission, Directorate General for Employment and Social Affairs, Social Security and Social Integration, Coordination of Social Security Systems, (ec.europa.eu).

For any questions regarding importing a car, contact your French Consulate General. For VAT inquiries contact the French Fiscal Attaché

■ CARS AND MOTORING

Getting around by car

Some people may want to import their car to France when they come. Procedures for this are covered in the chapter *Moving to France*.

Obtaining a *carte grise*

Procedures may vary slightly from region to region, but normally the first step is to contact either the *préfecture* (government authorities), or the Direction Régional de L'Industrie de la Recherche et de l'Environment (DRIRE) who will send a leaflet requesting the following documents.

■ *Demande de Carte Grise*: more formally known as *Demande de Certificat d'Immatriculation d'un Véhicule*

■ You will also have to purchase a *timbre fiscal* (tax stamp) from a *tabac* (tobacconist)

■ *Justification de l'origine du véhicule* (*certificat de vente*): The original bill of sale for the car. Although the French consulate specifies that you must produce this document, in practice not everyone can supply one, for instance if they have bought the car privately, secondhand. Apparently, if all other documents are in order, this will not cause problems

■ *Titre de circulation étranger*: Vehicle registration document from your own country

- *Quitus* from the French Inland Revenue: Even though there is no duty to pay on a vehicle being permanently imported this document is still required in order to prove that the vehicle is exempt from VAT. It should be obtained from the *Centre des Impôts* nearest to where you are going to be based in France
- *Rapport de Contrôle Technique*: The fee varies from issuer to issuer and also depends on the size etc of the vehicle but is usually around €70

Failure to pass any of the sections means that repairs/modifications have to be carried out. Almost always, modifications to the exhaust will be needed, and also UK headlamps need to be changed for driving on the right (temporary black tape stickers and yellow varnish will not do). You will also need a letter from the head office of the vehicle manufacturer confirming that the model and type of car has been approved for France. This involves writing to the head office in France. Brace yourself for a shock at the fee: some companies charge for this – in some cases as much as €150.

Once all the documents have been mustered you can take the vehicle to the nearest *centre de contrôle de véhicules* where the car will be thoroughly checked and tested and any remaining problems listed for rectification before all the paperwork can be finalised and taken to the *préfecture*. The *préfecture* issues the Certificat d'Immatriculation more commonly known as the *carte grise*. Before the *carte grise* is handed over, proof of identity and residence must be shown.

British expatriates should then write to the DVLA in Swansea advising them that the vehicle has been re-licensed in France; see www.dvla.gov.uk.

Driving licences

■ EU driving licence

Thanks to the EU directive on driving licences, if you are driving on a licence issued in one of the EU states then you need not exchange your licence for a French one within a year of your arrival. You can continue using it anywhere in the EU until it expires.

EU licences including those issued in France, are *permis à points* (penalty-point system) meaning that drivers begin with 12 points and lose points for each driving offence. If all the points are lost so is the licence to drive. The renewal period varies according to age and the type of licence.

■ Non-EU licences

Visitors to France from non-EU countries staying less than 90 days can drive with a certified translation into French of their national licence or an International Driving Licence. Foreigners from Australia, South Africa, Canada and certain US states (see below) who are staying in France can use their licence for up to a year but if staying on longer than that, they must have exchanged their licence for a French one before the start of their second year in France. Foreign students with a student card are allowed to use their national licences in France.

To apply for an exchange you must have an International Driving Licence, with an official translation in French. Some US states (Florida, Illinois, Kansas, Kentucky, Michigan, New Hampshire, Pennsylvania and South Carolina) have special agreements with France enabling them to exchange their licence automatically for a French one at the nearest *préfecture*. You should ask for the *service permis de conduire* or for a *demande d'échange de permis de conduire* (request for an exchange of driving permit). If your country (for instance New Zealand), or your US state (see list above) has no special agreement with France you will have to take a French driving test (regardless of whether you have been driving for one month or 20 years) which is laborious and expensive. Americans can check on the website www.americansinfrance.net for useful advice on the subject. For the verbal driving test, an interpreter may assist if needed.

Importing a car

The basic procedure for importing a car to France has already been explained in the chapter *Before You Go*. If you have bought and registered your car elsewhere in the EU, and appropriate taxes and VAT have been paid, there should be no problem importing the vehicle duty-free, assuming you are taking up permanent residence in France.

Once resident in France it is necessary to re-register the car and to have French number plates (*plaques d'immatriculation*) fitted. This procedure begins at the nearest *préfecture*. The documents required to do this may vary, and different offices may request different documents. However, at the very least your passport, *carte de séjour* (residence permit), and car registration document will be required.

It is also necessary to have vehicles inspected for roadworthiness; this is done at the *Service des Mines*. It is as well to obtain details of the test requirements, which are not especially rigorous, beforehand.

After this procedure has been completed you receive French registration documents. Once you have taken up permanent residence, you should amend your car insurance: you will probably have to change to a French insurance company (see below).

If importing a car to France, whether on a permanent or temporary basis, note that minimum tyre tread requirements are higher in France than in the UK. In addition, it is compulsory for foreign-registered cars to have a nationality badge, and right hand drive cars must be fitted with headlight beam converters.

Buying a car

◼ New cars

If you decide to sell your current car in order to buy a left hand drive one on moving to France, you will find that French makes, basically Renault, Peugeot and Citroën, dominate the market (just over 50% of market share). The advantage of a French make is that it is much easier and cheaper to obtain spares and to service them and although UK and other European cars are available, service facilities and the general level of garage know-how about them can be patchy. Ford and up-market German makes and Japanese cars are less common than elsewhere in the EU but are increasing market share.

French car prices are currently, overall, a little higher than in the UK. It is difficult to make a direct price comparison, however, as cars sold in France tend to include much less standard equipment than in otherwise identical models.

Those who wish to buy a new car can go to the appropriate franchised dealer. New cars are almost always sold at list prices, so, although it is still worth shopping around and asking for a discount, large discounts on the list price and haggling in the showroom are not customary. Most dealers have their own financing deals which generally involve a deposit of 20%–30% of the purchase price and the remainder in monthly instalments over three to five years; but the interest rates are high. You might do better getting a bank loan as the interest charged is generally lower. If you take out a bank loan to buy the car, make sure that both it and the bank loan are

FACT

◼ New penalties for polluting cars were introduced at the end of 2007, ranging from €200 to €2,600. Cleaner cars can get a bonus of €200 up to €5,000 (for electric cars).

insured. The supplying car dealer will arrange all the relevant paperwork including a temporary statement of ownership (*carte grise*).

Some French car-buyers avoid paying French dealer prices by using the newly sprung up specialist importers of European cars. With savings of up to €1,500, on French cars, imported from other European countries this is worth looking into.

▌Used cars

Used cars are also available from franchised dealers. These mostly only sell used cars up to one or two years old, and are usually a reputable source and offer appropriate warranties.

If you choose to buy a used car (*un vehicule d'occasion*) from outside the franchised dealer networks then some caution is required: this applies whether buying privately, perhaps from a newspaper advertisement, or from a dealer. Used car dealers in France have a very poor reputation, and despite recent legislation intended to prevent just this, dangerously defective cars are by no means rare. If there is a *garagiste* with a good reputation local to your property, it might be a good idea to try there first as if the *garagiste* knows they are going to see you regularly and get your business you might be offered a good deal.

Few dealers sell models more than five years old. The *préfecture* in the *département* in which the car is registered should issue the seller with a *lettre de non-gage* which means there are no outstanding debts (e.g. hire purchase) on the car. If the car is over five years old, the seller must provide evidence that the car has been checked and issued with a *contrôle technique* which lists the faults that need to be put right before the sale. The purchase of a used car must be registered at the *préfecture*. You will need to take with you a certificate of sale which is an official document supplied by *préfectures* to sellers; the cancelled *carte grise* (log book), and the *autobilan* (test certificate), as well as all your own identity documents are all required for this.

If you buy the car outside the area you are living in then you will need to get the car re-registered locally when you are back home.

A useful publication is *L'Argus* (www.argusauto.com), the French car guide. It provides details on how much you should pay for particular models and the purchasing process.

Running a car

Running a car in France, as in any other country, can be expensive and also requires a great deal of official documentation. Garage services, for both maintenance and repair work, tend to be expensive. In general, the French don't give such great

FACT

▌Note that cars don't necessarily need an annual safety test unless you are intending to sell them.

Electric cars   *i*

If you live in Paris, there is a special incentive scheme to encourage the purchase of electric cars, which are tax exempt and entitled to free parking. There is a network of 111 free charge-up stations in Ile de France, however this is still a very much under-used option.

importance to their cars as in many other Western countries. Petrol and diesel prices are comparable with for example prices in the UK.

Main documents required by car owners

■ Registration document (carte grise)

This is supplied when you register or buy a new or used car, and should be handed on to the buyer when you sell it. Cars are registered locally in France and if you move to another *département* then you must re-register your car at a *préfecture* there within three months: this involves obtaining a different registration number and new number plates.

In order to get a *carte grise* you will require the necessary documents including proof of property ownership, or a rental agreement or a French utility bill in your name. If you are renting from another owner and don't have any bills in your name then you will probably be refused a *carte grise*.

■ Insurance certificate

You will also receive an insurance sticker, which must be displayed on the vehicle's windscreen (*carte verte*).

Car insurance

Car insurance is comparatively expensive in France partly because all premiums include high taxes. Even higher *cotisations* (premiums) are charged for cities and areas notorious for their high crime rate. Another factor affecting insurance charges is the high collision rate (one every 85 seconds according to one estimate). It is particularly important to shop around and to find the best deal possible.

The basic legal requirement for French car insurance is third party *(au tiers)* liability, and many owners of what seem quite new cars risk taking out no greater cover than this, though most will also have cover for accidental damage to the vehicle. Comprehensive insurance *(tous risques)* is available which will cover most risks, including damage to your own car. It is particularly important to examine each policy and to see what is and what is not included, as various policies don't necessarily cover

the same risks (*conditions générales* and *conditions particulières*), and the insurance inclusions and exclusions will certainly vary from a UK or US comprehensive policy.

If you are taking up permanent residence you will require a new policy that complies with French requirements: ask various companies and/or brokers for quotes (*devis*) as they all compete against each other for business. If you are in France, it should be a simple matter to locate local brokers. Leading French insurers include AXA, AGF, CNP, Generali France and Groupama and a list of their regional agencies is usually given on the company websites (see below).

There are various peculiarities of French motor insurance. Firstly, the *bonus/ malus* system: although one gains a useful no-claims bonus and discount for not claiming each year, one also gains a claims supplement and loading if a claim is made (maximum 350%), which can make insurance very expensive. Basically, to get the maximum discount (50%), you need to provide the French insurance company with proof of no fault claims for 13 years. The other party may offer to settle with you directly if they have caused damage to your car and don't want to lose their bonus. If you decide to agree, make sure that you complete the *constat*

Insurance glossary

French	English
assurances touts risques/tous risques	comprehensive insurance
au tiers/responsabilité civile	third party liability
bonus	no claim bonus/discount
bris de glaces	windscreen damage
dommages a votre vehicule	accidental damage
franchise	policy excess
garantie conducteur	personal accident/bodily injury to driver
vol et incendie	theft and fire

Main points of motor insurance in France

- Compulsory cover for third party liability
- No restriction on drivers (vehicle can be driven by any driver with the insured's permission)
- The no claim bonus cannot be protected
- The maximum no claim discount is 50% (13 years with no liable claim)
- When taking out insurance with a French provider, the proposer must provide sufficient proof of his/her insurance cover 13 years back in order to claim the maximum no claim discount

à amiable (see below) in any case, so that you have this official document to fall back on if the payer defaults.

Another difference to be aware of is that many comprehensive policies will reduce cover to third party only, if any accident or damage occurs because the driver was breaking road traffic law. If you want a policy that is tailored to the usage of the car, it is possible to arrange insurance based on the car's mileage (*kilométrage*). It is necessary to carry proof of insurance *(une attestation d'assurance)*, which will be issued by the insurer. This should be kept in the car with your car registration papers. If you are unfortunate enough to be involved in an accident it will be necessary to complete a *constat à amiable* (agreed accident statement) which has to be signed by both parties after they agree the description of the accident. This is a standard form that is issued by the insurer. Don't sign anything you don't understand as signature is taken as proof. If the other car involved won't sign, be sure to take down its number.

As with house insurance, it is usually necessary to give a long period of notice (sometimes three months) before cancelling a policy and one is liable for premiums until that notice expires.

English-speaking insurance agents

Agence Eaton: Continent Assurances; ☎02 97 40 80 20; www.french-insurance. com. Bilingual insurance bureau. All types of insurance

British Insurance Brokers of Aquitaine: Gaye Galliver, Villaréal; ☎05 53 01 13 84; bibasarli@wanadoo.fr; www.ericblairnet.com. All types of insurance

Bruno Sellier: Cognac; ☎05 45 82 03 20; info@sellier-insurance.com; www. sellier-insurance.com. All types of insurance

Steen J B Andersen: AXA Assurances, Nice; ☎+33 673 04 60 57; info@ steenandersen.net; www.steenandersen.net. All types of insurance

Tredinnick Insurance: Cognac; ☎+33 (0)5 45 82 42 93; insure@tredinnick-insurance.com; www.charente-properties.com. Bilingual insurance bureau. All types of insurance

Useful websites – insurance companies

- ■ *AGF:* www.agf.fr (☎08 20 10 08 20)
- ■ *AXA Assurances:* www.axa.fr (☎08 11 90 11 01)
- ■ *AZUR Assurances:* www.groupeazur.fr (☎08 20 01 40 00)

Abolition of the *vignette*

The *vignette*, French car tax badge is not required as this tax was abolished in 2001 for most private vehicles and vehicles under three and a half tonnes. It is still required for commercial vehicles and the rules are quite complicated so check if you are in doubt.

- *GMF*: www.gmf.fr (☎08 20 80 98 09)
- *MAAF Assurances*: www.maaf.fr (☎08 00 16 17 18)
- *MACIF Assurances*: www.macif.fr (☎01 55 56 57 58)

Selling a car

You cannot sell or otherwise dispose of a car imported duty free within 12 months without paying the TVA (value added tax; VAT) on the import. As far as documentation is concerned, selling or part exchanging a car in France is probably more complicated than you are used to. You have to obtain the appropriate certificate of sale form from the *mairie* or *préfecture* and, to complete this in duplicate and then to send one copy back to the registration office. The other copy and the *carte grise* registration document go to the purchaser.

In France, if the car is five or more years old it must be submitted to a mechanical inspection (*contrôle technique*), after which, if successful, it will be issued with a test certificate (*autobilan*).No matter how recently another, similar test has been done on the vehicle, you must arrange and pay for this beforehand.

Roads

French roads are among the best in Europe and the motorway system, over 5,000 miles of it, largely constructed since 1969, is also excellent, if expensive. France and Italy are the two EU countries which charge motorists for using the motorways. French roads are classified as follows.

■ A – Autoroute (motorway or M grade road in UK; freeway/expressway in USA)

With few exceptions these are toll roads (*Autoroutes à Péage*). The autoroute network was recently privatised. Tolls vary but are usually in the region of €5 per 100km. You pick up a computer card when you join the motorway and you pay on exit.

Be aware that computerised tills introduced in late 1997 will deliver a printout that not only tells you how much to pay but also how fast you have been driving. If you have exceeded the speed limit a flashing red light on the till will alert the operator to summon *les flics* (police). The standard fine for high-speed offences is €1,500.

■ N – Route Nationale (A grade road in UK; arterials in USA)

These are usually quite good and single or dual carriageway (divided highway), but they usually pass through towns, which can slow a journey down.

■ D – Route Départementale (B grade road in UK; collectors in USA)

Overall, the road network is very comprehensive and there are autoroutes extending from Paris to every corner of France. For example, the A6 and A7 to Marseille and A1 Autoroute du Nord to the Belgian border. Newer stretches include the A75 (routed across the Massif Central) from Clermont-Ferrand to the Mediterranean, and in the north, the A16 from Dunkirk to Abbeville on route to Normandy. You can check the latest autoroutes being built at www.sanef.com/www.info-autoroute.com/www.autoroutes.fr. Note that roads may not be as well sign-posted as you are used to, so make sure you have good maps such as the Michelin 1:200,000 yellow series.

The French tend not to be great long-distance travellers so traffic is very often quite light, with the definite exceptions, however, of Paris and some major city centres and during the main holiday months. Since nearly all the French workers take a month's holiday in either July or August the worst days, such as 31 July and 1 August when departing holidaymakers meet returning ones, the journey between the Mediterranean and Paris can easily take 17 hours. On Bastille Day (14 July) it is nothing to have a tailback of more than 50km on the autoroutes going south from Paris. For nearly 20 years the French government has used a cartoon character called *Bison Futé* (Crafty Bison) to warn motorists, through the mass media, of impending bad traffic days and to advise, by means of maps, available at service stations, alternative secondary routes which are designed to circumvent the traffic jams.

Driving

Although the basic rules of the road are very similar in France to the rest of Europe, as are most road signs, there are some differences. It may seem needless to point out that in contrast with what has become a British peculiarity, the French drive on the right. The majority of accidents caused by Brits occur after they pull out from a picnic spot, hypermarket or petrol station and forget this vital fact.

Those particularly concerned about driving in France, together with those who cannot yet drive, can take lessons with a local driving school (*l'auto-école*). Before you can start with a driving school, you will need to produce some ID (e.g. *carte de séjour*) and proof of your address (you can use a receipt for rent, or an electricity or telephone bill), an excise stamp and four photographs.

■ Learner and young drivers

The minimum age for a learner's permit (*apprentissage anticipé de la conduite (AAC)* is 16. Beginners have a sign on the back of the car – a circle enclosing two people. Drivers who have had held a licence for less than one year are restricted to 90km/h (55mph).

You should have a copy of the French Highway Code. Some of the fundamental rules follow.

■ Speed limits

The speed limit on all autoroutes is 130kph (80mph); however, this reduces to 110km/h (65mph) in wet weather, and is 110km/h on non-toll autoroutes. The speed limit on dual carriageways is 110km/h and 90km/h (55mph) on single carriageways – both reduced by 10km/h in wet weather. A speed limit of 50km/h has been introduced for foggy conditions where visibility is reduced to 50m. *Rappel* means the restriction is continued.

The limit in towns varies between 45km/h (30mph) and 60km/h (38mph). Often a town name sign acts as the start of a speed limit and that same sign crossed through with a bar signifies the end of the limit.

■ The Priorité rule

One of the most important rules to remember when driving in France is the *priorité à droite* which means you must give way to traffic joining from the right from another road (but not driveway), however minor. Thus, you must stop, as

 ■ The French government's road traffic website is www.securite-routiere. gouv.fr.

More essential road signs	
attention travaux	beware road works
allumez vos feux	switch on your lights
bande d'urgence	breakdown lane
chaussée deformé	uneven road edges or temporary road surface
déviation	diversion
gravillons	loose chippings
ralentez	slow down
rappel	reminding you to heed the previous sign, usually in restricted speed areas
sens interdit	no entry
serrez à droit/gauche	keep to the right/left
vous n'avez pas la priorité	give way

emerging drivers will not and, similarly, they will not be pleased if you stop when it is your right of way. This rule generally applies in towns and on minor roads. It used to apply also on major roads but this is generally no longer the case. If a major road does have priority this will be indicated by a sign reading *passage protégé*: this right of way ends when the same sign appears crossed through with a black bar.

You must also be careful at all junctions to see who has priority. *Cédez le passage* means give way, but *Stop* means just that! Give way when entering a roundabout (at one time traffic on the roundabout had to give way).

The other main highway rules are:

■ *Minimum driving age*: 18

■ *Seatbelts*: seat belts must be worn by anyone travelling in the front or back of a car, and children under 10 are not allowed, by law, to be carried in the front of a car unless they are in an approved, rear-facing seat

■ *Parking*: parking (*stationnement*) is controlled by a *zone bleu* in many towns. This involves buying a parking disc (available from news stands and small shops) which displays the time of arrival and departure: parking is restricted to a maximum of 90 minutes. Yellow lines don't prohibit parking in France, instead this is usually indicated by a blue circle with red border and red diagonal slash often accompanied by the sign *stationnement interdit*. Other parking restrictions include *unilatéral* parking on one side of the street and *parcmètres* (meters). You may also see *parking souterrain* (underground car park) usually unlimited time-wise, but costly

Police and fines

Disregard for the various rules of the road is widespread in France, despite the reputation of French traffic police for being very strict, and the fact that more restrictive laws concerning driving are continually being introduced. Patrols and radar traps are commonplace in France and the breathalyser is also used widely: the penalties for exceeding the legal alcohol limit rise relative to the amount of excess alcohol. The legal blood/alcohol limit is 50mg per 100 millilitres of blood; slightly lower than the UK's 80mg.

The maximum fines for offences including illegal parking are usually rendered on the spot. Typically: €50 for not wearing a seatbelt and €100 for parking in a bus lane and €137.30 for being slightly over the alcohol limit (up to 80mg) and much higher for more serious offences. Disqualification from driving, for anything from a week to several years (for drunk driving) is more readily imposed than in other countries and in some cases it is possible to have your licence taken away at the roadside.

Being stopped by the police for exceeding a French speed limit has varying sanctions depending on the speed limit and the amount you exceed it by. This ranges from €35 up to €1500 and will lead to points being deducted from your licence or licence suspension for a varying amount of time up to 3 years. A serious second offence is liable to a three-month prison sentence and over €3,000 in fines. If the charges are the most serious ones, not stopping after an accident or manslaughter, there is an automatic court appearance and the maximum penalty is two years in jail and up to €35,000 in fines. While these are serious offences from anyone's point of view, the more controversial one is dangerous driving, a charge imposed at the magistrate's discretion if the motorist is deemed 'to have deliberately put the lives of others in danger'. There doesn't need to have been an accident, it is enough to have witnesses. This carries a maximum penalty of a year in prison and a fine of €1,750, and is additional to whatever other charges and fines the magistrate may have deemed appropriate.

It is advisable to carry all driving documents with you when motoring, this includes licence, registration document, insurance papers, and also your passport or *carte de séjour*, whichever is appropriate.

Breakdowns, thefts and accidents

There is no exact French equivalent of the AA or RAC operating on a national basis. However, there are motoring organisations you can join which will arrange for a local garage, rather than their own service vehicle, to attend the breakdown. You can extend your AA or RAC assistance cover to France, or you can join an international help organisation such as Europ Assistance.

Emergency telephones

Bornes d'appel d'urgence or emergency terminals (tall, orange pillars marked 'SOS') can be found on autoroutes and on some other major roads. On autoroutes they are spaced at approximately 2km intervals and about 4km on other major routes; there are even some at strategic points on *départmentales* (D roads). On motorways and major roads they are positioned opposite each other on both sides of the road so that people don't try to cross a fast road to reach one.

They can be activated by pressing and releasing the button marked '*pour demander au secours*' (to summon help) and then speaking into the large oval metal panel. Calls are answered by the local emergency services or police station. Each telephone is numbered and you should give this number to whoever answers and tell them the location of your vehicle. If the call is to report an accident, give as many useful details as possible: the number of the telephone, the number of

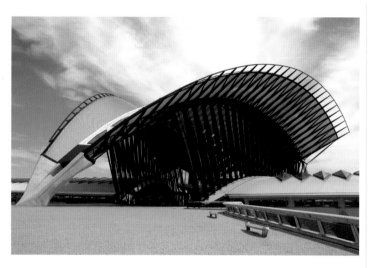

Gare TGV de Lyon, Saint Exupéry

vehicles involved and the state of any injured. Accident calls are relayed to the SAMU (*Service d'Aide Médicale d'Urgence*) and the *sapeurs pompiers* (fire brigade). If there is a language problem, try to get a French person to make the call. You should also display the red warning triangle from your car.

If your car has broken down, the emergency services will send out a *garagiste* although it is unlikely they will perform AA or RAC type roadside diagnosis and repairs. It is more likely that you will be towed to their establishment for a hefty fee.

It is compulsory for all cars to carry a red hazard warning triangle, which must be used in the case of a breakdown or accident and also to carry a spare bulb kit. You must stop if involved in any accident, however slight. French drivers tend not to call the police if possible and this is only usually required if someone is seriously injured.

France has a bad record in fatal motor accidents. The French Transport Ministry has bought in a barrage of regulations to improve matters over the last few years however, including licence penalty points and black human shaped signs beside the road where people have died. As a result figures have come down dramatically, from 7,643 in 2000 to 4,615 in 2007. The worst time for accidents is Sunday afternoon after the traditional Sunday lunch.

If you are involved in an accident then you have to fill in a report form, which should be supplied by your insurers and kept in the car at all times so that it can be filled in on the spot. This document is known as a *constat à l'amiable* and is a standardised form being used increasingly in various parts of Europe. In some cases, where there is disagreement as to who is to blame for the accident, it is usual to call a *huissier*, a legal official, who will prepare an official and impartial statement of facts for insurance or legal purposes.

As was highlighted by the car accident that killed Princess Diana in Paris, it is a criminal offence in France not to try to assist persons in danger, or if that is not possible to summon assistance. The maximum penalty is five years imprisonment and a fine of seventy thousand euros.

■ OTHER TRANSPORT

Air

Air transport both to and within France is efficient and reasonably priced. Owing to the size of the country it is also a service more regularly used than in most other European countries, although the expansion of the high-speed train network (see below) is proving tough competition on some routes.

The main airline Air France is a state company, which unlike many international airlines regularly shows an operating profit. It operates most international services and the major domestic ones. France has been experimenting with low cost airlines but the results haven't been impressive. Air Lib, the first French low-cost carrier formed only in 2001, went bankrupt at the end of 2003 and EasyJet and a Toulouse-based charter company Aeris took over its slots. Aeris then went under not long afterwards, followed by the budget airlines Air Littoral and Air Atlantique at the beginning of 2004. As one entrepreneur trying to start a cheap airline in France griped 'even if you have the money, they play a protective role towards Air France'. The said Air France has now taken over Régional Airlines, Proteus and Flandre Air, formerly independent budget carriers, which have now been merged under Air France with the brand name Régional. Air France also provides a shuttle air service (*La Navette*) between Paris Orly and Nice, Marseille and Toulouse. Once deregulation is underway in the French airline industry, more budget airlines may begin to emerge.

You can of course fly from almost every capital city in the world to Paris. In the case of the UK, it is possible to fly from nearly every regional British airport to Paris and to most major provincial cities such as Lyon, Marseille, Nice, Bordeaux and Strasbourg. For further information see 'Getting there' in the chapter *Before You Go*. Surprisingly, air tickets for travel within France can work out cheaper than driving (because of autoroute tolls and petrol prices) and on some routes the prices are competitive with rail travel. There are always special offers for limited periods and special fares for 'affinity groups' (under-26s, families, over 60s and students up to 27 years). Full details can be obtained direct from Air France in France. For a map of all the French airports visit www.aeroport.fr/site/fr/decouvrir/index.htm.

■ Useful contacts

Air France: www.airfrance.fr; ☎08 20 820 820 reservations

Nouvelles Frontières: www.nouvelles-frontiers.fr is a major French travel agent offering budget internal flights between Paris and provincial France and Corsica. Also does charters from Paris to the Caribbean (Martinique, Guadeloupe, St Martin); the Indian Ocean (Réunion, Mauritius and the Seychelles); the Pacific Islands (Tahiti, Noumea, Easter Islands). There are Nouvelles Frontières offices in Canada, New York and Los Angeles. To find the nearest office to you in France, go to the website and type in your address

Easyvols.com: website for comparing prices of flights and www.abm.fr/avion/gvadcomp.html gives A–Z addresses and telephone numbers of airline companies in France

■ Last-minute tickets and cheapest fares

Last-minute tickets (*vente de dernière minute* or VDM) are widely available on Minitel or by telephone. The website www.bourse-des-vols.com compares the fare

costs of different airlines and travel companies for a given journey and highlights the cheapest fares (from France) which you can book online.

Rail

France has an extensive rail system of 35,000km of line serving 3,000 destinations and part of it is one of the most modern in the world. Half of all long-distance rail traffic in France is high speed and 75% of all passengers are on the high-speed services. This model of a modern rail system is run by the Sociètè Nationale des Chemins de Fer Français (SNCF), a state-owned company in which a great deal of public money has been invested. State subsidy helps keep down customer charges but not running costs, and the level of deficit is billions of euros annually. Trains are generally punctual, which no doubt has something to do with a system of bonus reductions for drivers whose trains are late without cause.

◼ The TGV

The apogee of the rail system is the impressive 187 miles/300km per hour TGV (*Train à Grande Vitesse*) whose growing network currently links Paris to all south-east France as well as Bordeaux, Toulouse, Lille, Brittany and Switzerland. From Lille it links up with the Channel Tunnel. Using Eurostar from London, passengers can travel to Bordeaux, Nantes and Quimper without going to Paris, thanks to the 102km rail ring bypassing the capital through stations at Massy, Chessy and Charles de Gaulle Airport. The Lille connection also serves Lyon and the south. The Paris Lyon route, which is the busiest, sports the newer Duplex (double-decker) TGV, which is the nearest you will get to a flying sensation on land. There is also 156 miles of TGV line (which cost an average of 30 million euros a mile) between Valence and Marseille. You can travel by TGV from Calais to Marseille (via Lille) in four hours (or from London in six and a half hours). The cheapest return fares booked in advance from London to Marseille start at just under €100, or one-way

FACT

◼ All French towns and cities of any size are linked to each other by rail, although it is frequently necessary to travel between them through Paris. All the main cities have commuter lines and various types of trains are available.

from just under €50. The link from Paris to Strasbourg, home of the European Parliament, is now up and running. A map of the TGV network is at www.tgv.com/reseau/carte-aujourd'hui.jsp.

◼ Other services and discounts

The non-TGV express trains include those which travel to other European cities and local trains. Prices vary with the speed of the service and time of travel. There is a discount if you book your ticket eight days in advance. There is a range of reduced fare passes giving unlimited travel for a fixed period although you still have to pay for the obligatory advance booking on the TGV. Other discount deals of up to 50% are: the *Carte Senior* for senior citizens over 60; the *Famille Nombreuse* for families with three plus children 30%–75%; the Youth Card for 12–25-year-olds, which costs about €45 and gives 25%–50% discount on off-peak rail journeys for a year; and the *Carte Couple* for couples. Season tickets for commuters are also available but these are always changing and the structure is complicated. Make further enquiries at your local station.

On the Paris to Marseille route SNCF offers a service called iDTGV (*interactif-Détente Train à Grande Vitesse*) which competes with the no-frills airlines pricing system. The fare is €19 (one way) if you book early enough on the internet at www.idtgv.com. The nearer to departure the more expensive the fare. The train runs once a day from Paris to Avignon, Marseille and Toulon.

Paris rail terminals and the areas they serve	
Gare D'Austerlitz	South-west, Bordeaux, Spain
Gare de l'Est	Strasbourg area and Germany
Gare de Lyon	South-east, Lyon, Switzerland, Italy
Gare du Nord	North, Channel Ports, Channel Tunnel (see below), Holland, Belgium
Gare Montparnasse	West, Brittany
Gare St Lazare	Normandy

◼ Tickets

Train tickets can be bought at stations from machines (*les billetteries automatiques*) as well as the ticket offices. Some travel agents will also book train tickets. The SNCF has a computerised booking system at www.sncf.fr or www.voyages-sncf.com. It is also possible to book tickets via the telephone Minitel system. TGV seats must always be booked in advance and there is a supplement. Eurostar tickets can be bought at www.eurostar.com and Thalys International (Belgian high speed train) tickets for Paris to Brussels at www.thalys.com. Thalys also goes to Disneyland Resort Paris.

All rail tickets must be validated (*composté*) in the orange machines labelled *compostez votre billet*. The machines automatically date-stamp and clip tickets and are located at platform entrances. Ticket collectors don't appear on platforms, only on the trains. They will fine you 20% of the fare if your ticket is not *composté* and being a foreigner is not considered an excuse.

 Corsica Rail Travel: for information on the narrow-gauge railway linking Bastia, Ajaccio, Calvi and Corte go to www.ter-sncf.com

TIP

◼ For sheer scenic indulgence take the narrow-gauge Chemin de Fer Provence (www.trainprovence.com), which runs between Nice and Digne in Provence.

Le Poinçonneur des Lilas

Perhaps the most famous of all French transport employees is Le Poinçonneur des Lilas, the character from the song of the same name by Serge Gainsbourg who spends his days punching holes in travellers' metro tickets to validate them for travel. The song starts with the downbeat:

J'suis l'poinçonneur des Lilas
Le gars qu'on croise et qu'on n'regarde pas
Y a pas d'soleil sous la terre
Drole de croisière

But becomes gradually more psychotic as our protagonist repeats the chorus and we imagine him punching and punching away all day:

J'fais des trous, des p'tits trous, encor des p'tits trous
Des p'tits trous, des p'tits trous, toujours des p'tits trous
Des trous d'seconde classe
Des trous d'première classe

◼ Motorail

This service, by which it is possible to transport both car and passengers overnight by train, is particularly useful for those travelling from the north or from Paris to the southern regions of France. It is pricey, at about €600–€800 return for a family of four, but this has to be offset against the cost of going by car with autoroute tolls and higher petrol costs, and the boredom factor if small children are on board.

Paris transport

◼ Paris Métro and RER

The Paris Métro is an urban underground system that carries 5 million passengers a day plus another 5 million on the RER (Réseau Express Régional) regional network that links into the suburbs. Buying a *carnet* (book of 10 tickets) is cheaper than buying single ones. The price of a single ticket is the same wherever you go on the city of Paris. If you are staying in Paris for several weeks it is worth investing in a monthly ticket (*Carte Orange*), which covers the Métro, Paris buses and RER suburban trains.

Métro, buses and RER are run by the Régie Autonome des Transports Parisiens RATP, the Paris transport authority. See the RATP website (www.ratp.fr) for information on travelling in Paris.

The Paris Métro is well policed and is considered safe to use at night. Recent changes have extended running times of the metro on Friday and Saturday nights for one extra hour until 2am.

Coach and bus transport

France has a reasonable system of long distance coach services (*autocars*), some of which are operated by SNCF. The only effective way to obtain current details is to apply directly to tourist offices in France. Eurolines offer coach travel for journeys further afield than France (www.eurolines.fr).

In the major French cities the bus system is integrated and coordinated with the underground (Métro) and the commuter rail lines. For these, although one can pay in cash on the bus it is much easier, quicker and cheaper to buy an appropriate concessionary pass or to book tickets in advance.

Sea and river transport

For details of the sea crossings between southern and northern Britain and northern France and Belgium see the 'Getting there' section in the *Before You Go* chapter.

From France itself, the *Société Nationale, Maritime Corse-Méditerranée* (SNCM) operate ferries between Marseilles and Toulon and a choice of vessels to Corsica. The NGV *Asco and Aliso* are fast ferries which run from the end of March and can

i Detailed maps of the navigable waterways of France are available online at www.guide-fluvial.com

speed you from Nice to Corsica in two and three-quarter hours. Fares cost about €40 one-way per person and about the same for a car plus port taxes of €10 (per person) and per car. The vessel *Napoleon Bonaparte* (who else?) operates an overnight service between Marseille and Corsica. You can book in France (☎04 91 56 38 63; info@sncm.fr;www.sncm.fr) or London (☎020 7491 4968).

Useful contact

SNCM Ferryterranee: ☎0870 499 1305; www.sncm.fr. Year-round ferries from Marseille, Toulon and Nice to Bastia, Ajaccio, Calvi and Ile Rousse. Sample (special offer) fare Marseille to Ajaccio for car and two passengers €264. Also faster hydrofoils in summer only.

◼ Inland waterways

France's network of navigable waterways is a vast 5,600 miles (9000km). If you haven't taken your own cruising craft with you, then it is possible to hire boats of almost any size from cabin cruiser, up to converted commercial barges (*péniches*) which can sleep up to two dozen people plus several crew. The main canals are in the north where canals and rivers are linked and have to be shared with commercial traffic heading for the ports. Popular regions for pleasure cruising include: Burgundy; the great river Rhône; the Midi (the Canal du Midi connects the Atlantic with the Mediterranean); and Brittany and the Loire on the rivers Vilaine, Sarthe, Mayenne and Loire.

◼ TAX

Tax and the expatriate

In the future it is conceivable that tax systems throughout Europe may be completely integrated, but at present this is far from the case. As a result of the different tax regimens in different countries there are complications involved in a move overseas. This doesn't just apply to tax affairs in the host country. There are also tax implications in your home country. Tax regulations are more complicated if you are buying a second home (*une résidence secondaire*) in France because then you are obliged to become involved in two very different tax systems.

It is advisable to take individual and independent financial advice before committing yourself to a move to France. This will ensure that no unnecessary tax is paid, and should also minimise eventual tax bills. If you don't already have an accountant who is experienced in expatriate taxation then the addresses of Franco-British tax consultants can be obtained from the French Chamber of Commerce in Great Britain (☎020 7304 4040; www.ambafrance-uk.gov). The IRS also publishes a tax guide for US citizens resident abroad. Visit www.irs.gov. A list of tax advisers is given below.

The question of residence

Any person who spends more than six months (183 days) per year in France has to pay French tax on his or her worldwide income. This also applies if you spend more time in France than in any other country. Taxable income includes income from work, letting and leasing, trade enterprises, returns on investment, annuities and speculative capital gains (except, in certain circumstances, on the sale of a principal residence). Before moving to France it is therefore important to consider where your main residence will be for tax purposes. The important point to note is that you don't necessarily escape one country's income tax and become subject to another's just by moving there. It all depends on where the tax authorities consider you are resident for tax purposes, and also where you are domiciled – the two not necessarily being the same thing.

■ Procedure for residents of UK origin

The situation is reasonably straightforward if you are moving permanently to France. You should inform the UK Inspector of Taxes at the office you usually deal with, and you will receive a P85 form to complete. The UK tax office will usually require certain proof that you are leaving the UK, and thus their jurisdiction, for good. Evidence of having a sold a house in the UK and having bought one in France is usually sufficient. If you are leaving a UK company to take up employment with a French one then the P45 form given by your UK employer and evidence of employment in France should be sufficient. You may be eligible for a tax refund in respect of the period up to your departure in which case it will be necessary to complete an income tax return for income and gains from the previous 5 April to your departure date. It may be advisable to seek professional advice when completing the P85. Once HM Revenue and Customs has been satisfied that an individual is no longer resident or domiciled in the UK, they will close the appropriate file and not expect any more UK income tax to be paid.

France has a double taxation agreement with the UK, which makes it possible to offset tax paid in one country against tax paid in another. While the rules are complex, essentially, as long as you work and are paid in France then you should not have to pay UK taxes, as long as you don't spend more than an average of 91 days a year in the UK spread over 4 years. For further information see the HM Revenue and Customs Non-Residents section at http://www.www.hmrc.gov.uk.

■ Procedure for non-residents of UK origin

If you are buying a second home in France, whether for long holidays or retirement, etc., then the situation as regards taxation is more complicated in that you remain liable to UK tax but may also acquire liability for French tax. This may also be the case if you are maintaining any sort of financial connection with the UK, e.g. if one still owns and rents out a home in the UK, thus generating an income. If this is the case then an accountant in the UK must be consulted for individual advice, otherwise you may find that both the UK and French tax authorities will consider you liable for income tax on your income, no matter where it is earned. Some people who have moved to France but spend long holidays or business trips back in the UK have found that the UK Inland Revenue still consider them domiciled in the UK for tax purposes.

■ Aspects of tax residence

It is important to understand that the French authorities make no distinction between 'residence', 'ordinary residence' and 'domicile' in the way the British tax authorities do. In the British sense, the country where you have your longest-lasting ties is your domicile; this is a concept not defined in the UK Tax Acts, but rather based on precedent.

The French tax authorities define tax residence (*domicile fiscal*) differently from the British. If your household – *foyer fiscal* – is in France, e.g. your family lives there, then you are tax resident there. The other test of tax residence is where you have your principal residence – *séjour principal*. If you spend more than 183 days a year in France then you are tax resident. You may even be tax resident in France if you spend fewer than 183 days a year there, if you have spent more time in France than in any other country. Whether you have a *carte de séjour* or not doesn't enter into the assessment. If the main centre of your economic interests is in France, or your main employment is there, then you are certainly tax resident there.

Situations may arise where one married partner is tax resident in the UK and the other in France. Partners are considered separately as far as tax residence goes, even though the location of your household is the main criterion for establishing tax residence. In this case you have a choice between being taxed together in the usual way, or being treated separately, so that the resident spouse will declare their income to the local *centre des impôts* and the other to the *Centre des Impôts des Non-Résidents* in Paris. This is a possibility, since under French law, those married in the UK and USA are assumed to come under the regime of separate estates – *régime de séparation des biens*. It is advisable to make a declaration that you are married under the separate estates regime before a *notaire* (notary).

As a basic principle, tax is levied on a household as a whole – the *foyer fiscal* – rather than on separate persons. It isn't usual for a husband and wife to pay tax separately, unless they are in the throes of divorce and have separate households, or are married under the separate estates regime. If you have entered into a PACS – a civil partnership contract – you will have to wait for three years before you can be assessed as one household.

US citizens: US tax liability

US citizens receiving income in the USA, for example from investments, must file a US tax return. Any US citizen who is abroad on 15 April and knows they will be liable for tax should ask for Extension Forms so that they can avoid paying interest charges.

Unfortunately, IRS tax returns may not be filed with the IRS office in Paris. They should be mailed direct to The Internal Revenue Service (Austin, TX 73301 0215, USA; www.taxbrain.com/taxcenter/extensions/default.asp).

◼ Help and advice

Contact the IRS in the USA before you leave. For all the necessary details relating to your situation you can download the whole of IRS Publication 54 *Tax Guide for US Citizens and Resident Aliens Abroad* from the IRS website www.irs.gov, by looking under International Taxpayer. Assistance can also be requested from the IRS in Paris (office is in The American Consulate, 2 rue St Florentin and is open from 9am–12pm to personal callers), but they will refer you back to the IRS in Texas if they have too many enquiries to deal with. The mailing address for the IRS in Paris is c/o The American Embassy (2 Av Gabriel, 75382 Paris, Cedex 8; www.amba-usa.fr). You can also call 01 43 12 25 55. As there is a long wait time it might be better to fax your enquiry (fax: 01 43 12 23 03).

◼ Foreign-earned income exclusion

US citizens and resident aliens of the USA who live abroad can qualify for tax US tax exemption on foreign earned income up to the value of $85,700 (2007 income).This can apply to spouses individually. If your tax affairs are complicated you might prefer to use a firm in France that specialises in US expatriates' tax.

Types of income subject to *impôt sur le revenu*

bénéfices agricoles (BA)	agricultural profits
bénéfices industriels et commerciaux (BIC)	industrial and commercial profits
bénéfices non-commerciaux (BNC)	non-commercial profits
plus values à court terme	capital gains (short-term)
rémunerations des dirigeants de sociétés	certain directors' remunerations
revenus de capitaux mobiliers	investment income
revenus fanciers	property income
traitements, salaires, remunérations assimilées, pensions, rentes viagères	wages, salaries, remunerations, pensions, life annuities

The French tax system

Personal income tax

Known in France as *IRPP (Impôt sur le Revenu des Personnes Physiques)* this tax goes as high as 40% at the marginal rate, but this gives a somewhat misleading picture, as most tax is collected in the form of social security payments and VAT. While everyone pays social security contributions, only half of French families pay *impôt sur le revenu.*

Tax returns

There are several different types of tax returns – *déclarations fiscales* – for different types of income. The forms can be viewed on the government website www.service-public.fr, and can also be obtained at any time from your Centre des Impôts or *mairie*. The basic form is No. 2042, the *déclaration des revenus*. If you are self-employed, have capital gains to declare, or rent out property, you also have to fill in No. 2042C, the *déclaration complément*. For business, see below.

Calculation of impot sur le revenu

The basic 20% abatement for salaried workers was abolished in 2005 but at the same time the number of tax tranches was reduced from 7 to 5 and the rates and limits of the tranches were adjusted so that the abolition of the abatement did not translate into increased taxation.

IR is levied on a range of sources of income, whether you are salaried or non-salaried. Bank interest and income from some savings accounts and life insurance are taxed at source.

Benefits in kind are taxed at the same rate as wages, salaries, pensions and life annuities, according to their market value. Profits from running *chambres d'hôtes* and *gîtes* come under BIC (see below). Non-commercial profits – BNC – concerns income from liberal professions, i.e. doctors, architects, lawyers, and other services.

Property income concerns the letting of houses, offices, factories, etc., agricultural land, lakes, forests, as well as hunting rights.

Exemptions

Certain kinds of income are exempt from income tax, notably:

- Rental income, if you rent out rooms in your own home on a long-term basis, as long as the rent is considered 'reasonable'
- Income from certain savings plans, and investments in industry, under certain conditions
- Social security benefits, some maternity benefits, disability benefits, incapacity benefits
- Redundancy payments

Deductions

Before any tax is calculated you are entitled to certain deductions, notably:

- Maintenance payments to parents and children, including adult children, if they can be shown to be in need
- Child support and alimony payments to divorced partners
- Voluntary payments to children up to a reasonable limit
- Voluntary payments to persons over 75 living in your home
- Losses on certain business investment schemes, qualifying for tax breaks
- Accountant expenses

If your income falls under wages, salaries, pensions, etc. there are further items to deduct from your gross income before tax is calculated:

	Married couple	Single, widowed, or divorced
None disabled	2	1
1 disabled	2.5	1.5
1 dependent child	2.5	1.5
1 disabled dependant	3	2
2 dependent children	3	2
2 dependants including 1 disabled	3.5	2.5
2 disabled dependants	4	3
3 dependent children	4	3
4 dependent children	5	4

- Professional expenses – including travel to and from work, meals, hotels; these will be part of your business expenses if you are a non-salaried worker, otherwise you can claim a fixed 10% of your gross income
- The interest on loans contracted in order to invest in a new company can be deducted from the salary paid by the company
- Private pension contributions

Methods of calculation

The basis of the calculation is the total income of the household added together. In order to compensate taxpayers with dependants or low earners in their household,

Slice or tranche	Net income	
1	0–5,687	0%
2	5,688–11,344	5.5%
3	11,345–25,195	14%
4	25,196–67,546	30%
5	67,546 and over	40%

the French use a 'family quotient' system – *quotient familial* – calculating tax according to *parts* assigned to members of the family. The total income is divided by the number of parts, which has the effect of calculating the tax as if each member of the family earned the same amount. Once the tax has been worked out on a sliding scale, it is multiplied by the number of parts to arrive at the final figure.

As a single person, you have 1 *part*. If you are married then you have 2; if one partner is disabled the couple receives 2.5 *parts*; if both are disabled 3 *parts*. There are numerous different categories of *parts*. Dependants (*personnes à charge*) are (to put it simply) children under 21, students under 25 and disabled children whatever their age. They are only accepted as dependants if they are based at home and still require some support from you. In the first three cases they may be 'attached' to the household, even though they are living and working away from home, and you will receive an additional 0.5 *parts* for each of them. Since 2003, divorced or separated parents can receive 0.25% of the *parts* if they share custody.

The most commonly used *parts* are given below.

As a rule, each additional child or dependant gives a further 0.5 *parts*. Three children or dependants give 1 *part* apiece, plus 0.5 *parts* if one is an invalid. There is a limit to the amount that you can save with this system. If your saving is more than €2,227 (indexed) per half *part* above your base *parts*, then you don't qualify for the *quotient familial,* and your tax has to be calculated differently. Single parents and those with disabled dependants are treated more generously.

Tax calculation by tranches

The French tax system resembles other systems in that tax is calculated progressively on the amount per *part*. The amount per slice or tranche has to be multiplied by the *parts* to arrive at a final figure before tax credits and rebates are applied. The following figures apply to income earned in 2004. They are revised annually depending on inflation.

Main tax deadlines	
Declaration form	Payment
IR *Micro*	31 March No. 2042, 3 instalments/final payment 15 September
Réel simplifié BIC	30 April No. 2031 as above
Réel normal BIC	30 April No. 2031 as above
BNC	30 April No. 2035 as above

Tax credits

There are various tax credits and reductions, too numerous to go into in great detail. Note that these are all subject to conditions and limits. All are subject to having the correct paperwork. The more usual ones include:

- 50% of the cost of domestic help, child-minding, gardeners, cleaners, etc. up to a maximum credit for all employees of 50% of €15,000
- Child-minding expenses outside the home
- Charitable donations; within relatively low limits

Type of tax	
IR	Trésor Public
IS	Centre des Impôts
ISF (wealth tax)	Trésor Public
Taxe d'habitation	Trésor Public
Taxe foncière	Trésor Public
Taxe professionnelle	Trésor Public
Taxes sur les salaires (payroll tax)	Centre des Impôts
TVA	Centre des Impôts

- Renovations, extensions, repairs to the principal residence, and to tourist accommodation in certain rural areas, up to 15% of the purchase price of the property
- As part of the tax reductions introduced by Nicolas Sarkozy's government in 2007 (Law no. 2007–1223 dated 21 August 2007) known as la loi TEPA a tax credit of 20% (maximum of €7,500 for a couple) of loan interest on loans taken out to buy or build your main home
- A 25% tax credit for the costs of installing heavy equipment for the home
- Environmentally friendly vehicles
- Investments in small and medium-sized businesses

The décote

If your tax liability is below €814 (indexed) you are eligible for a rebate – *décote* – of the difference between €407 and half the tax liability. Thus if your tax liability is €700, you will have a rebate of €57 and your liability is reduced to €643. If your liability is under €407 you pay no tax at all.

◼ Other tax annex forms

There are a number of other tax forms that one may be required to fill in:

- ◼ No. 2044 for *revenus fonciers* – property income
- ◼ No. 2047 for foreign income
- ◼ No. 2049 for capital gains (IPV)
- ◼ No. 2065 for corporation tax (IS)
- ◼ No.1810 for fixed minimum corporation tax (IFA)
- ◼ No. 2074 for capital gains on investments

Social security taxes

The basic tax is the CSG (*Contribution Sociale Généralisée*) which is applied at a rate of 7.5% after a deduction of 5% for professional costs (i.e. 7.5% of 95% of gross income). All earned and unearned income is subject to this tax, which is in many cases a withholding tax. A contribution to repaying the social security system's debt, the CRDS or *Contribution pour le Remboursement de la Dette Sociale,* is levied at 0.5% on similar terms to the CSG. Most types of income are also subject to an additional 'social contribution', the *Prélèvement Sociale* at 2%.

Social security contributions are entirely separate from social security taxes and are dealt with below.

Paying in instalments

The French tax system works on the basis that you pay income tax (IR) in instalments on your income for the previous year, calculated on the basis of your income in the year before that. There is, therefore, a delay before a foreign resident starting work in France for the first time pays any tax. If you have been resident in France, there will be no break in your tax payments, unless you have been unemployed. You will be paying tax on your previous year's salary during the year that you start your business. If you come from abroad you will pay for the first time by September 15 in the year after you start up. You are then hit with the entire tax bill in one go for the previous year. Changes to this system are being discussed, with talk of introducing a withholding tax, more similar to Britain's PAYE system.

No tax is paid in advance (except for taxes withheld at source on savings etc.). If you work for an employer, tax can be deducted at source through the year. Businesses pay IR in three instalments in February, May and September – the *tiers provisionnels,* as do many salaried workers. Strictly speaking the first two payments are due on 31 January and 30 April, but it has become the custom to extend the deadline to 15 February and 15 May. Normally you will receive your final assessment during September. You cannot be required to pay your final instalment before 15 September. Since 2003 you are required to pay within 45 days of an assessment. If you fail to pay in time then there is a 10% penalty.

FACT

◼ If you file your tax return even one day late, you automatically receive a 10% penalty.

All French residents must be registered with the local *inspecteur des impôts*. You are liable for tax on your worldwide income from the day you arrive in France. It is up to you to request a tax return (*déclaration fiscale*) if you don't receive one automatically. Small businesses are given more time to submit their tax returns, as are those who submit their returns online. For the *micro* regime the final date is 31 March. For BIC and *déclaration controlée* (BNC) it is 30 April.

Wealth tax (ISF)

ISF or *Impôt de Solidarité sur la Fortune* only affects those with net assets over €760,000 (indexed) if they are resident or have assets in France on 1 January of any tax year. The tax is levied on the fiscal household, defined as:

- Single persons, divorced, widowed, unmarried or separated from their partners
- Married persons, including dependent children under 18
- Persons who are known to be living together (*concubinage notoire*), and children
- Those who have entered a PACS (partnership contract) and children

The household's net assets as of 1 January are calculated by the householder him or herself; they include the assets of everyone in the household. The declaration, accompanied by payment in full, is due by 16 July for EU citizens, and 15 June for French citizens. Other foreigners (e.g. US citizens) have until 1 September to pay. Variations in the value of your assets during the year can't be taken account when calculating your liability.

All your assets, including cars, yachts, furniture, etc. must be taken into account. You will need to produce receipts and insurance policies in order to justify your valuations. You are expected to calculate the 'fair market value' (*valeur vénale réelle*) of your property on the basis of prices in your area. The tax authorities have their own ways of assessing your net worth. Many items are exempt from wealth tax, of which a few are given here in a simplified form:

- Antiques over 100 years old
- Copyrights on works of art, literature, music
- Personal injury compensation
- Movable and sometimes immovable property that you require to carry on your profession
- Shares in companies of which you are a director, with more than 25% voting rights

It may be possible to have assets that you need to run *gîtes* (self-catering) or *chambres d'hôtes* (bed and breakfast) exempted from wealth tax. You are allowed a 30% reduction (increased from 20% by the *loi TEPA*) on the household's principal residence (not more than one house). Wealth tax is generally payable on shares in French companies and foreign companies owning property in France.

Since the basis on which ISF is calculated is your net worth, any debts can be deducted from the total. This includes any property loans. Any money you owe to builders or other tradesmen can be deducted, as can the taxes you owe for the previous year (including the ISF itself). Money that is owed to you is added to the total. There is a limitation on wealth tax, inasmuch as your total tax liability (including income tax) cannot exceed 85% of your net taxable income for the previous year. The ISF tariff ranges from 0.55% up to a maximum of 1.8% on assets above €16,020,000. It is not necessarily indexed every year.

■ Payment and penalties

Your wealth tax return and payment have to be made to the local Centre des Impôts by 16 July. If you are not resident in France contact: ☎0820 32 42 52; www.inpots. gouv.fr.

■ Inheritance taxes

These are dealt with in the chapter *Buying property*.

■ Useful addresses

Franco-British Chamber of Commerce: ☎+33 (0)1 53 30 81 30; www. francobritishchamers.com. Will provide a list of Franco-British tax consultants

French Fiscal Attaché: French Embassy, Tax Department: ☎0207 073 1000; www.ambafrance-uk.org

Direction des Résidents a L'Etranger et des Services Généraux: ☎01 49 25 12 45. Further tax information

Conseil Supérieur de l'Ordre des Experts Comptables et Comptables Agréés (CSOEC): www.oec-paris.fr. Chartered accountants professional organisation

■ Useful contacts – expatriate financial planning

Axis Strategy Consultants: ☎+33 (0)1 39 21 74 61; www.axis-strategy.com. Specialises in financial advice for expatriates living in France

Blackstone Franks LLP: ☎020 7250 3300; www.blackstonefranks.com. Also offices in France. Specialists in the expatriate financial sector

Blevins Franks: Specialists in the expatriate financial sector; tax advisory; ☎020 7015 2126; jane.hayward@blevinsfranks.com; www.blevinsfranks.com. Publishers of the book *Living in France*, available from Blevins Franks partners

Brewin Dolphin Securities: www.brewindolphin.co.uk. Services include international portfolio management with off-shore facility for those domiciled or resident outside the UK

Dixon Wilson: ☎01 47 03 12 90; ☎020 7680 8100; www.dixonwilson.co.uk. Chartered accountants, provide strategic financial and tax planning services to businesses, companies and high net worth individuals resident either in France or the UK (see advertisement above)

Hansard Europe Ltd: ☎01 624 688000; enquiries@hansard.com; www.hansard. com. Hansard has products aimed at the French market and designed to be tax efficient with regard to French tax and life assurance regulations

John Siddall Financial Service Ltd: ☎01329 239111; www.siddalls.net. Independent financial advisers providing expertise across a spectrum of investments, retirement and tax planning for private clients at home and abroad. Many years experience in assisting British nationals wishing to become resident in France with all aspects of their financial planning; part of the IFG Group Plc and Authorised and Regulated in the UK by the Financial Services Authority

PKF (Guernsey) Ltd: ☎01481 727927; admin.guernsey@pkfguernsey.com; www.pkfguernsey.com. Chartered accountants and French tax specialists

Smith and Williamson: ☎020 7131 4000; www.smith.williamson.co.uk. A UK chartered accountant, experienced in dealing with most tax matters relating to expatriates and non-UK residents

■ Useful websites

- ■ *www.impots.gouv.fr:* Government site, with tax simulation programme
- ■ *www.hmrc.gov.uk*: For non-residents info
- ■ *www.lesechos:fr/patrimoine/index.htm:* Finance website

■ THE LEGAL SYSTEM, THE POLICE AND COURTS

The justice system and courts

Of course, the modern French justice system is very different to the Napoleonic Code, but in terms of laying down the basic principles of French law (and that of

Civil & criminal courts

Civil courts	Deal with
conseils de prud'hommes	labour conciliation tribunals; deals with issues involving labour and apprenticeship contracts
tribunaux d'instance	small claims, rent, etc. and civil cases up to about €4,500
tribunaux de commerce	disputes between merchants or anything to do with commercial acts. are presided over by lay commercial judges (juges consulaires)
tribunaux de grande instance	civil cases not heard in special courts including divorce, adoption, etc. and some criminal cases.
tribunaux des affaires de sécurité sociale	disputes with the various social security agencies over payments for illness, pensions, etc.
tribunaux paritaires des baux ruraux	cases involving agrarian landlord-and-tenant disputes
Criminal courts	**Deal with**
cours d'appel for appeals there are 27 cours d'appel	the supreme court of appeal (Cour de Cassation), has the power to quash or annul sentences but doesn't consider the facts of the case, only whether the law has been correctly applied by the tribunaux and the cours d'appel. It will thus only exercise its power of annulment if it is deemed the law has been wrongly administered.
cours d'assises	serious criminal offences composed of a presiding judge and two assessors (professional judges) and nine jurors. Decisions from the assizes courts may not be appealed against; only points of law.
tribunaux correctionnels	more serious offences punishable by imprisonment of up to 5 years (longer for drug trafficking)
tribunaux de police	petty offences involving 1–2 days' imprisonment or fines ranging from a few euros to hundreds of euros

many other countries) the Code is highly influential. Napoleon himself considered it his greatest achievement. It was written very quickly in accordance with the principles of the French Revolution but also laid down the absolute right of property. It replaced old feudal and royal laws and stressed the importance of a clearly written and accessible code of law that took the lawmaking initiative away from the judiciary. Still today, there is no case law in France, however the decisions of the higher courts do offer important interpretations. Perhaps the greatest impact of Napoleon's Civil Code (as it was also know) is the way it structured the procedure of French life at a fundamental level. This has had a long-lasting impact on the French psyche. The reference points of society are authoritatively laid down and are regularly called upon to regulate all aspects of life. This, in some respects, is a key to understanding the French temperament.

In 1994, France's penal code was completely revised to take into account offences such as sexual harassment, crimes against gays and ecological terrorism and to introduce an offence of crime against humanity. Vagabondage and begging became legal. More conservative measures include 30-year prison sentences without parole for child murderers and stiffer sentences for drug trafficking. Nearly all the Britons held in French jails are there for this. The most unpolitically correct change was probably the plea of 'legitimate self-defence of property', which means that property owners are generally considered to be within their rights if they injure or even kill trespassers. There is also an article which makes it an offence for witnesses of a violent crime not to intervene to help. The same applies if someone is in need of medical help.

Some useful terms to know:

- *le débat contradictoire* is the opportunity to defend yourself
- *une contravention* is the lowest kind of crime (fines/short sentences)
- *un délit* is more serious (sentences less than ten years)
- *un crime* is the most serious offence category (rape/murder)
- *un magistrat* is a generic term for judges, as opposed to
- *le parquet* which refers to prosecutors who request enquiries to be made, bring accusations and also monitor court activity
- *publicité* except where government secrets are involved or victims are considered to need protection from additional trauma (rape, child cases), all civil, administrative and criminal cases are open to the public
- *siège* is the seat of the judge
- *le tribunal* is the court of first instance, appeals are taken to the *cour d'appel* and the *Cour de Cassation* may countermand appeal court decisions.

There has long been doubt about the independence of the French judiciary, not least because the Justice Ministry is responsible for appointing state prosecutors and for telling them when to instigate judicial enquiries. This means that when the enquiries involve political corruption, the party in power is inclined to appoint tame judges who will do as they are told, or who share their views.

Reforms have been made, not least measures to reinforce the presumption of innocence and stop trial by media, although some fear this will muzzle the press when they try to bring corruption stories to light. Anti-terrorism laws to increase video-surveillance and allow monitoring of the internet and mobile phones have been introduced for all British lines.

In France the judicial system is notoriously slow and cumbersome. For instance it can take minor civil disputes five months to come to court while those accused of more serious offences can wait up to three years to have their cases heard. The European Court of Human Rights has condemned French judges many times for failing to come to a decision within a reasonable time. One of the initiatives of the high profile Justice Minister, Rachida Dati (called *ma beurette*, my little Arab girl by President Sarkozy), has been to introduce measures to attempt to make the justice system more efficient and more transparent. This includes computerisation to allow lawyers and those subject to trial the opportunity to follow the progress of cases at the click of a mouse. Also, more controversially, this overhaul threatens to close 300 tribunals across the country. The accent has also been put on help to victims and the re-introduction of criminals into the community using an expanded electronic bracelet scheme.

FACT

It isn't unusual for people not to lock their homes or cars out in the deep countryside.

Crime

France has a crime rate similar to that of other highly developed European countries. However, the national crime pattern shows some uniquely French aspects as it tends to centre on particular urban districts, leaving the rest of France (especially rural areas) with contrastingly low crime rates.

In common with almost all capital cities with a constant throng of tourists, Paris has a high crime rate, as does the Côte d'Azur, particularly and unsurprisingly, of theft and burglary. Marseilles is a notorious centre of crime, including drugs and gangland activities although it has been trying to improve its image in recent years.

 It is helpful to find out which force is actually required before contacting the police on a routine matter. Dialling '17' will connect you with the appropriate police service (which arranges ambulances) in an emergency: dial '18' for the fire and rescue services.

A recent breakdown of crime figures shows that well over half of all crimes committed in France involved theft. Having said this, there are rural areas of France that are virtually crime free and this can be one of the attractions of living in such areas.

Recent statistics from the Interior Ministry (www.interieur.gouv.fr) suggest that in 2007 violent crime was down for the first time in 12 years. Drug usage (*les stupéfiants*) is still on the increase but road-related crime was down significantly.

France has over 180 penal establishments and a prison population of about 58,000 of which fewer than 5% are women. France has a much lower incidence of female

Riots in the banlieues: November 2005

In autumn 2005 in Clichy-sous-bois, a northern suburb of Paris, two young Arabs were accidentally electrocuted in an EDF high-voltage depot after they climbed a 3m, barbed-wire covered wall, trying to escape the police. This incident sparked a wave of rioting throughout France's *banlieues*, in which cars were burned and administrative buildings attacked every night for several weeks running (numerous amateur videos that can be viewed on file sharing sites on the internet document this as well as examples of police brutality). Nicolas Sarkozy, who was Interior Minister at the time, implemented a policy of zero tolerance towards the rioters, giving strong support to the police. The riots highlighted the situation of the young *banlieuesards*, the residents of troubled housing estates who feel they have very little stake in French society – unemployment among the young in these areas averages 40%.

imprisonment than the UK or the USA, and 36.11% of crimes are solved, with the figure at 60% for violent crime. Michèle Alliot-Marie, the Interior Minister, Rachida Dati and President Sarkozy have made it clear that security is high on their political agenda.

Police

French police are generally well equipped (and well-armed) to tackle the crime problem: they are strict, efficient and have far-reaching legal powers. The role of the police in the riots that spread through the *banlieues* (suburbs) of France at the end of 2007 is discussed below.

A popular misconception is that all French police (*agents de police*) are *gendarmes*. As their name (rough translation is 'armed men') suggests, the Gendarmarie Nationale is a paramilitary police force and comes under the control of the Ministry of Defence. It is the only police force evident in many quiet country areas. The Gendarmarie Nationale also patrols roads and undertakes other specialist duties including motorcycle escorts and sea patrols.

■ City police

Towns and cities have their own police (*police municipale/corps urbain*) which deals mainly with petty crime, traffic control and offences and road accidents. French police used to wear a military-style pillbox, peaked cap (*képi*), also worn by *gendarmes*, but this was abandoned years ago in favour of contemporary blouson jackets and ordinary peaked caps for men and a trilby-type hat for women.

■ Police Nationale

Police Nationale deal with crime on a much larger and more serious scale, crossing city and departmental boundaries.

■ CRS

Other divisions in the police force include the *Compagnies Républicaines de la Sécurité* or CRS (essentially riot police but often drafted to other less risky duties, such as patrolling the Côte d'Azur in summer).

■ Frontier/customs police

A special police division also patrols frontiers, acting in a customs capacity at land, sea and air frontiers.

The new Sarkozy government has introduced some limited measures to combat youth unemployment, but more importantly has shown that it is willing to break with the traditional French policy on the question of racial discrimination. Overly optimistic republican ideals promoting the idea that everyone is accepted as French under the universal principles of the revolution have meant that governments have ignored the institutionalised racism that exists in France. There has also been a policy of not collecting racial or ethnic statistics because of anti-Semitic crimes under Vichy France that were aided by detailed pre-war censuses.

Working in France

THE EMPLOYMENT MARKET

For anyone who isn't yet old enough (or rich enough) to retire, finding a job will be the most important part of going to live in another country. Working overseas, temporarily or permanently, can be a way of furthering your career by getting valuable experience, or a means of fulfilling an ambition to live abroad: this chapter aims to cover both situations.

Since the arrival of the European single market, there has been nothing to prevent any European Union (EU) national, in possession of skills and experience in demand, from working in France. The Treaty of Rome, which heralded the Common Market, guaranteed the free movement of labour and services in the countries of the EU. However, it wasn't until comparatively recently that a system was devised to recognise the qualifications obtained in one EU country and used in another. Initially, directives for the mutual recognition of qualifications were dealt with individually, for instance architects in 1985 and general medical practitioners (GPs) in 1986. It's estimated that only a couple of thousand GPs from the older EU Member States have taken advantage of the directive to work abroad but it is expected that many more from the accession countries will now do so.

In 1990, another directive ruled that all remaining professional qualifications not yet covered by EU directives, should be left to the discretion of individual national governments as to whether to allow nationals from another EU country to use them with or without a period of probation, or having to take a further examination before practising. In general, qualifications obtained in one member country are now recognised in another.

Residence and work regulations

EU nationals

Any EU national from the older EU countries can look for a suitable job in France. Once they find a job they can start paying social security contributions into the French system and ultimately, if they so wished, settle permanently there. A residence permit isn't required. For more details, see the chapter on *Before You Go*. There are, however, still some restrictions on work permits for nationals from accession countries in France (unlike in the UK, Sweden, Ireland, Spain, Portugal, Greece and Finland where accession country nationals have complete freedom to work). France has announced a progressive and controlled lifting of restrictions for nationals of Estonia, Hungary, Lithuania, Latvia, Poland and the Czech Republic and will do so after consultations with labour unions as to which occupations have recruitment pressures. If citizens of these countries wish to set up companies or work as self-employed, they must obtain a work permit (*permis de travail*) to do so. In any case, all work permit restrictions for EU nationals must be lifted throughout Europe by 2011.

Non-EU nationals

It's more difficult for nationals of non-EU countries to find work in France. For instance, Americans will find it more difficult to find employment than EU nationals. Non-EU nationals are supposed to:

ℹ ■ The network of *Centres d'Information et de Documentation Jeunesse* (CIDJs www.cidj.com) has some useful leaflets including *Séjour et emploi des étrangers* (No. 5.5701).

■ Arrange employment in advance of entry into France

■ Have their job arrangements approved by the French Ministry of Labour, and/or their employer should apply for approval to the Office des Migrations Internationales (☎01 53 69 53 70; www.diplomatie.gouv.fr)

■ Have a pre-arranged, long-stay visa for workers

The red tape can be much simpler if the applicant already has *carte de résident* and has lived in France for 10 years. Other exceptions are spouses of French citizens and students who have studied in France for two years and who have at least one parent who is a four-year resident of France. Also non-EU students are permitted to do some part-time work such as au pairing, or similar temporary jobs, if they have a definite job offer.

Needless to say, the regulations can also be negotiated more smoothly if the applicant has a desirable skill, or has been offered employment by a French company, or the French subsidiary of the company employing them. Without any of the above advantages, it could be an uphill struggle to first convince an employer to employ them rather than any other candidate from within the country or other EU countries. Even if this proves feasible, they won't be entitled automatically to the right of residence and it is now more difficult for non-EU citizens to move their dependants to France.

■ Useful addresses for Americans

Exchange Training Programs. ANPE – Espace Emploi International: ☎01 53 02 25 50; stageseei.omi@anpe.fr; www.emploi-international.org; a reciprocal agreement with ANPE (French national employment service) allows young workers with a minimum of a year's experience to do paid work in France for three to 18 months

Internships: Internships International LLC: ☎941 373 221; info@internships international.org; www.internshipsinternational.org; charges $1,100 for fixing up an internship in your selected field for up to three months.

Teaching: Franco-American Commission for Education Exchange: ☎01 45 20 46 54; cfa@fulbright-france.org; www.fulbright-france.org; teaching in French secondary education as an assistant and teaching positions at public universities as visiting professors, assistants or readers; the Franco-American Commission provides an information sheet *Teaching Positions in France*; for assistant posts in French secondary schools you can also contact the CIEP (www.ciep.fr)

Students: The French Embassy (☎212 439 1400), has an information sheet *Employment in France for Students*. For other addresses useful for Americans, see the section on 'Temporary work'.

Accommodation and job hunting

Landlords usually require a reference from an employer. Probably the best approach is to try to get lodgings with a friend and if necessary pay them rent or a contribution to live in their home until you find a job and can then look for a place of your

I hadn't thought about international organisations as an option but they can employ Americans.

> **Karalyn Monteil's story shows the sort of determination that might be required if, as an American, you wish to live and work in Paris.**
>
> I came to France without work papers or any knowledge of the language and without knowing anyone and quickly realised I didn't have many options. I was 27 and already had a career but I ended up taking a job as an au pair. I had time to do some freelance writing with Paris Voice.
>
> I wasn't paid (no papers) but they let me put free classifieds in for jobs I could earn money from. The problem was I couldn't get a bank account or a cell phone (at that time you had to show a carte de séjour before you could get a phone) so I got a pager and I used to get people to phone me at the phone booth down in the street. I did a lot of phone classes from phone booths in the street. I also used to do power walking classes, walking executives home from work and speaking English on the way or intensive business English lunches where I could eat for free!
>
> I was really tempted to go home several times. After a year and a half I met someone at a barbecue who worked for the OECD. I hadn't thought about international organisations as an option but they can employ Americans. I interviewed with the OECD and they offered me a secretarial job right away. That was the first time I had official papers. Up till then I'd been going to Switzerland or London every few months to get my visa renewed.
>
> I was still doing freelance writing for Elle.com. The job with the OECD was secure but I ended up taking a job with Elle because that was more the sort of work I wanted to be doing. Then they decided to move the English writing team to New York! At that point I realised my only option was in the international sector if I wanted to stay in France.
>
> Someone I knew knew someone working at UNESCO and they photocopied me the page of the contact numbers of people in the culture sector. I started calling at random and telling my story and how I really wanted to stay and work in Paris. Eventually I got some leads. Every Monday for two months I called the director of the World Heritage Centre. I'd get through to the secretary and the director would always be busy but eventually I spoke to him and went in for an interview.
>
> I thought I'd just get an unpaid internship but they gave me a one-month contract as editorial assistant on the World Heritage Review which kept getting renewed for two years until I got offered a temporary post co-ordinating the museum programme in post-conflict countries. UNESCO was never able to get me my carte de séjour for some reason and I finally only got one when I had a French baby last year.

own. Unless you are lucky enough to have a job lined up, you may have to accept that the home and job which you first take in France may not be ideal but are a necessary stepping stone. Then once you are established, it will be possible to set about finding better alternatives.

Unemployment

Unemployment (*le chômage*) was running at nearly 13% (3 million) in 1998. However, a variety of job creation schemes, especially for the under-25s, and the introduction of a 35-hour week in 2000, have reduced this to just under 8.7%. At 7%, the Eurozone average is currently at its lowest ever rate. GDP growth is, however, expected to be well under 2% in France for 2008 and unemployment may rise slightly during the year.

Jobs for younger and older people

Young people under 25 and those made redundant at age 50 or older, find it extremely difficult to find steady re-employment, unless they have a high level of prized skills, or are able to become self-employed. Newcomers to the job market tend to have a more precarious situation with over a third having fixed-term, temporary or subsidised contracts. The worst unemployment levels are in the *banlieues* (suburbs) where youth unemployment is running at 40%. At the time of going to press President Sarkozy had announced a diversion of €500 million to come from the current infrastructure budget in a plan to create 100,000 apprenticeships for the *banlieues*. However, there are no plans to set up independent funding of the programme as yet.

Demand for foreign staff

France has never been the easiest country for foreigners to find work in because of the wealth of well-qualified people to take professional jobs, and also plenty of blue-collar and unskilled workers. It has long been one of the very few major countries to have a self-sufficient labour supply. However, the common market has created new opportunities, particularly for foreign employees, many of which are outlined in this chapter. For those looking for temporary and short-term jobs, the reality is that now, more than ever, job finding has to be well planned and systematically carried out. This applies even to temporary jobs found on spec. For instance it's no good looking for a job in Paris in July and August when all the small businesses are

closed. However, it would be worth visiting potential employers in the Alps during the summer to fix up a job for the skiing season. There are also possibilities for self-employment, even in times of recession – skills such as nursing and services from hairdressing to financial advising will always be in demand.

French business and industry works very much to its own standards and specifications. Unlike many countries it doesn't always set out to follow the standards that are set by the USA. Nonetheless, over the past 15 years, France has entered foreign markets, realising that to succeed it must produce products for international tastes and not just for Gallic ones. Perhaps due to this recent international bias in industry, French employers are now willing to recruit internationally, providing opportunities in industry for British and American professionals among others. The French economy is soundly based thanks to the policies of recent governments. It will be helped by the country's continuing strong position within the EU and by the notable French ability to promote its own interests through EU policies.

Many people who holiday in France are immediately taken with the lifestyle and the air of affluence. However working there is quite a different proposition and it's useful to consider what France is like as a country to work in. As recently as the early 1980s, France attracted few foreign workers. Most industries were in a poor state, and rates of pay were abysmally low. Industrial relations were also notoriously bad and employees enjoyed very little job security. The France of the early twenty-first century offers a very different situation: high-tech industries are at the forefront of their field, and salaries in these, and the majority of other industries, have soared. Legislative reforms from 1983–86 resulted in not only relatively good industrial relations and professional equality between men and women but also increased rates of remuneration for employees. However, the French social security deductions and top band tax rate are higher than most of Europe, except Scandinavia. Needless to say, comparison with American salaries isn't impressive. Nevertheless the lifestyle, expertise and the character of France attract skilled workers from Europe and executives who, perhaps, once considered only Germany, Japan and the USA as the world leaders of industry.

The employment outlook

France is particularly strong in most areas of advanced technology. This includes all aspects of electronics, computing, and high technology manufacture. There is a regular need for computer engineers and there is an accelerated visa procedure for them. Tourism has long been one of the largest and most successful French industries. Nice alone has 8 million tourists a year, over half of them French.

Traditionally, France has not been a world leader in the professional services industries; this is, however, one area which is now developing and where expertise is required. Insurance, banking and advertising are all going through a period of expansion. It isn't just French banks that can offer employment to foreigners; foreign banks from other EU countries can now provide their services outside their country of origin, through branches throughout the EU without the need to obtain special licences. However, the most radical reforms are likely to be in the banking sector and in financial services – particularly those connected with the stock market, which is bustling with employees of newly created securities subsidiaries and in the areas of pensions and insurance.

France is also still home to many leading manufacturing industries, for example, motor vehicles, aerospace and defence equipment. The common assumption that the main demands for employment are in modern industries isn't necessarily correct. Although some of the traditional industries, e.g. steel production, have died out, others have been, or are constantly being, modernised e.g. wine production and agriculture. France is largely self supporting in foodstuffs as well as being a major exporter of them.

France offers potential employment to a wide range of skills and abilities and expertise. Thus, while a scientist or a computer designer may well find numerous job opportunities in France, there is no reason why, for example, a plumber or a hairdresser should not also have access to an equal number of job opportunities – this is the very nature of the EU freedom of movement of labour provision.

▇ FINDING A JOB

Evaluation of skills

At this stage, it's wise to decide on a target job. This means assessing the kind of job for which you are most suited and examining the feasibility of doing it in France. It isn't always a good idea to start a completely new career when moving to a new country although people have done so with, for instance, urban employees turning themselves into farmers. Anyone considering executive and professional positions may want to take advice from a professional career consultant while those with a skill or trade should seek preliminary advice from their trade association at home.

French employers are anxious to recruit anyone who has a particular skill or ability, which will ultimately further the interests of their company or organisation. This applies across the board from the most advanced technology projects to companies looking for sales representatives with a track record. French employers recognise all such skills and they are prepared to pay generously for them. Having proven skills equally applies to more mundane jobs. The majority of French workers, even those in quite basic jobs, have undertaken some form of apprenticeship or specialist training to qualify them for their position and they are known as *ouvriers qualifiés*. You will find that applying for positions for which you don't have the appropriate qualifications is far harder in France than in the UK or the USA. Experience alone isn't usually considered a substitute. This can be frustrating for those from an English-speaking environment where experience is valued as much, if not more, than qualifications.

If you are from the UK and you aren't sure how your qualifications correspond to French ones, the UK National Recognition Information Centre (UK NARIC; www.naric.org.uk) will advise you. The service is free of charge to students. For more information on UK NARIC, see below.

EC professional qualifications directives

The EC directive on the mutual recognition of professional qualifications (89/48/EEC) was notified to Member States in January 1989. This directive (usually referred to as the first diploma directive) dealt with professional qualifications awarded after at least three years of higher education (e.g. doctors, dentists, pharmacists, architects, accountants, lawyers, etc.). The second diploma directive (92/51/EEC) dealt with

TIP

■ Prospective job seekers are advised to consult the association relevant to their profession for the exact conditions for acceptance in France.

all qualifications that take less than three years to obtain. The second directive includes: qualifications achieved after post-secondary level education involving a course of 1–3 years (defined as diplomas); awards made on completion of a course following a minimum school leaving age qualification (defined as certificates); and work experience. This means that that UK's NVQs and SVQs and their equivalents are recognised by the EU. The Member States implemented the second diploma directive in 1994. This mutual recognition of qualifications may in some instances be subject to certain conditions such as proficiency in the language of the state where the professional intends to practise and length of experience. For a copy of the first directive, you can download *The Single Market, Europe Open for Professionals, EC Professional Qualifications Directive* from www.berr.gov.uk.

Although some professionals such as doctors and dentists have been able to practise in any EU state for several years, other professions have proved a stumbling block. For example, in France, the problem of recognising British ski instructor qualifications, which the French consider not as comprehensive as their own, has been solved with the introduction of the equivalence. For this another exam must, however, be taken in France (see below).

Certificates of experience

If you have experience but no skills, you can apply for a European Certificate of Experience. In the UK these are handled by UK NARIC; other countries will handle via their own organisation. Their role is to implement Directive 99/42/EEC (the so-called third directive) concerning the mutual recognition of experience gained in a profession in EU member countries. A certificate costs €105, £70 and takes 15 days to process. Download from www.certex.org.uk or contact UK NARIC (☎0870 990 4088; www.naric.org.uk)

 There is considerable information on professional bodies and EC directives on the EU website (www.citizens.eu).

Naric

UK National Academic Recognition Information Centre (NARIC) provides information on the comparability of overseas qualifications in each EU country. For France this is the NARIC based in Paris (www.education.gouv.fr/sup). You should go through your UK or French Employment Agency (ANPE in France) rather than contact NARIC directly, otherwise you will be charged for the service. You can look at www.naric.org. uk if you want more information in English, but you shouldn't contact the NARIC in the UK if you are going to work in France.

Sources of jobs

Newpapers

◼ UK newspapers and directories

The combined effects of the Single Market and the implementation of
the EC Professional Qualifications Directives (see above) are unlikely
to trigger a flood of transcontinental job recruitment, but mobility
has certainly become practicable for an increasing number of EU
nationals. It is therefore likely that UK newspapers will carry a
growing number of job advertisements from other member states
including France. Most British newspapers including *The Times,
The Financial Times* and the *Guardian* carry small numbers of job
adverts from other European countries regularly. Of course the
internet is gradually replacing printed newspapers and this is as much the case
for jobs sections than any other. All the main papers also have internet sites dedicated
to jobs. The Guardian jobs (http://jobs.guardian.co.uk) website is generally thought
to be the most comprehensive. The *Times Educational Supplement* (http://jobs.tes.
co.uk) is the reference for education jobs, including jobs abroad.

Alternatively, a wide range of casual jobs, including secretarial, agricultural,
tourism and domestic work, are advertised in the directory *Summer Jobs Abroad*
by David Woodworth and Victoria Pybus, while *Teaching English Abroad* by Susan
Griffiths lists schools worldwide which employ English language teachers each year
and *Working in Ski Resorts Europe & North America* by Victoria Pybus includes all the
main French resorts and tells you how and where to get jobs in them.

◼ International newspapers

International newspapers are a relatively new development in newspaper
publishing; these publications circulate editions across several national boundaries
and usually carry a modest amount of job advertising. The newspapers to consult
include the *Wall Street Journal, Financial Times* and *The International Herald Tribune*.
As well as employers advertising in these papers, individuals can place their own
adverts for any kind of job, although bilingual secretaries and assistants, marketing
managers and other professionally qualified people seeking to relocate abroad are
in the greatest demand. For details of advertising in the Paris editions contact the
classified advertising department of suitable newspapers.

◼ Useful addresses

The Financial Times (FT): www.ft.com; the FT is printed in English in the UK,
Germany, France, the USA and Japan and distributed worldwide; international
appointments appear on Thursdays in all editions

International Herald Tribune (IHT): www.iht.com; the IHT has a circulation in
France of 39,000

Wall Street Journal: http: //online.wsj.com; European edition published in Brussels

French newspapers

You can place adverts in French newspapers as well as use them as a source of
possible jobs. Keeping an eye on the jobs advertised in French newspapers could be
helpful but obviously the majority of posts are aimed at French nationals. The potential
for finding a job increases substantially if you are already in France, speak French and

Job hunting online

Logging on to job sites on the internet and then refining your search to France could yield some leads. Some of the current international and French job websites are:

- www.apr-job.com
- www.careerbuilder.com (international jobs website)
- www.overseasjobs.com
- www.init-emploi.tm.fr
- www.jobware.net
- www.michaelpage.fr
- www.monster.fr (thousands of jobs in France and career advice)
- www.phospore.com/statique/stagejob/home.cfm (aimed at young people this site offers paid jobs and traineeships in various sectors including museums, sales, administration, etc. and has some very useful contact addresses)
- www.webcible.com (very good site for jobs in specific fields eg IT, finance etc)

 Useful newspapers' websites

- *Le Figaro*: www.lefigaro.fr
- *Le Monde*: www.lemonde.fr.

have marketable skills and a track record. For jobs in Paris, the main newspapers to consult are *Le Monde* and the employment site it has set up jointly with Telerama at www.talents.fr. and *Le Figaro* (www.lefigaro.fr/emploi). Another publication worth consulting is the weekly journal *L'Express* (www.lexpress.fr). For regional jobs consult the regional newspapers in the area where you will be based. For more information on the French press generally, see the section on 'Media' in the chapter *Time off*.

British professional and trade publications

Professional journals and magazines are another possible source of job vacancies abroad, from British companies wishing to set up offices elsewhere in Europe and foreign firms advertising for staff e.g. *The Architects' Journal* (www.architectsjournal. co.uk), *The Architectural Review* (www.arplus.com), *Accountancy* (www. accountancymagazine.com), *Brewing & Distilling International* (www.bdinews.com) and *The Bookseller* (www.thebookseller.com) to name but a few. Some of these magazines are considered world authorities in their field and have a correspondingly wide international readership.

An exhaustive list of trade magazines can be found in media directories, for example *Benn's Media* and the *Writers' and Artists' Yearbook*, both of which are available in major UK reference libraries.

Professional associations

In the UK, professional associations are a useful contact point for their members with regard to practising elsewhere in the EU. During the negotiations involved in finalising the EU mutual recognition of qualifications directives, many professional associations negotiated with their counterparts in other member states and can therefore be helpful in providing contacts.

For details of all professional associations see the directory *Trade Associations and Professional Bodies of the UK*, available at most UK reference libraries. It is also worth trying to contact the French equivalent of UK professional associations: the UK body should be able to provide the address. Alternatively you can consult your trade union for information, as they may have links, however tenuous, with their counterpart organisation in France. A list of addresses of the more mainstream professional organisations is given below.

◼ Useful addresses

Architects Registration Board: ☎020 7580 5861; 020 7436 5269; info@arb.org. uk; www.arb.org.uk

Association of Professional Music Therapists: ☎020 84404153; www.apmt.org

Biochemical Society: www.biochemistry.org

British Computer Society: ☎020 7580 5530; www.bcs.org

British Medical Association: ☎switchboard 020 7583 6588; international info@ bma.org.uk; www.bma.org.uk. The BMA's International Department gives extensive help and advice to its members wishing to work elsewhere in Europe, and general advice to incoming doctors from other countries

British Dietetic Association: ☎0121–200 8010; www.bda.uk.com

Chartered Institute of Bankers: ☎01227 762600; institute@cib.org.uk

Chartered Institute of Building: ☎01344 630700; reception@ciob.org.uk; www. ciob.org.uk

Chartered Institute of Housing (CIH): ☎024 76851700; www.cih.org; the CIH may be able to help individual members further by putting them in touch with key people/organisations in the EU

Chartered Institute of Library and Information Professionals: ☎020 7255 0500; info@cilip.org.uk; www.cilip.org.uk

Chartered Institute of Marketing (CIM): ☎01628 427500; www.cim.co.uk

College of Radiographers: ☎020 7740 7200; www.sor.org

Faculty of Advocates: ☎0131 226 5071; www.advocates.org.uk; the Scottish lawyers association doesn't have a formal information service which helps members to find jobs abroad but it does maintain close links with other European Bars

General Council of the Bar (The Bar Council): 020 7242 0082; www.barcouncil. org.uk

General Dental Council: ☎020 7887 3800; information@gdc-uk.org; www.gdc-uk.org

General Optical Council: ☎020 7580 3898; goc@optical.org; www.optical.org

Institute of Actuaries: ☎01865 268200; institute@actuaries.org.uk; www. actuaries.org.uk

Institute of Biology: ☎020 7581 8333; www.iob.org; can give members advice/ contacts in Europe

- www.cadremploi.fr: Cadremploi (☎01 45 00 78 70; info@cadremploi.fr) is a career management website with free access for professionals at middle and top management level, used by 600 top recruitment consulting firms which regularly access the site to update their own entries; listings also come from *Le Figaro*, the top newspaper for jobs vacant and several other newspapers
  - www.phosphore.com: is aimed at students and young people and is good for contacts for work and training positions

Institute of Cast Metal Engineers: ☎01527 596100; info@icme.org.uk; www.icme.org.uk

Institute of Chartered Accountants in England & Wales: ☎+44 (0)20 7920 8100; international.affairs@icaew.co.uk; www.icaew.co.uk; Brussels Office ☎+322 230 3272; offers members advice on working within the EU

Institute of Chartered Foresters: ☎0131 225 2705; www.charteredforesters.org

Institute of Chartered Shipbrokers: ☎020 76231111; www.ics.org.uk

Institution of Civil Engineers: ☎020 7222 7722; www.ice.org.uk; also has an international recruitment agency: Thomas Telford Recruitment Consultancy (☎020 7665 2438)

Institute of Marine Engineers: ☎020 7382 2600; www.imarest.org; provides its members with contacts and information through its network of branches throughout Europe

Institution of Materials, Minerals and Mining: ☎0207 451 7300; www.iom3.org

The Institution of Engineering and Technology: ☎01438 313 311; wwwtheiet.org

Institution of Gas Engineers & Managers: ☎01509 282728; www.igem.org.uk

Pharmaceutical Society of Northern Ireland: ☎028 90326927; www.psni.org.uk

The Registrar and Chief Executive, United Kingdom Central Council for Nursing, Midwifery and Health Visiting: ☎020 7637 7181; www.ukcc.org.uk

Royal Aeronautical Society: ☎020 7670 4300; www.raes-hfg.com

Royal College of Speech and Language Therapy: ☎020 7378 1200; www.rcslt.org

Royal College of Veterinary Surgeons: ☎020 7222 2001; admin@rcvs.org.uk www.rcvs.org.uk

Royal Pharmaceutical Society of Great Britain: ☎020 7735 9141; www.rpsgb.org.uk

Royal Town Planning Institute: ☎020 7929 9494; online@rtpi.org.uk; www.rtpi.org.uk

Specialist French publications and websites

If you understand French you can use a range of specialist publications aimed at jobseekers. *Courrier Cadres* is published by APEC (*Association pour l'Emploi des Cadres*; www.apec.asso.fr), a national organisation funded by employers and trade unions for the placement of managers and executives. This publication is for those with *Bac* +4 or the UK/US equivalent (see the section on Education in the chapter Daily life) and is open to foreign job seekers. It is published weekly on Thursdays (price €2.50).

For the hotel and catering trade the French publication *Journal L'Hôtellerie* (☎01 45 48 64 64; lhotellerie@lhotellerie.fr; www.lhotellerie.fr) is published weekly

(€3 for a single issue) and has a large job section while *L'Usine Nouvelle* is for jobs in industry. *L'Etudiant* (www.letudiant.fr) magazine available on newsstands, has job opportunities for the summer vacation.

Employment organisations

Eures

EURES (short for European Employment Services, http://europa.eu.int/eures) is a computerised, pan-European job information network, which has specially trained EURES counsellors. In the UK, Ireland and other European countries, you can access the EURES network from national job centres. Job seekers can use EURES to find out about job vacancies in any member state plus some national background information including living and working conditions and taxation and social security. Advertising vacancies on the EURES network is free for employers, and all types of jobs from unskilled to executive and professional posts appear on the network (a total of about 1,300,000 vacancies are listed at any one time). Jobseekers can upload their CV (résumé) which are searchable by employers.

In France EURES centres are known as L'Espace emploi international (EEIs) (www.emploi-international.org) linked to the ANPE (www.anpe.fr) and the Agence Nationale de l'Accueil des Etrangers et des Migrations (www.anaem.social.fr). Each French region has its own EEI and you can source these on a map on the EEI site. They are not strictly relevant to foreigners wanting to work in France as they deal with French people wanting to work abroad.

Useful contacts

L'Espace emploi international Paris: www.emploi-international.org. The umbrella organisation of the ANPE and ANAEM services. The services are open to French citizens, EU citizens living in France and non-EU citizens living in France with official authorisation. The jobs found on the website don't include unpaid work such as voluntary, internship, au pair and training jobs for students. The website has a contact for each region of France

Overseas Placing Unit: Jobcentre Plus; www.jobcentreplus.gov.uk and www.europa.eu.int/jobs/eures. Central coordinating office of EURES, the European Employment Services Network. In the UK, in addition to the above websites, details of vacancies for work overseas including France are available from local job centres and via the Employment Service Direct enquiry line ☎0845 6060 234.

UK-based employment organisations

There are some employment agencies in the UK which specialise in finding overseas jobs for clients. In many cases these agencies deal with a specific sector e.g. electronics, secretarial, medical, etc. They tend to recruit only qualified and experienced staff, and deal mainly with regions of the world, e.g. the Middle East where there is still a shortage of home-grown specialists, rather than Europe. Most recruitment consultants are retained and paid by employers to fill specific vacancies and don't search on behalf of employees using them. An exception is agencies that recruit bilingual staff, mainly secretaries and personal assistants, and also receptionists, customer services employees, administrators, interpreters and translators, for France.

TIP

The ANPE has a specialised service for those with higher qualifications (but not necessarily graduates) seeking managerial posts. These are dealt with by the 18 or so ANPE *points relais cadres* located around France and there is a weekly guide of executive vacancies called *Atout Cadres* from the same organisation.

Useful addresses

Recruitment and Employment Federation: www.rec.uk.com. Can help locate employers by job sector

UK-based Sheila Burgess International: www.sheilaburgessint.fr; ☎01 44 63 02 57. In business over 12 years. Specialises in multilingual secretaries and personal assistants

French employment organisations

◼ Commercial employment agencies

Legal restrictions mean that French private employment agencies, as in Germany, are prohibited as such and function only as temporary employment bureaux (*agences de travail temporaire/agence d'intérim*) and most are chains with branches in several cities. The addresses of some major ones in Paris are listed in the section 'Temporary work'.

◼ The French National Employment Service

The *Agence Nationale pour l'Emploi* (ANPE) is the national government job service of France and as such has the monopoly on placements particularly in the Alps. The ANPE provides services to both job seekers and companies; it assists unemployed people in registering for social benefits and gives advice on career development and related issues. About 120,000 vacancies are registered daily on www.anpe. fr. The Agency has offices all over the country and 41 in Paris, among which four are specialised in professional and other executive level job opportunities (e.g. Espace Cadres Saint-Lazare, Paris; ☎01 53 21 80 50). Although most offices run a general drop-in, some specialise in particular areas of employment such as hotel and catering, or tourism. For instance ANPE (Albertville; ☎04 79 32 20 03; ale. albertville@anpe.fr) runs a special department for hotels and thermal institutions in the French Alps. In Paris ANPE also deal with *demandes d'emploi* (jobs wanted) through advertisements in *Fig-Eco* (a supplement of *Le Figaro*) for a journalist, graphic designer and a bilingual secretary. Yet other ANPEs are known as *antennes saisonnières* which are open during the summer or winter only. For example in the Alps there are extra winter bureaus (*antennes saisonnières hiver*) open from October/November to the end of February in most of the main resorts. In Annecy there is a year-round bureau (☎04 50 51 00 42). For further details of winter bureaus see the section 'Temporary work' (Ski resorts).

Useful addresses – ANPE points relais cadres

Alsace: Espace Cadre, 8 rue Adolphe Seyboth, 67000 Strasbourg; ☎03 88 15 46 60; esp-cadres-strasbourg@anpe.fr

Aquitaine: Ale Bordeaux Cadres, 1 Terrasse Front du Médoc, Tour 2000, 33076 Bordeaux; ☎05 56 90 85 10

Marseille: Marseille Cadres, 7–9 rue Jean Mermoz–13272 Marseille Cedex 08; ☎04 91 81 73 82

Midi-Pyrenees: Espace Cadres, 6A Place Occitane, B.P. 602, 31001 Toulouse; ☎05 61 12 59 59; esp-cadres-toulouse@anpe.fr

Orleans: Espace Cadre ANPE: 31 Avenue de Paris 45000, Orleans; ☎02 38 77 86 92

Nord/Pas-de-Calais: Lille Cadres, 12 rue de Jemmapes, Boite Postale 69, 50009 Lille; ☎03 28 52 20 20ale.espcadlille@anpe.fr

Rhônes Alpes: Espace Cadres, 89 rue General Mangin, 38030 Grenoble; ☎04 76 40 76 72

Rhônes Alpes: Espace Cadres Lyon, 7 rue Louis Guerin, 69628 Villeurbanne; ☎04 72 69 09 20

EU nationals from outside France are entitled to use the ANPE on equal terms with French nationals. In practice, ANPEs are primarily devoted to finding jobs for French nationals and can be difficult to negotiate for foreign job seekers. Of course, the staff are largely trained to provide help for those with French qualifications on the French job market, nevertheless resources such as career counselling are available to all through outsourced companies. Needless to say the greater your ability to communicate in French the better your chances generally of a positive response.

Offices don't usually deal with individuals by letter so you will usually have to apply in person. ANPEs are listed in the French Yellow Pages for each area under the classification *Administrations du Travail et de l'Emploi*. A list of ANPEs throughout France is available from the main office at ANPE, 4 rue Galilée, 93198 Noisy-le-Grand Cedex (tel: 01 49 31 74 00; www.anpe.fr) which also operates EURES (see above).

Embassies and consulates

Embassies and consulates won't assist members of the public to find jobs. Not only are they unable to deal with the amount of administration involved, but they are not keen to encourage foreign workers to take jobs away from nationals. However, they can be the source of some useful addresses. It may be worth contacting them by post, or in person, to see if they can assist. Most of them produce a few pages of information for foreigners about living and working in France which can be downloaded from their website. The French Consulate has information about employment in France and the British and American representations in France generally have some information for their citizens resident in France.

Chambers of commerce

Chambers of commerce serve the interests of businesses trading and they don't operate as employment agencies. However they may be able to offer background information which can be helpful in the job-hunting process; moreover, the French Consulate does propose the appropriate national Chamber of Commerce as a source of local information.

Perhaps the best way in which the national Chambers of Commerce can assist is by providing the names and addresses of member companies. Many of these companies are large organisations, which may well have current or prospective vacancies. Thus, it's worth enquiring on the off chance that there is a job available at the time at which you apply.

In addition to the national Chambers of Commerce there are local and regional branches all over France, in virtually every city and town. Many of these enthusiastically support local industries and companies and, on request, will supply details of them. It is unlikely, however, that they will know of actual, current vacancies, although information you can obtain from them could be a good pointer as to which areas to look at and which companies to approach. The addresses of the main Chambers of Commerce in each French region are listed later on in this chapter.

Useful addresses

Chambre de Commerce Française de Grande-Bretagne: ☎020 7304 7071; njoyce@ccfgb.co.uk; produces useful publications including: *Setting up a Business in France* (£16) and *Making Yourself at Home in France* (£20)

Franco-British Chamber of Commerce & Industry: ☎01 53 30 81 30; www.francobritishchambers.com

Assemblée Permanente des Chambres de Commerce et d'Industrie: ☎01 40 69 37 00; www.acfi.cci.fr

Placing employment wanted adverts

When seeking a job overseas it isn't always sufficient to rely solely on advertised jobs as a source of prospective employment. It can often be more successful to attract the attention of potential employers who may have a vacancy. Many employers are impressed by someone taking the initiative to make a direct application, and, of course, in some cases it is possible that an employer may need just the service which you are offering.

One of the easiest ways of canvassing potential employers is to place a employment wanted request (*demande d'emploi*) in the French press. Obviously, the advertisement should be written in French and a telephone/fax number for replies provided if possible. You can place advertisements directly with a French newspaper but if you are in the UK it's easier to use an advertisement agency. Your advert should highlight your skills and languages and request employment in France.

FACT

■ Non-commercial international organisations provide opportunities for transfers abroad.

Company/organisation transfers

The alternative to finding work in France by applying direct or in person, is to find

 In the UK contact *Mercury Publicity Ltd* (☎020 7611 1900): takes advertising for *Le Figaro* and French regional newspapers.

a position within a company or organisation in your home country which offers the possibility of being transferred to France. Currently, few companies will guarantee staff that they will be posted to a specific country after a certain period. However, both the request and the practice are becoming more common as companies take advantage of the single European market for goods and services by expanding their operations elsewhere in the EU.

The following types of companies and organisations can offer the option of working in France.

■ French companies operating in the UK

Over the past decade, a number of French companies have entered the UK market, often quite aggressively. For example, many food producers and distributors, e.g. Yoplaît, and also financial institutions, e.g. Crédit Lyonnais and the Société Générale Merchant Bank and AXA insurance. However, check first that the company you target is a French company. For example, French car manufacturers are very active in the UK market but the importing companies are essentially British, not French.

Paris financial district

◼ British companies operating in France

Despite criticism that UK companies have been slow to enter the French market, a number of British companies are now actively involved in France, including such household names as Tesco, Glaxo, Wimpey, United Biscuits, Courtaulds, KP Foods, BP and ICI. Many more UK companies including smaller ones are following the lead provided by the big companies. In the finance area, British banks such as Barclays or the Woolwich already have a significant presence in France. Altogether about 2,000 British companies have set up in France.

◼ International companies

An increasing number of multinational companies have branches and subsidiaries all round the world, and these can offer possible employment prospects. For example, Nestlé is essentially a Swiss company, but it has major involvements in both the UK and France. Many addresses of companies of a similar status can be obtained through the respective Chambers of Commerce, as discussed earlier. The company names may be different in each country and often a certain amount of detective work is necessary to discover the extent of a particular company's operation in the UK and France and the consequent potential for later being posted elsewhere.

 A useful publication in this respect is *Who Owns Whom* (see http://solutions.dnb.com/wow), which is available in main reference libraries and provides the names of British companies with French subsidiaries.

Few companies will recruit exclusively with a transfer in mind, but you can always discuss your aims at interview; senior staff will be in a much stronger position to dictate their requirements.

■ Worldwide organisations

Alternatively, there are jobs with worldwide organisations, such as the United Nations, UNESCO, the World Bank and UNICEF, all of which have offices in Paris. Transfers within worldwide organisations are available for those with suitable qualifications. Further details are given in the section on Permanent work. Where a posting abroad is actually made, it will usually include many financial increments and perks; salaries are often negotiated at the highest international rates, higher than either the UK or French equivalents. Fringe benefits may include relocation assistance, subsidised mortgages, accommodation, school fees, health insurance and pension plans.

Methods of application

Unsolicited applications

You may wish to compile a list of companies likely to have a use for your particular skills and/or qualifications. Possible sources of addresses include the Chambers of Commerce yearbooks, the French Yellow Pages (www.pagesjaunes.fr) and various professional and industrial directories and websites.

Unless you have a personal contact, applications should be addressed 'For the Attention of the Head of Personnel' (*A L'Attention du Chef du Personnel*), or the Head of Department (*Chef de Service*) or in the case of a multinational, Head of International Human Resources, and if you can discover their name by means of a quick telephone call or internet search, so much the better. It is now standard to send your application by email, including your CV (résumé). If necessary both can be professionally translated into French. A professional agency such as the Institute of Translation and Interpreting in the UK (☎01908 325 250; info@iti.org.uk; www.iti.org.uk) will charge in the region of £80 or €100 for one thousand words, but obviously costs vary depending on what is involved. In view of the high cost of professional translations, it's worth checking other possibilities, e.g. local colleges of further education or universities, for this purpose.

Note that such applications need not be restricted to companies, you can also apply to recruitment agencies (*cabinets de recrutement*) and search consultants (*cabinets de chasseurs de têtes*). You can also contact international recruitment agencies in your own country.

A directory of some of France's largest organisations and most important companies is provided at the end of this chapter and can be a starting point from which to begin targeting potential employers. You can also attend trade fairs in your own country or in France to collect the addresses and particulars of potential employers.

Personal visits

If you are in France and looking for a job, you may want to make enquiries in person as to the availability of employment. This involves not only responding to jobs advertised but also canvassing potential employers on the spot. Although usually an exhausting business entailing much wear and tear to shoe leather and the human spirit, it may still be possible to obtain a job offer this way. After all, all you need is one positive response so this technique is worth a try.

Before making an approach to a potential employer decide how you can best sell your skills, talents or experience. For example, those looking for casual work in the tourist industry could suggest that as native English-speakers they can improve the service that, for example, a hotelier or restaurateur offers to English-speaking customers.

When making impromptu personal visits to potential employers, ensure that you have a stock of CVs (résumés) with you and that you give a contact telephone number. If you hear nothing for a few days follow up your visit with a telephone call. Of course, you may be lucky enough to be telephoned by the employer, or in exceptional cases, offered a job on the spot.

Form, content and style of applications

In the vast majority of cases, no matter how one finds out about a job, it will be necessary to write a cover letter as part of your application. You should use the cover letter to explain why you are applying for the job and how you meet with requirements. The letter would usually be a single page, written formally and succinctly. It needs to be tailored to the company/type of job for which you are applying, and appear individually prepared. Clearly state your reasons for application and the relevance of your qualifications and experience to the employment available. Abbreviations should be avoided. It may be helpful to get the advice of a French friend or an advisor at the ANPE to help you produce an effective style in French, rather than simply getting translated what you would usually write in English.

Curriculum vitae (résumé)

A solid, well-formatted CV/résumé is essential. In France, education tends to be put first but there are now no hard and fast rules and most people tailor their CV according to their particular experience and the job they are applying for. Obviously the main areas are personal information, education and professional experience, with a personal interests/miscellaneous section at the end. Note that for a potential French employer the CV should be modified to remove any abbreviations and explain any qualifications, etc. which could confuse a foreign reader. Generally, it's better to provide a succinct CV that you may consider too short, rather than one which is comprehensive but which the employer will think overlong.

Interview procedure

If you are offered an interview, remember that first impressions and appearances are crucial. Check in advance that the travel costs will be covered, otherwise you will have to decide if the cost of the trip is justified. French employers tend not to offer interviews lightly, so the invitation to attend one is a positive sign. Those selected for interview tend to have been already short-listed.

The importance of the first impressions can't be stressed enough. As one expert put it 'the interview begins the moment you walk through the door' so it will be up to you to create the right ones based on your knowledge of the company to date. The interview may be with just one person or with a panel. It may be formal or informal depending on the job applied for and the style of the person interviewing you.

Obviously an interview in France will be as much a test of language ability as job

ability. This applies for more basic jobs as well as for executive positions. In particular, try to find out the correct pronunciation of names and titles beforehand. Styles have changed a great deal over the last few years and it's becoming less uncommon for people to call each other by their first names, even when they first meet in an interview situation, although the person interviewing you will indicate how they want you to address them. You can always fall back on '*Monsieur*' and '*Madame*'. Remember to use the more formal '*vous*' form of address throughout the interview unless, which is unlikely, an interviewer addresses you in the '*tu*' form.

◼ TEMPORARY WORK

This section deals with seasonal jobs in agriculture, childcare, tourism, as well as a variety of possibilities temping through agencies. Temping is something you might have to do before you find a long-term post. Teaching English as a foreign language is dealt with under 'Permanent work' although temporary posts are also available in this field.

Agriculture

Although the number of people working in agriculture is declining in France, there are still more livelihoods tied up with the land than in other, highly developed European countries. There are still thousands of temporary agricultural jobs throughout the year

Grape picking in France

and this can be considered a major source of temporary work. Some harvests are traditionally the preserve of itinerant workers from other Mediterranean countries: grape picking (*les vendanges*) is often done by Spanish, Portuguese and Moroccan teams who return to the same vineyards year after year. However, human pickers have given way to mechanical pickers in some areas.

Nearly every region of France has its agricultural specialities. The vineyards reach from the salt marshes of the Camargue in the south, north to the Loire and Champagne. There are luscious fruits including melons and peaches produced by the Mediterranean climate of Languedoc and apples and plums in the more temperate Dordogne. Other regions where the land is remarkably productive include the great Rhône valley which is a huge fruit and vegetable region, while the south-west around Bordeaux is where maize growing is concentrated. The Loire Valley, the Paris Basin, Brittany and Normandy are other areas with high volumes of agricultural produce. These are just some of the possibilities for harvest work, which can begin as early as mid-May in the south of France for strawberries to late October for grape picking. Jobs are found most easily by visiting the local ANPE or by going round knocking on doors. It is an easier task if you have your own transport.

TIP

■ Conditions of work vary, but many workers are expected to provide their own accommodation and food, so a tent is essential.

Useful organisations for casual farm work

Appellation contrôlée: based in the Netherlands, AC arranges for applicants to spend two weeks grape picking or working on a fruit harvest in the southern part of France. For further details see www.apcon.nl or email project2@bart.nl. Possibility for friends to work together on the same farm

Association des Faucheurs a la Faulx de Pont Salomon: the French association of scything by hand offers courses in this art, which is still used for clearing ground of undergrowth and for cutting on steep sloping fields; http://asso.faucheurs.free.fr

Sésame: a non-profit making association founded by French agricultural organisations and based in Paris (☎01 40 54 07 08; www.agriplanete.com). Sésame arranges for agricultural *stagiares* (trainees) to work on farms of all types, including fish farms, around France. They may also have some seasonal work such as grape picking but this isn't their main function. Length of stay varies depending on programme: Agri-découverte (up to three months), Agri-culture (six months to a year) and Agri-Echange (two to twelve months). Incoming trainees must have a basic knowledge of French as most French agriculturists don't speak foreign languages. Salaried trainees are paid the equivalent of the minimum legal salary (SMIC) in France from which the cost of meals and accommodation are deducted

WWOOF: this is a potentially useful (apart from the CDIJs and ANPEs) organic farm organisation whose members offer bed and board at a member farm in return for voluntary farm work. Over 250 organic farms, smallholdings and gardens in France belong to WWOOF. Visit www.wwoof.org where you can also see the types of farms to visit. Membership is €15 to download the addresses from the internet

SARL Anjou Myrtilles: ☎02 41 52 83 81; www.anjoumyrtilles.fr; Anjou Myrtilles employs approximately 450 people during the picking season (May to August) to pick and pack blueberries and other soft fruits. Campsite nearby

SCA soldive: ☎05 49 22 40 63; soldive@wanadoo.fr; the complete antithesis of WWOOF, this outfit employs over 1,000 farm labourers to harvest melons, plus tractor drivers and farm machinery mechanics. Work is between August and October

Au pair and nannying

Despite its potential drawbacks (the parents, the children, the sexploitation), being an au pair/nanny/mother's help, officially known in France as *stagiare aide-familiale* is probably still the best way (perhaps the only way if you are an American – see Karalyn Monteil's story earlier in this chapter) of learning the language and getting to know the country and is a good starting point for going to live and work there on a longer-term basis later. In Paris particularly there is no problem finding posts: there are dozens of agencies; also CIJ offices, and sometimes ANPEs have lists of families looking for live-in helpers. By arranging a job on the spot you get a chance to meet the family, inspect the accommodation and its proximity to amenities (isolation in the suburbs isn't ideal), and more importantly the children (and vice versa) before committing yourself.

Working hours are a five and half hours per day, Monday to Saturday with one full day off and no more than three nights babysitting per week. Although few au pairs actually manage to keep these hours, if the family is a good one and takes a genuine interest in the au pair and includes them in family life, it can still work out extremely well for both parties. Anyone who really wants to concentrate on studies in French should ask to be a demi-pair. This entails only 12 hours work per week in return for room and board but not pocket money. Au pair work should include only light household duties and normal childcare. An au pair isn't obliged to care for children with special needs or disabilities. Free meals and single accommodation should be provided even outside normal duty hours. An au pair should attend a language course as this is considered one of the main objectives of the arrangement. The salary is tied into the SMIC (see 'Employment laws') and is currently about €1,280 per month (152 hours' work).

There are also regulations for the family employing you: by law, they are obliged to pay monthly social security contributions to the local URSSAF office to cover the cost of emergency or routine medical treatment. Au pairs in or near Paris should get a monthly *carte orange* travel pass which is valid for most public transport.

It is also possible to find families who will offer a more informal arrangement such as several evenings of babysitting a week in return for board and lodging. Babysitting agencies in Paris you might be able to sign up with are listed below.

Although the majority of French families will expect their child helper to be female, the concept of the male au pair is spreading, so men should not be put off from answering advertisements if they are good with children. You should also put up your own: one male au pair got his job by putting a job wanted notice on the upstairs notice board of the British Church (just off the rue de Faubourg St Honoré) in Paris.

Au pair agencies

Note that agencies in France charge both applicants and families for their services; in the case of applicants charges can be as high as €120.

Accueil Familial des Jeunes Etrangérs (AFJE): ☎01 42 22 50 34; www.afje-paris.org

Accueil International: ☎01 39 73 04 98; au-pair@easynet.fr; www.accueil-international.com

Agence Nurse Au Pair Placement (NAPP): ☎01 45 00 33 88; nappsarl@aol.com

Anglo Nannies: ☎04 42 71 99 18; www.anglonannies.com

APITU: ☎02 99 58 22 36; www.apitu.com

Association Families Jeunesse: ☎04 93 82 28 22; info@afj-aupair.org; www.afj-aupair.org

Association Oliver Twist: ☎05 57 26 93 26; www.oliver-twist.fr

Au-Pair Azur: ☎06 61 98 81 81; www.aupairazur.com

Butterfly & Papillon: ☎04 50 46 08 33/04 50 67 01 33; www.aupairusa.multimania.com/www.butterfly-papillon.com

Euro Job France au Pairs: ☎05 46 23 99 88; www.eurojob.fr; places au pairs in Paris and other large cities in France

Euro Pair Services: ☎01 43 29 80 01; www.europairservices.com; places au pairs in Paris and other large cities in France

France Monde Au Pair–Eurojobs: ☎05 46 23 99 88; www.eurojob.fr

French American Center: ☎04 67 92 30 66; www.frenchamericancenter.com

Good Morning Europe: ☎01 44 87 01 22; www.good-morning-europe.com

Inter-Séjours: ☎01 47 63 06 81; fwww.asso.interséjours.free.fr; charges registration fee of about €130

Institute Euro-Provence: ☎04 91 33 90 60; www.europrovence.org; largest au pair agency in southern France

Interexchange.org: can place American au pairs in France

Les Enfants d'Abord: ☎04 72 73 11 46; www.lesenfantsdabord.org

Mary Poppins: ☎04 76 75 57 33; www.perso.wanadoo.fr/marypoppins.au pair; mostly in the Rhône-Alps area, particularly the city of Grenoble

Perlangues: ☎01 60 77 35 00; www.perlangues.com

Séjours Internationaux Linguistiques et Culturels (SILC): ☎0825 161 300/05 45 97 41 63; www.silc.fr; fee in France €236.

Soames Paris Nannies: ☎01 64 78 37 98; www.soamesparisnannies.com

Babysitting agencies in Paris

Ababa: ☎01 45 49 46 46

Allo Maman Poule: ☎01 45 20 96 96

Allo Service Mamane: ☎01 42 67 99 37

BabyChou: ☎01 43 13 33 23; contacts@babychou.com; www.babychou.com

Babysitting Service: ☎01 46 37 51 24

Home Service: ☎01 42 82 05 04

Kid Service: ☎01 47 66 00 52

123 Soleil: ☎01 43 57 44 53

Pro Sitting: ☎01 44 37 91 11; www.prositting.com

Business and industry

Private employment agencies

As already stated, French regulations stipulate that commercial employment agencies in France only deal with temporary work. They can offer a range of work in offices, shops and industry and you have to register with them in person. Among the largest are Manpower, Bis and France Select. The biggest in France is Adecco which has about 1,000 branches and covers more than 40 sectors of employment.

Agencies advertise in newspapers and weekly reviews and others may be found by looking in the *pages jaunes* (www.pagesjaunes.fr) under *agences d'intérim/ personnel intérimaire/travail temporaire*. There are dozens listed for the Paris region.

Note that employment agencies are required by law to request a social security number (*un sécu*), which means that you can only get employment through them if you have already worked legally in France. Some working travellers claim that they have managed to get on an agency's books without one, especially in Paris. Possibile jobs include: market research (*entreprises en recherche de marché*) for international companies, leaflet distribution (*distributeurs en publicité*), door-to-door seller (*vendeur porte à porte*), all of which usually require less adept French, probably the ability to learn a specialised terminology or a salesperson's or researcher's patter off by heart. If your French isn't up to even these jobs then you could try others where French is hardly required at all: domestic or office cleaner for contract cleaning firms (*entreprises de nettoyage*), house removals (*démenagement*), or even night security (*surveillance de nuit/agent de surveillance*).

Private employment agencies

Adecco: www.adecco.fr
Adia: ☎01 47 16 11 02; www.adia.fr
Eric Soutou: ☎01 42 61 42 61
Euristt: Groupe CRIT www.groupe-crit.com
GR Interim Temp agency: www.group-gr.com
Hays Personnel Interim: www.hays.fr
Hôtesse Secretaires: ☎01 42 96 34 80
Manpower (for Executives): Manpower Paris Cadres (Rive Gauche); ☎01 45 38 74 74; www.manpower.fr
Progressis: ☎01 44 55 05 45; www.progressis.com;Agency for secretaries and assistants
Vediorbis: www.vediorbis.com

Teaching English

Although this category of work is dealt with in greater detail in the 'Permanent work' section (see below), English teaching can also be considered a useful source of temporary employment. Once scornful of the mere suggestion of a need to speak English, the French have realised that for business and particularly for science and technology they can't do without it. Hence the spurt of language learning in schools which means that 65% of under-35s now claim to have a working knowledge of English, and a plethora of English language institutes, particularly in Paris and big cities. Many companies provide their employees with free language courses and thus business people provide the main source of clients. The clients are taught in schools or at their place of work. Although the majority of language schools prefer people to work for a year or longer contract, some companies, notably Berlitz have a high turnover of staff in their dozen or so Paris schools owing to the pressure many staff find themselves under. Another alternative is offering private language tuition. The going rate is €20–€30 (about £15–£20 an hour) but you can get more.

In some of the regions there are opportunities to teach English as a large number of *mairies* and Chambers of Commerce (*Chambres de Commerce et d'Industrie* or *CCIs*) have their own language study centres (*centres d'etude des langues*). It is also possible to exchange language tuition in return for a room and keep. Another possibility is telephone teaching. The pay rates are about the same as for private language tuition.

Americans may find that English teaching is one area where a long-stay visa isn't difficult to obtain as American English is considered fashionable and desirable in some circles. Note that many language institutes expect to hire foreigners already resident in France and with the appropriate working papers. Agencies advertise in newspapers and weekly reviews (www.fusac.fr) and others may be found by looking in the *pages jaunes* under *agences d'intérim/personnel intérimaire/travail temporaire*. There are dozens listed in the several directories for the Paris region.

Tourism

As one of the great tourist destinations of Europe, France has plenty of related temporary work to offer. This section covers most of them including Euro Disney and the adjacent Parc Walt Disney Studios, hotels and catering, holiday centres and campsites, ski resorts and holiday boats. Of course work in tourism need not be temporary; those interested in making a career in tourism will find that most big companies, e.g. Club Med, have career development opportunities.

Disneyland Paris and Walt Disney Studios

◼ Disneyland Paris

Despite initial financial catastrophes, which made pundits predict the folding of EuroDisney by 1994, it celebrated its 15th birthday in 2007. The enormous complex that comprises Disneyland Paris, 30km east of Paris, has nearly 6,000 hotel rooms, and an entertainment centre as well as the huge theme park. Overall about 12,000 employees service the complex during peak season on a mixture of long-term and short-term contracts. Seasonal positions are from March to October with a minimum availability of mid-June to the end of August. 'Cast members' (Disneyspeak for staff) must all have a minimum of conversational French and preferably a third European language. A nationality quota is operated to ensure that no one nationality predominates. The majority of jobs are in food and beverage, housekeeping, merchandising and custodial departments.

The minimum period of work in summer is two months, and your ability to speak French will be tested at interview. Monthly gross wages start at about €1,280 for a 35-hour week and there are deductions for social security. There is some staff housing

 Disneyland Paris: Service de Recruitment Casting (☎01 49 31 19 99; dip. casting.fr@Disney.com; www.disneylandparis.com.

Walt Disney Studios: further details from ANPE Project Eurodisney, 20 rue Pierre Mendès, 77200 Torcy, France; www.anpe.fr.

TIP

For companies providing campsites and mobile home sites see France Guide, the official French tourism website (www.franceguide.com) and Hôtellerie de plein air en France (www.site.ifrance.com/camping-car/campings.html), with useful links to campsites and caravanning in France.

on site but not enough to go round. Assistance is given with finding accommodation, and travel costs to and from Paris are reimbursed on contract completion.

Walt Disney Studios

The newest French theme park opened in March 2002 at the Disneyland Paris resort complex at Marne-la-Valléee east of Paris. It is aimed at older children and adults with attractions such as film studios, live stunts, interactive animation and a roller coaster with a rock 'n' roll theme. The Walt Disney Studios theme park has six hotels with 5,000 rooms. Recruitment for 3,500 staff for departments including retail, bookings, swimming instruction, dining room, kitchen, hotel, etc. began in 2001. Basic salary is about €1,280 with more paid to experienced and qualified staff.

Campsites and holiday centres

One of the favourite French summer pastimes seems to be camping, especially *en famille*. At the last count there were over 16,000 campsites in France, about 2,000 of which were small, basic, privately-run sites owned by families, farmers and even expatriates. Campsites are graded according to the facilities provided and there is an official rating system. At the top end, four-star sites have a range of amenities from tennis courts to indoor recreation areas. Some of the larger sites are run by holiday companies and are popular with the British, Dutch, Germans, etc.

British campsite companies in France

A number of British companies also run sites in France and employ summer staff as campsite couriers who welcome the holidaymakers on arrival, clean the mobile homes on changeover day and carry out general maintenance duties. Although many companies recruit students and those having a gap year between school and university, it's possible for older people to be recruited. NSS Riviera Holidays of Hull states a preference for mature, active couples aged 40+ with a pension or private income. You have to be prepared to work a spring, summer or autumn for nil payment but with many perks including no charge accommodation and facilities, plenty of free time and help with ferry crossing and insurance.

Les colonies de vacances

Outdoor activity centres in France may be commercially run, or *colonies de vacances* (summer camps for children or families), run by the French government or French non-profit organisations. There is a non-profit association called UCPA which runs over 50 adult (age 18–39) activity centres which need a range of staff including qualified sports instructors, bar and catering staff, nurses and possibly even language teachers. Some British companies, such as Discover, PGL and Acorn Adventure, operate summer activity camps for children and adults and are another possible source of temporary work.

Opportunities for Americans

The Alliance Abroad Group Inc. (☎1 8886 ABROAD; www.allianceabroad.com) offers jobs for three months in campsites and hotels or restaurants in Paris, Bordeaux, Tours, Montpellier, Nice and Toulon, 39–42 hours per week. Meals and accommodation are provided free by the employer plus €180 pocket money per month. Placement includes 15 hours of French language tuition.

Campsite and mobile home operators

Camping Club Mar Estang: ☎04 68 80 35 53; marestang@wanadoo.fr; www.marestang.com. Three-star, French-run site needs staff for seasonal contracts of two to six months. Jobs include receptionists, bar staff, swimming pool attendants, restaurant and kitchen staff, entertainment team, kids and teenager club staff, ice-cream attendant, ground and security staff, maids and a disc jockey. Salary of €1000–€1500 depending on schedule. Kitchen and pool staff need relevant qualifications. Apply to Laurent Raspaud

Carisma Holidays: ☎01923 287339; personnel@carisma.co.uk; www.carisma.co.uk; contact Chris Simpson; employs site managers, full season and high-season couriers for campsite/mobile home holidays on the west coast of France. Period of vacancies 1 May to late September or for high season in July and August. Up to €150 per week plus tips. Full training given on site

Chateau de L'Eperviere: ☎03 85 941 690; domaine-de-leperviere@wanadoo.fr; www.domaine-eperviere.com; needs a joiner, plumber and a manual labourer for a maximum of six months from early in April to late September also students to work on the campsite. Duties include bartending, waiting tables and reception. Must speak French and maintenance staff must have a driving licence

Haven Europe: ☎01422 203287; www.havenholidays.com. A self-drive, mobile home and camping company. Courier staff and children's couriers are employed at their French campsites from March to September

Matthews Holidays: ☎01 48 32 84 04; www.matthewsfrance.co.uk; couriers and campsite representatives are taken on from April to May to maintain and clean mobile homes at a site in western France; knowledge of French and aged at least 21; €160 per 35-hour, six-day week

NSS Riviera Holidays: ☎04 93 85 93 38; www.nssrivieraholidays.co.uk; prefer mature couples aged 45+ who are active, to work in a complex of 30 chalets, cottages and mobile homes on a four-star holiday village between St Tropez and Cannes doing DIY to a high standard three days a week in return for free accommodation, electricity and gas

Supersites (Canvas Holidays): ☎01383 629018; recruitment@canvasholidays.co.uk; www.gvnrecruitment.com or www.chooseacottage.co.uk; employs campsite couriers and children's couriers (must have formal childcare experience). Positions from March to October. Couples welcome

Vendée Loisirs Vacances: ☎02 51 58 04 02; v.l.v@wanadoo.fr; www.vlv.fr; job for two friends or a couple to welcome and check out guests and clean mobile homes

Activity holiday centres

Acorn Venture Ltd. ☎0870 121 99 54; personnel@acorn-venture.com; www.acorn-venture.com. Adventure holiday company offering group multi-activity holidays in Europe including two centres in France in the Ardèche and on the coast at Narbonne. Needs instructors with relevant qualifications and a qualified nurse plus catering, management and representative staff

Carisma Holidays: ☎01923 287339; beach site managers. For more details see Campsite operators above

Bombard Balloon Adventures: ☎03 80 26 63 30. This is an adventure centre that employs hot-air balloon ground crew for the season May to October. Americans can apply to the US head office (www.bombardsociety.com/jobs)

FACT

■ Jobs with French-run campsites and centres are more likely to help you integrate with the French, but all may give you the time to look around and arrange something more permanent.

Centre d'Echanges Internationaux: www.cei-frenchcentre.com; employs instructors in July and August to teach sports, dancing, music, crafts, etc. in international holiday centres. Pay of about €300 per month plus board and lodging. Applicants must speak French

Centre de Voile l'Aber-Wrac'h: ☎02 98 04 90 64; CVL@wanadoo.fr; http://pagesperso-orange.fr/www..perso.wanadoo.fr/CVL; sailing instructors and sailing camp leaders for Brittany sailing centre during July and August. Pay is €150 weekly plus board and lodging. Must be qualified

Club Méditerranée: ☎0153 35 35 53; www.clubmed.com; recruitment from the UK: Recruit.uk@clubmed.com or ☎08453 67 67 67 Mon to Fri; popularly known as Club Med and constantly revamping its image (which for some observers is firmly stuck in the 1970s) Club Med has 100 leisure villages in 40 countries, 12 villas, a cruise ship operation and a French tour operator which includes ski resorts. It employs thousands of staff including reps and ski instructors. You should speak a minimum of two languages including French. Its French operation includes seaside and ski side resorts; just over 20 'villages' in total

Discover Ltd: ☎ +44 (0)1833 744 392; www.discover.ltd.uk; Discover's field study and activity centre is in the south of France and employs a general assistant and a cook from 1 April to 1 October

PGL Travel: ☎0870 401 4411; pglpeople@pgl.co.uk, www.pgl.co.uk/people; runs adventure holiday centres throughout France: the Ardèche, the Alps, the Mediterranean coast, etc., and needs domestic staff, leaders, instructors, nurses and drivers between March and the end of September. Staff get pocket money and full board

UCPA: ☎02 04 71 47 93; www.ucpa.com; the national union of sports and activity centres has over 100 venues operated on a seasonal basis: some have both a summer and winter season, but most are for summer only. Each centre caters for 200–300 adults and employs 12–20 qualified sports instructors, music and theatrical events leaders plus catering staff

VFB Holidays Ltd. ☎01452 716 840; www.vfbholidays.co.uk; recruits representatives for the summer season in Corsica. Representatives with at least two seasons experience under their belts to work from April to October. Applicants should be bilingual English/French and a first aid qualification is useful but not essential. Recruitment takes place in January for the following season. Four or five positions available per season

Fédération Unie des Auberges de Jeunesses (FUAJ): ☎01 48 04 70 30; Administration Office; ☎01 44 89 87 27; centre-national@fuaj.org; www.fuaj.org. Produces a guide to 200 youth hostels, which employ hostellers for short periods to work in the kitchen, reception and as sports monitors

Hotels and restaurants

Most people get jobs by asking in person. Wages are at the SMIC rate. It is possible to arrange work in advance from your own country, either by contacting hotels directly (proprietors' names and email addresses can be obtained from a tourist guide) or through the handful of agencies such as the UK Overseas Handling agency (see below). Alternatively, *The Directory of Summer Jobs Abroad* (Vacation Work, Richmond) is an annual publication with lists of employers and details of their precise terms and requirements.

FACT

■ Hotels and restaurants are probably the easiest places to find temporary work, especially on the spot if you choose a thriving tourist region in high season.

A snow machine working in a ski resort

A good website for hotel jobs is www.lhotellerie.fr which gives details of jobs in the hotel sector throughout France, searchable by geographical region. The agency Selectis (☎01 40 05 00 50; selectis@restoemploi.com) recruits for more than 200 employers in Paris (restaurants, hotels, night clubs, cafés and brasseries) while the ANPE in Nice has a specialised *hôtellerie* section (☎04 93 97 90 00; ale.nice-hotellerie@anpe.fr) which handles vacancies in the whole region.

Ski resorts

There are hundreds if not thousands of possibilities for those looking for temporary work in the Alps. You can either work for the French, in which case you will need to speak the language. You will also receive a reasonable wage based on the French statutory minimum. The disadvantage is that in some cases you would have to find your own accommodation. Alternatively, you can work for a British company, receive only pocket money and free board and lodging, look after British punters and learn less about the French, but a lot about skiing. The types of job available working for the French include all types of hotel, catering and bar jobs, nightclub coat check, night watchman, cleaners, letting agency receptionists for self-catering apartments and ski shop assistants. There has been a problem with British ski instructor qualifications being accepted in France, unless British qualified instructors pass a very competitive French exam the *equivalence* which involves a slalom against the clock. Even so with too little work all the time for all the instructors, work is by no means guaranteed.

If you hold professional qualifications in hotel catering or tourism, you could try the ANPE in Albertville (☎ 04 79 37 87 80) which has a centralised placement service for vacancies in: Morzine, Avoriaz, La Clusaz, Chamonix, Megève, St-Jean-de-Maurienne,

> ## Tamsin Williams spent the winter of 2006/7 in Morzine and is back there for 2007/8
>
> I'd been on holiday there and I knew it had an English support network. It's good for someone who doesn't speak good French. I went out there for snowboarding and just decided to grab work as I could. I met someone who had a niche in cleaning chalets. There's a lot of info on the net for younger people who want to find work, 18–24 holidays, but at the same time there are a lot of people who've been out there doing the season for 15 years or more. There's work available doing transfers, kitchens, changeovers and even shop work. A lot of English have set up there. I stayed for four or five months but some people I met there stay out there the whole year, do building work in the summer and use the winter to board. There's a whole age range.
>
> You can find a lot of contacts through forums to help find places to live. You don't need much documentation. The estate agents took our passport details and we paid a deposit and paid for the electricity when we left. We had a two-bedroom apartment with a lounge and a balcony, five minutes by bus from the slopes. It cost us €6,000 for five months. If you can prove you're a resident you can get a reduction on ski passes. Morzine's very sociable, good for après. There's the Dixie bar and the Cavern and a couple of trashy Euro clubs. It's easy to get to know people. Café Chaud has French staff with live French rock. Most of the places have English staff and English customers, so when you feel you're cheating too much you go to Café Chaud.

Bourg-St-Maurice, Les Arcs, Tignes, Val d'Isère, Les Deux Alpes, Courchevel, Méribel, Chamrousse and L'Alpe d'Huez. The Albertville ANPE also operates in the summer as well for a different selection of resorts including thermal spas like Thonon-les-Bains and Aix-les-Bains.

Agences locales pour l'emploi (French work bureaus)

Opening periods may vary, except year round offices.

Savoie

Agence d'Aix les Bains: ☎04 79 88 48 49; www.anpe.fr. Open all year
Agence d'Albertville: ☎04 79 32 20 03
Agence de Chambéry: ☎04 79 60 24 70
Agence de Montmélian: ☎04 79 84 78 20

Ski Staff: ☎ 04870 432 8030; work@skistaff.co.uk; www.skistaff.co.uk; all kinds of ski jobs. Specialists in placing all levels of winter staff with English companies in the French Alps. Apply online direct to ski companies or apply to Ski Staff

Antennes saison hiver (Seasonal work bureaus for winter jobs)

Opening dates may vary from year to year.

Bourg Saint Maurice: ☎06 22 85 15 07; www.saisonniers-basin-arcachon.com

Courchevel: ☎04 79 00 01 01; www.mairie-courchevel.com

Les Menuires: ☎04 79 00 23 20; www.mairie-smb.com; open November to the end of April

Méribel: ☎04 79 08 60 01; www.meribel.net. Open from the beginning of October to mid-December

La Plagne: ☎04 79 09 20 85; saisonniers.laplagne@wanadoo.fr; www.saisonniers-basin-arcachon.com; open from the beginning of October to mid-December

Tignes: ☎04 79 40 09 89; www.saisonniers-basin-arcachon.com. Open from beginning October to mid-December

Val d'Isère: tel: 04 79 06 84 78; www.association-vievaldis.org. Open from the beginning of October to the end of March

Val Thorens: ☎04 79 00 08 08; www.mairie-smb.com. Open from the beginning of October to the end of March

A useful publication is Vacation Work's *Working in Ski Resorts Europe and North America* which describes all the main French resorts and how, when and where to get jobs in them. British tour operators who go to France are also listed in this publication as are their precise requirements.

Useful addresses

Club Méditerranée Human resources: ☎08453 67 67 67; recruit.uk@clubmed. com; www.clubmed-jobs.com. Apart from its sun-soaked holiday villages worldwide French company Club Med operates ski resort hotels (also called 'villages') in l'Alpe d'Huez, Les Arcs, Avoriaz, Chamonix, Flaine, Les Deux Alpes, Les Menuires, La Plagne, Tignes Val Claret, Val d'Isère and Val Thorens and employs over a thousand staff for the winter season including 400 chamber staff, 300 waiting staff, 100 maintenance personnel, 30 children's helpers and 40 bar staff. If applying within France, the recruitment is done via the Club Med Centre d'Appel, Service Recrutement; cmcae. recrutement.clubmed.com

Natives.co.uk: ☎08700 463377; jobs@natives.co.uk; www.natives.co.uk. Natives is a seasonal workers' job site with a ski jobs section featuring hundreds of jobs in the Alps with UK tour operators

Pierre & Vacances: ☎01 58 21 58 21; www.pierrevacances.com. Real estate and property company that has hotels and self-catering apartments in many French ski resorts. Applicants must be fluent in French

Snow-Fun: ☎04 79 41 14 76; shop@snowfun.fr; web: www.valfun.com. Snow Fun is a French company with a chain of seven ski shops also ski schools in Val d'Isère and four shops in Tignes. They employ about 50 shop staff and 60 ski instructors in Val d'Isère and 60 shop staff in Tignes

Nanny for a ski company

Another possibility is to approach ski companies, which employ nannies to look after clients' children in the resort. An NNEB qualification or similar is normally required. The following companies offer such positions: Crystal (020 7383 1975; www. shgjobs.co.uk); Esprit (01252 618318; www.esprit-holidays. co.uk); First Choice (0800 169 5692; www.firstchoice4jobs. co.uk); Crystal Finest (020 8541 2223; www.crystalfinest.co.uk) and Ski Beat (01243 780405; www.skibeat.co.uk).

Sogimalp SA: ☎04 50 21 04 98; fax 04 50 21 28 43; www.sogimalp@wanadoo. fr. Estate agent letting apartments in ski resorts; employs seasonal workers (approximately October to mid-May) to deal with clients in the resort

UK Overseas Handling (UKOH) International Recruitment: ☎0870 220 2148; www.ukoh.co.uk; UKOH recruits for French-owned tour operators and accommodation management companies in the Alps and on the coast and clients include Eurogroup. Positions are mainly in the Trois Vallées, including the resorts of Tignes, Val d'Isère, La Plagne and Les Arcs and with Eurogroup, which owns and operates hotels, restaurants and nightclubs in Méribel, Courchevel and Val d'Isère. Applicants must speak very good French. Salary package includes full board and shared accommodation. Staff are also required for summer season (May to October) for hotels and tourist residences in French coastal resorts in the south and west.

Voluntary work

Those who can offer their services free and in many cases pay a small daily fee for board and lodging (though occasionally this is provided at no cost), will find a wide range of opportunities available. This is a good way to make French contacts and improve your French, but not usually a way to support yourself once you are in France. In some instances board and lodging and sometimes pocket money are provided. However, if you happen to be a qualified archaeologist or a stone mason, etc., and you join a summer camp you might manage to extend your stay on a remuneration basis to work on a long-term project. CIDJ (see below) has a free leaflet *Chantiers de jeunes bénévoles* (Voluntary Work Camps) that lists most of the organisations in France offering this kind of work. Many are connected with the preservation and maintenance of France's architectural and historical heritage, but social programmes are another possibility.

Architectural and historical heritage

Les Amis de Chevreaux-Chatel: ☎03 84 85 95 77; accjura@free.fr; http:// accjura.free.fr.w.volontariat. The Chateau of Chevreaux is situated in a hilltop village above the Bresse Plains. Les Amis de Chevreaux is a place where young people of different nationalities can meet and spend time together. The work site in the Jura requires willing volunteers to help with the restoration of the 13th-century castle of Chevreaux. Volunteers stay for the last three weeks of July and the first three weeks

of August and stay on site at the castle in tents with camp beds and sanitary and kitchen facilities. Age 18 plus.

APARE: Association Pour la Participation et l'Action Régionale, Campus Européens du Patrimoine; ☎04 90 85 51 15; apare@apare-gec.org; www.apare-gec.org. Created in 1979 by a group of Provençal dry stone architecture enthusiasts, Apare organises local development projects for all ages on heritage sites. Volunteers of all nationalities can spend two or three weeks between June and October on such camps. Technical advisors instruct volunteers in traditional techniques such as dry stone walling, stone dressing and lime facing. The registration fee of €250 (three weeks) covers food, lodging, insurance expenses and leisure. Minimum age 16; no upper limit. Apare also runs training courses for qualifications in work camp leadership and technical instruction but you must speak French to enrol.

Château de St-Ferriols: 11500 Aude, Languedoc; ☎+33 (0)4 68 20 11 42; sophie@st-ferriol.info; www.st-ferriol.info/. Privately owned château that welcomes volunteers from time to time to help with gardening, woodland, restoration, archaeology, historical research and fund-raising. People with experience of stonemasonry, dry stone walling, working with lime, woodworking, blacksmithing, leaded glass making, heraldic artwork, historical research, excavations, herbalism and organic gardening and less specialised skills like labouring and gardening welcome. Volunteers usually five hours and day, five days a week and are well fed. Beautiful location and comfortable accommodation can be arranged in a nearby village or a caravan provided or camping.

GEC: Grouping of European Campuses; ☎04 90 27 21 20; gec@apare-gec.org; www.apare-gec.org; non-government organisation for the preservation of environmental and cultural heritage. Organises a mixture of academic and practical 'campuses' in several countries including France. Employs volunteers to take part in over 20 summer work camps in Provence, mainly restoring ancient buildings. Work camps last a month. The participation fee is €60. Travel expenses to and from the campus are the volunteers' responsibility.

RIVE Programme: International Network for the Environment (same co-ordinates as GEC above), organises longer duration campuses for one to three volunteers allowing the subject of work to be dealt with in depth. The projects are mostly social and humanitarian and the costs of the volunteer are borne by the host organisation which also provides a representative responsible for the training and personal support of the volunteers. Ages 18–25.

Jeunesse et Reconstruction: ☎01 47 70 15 88; info@volontariat.org; www.volontariat.org; requires volunteers for projects all over France. Type of work varies depending on the camp but may include constructing community centres or digging drains in wet areas. Board and lodging are free. About seven hours work per day, five days weekly. Volunteers are international. Those who commit themselves for three months receive pocket money.

Rempart: ☎01 42 71 96 55; www.rempart.com; Rempart needs volunteers to work for various archaeological and heritage sites all over France. Wide range of projects includes, castles, chapels, abbeys, ancient villages and Gallo-Roman sites. Techniques used are masonry, carpentry etc. Board and accommodation normally cost €7 daily. No skills required. 30–35 hours work weekly, free time for recreational activities to discover the area. Basic knowledge of French is desirable.

La Sabranenque: ☎04 66 50 05 05; info@sabranenque.com; www.sabranenque.com; restoration organisation that needs helpers to work on villages, sites and simple monuments using traditional building methods. Two weeks minimum between 1 June and 30 September.

Social programmes

Associations des Paralyses de France: ☎01 40 78 69 00; www.apf.asso.fr. Employs assistants to work in holiday centres for handicapped adults for 15–21 days during summer. Pocket money, board, accommodation and expenses are provided. Applicants should be able to speak a little French. Applications to APF Evasion at the above address.

Cotravaux: ☎01 48 74 79 20; informations@cotravaux.org; www.cotravaux.org. Cotravaux is the co-ordinating body for voluntary work organisations in France. It aims to develop the services provided by work camps and to find new work camp opportunities. Members of Cotravaux include Concordia, Neige et Merveilles, Service Civil International, Jeunesse et Reconstruction, Alpes de Lumière, Compagnons Bâtisseurs, Union REMPART, UNAREC, Fédération Unie des Auberges de Jeunesse (FUAJ), Solidarités Jeunesse, Action Urgence International (AUI).

Espaces-Chantiers Environment Local (ECHEL): RICA (www.frenchfoundation.com) can arrange for US volunteers to work in a variety of social projects in France for eight weeks from early July. Conditions for participation, type of accommodation provided and expenses paid obviously vary from organisation to organisation. Volunteers should apply to the individual organisations for information; addresses can be obtained from Cotravaux. Note that most French voluntary organisations have partners in other countries which can receive applications. Cotravaux can give you a list of such organisations in your country.

Solidarités Jeunesse: ☎01 55 26 88 77; www.solidaritesjeunesse.org. Organises long-term (minimum six or nine months; maximum 12 months) voluntary work with disadvantaged adults and children and young people in rural areas. Volunteers' work varies depending on the project and may include some of the following: help with leading work camps, joining in activities, helping with renovations of buildings, vegetable growing, animal husbandry, organising training sessions and collective life. Volunteers should be aged 18–25 and return travel is reimbursed. Free board and lodging are provided.

Jeunesse en Action: ☎02 35 70 61 70; www.crajep-hn.org. This is a new programme funded by the European Commission aimed at promoting a feeling of citizenship and particularly European identity and furthering solidarity among young people aged 15–28. They offer voluntary service in many different areas of work, involving a large number of different countries.

Training and work experience

One of the problems for those leaving school or university is that when they begin to look for work, they find that they are up against those with a proven track record, who understandably have greater success than those with no experience in the work place. The EU has come up with various schemes for young people aimed at giving them an advantage with regard to European job opportunities. The most ambitious of these schemes is Leonardo.

French government programmes for Americans

Ambassade de France aux Etats-Unis: ☎202 944 60 11; www.info-france-usa.org. For all information on long and short-term internships in France and an application form, you can contact the above address or use the contacts below.

CEI Paris Work in France Department: ☎+33 (0)1 40 51 11 81; www.cei4vents. com. Scheme that allows university students to get a temporary work permit during college holidays. There is a self-placement scheme, and a job and internship programme. CEI inscription fees range from €330–€450. Some schemes open to young graduates also. Many jobs are in hotel and catering and internships are in any field related to students' studies. Usual length of job in three months. Internships can

Independent programme

Horizon HPL: Paris Office: ☎+33 (0)1 40 01 07 07; www. horizonhpl.org; also has offices in Aix-en-Provence and Dublin. Horizon is a private French/British organisation that organises work experience placements in hotels and businesses for those who wish to improve their languages. Work placements of three to 12 months are combined with French tuition. Horizon charges fees for 'enrolment and acceptance' and for tuition and training while in France. Hotel trainees get accommodation and wages. Age17–50 years.

last longer. Pay is at the minimum wage (approximately €8.40 per hour). For further details contact the above contact details.

French Embassy, Cultural Service Internship Programme: ☎202 944 60 11; www.diplomatie-gouv.fr; collects information on short-term internships in France and long-term internships in the public sector and NGOs.

French-American Chamber of Commerce: ☎212 765 4460; www.faccnyc.org; oversees an Exchange Visitor Programme. Internships are generally open to graduates with the relevant experience. The visa is for six months and can be renewed twice.

European Union programmes

Socrates-Erasmus Council: ☎+44 (0)2920 397 405; www.Erasmus.ac.uk; Erasmus is part of the Socrates programme. Options include allowing university students and academic staff to study/teach at a university in another EU country.

Lifelong Learning Programme (Programme education formation tout au long de la vie): www.europa.eu. Brought out in 2007, this programme should replace the previous Socrates, Leonardo and e-learning Minerva and Lingua. Lifelong

 Bursaries for Socrates-Erasmus intended to help with costs are available depending on the location and length of the placement (☎01227 762712; www.erasmus.ac.uk)

Learning aims to build a European universal education space and make Europe a society of knowledge with durable economic development. It is divided into four sectors: Comenius which deals with secondary school education and teacher training; Erasmus still encouraging mobility in Europe and providing the means for intensive stays in other EU countries; and professionals training from Leonardo da Vinci and Grundtvig providing education for adults

Leonardo da Vinci: ☎020 7389 4389; leonardo@britishcouncil.org; www.Leonardo. org.uk and www.britishcouncil.org; Leonardo is the EU vocational training programme. It enables people in initial vocational training, higher education students, young workers and recent graduates as well as trainers, to take part in work placements or exchanges in other European countries. The length of placement varies according to the type of participant, but can be from three weeks to 12 months. There is a separate strand, Youthstart, for young people under 20 years, in particular the unemployed and unqualified

Lingua: www.lingua-institut.com; set up in 1990, Lingua is aimed at, among others, foreign language teachers. Under the scheme teachers can spend time in the country whose language they propose to teach. Lingua funds scholarships and exchange visits for students and teachers of modern languages. Options include language teacher training and assistantships for future language teachers. Lingua candidates can't apply as individuals, they have go through an organisation.

Companies that recruit trainees (stagiares)

- **Citroen:** ☎04 47 48 35 63; www.citroen.fr; contact: Pierre Eric Billaut
- **Dassault Systems:** ☎01 40 99 40 99; www.3ds.com; information technology
- **EADS:** www.eads.com

- **Groupe Danone:** ☎01 44 35 20 20; www.danonegroup.com and www.danone. fr; food Industry including dairy, beverages (including Evian) and biscuits
- **General Electrique:** ☎01 30 70 40 40 (*recrutement et stages*); www.ge.com; diverse: everything from jet engines to power generation
- **Hewlett Packard:** www.France.hp.com; computers
- **Groupe Mars:** ☎0238 59 61 61; www.danone.com; confectionery, food and food products, pet foods
- **Plastic Omnium:** www.platicomnium.fr; containers
- **Procter & Gamble:** ☎01 40 88 55 11; www.pg.com; consumer products including food and healthcare
- **RATP:** www.ratp.fr; Paris transport
- **Renault:** www.Renault.fr
- **Schlumberger:** www.slb.com; Oilfield services
- **Semagroup:** www.semagroup.com; Information Technology
- **SGN:** www.sgn.areva-nc.fr; ☎01 39 48 68 80
- **Shell:** ☎01 47 14 84 71; http://www.shell.com/home/Framework?siteId=fr-fr
- **Solvay:** ☎01 40 75 80 00; www.solvay.fr; chemicals
- **Thales:** ☎01 53 77 86 59; www.thalesonline.com; military electronics
- **Usinor:** stages 01 41 25 90 12; www.usinor.com; steel

Centres d'information jeunesse

There are about 30 CIDJs in France, and are a useful source of information particularly for foreign students. Although it's by no means their main function, they can help people find jobs, particularly seasonal agricultural work and other part-time and temporary possibilities for the summer and winter. In addition they can provide leaflets on the regulations that affect foreign students (www.cidj.com). Some CIDJs just display vacancies on notice boards in their offices, while others have a more formal system run in conjunction with the local ANPE.

The CIDJ in Marseille (☎04 91 24 33 50; www.crijpa.com) is particularly useful for agricultural jobs and for *animateurs* (children's summer camp monitors), while the Nice CIDJ (19 rue Gioffredo, 06000 Nice; ☎04 93 80 93 93; www.crij.ca.frpr) has plenty of catering jobs. Mother's help jobs are also available through some CIDJs.

FACT

There are CIDJs in Amiens, Bastia (Corsica), Besançon, Bordeaux, Caen, Cergy Pontoise, Dijon, Evry, Grenoble, Lille, Limoges, Lyon, Marseille, Melun, Montpellier, Nancy, Nantes, Nice, Orléans, Poitiers, Reims, Rennes, Rouen, Strasbourg, Toulouse and Versailles.

■ PERMANENT WORK

The details and information in the 'Finding a job' section will be useful reading for those looking for long-term and permanent work in France. This section deals with individual areas of work such as teaching English as a foreign language (TEFL), information technology, bilingual secretarial work and working for the institutions of the European community.

Computers/information technology

Apart from specialised jobs in the computer field, those with computer expertise could consider working as an IT trainer. Many companies offer their staff on-going

> **Rajaneesh Dwivedi studied Music and IT at Keele University and decided to move to Montpellier a couple of years after graduating.**
>
> I was able to use my IT skills to get work, though it did take time and a few mauvais plans (dodgy situations) to get something satisfactory. It's not easy to find work in Montpellier as there's a fairly high unemployment rate, though I'm lucky in that there are a number of high tech businesses that have established themselves here. I started out as a programmer on a team of software designers a few years ago but as the company I work for has a lot of international clients, I have now taken on the role of product trainer.

FACT

■ Those who work in computing and can speak another European language can almost always find jobs in the EU.

voluntary training schemes, of which the most popular are English (see below) and computer studies. If you have any experience in this field and speak good French, you could try contacting companies direct. If you are concerned that you might need a specialised technical vocabulary, the following glossary of French computerese may reassure you: browser (*le browser*), computer (*l'ordinateur*), email (*l'e-mail*, or *la messagerie electronique* if the Academie Française are listening), the internet (*le net*), software (*le logiciel*), webcam (*la webcam*), web surfers (*les surfers du web* or *les internautes*).

Useful addresses and publications

Computing: ☎020 7316 9000; www.vnuservices.co.uk; magazine published by VNU Business Publications. Regular job adverts from IT recruitment consultancies, which can place computer personnel in France

Computer Futures: ☎020 7446 6666; contract@computerfutures.com (for contract work); permanent@computerfutures.com (for permanent work); www.compfutures. com; in France: ☎+33 (0)1 42 99 83 33; france@computerfutures.com (contract work); recrutement@computerfutures.com (permanent work). A leading supplier of IT personnel worldwide. Ring for an appraisal of the demand for your skills or deposit CV (résumé) online

EBM Recruitment Agency: ☎+33 (0)1 42 44 23 35; ebmrh@ebm.fr; www.ebm-fr.com. European Business Management (EBM) specialises in recruiting human resources for the IT sector

Hewlett Packard: www.france.hp.com

Modis Head Office: ☎+44 (0)20–7083 6400; www.modisintl.com Permanent and contract IT recruitment for software and communications projects in France and worldwide

Unilog DRG: ☎+33 (0)1 58 22 40 00; recrutement@unilog.fr; www.unilog.fr. French IT company that employs graduates with or without computer science qualifications as long as they are motivated to acquire computing expertise. Applications must be in French and addressed to the recruitment department

Secretarial

There is a great demand for bilingual secretaries in France and Paris is one of the most fertile hunting grounds for this type of work. Emma Corney, a graduate in French and management studies, decided to move to Paris on completion of her degree. Having already spent a year during her studies living there and working in a marketing placement programme with an international IT company, she wanted to go back. She got a job through the secretarial recruitment company Sheila Burgess and then got a job working for them as a recruiter.

Useful addresses

Boyce Bilingual: www.boycerecruitment.co.uk; ☎020 7611 3999; Recruits secretaries for Paris and the Paris area.

Insead: ☎01 60 72 40 00; www.insead.edu; the renowned MBA college regularly recruits administrative, technical and secretarial staff to work on campus. Must be bilingual/multi-lingual

Sheila Burgess International: www.sheilaburgessint.fr; ☎01 44 63 02 57; in business over 12 years. Specialises in multi-lingual secretaries and personal assistants for international companies in Paris. Clients include international companies and firms and EU bodies and international organisations. Please note jobs are not temporary or of a short-term nature

Team RH: ☎01 42 33 26 12; jobs@teamrh.com; www.teamrh.com; recruits bilingual or trilingual administrative assistants for international companies in Paris. Most jobs are long-term

TEFL and teaching English in French schools

There is a continuing demand for English language tuition in France, particularly from the business sector. Larger French companies are encouraged to set aside part of their annual budget for staff training under the *Droit de Formation Continue*. The most popular *formations* are English and computer studies. In some cases American English is considered more useful and so there are opportunities

> ❝
> **Emma Corney says the biggest challenge of living and working in Paris is the social one and you have to make a huge effort.**
>
> I love everything about Paris from the bustling streets to the beautiful architecture. I could quite happily pass the time wandering through the various quartiers and watching the world there go by. Even though Paris is a fantastic city for young people to live in, where there is something for everyone, it can also be quite daunting to know where to start making new friends. Paris is a big place and Parisians can be quite reticent about welcoming foreigners into their well-oiled social circles. It is all too easy for you stay within your expatriate group. I recommend taking up every invitation that comes your way as you never know who you might meet.
> ❞

also for American TESOL (Teaching English to Speakers of Other Languages) teachers. The work permit regulations are more complex for non-EU citizens (see the chapter *Before You Go*) and so if there is a demand for a teacher in American English, it won't be difficult to find one.

Teaching jobs in France sometimes appear in British newspapers and the relevant journals: regular standbys in this respect are *The Guardian*'s Education Section (http://education.guardian.co.uk) which appears on Tuesdays and *The Times Educational Supplement* (www.tes.co.uk) published on Fridays. More specifically, the monthly 'trade' newspaper *EL Gazette* (ww.elgazette) is available on subscription. It is a useful source of job possibilities. A comprehensive guide covering all the practicalities of TEFL teaching with listings of schools and their requirements worldwide is *Teaching English Abroad* (Vacation Work).

For qualified American TEFL teachers, the *TESOL Placement Bulletin* from TESOL (☎703 325 0885; www.tesol.org) is published six times annually and is sent to TESOL members who register for the Placement Service; careers@tesol.org/www.tesol.org. Another relevant North American publication is *The International Educator* (www.tieonline.com) which concentrates on jobs in international, English-medium schools, most of which follow either an American curriculum or the International Baccalaureate (IB).

The schools may or may not help you find accommodation, you have to be flexible about working hours, and the contracts last from nine months to two years. Shorter contracts are also available at some schools. In some cases you will need your own transport, for instance if teaching is carried out at business premises or on a one-to-one basis in clients' own homes. All these details, and the conditions of employment should be gone into with the school concerned before you accept a job.

FACT

■ There is considerable variation between schools regarding teaching jobs.

Conditions of work for TEFL teachers

However careful you are though, it seems to be the opinion of the majority of those who have taught English abroad that language schools tend to regard their teaching staff as expendable, often overworking them and expecting complete flexibility (i.e. to take on extra classes at the drop of a hat). Consequently, there is usually a fairly rapid staff turnover as teachers can't take the stress on a permanent basis. All you need is a good education, preferably to degree level, excellent communication skills and preferably one of the recognised English teaching qualifications. It is also one of the best possible ways to meet a wide variety of French people and there is considerable job satisfaction to be had from watching your class or students improve. If you decide to take up TEFL as a career after establishing yourself in one city or another, you could consider opening your own language institute (see the section 'Starting a business').

One of the improvements for teachers of English in France in recent years is that their conditions of employment have become regulated. This means that for salaried teachers, formal contracts and the regulation benefits, sick pay, etc. have to be provided by the employers. (see the section 'Aspects of employment', below). Legislation also applies to wages which are between €1,500 and €2,000 monthly.

TEFL training courses

For details of many courses and possible TEFL qualifications, consult *Teaching English Abroad* (see above). If you are in the UK, you can also obtain a free list of the main (RSA/UCLES) courses with their addresses only, from the British Council Information

> ## Claire Oldmeadow runs The Language Network (see below) in Paris. This is what Claire has to say about English teaching in France.
>
> If you want to live in France, teaching English is one way of making a living. However, you should bear in mind that you'd have to work very hard to make ends meet and that you might not have a regular income. On top of that, if you chose to live in the Paris area, you could find that your meagre income barely covered your living expenses, even if you lived frugally. However, by being creative, proactive and open to change you should be able to find ways of increasing your hourly rate of pay and possibly even achieve more stability. You might have to start off in one of the private language schools paying as little as €12 net/hour (before tax), but if you played your cards right, you could quickly progress to working part-time for a university paying €30/hour – if you didn't mind waiting months to get paid! If you were even luckier you might be able to find work in a private higher education establishment paying up to €38/hour. Alternatively, you could become self-employed and find your own work in companies. However, to do this successfully, as well as having a good grasp of the French language and culture and a flair for business, it helps if you also have a network of contacts to give you an introduction into companies you are targeting.

Centre in Manchester(☎ 0161 957 7755) which also distributes and information pack *How to Become a Teacher of English Abroad*.

If you are applying on the spot, you will find language schools listed in the French Yellow Pages under *Enseignements Privé de Langues* or *Ecoles de Langues*. There is also a comprehensive list of Paris language schools on the website www.paris-anglo.com.

Useful contacts

The Franco-British Chamber of Commerce and Industry: ☎ 0153 30 81 30; www.francobritishchamber.com. Self-employed teachers can join the Chamber and attend events gathering people from the Franco-British business community

The Language Network: ☎01 44 64 82 23; claire@thelanguagenetwork.fr; www.thelanguagenetwork.fr. An association for EFL teachers in France which advises teachers about all aspects of teaching in France. It also collects and diffuses EFL job offers

Tefl Jobs In France: www.tefljobsinfrance.com

TESOL France: www.tesol-france.org. Organises seminars and workshops for EFL teachers

TOEIC or Test of English for International Communication: ☎01 40 75 95 20; www.toeic.eu; TOEIC measures proficiency in business English at intermediate and advanced levels. Currently over 4.5 million people take the test every year making it the standard test of workplace English language proficiency worldwide

EU scheme

◼ EU Lingua scheme

The Lingua scheme is aimed at promoting language teaching of all the languages in the EU as a foreign language. It also enables teachers of foreign languages to train and study in the country whose language they are teaching. In its first year of operation (1991) 516 teachers from the EU received grants. Now thousands of teachers take part in the scheme annually. France is very popular country in which to be a Lingua scheme participant. For further details of the Lingua scheme, see 'Training schemes' above.

Addresses of language schools

Inlingua: ☎01 45 51 46 60; rivegauche@inlingua-paris.com; www.inlingua-paris. com; an international chain of language teaching schools of which there are 29 in France. A minimum of two years' teaching experience is required. You can approach the schools direct. Further details in the UK can be obtained from Inlingua Teacher Training and Recruitment (☎01242 253 171)

Audio English: ☎05 56 44 54 05. Applicants must have a BA or equivalent and good French. The minimum contract is 10 months. Minimum pupil age: 6 years

University of London: ☎01 44 11 73 83; c.campos@biparis.lon.ac.uk; www.bip. lon.ac.uk. High level TEFL qualification required and at least five years' teaching experience. Preferably French speakers

Centre d'Etude des Langues: ☎03 21 93 78 45. Minimum contract 9 months. Adult and child classes

Demos Langues: ☎04 72 61 99 67; www.demos.fr. Also at Grenoble ☎04 76 49 96 19 and Paris ☎01 44 94 16 32. Takes British and American teachers with a BA and 1 year's experience in TEFL, or RSA certificate. Contracts are usually for an academic year, or January to June. Students are mainly adults of all ages

Fontainebleau Langues & Communication: ☎01 64 22 48 96; bente.evans@ calv-flc.com; www.flc-int.com. One year minimum. Majority of teaching takes place on company premises so own transport necessary. Applicants must have TEFL training. Minimum contract is a year

Julie Legree: ☎02 51 46 45 45; Employs four TEFL teachers to teach English in primary schools around the Vendée from October to May. Also a TEFL teacher to teach ages 14–21 in a college and lycée as an assistant. All posts involve 20 hours per four-day week. Free board and lodging with local families and a monthly allowance

Linguarama: ☎01 47 73 00 95; defense@linguarama.com; www.linguarama.com. Full-time teachers. 25 hours a week, September to June. Part-time teachers work flexible hours. Business English taught at company premises or at the school. Advice on finding accommodation

TEFL Jobs in France: ☎06 75 49 35 92; contact@tefljobsinfrance.com; website www.tefljobsinfrance.com. Minimum contract one year. 25 hours a week with some evening work

Telab Language Courses by Telephone: ☎03 85 50 58 58; s.evans@telab.com; www.telab.com. Language teaching qualifications and at least two years' experience of teaching business clients and knowledge of a particular field: financial, medical, technical, etc. Teachers work from home

Wall Street Institute: ☎04 50 10 10 00; wsi-annecy@wanadoo.fr; www.wallstreetinstitute.fr. Permanent contract teachers work part-time or more if necessary

Wall Street Institute, Nantes: ☎02 40 35 08 70; wsi-nantes@wanadoo.fr; www.wallstreetinstitute.fr. St Nazaire: ☎02 51 10 06 36; wsi-stnazaire@wanadoo.fr

English assistant

Working as an English assistant in a French school is a great introduction to French daily life and culture. You don't need to speak French fluently as it's your ability to speak and teach English that is very much in demand by the French Ministry of Education to promote English teaching in French schools at all levels from kindergarten upwards. Several English-speaking nationalities are eligible and for Americans particularly it's one of the easiest ways to fast track your way to a job in France provided that they have completed a minor or major in French and are not over 29 years of age.

Further information about the assistant programme can be obtained from the Centre international d'études pédagogiques/CIEP (contact@ciep.fr; www.ciep.fr/assistantetr/index.htm).

Useful contacts

Association Pour l'Emploi des Cadres (APEC): ☎01 40 52 20 01;www.apec.asso.fr. A private organisation financed by subscriptions from private companies which specialises in managerial staff employment

Don't expect everything to be planned for you. You may have to wait a long time to even hear if you are accepted.

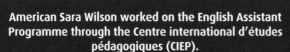

American Sara Wilson worked on the English Assistant Programme through the Centre international d'études pédagogiques (CIEP).

Your ability to speak English fluently is in such high demand that the normal problems of obtaining a work visa are waived. The contract is from October to the end of April, with three two-week breaks in between. The breaks are a wonderful opportunity to explore outside of France. I came home for the Christmas break and travelled to Egypt and Ireland during the winter and spring breaks.

Don't expect everything to be planned for you. You may have to wait a long time to even hear if you are accepted. I applied in February and didn't receive the acceptance letter until July to start the job in October. Finally, the location of your school and your responsibilities are not up to you. The French Ministry of Education hires for schools throughout France, so you may not get your first choice. Also, there seems to be a lot of uncertainty about what the English assistant's role really is within the school. For example, I rarely had the opportunity to teach, and when I did, it was always with the primary English teacher by my side. Some of my friends, on the other hand, were solely responsible for their classes.

> Robert Hoehn (www.roberthoehn.fr) runs the site www.parisfashionweekly.com, which profiles new up-and-coming artists in the world of cinema, fashion shows, photo shoots and commercial work.
>
> I came to the city to find work as an actor. I had a real hard time getting started in the French theatre world, which is very closed. If you do get a job there, it's pretty much by accident. I've had a few French roles and I've been on a TV show. But where I really got started was with a voiceover demo I made on request for a company that shoots corporate videos that a friend of mine who works in pizza restaurant put me on to. Since then voiceover's taken off for me. There're only a few films that get dubbed into English every year but I get commercial work all the time. It's work I would never have got in the States but here there's far less competition.

Bilinguagroup: ☎020 7493 644; Paris@bilinguagroup.com; www.bilinguagroup.com. Recruits all types of bilingual staff including secretarial, legal and executive. Send CV by email

Dorothy Danahy: ☎01 47 20 13 13; recruitment@dorothydanahy.com; www.dorothydanahy.com. Recruits all types of bilingual staff including secretarial, legal and executive. Send CV by e-mail

Euro London: ☎01 53 43 94 52; paris@eurolondon.com; www.eurolondon.com. Recruits multilingual personnel through all industries in Paris area

Femmes et Carrières: ☎01 44 51 63 33; mail@femmesetcarrieres.com; www.femmesetcarrieres.com. Recruits all types of bilingual staff including secretarial, legal and executive. Send CV by email

1001 Talents: ☎01 42 70 34 12; contact@1001talents.com; www.1001talents.com. Recruitment/executive search agency operating in several areas: hi tech (IT, telecoms, electronics, internet), insurance and food services. Most jobs are in the Paris area

■ EMPLOYMENT REGULATIONS AND CONTRACTS

Salaries

At first glance French salaries compare favourably with others in Europe and most people moving from the UK to an equivalent job position in France, at whatever level, will expect to receive a higher salary there. However, they may be disappointed. The reason why French salaries *seem* attractive for executive and professional jobs but are not, is mainly to do with taxes and deductions. If you add together social security deductions, income tax (which however has recently been reduced to a top rate of 40%) and a high level of indirect taxation, the burden of tax overall is greater than in the UK or the USA. This is offset, particularly in the case of executives, by a generous range of company benefits and schemes from which may be derived fiscal or financial benefits (see 'Benefits' below). It is generally the self-employed who are worst off in France, as they don't have access to the range of benefits and perks and are likely to pay considerably more tax and 'social contributions' than anyone else. Employees will no doubt look to the attractions of France itself and the compensations of a shorter working week and longer holidays for the main benefits of working in France. At least in France there is less chance of the burnout to which Americans and Japanese are prone. Note that both salaries and living costs will be higher in the largest cities.

Most salaried jobs are covered by collective bargaining agreements (*conventions collectives*) between employers' and employees' bodies nationally or regionally. This effectively means that wage rates for different jobs are fixed, but it also means that wages tend to keep pace with the cost of living generally. Employers must, by law, offer at least the minimum wages, which have been negotiated.

One of the points to note about French salaries, as with many other countries, is that there is a greater differential than in the UK between unskilled or semi-skilled and professional jobs.

Le SMIC

France's official minimum wage is the *Salaire Minimum Interprofessionel de Croissance*, usually referred to as *le SMIC*. The rate increases more than once a year and is indexed to the cost of living. The gross rate is currently €8.44 (about £6.30) per hour or €1,280.09 monthly (for 152 hours of work) with slightly more for those doing a 39-hour week. Something like 2 million employees in France receive the SMIC.

Social security contributions

French *sécurité sociale* contributions are compulsory for employees and the self-employed. Often referred to colloquially as *la sécu*, contributions cover a comprehensive range of cradle to grave benefits including sickness and maternity, unemployment, work injury and old age benefits. The generosity of these benefits doesn't come cheap and contributions are correspondingly high – often 50%–60% of gross pay, the lion's share of which (about 40%) comes from the employer. The self-employed are responsible for their whole contribution and so for them the cost is fairly punitive.

National Social Security funds

The central agency responsible for collecting social security contributions is URSSAF (*Union de Recouvrement des Cotisations de Sécurité Sociale et d'Allocations Familiales*) www.urssaf.fr, from where it's filtered to various funds known as *Caisses* through ACOSS (*Agence Centrale des Organismes de Sécurité Sociale*). There are national healthcare caisses for different categories: e.g. the liberal professions' is CNAM, (*Caisse National d'Assurance Maladie des professions indépendent*) and for salaried employees it's CMAMTS (*Caisse National d'Assurance Maladie des Travailleurs Salariés*), etc. On a local level, you deal with the *Caisse Primaire d'Assurance Maladie* (CPAM), which reimburses the cost of medical treatment. Your local office can be found by logging on to www.ameli.fr.

Foreigners working and residing in France continuously for at least three months get basic, comprehensive health cover (*Couverture Maladie Universelle* or CMU) which is also free to low earners (under €6,400 a year). Once you have a social security number and a French employer, you will then have the contributions deducted from your salary.

For further details on using the French health service see the section 'Health' in the *Daily life* chapter.

Contributions for the self-employed

Anyone who is self-employed has to register directly with URSSAF. Self-employment contributions go to regional *caisses* called Caisses d'assurance Maladies, Régional (CMRs) which come under the umbrella of CNAM (see above).

Contributions from the self-employed are calculated on an annual basis but can be paid in four instalments per year. For the first two years before a pattern of earnings has been established the rate is calculated on a *base forfaitaire* (flat rate) which varies. You can be exempted from most contributions if you earned less than the tax threshold in the previous year.

Association pour la Gestion de la Sécurité Sociale des Auteurs (AGESSA). If you are a writer, composer, librettist, website designer, translator, illustrator, etc. and are paid in royalties you can register with AGESSA. Contributions to AGESSA entitle you to social security reimbursements, but you need to have achieved a certain level of royalties to qualify. For further details check out (www.agessa.org).

■ ASPECTS OF EMPLOYMENT

Benefits and perks

As mentioned earlier, there is a tendency for French salary figures not to represent the bottom line or actual financial package offered. You should expect various benefits and perks to be included in a salary as a matter of course. Often, senior and middle management receive a bonus, perhaps linked to the profits of their company, of 10% or even 20% of their salary. In addition, profit-sharing schemes (*Participation des salariés aux résultats de l'entreprise*), which also entitle one to various tax benefits, are becoming more common in France as are company investment securities schemes (*plan d'épargne d'entreprise*) whereby the company holds an investment portfolio on behalf of its employees. Another possibility sometimes offered is share option schemes (*options sur actions*).

Company cars aren't the norm in France as elsewhere. The most frequently offered benefits are private health plans (*mutuelles*) either contributory or wholly paid by the employer, which top up the amount of health insurance above that provided by the state. Such benefits are of real value when one considers that *sécurité sociale* pays a maximum of 75% towards non-emergency hospital treatment. Other benefits may include everything from all expenses paid holidays to rent-free accommodation.

FACT

■ The vast majority of employees, even those in the most mundane jobs, receive an extra month's salary at Christmas; this is known as the 13th month (*13ème mois*) payment. Some organisations also give a 14th month bonus prior to the summer holiday period.

Working hours and holidays

The regulations governing working conditions in France are set down in the Employment Charter (*Code de Travail*). The greatest change in the French working week (since the introduction of the 40-hour week in 1936), was *La Loi Aubry*, which introduced the 35-hour week (for companies employing more than 20 staff) in 2000. The full introduction of the 35-hour week was staged. Smaller companies with fewer than 20 staff were given an extra two years to help them make the adjustment. Companies can extend their working hours above 35 hours by collective bargaining or company agreement and pay overtime rates or compensatory time off, and this practice will probably increase under Sarkozy as tax breaks are offered for overtime worked.

The normal working day is generally 8.30am to 5.30pm Monday to Friday with a long lunch break. The long lunch break of up to two hours, used to be sacrosanct but

The 35-hour week

The 35-hour week was a core strategy of Lionel Jospin's government (elected in 1997) to deal with France's serious unemployment. The reduction in hours has created about 300,000 new jobs and helped to reduce unemployment from nearly 13% in 1998 to under 9% now. The fears of reduced productivity as a result of the 35-hour week were not realised. The legislation has built-in flexibility so that for instance a wine producer can have their staff working 38 hours a week at busy times such as the harvest, and 32 hours at other times when there is less work. The main beneficiaries of the 35-hour week are employees of larger organisations and most manual workers. Otherwise the tendency and legality to work longer hours among particular professions and types of worker with special working conditions (concierges, sales reps, company managers, etc.) seems to be increasing again. Even before the introduction of the new working hours, French employees were already working less than their counterparts in Britain, the USA, Japan and Germany. In practice, the majority of French executives regularly work well in excess of 35 hours weekly. After several high profile 'busts' by inspectors staking out company car parks at premises including Carrefour and Thomson CSF (so they could see what time workers left), a number of prosecutions took place. On factory production lines the new ruling generally translates as working three days on and two days off, which means the weekends are treated like any other day as regards payment.

FACT

■ It is usual for some businesses, especially factories, to close down during July or August so total flexibility as to holiday dates may not always be possible.

there is a tendency to have shorter lunch breaks. In Paris lunch is generally from 1pm or 2pm whereas in the provinces it is more likely to be from midday or 12.30pm.

Holidays

By law, all employees are entitled to a minimum of 30 days *congés payés* (paid holiday) per year, plus 11 different *jours fériés* (public holidays). In some jobs more may be offered. To put it in relative terms the average American worker will spend a decade longer working over a lifetime than his or her French counterpart. In some French companies the 35-hour week has been translated into extra holiday sometimes knows as RTT (*Réduction du temps de travail*) which can amount to as much as 15 extra days a year. However, the company usually says when the holiday can be taken and if not used at the stated time it may be forfeited.

Sick leave

Authorised sick leave (*arrêt de travail pour maladie*) is normally required after three days of sickness. A doctor will issue a sickness leave form (*un avis d'arrêt de travail*), which has to be completed and sent within 48 hours to the social security agency (parts 1 and 2 of the form) and the employer or ANPE office (part 3 of the form). Employees on sick leave may not work and have to comply with authorised times for leaving the house (usually 9am–11am and from 2pm to 4pm). A good site to consult for more information on this is http://vosdroits.service-public.fr. It is an offence to work while on authorised sick leave and not to comply with the times for leaving the house.

Women and work

Women intending to build a career in France will probably find the notion of sexual and professional equality stronger in Paris than in the provinces, although other career factors favouring Paris for foreigners are far more significant, such as the fact that Paris is more international.

Maternity benefits, parental leave and employment rights

French maternity benefits are extremely generous, which is sometimes held up as a reason for French employers not to promote women to positions of power and responsibility, i.e. because women are likely to cost them more in benefits than a male employee. Pregnancy (*la grossesse*) is profitable for many families since the social security system encourages it.

French companies are generally quite progressive in providing crèche and other child care facilities which allow flexibility in hours for working mothers.

Maternity leave

Women are entitled to 16 weeks maternity leave: six weeks prior to the birth (*repos prenatal*) and the rest after the birth of the first child (*repos postnatal*). The mother (or it can be the father) who stays at home is provided with an allowance for each of the first three children. This is in addition to 10 weeks post delivery at 90% of their normal salary. If more leave is advised by a doctor then this must also be allowed at full salary for up to six months. You may shorten your maternity leave but eight weeks is compulsory. Other maternity benefits are related to the term of employment. French women are positively encouraged to have more babies as the government introduced a scheme in 2004 which now pays them €800 for the first child. This is in addition to the generous allowances, universal nursery schools and tax concessions for childcare, so it is no wonder that France has one of the highest birthrates in the EU.

Parental leave

Both parents are entitled to an additional year of unpaid parental leave (*congé parental*) after which the employer is obliged to re-employ them in their former job at the same salary, or a higher one if wage/price index increases have occurred in the interval.

Paternity leave

- Fathers are also entitled to six months paternity leave

Adoption

- All the above rights are also applicable in the case of adoption

Trade unions and conditions of work

The power of the trade unions (*syndicats*) in France has declined since the decade of the 1970s when labour disputes and strikes were the norm. Since then the membership of the largest and most influential union, the CGT (see below) has fallen by half from the over 2.5 million members it had then. One of the reasons for the unions' decline is recent legislation which has encouraged, even forced employer and employees, with or without unions, to talk and negotiate wages and working conditions. This has helped to avoid many of the traditional problems between

FACT

- The government actively encourages the provision of childcare by companies, for instance by offering companies a 60% tax credit for offering family-friendly facilities.

319

workers and management. Despite this reduction of influence it is estimated that around four million French wage earners are unionised in a veritable alphabet jungle of acronyms, which in turn are grouped in confederations. Unions tend to be strongest in the older, traditional industries, and hold little sway in the new, high-tech ones. They also usually operate on a regional basis rather than nationally with the exception of the notorious French lorry drivers' union. Some of the main unions you are likely to come across are listed below.

Confédération Générale du Travail (CGT): www.cgt.fr. The largest trade union and traditionally controlled by Communists, the CGT's main territories are the two largest cities, Paris and Marseille. Its main support is found among heavy industries, mining, docks, electricity, newspaper printing and railways.

Confédération Générale du Travail-Force Ouvrière (CGT-FO): ☎01 40 52 82 00; www.force-ouvriere.fr. With an estimated membership of more than 750,000 the CGT-FO should not be confused with the CGT from which it split in 1948. The CGT-FO, often just referred to as *Force Ouvrière* is affiliated to the International Confederation of Free Trade Unions (ICFTU) and the European Trade Union Confederation (ETUC). Traditionally, the bulk of its support came from nationalized industries and the civil service.

Confédération Française Démocratique du Travail (CFDT): ☎01 42 03 83 10; www.cfdt.fr. The CFDT came into being in 1964 when the majority of the members of the *Confédération des Travailleurs Chrétiens* (CFTC) wanted to emphasise their secularism by changing the union's name. It has about 800,000 current members from all public and private sectors.

Confédération Française des Travailleurs Chrétiens (CFTC): ☎01 44 52 49 00; www.cftc.fr. Founded in 1919, the CFTG is an offshoot of the CFDT – it broke away in order to promote the idea of Christian Unionism based on Catholic doctrine and the notion of the Church and State working in harmony and recognising the problems of the working class. It has a nationwide membership of about 250,000 (including 60,000 pensioners) representing a variety of industries.

Confédération Française de l'Encadrement Confédération Générale des Cadres (CFE-CGC): ☎01 55 30 12/59; Founded in 1944. Originally a military term for officers of the army, *cadres* has come to mean any type of executive or manager. CGC adherents include engineers, workshop supervisors and technicians as well as sales representatives and agents.

The Conseil National du Patronat Français (CNPF): ☎01 40 69 96 00. This is one of the employers' unions (*syndicats patronaux*) and was formed in 1946 at the instigation of the government. It represents the majority of firms, except SMEs which have their own union, the CGPME (see below). The CNPF represents employers in their dealings with the state. The CNPF has a strong influence on the economic and social policies of its membership which is drawn from the ranks of business, industry and banking.

Confédération Générale des Petites et Moyennes Entreprises (CGPME); ☎01 47 62 73 73; www.cgpme.org. The CGPME split away from the CNPF in 1948. Comprising 400 or so federations it brings together some 80% of the professional classes found in SME's in industry, trade and services and 256 inter-professional structures found in the départements and regions. Membership totals about 1.5 million firms.

Fédération Nationale des Syndicats d'Exploitants Agricoles (FNSEA): ☎01 53 83 47 47; www.fnsea.fr. The farmers' union.

Féderation Syndicale Unitaire (FSU): ☎01 44 79 90 30; Teachers union.
Union Nationale des Syndicats Autonomes (UNSA): ☎01 40 16 78 00; www.
unsa-education.org. Founded in 1928 it was part of the CGT but left to become
independent in 1948. Currently the umbrella organisation for about 50 teaching
unions it has a membership of about 150,000.

Representative committees

With the decline of working class consciousness, which led directly to the creation
of trade unions and gave them momentum, has come a decline in militancy
and consequently memberships have fallen. More recently there has been a
trend towards the formation of representative committees (*coordinations*) and
autonomous unions, which focus on specific sectorial demands such as teachers,
nurses and students. Representative committees however, still need the power of
the trade unions behind them to enhance their chances of a satisfactory outcome
to disputes.

Employees' councils

Companies with more than 10 employees are required by law to appoint
representatives or employees' councils. These bodies are entitled to certain
information from the management of a company, which must also consult them
on certain matters relating to pay and working conditions. The councils, of course,
do not have legal powers to change management decisions but this is still an
arrangement, which has helped to avoid disputes.

Contracts of employment

If you are offered a job and decide to accept the pay and conditions offered, it is a
legal requirement to sign a contract of employment (*contrat de travail*). There are a
number of different types of contract, all of which have varying implications. There
are, however, two main types.

Fixed-term contract (Contrat à durée déterminée/ CDD)

Fixed-term contracts must be in writing and the date for termination must be given
in the contract. This contract can be for temporary employment if for a specific
purpose but fixed term generally means for a maximum period of 18 months. After
this employment either ceases or the employee is transferred to a CDI. The contract
may be renewed twice, but not for a period exceeding the original contract or 18
months total. There is no minimum period for the contract.

■ Indefinite-term contract (Contrat à durée indéterminée/CDI)

This is the usual type of contract for permanent employees. Unlike the *contrat
à durée déterminée*, it does not have to be in writing. However, it is obviously
sensible to insist on having it in writing for future reference. Most indefinite-term
contracts include a trial period, usually three months, after which the contract
becomes binding on both parties.

A contract can sometimes be very complex; French business people often have
a very detailed understanding of the law. Even if your French is good, it may be
advisable to engage professional help in understanding a contract. One of the most

FACT

■ A contract of
employment
should detail, at
the very least, the
job title, duties and
responsibilities,
hours of work, rate
of pay and terms of
dismissal involved in
the position.

A closed factory in Boulogne

important stipulations of French employment law is that an employee can only be dismissed or made redundant in very specific circumstances (see below). The Agence Nationale pour l'Amelioration des Conditions de Travail (ANACT; www.anact. fr/index.html) and the Observatoire Européen des Relations Industrielles (EIRO; www.eiro.eurofound.eu.int/) both work towards improving living and working conditions in France and have informative websites.

End of contract bonus

If a contract has run to its full course, the employee is entitled to an end of contract bonus (*indemnité de fin de contrat*) which amounts to 5% of the salary plus any other bonuses granted by the employer. An *indemnité de fin de contrat* is not payable in the case of seasonal or temporary work.

Rights of temporary and seasonal workers

There are separate contracts for seasonal workers (*saisonniers*) and temporary employees (*travailleurs temporaires*), but these afford few rights to employees while embroiling employers in the social security system.

Employers who want to take on part-time home helps/au pairs, etc. have to pay employee social security contributions. Once employment has been formalised, employers have to observe the complex rules of dismissal, which is why many families employ home helps and baby-sitters on an informal cash-in-hand or exchange for room and board basis. There is a system of payment for home helps called *cheque emploi* service which allows the employer to offset the amount paid against tax.

A contract of employment must be presented when applying for a residence permit (*carte de séjour*), in France. It may also be required on other occasions – e.g. pay slips aren't sufficient proof of holding a job but a contract of employment, obviously, is. Note a residence permit is no longer required for EU nationals.

France does have a sizeable black market workforce who work without any form of employment contract and consequently without the benefit of *sécurité sociale* or the substantial legal protection to which all employees are entitled. The size of this workforce is not as great as in for example Italy, but it is not uncommon for people to be asked to work 'unofficially' in seasonal jobs such as tourism or agriculture.

Termination of a contract

If you have a *contract à durée déterminée*, i.e. with a date of termination, it can only be terminated before that date if specific circumstances arise. If one of the parties has committed a *faute grave* (serious fault), or through *force majeure*, events or circumstances occur which are beyond the control of either party. For various reasons the regulations governing termination and dismissal are very formal and precise and non-observance of the step-by-step rules for dismissing employees can lead to the dismissal being invalid.

◼ Termination by the employer

If the employer terminates the contract prematurely, compensation payable amounts to the total remuneration due until the contract expires. If the employee is dismissed for *une cause réelle et sérieuse* the employer must summon the employee, by registered letter (*lettre recommandée*) to attend a formal meeting during which the reasons for dismissal will be clearly stated. Within 24 hours the employer must send a further registered letter notifying the employee of his or her final decision and the reasons. If the employer fails to take these steps, the dismissal will not be valid.

◼ Termination by the employee

If, however, the employee defaults on the contract or commits another *faute grave*, he or she will have to compensate the employer. If the employee simply wishes to terminate the contract, notice should be given in writing and sent by registered post, and no reason need be given. The amount of notice depends on the category of job: factory workers have to give a week's notice, white collar workers usually have to give a month while senior employees (*cadres*) are expected to give two or three months' notice. An employee who has not committed any *faute grave* is entitled to an *indemnité compensatrice de congé payés* (payment in lieu of holiday entitlement due up to the time of leaving).

Force Majeure (the occurence of events beyond the control of either party), absolves either party of the obligation to pay compensation.

◼ Serious dispute with the employer

In the event of there being a serious dispute between employee and employer you can contact the Prud'homme organisation in Paris (☎ 01 40 38 52 00) set up to help employees whose interests have been threatened and to protect their legal rights. If they decide you have a case it can take about six months to come to court. You will need a lawyer and in a straightforward case this can cost in the region of €600–€900. If you win, you can expect to be awarded a sum of money depending on the facts of the case.

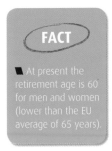

French pensions

The French pension system is generous although the government has been introducing reforms in the face of rocketing costs of providing social security in France. In 2003 the law was on pensions was changed so that instead of working for 37 and a half years and earning a state pension of 50% of their annual salary in their 10 highest earning years, the French now work 40 years for a state pension of 50% of their 25 highest earning year. This reform has come in gradually since 2003 and is now fully in force. The French pension system depends on those who are working paying into a state fund, the Caisse de Retraite, which in turn supports those on a pension. Because of France's ageing population (16.5% of the population are currently over 65 and this is expected to increase to 25% by 2030) the pension system runs up an annual deficit of billions of euros.

Useful contacts

CNAVTS: ☎01 55 45 50 00; www.cnav.fr/. Social security general scheme
CCMSA: ☎01 41 63 77 77; www.msa.fr/. Farmers social insurance
ARRCO: ☎01 71 72 12 00; www.arrco.fr. Supplementary pension for workers
AGIRC: ☎01 71 72 12 00; www.agirc.fr/. Supplementary pension for executives
ORGANIC: ☎01 40 53 43 00; www.organic.fr/. National old-age, disability and death insurance for shopkeepers and industrialists
CANCAVA: ☎01 44 37 51 00; www.cancava.fr/. National scheme for craftspeople
CNAVPL: ☎01 44 95 01 50; www.cnavpl.fr/. National scheme for liberal professions

British expats: continuing contributions to UK managed pension funds

Up until April 2006 most British expats were excluded from contributing to UK approved personal pensions unless they had earnings subject to tax in the UK or were allowed to remain members of UK approved employer's schemes. The change means that any UK citizen is able to join any type and any number of pension schemes at the same time, subject to certain restrictions. For many people the security of dealing with approved UK institutions is a major benefit. You should consult an independent financial advisor to explore this option further.

French labour relations

Throughout the 1980s a much more balanced and satisfactory relationship developed between employers and employees. This was in large part due to the periods of power enjoyed by both socialist and right wing governments, who managed to introduce legislation favourable to both workers and employers. In addition, some state industries have been privatised, which has helped present the state and the law as a mediator rather than just an employer.

Of course, labour disputes and strikes still occur, but current legislation is designed to channel employees and employers into negotiations thus providing greater potential for defusing disputes. Generally, French employers are now more sympathetic to their employees' demands for a good standard of living and more willing to share the financial success of their companies. At the same time, employees have become more aware of the need for quality, competitiveness and the financial success of the company for which they work, especially if they have a stake in it.

Employers' expectations

French employers tend to resemble those found in the USA in that they demand a very high standard of competence and are also often impatient and intolerant of mistakes. For these reasons most modern French companies are both efficient and motivated. Employers are often willing to consider new ideas from their employees, and, in the case of a foreign employee, much headway could be made by suggesting alternative practices or helping to develop a market, where appropriate, in the new country. Most employers will expect a certain degree of determination and initiative from their employees, confounding, to some extent, the traditional image of a relaxed business atmosphere.

Promotion

At one time the system of employee progress up the promotional ladder was almost rigidly predetermined in the majority of French businesses. It was extremely difficult to advance one's career at a faster rate than that dictated by the company for which one worked and employees tended to stay within one organisation, rather than switch to a competing firm in search of better prospects. Nowadays, most companies prefer to single out employees who show particular ability and reward them financially and with promotion rather than watch them take their talents elsewhere. This is a trend, which has brought about the evolution of the French equivalent of yuppies. The current situation is therefore beneficial to the able, and there is awareness among employers that fast-lane promotion should be allowed when merited.

The promotion disadvantages for foreign employees are therefore likely to be caused by other factors. One possible problem which foreign employees may encounter when working within a French company is that their level and breadth of education is different to their French counterparts. In some ways it may exceed the other, in others it may fall short. Many senior French business people, for example, have trained in the legal profession, even though they may never have had any intention of pursuing a legal career.

Another possible problem for anyone working in France who is poached by a rival firm or simply wishes to transfer for career reasons is that they may have to sign a *clause de non-concurrence* to prevent them from divulging the business secrets of one company to another. This occurs particularly in the sphere of high technology.

Such clauses are enforceable under French law and you should be aware of them, as it is a serious offence to be convicted of breach of confidentiality.

European business studies

One possible solution to the problem of discrepancies in education and business background is to take a postgraduate course at the College of Europe in Bruges (☎+32 50 47 71 11; info@coleurop.be; www.coleurop.be). Applicants require a BA and courses are in administration, economics or law. A number of scholarships are awarded each year through the cultural department of the Belgian Embassy in London.

■ WORKING CULTURE AND ETIQUETTE

There are major differences in the approach to work between France and the English-speaking world. The first point that will be noticed by anyone looking for work in France is the emphasis put on qualifications. It seems as if you can't do even the most mundane of jobs without having a relevant professional qualification. Part of the reason for this is the high levels of unemployment in France over recent decades which have meant that the government has encouraged the workforce, and especially the young, into gaining training to remove this section of the population from unemployment statistics. The other reason is that, traditionally, the French economy has been far more planned than the UK or the US economies with less opportunity for entrepreneurial activity.

The emphasis on qualifications affects schoolchildren from a very young age and creates a deterministic mentality among the French when it comes to work and looking for work. This means that a person will be qualified for a particular area of work and will have a highly developed sense of their responsibilities in this area and what they can and cannot do, or perhaps are willing, or not willing to do. Needs, then, are assigned functions that are taken on by those expressly qualified to fill them. This creates less fluidity on the job market than you might be used to and, indeed, the French tend to stay in the same post/company far longer than the British or Americans, who have less loyalty to the companies they are working for and develop in a far more goal-driven environment.

As mentioned elsewhere, the typical French working environment is hierarchical and this is reflected in the different work regimes. All employees are either cadres (executives/managerial staff) and non-cadres (non-executive/non managerial). These labels have a legal status and different tax, pension and social security regimes attached to them. A certain qualification/education level is generally required to become a cadre although experience can qualify non-cadres for an upgrade. By the same token, the most senior positions in both the public and private sectors would seem to be reserved for those educated in the *grandes écoles* (elite higher education colleges). Indeed, there is certainly less differentiation at the highest level between the public and private sectors, with top managers taking up positions alternately in one and then the other. This system, putatively based on merit, works to exclude those who have been unable to gain access to the right qualifications. This is one of the main reasons for the feelings of disenchantment among the generally unqualified young unemployed from the *banlieues* (suburbs). New immigrants from other EU countries may also find themselves victims of not having the required qualifications and this can be a real obstacle to finding satisfactory employment in France.

In addition many well-qualified young French complain of the lack of opportunity for advancement within French companies. The large French population in London is to a large extent a result of this feeling among young French. The British economy is seen as providing more equality of opportunity for those who are well-qualified and wish to move forward in their careers. In France there seems to be something of a bottleneck, with many older members of the workforce occupying positions of responsibility that will not become available for some time to come. Nevertheless, there is perhaps a more balanced attitude towards work in France than in the UK or the USA. In Britain nearly half the workforce works more than a 40-hour week and the average hours worked per year is 1,708. In France, the 35-hour week has been in force for almost a decade and although the present right-wing government is introducing measures to allow employers to pay employees for overtime (which will be untaxed) rather than for employees to be forced to take this time off in lieu it is unlikely to change the principle. (The new measure is one of the measures aimed at increasing purchasing power and will make the law more flexible so that people can work longer hours if they wish. More information on working hours can be found at www.35h.travail.gouv.fr.) In addition, in France 72% of the workforce takes more than five weeks' holiday a year. This is considerably more official holiday than Britons or Americans have from work.

The way in which business is conducted may at times, especially in the south, seem casual, but it has nonetheless produced results. Productivity levels are very high in France. The free market economy is also one which receives close guidance and enthusiastic support from the state.

The potential shown by French industry in recent years should serve to remind foreigners that the country is attractive not only on the basis of its scenery, weather, food and culture but also on the basis of the opportunities to work in a dynamic environment with good conditions of employment. Perhaps the secret to making the most of the employment situation in France is to think long term. Because of the heavily structured system, it can be frustrating to those looking for quick results and it can feel a bit like you are banging your head against an unsympathetic wall. Nevertheless, if you are prepared to take the time to find out what the requirements are for your particular goals, it can also be rewarding.

FACT

■ The average number of hours worked per person in France per year is 1,650 (2006).

◼ BUSINESS AND INDUSTRY REPORT

The Organisation for Economic Co-operation and Development (OECD) ranks the French economy sixth of the world economies in terms of gross domestic product (GDP) (behind Germany and the UK), with GDP per capita at an annual $35,000 USD (again just behind Germany and $5000 behind the UK). Industry makes up about a quarter of the total with services almost three quarters and agriculture at just 2.7%. Agriculture does, however, have an important place in the French economy historically, with, still in 1940, about half of the French population living off the land. GDP growth in volume over the last few years has been around the 2% mark annually and inflation is currently running at just under 2% (affected by the worldwide rise in oil and food prices). The labour force is around 28 million, with again a quarter employed in industry, just over 70% in the services sector and just under 5% in agriculture. Unemployment is 8.7% and only 6.2% of the population lives below the poverty line (this is one of the lowest in the world; 15% in the UK). Nevertheless 10% of households control 46% of the total wealth.

Since 1991, the proportion of people employed at the minimum wage (SMIC) has increased from 8.1% to over 15%. According to INSEE, 27% of full-time employees earn less than 1.3 times the SMIC. At the same time, the wealthiest sector of the population has seen it's revenue increase significantly over the past 10 years. The weight of forced expenses (accommodation, insurances, credit, taxes and so on) has doubled in the last 50 years, which is why purchasing power is such an issue in France right now, with the recent relaxation in the 35-hour working rule and the introduction of untaxed overtime by the Sarkozy government aiming to allow workers to increase their take-home pay.

Industries in France

The main industries in France are machinery, chemicals, automobiles, metallurgy, aeronautics, electronics, textiles, food processing and tourism, with Germany the main export market for French goods (14.7% of exports), followed by Spain (9.6%), Italy (8.7%), the UK (8.3%) and the USA (7.2%). France's main economic partner is clearly Germany with 18.9% of imports also coming from there (10.7% from Belgium, 8.2% from Italy, 5.9% from the UK and 5.1% from the United States, not a major trading partner for France). Public finances are in deficit to the tune of $1.25 trillion or around 65% of GDP and this is rising by several billion every year.

Although there has been significant liberalisation of the economy over the past 20 years with many of the previously state-owned companies having been privatised (EDF, France Telecom, Air France and so on), the government still plays an active role in the economy. Government spending is higher than any other G7 country and the government still holds shares in corporations in a range of sectors, including utilities, transport and banking. In spite of the popular misconception, French unions are in fact fairly weak, with only 10% of the workforce being unionised. However, the heavily unionised sectors, such as transport, have the power to cause maximum disruption and have therefore often been successful in attracting media attention for their demands over recent years.

Unemployment is such an issue in France, partly because it is so high among the over-50s and the young immigrant populations. Successive right-wing governments have tried to stimulate employment by lowering payroll contributions and weakening workforce legislation. They have also tried to help small businesses that traditionally have struggled with financial disincentives to entrepreneurship. There have been income tax cuts, financial rewards to the long-term unemployed who get back into work, reductions in social security contributions for businesses getting involved in training schemes. Social security contributions remain high however for most employers and are a real disincentive to employment. One of the main areas where successive governments have tried to cut social security costs is in unemployment and retirement benefits. This means that the retirement age has been raised and that state unemployment insurance is no longer so generous as it once was.

France has a large and diversified industrial base, with strengths in telecoms, aerospace and defence, shipbuilding, pharmaceuticals, electronics, construction and automobile production (French people mainly buy French cars). France has the third largest arms industry in the world with its own government being its main client. Defence spending went up a lot during Chirac's presidency. It also exports arms heavily to the Middle East. R&D spending is also high in France at 2.3% of GDP, third highest in the OECD. France is the second-largest trading nation in western Europe after Germany, with, until recently, the economy showing a trade surplus. France relies heavily on nuclear power (almost 80% of the country's electricity). There is also significant hydroelectric power generation (11.1%). France is the EU's leading agricultural producer, with production concentrated in wheat, dairy, wine, pork, beef, apples, fruit and vegetables. The agricultural sector is heavily dependent on subsidies from the EU and 70% of exports go to EU countries. France is also the most visited country in the world with 75 million visitors annually.

The economy is fairly equally spread between the different regions of France and doesn't show the disparities seen in Germany or Italy. The Nord-Pas-de-Calais, Picardy, Languedoc-Roussillon and Corsica are the poorest but the differences aren't extreme. Ile-de-France is by far the most powerful, followed by Rhone-Alpes (industry, services, high-tech) and PACA (services, industry, tourism, wines). The government has made great efforts through a programme of decentralisation to ensure that wealth is well spread throughout the regions.

FACT

■ Much emphasis is placed on tourism and preservation of the nation's heritage.

■ REGIONAL EMPLOYMENT GUIDE

In the first chapter in this book, the main cities and regions of France were discussed with a view to residence. In this section the same major cities and regions are covered, but now with a view to indicating the main possible sources of employment.

The information provided gives some idea of the industries, which are dominant and the types of jobs, which are most readily available in each area. In each case, sources of further information on the region in question are given. The press listing is for the regional newspaper in that area which may be a source of jobs and information; other local newspapers may also be useful. The Chamber of Commerce in a region may be able to provide information as discussed earlier in this chapter and the listing usually gives the address of the largest branch in that region – there will be others in adjacent towns.

Alsace

Départements: Bas-Rhin (67), Haut-Rhin (68)
Main cities: Colmar, Mulhouse, Strasbourg
Regional newspaper: *Dernières Nouvelles d'Alsace*

Chamber of Commerce: ☎03 88 75 25 25; www.strasbourg.cci.fr; information@ strasbourg.cci.fr

Major employers: CEPL (logistics); Daimler Chrysler, PSA Peugeot-Citroën (automotive); Gerriets (textile)

Employment prospects

Strasbourg is a major administrative centre for the EU and seat of the European Parliament. It also has a very important university and is an academic and financial centre. Outside Strasbourg the main industries are minerals, heavy engineering, automotive, textiles and brewing and wine production. Mulhouse is a heavy industry area and the wine production is centred on Colmar. Other industries include cotton and linen textiles, electrical appliances and chemicals.

Employment prospects were quite good until the past few years when unemployment has risen faster in Alsace than the national average and is now at 7.5% for the Bas-Rhin and 8% for the Haut-Rhin. This has been the result mostly of cutbacks in the industry sector and especially the automobile sector. Decline in the German economy has had a depressing effect on the local economy and in the area of temporary jobs there has also been a marked decline. One quarter of workers work for a foreign business which is 11% more than the national average. The hotel trade has bucked the trend by expanding thanks to a thriving tourist industry.

FACT

■ Employment rates are higher in the tourist sector.

Aquitaine

Départements: Pyrénées-Atlantiques (64), Landes (40), Gironde (33), Lot-et-Garonne (47), Dordogne (24)

Main cities: Agen, Bayonne, Biarritz, Bordeaux, Dax, Mont de Marsan, Pau, Périgueux, Villeneuve-sur-Lot

Regional newspaper: Sud Ouest, Paris papers also relevant

Chamber of Commerce: ☎05 56 11 94 94; CRCI@aquitaine.cci.fr; www.aquitaine.cci.fr

Major employers: 96% of Aquitaine's 16,583 companies are SMEs and 85% of these have fewer than 10 employees. The agro-food industry is the region's biggest employer and companies such as Labeyrie, Fromarsac, Fromageries de Chaumes, and 3A employ a total of 30,000 staff. There are 200 SMEs acting as subcontractors. SNECMA, EADS, SNPE, Establissements de la DGA (aeronautics). Smurfitt, Group Gascogne, Capdeville, Williamete (wood and paper). Total, Turbomeca, Thales, CEA, Ford France and Fayat are also all major employers

Employment prospects

Aerospace, aeronautics, electronics, agri-foodstuffs, wine and wood pulp are Bordeaux's main industries along with chemical and pharmacy. It is also a base for high-tech manufacturing of various kinds. Bordeaux is also an important port, both for imports and exports. Agriculture and forestry cover about 90% of the region and its products are gastronomically prized: wines, and pâté de foie gras (made by force-feeding ducks and geese) are internationally consumed. Aquitaine is also the biggest corn-producing region of France. About half the jobs in the agriculture sector are seasonal or temporary

Aquitaine's unemployment at 9.6% is higher than the national average which is in part due to lack of direct foreign investment and a lack of entrepreneurs

FACT

■ Wine production is a major industry on which Bordeaux will continue to thrive thanks to its great name vineyards.

as well as insufficient transport infrastructures. This is in spite of a year on year growth in job creation. Reasons for such high unemployment include the fact that many people are attracted to live in the region because of its quality of life and so more people are entering the workforce than are leaving it. The GDP, however is well above the national and European average at 3.1%. There are some categories with excellent job prospects: commerce is a thriving sector and a source of 150,000 jobs. Tourism offers an excellent source of seasonal jobs 30,000–50,000 depending on the season. Large tourist centres include Dax for its spa cures and Lourdes for pilgrimages, and also on the coast (e.g. Biarritz, St. Jean-de-Luz, Arcachon).

Auvergne

Départements: Allier (03), Cantal 915), Haute Loire (43), Puy-de-Dôme
Main towns/cities: Ambert, Aurillac, Brioude, Clermont-Ferrand, Montluçon, Moulins, Riom, Thiers
Regional newspaper: *La Montagne*
Chamber of Commerce: ☎04 73 40 65 65; web@debussac.net: website: www.auvergne.cci.fr
Major employers: Limagrain (agri-industry), Michelin, Goodyear-Dunlop (tyres), Aciéries Aubert et Duval (iron and steel forgings), Atelier Industriel Aeronautique, Trelleborg, Capgemini and Scorpa (aeronautics), Péchiney-Rhenalu (aluminium workings), Volvic (spa water)

Employment prospects

Clermont-Ferrand is an important academic town and also has a wide range of light manufacturing industries in addition to the major industrial presences of the Michelin tyre company and the headquarters of another international group: Limagrain, which is ranked the 3rd sowing industrial in the world. Other than Clermont-Ferrand, St Etienne is a major, heavy industrial and mining town in the old style. Industry accounts for 22% of jobs compared with the national average of 18% and Auvergne is in the top third of industrial regions in Europe. Traditional industries for the area including agriculture, industry and construction are cutting back employee numbers. Metal industries, mineral water and meat and dairy foods are maintaining job levels. Agriculture makes up about 7% of jobs compared with 3.85 in the rest of France. The rest of the region is largely agricultural centred on beef cattle and cheese production. The area includes various spa towns, such as Vichy, where some, mainly domestic, tourism exists and there is the possibility of seasonal hospitality jobs. The region is hindered by lack of qualified workers and very high turnover, while falls in population could lead to an even bigger lack of workers, which would be detrimental to regional industry.

Bretagne (Brittany)

Départements: Finistère (29), Côtes-d'Armor (22), Ile-et-Vilaine (35), Morbihan (35)
Main cities: Brest, St Malo, St Brieuc, Rennes, Vannes

Regional newspaper: *Ouest France, Le Télégramme*
Chamber of Commerce: ☎02 99 25 41 41; crci@bretagne.cci.fr, www.bretagne.cci.fr
Major employers: Leclerc, Les Comptoirs Modernes (distribution)

Employment prospects

Rennes is the industrial hub of the region and companies there are involved in printing and publishing, motor and automotive manufacture and telecommunications. Rennes is also an academic and administrative city, and as such is a centre for research and development of all kinds. The port of Brest has recently developed industries in engineering and electronics.

Historically, Brittany's economy is based on agriculture and food processing, especially the meat (pigs) sector which employs half the labour force. Shipbuilding, fishing and seafood processing, marine research and marine biotechnology are the other main activities. It is also one of the leading French vegetable-producing regions. There has been a downturn in the industrial sector, particularly in the area of electrical and electronic equipment and shipbuilding is in decline. The construction sector is creating an increasing number of new jobs as is the services sector in retail trade and personal and domestic services. The tourist trade brings a lot of seasonal work, especially on the coast. During the latter part of 2004, unemployment was high at 8% but it reached its peak in 2004 and has been falling since then.

Bourgogne (Burgundy)

Départements: Côtes d'Or (21), Saône-et-Loire (71), Nièvre (58), Yonne (89)
Main cities: Auxerre, Dijon

Regional newspaper: see Paris press
Chamber of Commerce: ☎03 80 60 40 60; www.bourgogne.cci.fr
Major employers: Unilever-Amora, Enckes-Granini, Nestlé, Senoble (agri-food), Essilor, GEC Alstom, TPC, Schneider, Thomson (electricity/electronics), Gates, Koyo-Peugeot, Michelin, Plasto, Valéo (automotive), JC Boisset, Kriter, Cottin Frères (wine)

Employment prospects

Well known for wine and food production, Burgundy has a reputation for mass production of many of its wines, unlike many areas of France. Traditionally the region's prosperity came from heavy industry, which has now declined leaving food, wines and agriculture of greater economic importance. Still prominent industries include iron and steel, engineering, glass, ceramics, motor manufacture. Mâcon and Bourg-en-Bresse are more industrial than Dijon, as the proportion of industry is greatest in Saône et Loire as well as the North of Yonne and the South of Nièvre. Industry accounts for 23% of regional workers, however, industrial work has been on the decline since 2001. Tourism, based on the region's gastronomy and architectural heritage, is also fairly important. Employment is high in the Saône-et-Loire and in Nièvre because of the manufacturing concentrated there. Building and construction enjoyed a recent boom with a recruitment drive for civil engineering and building staff. There is plenty of seasonal work available in the tourist industry, particularly hotels and catering.

Champagne-ardenne

Départements: Ardennes (08), Marne (51), Aube (10), Haute-Marne (52)
Main cities: Châlons-sur-Marne, Charleville-Mézières, Chaumont, Reims, Troyes
Regional newspaper: *L'Union* and see Paris press
Chamber of Commerce: ☎03 26 69 33 40; crci@champagne-ardenne.cci.fr www.champagne-ardenne.cci.fr
Major employers: La Fonte Ardennais, Forges de Courcelles, GHM, Pum, (metals); Petit Bateau (textiles), Vistéon (automobiles), Groupe Soufflet, Lang Ferry

Employment prospects

By far the leading regional employer is the metallurgy industry particularly well established in the Ardennes with nearly half the nut and bold production of France being carried out there. Traditionally, the area had much heavy engineering, steelworks, mining, textiles, etc. which are gradually being replaced by new industries including electronics and agri-foodstuff production. Agriculture, primarily cereal crops, continues to be an important industry, although the region's riches derive directly from champagne, an industry in its own right, centred on Epernay. Unemployment is currently at 10.1%, well above the national average, which is not helped by the fact that Ardennes is one of the worse affected departments in France.

La Corse (Corsica)

Départéments: Haute-Corse, Basse-Corse
Main cities/towns: Ajaccio, Bastia, Calvi
Regional newspaper: *Corsican*
Chamber of Commerce: ☎04 95 54 44 44
Major employers: Corse Composite Aéronautiques, Société Ajaccienne des boulangerie Miniconi et Fabbri Gino, Sagem SA, SARL les Poulets Bastiais, Corsetyrene, Société Fromagère Corse

Employment prospects

Corsica, although technically part of metropolitan France, is industrially and commercially as separate as it is geographically. It has a small population, owing to emigration, no heavy industry and only limited agriculture, mainly vineyards and sheep. The island is, however, famed for its magnificent coastline, and tourism, mainly domestic, is the principal source of revenue. About 2 million tourists a year visit Corsica giving rise to an estimated 30,000 seasonal jobs indirectly or directly related to the tourist industry. Out of season, most of the jobs are in Ajaccio and Bastia where about 6,000 islanders commute daily. The other large town, Calvi, has a population of 5,000. The total population of Corsica is about 260,000 and unemployment follows the seasons with about 9,000 people unemployed in summer, rising to about 15,000 in winter.

Franche-Comté

Départements: Haute-Saône (70), Territoire de Belfort (90), Doubs (25), Jura (39)
Main cities: Belfort, Besançon
Regional newspaper: *L'Est*
Chamber of Commerce: ☎03 81 47 42 00; crci@franche-comte.cci.fr; www.cciexpert.net
Major employers: PSA Sochaux is the largest employer (automotive); Alstom, General Electric (electronics), Geodis, Gefco, Easydis, Intermarché, Peugot (logistics); Solvay, Vetoquinol, V33, Cerp (chemicals); Guillin Emballages, Plastival (plastics); Smoby, Berchet group (toys)

Employment prospects

This region has a higher percentage of its population working in industry than any other region of France. Principal industries are light and heavy engineering, light assembly, textiles, mining and minerals. Appropriately enough perhaps for an area that borders Switzerland, Besançon is the clock-making centre of France and is famed for high-precision engineering. Montbéliard-Sochaux is the base of the Peugeot car company and other parts of the region produce small amounts of cheese, woodwork and artisans' products. In addition, Besançon has become a centre for micro-technics and many small firms there are at the cutting edge of this industry. Franche Comté also attracts a modest number of tourists. Regional unemployment at 7.8% is below the national average.

Languedoc-Roussillon

Départements: Lozère (48), Gard (30), Hérault (34), Aude (11)
Main cities/towns: Alès, Carcassonne, Mende, Montpellier, Nîmes, Perpignan, Séte
Regional newspaper: *Midi Libre*
Chamber of Commerce: ☎04 67 13 68 00; crci@languedoc-roussillon.cci.fr; www.languedoc-roussillon.cci.fr
Major employers: Nestlé, SNCF, the hospitals, La Poste, Carrefour, France Télécom, Crédit Agricole, Hérault General Council, EDF, Caisse d'Epargne and France Telecom

Employment prospects

Languedoc is one of the newest and fastest economically developing areas in France, it also has an important academic and research centre in the old university city of Montpellier; however, unemployment lies at 12.4%, one of the highest in France. Prominent industries, in both the city and the rest of the region, include computers, electronics, medical equipment and research, telecommunications. Other main cities, Perpignan and Nîmes are similarly high-tech-based and as a result of the above-mentioned economic boom, construction is also a major industry. In the summer, tourism provides a useful boost to the economy along the now highly developed coastal stretches while wine production and agriculture (Mediterranean fruit and vegetables) predominate inland. Despite some cutting edge technological industries, Languedoc-Roussillon is one of the least-industrialised regions of France; only 21% of its GDP comes from industry while nearly 70% of the workforce is employed in service industries. The region is experiencing the highest migration trend in France and as a result has a high level of unemployment mainly because people are attracted to the lifestyle of the region faster than jobs can be created for them. It is also especially popular for pensioners.

Limousin

Départements: Corrèze (19), Creuse (23), Haute-Vienne (87).
Main cities/towns: Brive-la-Gaillarde, Guèret, Limoges, Oradon-sur-Glane, Tulle
Regional newspaper: *Sud Ouest* (Bordeaux) and *La Dépêche* (Toulouse)
Chamber of Commerce: ☎05 55 04 40 00; www.limousin.cci.fr
Major employers: Legrand Group, Sicame, Schneider, Thomson (electronics); International Paper, Smurfit, CGCO (wood and paper); Unilever, Danone, Madrange, Charal, Bizac, Pierrot Gourmand (food), Bristol Myers Squibb, Boiron, Pharmacia France (health and medicine), Deshors, Mecalim, Dito Sama, Valéo (metal and mechanical)

Employment prospects

The majority of companies in Limousin are small and medium-sized but they are working on precision and high-performance products. These businesses cover most types of products from pharmaceuticals to cutting edge technology. In Limousin, 78% of companies employ fewer than 50 people; only 52 companies have a workforce of more than 200 including Deshors, which employs 450 and Sum which has about 600. In many ways Limousin encapsulates rural France at its most tranquil, the main way of life being agriculture, mostly small-scale cattle farming. Agri-foodstuffs and leather products are also important. In addition, there are local, cottage industries in metalwork, glass, etc. and Limoges porcelain is known worldwide and is probably the region's most famous industry. Unemployment is also well below the national average after decreasing steadily for the past few years it now sits at 6.5%. A worrying trend, however, is the number of qualified young people moving away from the region as youth (and 50+ workers) unemployment is actually higher than national average.

Loire-valley/Centre

Départements: Cher (18), Eure et Loir (28), Indre (36), Indre-et-Loire (37), Loir et Cher (41), Loiret (45)

Main cities/towns: Blois, Bourges, Chartres, Chateauroux, Montargis, Orléans, Tours

Regional newspaper: see Paris press

Chamber of Commerce: Saint Jean de la Ruelle ☎02 38 25 25 25; Orléans ☎02 38 77 77 77; www.loiret.cci.fr

Major employers: Christian Dior, Abbott, Pfizer, Michelin, Hutchinson, MBDA, Philips, Alcatel, ST Microelectronics, Thales, John Deere, Valéo, Mecachrome, Harry's, Louis Vuitton, Tupperware, Weinberg, Guerlain, Renault, Cadbury, IBM, Vivarte, Bouygues Telecom

Employment prospects

The Loire valley, in effect a sub-region of the Loire region, is now an important commuter area serving Paris, as well as a popular tourist centre. Other main industries are pharmaceuticals, cosmetics, agriculture and, food manufacture and processing as well as occupying a key position in logistics and call centres. It is the fifth biggest industrial region in France. Unemployment is continuing to remain low at below 7%.

Pays de Loire

Départements: Loire-Atlantique (44), Maine et Loire (49), Mayenne (53), Sarthe (72), Vendée (85)

Main cities/towns: Angers, Anjou, Maine, Nantes, La Roche-sur-Yonne, Laval, Le Mans, St Nazaire

Regional newspapers: *Ouest France* and *Presse Océan*

Chamber of Commerce: ☎02 40 44 63 00; www.paydelaloire.cci.fr

Major employers: Bull (SA), Thomson, NEC computers Motorola (information and communication technology), Bosch, Scania, Valéo (automotive construction and components), STMicroelectrics, Renault Industrie, Chantiers de l'Atlantique,Manitou BF, Charal, Michelin

Employment prospects

FACT

■ Pays de Loire is also experiencing a low unemployment rate of under 7%

The industrial hub of the whole Loire region is the Nantes-Saint Nazaire port complex, the fourth largest port of France. Nantes is linked to Paris by high speed train (TGV) which takes two hours. The region's industries include electronics, engineering, garment and footwear manufacture. Other regional industries are traditional, including food processing, maritime industries, fishery, agriculture, and wine production. New industries are also being established in research and development services and telecommunications. The Pays de la Loire (as Loire West is otherwise known) has been a job hotspot for the last few years thanks to its many investment projects. One in four employees in the area is set to retire in 2010 and one-third of the vacated jobs will be in health, social work and the public sector, further enhancing employment prospects.

Lorraine

Départements: Meuse (55), Meurthe-et-Moselle (54), Moselle (57), Vosges (88)

Main cities: Metz, Nancy

Regional newspaper: L'Est Républicain
Chamber of Commerce: ☎03 83 90 13 13; www.lorraine.cci.fr
Major employers: Saint Gobain (cast iron); SOVAB (automotive); Danone-Malteurop, Neuhouser, Vittel, (foodstuffs); Sollac/Usinor (steel); Altofina, Air Liquide, Solvay (petrochemicals); Leach International, Toshiba, Minolta, Daewoo, Philips (electronics); Baccarat, Daum, Saint-Louis (handmade crystal), Sollac, Ascometal, Smart, PSA, Ispat Uni-metal, Contrexeville

Employment prospects

Unemployment was very high in previous years, reaching 9.4% in 2006, but has since lowered again to 8.6%. The wealth of this region once derived from old heavy industries connected with iron, steel and coal production but these, to a large extent, have ceased to exist. The region is now undergoing a period of industrial reconstruction and conversion ('technical transfer') as can be seen from the diversity of its commercial enterprises. It has an abundance of natural resources. Nancy is an important academic city, as well as being an administrative, business and commercial centre. Other industries in the city include finance, banking, electronics and computers. The region, as opposed to the city, is important for agriculture, food processing and textiles. But most people are employed in the metal sector: iron, steel, smelting and precision mechanics. The economy has fallen off in the past two years and there is much competition for low-skilled jobs from a large group finding it difficult to get work despite a considerable improvement in the labour market over past few years.

TIP

■ You need to research the possibilities carefully if you are hoping to work in Lorraine.

Nord-pas-de-Calais

Départements: Nord (59), Pas-de-Calais (62)
Main City/Towns: Lille, Dunkirk, Calais, Boulogne-sur-Mer. All are ports as well as Roubaix, Valenciennes, and Arres
Regional newspaper: La Voix du Nord
Chamber of Commerce: ☎03 20 63 79 70; www.nordpasdecalais.cci.fr
Major employers: Cousin, Dewarin, DMC, Doublet (textiles); Daniel Ferry, d'Haussy (printing/publishing); PSA, Renault, Toyota (automotive); Air Liquide Chimie Dérivés (chemicals); Boel, Textron (engineering), LaRedoute. Also headquarters of Auchan, Boulanger, Castorama and Match (retail chains)

Employment prospects

Traditionally a tourist haven, it suffered a decline in industry, though industry is growing again and employment with it. This region is one whose importance was traditionally based on heavy industry including mining and steel production, which have declined considerably in recent years, and have been replaced with some high-tech businesses. Major industries include heavy engineering, mining and mineral exploitation, electronics, transport and distribution and energy industries. The area is currently experiencing a boom in development as a result of government incentives for inward investment and the increased opportunities afforded by the Channel Tunnel and the TGV high speed link to Paris, Lille, Brussels, etc. Nord Pas-de-Calais is a major area for foreign businesses of which there are more than 1,400 in the area employing a total of nearly 130,000 staff. It may therefore be feasible to first get a job with a British business and try to get a posting to this area. British companies include Whessoe, BP, Courtaulds, KP Foods and P&O. However, be warned that such an industrial area with large employers is subject to fluctuations in employment which reached a very high 12.5% in 2004. It is currently well above the national average at 11.5%.

Normandie (Normandy)

Départements of Upper Normandy: Eure (27), Seine Maritime (76)
Départements of Lower Normandy: Calvados (14), Manche (50), Orne (61)
Main cities/towns: Rouen, Evreux, Giverny, Dieppe, Le Havre, Bayeux, Caen, Cherbourg
Regional newspaper: *Paris-Normandie*; also Paris press
Chamber of Commerce: Rouen ☎02 35 88 44 42; Caen ☎02 31 38 31 67
Major employers: Renault Group, PSA Peugot-Citroën (automotive); Snecma, Hurel-Hispana, EADS Revima (aeronautics); Philips, Alcatel, Thalès, Digital Airways, Stepmind, Sagem, Bosch (electronics/IT); Altofina, Total, Shell, Exxon-Mobil, Chevron-Texaco (oil/petrochemicals); Danone, Legal, Nestlé, Ferrero, Maîtres Latiers du Cotentin, Segafredo (agri-foods); Aventis, Oril, Glaxo, Janssen, Sanofi, Upjohn (pharmaceuticals)

FACT

■ There is a fair range of seasonal employment connected with the tourist industry.

Employment prospects

Upper Normandy includes Rouen and the Seine valley, which comprises a heavy, industrial area with two major ports: Le Havre and Rouen. Industries include heavy engineering, metal industries, motor manufacture, chemicals, petrochemicals, pharmaceuticals and plastics. New industries include electronics and telecommunications. Jobs in agriculture are on the decline although agri-food is generating jobs. It's unemployment rate remains fairly high at around 9%. Lower Normandy is largely rural and agricultural (livestock, dairy products and fruit), and also, through the summer months, an important tourist region. Paris is easily accessible. Jobs in the industrial sector are holding steady but not generally increasing. In the agri-business sector employment is increasing, except meat businesses where falling consumption is causing cutbacks in jobs. There is a fair range of seasonal employment connected with the tourist industry. Unemployment tends to be higher than the national average overall, because of fluctuations in employment requirements for the many large industries in upper Normandy. However, salaries are also above the national average.

Paris/Ile de France

Départements: Ville-de-Paris (75), Seine-et-Marne (77), Yvelines (78), Essonne (91), Haute-de-Seine (92), Seine-Saint-Denis (93), Val-de-Marne (94), Val-d'Oise (95)
Main cities/Towns: Evry, Fontainebleau, Mantes, Meaux, Orly, Paris, Pontoise, Roissy, Versailles
Regional newspapers: Paris press – see section on newspapers in the chapter *Daily life*
Chamber of Commerce: ☎01 53 40 49 61; www.ccip75.fr.

Major employers: A huge number of industrial companies operate in the Paris area and Sony, IBM, Hewlett Packard France, Siemens and Motorola are among the foreign companies with bases in the capital, Paris. The majority of high-tech companies which have seen an immense boom in the past decade or so, are in the *départements* of Hauts-de-Seine, Yvelines and the northern part of Essonne

Employment prospects

Needless to say, most industrial and commercial sectors are represented in Paris and its hinterland, which contain some 20% of the total population of France. The majority of jobs in the capital are in public administrations since Paris is the seat of all the machinery of government and its higher functionaries are based in Paris. Unusually, some heavy industry (notably motor manufacturing) still exists in the capital itself. Paris is also one of the most famous tourist cities in the world and there are thousands of jobs connected with this area. International organisations including UNESCO and OECD also have their seats there. There is also a huge service industry in and around Paris including financial services, company services and real estate services. The hinterland is important for agriculture and is a very fertile area. Important business and commercial areas outside central Paris are La Défense to the west and Quai de Bercy in the south-east. Some of the outer suburbs of Paris are business and commercial centres in their own right, for example, the new town of Marne-la-Vallée to the east.

FACT

Paris is the number one economic region in France as well as being one of the leading ones on a European level.

Picardie (Picardy)

Départements: Somme (80), Oise (60), Aisne (02)
Main cities/towns: Abbeville, Amiens, Beauvais, Chantilly, Compiegne, Laon, Pierrefonds, St Quentin
Regional newspaper: *Le Courrier Picard*
Chamber of Commerce: ☎03 22 82 80 80; www.e-picardie.net
Major employers: The majority of businesses comprising one of Picardy's two main industries, mechanical engineering, are SMEs. The other main industry is agri-foods supported by the 18,000 plus farms of the region, which are primarily arable but also produce beef and dairy products. Findus frozen foods is a large employer in the area, as is Herta which specialises in pre-packaged convenience foods. The service industry for enterprises and individuals is also a large employer

Employment prospects

There is approximately 10% unemployment in Picardy which is only a fraction above the national average. Some heavy industry, generally iron and steel based, exist throughout the region alongside chemical, tyre manufacturing, engineering and textile industries. Agriculture and food production (cereals and industrial crops) are also important and there have been developments in the agri-foodstuffs industry. Transport/logistics is a growth area and tourism is also expanding. The proportion of temporary employment in Picardy is very high.

Poitou-charentes

Départements: Charente (16), Charente-Maritime (17), Deux Sèvres (79), Vienne (86)

Main cities: Angoulême, La Rochelle, Niort, Poitiers
Regional newspaper: *Sud Ouest and Ouest France*
Chamber of Commerce: Limoges ☎05 55 04 40 00; www.limoges.cci.fr; Poitiers ☎05 49 60 98 00
Major employers: Poitou-Charente is a region of small businesses. Fewer than 24 businesses in the region have 500 or more employees and there are over 5,000 employing fewer than 20. The biggest employers are Heuliez (heavy goods vehicle manufacture), Leroy-Somer (small electric motors), Rullier Bois Import and SCE (wood and wood products) and Macif, Maaf, Maif (mutual insurance)

Employment prospects

Poitou Charente has some of the lowest salaries in France because it's largely dependent on its agriculture and fisheries, particularly its oyster beds, beef and veal production, butter and cognac. It is also the largest cereal growing region after the Parisian Basin and contains a third of France's goat flocks. Poitiers is a localised business and commercial centre while La Rochelle is one of France's leading resorts and the region is popular with tourists generally. Seasonal jobs are the most likely form of employment including at the Futuroscope theme park at Poitiers. Unemployment varies depending on the *département*. It is highest in Charente Maritime and lowest in Deux Sèvres. Building work has been one of the drivers of economic activity in Charente Maritme but with the downturn on the property market because of the sub-prime crisis and the change in healthcare regulations for expats, the building sector is showing signs of slowing.

Provence-Alpes-Côte d'Azur

Départements: Vaucluse (84), Bouches-du-Rhône (13), Var (83), Alpes-de-Haute-Provence (04), Haute-Alpes (05), Alpes Maritimes (06). The first four of these departments comprise the region of Provence
Main cities: Antibes, Aix-en-Provence, Arles, Avignon, Cannes, Dignes, Gap, Grasse, Marseille (regional capital and home to most of the largest companies), Nice, Toulon
Regional newspaper: Paris newspapers and *La Provence, La Marseillaise*
Chamber of Commerce: Marseille ☎04 91 14 42 00; Nice ☎0820 422 222; www.ccinice-cote-azur.com

Major employers: Eurocopter (aeronautics); Hemosystem, Naturex, Innata Pharma, Nicox (biotechnology and pharmaceuticals); Pernod-Ricard, Dole (foods); Atmel (micro-electronics); Suez (water treatment and distribution), Peugot (automotive); Alstom (transports and energy)

Employment prospects

As in Languedoc there is a lot of inward migration to the PACA region. This was fuelled by the employment boom which lasted until 2002. Unemployment is currently about 10.8%, and falling. The services sector is predominant and the construction sector is strong. Out of a population of 4.6 million, the active population is just 2 million. Marseille is fast becoming the centre of a vast free trade area distributed around the Mediterranean basin. Business start-ups for micro-companies are fostered locally as they are seen as a way to boost employment. The area is also a boom area for high-tech companies and biotechnology for which PACA has achieved a cutting edge reputation. Marseille is traditionally a heavy industrial area, most of which still exists, albeit on a smaller scale than before. Other industries include chemicals, oil, textiles, pharmaceuticals, heavy engineering, iron, steel and shipyards. Marseille and Toulon are major merchant port and distribution centres involved in maritime and shipping services and research. New growth industries in Marseille include electronics, computing, aerospace and light, high-tech manufacturing. Nice in Provence and its environs are world famous for their fashionable resorts and tourism which gives rise to a large number of seasonal jobs. However, other high-tech industries also flourish there including electronics and computing, telecommunications and marine industries. Sophia Antipolis near Nice, is one of the most important high-tech centres of France with a large number of factories dedicated to its production. More non-tourist industry is to be found at Cannes and Menton. The rest of Provence is largely agricultural, growing Mediterranean produce: both the coast and the Alps are important tourist areas.

Pyrénées

Départements: Ariège (09), Haute Garonne (31), Haute Pyrénées (65), Gers (32), Tarn (81), Tarn-et-Garonne (82), Aveyron (12), Lot (46)
Main cities/towns: Albi, Cahors, Castres, Montauban, Rodez, Tarbes, Toulouse
Regional newspaper: *Dépêche du Midi*
Chamber of Commerce: Blagnac ☎95 62 74 20 00; Toulouse ☎05 61 33 65 00;
Main Employers: Groupe 3A, SA des Caves et Producteurs Réunis de Roquefort, Groupe RAGT, Andros Danone, Polainat, Poult Biscuits, Syngenta Seeds, CRT (agrifood); Airbus, EADS, ATR, Liebherr Aerospace, Ratier Figeac, Latecoere, Thales Avionics, Air France Industries, Blanc Aero Industries, Rockwell, Collins France (aeronautics); Fegeac Aéro, STTS, Mecaprotec Industries, GIAT Industries, Comau Systeme France, Filtrauto, Cinetic Machining, Forest Line Capdenac, Flow Control Technologies, SOFOP (metallurgy); Pierre Fabre, Sanofi Synthe Labo, Syngenta (Biotech)

Employment prospects

There is a great deal of industry in the Midi-Pyrénées as this region is generally known. Aerospace is a huge employer as the European Airbus is built in Toulouse. The other big industries in the region are biotech industries, electric and electronic equipment, metallurgy and metal fabrication. The main problem has been the creation of sufficient technology jobs fast enough to replace the job losses caused by the decline in the manufacturing industry (textile, clothing and leather). Toulouse is very much a boom city economically and all its industries are high-tech, including aeronautics, aerospace, aviation, electronics, data processing, computers and robotics. Toulouse also boasts many academic and research facilities as well as government offices. The Pyrénées area generally tends towards traditional agriculture and wine production and is very much in contrast to its thrusting capital city. Health and health provision is another area where there are good employment prospects.

Rhône-Alpes

Départements: Rhône (69, Loire (42), Ardèche (07, Drôme (26), Savoie (73), Haute-Savoie (74), Isère (38), Ain (01)
Main cities/towns: Annecy, Cluses, Grenoble, Lyon, Roanne, St Etienne
Regional newspaper: *Progrès de Lyon*; also Paris press
Chamber of Commerce: ☎04 72 11 43 57; www.rhone-alpes.cci.fr
Main employers: Aventis, RVI (conglomerates); Naf Naf, Zara, Etam, La Redoute (fashion); Badoit, Candia, Nestlé, Justin Bridou, Weiss, Cémoi (food); Easygis (logistics); SNF Floerger, Desjoyaux (water and environment)

Employment prospects

The Lyons region is France's second largest industrial region after the Ile-de-France region. Mechanical engineering, chemistry, pharmaceutical and healthcare industries are pre-eminent in the area. Unemployment is below the national average at 8.8%. This is a growth area including many start-ups, but most of the vacancies on offer are for casual and part-time jobs. The region has the highest number of seasonal jobs in France including winter sports jobs. Despite the heavy industry in Lyon, the area also has agriculture and vineyards and there are many seasonal jobs connected with this.

FACT

■ Lyon is also a capital of gourmet cuisine.

Savoy and Dauphiny

Départements: Drôme (26), Isère (38)
Main cities: Aix-les-Bains, Chambéry, Charbonnières-les-Bains, Grenoble, Valence
Regional newspaper: *Dauphiné Libéré* and Lyon press
Chamber of Commerce: Grenoble ☎04 76 28 28 00; www.grenoble.cci.fr
Major employers: RES Groupe, TCI Groupe, Varvat Metallerie EURL (metal working); Alpes Confection Industrielle (textiles); Bellemin Robert SARL, Bovagnet Scierie, Les Charpentiers du Guiers, Most Emballages, Pic Bois Gravures (wood and wood products)

Employment prospects

Grenoble is one of the booming new French techno-cities. Its industries are almost all high-tech and include computing, electronics and telecommunications. The area is also the centre of the substantial French nuclear industry and Grenoble is an important academic, scientific and research centre, which boasts a famous university. Traditional industries include engineering, mining/minerals and textiles. A substantial tourist industry exists within the region all year round, although principally in winter as most of the French Alpine resorts are to be found here where a great deal of winter work is available.

■ DIRECTORY OF MAJOR EMPLOYERS

The directory lists the major employers in France, and the respective industries in which they are involved are also given. Employee numbers range from 600 (Gecina) to over 117,000 worldwide (EDF).

Air France-KLM: www.airfrance.fr. Now only 25.6% state-owned

L'Air Liquide: www.airliquide.comfr.; Chemicals

Alstom: www.alstom.com. Business equipment, transport (creator of the TGV)

Areva: www.areva.com. Nuclear power production

Assurances Générales de France (AGF): www.agf.fr. Financial, insurance. Majority owned by Allianz (German insurer)

Aubay: www.aubay.com. Computer software and services, IT consulting services.

Auchan: www.auchan.fr. Superstores.

AXA Assurances IARD SA: www.axa.com. One of the world's largest insurers. It has more than 50 major subsidiaries in France and operations include US-based AXA Financial

BNP Paribas: www.bnpparibas.com

Bouygues: www.bouygues.com. Telecoms and media, services, construction

BP: www.bp.com

Carrefour: www.carrefour.com. Retail

Groupe Casino: www.groupe-casino.fr. Superstores

Christian Dior: www.dior.com

Club Méditerranée (Club Med): www.clubmed.fr. Holiday operator has 150 leisure operations in 40 countries, including 120 resort villages 12 villas, a cruise ship and a French tour operator

Compagnie Française Philips: www.philips.fr. Electrical

Compagnie Générale des Eaux (now Veolia): www.generale-des-eaux.com. Water utility with 2,600 subsidiaries ranging from catering to cable television

Compass Group France: www.compass-group.fr. Provider of food and related services in 98 countries; 20,000 employees and 3,000 restaurants in France

Cora: www.cora.fr. Hypermarkets

Groupe Danone: www.danone.fr. Food Industry including dairy, beverages (including Evian) and biscuits

Electricité de France (EDF): www.edf.fr

ESSO-SAF: www.esso.com. Petrochemicals

Euromarché: www.euromarche.com. Distribution

France Télécom: www.francetelecom.com. Telecommunications

Gaz de France: www.gazdefrance.fr. Gas utility

Gecina: www.gecina.fr. France's largest publicly traded real estate firm. More than 90% of its holdings are in Paris and some in Lyon

Hachette: www.lagardere.com. Part of Lagardere media group (see below). Publishing

Havas Advertising: www.havas-advertising.com. Advertising

IBM France: www.ibm.com/fr/fr. Office systems and computing

La Française des Jeux: www.francaisedesjeux.com. Lotteries

Lagardère: www.lagardere.com. Media group

Leclerc: Association des Centres Distributeurs E Leclerc; www.e-leclerc.com. Large food retailer supports 550 individually owned superstores mostly in France, under the Galec brand

Louis Vuitton Moet Hennessy (LVMH): www.lvmh.com. Accessories, leather and luxury goods

Michelin: www.michelin.fr. Tyres, publishing

Groupement des Mousquetaires: www.groupedesmousquetaires.com. Stores

L'Oréal: www.loreal.com. Cosmetics, pharmaceuticals

PPR (Pinault-Printemps-Redoute): www.ppr.com. Retail businesses and luxury goods

Pierre & Vacances: www.pv-holidays.com. Holidays

La Poste: www.laposte.fr. Postal and banking services

PSA (Peugeot-Citroën): www.psa-peugeot-citroen.com. Cars, commercial vehicles, engineering

Renault: www.renault.fr. Motor industry

Shell France: www.shell.com. Petrochemicals

SNCF: www.sncf.fr. Passenger and freight transport

Suez SA: www.suez.fr. Water, gas and electricity

Tereos S.A.: (formerly Béghin-Say) www.tereos.com. Sugar

Thales: www.thalesgroup.com. Aeronautics, defence, technology and information services

Total: www.total.com

Valéo: www.valeo.com. Cars

Vivendi Universal: www.vivendi.com

British companies and organisations offering employment in France to UK graduates

ALCAN: www.alcan.com. Marketing, selling, distribution, support and repair of advanced technology products

Arjo Wiggins Fine Papers Ltd: www.argowigginsfinepapers.co.uk. Wholly French-owned company. Paper manufacturers. Technical, engineering staff for French parent company

Barclays Bank: www.barclays.fr. For jobs in France you should contact Barclays International in France as the opportunity to transfer abroad from the graduate recruitment programme in the UK is no longer offered

Booz Allen & Hamilton: www.boozallen.com. Business analysts and consultants. Usually recruits graduates pre-MBA

Boston Consulting Group: www.bcg.com. Management consultants. Paris office recruits for France (☎01 40 17 100)

British Council: www.britishcouncil.org. Promotes all aspects of British culture abroad. Enquiries to UK office or British Council offices in France

Choice Hotels Europe: www.choiceHotelsEurope.com. Owns, manages and franchises over 500 hotels in 13 European countries. Some opportunities in France (mainly Paris) for those with relevant background. Fluent French or good working knowledge required. Minimum six months' employment. Applications by e-mail to careers@choicehotelseurope.com

Clifford Chance: www.cliffordchance.com. Global law firm. The Paris office carries out recruitment for vacancies in France (☎01 44 05 52 52)

First Choice Holidays: www.fcski.co.uk. Has details of ski jobs and you can download application forms. The website also has link to summer jobs. Leading tour operator with opening abroad and in France in winter and summer

Freshfields, Bruckhans, Deringer: www.freshfields.com. Lawyers. Paris office ☎01 44 56 44 56

Huntsman Tioxide UK Ltd: www.huntsman.com. Chemical, mechanical engineering. Office in Calais

Inlingua Teacher Training and Recruitment: www.inlingua-paris.com. Various schools in Paris. Runs 250 language schools worldwide

International House: www.ihworld.com. Runs 95 English language schools in 20 countries and internationally recognised training courses for TEFL teachers

Kier Construction: www.kier.co.uk. Construction

Kimberley Clark Ltd: www.kimberley-clark.com. Soft tissue and allied products. The company has a policy of making transfers to France and other EU countries available to all the workforce

Mars Drinks: www.marsdrinks.co.uk. Has recruited from the UK for marketing and sales in France

Slaughter & May: www.slaughterandmay.com. Lawyers. Can be seconded to offices in Paris

American companies

For details of American companies which operate in France see *The Guide to Doing Business in France* published by the American Chamber of Commerce in France (☎01 56 43 45 61; amchamfrance.org; www.amchamfrance.org).

Other possibilities

The French Cognac company, Hennessy, based in Cognac, employs some bilingual staff and a dozen or so summer guides to show coach parties and tourists round the Hennessy production premises.

■ RETIREMENT

Overview

France has been popular with foreign visitors since the 19th century, but it has been the development of mass tourism that has made French life and culture so accessible.

Useful publications and resources

- *Making a Living in France* (2005) and *Culture Wise France* (2007) by Joe Laredo. For anyone planning to live or work in France. Also *The Best Places to Buy a Home in France* (2007) by same author
- *International Employment Gazette*: www.intemployment. com. American online subscription magazine with details of professional jobs worldwide with a European section
- *Taxation in France, a Foreign Perspective* (PKF) by Charles Parkinson of PKF (Guernsey) Ltd. Very detailed handbook by an expatriate tax expert

Many people buy holiday homes when they are still living in their own country with the expectation of retiring to France when the time comes. Until recently, Spain had the largest colony of expatriates over 60, but rising prices and complications with property purchase and sales left many people there disillusioned, if not hard put to make ends meet. France will never be as popular as Spain with those looking for a warm retirement spot, but nonetheless, pensioner numbers retiring to France have increased in the past decade thanks to low property prices in many areas, less sharply rising prices generally and the beauty and diversity of the rural regions.

If you are discriminating about the area and location you choose, there will be all the benefits of Spain, such as good weather and a substantial expatriate population of a similar age group, with the added benefits of novelty, a new culture and a different way of life. Additionally, although property prices vary greatly between different parts of the country (and even within them), it's possible to buy a property to retire to in France at a lower price than the equivalent in Spain. Finally, although many parts of this book apply equally to those wishing to retire and to work in France, this section aims to draw attention to the procedures and decisions which apply specifically to those planning their retirement in France.

The decision to leave your own country

Mention retirement in France and most of us visualise warm, sunny weather, café au lait and croissants, buying wonderfully fresh produce in the market, eating in little bistros, and having the leisure to appreciate the changing of the seasons. However, such a move has other realities such as coping practically and emotionally with such as move and the consequences. For instance, the prospective emigrant must be able to afford the move financially, and also be willing to improve the quality of his or her French, if not to learn from scratch a new language (see Abraham Paris' comments below). You'll need energy and enthusiasm to move and set up home in a new country and make new friends, and being prepared to leave your former home permanently, and thus to see much less of your family members and friends can be a wrench.

Many people who retire abroad have what it takes to make a success of the move and are perhaps more committed to the venture than many younger people. However, decisions to move are often born out of a love of the country discovered through past holidays, work, cultural exchanges, etc. As living permanently somewhere is not the same as spending short periods there, it may be a good idea to consider a long 'try out' holiday, of say six months. Alternatively, you could buy a second home in France (if finances permit) and spend several months there annually over several years and finally make a permanent move to France, selling your home only when you feel certain that it's right choice for you. Seeing your favourite area of France at different seasons is also important as many parts of France are bustling and cheerful in summer, but deserted and desolate in winter.

There is a popular misconception that because property is cheaper in France, that living costs generally are cheaper but this is not in fact the case: many things including meat, utilities and insurance are more expensive and many useful things

> **Abraham Paris spent most of his working life in the UK and moved to Saumur to retire. This is his experience of learning French as a senior.**
>
> It's not easy for my age group! But it can be very interesting for those of us who have the drive, desire and power to learn the language and understand the French. I find it very difficult. French people speak very fast (I tell them they speak like the TGV). On the positive side, it does certainly occupy the brain and those times that are wasted doing nothing! It can really be a fulfilling challenge for an older person.

Advantages of moving to France at retirement age

- Property costs can be up to 50% lower in some areas of France than for an equivalent property in the UK or the USA
- Current UK and US property prices should enable many people to sell their UK home, buy a French one and have money left over
- The quality of life offered is often calmer and of a higher standard in France than in some other countries
- Some rural areas are virtually crime-free
- The climate in many regions is more temperate
- The challenge of adapting to a new culture and way of life may bring a renewed zest to the lives of older people
- You would not forfeit any UK or US earned pensions by a move to France as company and/or state pensions can be paid there (details later in this chapter)
- You need not feel isolated or lonely if you are determined to speak French, as knowledge of the language will act as a key to making friends and coping with all aspects of daily life
- Family and friends who were previously 'irregular' in their visits may perhaps show a sudden (and presumably not unwelcome) enthusiasm for visiting you once you have moved to your retirement property in the Languedoc or Brittany

> ❝
> **Charles and Kath Dunstan live in Neulliac in central Brittany. They decided to retire to France back in the 1980s, bought in 1991 and have been living there for the last eight years. They both speak good French and are well integrated into village life.**
>
> Neulliac is a lively village with 1,500 residents. We're well accepted and are members of the Comité des fêtes and the local Club des retraités. We play boules there on Thursday afternoon and do a walk with them once a week. Afterwards we usually go back to the clubhouse for cake and wine. The farm next to us is not a working farm and, something that we're quite proud of, whenever there's a death in the village we get called and it's our responsibility to go to the chapel next door to ring the bell for five minutes every day before the funeral. We mix with both French and English out here. Sometimes we have a dinner party and it'll be all French, sometimes all English and sometimes a mixture.
> ❞

including books and clothes carry VAT. Two of the few commodities, which are cheaper are wine, and quality eating out.

It would be an unbalanced assessment, not to mention some of the real advantages which can be derived from a move to France at retirement age.

Residence in France for EU nationals

In a departure from the *Loi Sarkozy* of 2003, which waived registration altogether, *Loi Sarkozy II* requires EEA/Swiss nationals who move to France to register their intention to stay at their local *mairie*. Although the administrative framework for registration, *la declaration d'enregistrement*, is not in place at the time of writing, it's imminent. As part of the declaration, you will need to state whether you are coming to France as a professionally active person, as a student, as a retiree with the means to support yourself or whether you are without a professional activity but with the means to support yourself.

Special considerations

Note that this measure is, in part, a response to the large numbers of EU nationals coming to France to benefit from the particularly well-funded welfare system, including so-called health tourists. Health reforms introduced in autumn 2007 indicated that the French government were no longer going to allow EU retirees of active age access to the French healthcare system. After pressure from British officials however, the French health minister announced that those who were resident before 23 November 2007 would still qualify for healthcare.

If you are from the UK

These negotiations are part of EU government jostling that has been going on for some time on this issue. A few years ago the British government began clamping down on 'health tourism' and brought in changes to reduce British national health service obligations to pensioners living abroad. This meant that Britons who retired abroad could no longer return home to Britain in order to receive free medical treatment if they lived in other European states for more than six months a year. Although this measure also caused a mini-panic wave, it was in fact nothing new. John Major's government passed a vaguely known law to the effect that pensioners who lived abroad for more than three months of the year should no longer automatically receive free health treatment on returning to Britain, but there was never any will to enforce it. By extending the period from three to six months, the idea was that it might seem more reasonable to enforce it.

The procedure for those who don't fit exactly into the categories envisioned by the French and British governments is in the process of being defined. If any unusual circumstances apply to your situation, it will very much be a case of feeling your way through the procedure. If, for example, someone is working in the UK and buys a holiday home in France which is later to become a permanent residence, they should be able to live there for up to six months in a year while still working and still return to Britain for medical treatments. However, once retired and residing in France they should ensure that they are entitled to the benefits of the French health service and are insured for the portion not paid by the state. For more on this see the 'Health' section in *Daily Life*.

Residence in France for non-EU nationals

The procedure for non-EU Nationals proposing to retire to France is broadly the same as that outlined in the chapter *Before You Go*. However, there is an element of discretion involved on the part of the French immigration authorities concerning applications from non-EU nationals, providing that all their documentation is in order.

Americans wanting to reside in France for longer than three months for purposes other than tourism have to apply for a long stay visa/*visa de long séjour* at a French consulate in the US before they arrive in France. Anyone arriving in France with a *visa de long séjour* stamped in their passport has to apply for a *carte de séjour* immediately on arrival.

Possible retirement areas

Aquitaine

◼ South-west France

This area includes the attractive Dordogne river valley and, a little further east, the popular Lot département. Bordeaux is a major city in the region but most other areas are quiet and rural. For more information see the regional website www.tourisme-aquitaine.fr and www.bordeaux-tourisme.com.

Languedoc-Roussillon

Although geographically positioned in the south of France, Languedoc-Roussillon is in many ways the quieter and slightly less fashionable, and thus less expensive, part of the Midi. It's possible to live quite near to the Spanish border (around Perpignan) and hence to enjoy the benefits of both France and Spain: Barcelona is approximately 100 miles (160km) away. Foreign residents have been flooding into the departments of Hérault, Aude and the Gard. For more regional information, see www.sunfrance.com.

Where to retire: things to think of

Those who have already visited France may have some idea of where they would like to retire to, while those who have not should plan a preliminary visit before committing themselves to any specific region. Many factors are involved in the property buyer's choice. Climate, scenery, available facilities and transport connections are key considerations. While many people planning their retirement purposely choose a quiet area, the holiday and resort regions of France are very popular and thronged in summer and desolate in winter. Property in holiday areas is inevitably more expensive than elsewhere. Whilst there are a good many expatriates and retired expatriates in France, however, there is no one area (like the Costas in Spain, for example), which have become a haven dedicated to the needs of a specific group. The nearest equivalent in France would probably be the Dordogne. The following is a brief guide to the areas of France traditionally popular with British retirement buyers.

FACT

■ The Côte d'Azur is still the most upmarket area of France.

Provence and the Côte d'Azur

These regions usually referred to as PACA (short for Provence-Alpes-Côte d'Azur) make up what is traditionally understood as being the south of France, running from Marseille to the Italian border: the further east one goes the more fashionable the resorts become. This region is very popular for retirement, due to year-round good weather. However, property is very expensive in both areas. More information is available from www.visitprovence.com.

Poitou-Charentes

This is an attractive area in western France with a coastline to the Atlantic, and subsequently a popular spot with holidaymakers in summer, but quiet in winter. Property prices increase towards the coast; La Rochelle is an especially attractive resort. For more regional information, see www.poitou-charentes-vacances.com and www.tourisme-atlantique.com.

Pays de la Loire

The area surrounding the Loire river is so large that it's usually considered as two regions of France – the Loire Valley and the Loire-West. The east of the Loire is convenient for Paris while the west offers access to the Atlantic coast and Brittany. However, as approximately 30% of the total population of the Pays de la Loire are under the age of 20 it may not be the ideal retirement spot for those who aren't especially enthusiastic about the younger generation. On the plus side however,

Nantes, the main town has a retired population of 50,000 and makes special provisions for its senior citizens over the age of 65, including letting them use public transport free of charge. There are at least 80 clubs in the city aimed at the retired. You would need to speak French to get the most out of such an abundance of mature conviviality though. This region also includes the popular department of the Vendée which has flat sandy beaches and excellent golfing facilities (but the coast has been overdeveloped), whereas the Mayenne (www.tourisme-mayenne. com), which is wild and somewhat thinly populated, may be rather too isolated for retirement purposes. For more regional information, see www.enpaysdeloire.com; www.paysdelaloire.fr.

Brittany, Normandy and Nord-Pas-de-Calais

◼ Brittany

Brittany, famed for its unspoilt countryside, has become more popular as the region's accessibility to other parts of France has improved. Brittany has however managed to retain its own very strong sense of individual identity, and its people, proud of their Celtic origins, have perpetuated many cultural traditions to which they are deeply attached. Many Britons are attracted by Brittany and have bought properties there. For more regional information, see www.tourismebretagne.com.

◼ Normandy

Although Normandy has a rate of unemployment considerably above the national average, it also offers the lowest rate of local taxation per head outside the Paris region. It has a wealth of history on offer: Mont-St-Michel, the Bayeux tapestry, sites of the D-Day landings and the eerie stillness of the vast cemeteries from both world wars. Although many of Normandy's historic towns were devastated in the Second World War, extensive renovation and modernisation has not destroyed the essential character, which the area retains. A final point to remember is that Normandy ranks fourth among French regions in terms of tourism and the seafront includes some of the most fashionable resorts along the north coast. Inland there is much attractive countryside, especially in lower Normandy. For more regional information, see www.normandy-tourism.org.

◼ Nord-pas-de-Calais

This region is one of the smallest regions in France but possesses the greatest population density outside the Paris area. The region includes some of the least inspiring scenery to be found throughout the country. Much of it is flat and the Nord is virtually one long industrial conurbation. However, having said that, the main industrial city of Lille has experienced something of a renaissance in recent years. Property prices are low but the area is becoming more sought after by Brits commuting back home using the Channel Tunnel, which has boosted the economy and general affluence of the area.

In all three regions the weather is similar to that in the UK, and although some towns may be very busy in the summer, others are quite remote, and all areas are generally much quieter during the winter months. For more regional information, see www.northernfrance-tourism.com.

FACT

◼ All three regions have attracted a lot of interest from retirement buyers in recent years due to the comparatively low property prices and because of their accessibility to the UK.

Pensions and finance

UK state pensions

There is no reason why a move to France should affect the provision or rate of state pension for the vast majority of people. Whether or not it works to your advantage will depend on the current costs of living in France and currency fluctuations against the euro. At the time of going to press, Britain's position on joining the single European currency hasn't changed. The value of the euro is going up against sterling making the cost of living in France higher, relatively speaking.

If a pension is paid in France but sourced from the UK it is index-linked and will be up-rated in line with levels in the UK. This is unlike the situation for British pensioners in some other countries, notably Canada and Australia, where UK pensioners receive pensions frozen at the level when first claimed. This is one major advantage of retiring to a EU country.

Both those who have yet to claim and those who are already claiming a state pension should contact the Pension Service International Pension Centre (IPC) (☎0845 60 60 265 or +44 191 218 7777 from abroad; www.pensionservice.gov.uk) for details of payment arrangements for UK state pensions. For those who don't plan to spend periods longer than three months at any one time in France, the easiest course of action is to leave the state pension to mount up in the UK and to cash it in on returning. In the case of a longer or permanent stay, in France a pension can still be paid to a UK bank account or to an agent or friend in the UK. Alternatively, it's possible to have the pension paid in France, usually on a monthly or quarterly basis by filling in form E121 issued by the Department of Work and Pensions in Newcastle-upon-Tyne.

As stated, a UK state pension will be paid at UK rates and also in UK currency as long as any contributions still due are paid up: consider this point carefully in the case of early retirement. For information on French pensions see below.

UK personal pension plans

Those with personal pension plans should contact the company or financial consultant concerned for details of how the money can be paid in France. Usually the money will be forwarded in sterling, but some of the larger personal pension plan insurers can send euro currency cheques, though an annual fee will be charged. You will need to ascertain the most financially advantageous way for receiving payment of the pension. If it can't be paid in France you may need to maintain a UK bank account and stand the cost of currency exchange yourself.

For information about the reduction of restrictions of continuing contributions to a UK pension fund when you are working abroad see the section on 'Continuing contributions to UK pension funds'. Expatriates can also invest in offshore pension plans run from offshore financial areas including the Isle of Man and the Channel Islands of Guernsey and Jersey. There would be no UK tax demands on the interest on such pensions, which would be paid in full, but they would almost certainly attract tax in the country where they were being paid.

US pensions and social security

Americans who retire in France will have their pensions dealt with through the Social Security department of the French Embassy in Paris, which handles pensions

and other social security benefits such as disability allowances being paid to Americans living in France. It's advisable to apply several months in advance for your pension to be paid in France as the paperwork has to be sent to the USA. The pension and or other benefits are paid direct into a personal bank account in the USA.

Note that overseas regulations imposed by US Social Security are different if you were retired in the USA. If you intend to do some part-time work in France after your retirement from regular work, you should check with US Social Security as to how many hours you can work a month and still claim your benefits. Otherwise, you may loose some of them if the US Social Security doesn't consider you retired.

Claiming US pensions and benefits in France

US citizens who are planning to retire in France and who have queries about claiming US disability benefit, pensions, etc. in France can contact the Federal Benefits Unit of their Embassy in Paris or the US Consulate in Nice.

- **Federal Benefits Unit**: American Embassy, 2 rue St. Florentin, 75382 Paris Cedex 08; ☎01 43 12 47 05
- **Federal Benefits Unit**: American Consular Agency, 7 Avenue Gustave V, 06000 Nice; ☎04 93 88 89 55

French pensions

For many years France has had the reputation of treating its retired people more than fairly. Whereas in the UK pensions are paid at a basic flat rate, in France, rather like SERPS (state earnings related pension scheme), the pension is earnings related. There are also generous tax exemptions on compensation paid by employers when workers over 60 are forced to retire (in fact often voluntary retirements deliberately disguised as compulsory). There are other incentives to retire early and those over 57 receiving unemployment benefit are under no obligation to search for work. Then there are the famous *régimes spéciaux* (covering employees of current or former public sector companies), an attack on which were the source of transport strikes in autumn 2007.

The problem is that this high rate of pension payment has proved unsustainable. The system relies on those in work paying into the *Caisse de Retraite* (state retirement fund) now, to fund those who are elderly now. The problems are that not only is unemployment still relatively high, but the population is also getting top-heavy with older people. Currently the French pension fund is running at an annual deficit of billions of euros. Previous governments have been wary of tackling the problem head on although a reform in 2003 linked pensions to life expectancy, lengthening the time people must work in order to be entitled to a pension, which is gradually being raised from 37.5, and will go up to 40 years by 2008. President Sarkozy is likely to continue to gradually try to eliminate the privileges of the 'special' regimes and repeal incentives to retire early.

For those French pensioners (usually farmers and women) who fall below the *minimum vieillesse* (minimum income level) there are additional benefits, which are means tested.

The most radical reform of the French pension scheme is the introduction of private pension schemes. These were almost unheard of prior to a new law passed in June 1997. A private pension plan is known in France as a PER (*Plan Epargne de Retrait*). If you are planning to retire in France, but are still working in your own country it makes sense to create a pension fund based on French-based funds and to receive the income in euros in order to avoid possible currency fluctuations. The following companies offer independent financial advice and tailored packages for expatriates in France.

■ **Dixon Wilson**: ☎0207 680 8100; www.dixonwilson.co.uk; Paris office ☎01 47 03 12 90

■ **Siddalls**: ☎05 56 34 75 51 (Poitou-Charentes but there are several other French offices). In the UK: ☎01329 239111; www.siddalls.net

Finance

Anyone considering retiring to a foreign country should take specialist financial advice regarding their situation. Most people in a position to retire overseas have an amount of capital to invest, or will have when they sell their home, and it's essential to take good advice on how and where this may best be done. Moreover, those who intend to maintain connections with both the UK and France need to take advice on how their taxation affairs can be arranged to their own greatest advantage. Unless professional advice suggests otherwise, there is no reason why you can't continue with bank accounts or investments already established in the UK. In most cases it's possible to earn interest on deposits paid without deduction of tax where you are non-resident.

Taxation advice for UK businesses

This section is for readers from the UK. Readers from elsewhere should check the situation in their home country.

The matter of taxation is inextricably linked with investment considerations. Reasonably impartial advice can be obtained from the UK Inland Revenue, which should be able to advise you on what constitutes income to which it has no entitlement. It will in any case probably be easier to deal with than its French equivalent. Those in need of taxation advice should contact the Inland Revenue Office which they last dealt with.

For those intending to move permanently to France and to sever all financial connection with the UK (except for any pensions, etc.) the situation may be quite straightforward in that they will be liable for French income tax. Note also that someone becomes liable for French income tax just by owning a property in France, even if not resident there. Non-residents must register their French property with the Centre des Impôts des Non-Résidents (www.impots.gouv.fr) and will be charged tax based on an estimated letting value. This doesn't necessarily mean, however, that one will pay any or much more, tax.

A more complex situation arises if you intend to divide time between the UK and France. In this case, it's advisable not to approach either the UK or the French tax authorities until you have taken specialist advice. It will be necessary to decide which income is taxed where and this will depend on where you are considered both resident and domiciled. Generally, you can't totally escape UK taxes if you spend more than 183 days in the UK in the first year of possessing a residence abroad.

Finally, because the UK tax year runs from April to April and the French year runs from January to December there are advantages and disadvantages, from a tax point of view, in choosing a particular moving date. Whereas employees will not usually have much choice when they move, the retired person should make the most of the advantage of choosing a particular date.

In general, if their affairs are properly managed most people will not be substantially better or worse off under a French tax regime than a UK one: note, however, that in France there are tax allowances for the elderly and also for dependants.

◼ Useful publications

◼ ***Taxation in France 2004:*** (£25) by Charles Parkinson. The author is an English chartered accountant and barrister who has specialised in French tax and estate planning for many years. See www.pkfguernsey.com

◼ ***Living in France:*** available from www.blevinsfranks.com

 ◼ See the website of the Caisse Nationale d'Assurance Vieillesse, www. cnav.fr, the organisation dealing with pensions of salaried workers for the French government's information on French pensions (in French).

French versus UK pensions

This section is for readers from the UK. Readers from elsewhere should check the situation in their home country.

If a UK national moves to France while working and then later retires, he or she will then be entitled to a French state pension, in proportion to the number of years that he or she has worked there. Such a person will also qualify for the state pension from the UK, depending on whether the claimant has paid enough National Insurance contributions before leaving the UK. It's wise to consult the Pensions Service in the UK first about whether it is necessary to continue to pay National Insurance contributions, even though you are living in France, in order to acquire entitlement to a full UK pension. Otherwise the amount could be very small. While the UK state earnings related pension scheme, or SERPS, was out of fashion for a while, many people have now opted in again, as it's at least guaranteed to pay out a certain amount.

Pensions organisations in France

While working in France you pay contributions towards your old-age pension (*assurance vieillesse*) to the state social security organisation URSSAF, which entitles you to a basic pension (*retraite de base*) and the supplementary pension (*retraite complémentaire*). Contributions to the basic pension are more or less the same for salaried workers, *commerçants* and artisans (16.35% of the social security threshold), but less for liberal professions. The intention is that you will be able to receive 50% of your average salary for your highest earning years at the age of 60 or 65. Entitlement is based on the number of *trimestres* or three-monthly periods you have contributed for. At the current time the number of qualifying *trimestres* is being progressively increased from 150 to 160 in 2008 (i.e. a full 40 years). From 2008 your pension will be calculated on the basis of your 25 highest-earning years, whereas in the past it was based on your 10 highest-earning years.

There is a multitude of organisations dealing with your *retraite complémentaire*, depending entirely on what kind of profession you exercise. Once you have registered with the social security authority, URSSAF (which is done for you as an employed person), the necessary information will arrive without much delay. Only non-salaried self-employed people categorised under *commerçants/industriels* are exempt from paying into a *retraite complémentaire*. If you are self-employed, you have to pay contributions to cover incapacity (*invalidité*), and towards *capital-décès*, a lump sum paid to surviving dependants when you die. The following table will give you some idea where to look for information.

Artisans	Commerçants/ industriels	Liberal professions
RSI	RSI	CNAVPL
www.le-rsi.fr	www.le-rsi.fr	www.cnavpl.fr

Paying tax on your UK pension

This section is for readers from the UK. Readers from elsewhere should check the situation in their home country.

The basic French state pension is paid tax-free. You will still have to pay tax on all other sources of income, for example, UK pension. Private pensions, foreign pensions, etc. attract an additional abatement of 10%. There are further abatements for persons aged over 65.

If tax is or will be deducted at source in the UK from your pension, you need to contact the Inland Revenue's Centre for Non-Residents and ask for Form FRA2/INDIVIDUAL. Once the French tax office has stamped it and you have returned it, the Centre will instruct your pension provider not to deduct tax at source. You will then pay French tax on your pension. Contact the Centre for Non-Residents, St John's House, Merton Road, Bootle, Merseyside L69 9BB; ☎0151 210 2222; non-residents@inlandrevenue.gov.uk; www.inlandrevenue.gov.uk/cnr.

Healthcare

Healthcare is an important consideration when making a move to a new country in retirement. While many parts of southern France enjoy a mild climate which offers a positive health benefit it would be inadvisable to bet the preservation of your health on it. If you find yourself with the prospect of using French healthcare you can be assured that health facilities are generally good anywhere in France, and some excellent private hospitals exist for those who wish to pay for their own treatment. General practices, dental offices, clinics and hospitals, which provide state healthcare treatment are generally reliable institutions. In addition, if you have to see a specialist you will probably find the wait isn't that long. In general, all the medicines and procedures found in some other countries are available in France, merely under different names.

The most likely problem could be finding an English-speaking doctor. Therefore, unless your French is good you may feel more comfortable selecting a location where English-speaking facilities are available, especially if you have a recurring medical condition (a list of English-speaking doctors is available from the British

Consulates). This may mean using private facilities, or alternatively, returning to your own country, with the extra expense that this involves. However, it's often quite practical to rely on *sécurité sociale* for medical care. Note that under this system a patient's contribution of about 30% of the total treatment costs may have to be met. The cost of this, or the insurance to cover it, has to be budgeted for. As discussed above, those who have worked in France and paid into a private 'top-up' scheme, as most people do, have the bulk of this contribution covered: those who are retired and move to France, however, may not and should consider joining a French insurance scheme or a private healthcare plan (see below). For further details on the health system in France see the section 'Health' in the chapter *Daily life*.

Securité sociale and health benefits

Although the French social security system is covered in detail in the chapter *Daily life*, the aim of this section is to outline the range of health care benefits available specifically to those in or approaching retirement.

As already mentioned, the changes in the rules governing EU expat access to the French health system are covered in full in the section on Health in the chapter *Daily life*. The main thing to know is that any EU national who moves to France and is of retirement status is entitled to the health benefits of *sécurité sociale* mainly free of charge. This assumes, however, that you are entitled to, or claiming, a pension in your own country, so, for example, someone who had retired before retirement age would not be covered. To claim free entitlement to *sécurité sociale* you must first complete form E121, available from the Department of Work and Pensions (☎0191 218 7777; www.dwp.gov.uk) and then register with *sécurité sociale* in France. You do this by going to the local branch of the Caisse Primaire d'Assurances Maladie (CPAM) in France and handing over the document sent to you by the UK DWP. You will then be given a *carte vitale* (health card) which should be carried with you at all times as it allows you among other things access to health care and hospital treatment (although a financial contribution of about 30% is generally required – see the chapter *Daily life*). For this contributory charge you can take out a supplemental insurance policy (*complémentaire/mutuelle*). These are sold by insurance companies all over France, but it's important to get several quotes and check the details of what is covered carefully, to ensure you are getting what you want. Another point to note is that the cover doesn't usually become active until up to three months after you have signed up for it. If you aren't of retirement age and don't work, you do qualify as long as you were resident before 23 November 2007. Otherwise you will need to take out full private cover.

Other benefits provided by the *carte vitale* include visits to doctors and dentists, glasses and medicines. For life-threatening conditions almost everything involved with your treatment and care is 100% free.

Wills and legal considerations

Most people approaching retirement either have already made, or intend to make, a will. Such a step assumes even greater importance and complexity if you intend to move abroad. If a will has not been made then take advice from a solicitor with experience of French law; even if a will has been made it must be reviewed before the move takes place.

Generally, the disposal of property held in France after death is governed by French law (*droits de succession*) whether you are a resident of France or elsewhere. As French law is quite different from Anglo-Saxon law in this respect, a careful consideration of the options available for avoiding it should be made. A fuller explanation of the French inheritance laws (including the recent changes brought in by Sarkozy such as the higher tax free band for inheritance) can be found in the chapter *Buying property*. For possessions other than property you can elect that any disposal is governed by law from your home country, whether you are resident there, or living as a French resident. If your will doesn't dictate this, then French law will automatically apply.

The main difference between French and Anglo-Saxon law is that in France, you aren't allowed to dispose of your estate to whom you wish. There is a strict code, which governs who the estate may be left to and in what proportion. It's sometimes possible to bring legal instruments to bear on this regulation, but it may result in greater taxes being payable on the inheritance.

In general, spouses under French law gain their inheritance rights under the French laws relating to marriage, not to those pertaining to inheritance itself. This recognises that a husband and a wife have both individual and communal possessions (e.g. a house would be a communal possession). On death, the surviving partner is entitled to all his or her individual possessions, but not necessarily in property. This is usually divided equally to any children. For example, if there are two children then each child will receive one half of the estate. In other words, a wife doesn't receive all her husband's estate on his death as is quite usual in the UK and the USA.

Many couples feel that their surviving spouse should receive all their own estate on their death and that children don't need a share in this. However, if individual arrangements aren't made then, on the death of the estate-holder, the estate itself may be divided up contrary to the wishes of the deceased.

Death

This, like taxes, is something which inevitably affects us all. Initially, consider what the situation would be if your spouse should die after moving to France. It may well be that the survivor would want to return to their own country to be closer to family and friends: provision should be made for this at the outset, perhaps by arranging life assurance which will cover the costs of returning home. In a forced situation these costs could be much greater than those involved in the original move out.

Deaths in France must be certified by a doctor and registered within 24-hours at the *mairie* with the death certificate and proof of the deceased's identity. A funeral cannot take place until the *mairie* gives its approval. If you don't know of a reliable funeral director who will take care of all the formalities, you can contact the Association Française d'Information funeréraire (www.afif.asso.fr), which represents the funeral trade in France. You will probably be invited to view the body and to witness the sealing of the coffin with a red seal in the presence of a police official as is customary in France.

Note that as France is predominantly a Catholic country, burial facilities for other faiths are comparatively rare; the nearest British Consulate will provide the address

of a Protestant church or synagogue. Cremations are less usual in France than elsewhere, but are becoming more common; a request previously signed by the deceased or by the person dealing with the ceremonies is required for cremation. It frequently happens, despite the expense of such an undertaking, that a spouse and family prefer their deceased relative to be buried or cremated back in their country of origin. If this is the case, then the nearest consulate should be contacted as soon as possible for information and guidance on the appropriate way to carry out this procedure. A list of UK and US Consulates is given in the Appendix 4.

Embarking on a new lifestyle

One reason for retiring to France is to build a new lifestyle and embark on an new challenge at the stage in life which the French call *le troisième âge* (the third age). France definitely offers this opportunity, but at least for British expats it's near enough to the UK to make visits with family and friends practical and soften any

 The Association Française d'Information Funéraire (AFIF) (☎01 45 44 90 03; www.afif.asso.fr) is an independent, non-profit organisation that aims to provide answers about funeral arrangements in France. The website has a directory of funeral directors all over France arranged by region.

initial homesickness. (Culturally, though, the two countries could be continents rather than one short stretch of water or tunnel apart, and it's often just this difference, which attracts culture-starved Francophiles).

Most people retiring to France opt for a fairly quiet life, either in rural countryside or close to scenic parts of the coast. These areas can, however, seem remote, especially through the winter, and you'll often have to organise your own entertainment, if you are to avoid becoming a recluse for six months of the year. Proportionally, the percentage of those aged 60+ is growing in France as in other Western economies. The over-60s can expect a healthy and active participation in the life of a community.

Of the 12 million or so people aged 60+ in France, more than a quarter live alone. The French resist formally organised social events and entertainment so you might need to take an adventurous social attitude. The over-60s in France have a role in the community; many belong to associations that organise everything from prison visits to a counselling service for small businesses or school support groups. It can be difficult for a foreigner to get involved. Most communes organise free meals for the elderly on a regular basis.

If you aren't integrated socially with your local French community, you may want to pursue hobbies and interests that you can carry on with in France. For example, France has an ideal climate for gardening. Some towns, such as Amiens or Bourges have very picturesque networks of allotments that are attractions in themselves. Sports facilities are good, with golf, tennis and riding widespread. Charles and Kath Dunstan are very impressed at the sporting facilities in their commune of 1500 people. This may also be the ideal time to take up a new pastime, such as painting or walking,

TIP

■ If you don't speak the language you will find it harder to meet people of your own age.

to take full advantage of scenic surroundings. As far as reading is concerned, internet ordering is the best way to obtain books in English. Otherwise the lack of literature in English can act as an incentive to work on your French. Many universities offer courses aimed at older people or you can study with the University of the Third Age.

France is an ideal country for travelling and sightseeing and you could easily make history and culture your main interest. More on the museums, chateaux and monuments of France at www.francetourisme.com. There are great facilities for camping and caravanning and most public transport, museums, historic sites and leisure facilities offer discounts (often 50%) for retired people. Of course, food and wine can also be absorbing interests.

Having said all this, retirement needn't be crammed with activity. In most cases it's quite practical to take a job, perhaps part-time or on a consultancy basis, or to start a small business. Check the position as regards the documentation required to do this in the 'Starting a business' section of this chapter.

Vacation villages

Vacation villages are very popular in France and there are over 700 of them where whole families, singles or retired people can go and have a holiday with activities. Most of the 700 vacation villages can accommodate seniors and provide activities: dances, spas, games of pétanque, painting, gastronomy and a range of more dynamic activities. Younger seniors will probably want golf, cycling, walking etc. The Vacanciel brand (☎0825 12 45 45; www.vacanciel.com) of holiday villages offer special grandparents and grandchildren packages where both generations are catered for at the same time. Other brands are ValWf (☎0825 003 211; www.valvf. fr), BelambraVvf (☎0825 12 13 14; www.belambra-vvf.fr), Renouveau Vacances (☎04 79 75 75 75; www.renouveau-vacances.fr).

Useful addresses

■ **The American University in Paris:** Division of Continuing Education (☎01 40 62 07 20; www.aup.fr) offers courses for adults in a variety of technology and technical courses, translation, etc.

■ **Elderhostel:** www.elderhostel.org. Non-profit. Offers learning opportunities for the over 55s in 70+ countries. Ask for details of courses in France.

Starting a
Business

■ OVERVIEW

Until recently, most people taking up residence in France did so for career reasons, or to retire there. However, these are by no means the only options available; for some, the intention of starting or buying a business in France is reason number one.

Operating a business abroad is not only for established business people or multinational companies. In addition to the traditional large-scale opportunities, recent administrative developments within the EU have made a point of encouraging small and medium-sized businesses and individuals to set up enterprises in other EU states. Apart from manufacturing, business ventures can take almost any form. Running a small shop, art courses, letting agencies, consultancies, hairdressers, bookselling, running a bed and breakfast, building, surveying and plumbing services are some already in existence. Other professional services from farming and landscape gardening to running bars and franchises also offer potential livings.

Inevitably, the cultural differences between France and other countries will complicate an already nerve-racking undertaking for someone determined on setting up a new business. Such a venture is risky enough in your own country and many new companies go to the wall within their first year. In France, the failure rate is about one in three. Although the statistics may offer better odds for the survival of small businesses, this should not belie the extra difficulties caused by unfamiliarity with foreign business procedures and a lack of personal contacts, the absence of which could prove serious drawbacks. Having a French business partner or company with compatible interests may help to sidestep some of the bureaucratic processes involved in creating a business from scratch. If this is not possible then you may need to consult a *boutique de gestion* – a partnership of accountants and other professional business advisers – whose expertise lies in launching new businesses and providing financial and other services. Controls on foreign investment in France were eliminated early in 1996 and tax legislation for foreign businesses is competitive with some northern European countries.

Despite hundreds of thousands of small businesses (*fonds de commerce*) in France, the French are regarded as far less of a nation of entrepreneurs than the British when it comes to the small business sector. Small businesses tend to have been established for several generations and to be run along traditional lines. Since the early 1990s business creation has declined progressively in France, which now has one of the lowest rates of business creation in the EU. However, the current right wing government is committed to reducing the overwhelming cost of social security and other taxes on businesses.

Financial and linguistic considerations

Anyone intending to start, or buy, a business in France should initially consider what kind of scale it will be on, the level of personal investment and whether outside finance will be required. For instance even a very modest business would probably require a minimum sum of €50,000 cash to buy, or €80,000 cash to start, and twice these amounts is preferable. If you need additional finance from a bank then you will need to draw up a very detailed business plan. This needs to include items such as whether the business will be run from your own premises or leased ones,

The full implications of the single EU currency, the euro, are evident now that it has been in use since January 2002. The various economic pundits who predicted that the union of the Eurozone with a single currency would result in historically low interest rates in most European countries have been proved right.

whether you are starting from scratch or acquiring an existing business, what legal form the business will take and what activities it will engage in. Profit projections will be required.

Other considerations for running a business in France are: to be fluent in the language, or a willingness to become so; and expertise and experience of a popular profession or trade, e.g. farming, catering, interior decorating, hairdressing, etc.

Regulations for entrepreneurs

EU nationals are entitled to move to France to set up, or buy, a business without any prior authorisation. The regulations for those wishing to take up residence in France in order to buy or start a business are broadly the same as for those wishing to take up employment or retire there, and are referred to in the chapter *before You Go*. A residence permit is no longer required for EU nationals whether they are starting a business or not.

Non-EU nationals may, however, require a visa and should consult the French Consulate about this. Generally, non-EU nationals are expected to make a more substantial business investment to gain admittance to France, whereas EU nationals are accepted no matter what the scale of their proposed business activities. Non-EU nationals will also need to get a special foreign merchant's permit (*carte de commerçant étranger*) which can take up to six months to obtain.

Business registration (*immatriculation au registre du commerce*) is in any case compulsory and involves registering with the local Chambre de Commerce (or Chambre des Métiers if you are a self-employed tradesperson). Farmers should register with the Chambre d'Agriculture. You can find the appropriate address from the local library, *mairie* or the Assemblée des Chambres Francaises de Commerce et d'Industrie (ACFCI).

This procedure should be followed by anyone who is self-employed, or who runs a company which they own but of which they are also an employee. Whatever entity the company takes e.g. a EURL SARL or SCI (see the section on 'Business structures' below), the legal, financial and registration formalities involved can usually be dealt with in a few weeks. If you wish to set up a business in France but not actually to become a resident there, then enquiries should be made to the French Consulate, as it may be necessary to seek approval from the Ministry of Finance. Such a procedure is not necessary for businesses based outside France merely doing business with France.

■ PROCEDURES INVOLVED IN BUYING/CREATING A BUSINESS

Creating a new business

Starting a new business will almost certainly require more capital than buying one, and consequently constitutes a greater risk. If you have to take out a loan, you will have to have a well thought out business plan. It is also advisable to ensure you have enough capital to keep the business going until it turns a profit, which may be several years. However, once you have built up a successful business there is a potential financial gain from selling it on.

Anyone aspiring to this kind of venture will need a sound knowledge of business management in general, and to have pinpointed the type of business for which there is already a demand which has not yet been saturated. Finding a gap in the French market, which you feel you can fill is another entrepreneurial possibility. Such a 'gap' is likely to be a product or service, which does not exist in the host country. Again, there is an element of risk – remember that even with a good idea, the break-even point will probably take longer to reach in France than in the UK or the USA: it may take four years to return any profit.

Some people test the waters by registering their company in the UK and then

An alpine chalet business

operate in France for a while semi-legally. Once you are officially working in France you have to pay social security contributions, health insurance mainly. If you register with the ASSEDIC (the unemployment benefit organisation) before you start, there are incentives for the unemployed to start a business, such as reductions in social security contributions. You can also register with the ANPE. When it's time to start the business, you can make a claim under the ACCRE scheme to help with your business. The percentages and types of incentive change every year.

Buying an existing business

Generally, the cost of buying small enterprises is much less in France than in the UK: property and land are also cheaper. Many people wanting to buy a business have found they can do so in France, whereas a similar type of business in the UK would be totally beyond their reach.

One problem with buying in France is that there is often not a wide choice of businesses for sale in any given area, as family enterprises tend to remain within the family or to be sold by word of mouth, rather than to be advertised. The French magazine *Pic International* (www.pic-inter.com), a monthly magazine giving listings of all types of small businesses for sale everywhere in France. It is also available on subscription.

Another fact to bear in mind is that many small businesses exist at subsistence level, rather than generating a rising profit. This tends to be because a typical proprietor sees his or her business as a way of life, rather than a streamlined system geared to making profit. This type of concern may suit those from the UK who are looking for a sideline or semi-retirement business, but obviously not those who have a more financially ambitious idea of business. This is not to say that the concept of getting rich quick through a timely business enterprise is unknown in France – it's just that it isn't a generally anticipated consequence of commerce.

Those looking at advertisements of businesses for sale will see that some give the price for *fonds* and some for *fonds et murs*. This is because the French make a distinction between the physical property (*les murs*) and the business including goodwill, the trading name, and other tangible and intangible assets which comprise *les fonds or les fonds de commerce*. This means that buying an existing business usually involves two transactions: buying the business (*fonds*), which includes the goodwill, the clientele, the fittings and fixtures, and purchase of the existing stock. The premises may either be bought outright, or rented. The former involves a similar procedure as for residential property (see the chapter *Setting up home*). The main difference between the two is that the fees involved, which cover the notarial charges, expenses and taxes, etc. may be rather greater for a business. These can be in excess of 20% of the purchase price: always ask for a quotation beforehand. Renting is often a cheaper alternative under a commercial lease, *le bail commercial* (see below).

Starting a business

Obviously, the final decision whether to create or whether to buy a business will depend on financial considerations rather than personal inclinations. However, if you are contemplating starting a business of a type already present in France look at as many similar businesses as possible and find out as much about running costs and tax and other charges as you can and compare them with your own country. You will also need to carry out a thorough feasibility study which might include: taking into account the number of similar businesses in the area; the size of the local population or expected itinerant business; and thus whether the area can support another business of a similar kind. If you employ people to work for you, you will have to fulfil stringent legal and financial obligations under France's complicated employment laws. Even if you rent premises rather than buy them, and work on your own, you can pay up to 65% of your income in social security charges, which is why many French people claim they are working part-time.

The cost of buying a business

The following list provides some examples of the types of business for sale in France. Prices are for the business and freehold, excluding stock unless stated.

A range of business purchase costs		
Business	**Area**	**Price**
Bar/rest, village centre	Allier	€97,000
Auberge in village	50km Grenoble	€270,000
Boulangerie	Evreux, primary position	€278,000
Bicycle/sports hire (seasonal business, only) kiosk and stock	Languedoc	€15,000
Fully-equipped *garagiste* (business and property on lease, prime position)	Lot Valley	€250,000
Automated strawberry farm, 9 hectares	Aquitaine	€1,000,000

Finding a business

In theory there is no reason why buying a business in France should be any more complicated than buying one anywhere else. However, very few foreigners have bought businesses there in the past, and business creation has tended to be the more popular alternative.

Businesses for sale can be found through both specialist business agents and estate agents. Undoubtedly, the easiest way is to search on the internet for *immobiliers*. Major French newspapers also include business for sale advertisements: these newspapers are listed region by region in the chapter *Daily life*. Although some preliminary research and investigation can be done from outside France, in order to prepare any sort of valid shortlist it's essential to visit the country for at least one inspection trip.

To work out the feasibility of any business you need to build up a detailed knowledge of the trade or area in question. In particular, take into account location, local competition, previous results and profits, etc., very much as you would expect to do anywhere. A survey of small businesses showed that:

▪ the most popular region for private enterprise was Paris (28%) and then the Rhône-Alpes (12%)

▪ over 47% of private entrepreneurs were in services, 36% in industry and commerce and 9% in cottage industries

▪ 48% of these entrepreneurs were age 30–40 and 27% age 20–30

If you are considering the purchase of any business connected with tourism or leisure (as many expatriate businesses tend to be) it's particularly important to see how the business varies seasonally. In some areas businesses survive on the income generated by summer tourism, while others have year-round tourism potential.

The French publication *PIC International* (*www.pic-inter.com*) is an invaluable specialist publication for those wishing to buy a business in France. British publications which may contain some businesses for sale adverts include *French Property News* (*www.french-property-news.com*) and *Living France* (www.livingfrance.com). In addition many of the UK-based estate agents who deal in French property generally have some small businesses on their books, often as part of a residential property.

 Useful contacts
- www.axxis.fr – company describes itself as 'one stop shop to business acquisitions'
- www.demain.fr – offers existing businesses for sale

Raising finance

Many people find they can raise capital by selling up in their home country, as even after buying a French one of similar standard there is, at current property prices, likely to be a surplus which can be used for business purposes.

If necessary a loan can be raised from a financial institution. Most French banks will consider applications for finance from those wishing to set up business in France and can be approached initially through their offices in your own country, who may assist in setting up a loan with their relevant branch in France, or at least provide an introduction.

The terms on which a bank provides finance for buying or starting a business abroad are broadly similar to those you would expect in the UK or USA. You have to demonstrate some business ability, have a well thought out business plan and be able to offer some security. It is unlikely that a bank will provide a sum in excess of the amount which you are able to inject in cash: such a loan would usually need to be repaid over between five and seven years.

The French government and EU incentives

It may be worth investigating the financial incentives provided in France for the purpose of encouraging investment of all types. Some are suitable for single traders, some are for farmers, whereas others, such as EU regional aid programmes and those run by the French Industrial Development Board DIACT (previously called DATAR; see below) are geared to small and medium-sized businesses engaged in industrial production. Incentives include subsidised loans and grants and tax incentives for starting businesses in special development zones. Some of these are applicable to craftspeople and traders with evidence of trading or a qualification. Tax incentives are also offered by the French state in certain circumstances of business creation.

One alternative worth considering as a means of raising business finance is to mortgage any property you buy which is also sufficient to provide business start-up or purchase capital. This allows for a longer repayment period and removes the need to make a case out for your proposition.

SOS Villages scheme

In the SOS Villages scheme, *mairies* of depopulated villages of 2,000 inhabitants or fewer buy up defunct business premises and let them to village-type businesses (butchers, bakers, hairdressers) and professional services (e.g. doctors) at very favourable terms; this initiative is known as service installation. You can get more information from the website www.sos-villages.asso.fr.

An important organisation that can advise you where to look for loans and other assistance is France Initiative Réseau (www.fir.asso.fr), which runs 242 Plates-Formes d'Initiative Locale (PFIL). Micro Credits (www.adie.org) is an EU-backed loan scheme to very small businesses. If your business is a legally registered company (i.e. not sole trader) and in a special development zone you may be eligible for a grant from the European Social Fund. The local Euro Info office can help you to find out if you qualify (www.fse.gouv.fr or www.eic.minefi.gouv.fr).

DIACT

The French government provides enthusiastic support for new business and industry. This includes investment and business ventures from overseas countries, and within Europe, France is one of the leading countries for attracting such ventures.

The development of business and industry is under the overall control of a

Secondhand shop in Vertieillac

special development governmental organisation called DIACT (Délégation Interministérielle à l'Aménagement et à la Compétitivité des Territoires; www.diact.gouv.fr – this organisation has recently changed its name from DATAR). DIACT's sister organisation, Invest in France (www.invest-in-France) has offices in various foreign cities, including London (☎020 7823 0900), which can provide extensive information on the processes involved in doing business in France. It produces periodic reports concerned with actually doing business in France, the French system of taxation, tax incentives, company law and other business-related subjects. These publications are primarily focused on those who intend to buy or start up a business in France.

The agency can also advise on grants and incentives for which owners of new businesses in France may be eligible, as well as providing details of contacts in particular regions and industries of France who will be able to provide further assistance. DIACT also has offices in the areas of France, which have been identified as requiring special attention and have subsequently been designated enterprise zones by the French government: such areas include Lille, Rouen and Clermont-Ferrand.

According to Invest in France, just under 35,000 jobs were created by foreign investment in 2007. This was the third best year in terms of foreign investment and job creations since 1993. This means that the investment climate is currently very good. The real growth area, according to these figures, was in small projects in the service sector.

Chambers of commerce

The French CCIs have a high profile and are regarded as the place to go for information and help. Chambers of commerce exist in all French towns of a reasonable size and should be any prospective entrepreneur's first port of call. There are Chambres de Métiers for artisans and the Chambres d'Agriculture for agriculteurs. Lists of all the Chambers of Commerce and similar organisations can be found on the website www.apce.fr by clicking on 'e-mail', via which you can contact the CCI of each département. Also contact the regional development association, Agence Régionale de Dévelopement, which also exists throughout France. Both of these institutions are able to help and advise on business start-up and purchase procedure.

Legal and financial advice

It is advisable to obtain an independent valuation of the business to ensure that the price being requested is fair and reasonable. When buying in France it's essential to take professional advice both on the viability of the business and the purchase procedure. To do this you should retain an accountant, a lawyer and your own estate agent or *notaire* (notary) as a consultant. The best way to find a lawyer with the appropriate experience is probably by personal recommendation if at all possible. Otherwise, contact several and be very probing about their credentials, particularly their experience of French procedures and laws. Obvious positive signs are that they have a French partner (either a firm or an individual lawyer), and that they are knowledgeable about and experienced in the relevant French legal procedures. Any reputable firm will be happy to go to lengths to reassure you about having appropriate credentials. If you are from UK you can look at the adverts in *Living in France* magazine (☎ 01234 240954) and in the French Chamber of Commerce in Britain's publication *Setting up a Business in France* for both French and British accountants and solicitors with appropriate experience (see below for address).

Useful addresses

Bright Jones: Cabinet d'avocats, Montauban (nr Toulouse); ☎+33 (0)5 61 57 90 86. Sarah Bright Thomas and her partner are both qualified French lawyers but have the advantage of being English mother tongue speakers and can therefore advise on many aspects of moving to France and setting up there

French Chamber of Commerce in Great Britain: ☎020 7304 4040; www.ccfgb.co.uk

French Lawyer: ☎0845 644 3061; info@french-lawyer.com; www.french-lawyer. com. Contact Isabelle Cès: French property law specialists can help with company formation, commercial property and more

Holman Fenwick and Willan: ☎020 7488 2300; holmans@hfw.co.uk; website: www.hfw.com; in Paris: ☎01 44 94 40 50; holmans@hfw-france.com. Also offices in Rouen and Nantes. Solicitors experienced in business start-ups in France

International Property Law Centre: ☎0870 800 4565; www.internationalpropertylaw.com

Jeffreys Henry: Chartered accountants; www.jeffreyshenry.com. Has offices in Paris, Lille and Nice. Specialist tax and financial advisors to companies and individuals considering setting up business in France

International Law Partnership: ☎020 7061 6700; www.lawoverseas.com. Team of English, French and dual-qualified lawyers specialising in foreign work

Prettys Solicitors: ☎01473 232121; www.prettys.co.uk. Offers a bilingual business service in conjunction with *notaires* and *conseillers juridiques* (legal advisors) on all aspects of setting up and operating a business in France

Russell-Cooke: ☎020 8789 9111; www.russell-cooke.co.uk. Large firm with French law and property department, headed by Dawn Alderson, qualified in both English and French law and member of the Bordeaux bar

Stephen Smith (France) Ltd: ☎01473 437186; www.stephensmithfranceltd.com. Stephen Smith is the author of *Letting Your French Property Successfully*, published by PKF (Guernsey) Ltd.

Templeton Associates: UK ☎01225 422282; www.templeton-france.com. French mortgage and finance experts. Offices in France

The purchase procedure

The purchase of a *fonds de commerce* should involve the drawing up of contracts for both parties (i.e. the buyer and the seller), by either a *notaire* or a legal consultant (*conseillers juridique*). The contract must include details such as the turnover (*chiffres d'affaires/ca.*) and profit or loss of the business and the title to the property in which the business is conducted. French law also requires that two notices of sale should appear in the legal announcements pages of the *Bulletin Officiel des Annonces Civiles et Commerciales–BODACC* (Bulletin of Civil and Commercial Notices; http://bodacc.ort.fr). This is to ensure that any creditors know of the state of business and can therefore claim any outstanding dues. Creditors' claims are taken from the sale price which the buyer lodges with the notaire in a stakeholder account (*compte séquestre*).

Other procedures connected with purchase include the payment of transfer tax (*droits d'enregistrement*) which varies according to the estimated value of the business, but can amount to about 14% on a business with a transfer value exceeding approximately €45,700.

If the buyer is obtaining a business with existing employees, he or she must comply with French labour legislation, which requires that the workforce will have been consulted prior to the sale.

Glossary of terms and abbreviations for business purchase

French	Abbreviation	English
affaire	aff.	business
carte de commerçant		trader's card
centre commercial	ctre.cial.	shopping mall
cession		sale/transfer of a business
Chambre des Métiers		chamber of trades
chiffre d'affaires	ca.	turnover
code du travail		labour laws
conseil juridique		legal consultant
courtier		broker
couverts	cvts.	seating capacity
droit au bail		right to lease
fonds de commerce		business + goodwill, lease, trade name and marks
franchisé		franchisee
franchiseur		franchisor
matériel complet	mat. pro.	office equipment pour la profession
Registre du Commerce et Commercial and des Sociétés Companies		Companies Register
surface commercial	surf.ciale.	area of commercial premises

Once the business has changed hands, the name and particulars of the new owner have to be entered in the Commercial and Companies Register (*Registre du Commerce et des Sociétés*).

■ RENTING COMMERCIAL PROPERTY

It is quite common in France to have two options, when acquiring a business; either to purchase the property outright or to rent it. Renting the property is obviously cheaper, in the short term.

The protections afforded by law to domestic tenants may not apply to a commercial lease (*le bail commercial*). Thus, it's essential to take legal advice to ensure that the lease is satisfactory: such advice can be obtained from an independent estate agent or notary. However, as with domestic leases, business leases usually include a right to rent clause which is obviously essential to protect the future, and future value, of the business.

The law governing commercial leases says that the lease must be in writing, and a minimum of nine years' duration, with a possibility for the tenant to terminate the lease at the end of each three-year period. However, if the business person or company requires a lease for a shorter duration, two-year leases, or a lease terminable by either

FACT

■ Quite often in advertisements for businesses for sale you see: *Bail: 3-6-9, reste 4 ans*, or *6 ans, 7 ans etc: reste* refers to the period remaining on the lease.

party at any chosen moment (*convention d'occupation précaire*) are also possible, but there is no accompanying protective legislation or tenant right to renewal.

The rent may be subject to negotiation by both parties. Under present law a sliding scale clause may be inserted into the lease by which the rent can increase in conjunction with the quarterly index of the cost of housing instruction (*indice INSEE*) but if the rent increases or decreases by more than 25%, it's the market value, rather than the indexed sliding scale which prevails. Landlords can legally countermand this regulation by claiming that substantial improvements have increased the value of the building by more than 10% since the lease was signed, in which case the rent may exceed the maximum increase imposed by the index.

Pas-de-porte

Sometimes in advertisements you will see *pas-de-porte* mentioned. This is a lump sum, payable to the landlord when entering into a commercial lease. It is also possible for the landlord of a commercial property to demand a deposit of three to six months' rent. When buying a *fonds de commerce*, you should check for restrictive clauses in the seller's lease. For instance it will probably be necessary to engage a notary to draw up the deed of transfer and the landlord will have to be present when the parties sign.

Renewal of lease

When a tenant wishes to renew the lease he or she should inform the landlord six months in advance. The rent will be reviewed and fixed according the *indice INSEE*, the market value, or some other private arrangement. The conditions for renewal are that the tenant must have been operating the business for a minimum of three years and be the owner of the business. These regulations apply to EU nationals only. Should the landlord not grant renewal, the tenant is entitled to compensation (*indemnité d'éviction*) on reasonable terms, which may include the market value of the business and the cost of removal and relocation. However, if the tenant is the subject of an eviction order for non-payment of rent or change of use of premises, or is in contravention of other terms of the lease, the landlord will not have to pay compensation.

■ IDEAS FOR NEW BUSINESSES

Those who decide to start a small business from scratch will need a very good and sound business idea plus the flair and determination necessary to get it off the

Sub-letting

Sub-letting is not permitted without the prior consent of the landlord. The sub-let should be formalised in writing and authorised by the landlord so that when the main lease terminates, the sub-letter can request renewal.

ground and most importantly, a proper marketing strategy and business plan. As mentioned, there are two routes to follow; one is to jump on the bandwagon of an existing French business idea that is proving lucrative and the other is to find a gap in the market that your talents and business can fill. In either case you will need to do some research in France itself.

Specialising in delicacies from your home country can be a good business idea. For example, there is no reason why some British-flavoured businesses should not be exportable to France, just as some French businesses have been imported successfully into Britain. French bakeries and patisseries, chocolatiers, etc. are a booming market in particular areas of the UK. The agency Leisure & Land (www.leisureandland.co.uk) specialises in the sale of income-producing properties including hotels, vineyards, equestrian centres and other leisure projects in France.

Finding a gap in the market

Looking for a gap in the market can be a more risky, but ultimately perhaps, a more rewarding venture if the idea takes off. In some cases, a hobby could translate into a French business, although you would need to be very knowledgeable in the chosen area, for example, there are very few antique shops in France. It may also be possible to transfer a current business or trade to France. For example, plumbers , builders, hairdressers, small garages, etc. are needed in France, as in any other country. Other businesses can exploit traditional French tastes: for example running a vineyard or a snail, oyster or truffle farm. However unlikely it may sound, there are such foreign-owned enterprises in France. One small company has even started a brewery (*une brasserie artisanale*) in Normandy and a dozen others run English-style pubs with their own micro-brewery attached. There is increasing scope for herbalists and naturopaths as long as they are members of a recognised professional association as they are strictly regulated in France. Another growth area is for chiropractic and osteopathy.

Choosing an area

The best way of approaching setting up a business is to identify an area of France, which you like and look to see how your idea could adapt to that area. Regional and local differences may mean that an idea may work in some parts of France but not in others, thus necessitating some market research.

- Is there a demand for your product or service?
- What is the competition?
- Could you obtain supplies easily?
- Are staff easily available and can you afford them?
- What are the legal and licensing formalities involved, and what implications do these carry?

Some ideas for potential businesses may be gathered from the following run-down on the types of business that have recently been started by foreigners moving into France.

Shops

From an administrative point of view, shops are one of the simplest businesses to start. In addition, the French particularly appreciate small shops offering quality goods and personal service, in spite of the large number of hypermarkets. These shops can range from being simple grocery stores to specialist shops, such as the enterprising surf shop which opened in Biarritz. There are also possibilities for mobile shops. Marmalade, tea and English bread (which makes better toast than the French version) are just some of the items for which the French have developed a liking. It is possible to sell from the mobile shop in markets on market day.

There is a trend in France, similar to that in Spain, towards opening English-style shops (such as English bookshops, bakers, video-markets, etc.) in areas with expatriate populations. This may be a continuing possibility, provided that the market in some areas is not already saturated. It is worth remembering, however, that there aren't as many year-round expatriates in France as there are in Spain so you would almost certainly have to cater for a partly French clientele as well.

Bars and cafés

Running a sociable watering hole in a seaside place or a pretty village is one of the more idealised business ideas, and applies to France no less than in other lands. Almost every French village already seems to have several bars and cafés. However, such enterprises aren't necessarily large income providers and the clientele may be limited. For this reason, many people also consider opening a bar or café as a retirement business.

Moreover, setting up such an establishment is often not as simple as it appears. One drawback is that these businesses can involve long working hours, with little free time. In addition, competition is tough and the bureaucracy involved in obtaining a licence to sell alcohol is considerable, although this should not be a problem if one is buying a going concern which is therefore what most bar owners do. Many bar owners theme their enterprise for which you need to get together a collection of authentic paraphernalia such as objects, equipment and pictures or photographs for the walls and décor.

Drinking establishments are defined under French law as *débit de boissons* and the licence required comes in four variations depending on the categories of beverages served:

1	For non-alcoholic beverages
2	For 1 and also drinks no more than 3% proof spirit
3	For 1 and 2 and also drinks having an alcohol content of 18% proof
4	For 1, 2, and 3 and also all other liquors and spirits not prohibited by French law.

FACT

■ If you want to sell tobacco a licence is also required from the Direction Régionale de Douanes.

The procedure for opening, or acquiring a drinking establishment involves providing the local authorities (usually the *mairie*) with written notification of your intention, at least three weeks in advance.

Restaurants

There is always plenty of custom in France for good restaurants, whether grand ones with table linen and uniformed waiting staff, or small informal bistros. However, something that all these establishments share is the serious attention to detail and the quality and presentation of the food. Because of client expectations the restaurants in France, even basic, inexpensive restaurants must offer good food to survive.

There is a distinction in law between restaurants and bars. Restaurants are regarded as places where drinks are served as an accompaniment to food and less stringent regulations are in force for eating, as opposed to drinking establishments.

Tea shops

A way round the alcohol licence rigmarole might be to open a tea shop serving English-style bread, cakes, muffins and scones baked on the premises. There could be a lunchtime sandwich service and afternoon teas with a range of tea flavours. See Stephen Clarke's *A Life in the Merde* for an entertaining take on setting up a chain of tea shops in Paris.

Hotels

As with restaurants, good hotels in France (in any price range) are always popular and can be very profitable enterprises. It is essential to choose the location of the hotel with care, and to either have or gain experience of the trade before embarking on this kind of enterprise. There are an increasing number of hotels run in France by foreigners.

Probably the main advantage of entering this business is that hotels and properties for conversion can be purchased very cheaply. However this must be balanced against the notarial charges, which are higher for hotels than for non-commercial property. Any establishment with more than six letting bedrooms is classed as a commercial hotel business and the notary charges 21% on top of the agreed purchase price. So a 16-roomed hotel for €150,000 may not be quite such a bargain after all. On a more modest level, there is also scope in France for guesthouses and bed-and-breakfast type accommodation, perhaps within one's own home (see below).

There are very strict regulations governing both hotel and restaurant premises, the majority of which are related to the protection of human life against the risk of fire and other emergencies, which could result in panic. The formalities involved in setting up a hotel involve compliance with the classification standards, depending on what category (no star, one star, two star, etc) you are intending to register in. The hotelier also has to complete a barrage of forms to be returned to the *mairie* to verify compliance with the required standards. The operator must register the establishment on the Commercial and Companies Register and submit to a departmental inspection before consent to open as a business is granted.

Providing residential activity holidays and holiday accommodation

Residential activity holidays

France's substantial tourist industry means that residential activity holidays (e.g. art courses, sports, yoga, etc.) and holiday accommodation, particularly apartments or cottages, are in high demand. The business is usually seasonal and profits in most cases not high; but again the lower prices of property make the idea more viable.

Bed and breakfasts

These are usually advertised with handmade signs by the wayside reading *Chambres d'Hôtes*. No prior authorisation from the authorities is required but a provider must register with the *Registre du Commerce et des Sociétés* (www.infogreffe.fr) already mentioned.

If an evening meal is also provided a licence 3 (see drinking establishments above) is required in order to serve drinks with the meal.

Gîtes

This word has by now become familiar at least to many Britons, not least because some of the estimated 60,000 privately owned self-catering homes available in France are run by them. A *gîte* is a low price, rurally located, simple self-catering accommodation rented to holidaymakers. Various companies including Brittany Ferries will take over the marketing of such properties (www.britanny-ferries.co.uk), while you might find one to buy at www.gites-for-sale.com. To qualify as a *gîte rural*, holiday rental properties should be registered with the national organisation of *gîtes*, Gîtes de France (GdF). The requirements are for certain standards of decoration and equipment to be maintained, and that the property is available to rent for at least three months a year and that the

> ### Charles and Kath Dunstan run a *gîte* in Brittany. It's competitive but they make a living.
>
> Brittany is becoming over gîted and you need to make sure your place stands out. That's why we put in the swimming pool that meets all the French regulations and is heated and last year we put in wireless internet throughout the property, which attracted clients immediately. We keep the place to a high standard with nice furniture and objets d'art and we advertise with Brittany Ferries, which gives us a cushion. We get bombarded by people who build tourist sites on the net. They always give you a free trial and if we pick up clients through their site then we subscribe the following year. We get a complete mix of nationalities: French, Brits, Americans, Italians, Dutch.

FACT

There is a separate GdF guide for Gîtes d'Etape and Gîtes de Refuges. This is for *gîtes* that are specifically aimed at those wanting outdoor sporting activities especially hikers and climbers.

Ski resort chalets/apartments

Those with alpine property can let it out in both winter and summer. The potential for winter letting in fashionable French ski resorts like Val d'Isère, Méribel and Courchevel is prodigious as tour operators usually want to secure suitable accommodation on five-year contracts. Private owners with prime and well-positioned property on the slopes can recoup a year's running costs from a three-week let around February half-term. Alternatively, purpose-built studios in a popular resort such as Les Menuires can be let to young travellers who are notching up a season working in a ski resort. Some also organise commercial skiing packages including catered chalet accommodation, from what is essentially their own holiday home.

owners live close by. The advantage to be gained is that a *gîte rural* qualifies for a lower rate of tax to be paid by the owner than either bed and breakfast or guesthouse accommodation. Also that by appearing in the GdF organisation's handbook, publicity is laid on and there is a reasonable chance of a steady influx of customers, though this generally only happens in the most popular holiday regions. However, membership of GdF entails paying 12%–15% of your takings to the organisation.

Short lets of furnished property

Many people with a holiday home in France help pay for it by letting it out for short periods, a few weeks or months at a time, to holidaymakers. No prior authorisation is needed, but the owner must pay a small businesses income tax (*Impôt sur les bénéfices industriaux et commerciaux*, BIC) unless it's their main residence, or part of it.

Other types of activity holiday being offered from private homes in France include painting, photographic, cookery and craftmaking courses.

The renting of unfurnished property is much more strictly regulated and leases aren't normally for less than three years. For further details, see the chapter *Setting up home*.

Useful websites

Several websites advertise *gîtes* and other properties for rent on which you may aim to get yours on, depending on suitability.

- www.francedirect.net – all kinds of rentals from *gîtes* to *châteaux*
- www.gite.com – charming and traditional holiday homes
- www.villarama.com – enables the customer to book direct with owners
- www.abritel.fr – the ex-Minitel site now on the web. Used by the French
- www.vintagetravel.co.uk – villas in France and elsewhere
- www.hhfrance.com – self-catering properties direct with owners
- www.holiday-rentals.co.uk – properties in several countries

- www.renting-abroad.com – properties in several countries
- www.villaholidaycentre.com– rural and coastal rentals

Tax relief and grants on rentable property

If the intention is to buy a property and then let it there are a number of important considerations in addition to those mentioned above. These mainly concern the treatment of income for tax purposes and the availability of grants.

If you are from the UK and declare the rental income in the UK, then you will have to pay tax to the Inland Revenue. The tax rate depends on your own tax rate, but the main point is the allowance given for overseas investment. Each individual tax inspector has discretion as to whether you can claim interest paid on a loan as an 'expense'. There are virtually no other allowances given in the UK. However, if you declare the income in France, you have to pay 5.5% TVA (value-added tax; VAT) on the gross amount, and you are then allowed a number of allowances under French law. These include:

- Interest on a euro loan taken out in France: depreciation at the rate of 4% of the value of the property per annum.

- Management charges: charged by an agent handling the rental, or to cover your costs in advertising, etc. These can be 10% for country property and 15% for town property.

- Maintenance and cleaning costs: may include repairs to the property; you may even be able to claim for inspection trips to the property.

If you are claiming French allowances you will almost certainly need a French accountant to complete the returns for you and pay the income into your French bank account. It also makes even more sense to have a Euro loan. If you intend converting barns, stables, etc. into *gîtes* or letting units, you may be eligible for a grant of some kind. This would come from the *département*, region, state, or even the EU. The mayor of the commune is all-powerful, and he or she decides whether or not to give planning permission. The *mairie* will also point you in the direction of the right person for a grant. The GdF is gives grants towards the cost of renovation; but you are tied to it for letting for 10 years.

Franchising

If you are tempted by the idea of running your own business, but are deterred by the high failure rate, you

Beginning renovating a property

Sports and fitness

Sporting activity is not yet that popular in France. Nevertheless, it's a growing industry, which carries strong business potential for those with qualifications or experience. Possible openings include sports, squash and golf clubs, tennis and fitness centres and riding schools. Fortunately, with the exception of water sports centres and ski schools, and the big towns along the med, there is not a great deal of commercial competition in this field at present.

may consider taking on a franchise. According to the L'Association Française des Chambers de Commerce et d'Industrie, the number of Franchises in France has doubled in 10 years and the sector employs 400,000 people. Under this system, a company authorises the franchiser to sell that company's goods or services in a particular area, usually exclusively. Franchising is well known in the USA and UK, and was introduced into France in the 1980s. Franchising covers all kinds of products but one of the most popular is clothing including Petit Bateaux and Séphora.

Franchising brings with it several advantages. Usually in the first year of business, many small companies experience difficulties while establishing a reputation and building up a clientele. With a franchise, the franchiser is selling a name that already has a reputation, and whose products are in demand through national advertising. The company offering the franchise will also help the franchiser to obtain, equip and stock the premises, and will handle the accounting. In exchange, the franchiser pays royalties, which are proportional to the sales.

Some French franchises

Alpha Beauté: ☎01 44 70 18 85; www.alphabeaute.fr. Perfume and beauty products

Astarte: ☎01 42 74 61 44; www.astarte.fr. Costume jewellery and accessories

Bookan: ☎02 51 77 88 30; bkfrance@free.fr; www.bookan.fr. Books

Car'go Location Vehicles: www.cargo.fr. Care rental chain in the process of expansion

ChocoClic: www.chococlic.com. Chocolate franchises in France

Easy Cash: www.easycash.fr. Secondhand goods shops (buying and selling)

Icolandia: www.icolandia.com. Children's play centres

Le Jardin des Fleurs: www.florapartner.com. Florists

Farming

Farming has been one of the most popular business activities for foreigners moving to France in recent years. British farmers emigrating are helped by large French subsidies (partly funded by France through ADASEA (www.adasea.net), a government quango, and partly by the EU). This exodus is also promoted by the comparatively low cost of both land and property in France.

SAFER first

The downside to buying a farm is that while it may seem a straightforward operation, there is no certainty that you will actually be permitted to buy because of the existence of the organisation called SAFER (Société d'Aménagement Foncier et d'Etablissement Rural) which can either be your foe or your friend. SAFER (www.proprietes-rurales.fr) is the place to go if you need help with any rural matters from livestock to gîtes. SAFER will also help those trying to set up a business in a rural area to find an appropriate property. However, it also has the right to match the highest bid on the price of farmland. Farmers can also sell their land direct to SAFER, which will then sell it on at the same price, with a small administration charge added. No farmland can be sold in France unless SAFER has been given the option to buy it first. Once SAFER has assured the seller that it has no interest in buying the land, the sale can be finalised. An article in the *Sunday Times* 'French Mistress' series in 2004, told how one British family lost their property when Safer decided to buy it, after they had moved in: 'Six weeks after they moved in, the Kennys received a letter from Safer telling them it was buying their home, claiming it had advised the *notaire* of its intention (which he denies). The Kennys were given six months to find somewhere else to live. They will get back the purchase price plus legal costs, but the turmoil it has caused is hard to put a price on.'

TIP

■ Be warned: farming is not for the faint hearted, and a knowledge of French is pretty much essential if you are to make friends.

Who is eligible?

The French government is generally keen to encourage foreigners to farm in France. It may grant financial aid to farmers under 40 or to those in possession of a diploma recognised by the French Ministry of Agriculture. Those who plan to farm in less popular or depopulated regions may also be eligible for help with farm modernisation and other financial incentives from government agencies. To qualify for such incentives such as interest free loans and grants available any time in the first 10 years of starting up, experience in the work is essential. French agricultural colleges in some areas (e.g. Limoges) also offer short courses for farmers. Further information for farmers and details of possible grants can be obtained from the Association Départementale pour l'Aménagement des Structures des Exploitations Agricoles (ADASEA; see address below). You can also check out the website www.eurofarms.com, run by George Lidbury, who is half French and has been helping British farmers settle in France for over a decade.

You also need permission to run a farm. This comes from the département which decides who can farm and where. You have to fill in an application form (*Demande d'autorisation d'exploiter*), which is submitted to the Direction départementale de l'agiculture et de la fôret (DDAF). A complete form including the letter you need to send to the DDAF can be found at www.service-public.fr/formulaires/index.html. There are regional variations in the application forms.

Vineyards

Wine-producing by the British in France has a long and mostly honourable history as the names of some of the top-notch Bordeaux châteaux remind us. At one end there are the multinational and tycoon investors such as Pearson and George Walker and in the middle are the owner-grower viticulteurs Britanniques, the likes of which run châteax Méaume, du Seuil (Graves) and Bauduc (Entre-Deux-Mers) as well as others. At the bottom end are those who send their crop to the local cooperative to be turned into the local plonk. A fully-fledged château vineyard doesn't come cheap. Whereas agricultural land may seem cheap, the unique and proven soil and conditions for optimum wine-producing are anything but that. Buying a château and turning it into a château labelled wine then costs even more since you have the outlay on equipment such as a wine press and metal tanks and barrels. You would need an *oenologue* (expert freelance wine expert) to assess the potential of the land for producing a good wine; this would include soil content and its suitability. The micro-climate is also crucial, particularly the likelihood of frosts. Not least would be the status of your own skills (or lack of them) as a wine maker. It is possible to study oenology at a French university and become an apprentice; it's also possible to teach yourself the basic principles.

Market seller

Market sellers are known as *commerce ambulant* in France. Markets are very popular (more so than in the UK) despite the competition from supermarkets, and a weekly limit of two days that shopping centres can rent out stands to market traders. Selling in markets can be hard going as you need to be up at the crack of dawn to reach the market in time to set up your stall early and the profits aren't usually that great. The kinds of goods foreigners sell in markets include produce such as fruit, vegetables, eggs etc, secondhand goods and bric-a-brac (*brocante*), English books and videos and handcrafted items. Selling takeaway food is bound by many food safety and hygiene regulations necessitating dealings with the Direction départementale des affaires sanitaires et socials, and so is only for the very keen.

APCE statistics say that some 60,000 market enterprises exist in France and about 7,000 new ones are launched annually. Market traders need to obtain a carte *professionnelle non-sédentaire* (renewable every two years) from the *préfecture* (local government office) for which various documents including proof of civil and liability insurance have to be produced. Market trading has to be registered as a business at the Chambre de Commerce, or if you are a maker of the objects you sell, at the Chambre de Métiers. The *placier* is the person you pay for the hire of the stall. Markets themselves are usually run by the *mairie*, or a concessionaire which can be a specialised company. Market traders pay social security charges and *taxe professionnelle* in addition to income tax. You can also sell at the roadside or in hotels and other public indoor venues.

Property dealing

In the chapter *Setting up home* the procedures for the acquisition of property in France and the possible advantages were discussed in relation to whether the property was for permanent or holiday use. Another possibility exists – that of speculating in French property. This is largely possible because of the disparity in prices between the countries.

A few expatriates have moved into this business by buying, renovating and then reselling properties. This is usually done direct into the UK market, as holiday property, to reach the higher prices that are usual for such property. A business in property renovation would require higher than average capital (because of financial liability for taxes and debts), as well as some experience in the purchase and conveyancing procedure, and building works. This might be obtained from initially purchasing and restoring a property of your own.

Once you have gained experience, and have bought another property through a *notaire*, he or she will can help you set up a real estate company (*société civile immobilière/SCI*) (see business entities below).

Building services

Working as a builder in France has become a well-known way to make a living. Many builders find they can make a profit working for Anglophone clients. Customers are obtained by word of mouth so fly-by-night operators shouldn't survive long. Note that property magazines will only accept paid adverts from builders who are properly registered. Apart from experience and or qualifications, it's most important

> ### Cambridge-based French estate agent Islay Currie ran a building company in the Dordogne for several years
>
> In the 1980s I had made some profit from selling a share in a house in Cambridge, so not having any other projects, I decided to buy a pile of stones in France. After working on the house in the northeast Dordogne, I had made contacts with tradesmen, builders merchants, etc. so I started to do some work for a friend. I then registered with the Chambre de Commerce who sent me on the compulsory training course you have to do. This was very practical, but of course a lot of Anglos don't understand what is going on. So, I was set up with a trading name (Construction Currie) and a VAT number and off I went.
>
> There was a tricky moment when the Chambre de Métiers asked me what experience I had of building, so I told them I had a degree in civil engineering and 11 years as partner in a building firm and they were quite happy with that. I had actually worked for some years in Cambridge in a building cooperative.
>
> Once you are properly registered you receive a business number (SIRET) which legally entitles you to trade. This must be printed on your letterhead and on the devis (estimate). The devis is a contract; you cannot charge more if you do work that is not on the devis. Where you cannot actually know how much the work is going to cost (e.g. foundations for a house), you can give a devis provisoire (non-binding estimate).

to be able to formulate an estimate (*devis*) accurately, as in France this is a contract and the price given for the work specified cannot be increased. All tradespeople also need professional insurance to guarantee their work for 10 years (*garantie décennale*) or other statutory period.

Exporting

In the UK, the Department for Business Enterprise and Regulatory Reform (the BERR used to be theDTI) and the British Embassy and Consulates General in France often hold a range of promotional activities, which include the sectors recommended as having potential. Some of these are listed below. The BERR suggests that export activities could be carried out via a representative (importer, commission agent or stockist/distributor), selling through a manufacturer of complementary products with an established network, setting up a branch office or subsidiary or by establishing a company in France.

- Automotive components
- Boats and boating equipment
- Bridal wear
- Design
- Environmental goods and services
- Food and drink
- Gardening equipment and supplies
- Home and professional interiors

- IT and software
- Medical equipment
- Pet care
- Telecommunications

Useful contacts

The following can provide advice, details of the regulations, legal services, and in some cases, provide grants for individual businesses. Some are general and some are specific, for instance hotels and farming organisations.

Agence Nationale Pour la Création d'Entreprises (APCE): www.apce.com. The Business Creation Agency is responsible for entrepreneurship business creation and in the development of newly-founded companies. It detects and develops new products and services to help creators, operators and the public authorities in their objectives. APCE's multi-language website is very useful and you can download all kinds of useful information about starting a business in France from marketing tips to what kind of legal structure to adopt. It's linked to another site www.jobscout24.fr where you can advertise for staff in French.

Centre National pour l'Aménagement des Structures des Exploitations (CNASEA): www.cnasea.fr. Gives information and advice to farmers. Also agriculture grants

Centre National des Jeunes Agriculteurs CNJA: www.cnja.com. Organisation for young farmers

Confédération Générale des Petites et Moyennes Entreprises (CGPME): www.cgpme.org. Employers' organisation for small and medium-sized businesses

Conseil National des Professions de l'Automobile (CNPA): www.cnpa.fr. Information about regulations for automobile repairers and traders

Entente des Générations pour l'Emploi et l'Entreprise (EGEE): www.egee.asso.fr. All kinds of advice and guidance for starting new businesses and business queries

Fédération Nationale des Sociétés d'Aménagement Foncier et d'Etablissement Rural (FNSAFER): www.safer.fr. Information about SAFER, the French land commission agency which can both exercise a preemptive right to buy agricultural land for sale but also sells land. There is a special section called *Terres d'Europe*, which deals with foreigners (see address below)

Invest in France: www.invest-in-france.org

Terres d'Europe: www.safer-fr.com. Helps foreigners wanting to buy farm land or rural estates

SOS Villages: www.sos-villages.asso.fr. National association that promotes the continuation of village life by encouraging small business start-ups by buying up property in villages and renting it out cheaply to suitable small businesses (hairdressers, flower shops, farmers, internet based companies, etc.) and using funds generated to create local amenities such as swimming pools, retired people's social centres, youth clubs, music schools, libraries etc. It also buys

> **Magalie Morel, a business consultant working on the Côte d'Azur, explains that prospective entrepreneurs need to give careful thought to their choice of business form.**
>
> The first and most important decision is to decide how big you want your company to be. If you start out as a limited company, a SARL or EURL, then you are aiming to be quite big. Otherwise it is best to start as an entreprise individuelle, as a one-person business. If you make a mistake at the beginning about the form of your business you can have a lot of difficulties later on, so you need to get it right. For example, I have a Dutch-Indonesian client who imports furniture from Indonesia, and she is an entreprise individuelle. Another client who imports Jacuzzis from the USA has been a SARL right from the start. You also need to decide on your tax regime: Micro-Entreprise, régime simplifié, régime réel; this is nothing to do with the legal form of your company, but the basis on which you are going to be taxed.

residential property in the village and construction sites and sell them off at a loss for new residents to build homes

Union des Métiers des Industries de l'Hôtellerie (UMIH): www.umih.fr. Information on regulations governing the hotel industry

■ BUSINESS STRUCTURES AND REGISTRATION

There are various legal entities which a business can form though there is perhaps a greater diversity of types in France than in some countries, with strict rules applying to the operation of each type of business.

Bureau de liaison/bureau de représentation

A liaison office (*bureau de liaison*) is the minimal type of business foray. It essentially provides a shop window for foreign companies to communicate with potential customers but is not a business entity in the sense of having a legal relationship with customers or third parties. It may carry out assessments of the market and promotional activities. The main obligations of a *bureau de liaison* are to conform with French regulations on publicity and advertising materials. Any company dealing in comestibles should note that foreign foodstuffs may not be advertised on French television. Liaison offices must be registered with the Register of Companies.

Entreprise individuelle (sole trader)

This is a popular form of business for the self-employed with a modest turnover, who do not engage in any large financial activities, since in the event of problems, personal liability is unlimited. It's suitable for a sole trader and requires no start-up capital. There are three types of *entreprises individuelles*: *profession libérales* (e.g. doctors, accountants, lawyers, etc.), *commerçants individuels* (shopkeepers and other traders) and *artisans* (craftspeople). Social security deductions are very high in France for the self-employed and represent about 35%–40% of total earnings before taxes are deducted. They are also compulsory regardless of a lack of profit, or if losses are being incurred which is not uncommon in the first couple of years of business.

A law (*Loi Dutreil*, article 8) came into force on 1 January 2004 which means that an *enterprise individuelle* can now make a declaration of non-seizability (*declaration d'insaississabilité*) in the presence of a notary which will render your principal residence safe from creditors. The declaration is registered with the Bureau des Hypothèques (land registry) and must be published in the local newspaper. If you don't fulfil these conditions your home can still be seized by creditors.

Société à responsibilité limitée (SARL)

A SARL is the most common form of limited liability company and is suitable for small and medium-sized businesses. However, the extra costs in annual social security payments and business taxes can be extortionate, even if only a handful of staff are employed (see 'Employing staff' below). A SARL may be formed with between two and 50 shareholders of which a three-quarters majority is needed to alter the company's constitution and expand or decrease the capital. Shareholders may be of any nationality. To set up an SARL you used to need a minimum capital of about €7,620. However this is no longer the case. A law to encourage economic initiative that was brought in 2003 removed the obligation of a capital minimum to €1. A SARL may have one or two managers (*gérants*) categorised as salaried employees for tax and social security purposes. An annual audit by a statutory auditor (*commissaire aux comptes*) is not required unless turnover and/or employee numbers exceed certain limits. An AGM must be held to approve the financial statements before the end of the financial year.

Société par actions simplifié (SAS)

A SAS is a simplified version of the SA introduced in 1994 in response to a need for a more flexible structure to facilitate cooperation between businesses. The minimum corporate share capital of the shareholders must be €37,000 (or the foreign currency equivalent), half of which must be paid when forming the company and the rest within five years. The SAS cannot issue shares publicly.

Entreprise unipersonelle à responsibilité limitée (EURL)

An EURL is another limited liability entity and is basically a SARL adapted to a sole person with the same amount of start-up capital.

Société anonyme (SA)

An SA is appropriate for larger, more prestigious concerns. It requires more capital than a SARL and includes more formalities than a SARL. An SA also demands a minimum seven shareholders and is run by a board of 3–18 directors (*conseil d'administration*), who must be shareholders and who are appointed for a maximum of six years and a *président directeur générale* (PDG).

If the start-up capital (minimum is €37,000) is subscribed in cash, at least half the capital must be paid when forming the company and the rest within five years. Shares which are subscribed in kind must be entirely paid up and the contributions are subject to appraisal by the *Commissaire aux Apports* (Contributions Auditor) to assess their value. An SA must have an annual general assembly of shareholders and external auditors.

Partnerships

The laws of partnership in France are complicated as so many different forms exist. Expert advice is essential for those proposing any form of partnership. Some of the types are listed below.

Société en nom collectif (SNC)

This is a General Partnership which must have at least two members with no minimum capital restriction. The shareholders have joint and several unlimited liability for the company debts. For tax and social security purposes, the member shareholders are categorised as individual traders.

Société en commandité simple (SCS)

The SCS is a limited partnership. There is also a *Societé en Commandité par Actions* (*SCA*). This is a joint stock company whose active partners have unlimited liability and sleeping partners whose liability is limited to their stake in the company.

Société civile (SC)

A Civil Company may only deal in civil (i.e. non-commercial) matters which include, agriculture, building, and the professions. An SC has several forms and a minimum of two shareholders. For instance an SCI (*Société Civile Immobilière*) is a form commonly used for a real estate holding company, also for managing real estate, letting and property purchase. It's therefore useful for groups of expatriates buying property together to form or join an SCI. In this form, the SCI is registered as the owner of the property or properties and it can be a useful way of bypassing French inheritance laws (see the chapter *Setting up home*). In the SCI form it's similar to a partnership as individuals are taxed individually on their capital gains when they sell, gain income, or incur losses. An SCI cannot be used for commercial purposes but may be transmuted into a SARL. It's possible to create a SARL which rents the property from the SCI thus protecting the stakeholders and their property from personal liability in case of financial or tax problems. There are, however, tax liabilities involved in changing from an SCI to SARL (or indeed from any business entity to another) so it's advisable to take expert fiscal advice at the outset.

Succursale

A *succursale* is a branch office. These aren't legally separate from the parent company and thus all business must be concluded with the parent company, which is likewise responsible for any debts incurred by the branch office.

A branch office has more powers than a liaison office because it can conduct business in its own right (subject to the above). Note, however, that for tax purposes it's treated as a separate entity from the parent company. It must therefore keep its own company books.

If you are buying a business then its legal form will have important tax implications. For example, the purchase of a company involves extra purchase taxes and duties.

Procedure for registering a company

All SARLs, SAs, *Commandités* (partnerships) and other business entities must be registered with the Commercial Register (Registre national du commerce et des sociétés; www.infogreffe.fr) and the Chamber of Commerce.

There are several important procedures for registering and incorporating businesses set up in France, which must be executed within two weeks of beginning operations there. It's advisable to initiate the procedures at the CFE (*centre de formalités des entreprises*), at the local Chamber of Commerce as soon as you arrive. The business must be registered on the *Registre du Commerce et des Sociétés* which will be done by the CFE locally with the *Greffe* (clerk) from the *Tribunal de Commerce* (commercial court). Failure to register within the time limit's subject to penalties.

As with all bureaucratic procedures a barrage of personal documents is required including a copy of a birth certificate issued within the last three months and an accompanying official translation. If a foreign company is being registered then a copy of the memorandum and articles of association (*les statuts*) with a professional French translation will be required. The company registration number allocated by the *Registre de Commerce* is then relayed to the company's French bank the tax office and social security offices and any other relevant authorities including the *Institut National des la Statistique et des Etudes Economiques* (INSEE) which will issue the company with a NAF, SIREN and/or SIRET number.

The CFE, which handles all the administration involved in registering new businesses is usually the local chamber of commerce and industry. For instance if the traders, merchants and other businesses come under the following categories: *Répertoire des Metiers* (Trade Register) or *Les Groupements d'Intérêt Economiques* (Common Economic Interest Groups) and *Sociétés de fait* (de facto companies). There are however other CFEs (see box).

Setting up company banking and accounts

When opening an account you will need to be present in person and to provide proof of personal identity including a passport, birth certificate, translated memorandum and articles and certificate of incorporation. When setting up a company, the share capital will be held in a blocked account until the company registration formality has been completed. Other company banking facilities, loans, overdrafts, etc. will have to be negotiated on an individual basis.

For company accounts, you will almost certainly require a French accountant to set up the books and accounting system as it varies from the British system. If the books don't conform to French auditing requirements they will have to be

FACT

■ *Chambre des Métiers* (Chamber of Trades) for craftspeople who are self-employed or with a firm.

■ *Greffe du Tribunal du Commerce*: (Clerk of the Commercial Court). For sales representatives.

redone, which for several years' accounts would be very expensive. The annual publication *Mémento Comptable*, published by Editions Francis Lefebvre and written by PriceWaterhouseCoopers, is the main reference accounting manual.

■ RUNNING A BUSINESS

Running a small business in France tends to be a more easy-going and relaxed affair than in the UK or USA. Business procedures can be fairly informal, especially in the south where a Mediterranean attitude prevails. As already mentioned, running a business can become a way of life rather than a purely profit-driven exercise.

Small, privately-owned businesses, by their very nature, demand much hard work, long hours and little free time. Much emphasis is placed on offering a personalised service and a high level of customer care, since establishing a good reputation and relationship with the customers is vital for the survival of a business. Formal advertising and marketing tend to be less important, and beyond the financial range of most small businesses. Nevertheless, dealing with suppliers and other contacts will demand the full extent of one's persuasive skills and negotiating techniques.

However, the relaxed attitude described above is not applicable to official bureaucracy. In addition, some types of businesses may find themselves up against the ever intrusive, and occasionally bizarre-seeming, regulations that emanate from Brussels. In France, accounting and other official procedures are often very complex and professional advice in matters such as taxation will be essential.

Employing/dismissing staff and employer contributions

Nearly all businesses employ staff, whether part- or full-time. Employees are usually taken on for a three-month trial period. During this time employment may be terminated by either party without any notice being given. If the trial period proves successful, then a contract of employment will be drawn up. This should always be in writing and a copy retained for future reference along with any correspondence with the employee. The different types of contract are dealt with fully in Employment laws and rights.

The rules which govern relations between employers and employees in France are embodied in the detailed statutory regulations known as the *Code du Travail* which among other things sets out minimum wages and working conditions, hours of work, amount of paid holiday allowed per year etc. Some sectors of industry have their own collective bargaining agreements (*conventions collectives*) forged between the labour force and managements which come into effect the moment employment is offered. For other sectors, there is a statutory minimum wage (SMIC), which is indexed to the cost of living.

The discharging of employees is governed by a strict set of procedures, which if not followed, may result in penalties for the employer and/or reinstatement of the employee. If the proposed dismissal results from the serious malconduct of the employee, he or she must be summoned prior to the dismissal and the reasons for the notice given in full. Other procedures must also be followed further details of which are given in the section on Employment. If employers wish to make staff redundant for economic reasons, then it's a lengthy process hedged about with

FACT

■ A good way of integrating into the local community is to employ local people as staff. The local ANPE office will usually be pleased to help with staffing requirements and to advertise these free of charge.

restrictions. Among other things, the employer will have to pay compensation, *indeminité de licenciement* the amount of which is fixed by law.

Under the *Code du Travail*, employers must pay mandatory social security contributions for their employees. These contributions, together with payroll taxes add 60% to the payroll costs. The employer contributes 45% and the employee 15%. There are also supplementary pension schemes run by employers usually jointly with the unions. As the employer's social security contributions for employees are much higher than employee contributions they add considerably to the financial burden inflicted on small businesses.

◼ TAXATION

Main business taxes

If you run any kind of business, you will need to choose a tax regime; this is also relevant to those who run *gîtes* or *chambres d'hôte*. It's advisable to talk to an accountant or tax lawyer when making your choice, because making the wrong choice can leave you worse off.

Assuming that you choose to pay income tax (IR) rather than corporation tax (IS), you will need to choose between three types of regimes: *micro-entreprise*, *régime du réel simplifié* and *régime réel normal*. There are two versions of the *micro-entreprise* regime. *Micro-Bénéfices Industriels Commerciaux* only applies to commercial professions. Liberal professions can use the *Micro-Bénéfices Non-Commerciaux* regime. If you are taxed as a *micro-entreprise* you also fill in form no 2042P. If you run more than one business then you will fill in a form for each.

Micro-BIC

The basic idea is that you accept a fixed deduction from your turnover, in exchange for a super-simplified bookkeeping regime. The thresholds depend on what type of business you run. If you sell goods or provide furnished lodgings (which includes running *chambres d'hôtes/gîtes*), and your pre-tax turnover is under €76,300 annually, then you can choose to be taxed on turnover after an abatement of 68% is taken off. You effectively pay IR on 32% of your turnover. Capital gains aren't included in the calculation. Commercial services can choose to be taxed on their turnover (*chiffre d'affaires*) after an abatement of 45%, but their turnover is limited to €27,000. This regime is not obligatory – you can choose to be taxed on your real income (*régime du reel simplifié* or *reel normale*). It's important to realise that because you are only taxed on a fixed percentage of your turnover, you will pay very much smaller social security contributions and tax than someone who chooses to deduct their real expenses from their turnover and who is then taxed on the remainder. However large your expenses may be you will still win out as a *Micro-entreprise*. Another great advantage is that you only need to keep a very basic record of all your expenses and income, in a standard daybook, but you don't have to present full accounts at the end of each year. You simply enter your total turnover on form no. 2042C, and the type of services supplied at different locations. If you exceed the limit during one year, then you are taxed on the excess at the usual IR rates. In the year after you will no longer qualify for *Micro-BIC*, unless the two years taken together average out at less than the *Micro-BIC* threshold.

As regards *gîtes* and *chambres d'hôtes*, if the net income from rentals exceeds €23,000, or constitutes more than 50% of your household income, then you are considered a professional landlord; you will be required to register as a business and you will pay higher social security taxes on the income. If the property is sold the capital gains will be treated as business rather than private gains.

The *micro* regime is not only related to your turnover. If you opt to make TVA declarations then you are excluded from the *micro* regime. Companies that pay IS are always excluded, as are companies where the partners pay IR on their income, such as SARLs *de famille*. You cannot declare a loss under the *micro régime*, neither can losses be carried forward. If you start your business in the middle of the year then you are assessed pro rata, on a proportion of €76,300 or €27,000, as the case may be.

Micro-BNC

This is open to liberal professions and is also called a *déclaration spéciale*; you are taxed on turnover minus 37%. Your turnover cannot exceed €27,000 per annum to stay in this category. Liberal professions don't have the option of choosing the *régime simplifié* or *régime réel*. The next step up is a *déclaration controlée*.

Micro-BA

Farmers have their own *Micro* regime, otherwise called a *BA forfait*. To qualify your turnover has to be below €76,300. The *forfait* or fixed sum on which you are taxed is

Régime réel simplifié and *Régime réel normal*

Where your turnover before taxes exceeds €76,300 (commercial), or €27,000 (services and liberal professions), you have no choice but to move to the *régime simplifié*. You have the option of moving up to the *régime réel* (i.e. *réel normal*) if you want. You will be required to make a TVA declaration at the end of each year, and to make three-monthly estimated TVA payments. You can pay IR on your real income, and deduct your real expenses. You are required to keep accounts. The tax annex form you require is no. 2031 for BIC or no. 3035 for BNC. You can still belong to a CGA and claim your 20% abatement.

Once your turnover exceeds €763,000 (commercial) or €230,000 (services) you are in the realms of the *réel*. Here you need to hire an accountant (unless you are an accountant yourself), maintain full accounts, and publish annual balance sheets. You are also required to make monthly TVA payments and declarations. In other respects there is not that much difference between the *réel* and *simplifié*, just more paperwork. Your tax annex form is No.2031.

calculated according to standardised figures of production per hectare. If you have no revenues other than those coming under *bénéfices agricoles* you can fill in the basic tax declaration no. 2042. Most farmers are involved in some form of commerce and have to fill in no. 2342 as well. There is a scheme in place for young farmers who don't subscribe to *Micro-BA* whereby they can be taxed on only 50% of their annual income for the first five years.

Micro-foncier

This is more correctly called the *régime simplifié de déclaration des revenus fonciers*. It enables you to put your income from letting unfurnished property directly into the basic tax declaration form no. 2042, instead of using form no. 2044. It only

applies to landlords who earn less than €15,000 net in one calendar year from their lettings. You are given an automatic 14% deduction from the gross letting income for the year. If your real expenses add up to more than 30% of letting income during the year you will be better off with the normal *foncier* regime (i.e. you simply file tax annex form no. 2044). There is a useful calculator for *micro-foncier* on the site www.patrimoine.com. Once you opt for the normal *foncier* regime you are obliged to remain in it for five years.

Impot sur les societés

This is the French equivalent of corporation tax, and is known as IS. In very general terms, most French companies pay IS. The list of those that don't is given above under Impôt sur le Revenu. IS is levied at two rates:

- 33.33% + a non-deductible 1% contribution = 34.33%
- 15.45% on the first €38,120 profit as long as the company's capital was paid up in full at the time of incorporation, and at least 75% of the shares are held by natural persons (i.e. not other businesses). As a measure against tax avoidance, companies subject to IS are required to pay a graduated basic minimum of €750 on turnover above €76,000 which can later be claimed back if they actually pay IS. This is the *impôt forfaitaire annuel*. New businesses can in some circumstances claim exemption.

Companies are expected to calculate and pay their IS themselves without any demand from the tax office. There are numerous deductions of costs and expenses to be applied. Salaries paid to directors or partners can be deducted from the company's IS bill. The directors and partners then pay IR on the salaries and dividends they receive. You also have the option of carrying over losses, using depreciation and provisions for debts and a great deal more to reduce your tax bill.

Value added tax (TVA)

The French invented TVA; the *taxe sur la valeur ajoutée* generates 45% of the state's tax revenues. Most businesses are required to collect TVA and make payments to the Centre des Impôts. At the same time you deduct the TVA you pay on your purchases from the total you collect. You have the right to opt out of TVA if you are a *micro-entreprise*. The rates in continental France are:

- 0% TVA is payable on residential lettings
- 2.1% on medicines refunded by the social security system, newspapers, TV licences, etc
- 5.5% on agricultural and fishing products, water, hotel accommodation, books, medicines not refunded by social security, renovation expenses on residential properties, etc
- 19.6% charged on all other items.

Other business taxes

There are a number of sundry business taxes, mostly payable by companies with 10 or more employees, and which are calculated from the total salaries paid:

Taxe sur les Salaires (payroll tax): Levied on employers not liable for VAT. The tax varies according to the annual salary of the employee

Participation construction: Compulsory Construction Investment Tax. Levied at 0.65%

Participation formation continue: Training tax. Levied at 1.2%

Taxe d'apprentissage: Apprentice tax. 0.6%

Finally there are taxes on real estate (*taxes foncières*) which are calculated on the supposed rental value of developed and undeveloped land.

Accountancy advice

Businesses must prepare accounts each year, and in the case of partnerships, SAs and SARLs these must be supplied to the Commercial Registrar; they must also follow a prescribed legal format.

Accountancy advice is readily available in all parts of France: one should approach several firms and engage the one which takes an interest in and seems equipped to advise on the business's accountancy requirements. Accountants (*experts comptables*) aren't allowed to advertise, but listings can be found in the telephone directory.

French accountancy practices differ from those in other countries. Accountancy and audits to prepare the accounts are separate functions. Therefore you will require an accountant to give accountancy and tax advice, but a separate firm of auditors to prepare the annual accounts. Although there are a few UK accountants with experience of French procedures, most business people choose a local French financial adviser. Alternatively, various international firms of accountants have offices in both countries.

Useful addresses

International and UK chartered accountants with French associates:

Cabinet Henderson: ☎05 53 23 44 52; . Bilingual accounts with experience of handling the tax affairs of small to medium size, British-owned businesses

Dixon Wilson: ☎01 47 03 12 90; www.dixonwilson.fr. Chartered accountants, provide strategic financial and tax planning services to businesses, companies and high net worth individuals resident either in France or the UK

JPA International: JPA-Bourner Bullock; www.jpainternational.com. About 15 branches in France

Bentley Jennison Accountants: www.bentley-jennison.co.uk

Legal advice

The prospective businessman in France is almost certainly going to need specialist legal advice, both in the setting up or purchase of the business, and in future operations. This applies no matter how small or large the business is. French law originates from Napoleonic times and is very different to the Anglo-Saxon law of northern European countries.

Some UK law practices have specialists in French law, and these can be approached for advice. Some international law firms with offices in France specialise in giving both legal and financial advice. However, small businesses can also consult a local French practice particularly if recommended by other clients; such firms aren't hard to find but your French will have to be good, otherwise you will need an interpreter as English-speaking French lawyers are fairly rare.

French lawyers tend to work together in practices made up of a handful of lawyers. Therefore one firm can deal with most matters, be it contract law, employment law or litigation, etc. Not all lawyers (*avocats*) are qualified to act in a court.

Useful addresses

Holman, Fenwick & Willan Solicitors: www.hfw.com. Offices in London and Paris

Lefèvre Pelletier et associés, Avocats: ☎01 53 93 30 00 www.lpalaw.com.fr. French commercial law firm that specialises in foreign clients

Templeton Associates: ☎01225 422282www.templeton-france.com. Advice on acquisitions and setting up a business in France

◼ BUSINESS INSURANCE

French insurance commands a large market and is subject to legal regulatory control under the *Code des Assurances* and all insurance companies of whatever kind in France come under the scrutiny of the Direction Générale des Assurances. When choosing an insurance company many companies deal with a broker specialising in their field. Insurance in France is expensive as it's subject to tax from 7% to 30% depending on the type of insurance. Owners and tenants of business premises will require insurance against property damage and the subsequent financial losses incurred, and against legal liability to another party.

In addition there are special policies for hotels, restaurants and bars. Insurance companies will be particularly concerned that proprietors of such establishments observe the rigorous safety standards and provisions for the security of the property of guests anywhere on the premises including the car park. This is because in France proprietors are legally responsible for guests' property.

Anyone dealing in motor vehicle repairs or sales is under a legal obligation to protect the vehicles not only while on the premises but in their charge outside the premises, for instance when on tow etc.

FACT

◼ The essential difference between lawyers and *notaires* is that the latter are usually only involved with the law as it relates to contract, and also property matters.

It's compulsory for anyone operating in a professional capacity to be insured. For builders, there is a 10-year legal liability for work carried out. Owing to the extensive litigation possibilities to which this exposes the practitioner, it's advisable to find an acute and experienced insurance broker who can devise a very intricate insurance cover.

Useful addresses

Centre de Documentation et d'Information de l'Assurance (CDIA): ☎01 42 46 13 13; www.ffsa.fr. General enquiries from the public about insurance in France

Commission de Contrôle des Assurances: ☎01 55 50 41 41 www.ccamip.fr

Fédération Françaises des Sociétés d'Assurance (FFSA): ☎01 42 47 90 00; www.ffsa.fr

Miscellaneous

Registering rights over industrial property

Foreign business people should register their industrial property rights (i.e. patents) which can thereby be protected for exclusive exploitation for 20 years while trade marks (marques) can be protected for 10 years. This should be done at the Institut National de la Propriété Industrielle (www.inpi.fr.)

Incorporation fees

There are certain reasonably modest costs incurred for the registration of a company on the Commercial and Companies Register. Additional fees are needed to cover the printing of legal announcements and tax on the start-up capital. The total would come to about €500 for a limited liability, plus any legal or accountancy fees.

Siège social

Siège social is registered office. It's obligatory for all French companies and branches of foreign companies to have a registered address that is not just a post box number, but a genuine office from which it can carry out commercial business. The address must be registered with Register of Companies at the same time as the business. In large towns and cities it's possible to find agencies that can provide a *siège social* and other facilities for smaller businesses.

Statuts (company statutes)

These are the memorandum and articles of incorporation required by all French companies prior to registration. They should embody the details of the company including the form, name, *siège social*, aims, total capital, share value and restrictions on share transferability and the powers and limitations of named persons representing the company, etc.

Doing business with France without forming a company

Apart from the Bureau de Liaison, all forms of company already mentioned incur French tax liability. Likewise the appointment of a dependant agent or a resident salesperson with authority to make contracts, or the establishment or premises will also lead to French tax liability. There are some methods of trading however, which don't normally lead to liability for taxation in France.

- Distribution agreement: Under such an agreement, a distributor is allowed a gross margin on sales by the company for which he or she is distributing in France.
- Commercial agent: This is a popular form of distribution agreement in France. The Commercial Agent is an independent contractor who courts orders from clients on behalf of the manufacturer. For this service the agent is paid commission, normally a percentage of the total sales. Note that under French law, undue termination of such an agreement with a commercial agent can result in a settlement for damages in favour of the agent who is deemed to have been unfairly treated and the amount can total twice the gross annual remuneration earned by the agent.
- *Commissionaire à la vente*: Similar, but less formal than a commercial agent, in that the *commissionaire à la vente* orders from the supplier on an ad hoc basis.
- Franchises: A franchise agreement is where the franchisor agrees with the franchisee to allow him/her the right to run a franchise for the sale of goods or services to clients in return for an agreed system of remuneration.

■ SUMMARY

Just as the French are eagerly taking up the business opportunities that are now available to them in other EU countries, France itself is already very much open to foreigners wishing to start or buy a business there. Although the French have never been very keen on foreign business people entering the French market and making profits for foreign companies, they are very enthusiastic and supportive of anyone wishing to invest in France with a French business or company. This doesn't mean, however, that setting up any business in France is easy. Inevitably, it will be a more difficult process than in your own country. The rewards themselves may not be any greater than those, which could be achieved elsewhere, but the setting-up costs are frequently less.

Business glossary

French	English
acte de commerce	commercial act
cession	sale/transfer of a business
commissaire aux apports	auditor for contributors
compte séquestre	stakeholder account
concessionnaire	distributor
courtier	broker
Direction du Trésor	Treasury Directorate
gérant	legal manager
intérêts des prêts	interest
filiales	subsidiaries
franchisé	franchisee
franchiseur	franchiser
huissier de justice	bailiff
lettre de change	bill of exchange
mandat	power of attorney; proxy
moins-values	losses
plus-values	capital gains
redevances et honoraires	royalties
report des pertes	losses
retenues à la source	withholding taxes
tacite reconduction	automatic renewal of a contract
société-mère	parent company
travailleur indépendant	self-employed person

TIP

Proceed very much in the same way as you would if you were starting or buying a business elsewhere. Make use of all the support you can get and take expert professional advice on dealing with the French law and business practices.

■ MAIN RECEPTION ORGANISATIONS AND INFORMATION NETWORKS FOR NEW BUSINESSES

The American Chamber of Commerce in Paris: American Chamber of Commerce in France; ☎01 56 43 45 67; www.amchamfrance.org

Assemblée des Chambres Françaises de Commerce et d'Industrie (ACFCI): ☎03 20 63 77 77; www.grand-lille.cci.fr. French Chambers of Commerce Network can supply a list of Chambers of Commerce throughout France. Local Chambers of Commerce vary in the quality of their business start-up services as not all chambres have specialised staff. However they will provide contacts including notaires, lawyers specialising in businesses, accountants, etc. They also offer

seminars and courses where entrepreneurs can discuss the feasibility of their projects with experts

Chambres de Métiers et de l'artisaat (APCM) (Chambers of Trade Network): ☎01 44 43 10 00; www.artisant.fr. Can be contacted for a national list of Chambre de Métiers. Chambres de Métiers are often overlooked as they do much the same job as chambers of commerce. However, they are an invaluable local source of help to individual artisans who can request an individual appointment if needed

Le Réseau des Boutiques de Gestion: www.boutiques-de-gestion.com. 124 independent management shops, the BGs (*Boutique de Gestion*) provide comprehensive guidance in all matters relating to business start-ups and also post creation follow-up. Individually tailored service provided

Confederation of British Industry (CBI): www.cbi.org.uk. Information

DIACT: ☎01 40 65 12 34; www.diact.gouv.fr /www.investinfrance.org. Help and grants for manufacturers wanting to set up in France

Department for Business Enterprise and Regulatory Reform (used to be the DTI): ☎020 7215 5000; www.berr.gov.uk

European Commission: The European Commission has set up various EU wide business cooperation schemes, networks of business consultants and economic development agencies supported by the Commission. These have the task of assisting and give advice to SMEs (small and medium-sized enterprises) in particular for their search for cross-border cooperation partners. Further details from: The European Commission in the UK (☎0207 973 1992; ec.europa.eu/ unitedkingdom). European Commission representation in Scotland: ☎0131 225 2058; Wales 029 2089 5020; Northern Ireland 028 9024 0708

European Information Centres (EICs): provide information on EU issues for to small and medium-size businesses. EICs have a continuous flow of information on Europe and have access to EU databases which can assist companies looking for business partners in Europe. Not all services can be provided by all EICs and some charges may be made for some services. Further information at: www.euro-info.org.uk

France Initiative Réseau (FIR): ☎01 40 64 10 20; www.france-initiative.fr. Describing itself as the 'Salon des Entrepreneurs', The France Initiative Network is represented at local level by 240 *plate-formes d'initiatives locales* (PFILs), which offer various aids to new businesses: particularly interest free loans and also sponsorship (*parrainage*) of entrepreneurs by established heads of companies prepared to lend their expertise

UK Trade and Invest: ☎0207 215 8000; www.uktradeinvest.gov.uk. Further research on the French market can be undertaken at the Trade and Investment website

Franco-British Chamber of Commerce and Industry: ☎01 53 30 81 32; www.francobritishchamber.com

Relevant publications

The Agence Pour La Création d'Entreprises (APCE) publishes a range of guides under the generic name *guide metier* on starting and running various types of business including *Ouvrez un restaurant!, Ouvrez un gîte rural!, Créez votre Net-entreprise!, Devenez consultant!* and *Devenez artisan du bâtiment!*. In the same series are how to guides (*guide méthode*) including *La micro-entreprise de A à Z* and *Financer votre project d'entreprise*. They are clearly written and designed to be understood easily. Contact www.apce.com, www.editions-organisation.com.

Directory of European Industrial and Trade Associations: published by CBD Research Ltd. ☎0871 222 3440; cbd@cbdresearch.com; www.cbdresearch.com. At around £200 €300) (new edition, 2008), this is probably one to consult in a library. CBD also publishes *European Companies: Guide to Sources of Information*, which includes detailed information on how to form a company in each country

EU Policies: *A Guide for Business*: published by the American Chamber of Commerce in Brussels. The book deals with specific sectors of EU policy from competition to environment and from industry perspectives to the economy with reference to current EC legislation and policies and offers analyses of their impact on businesses. Can be ordered online at www.eucommittee.be

Franco-British Trade Directory: published by the French Chamber of Commerce in Great Britain:www.investinfrance.org. The CCFGB publish the *Franco-British Trade Directory*

Intrastat Classification Nomenclature (ICN): A 650-page guide for businesses doing interstate business in the EU and turning over more than €180,000 a year. It gives the vital EC code number for every possible item traded in the EU from artichokes to zips. Without such a code number, a business person will not be able to complete a Supplementary Statistical Declaration, SSD (in quadruplicate) which will make you liable to a fine (see TVA above); www.uktradeinfo.com

Starting and Running a B&B in France: *Daily Telegraph* books, Deborah Hunt, £14.99

Starting a Business in France: by André de Vries, published by Vacation Work, £12.95. A comprehensive guide to starting all kinds of businesses in France and the processes involved.

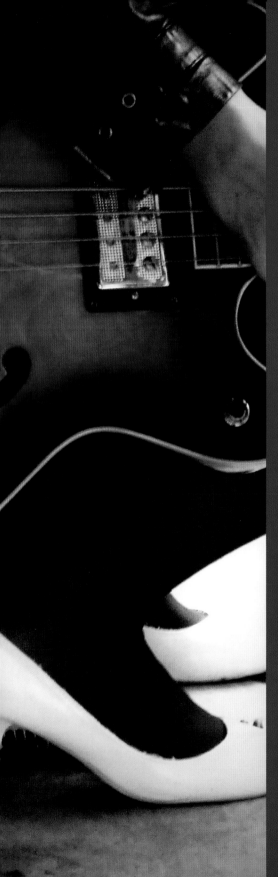

Time Off

■ INTRODUCTION

C harles de Gaulle once asked how you could rule a country with 500 cheeses – and part of what makes France so rich are the regional variations in landscape, specialities in food and wine and the people. Getting to know the particularities of your new French region, the countryside, communities and customs can be a truly absorbing activity, although, in some ways, now that the vast majority of French live increasingly similar urban lives, also a historical one. Nevertheless, a great deal of time and effort is spent in trying to preserve the knowledge of old traditions and keep the countryside alive. Grants are made available to people wishing to pursue, for example, old artisan techniques, and moving to rural France presents many opportunities for learning about and participating in this sort of activity.

Pottery in La Borne

The village of La Borne (www.laborne.fr) is in the Cher, in the Centre region. There has been a tradition of pottery there since the 16th century and today it's a centre for a great variety of contemporary potters. An association, the Centre Création Céramique (CCC; www.ceramiclaborne.org) organises exhibitions of the work of contemporary potters and educational visits to some of the old kilns in the village. There are opportunities to learn the art of ceramics yourself. The village is set in some gentle countryside and you can eat al fresco among the fruit trees of the garden of an organic restaurant at the crossroads in the village.

La Borne is just one example of how, when you live in rural France, you have the opportunity to take further activities you may just taste as a tourist. And, if they're part of your leisure time, they don't have to be expensive. Government finance is available for *la vie associative* and joining an association such as the CCC is a way of getting involved in these interests relatively cheaply. Associations are also structures you can pursue professional activities through. There are about 800,000 associations throughout France involved in activities from ceramics and theatre to sport and politics.

To continue with this particular regional theme, *Le Berry*, the old name for Centre is also a part of France where you can take part in traditional music and dancing at *les bals* (dances), where you can find people of all ages enjoying an evening out. Again, this activity isn't by any means limited to this region, but just an example. Further south in Le Berry, at St Chartier, a unique music festival is held each year where there is no amplified sound. People come from all over Europe with their instruments and spontaneous orchestras strike up all over the village. St Chartier is near Nohant, where Georges Sand, the author of rustic novel, *La Mare au Diable* is from.

In many ways, contemporary French culture does struggle to throw off the weight of this rich past and the cultural vitality of the present may seem to be held back by this heritage. Nevertheless, because the national identity is so dependent on cultural values, the state and local government are very active in promoting all sorts of cultural events. Participating in these is one way of getting a feel for the French sense of community. The *Nuits Blanches* and *Paris Plage*, innovated by the current mayor of Paris, have already been mentioned. Another very successful example of this is the *Fête de la Musique*, inaugurated under President Mitterrand by the popular Minister of Culture Jacques Lang. It takes place on the 21 June each year and for that night only, anyone can set up anywhere in the street anywhere in the country and play music. The cities, towns and villages of France are full of people wandering around and taking in whatever music comes their way. Many of the municipalities also commission big name musicians to play in open air concerts on public squares.

One of the major obstacles to taking full advantage of local opportunities may well be that because France has such a strong cultural identity, which is so heavily supported by the state, it is easy (not least for the French themselves) to take for granted what is potentially one of the most participatory cultures in the world. Just because the state itself is so active, individuals do not necessarily feel the need to take initiative themselves. Nevertheless, the tools are there if you wish to use them.

It is easy to talk too much about the French way of doing things, and as someone from elsewhere it's natural that you'll be sensitive to the differences and national characteristics of all aspects of life. However, life goes on an individual level in France, as it does anywhere, and you'll soon find there's no shortage of opportunity for making contact with passionate, lively, entertaining people who are full of character and interest. At the end of the day, surely what makes a place is its people. Here's an anecdote from an English friend about a summer holiday she took in the Dordogne as a child. She was standing on a bridge on a quiet country road, high up above the Dordogne river, trying to psych herself up into following her brother who had already made the long leap down into the water. There had been no traffic but suddenly a car appeared on the road and pulled up beside her. A French family got out and started clapping and cheering to encourage her to jump. Of course, she no longer had any choice but to disengage from her fear and step off the edge into the air.

■ PUBLIC HOLIDAYS AND FESTIVALS

Compared with Britain and the USA, France has a great number of public holidays, *les jours fériés*, and they are taken seriously with all shops, etc. firmly closed on the appropriate day. There is a widespread French custom known as, *faire le pont* (bridging the gap), of taking off the day in between a *jour férié* and the weekend. Businesses and shops aren't closed on these days but it gives individuals the chance of extending their weekend.

Public holidays in France	
1 January	New Year's Day
Easter Monday	varies, as UK
1 May	Labour Day
8 May	Victory in Europe Day
Ascension Day	varies
Whitsun (Pentecôte)	varies
14 July	Bastille Day
15 August	Assumption
1 November	All Saints' Day
11 November	Remembrance Day
25 December	Christmas Day

Holidays

The introduction of the 35-hour week has meant that in addition to the five-week annual holiday entitlement plus 12 days of public holidays, many employees now have extra days off, in lieu of overtime worked. There has been a lot of debate about the merits/disadvantages of the 35-hour week since Lionel Jospin's government introduced it as a measure to   reduce unemployment. The idea was to limit working hours so that companies would employ more people. The economic issues of the 35-hour week legislation and changes to it introduced by the new government are discussed in more detail in the chapter *Working in France*. Nevertheless, the measure has had a considerable impact on people's lives in France.

It's also usual to take three or four weeks in July or August and then one week at Christmas and/or Easter. As a result, many firms and small businesses close completely for a month in summer. Paris and its suburbs are almost deserted by the Parisians in August. The vacuum in the capital is filled by foreign tourists, while French holiday resorts and the roads to them solidify with the French.

This arrangement seems bizarre and lemming-like to the British worker used to two weeks away in the summer and lots of long weekends, or the American worker who has hardly any holidays at all. However, to the French it's a civilised

habit that recognises the importance of the quality of life. Older holidaymakers tend to stay within France, usually in the south (although the Atlantic coast and Brittany are also popular). Only the more intrepid investigate neighbouring countries on motoring holidays, and an even smaller number fly off to their holiday homes in Corsica, northern Italy, and the Spanish islands. The younger French are great travellers like the rest of their generation elsewhere, usually armed with the relevant *Guide du Routard* (the French equivalent of the Rough Guides). Many favoured destinations are the Mahgreb countries of north Africa, former French West Africa, the Francophone Caribbean and Vietnam.

A country of second homes

A staggering one in five French households owns or has access to a second home (*une résidence secondaire*) in France – a greater proportion than any other country in the world. These flats or houses are mostly situated in seaside resorts, mountain regions or in rural countryside. They are used as holiday homes, for long weekends and frequently intended as retirement homes for the largely urban population of France whose romance with the rural idyll is at least as strong as that of the British, Italians or Germans. Owning a secondary residence has come to constitute what amounts to a French national characteristic, and is not restricted only to the affluent. Camping vans and caravans account for 9% of secondary residences in France, which is an indication of the strength of the urge to get back to nature, which in France manifests itself through numerous caravan parks and campsites, and the quaint beach cabins on stilts of Narbonne Plage in the Languedoc.

Festivals

From the huge Avignon theatre festival that takes over the town for three weeks every July, to smaller street theatre *manifestations* that happen regularly along the Canal

St Martin in Paris, from the Carcassonne Cité Festival with dance, opera and classical concerts to the Montreux jazz festival and rock festivals such as *La Route du Rock* (which is set in a fort near St Malo) or *Le Printemps de Bourges* (which actually takes place at different venues within the town itself), from the *Festival de Cannes* to Clermont Ferrand's short film festival (Festival du Court Métrage) or from Nice's Carnaval to the Paris Gay Pride, there is an endless number of festival events taking place all over France throughout the year. Festivals aren't limited to performance or street gatherings either. The *Festival International de la Bande Dessinée* (The International Comics Festival – there is a very strong tradition of comics in France) is held in Angoulême every year and the *Rencontres d'Arles* is France's high profile photography festival, running from July to September. Whatever part of the country you're in, you'll have a great choice of local happenings focusing on different aspects of the arts, often very international in flavour, as well as more general municipal festivities where town and village squares are given over to music and stalls selling wine and food.

The great national festival is 14 July, which commemorates the storming of the Bastille prison in 1789. This event marked the beginning of the French Revolution and is known as Bastille Day in English but usually simply *le 14 juillet* in French. The biggest celebrations take place in Paris over three days involving firework displays, open-air balls and dancing through the city streets. Bordeaux has its *Fête le vin*, when you can taste the wines of the region, either in the city centre or in the vineyards (*les vignobles*). The Fêtes Medievales du Dauphin d'Auvergne is a gigantic medieval fair where the medieval era is recreated and brought to life. The Feria de Nimes is famously raucous and has revived the sport of bullfighting in the south. The *Festival du Cinema en Plein Air* is a free film festival held on an open grass space near La Vilette in Paris in July and August – Parisians generally turn up with their picnics and rugs so they can eat before the films start; on the odd occasion that it's too windy or if there is a summer storm, the pneumatic screen is deflated and the screening cancelled.

It would take several pages to give details of even a small percentage of all the festivals that are held around France. A good source of information is your local tourist information website or office, or the local press, or simply word of mouth. The websites of the festivals mentioned here are listed below.

 One useful site for sourcing music festivals by style, date and region is www.francefestivales.com.

- www.rencontres-arles.com
- www.festival-avignon.com
- www.bdangouleme.com
- www.bordeaux-fete-le-vin.com
- www.printemps-bourges.com
- www.festival-cannes.fr
- www.carcassonne.org
- www.montferrandmedieval.com
- www.montreuxjazz.com
- www.arenesdenimes.com
- www.laroutedurock.com

■ ESTABLISHING A SOCIAL LIFE

France offers a rich and colourful ambiance and the general atmosphere, temperament of the people and the favourable climate make for a great social life. It's not that the French don't work hard but they value their time off too. As already mentioned, the 35-hour week has been welcomed by most people who benefit from the extra days off, adding to their quality of life, giving more time for sport and other activities.

Much of the social life in France is based on, or starts with, a meal with friends, so accepting invitations to dinner is a good place to start. The French have a strong sense of what is appropriate when (how to cut the cheese and so on!) and have more of a structure to their customs and habits than does the deconstructed English-speaking world. However, this doesn't mean that they're judgemental or censorious. In fact they often show admiration for extreme behaviour, seeing it as courageous and examining the phenomenon rather than rejecting it on a moral basis. The French may seem serious at first and it isn't considered impolite to express your feelings on almost any matter. They certainly don't feel the need to make jokes constantly, as the English do, and in this way are perhaps more like the Americans in terms of temperament.

Obviously a great introduction to France and the French can be to have a romance with a French man or woman. The idea of the couple (*le couple*) is very strong and couples continue to preserve their time together whether they have had children or not, putting great value on romance and their independent relationships. In general, although affected by the worldwide individualisation of modern society, the French are a lot less promiscuous than stereotypes give them credit for. Getting together

> **Robert Hoehn, an American actor who lives in France and has a child by a French woman says:**
>
> Procreating with a French woman added a complexity to my life like playing four-dimensional chess. It stole my liberty in exchange for the incomparable joy of the birth of my son. When I asked an older American friend, who has been living in France for years, for some advice on the deteriorating relationship with the French mother of my son, he told me, 'First of all, no American man has any business being with a French woman.'

with a French man or women is how and why many people arrive in France in the first place or why they choose to stay. Watch out for those cultural differences however! We all know how hard it can be when you get close to another human, wherever they're from, and cultural differences can make the usual communication problems that little bit harder.

Gay life in France is inevitably centred on Paris. Listings can be found at www. paris-gay.com. Expat gays say that the scene is less mature than in London, New York or San Francisco. One struggling American says, 'In Anglo relationships there's a point where you have no limit on openness, but with the French you have the feeling you'll never really know certain aspects about the person. You feel that you're talking to a representative of the person you're dating rather than the person themselves. French men are some of the best looking in the world but there's always this thing about making yourself hard to attain. And being intelligent, the more intelligent you are, the harder you are to attain.'

The gay scene is known to be a good place to create professional relationships with other English-speaking men.

Expat communities and how to find them

You're far from alone as an expat in France and it will inevitably be easier, at least initially, to make friends with expatriates of any nationality who are in a similar position to yourself. There is a big community of English-speakers in Paris and notable but small Anglophone expat communities in Brittany, the Côte d'Azur, Provence, Poitou-Charentes, Languedoc, Nord-Pas-de-Calais and Normandy. The technopole city of Toulouse has a sizeable Anglophone expatriate community dominated by Americans who run the network Americans in Toulouse (AIT; www. americansintoulouse.com) which is open to all expats. Contact can be made through the web. There is a monthly newsletter detailing events for the coming months. The Federation of American Women's Clubs Overseas (FAWCO) has several branches around France (www.fawco.org).

A listing of British and Franco-British clubs and organisations and American clubs and organisations in France is available from embassies and consulates in France. The Anglo-French one is issued every year by the British Community Committee and is obtainable from their website (www.britishinfrance.com).

> ## Jeff Gross is an American novelist and screenwriter who has lived in Paris for the last 26 years.
>
> I came here in '82, inspired by Henry Miller, inspired by that whole lifestyle. When I came over I was part of a group of people involved in street theatre at Beaubourg. The level of talent of the clowns, mimes and so on was so high that often you'd have 2,000 people watching the shows and they'd come back day after day, because there was nothing else happening that was so funny, so alive. It was a nucleus of colour in a grey city. There was a sense you could create magic any minute. Aquarian guerrilla theatre. A lot of the guys who were involved went off to work with Cirque du Soleil.
>
> I've written a book about it, that time: World of Midgets. In the book I tell how I got papers. I was pretty much living hand to mouth at the time, living on 20 francs a day. Rents were cheap so you could do that. The police started tightening up on things after the bombings in '86. I would've had to go back to the States but I was fortunate enough to meet a publisher who knew François Léotard, the Minister of Culture. Léotard wrote this letter to the Ministry of Interior saying how I was a cultural asset to France and that I was attracted to France by it's climate of freedom and cultural expression. French people can be pretty pessimistic. They say nothing's possible but just about everything's possible here if you speak to the right people. Anyway, here I am, still struggling to get by, struggling to get my books published.
>
> I would say Paris is culturally moribund right now. In 26 years, I've hardly met any writers or artists who show as much devotion to their art, as to what they can get out of the system. Look at the intermittents. For me the idea of artists going on strike is completely absurd.

Useful expatriate websites

- **www.americansinfrance.net** – a resource for anyone wanting to live or travel in France
- **www.americansintoulouse.com** – AIT welcomes all English-speakers of whatever nationality living in or visiting the Toulouse area
- **www.amb-cotedazur.com** – a guide to the French Riviera, for those who work, retire or take a holiday there

- www.angloinfo.com – everyday life in France for those living in or moving to France
- www.craigslist.org – worldwide classifieds. Excellent resource for jobs and housing
- www.expatfocus.com – general expat site with large France section
- www.expatica.com – general expat site with large France section for those living in, moving to or working in France
- www.frenchentree.com – excellent practical information on all aspects of moving to and living in France
- www.intransit-international.com – Paris and France executive relocation
- www.justlanded.com – website dedicated to expats in European countries including France who are working, living or studying in those countries and want information, products and services, especially those that save money
- www.newcomersclub.com/fr.html – American site that has a directory of clubs and organisations in major French towns to give people new to France the opportunity to meet other expatriates in their area
- www.skovgaard-europe.com – relocation agent website with useful information and a forum for expats in France

■ MEDIA

Television

Like the rest of the world, France has embraced reality TV. There were objections about its degrading nature when *Loft Story*, the French version of UK's *Big Brother* first hit the screens, the house being stormed twice by protesters. *Star Academy* (known as *Star Ac*), the French *X-factor*, is now into its seventh season. Programming also includes all the formats that are popular elsewhere but with, of course, the local slant. One imported game show that has had success is *Le Maillon Faible*, a franchise of *The Weakest Link*, copied exactly and with a younger, butcher version of Anne Robinson. To those familiar with these programmes, French versions can make for quite surreal viewing, an anthropological experiment in observation of cultural differences where the control group is the format. There must be the odd PhD thesis knocking around!

La Roue de la Fortune (The Wheel of Fortune) and *Question pour un champion* (try this link http://www.youtube.com/watch?v=h0GfqLw5q8) are two of the most popular game shows. The highest viewing figures for any programme in 2007 were for the France/England rugby match during the Rugby World Cup. Sales of plasma screens also rocketed.

Main French terrestrial channels (chaines):

- TFI – the most popular channel with 27% (but falling) of viewing figures in 2007
- FR2 – state-owned FR2 and is often rated better than TF1
- FR3 – state-owned regional programming

- **Canal Plus (Channel 4)** – privately owned European-wide subscription channels based around movies and sport with a satirical and humorous output – a special decoder is required
- **Arte** – funded jointly by France and Germany and broadcasts from 7pm to just after midnight. Mainly cultural programmes
- **TV5** – international Francophone TV channel from France, Belgium, Swiss and Canadian public broadcasting
- **M6** – light entertainment/music

Le doublage (dubbing)

American and British series are also often dubbed into French (one of the main reasons for the nation's lack of progress in English), with *Friends*, *Sex in the City* and *Desperate Housewives*, just as popular in France as elsewhere. It can be disconcerting when familiar actors appear on screen with someone else's voice lain over the top. Dubbing is unlikely to end anytime soon, however, as it provides employment for a large body of unionised French actors. Once the French professional doing the dubbing has lent their voice to a particular actor or actress they tend to get recommissioned for all that actor/actress's roles. Disconcerting or comical as it may be to English-speakers, the art of *doublage*, as dubbing is known, is the source of a great deal of self-congratulatory discussion, with whole programmes on TV and radio being dedicated to it.

Talk shows

The French love for analysing and opening up a subject can also be experienced on the large number of narcissistic talk shows with French stars from different areas of the media generally joining a panel of other stars to discuss themselves and each other. Great for brushing up on your knowledge of French celebs. Talk show presenters are almost always men. The two I've found most entertaining are the rebellious, energetic Thierry Ardisson and the flirtatious, articulate and talented self-propagandist, Marc-Olivier Fogiel. Cauet can be engaging on a good day.

Satellite

It's estimated that half the viewers of satellite TV are immigrant families (who can receive broadcasts from their own countries and channels such as Al Jazeera). To access British TV channels in France you'll need to invest in a satellite receiver. If you are not much of a television watcher, then any digital satellite receiver will get you the basic BBC radio and television channels and some international news channels. For the full spectrum of channels you will need a Sky Digibox and a viewing card. The viewing card has to be activated by a subscriber with a UK address; some expats ask a friend in the UK to do this for them. Brittany Satellites (www.brittany-satellites.com) supply digital satellite equipment all over France and help with installation. There is also a useful fact sheet you can download from their website.

FACT

- There is a lot less comedy on French TV, and any joke that is cracked will be examined from all angles to assess the intelligence that lies behind it.

Cable

Many French towns are cabled, offering a range of programmes from French, Arabic, Italian, CNN (American) and Spanish networks. Cable subscribers pay a monthly fee.

Television licences

An annual television licence (*la redevance télé* or *une redevance*) is required for individual households and is currently €116. There are certain exemptions including those over 64 years of age and those on low incomes below the taxable threshold. The licence fee is collected with the *taxe d'habitation*.

Radio

Radio in France is divided into the public sector, run by *Radio France* (www.radio-france.fr), the national company, and RLPs (Radio Locales Privées, also called *radios libres*), private stations. Most stations stream live on the net (see www.listenlive. eu/france.html).

National radio stations

The selection of national radio stations caters for all tastes and like the BBC in the UK it's also public service broadcasting. National stations include:

- **France Inter** – www.radio-france.fr/inter; the oldest radio station, of general interest; also has news and topical debates
- **France Culture** – www.radio-france.fr/culture
- **France Musique** – www.radio-france.fr/musique
- **Radio Bleue** – www.radio-france.fr/chaines/france-bleu – special service for older people
- **France Info** – www.radio-france.fr/france-info; continuous news channel covering all France
- **Radio France Internationale (RF1)** – France's world service for the international community which is on the air 24 hours and broadcasts in 19 languages to all five continents

There is also a network of nearly 50 local radio stations, including FIP, which plays an anachronistic but relaxing juxtaposition of varying styles of music only interrupted once each hour, at ten to, by soothing female travel presenters.

Private radio stations

There are several private radio stations that are very popular but which originate from outside France. These include *Europe I* (www.europe1.fr), which belongs to the Hachette multi-media group and *RMC* (*Radio Monte Carlo*).

Since deregulation, the FM band has been crammed with private local radio stations – one estimate put the number at 1,500. The surviving stations are mostly music channels with national networks: *NRJ* (www.nrj.fr), *Nostalgie* (www.nostalgie. fr) and *Skyrock* (www.skyrock.com), are some of these. Minority interest stations also exist.

English-language radio stations

It's possible to receive various English-language stations throughout France, including the BBC World Service (www.bbc.co.uk/worldservice). In northern parts of France, the BBC national radio stations can sometimes be received, depending on the local terrain, weather conditions and time of day. The growth in the number of expats in France has led to the founding of radio stations to broadcast to them locally. The internet station Paris Live Radio (www.parislive.fm) no longer seems to be broadcasting. South of France stations include Riviera Radio (106.3 to 106.5FM; www.rivieraradio.mc).

Going digital

France has been quite late in the deployment of digital terrestrial TV, known as TNT (*Télévision Numérique Terrestre*) but it now supports many new channels as well as the older terrestrial television channels. Most broadband providers (ADSL) offer digital packages through triple play boxes (telephone, internet and TV). See the section on 'Utilities, phone and internet' in the chapter *Setting up home* for more information on providers.

For digital radio, French broadcasters have chosen the DMB format rather than DAB (chosen in Britain) or DAB+ or even DRM+ (the most efficient format). DMB allows you to broadcast pictures or low bit rate video or interactive graphics alongside radio.

FACT

■ You can listen to pretty much any station, as you can anywhere in the world, over the internet.

Newspapers and periodicals

The French newspaper industry, like the newspaper industry the world over, is suffering from a financial crisis brought on by a decline in readership and a falling off of advertising revenues. The growth of the internet and also the free press (Metro has the highest circulation figures in France) have hit traditional papers hard. French national dailies are not as popular as the British press, for example, and even the biggest sellers such *Le Monde* and *Le Figaro* have low circulation figures (about 340,000 down from 600,000 in the early 1990s) compared with the UK's national dailies, such as *The Guardian* or *The Telegraph* (roughly around the million mark). Subsidies do not make up for the fact that the distribution system is archaic and that papers are frequently held to ransom by print unions. The biggest selling national newspaper is the sports daily, *L'Equipe*, and *The International Herald Tribune* sells well in Paris.

The papers mentioned above are, strictly speaking, the Paris press as they are printed and distributed there rather than in the provinces. The regional press, printed and distributed locally is far healthier and is a reflection of the size and diversity of France. Some of the most important regional papers are *La Voix du Nord* (Lille), *Le Progrès* (Lyon) and *Ouest-France* (Rennes). *Ouest-France* has a far higher circulation (750,000) than the Parisian dailies and has 38 local editions covering the *départements* in western France.

The urban French seem to prefer their news in the form of current affairs and general information weeklies such as *L'Express, Le Point, Le Nouvel Observateur* and *Paris-Match*.

Main newspapers

■ **Les Echos:** second most popular financial daily after *Le Figaro*

■ **Le Canard Enchaîné:** satirical/scandal rag

■ **Le Figaro:** politically right wing, includes a lot of business and economic coverage

■ **Le Parisien:** Paris daily which also has a provincial edition

■ **France-Soir:** evening newspaper, mostly light news and chat

■ **Le Monde:** reputation for in-depth, high-brow reporting, politically centre left

■ **Libération:** former socialist newspaper founded by Sartre

Magazines

While newspaper readership may be declining, the magazine market in France is buoyant. The French read more magazines per head than any other nation. There are a huge number of titles to choose from (4,000). A large part (1,300) are technical and professional magazines; about 500 deal with general information and politics. Others which are big business include leisure titles dealing with special interests, (sports, hobbies, women's magazines). Purely society and people interest magazines are also popular: *Point de Vue* and *Gala* are two of the most popular.

English-language newspapers and newsletters

Newspapers in English, but based in France, include the *International Herald Tribune* (www.iht.com). A handful of English-language newspapers are published in France for the British and American expatriate communities. One of the best known is *France-USA Contacts* (☎01 56 53 54 54; www.fusac.org), which comes out every other Wednesday in Paris. It's a free newsletter, which comprises mostly classified adverts for accommodation, jobs, services and a social calendar, and is distributed to all the regular ex-pat gathering places in the capital. You can also place an advert asking for work and or accommodation in FUSAC, before your arrival in France.

There is also the monthly *French News* (☎05 53 06 84 40; www.french-news.com) 'for residents and lovers of France'.

UK newspapers

For those addicted to the UK press, it's fairly easy to get hold of English newspapers like *The Times* or *The Guardian* on the day of publication. A cheaper alternative is to subscribe before you move or follow newspaper websites.

French lifestyle magazines for English residents of France

There is a range of glossy and not so glossy publications which carry articles on France, French property adverts and advice, as well as useful information for daily life in France. These include:

■ **France Magazine:** ☎+44 (0)1242 216087; www.francemag.com

■ **French Property News:** www.french-property-news.com; started 1989; 11 issues annually; subscription costs £30

■ **Living France:** ☎+44 (0)1242 216087; www.livingfrance.com; same publisher as *France Magazine*; published monthly

Books

French-language publishing obviously does not have as wide an international market as that of English. The strong literary tradition of France means there is no shortage

Secondhand books for sale

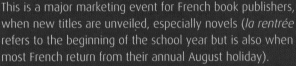

La rentrée littéraire

This is a major marketing event for French book publishers, when new titles are unveiled, especially novels (*la rentrée* refers to the beginning of the school year but is also when most French return from their annual August holiday).

In 1998, Michel Houellebecq launched a wholesale critique of post-war France and left-wing French sociology in his landmark, essay-like novel, *Les Particules Elémentaires* (translated as *The Elementary Particles* in the USA and *Atomised* in the UK). The success of this work abroad forced the French literary establishment to sit up and take note of an outsider who was simultaneously laying claim to his own Frenchness. Another novelist, less-internationally known but equally important in France, is the instinctive and personally political, Christine Angot, whose work is pioneering and ambitious in its use of language in an obsessive, microcosmic examination of the possibilities of autobiography. Her *chef d'oeuvre* is *L'inceste*, which made a great splash at *la rentrée* of 1999.

in the classical and historical departments. Gardening and DIY books are not big sellers. Books in France are expensive by UK and US standards, as they carry TVA (value-added tax (VAT)). English-language books are not necessarily easy to come by but there are many English-language bookshops in Paris including W H Smith on the rue de Rivoli. Another, Shakespeare & Company (see below) incorporates a writer's guest house and is a well-known source of temporary employment.

Amazon can keep you up with English-language publishing. Alternatively, you could join a book club. The Good Book Guide (www.thegoodbookguide.com), produces a review magazine containing a wide-ranging selection of books and videos, etc which can be mailed anywhere in the world.

English bookshops in Paris

The Abbey Bookshop: 29 rue de la Parcheminerie, 75005 Paris; ☎01 46 33 16 24; Canadian bookshop. British and American fiction

Attica: 64 rue de la Folie Méricourt, 75011 Paris; ☎01 49 29 27 27; www.attica.fr. A language specialist

Brentano's: 37 avenue de l'Opéra, 75002 Paris; ☎01 42 61 52 50. English and American books, magazines and newspapers

Galignani: 224 rue de Rivoli, 75001 Paris; ☎01 42 60 76 07; galignan@wanadoo.fr. Nearest métro: Tuileries. Famous English bookshop opened at the beginning of the 19th century. French and English books and English translations of French classics

Red Wheelbarrow Bookstore: 22 rue St Paul, 75004 Paris; ☎01 48 04 75 08; good. reading@wanadoo.fr. General literature and a large selection of children's books

San Francisco Book Co: 17 rue Monsieur le Prince, 75006 Paris; ☎01 43 29 15 70. American and English secondhand books

Shakespeare & Company: 37 rue de la Bûcherie, 75005, Paris; ☎01 43 25 40 93; www.shakespeareco.org. As featured in the 2004 movie *Before Sunset* starring Ethan Hawke and Julie Delpy.

Tea and Tattered Pages: 24 rue Mayet, 75006 Paris; ☎01 40 65 94 35; secondhand books and American cookies

W H Smith: 248 rue de Rivoli, 75001 Paris; ☎01 44 77 88 99

FACT

STEVEN CLARKE AND *A YEAR IN THE MERDE*

■ Steven Clarke is now on his fifth *Merde* novel, has sold film rights to his work and is worth millions. He originally self-published *A Year in the Merde* and wheeled it round Paris, delivering it to bookshops from a supermarket trolley.

■ SPORT AND FITNESS

France is a strong sporting nation as fans of football and rugby know. Rugby is particularly strong in the south-west. The success of French teams in successive World and European cups held in France over the past decade have raised the profile of the national teams. Large screens are put up in public squares and women and men come out to watch the matches in a convivial, party-like atmosphere. Participation in sport has more than quadrupled in the past 25 years. This trend is reflected in the increase in the number of sports clubs and facilities to be found throughout France.

Watersports and skiing are the most popular participant sports, which is hardly surprising when you consider the climate and natural facilities offered in large parts of the country for these activities. Swimming and waterskiing, sailing and windsurfing are all popular. The area along the coast near Leucate, north of Perpignan, is particularly popular among windsurfers because of the high winds that blow across the Mediterranean, also powering an extensive field of wind turbines in the hills just outside Narbonne. Fresh water, sea and deep-sea fishing are also favourite pastimes. Ski resorts, scattered throughout the Alps and the Pyrénées, are frequented by millions of French people each year. For the French, skiing is not an elitist sport, despite some alpine resorts, notably Courchevel, Les Arcs and Megève, having a reputation for being ultra ritzy. There is also cross-country skiing in the Vosges and the Massif Central. Parisians drive regularly to the Alps for skiing weekends.

Other popular sports include tennis and of course cycling, which is followed closely in the bars throughout the country during the Tour de France, in spite of the drug scandals that hit the sport every year. Cycling is also a popular participatory sport and you'll see no shortage of brightly-dressed cyclists on the roads at the weekends. There are many judo and other martial arts aficionados in France. Rollerblading is a much favoured way of getting around in the crowded streets of Paris and every weekend, thousands of rollerbladers get together and skate on a different course round the capital. Golf is expensive and exclusive. Cricket is played in English expat areas with some French participants. Traditional blood sports, such as hunting (with deer and wild boar, particularly in the Sologne, just south of Paris), shooting and fishing have a following, as do other traditional, but less aggressive pastimes. *La pétanque* (or boules as it's known in Britain) is played by all ages, in public spaces under the trees for shade, often beside an outdoor table-tennis table. Sports facilities are generally well-funded and even the most modest town will have a public swimming pool (*une piscine*).

Apart from approved sports facilities in towns, governments have promoted *colonies de vacances* where less well-off families who can't afford to go on holiday can at least

Parkour

Les parcours sportif are specially constructed courses found on the edge of French towns, often in a wood and are made up of a series of obstacles or pieces of equipment that exercise different parts of the body. On a *parcours sportif*, you'll find yourself doing a series of jumps, hurdling, running and pull-ups. They can be a source of great entertainment when you're taking a post-lunch walk with family as individuals try themselves out in front of the watchers.

David Belle invented a sport called Parkour in France in 2001, where a *traceur* (as *parkour* practitioners are known), often in an urban environment, performs a series of leaps, vaults and rolls to avoid or surmount whatever lies in their path. It has spread mainly by videos on the internet and been embraced by martial arts adepts and thrill seekers. The recent Bond movie, Casino Royale, begins with a *parkour* chase. To view David Belle doing his moves, visit YouTube: www.youtube.com/watch?v=x98jCBnWO8w&NR=1.

A hiking trip in the French mountains

send the children away for a subsidised holiday run by qualified *moniteurs*. It's estimated that such colonies provide holidays for a million children a year.

The French passion for climbing has been well publicised, but there is also great interest in rambling and hiking, which has rocketed in 10 years from being one of France's least popular sporting activities to one of the most popular. The Poitiers region alone has dozens of official hiking clubs. The governing organisation is the Fédération Française de la Randonnée Pédestre based in Paris (www.rando-paris.org) which comprises 2,800 associations in France and oversees 180,000km of paths. France's main hiking paths are called Grandes Randonnées (GRs) and these include GR20 which winds through the Corsican mountains and Gr58 in the Queyras (in the south-east) and the GR65 pilgrim route to Santiago di Compostela, and the GR10 in the eastern Pyrenees. There are also day-circuit routes (GR de Pays) which are marked with red and yellow painted slashes. Around towns and villages are the shorter promenades (PRs) with yellow signposts.

Information on all sports is available either from tourist offices, or the Ministry of Youth and Sports (Ministére de la Jeunesse, des Sports et de la Vie Associative, Direction des Sports; ☎01 40 45 90 00; www.jeunesse-sports.gouv.fr): Information on all aspects of sports including their organisations and sports holiday centres can also be found on the website.

Useful contacts

Fédération Unie des Auberges de Jeunesses (FUAJ): National Centre FUAJ; ☎01 44 89 87 27; www.fuaj.org

Fédération Française de Cyclotourisme: ☎01 56 20 88 88; 88; www.ffct.org

Fédération Française de Montagne et Escalade: ☎01 40 18 75 50; www.ffme.fr. Mountaineering and rock climbing

Fédération Française de Randonnée Pédestre: www.ffrandonnee.fr

FACT

Sunday is the main day for eating out and restaurant meals are very much a family affair.

■ ENTERTAINMENT AND CULTURE

Perhaps the most popular entertainment, and one which is also considered part of the country's culture, is eating – preferably at restaurants or bistros. Eating out, whether for little more than a snack and a drink or a full meal, is the basis of much French entertainment and social life. Every city, town and village has bars, cafés and restaurants in abundance, and standards are usually high and prices low in all but luxury establishments. Restaurants almost always reflect regional character.

Of course, Paris is an acknowledged European centre for theatre, opera and ballet and is also where many world-famous art galleries and museums are situated. However, there is often a considerable choice of all the above in other large cities and even small towns and rural areas have their own theatres and music and arts festivals (see section on 'Festivals' above). Check with your local *mairie* (town hall) or *syndicat d'initiative* (tourist office). Most regions of France have an extraordinarily rich patrimony, a large part of which is completely unknown to most foreigners. Museums, ancient sites, historic houses, fortified towns, magnificent architecture and art galleries are to be found throughout the country and are a good means of familiarising oneself with the culture, language and people of France.

A wealth of information is available on entertainment and culture in France and of course many events and venues are particularly popular with tourists (Le Moulin Rouge, etc.). There will be no attempt here to give comprehensive coverage of everything that's available but just an outline of some currents in entertainment and a few pointers to get you started.

Nightlife and the music scene

Night time entertainment is as various as the regions of France. In small towns, nightclubs and discos tend to be on the outskirts. In small coastal tourist towns the casino is often the centre of night life, combining gambling with a disco playing kitsch French pop. Paris and other big towns have some interesting clubs and venues, ranging from upmarket such as *Les Bains* to far more grungy (try the late night *L'Abracadabar*, ae. Jean Jaurès, Paris). The electronic music scene is strong with live acts and DJs that are well known all over the world. Nevertheless, you are sure to find it more restrained than in the UK or the USA with the emphasis as much on style as on letting your hair down. Among French DJs, probably the best known internationally is Laurent Garnier.

There is a vibrant live music scene, with a lot of interesting home-grown talent that is rarely heard in English-speaking countries. Three genres that are particularly strong are rap (MC Solaar, DJ Mehdi, NTM, 113, Diams, etc), *la chanson francaise*, which is text driven and founded in the traditions of Brel, Piaf and Gainsbourg and has seen a recent resurgence of young talent (Philippe Katerine, La Grande Sophie, Vincent Delerme) and, lastly, French electro which is the best exported (Justice, Air, Daft Punk). You'll also find a great variety of world music in France, due partly to the west African influence. This includes big international stars like Yousou Ndour as well as local talent such as Fanga who are innovating their own afrobeat (Fela Kuti) sound. Of course Paris is still one of the European and world centres for jazz, with international and French artists appearing regularly in venues such as New Morning or the Duc des Lombards.

French rap deserves a special mention as the most interesting, exciting and innovative rap scene outside of the United States. Obviously, the language barrier means that French rap is little heard elsewhere (though the father of French rap, MC Solar – *Qui seme le vent récolte le tempo* – has collaborated with American artists such as Guru). Nevertheless it has a strong tradition and a mature, varied output. As many of the proponents are second or third generation immigrants, content tends

TIP

■ For a list of some of the top Parisian nightclubs go to www.10best.com

■ For a complete listing of what's happening in hundreds of venues round Paris on any particular night, pick up *Lilo*, a free listings booklet available in bars and clubs all over town

to be inspired by life in the *banlieues* (suburbs) and the social problems and lack of opportunity there. Linguistically, there are many artists who have used the slang of the ghettos to bring the French language alive in truly poetic ways. One of the recent stars is *Diams*, a female artist who combines a cutting and powerful political critique with a distinctive, intelligent delivery and also the ability to hit a more tender register (look out for Diams' *Dans ma bulle*). The spoken word poetry scene has also grown recently, led by *Grand Corps Malade*.

Circus, mime, dance and physical theatre

France has a very strong tradition in circus, mime (Marcel Marceau) and physical theatre, with the Ecole Jacques Lecoq in Paris a world-renowned centre for this. Simon McBurney (*Last King of Scotland*) is one of the best-known alumni. Names to watch out for on tour in your area are *Les Arts Sauts* (trapeze), *Que-Cir-Que* (acrobats), *Les Nouveaux Nez* (clowns) or *Zingaro* (dancing horses). Two festivals held on this theme are the Festival Mondial du Cirque de Demain (Paris, December) and Festival International du Cirque de Monte Carlo (January).

Cinemas

Cinemas are widespread throughout Paris, which has a couple of hundred of them (more than any other city in the world) with foreign films often being shown in

66

Here's what cinema critic Marc Vervel (contributor to *Le Dictionnaire de la Mort*, with articles on some of the greats of France's cinematic past) has to say about it

French cinema is in the image of the rest of French culture, that is to say that it's prestigious past weighs on its present. If we put big budget movies to one side, there are essentially two currents. On the one hand, films that recall the great tradition of Duvivier, Clair and so on, emphasising a nostalgia for pre-war France (Amélie Poulain by Jeunet is in this vein). On the other, a cinema that is directly related to the Nouvelle Vague and strongly influenced by Truffaut (Huit Femmes by Francois Ozon), Chabrol (Harry, un ami qui vous veut du bien by Dominik Moll), Godard (La Vie des morts by Arnauc Desplechin) or Deny (Les Chansons d'amour by Christophe Honoré). In spite of some interesting work (such as the films mentioned here), this recent tradition has a tendency to produce slightly insipid and narcissistic dramas, with the marked exception of this year's Palme d'Or at Cannes (laurent Cantet's Entre les Mis or The Class as it is entitled in English). Contemporary French cinema would seem to be struggling to come to terms with its own era: the most impressive films of the last few years are often inspired by foreign filmmakers (the Dardenne brothers or Abdellatif Kechiche). In spite of a great deal of talent, the young generation has found it hard to emancipate itself from its too prestigious ancestry.

99

their original language. There is often a good choice of interesting films at your local *Maison de Culture* (arts centre). Of course, French cinema is admired all over the world, but perhaps more for its past than the present.

Useful contacts

- **www.parisinfo.com:** useful information on all aspects of the capital's culture and museums
- **www.monuments-nationaux.fr:** the chateaux of the Loire and much more.
- **www.timeout.com/paris**

Courses

As already mentioned, many courses are available through the large network of 'associations' that exist all over France in all sorts of interest areas. 'Associations' has a legal status as set out in a law enacted in 1901 and often receive government funding to carry out their activities. They are also funded through their members (*adherents*) who pay a yearly membership in order to be able to participate in activities they organise. Associations are non-profit organisations but can have employees. If you, yourself, are considering setting up an organisation providing cultural, artistic, sporting or other activities, a tax efficient way of doing this might well be through an association (or *assoc* – pronounced 'assoss'). You can find out about the associations that exist in your area by contacting your local *mairie*.

Mairies themselves provide courses in many different disciplines. Again you should get in touch with your local town hall for more information on what is available. You will find French courses are widely available. Although these courses are often crowded, they are cheap and can be a good supplement to other tuition that you are following. It's important to contact your *mairie* before the beginning of September to find out when courses open for inscription as places are limited and courses often fill up fast. You will probably have to go in person to sign up. Also, it's worth investigating courses that are provided through the organisation known as GRETA, a branch of the education ministry (www.education.gouv.fr), which promotes continuing education.

Of course many universities and higher education institutions offer courses for continuing education. See the section on 'Education' in the chapter *Daily life* or contact your local university to find out more about how you can go about benefiting from these. The Ecole du Louvre is particularly renowned for its courses in all aspects of art history, architecture, film and photography.

In addition to these avenues, it's also worth checking with your nearest Maison de la Culture (arts centre) as not only do they provide access to a whole host of arts related events, such as theatre, dance, exhibitions and conferences, but they also serve as a forum for arts in the local area. A selection of leaflets from organisations and individuals providing courses or arts-related events will be available there. As

■ A directory of existing associations is available at the site www.loi1901. com. Complete information on setting up an association is also available through this site.

■ For more information on courses and entry requirements visit www. ecoledulouvre.fr

mentioned at the beginning of this chapter, many craftspeople and artists provide opportunities for others to learn in their workshops. It's always worth asking local artists if they provide individual courses.

Lastly, many residential courses are organised throughout France in artistic disciplines. Details of some of these will be available through expatriate forums.

Public libraries

Libraries, *les bibliothèques* or *les médiathèques* are listed in *Le Catalogue collectif de France* (www.ccfr.bnf.fr) – an online resource with a dedicated search engine for all sorts of written and audiovisual documentation (including books, CDs, DVDs and digital information). You can search for libraries by region, department, town, type of library and area of interest. Public libraries in France are well funded with modern facilities, allowing you to use the internet, view audiovisual documents, listen to music and so on. They are well staffed and staff will be able to aid you with any enquiries you may have. Many educational activities are organised through libraries for both adults and children.

The national library, La Bibliothèque Nationale de France (www.bnf.fr) is situated at La Bibliothèque Francois Mitterrand (12, quai, Panhard-Levassor, Paris 13th, metro Tolbiac). The library, designed by Dominique Perrault, is a modern building made of glass, steel and wood and was the last of Mitterrand's Grand Projets (a series of modern monuments to symbolise France's central role in art, politics and the world economy). It's in the form of four 25-storey towers each in the shape of an open book.

English-language libraries

Many public French libraries have an English-language section. In addition there are a number of dedicated English language libraries throughout the country. The biggest are:

- ■ **English-Language Library in Angers** ☎02 41 24 97 07; www.ellia.org
- ■ **The American Library of Montpellier** ☎04 67 13 43 99; www.bibliotheque-americaine.com
- ■ **The American Library in Nancy** ☎03 54 50 54 27; www.europole.u-nancy.fr
- ■ **American Library in Paris** ☎01 53 59 12 60; www.americanlibraryinparis.org

These libraries offer a range of short-term and full individual and family memberships at reasonable rates (full one-year individual membership at the American library in Paris is €50).

■ MARRIAGE

Les union libres and PACS

The number of civil law marriages taking place in France is declining whereas common-law marriage (*union libré*) is widespread. Long-term relationships carry equal social status with marriage.

Le PACS

Same sex couples as well as adults of different sexes living together can legally register *Un Pacte Civil de Solidarité* (*PACS*). This says they agree to '*aide mutuelle et matérielle*' (mutual and material support) and that they are '*tenus solidairement des dettes contractée par l'un d'eux pour les besoins de la vie courante*' (jointly responsible for debts contracted for the needs of daily life).

PACS came into force in France at the end of 1999. It was conceived as a measure to allow homosexuals a legally recognised union. It was broadened to include domestic live-in relationships of different types except relatives: parent and child, brother and sister, niece, uncle, etc. are all excluded. It has been dubbed *le marriage lite* and predictably it's opposed by the Roman Catholic Church. Partners simply register their *PACS* at the court. A *PACS* can be dissolved by the couple. They must inform the authorities and wait three months for the dissolution. If one partner objects to the dissolution, the other has to have a bailiff's letter served on them.

A *PACS* confers most of the legal benefits of marriage, without the need for solemn exchange of vows in front of the mayor. Some see it as a pragmatic approach to domestic arrangements in the post-marriage society where clearly alternative domestic arrangements have to be catered for. However, it has not pleased the one group it set out to: homosexuals feel they are being short-changed in being denied full and equal marriage rights. A *PACS* couple, for example, can't adopt a child.

PACS confers legal rights including immigration for a partner, and tax, social security, housing and inheritance benefits. Couples can now file joint tax returns immediately they have entered into a *PACS* (formerly a wait of three years was required).

For other details contact a specialist lawyer and see 'Matrimonial regimes' in the chapter *Buying Property*.

■ For background details on *le PACS* see www.info-france-usa.org/atoz/pacs.asp; for the text of the Act go to www.legifrance.gouv.fr.

About France

■ THE PEOPLE, THEIR MANNERS AND CUSTOMS

The French people

Although it is fair to say that it is not the custom of the French to offer an exuberant welcome to foreigners as is typical of say Americans, neither are they unfriendly and xenophobic. Having said this, it is a commonplace observation that Paris has the reputation of being the coldest and most unwelcoming city in Europe for any foreigner. However, this is not true of the country as a whole and, certainly in rural areas, people are often very welcoming and helpful.

That the French are a nationalistic and proud race, however, is a generalisation difficult to refute. From time to time, concern among the French that their patrimony is being sold off piecemeal to Britons and other foreigners manifests itself, chiefly through the strident declarations of the right wing nationalists. The reputed hostility between the French and the English is more often than not an amiable rivalry, and although, politically, the French are clearly anti-American, this is a general notion and not transferred onto their relations with individual Americans in France.

Social attitudes

After a lapse in the 1960s, the family unit is currently enjoying an increased popularity in France and family members are likely to keep in quite close touch although extended families are now largely a thing of the past. Despite this

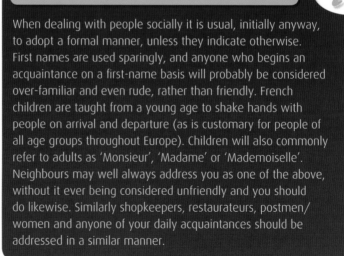

Forms of address

When dealing with people socially it is usual, initially anyway, to adopt a formal manner, unless they indicate otherwise. First names are used sparingly, and anyone who begins an acquaintance on a first-name basis will probably be considered over-familiar and even rude, rather than friendly. French children are taught from a young age to shake hands with people on arrival and departure (as is customary for people of all age groups throughout Europe). Children will also commonly refer to adults as 'Monsieur', 'Madame' or 'Mademoiselle'. Neighbours may well always address you as one of the above, without it ever being considered unfriendly and you should do likewise. Similarly shopkeepers, restaurateurs, postmen/women and anyone of your daily acquaintances should be addressed in a similar manner.

resurgence of family values, however it is estimated that about 50% of children are born to non-married parents and 22% of children are reared by single parents.

France harbours all the social problems which exist in any developed country and, as elsewhere, a tendency persists to ignore these problems until they flare up in a major incident. On-going social problems include problems with immigrants and youth unemployment, which successive governments have been trying to handle with job creation schemes and other programmes involving extensive government subsidies (see the chapter *Working in France*).

The aristocracy, bourgeoisie and working classes still exist in France, although distinctions between the three are less pronounced than ever before. In particular, traditional bourgeois values are now less endorsed and less prevalent than at any time in the past – with the exception only of the French Revolution.

Women in France

In as much as there is a high profile women's movement in today's post-feminist France you would have to say that Fadela Amara's *Ni Putes Ni Soumises* (Neither Whores Nor Submissives) organisation is at the forefront in terms of media attention. The movement's slogan is meant to both shock and mobilise. It was set up by a group of young French Muslim women in 2002 in response to the relatively high rates of violence and rape directed against them in the banlieues (suburbs) of large French towns. In May 2007 Fadela Amara was appointed as Urban Affairs Minister in Francois Fillon's new right-wing government. It is worth mentioning here the dispute over the wearing of the *voile*, the Muslim veil, by Muslim girls in state schools. During Chirac's presidency, the decision was taken not to allow this practice. It was decided that no sign of religious affiliation could be worn in French schools. The championing of Fadela Amara should be seen in this context and in the context of the much higher achievement rates of Muslim girls than boys in the French education system and the employment market (for more on France's immigrant minorities and the situation in the *banlieues* see the section The legal system in the chapter *Daily life*).

Fadela Amara was not the only high-profile woman to be appointed to Fillon's government. She was appointed along with more women ministers than had ever been appointed before, with Nicolas Sarkozy keeping his election promise of equal numbers of French men and women in his cabinet. Of course, his main opponent in the Presidential elections was the youthful and good-looking socialist female candidate, Ségolène Royal.

Christine Lagarde, the first female Finance Minister of any G7 country, and Rachida Dati, the glamorous Justice Minister are two of the stars of Sarkozy's government. There is also Michèle Alliot-Marie, the first French female Interior Minister. Christine Lagarde is the former head of a global Chicago-based law firm and has begun her work as Finance Minister by introducing reforms to the 35-hour week to allow workers to be paid for overtime rather than be forced to take it as holiday. She is also working on other ways of liberalising the French labour market. Rachida Dati, one of the ministers closest to Sarkozy, who holds dual French/Moroccan nationality, has been criticised for combining a sexy image (Dior dresses and high-heeled boots) with a post that many in the legal profession believe should be treated with more

Ministère de la Justice

Vœux du Garde des Sceaux

Paris le 17 janvier 2008

© B.LEMAIRE

French politician, Rachida Dati was a spokeswoman for Nicholas Sarkozy

solemnity. This criticism may well also be negatively motivated by her measures to streamline the justice sector.

The Sarkozy women story does not of course end there. More than any previous president, he has used his private life to help create his public image. The well-documented divorce from his previous wife, Cécilia, who did not vote in the presidential elections in 2007, had no sooner been made public than the President began dating the French Italian former model Carla Bruni, who he has now married. Jean Paul Gaultier has said, 'I loved the Chiracs, but politics are like fashion: it's about change and there has to be a first lady in a place like the Elysée Palace. Why not such a beautiful one?'

Gaultier is right to point out the differences with the Chirac regime, but what does all this mean in terms of the status of women in France? No doubt Christine Lagarde, Ségolène Royal and Rachida Dati are doing a lot to redress previous gender imbalances in the political world. Perhaps these role models will also have an impact in business, where women are still under-represented in top jobs. Still, also, many more men than women set up companies in France.

In terms of salaries and the workforce, a higher proportion of men are in active employment than women, although women make up only slightly less than 50% of the workforce. There is a salary difference of 25% between men and women. This is partly due to the fact that 30% of women in work in part-time posts (this is by choice for 70% of them). When you compare like with like in terms of equivalent posts, women do still fall short of men's salaries by 7%. The fact that 30% of women choose to work part-time is a reflection of the dominant role women still have in the family, though a high proportion of recent mothers work in France in comparison

i For more gender-based statistical analysis, visit www.insee.fr (the French office of national statistics).

with other European Union (EU) countries (a reflection of the extensive nursery care provided by the state in France – all children aged 3 and over have the right to a nursery place and often they start aged 2). In the past 15 years, numbers of marriages have been relatively stable. The average age for a women to get married is 29 and the number of 30–34-year-old and 35–39-year-old women having children has risen enormously, with increases of 30% and 40%, respectively, for the two age groups. The numbers of women aged 20–24 having children is down slightly and the number of teenage pregnancies in France remains low and stable. More girls than boys sat and passed the *baccalauréat* in 2007. There are many more girls doing the *bac littéraire* (arts based) than boys and slightly more boys than girls doing the scientific *bac*, although far more girls do a scientific than an arts-based *bac*.

Useful contacts

- *Alliance des Femmes pour la Démocratie*: ☎01 42 60 22 68; www.alliancedesfemmes.fr
- *Bibliothéque Marguerite-Durand, BMD*: ☎01 53 82 76 77. Library/archive for the history of women in France and abroad. Important collection of feminist documents, letters, manuscripts, etc. Open Tuesday to Saturday inclusive, 2–6pm
- *Centre National d'Information et de Documentation des Femmes et des Familles (CNIDFF)*: ☎01 42 17 12 00; cnidff@infofemmes.com; www.infofemmes.com. Provides information on women rights, employment, professional and daily life. Can help with training schemes, enterprise creation, marriage counselling, health, sexuality and family advice
- *Choisir la-cause-des-femmes*: ☎01 47 05 21 48; www.choisirlacausedesfemmes.org. Defends the rights of all women to contraception and abortion, struggles against violence perpetrated on women, and campaigns for parity of representation for women in all elected assemblies
- *Gay Paris*: www.gay-paris.com. This site explores many aspects of life for lesbians and gays in Paris, including listings of useful lesbian and gay groups. Paris does, of course, have a much larger lesbian and gay community than any other city in France
- *La Ligue du Droit des Femmes: LDF: Permanence téléphonique* (24-hours) ☎01 45 85 11 37. Administration of the Centre d'Accueil Flora-Tristan for battered women: ☎01 47 36 96 48; www.ldif-fr.org
- *Maison des Femmes*: ☎01 43 43 41 13. A well-known centre in Paris, including a resource centre and lending library specialising in lesbian cultures and research. Has a network of contacts in other cities, hosts meetings and produces the magazine *Paris Féministe*
- *Ni Putes Ni Soumises*: ☎01 53 46 63 00; www.niputesnisoumises.com
- *Union Féminine Civique et Sociale, UFCS*: ☎01 44 54 94 49; ufcsnational@wanadoo.fr; www.ufcs.org. Feminist association, training organisation, organisation for the protection of the environment, consumer organisation, civic association. Publication: *Dialoguer* (quarterly) and a newsletter from the website.

FACT

Britain has had connections with many countries from Norway to North America and from Palestine to India, but the French connection through geography and history, is the most enduring.

■ A BRIEF HISTORY

England and France

The Norman invasion of England in 1066 began a thousand years of antagonism and rivalry, conflict, and curmudgeonly cooperation that is the history of relations between Britain and France. In the 11th century, England, through the Norman invasion, became an extension of Normandy, to which was later added Gascony, acquired through dynastic marriage, and Picardy and Flanders. The French lands thus linked to the English crown in the 12th century, amounted to the western half of what is now modern France. The Normans brought with them to England their culture, which included the French language, Romanesque and Gothic architecture and chivalry, mainly in the form of the knightly tournament. The exchange was however a two-way street: English style went south to France, particularly south-western France, which remained under the English crown for about the next three centuries. This long period of association saw the rise of the popularity of Gascony wines, shipped to England's ports in annual bulk consignments, and a glance at the history of some of the most illustrious Bordeaux *châteaux* (e.g. Cantenac-Brown, Lynch-Bages) reveals their English (or even Irish) origins. World famous Châteaux Margaux was originally the property of the English crown. In 1337 the English king, Edward III claimed the French crown and began the 'Hundred Years' War' of which Calais was one of the spoils – it remained in British hands for over 200 years. Henry V, glorified by Shakespeare and Kenneth Branagh, pursued the British claim to France's lands, and Shakespeare's eponymous play ends on the high note of his era, the victory over the French at Agincourt in 1415. After that it was downhill for British claims to France. In 1429, with Henry VI on the English throne, a peasant called Jeanne heard angelic voices telling her to throw the English out of France. Such was her rallying effect on her countrymen, that in less than four months the English were on the verge of defeat from the armies of Jeanne d'Arc. The English occupation of France was more or less ended when the British lost the battle of Formigny in 1450, and with it Normandy. This was followed by defeat at Bordeaux in 1453 and the countries were finally separated.

Influence of the monarchy

France's feudal economy was gradually transformed and centralised around a powerful absolute monarchy. The long Italian Wars in the 16th century coincided with an alliance with the Ottoman Empire as well as the Protestant Reformation which challenged the power of the Catholic Church. This was also the time of Habsburg and Spanish dominance. Charles Quint encircled France and controlled Spain and Austria and a number of other kingdoms across Europe. French developed as the international language of diplomacy and the French language was reformed and regulated on several occasions. François Rabelais is credited with developing French as a literary language, emphasising the use of Latin and Greek words. The Religious Wars of the late 16th and early 17th centuries saw the rise of the powerful Cardinal Richelieu as chief minister of France. Louis XIV acceded to the throne a year after Richelieu's death and his long reign was characterised by many wars against other European powers, including Spain, Sweden, the Netherlands and England. The Sun King's military architect, Vauban, built a system of fortresses that France relied on for defence right up to the First World War.

The French Revolution

The next big era of conflict between England and France was the one for the colonies of the New World and the East. France took the opportunity presented by the American Revolution to attack England's positions in the colonies but bankrupted herself in the attempt to contend with wars both in Europe and overseas. The resulting over-taxation of the peasantry was one of the direct causes of the French Revolution in 1789. Prior to the Revolution there was a great flowering of new ideas from French intellectuals, philosophers and scientists in the era known as the *Siècle des Lumières* or the Enlightenment. Voltaire, Diderot, Rousseau and Montesquieu gained prominence. Louis XVI's ineptitude and inability to recognise the reality of his time eventually led to the riots and anarchy that culminated in the storming of the Bastille prison on 14 July 1789. A period of intense and bloody class conflict ensued. In August 1789, the National Assembly adopted *The Declaration of the Rights of Man*, which was based on the US Declaration of Independence and the doctrine of natural rights. The King remained as a figurehead but after the rise of the Jacobins and the Paris Commune, the Assembly suspended the monarchy and the King was tried for treason and executed, followed a few months later by Marie Antoinette ('Let them eat cake'). Robespierre now presided over the one-year Reign of Terror from his position at the head of the Committee of Public Safety, and 18,000 people were executed under the guillotine. Robespierre himself was also eventually executed along with many other Jacobins.

Influence of Napoleon

The French Revolution proved a mere hiatus in Franco-British rivalry as the British, Spanish, Dutch, Austrians and Napolitans joined forces to try to contain Revolutionary France. The rise of Napoléon Bonaparte and his plans for an Empire in Europe included designs on Britain. His ambitions were finally thwarted, as most British schoolchildren learn, on the plain of Waterloo in Belgium, but not before he had established control over most of the European continent. Napoleon's military genius was equalled by his administrative energy and he recognised the importance of logistics in both civil and military life. He consolidated the achievements and developments of the Revolution through the Napoleonic Code (see the section The legal system in the chapter Daily life). He established the bank of France and created a system of *lycées* to train a political and administrative class. He also put

a cap on the price of bread and invented the baguette. Quotes from the great man are at least as entertaining and impressive as Churchill's:

■ 'The art of governing consists in not letting men grow old in their jobs.'

■ 'The military are a freemasonry and I am their grand master.'

■ 'What is history but a fable agreed upon?'

Economically exhausted, France never realised her industrial potential in the 19th century, despite producing some of the world's best engineers like Monsieur Eiffel who built notable bridges (including one in Corsica) as well as the eponymous tower in Paris, and Ferdinand de Lesseps of Suez and Panama Canals fame. France in general and Paris in particular did, however, become synonymous with luxury goods, particularly fabrics for clothes and furnishings and household goods while Paris itself became a byword for fashion, luxury and elegance – a reputation it still lives on today.

The 19th century saw the return of the monarchy and then the Second Empire, established under Napoleon III. After the defeat of France by Prussia and the bloody repression of the Paris Commune of 1870, the Third Republic was established and lasted right up until the Second World War.

France had lost the provinces of Alsace and Lorraine to Prussia and was motivated by a desire for revenge. At this time came the political scandal with anti-Semitic overtones known as the Dreyfus Affair in which a young Jewish artillery officer in the French army was wrongly convicted for treason. The case split France and in his open letter to the President entitled *J'accuse*, Emile Zola expressed his disgust at the conviction of Dreyfus as a scapegoat behind which the military and political establishment were hiding.

Fashionable France

The dawn of the age of travel as a form of pleasure (at least for the wealthy), saw the English begin the habit of taking French holidays. Several Normandy seaside towns and Biarritz and Nice became very fashionable with 'Les Anglais'; while Paris attracted the highest society of all including British royalty. With this closer, sustained contact of the French and English, the French were able to reinforce their prejudices about the English and comment on their lack of sartorial style and physical disproportions, their gluttony and their inelegant manners. The English, it was said, went to France for pleasure, the French went to England for business (or as exiles from the various downturns of fortune inflicted on the royal and imperial dynasties). It became expedient, if not mutually comfortable, for the two nations to form the *Entente Cordiale*, a kind of alliance against the burgeoning power of a united Germany, and of Russia, which was also looming on the horizon.

At the beginning of the 20th century too, with the arrival of Gertrude Stein in Paris, America's literary romance with France, and particularly Paris, began. Stein's *The Autobiography of Alice B Toklas* tells the story of her discovery of and life with some of the great painters (Picasso, Matisse, Braque, Cézanne) who were working in Paris at the time, which, since the birth of impressionism had been at the centre of everything that was innovative in contemporary art. Stein was extremely influential with a whole generation of young American writers, including Sherwood Anderson, Hemingway and Faulkner. With *A Moveable Feast* Hemingway recalled the years he spent in Paris at the beginning of the 1920s, including uncharitable comments on many of the artists and writers he associated with at that time. Later, of course, there was Henry Miller.

Effect of the wars

During the wars fought as allies, both France and Britain talked up their own contribution at the expense of the other. The First World War was won by the Americans turning up in vast numbers just in time, but to the French it was won at Verdun. The British meanwhile having lost a generation of manhood at Mons, the Somme and the other battlefields, regard it as a victory won by their great sacrifice. In the Second World War, the French were contemptuous of the British tactical retreat at Dunkerque (Dunkirk), while the British condemned the French for cooperating in part with the Germans, when France split between Free France and Occupied France. This, if anything, reinforced the British prejudice that the French were treacherous. Those of the Free French who had dealings with the British see it from another more friendly point of view, as an era which forged many bonds of friendship and a French affection for many things British, including the British character.

Gertrude Stein's remarks on the difference between the American soldiers she saw in France in the First World War and those she saw at the end of the Second World War are illustrative of how the United States became comfortable in its status as a leading world power between the two wars. The GIs Stein describes in the First World War were far less articulate and confident in themselves than those in the Second World War.

France today

In the post-war years, France overtook Britain economically and in world influence. This is arguably a position she still retains today, despite the drawbacks of a lack of natural resources. After the failure of the Fourth Republic brought on by the colonial crisis in Algeria and the return of Charles de Gaulle in 1958, the Fifth Republic was established under a constitution that gave the President the considerable powers that that the French head of state still enjoys today. De Gaulle was strongly pro-European and anti-American (taking France out of the North Atlantic Treaty Organization (NATO)) and established the alliance between France and Germany that until recently controlled the destiny of the European Union – another source of contention between Britain and France.

The actual and symbolic linking of Britain and France by the Channel Tunnel has gone some way towards ending the rivalry of France and England and benefits both countries through inextricably linked mutual interests. The initial frictions resulting from refugees using the Tunnel to enter England illegally after escaping from loosely guarded camps sited very near the Tunnel's French end were resolved with the closure of the camp at Sangatte in 2003.

◼ GEOGRAPHICAL INFORMATION

Area and main physical features

France is the largest country of the EU and has a surface area of 544,500sq km. However, with an average population density of approximately 49 people per sq km, it's markedly less populated than the UK, Belgium, Germany, the Netherlands or Italy. The borders of France are largely defined by physical barriers: the Channel (*la*

FACT

◼ In *Wars I Have Seen*, Gertrude Stein left a very absorbing account of life in France at the time of the two world wars.

The Loire River

Manche), Atlantic Ocean, Pyrenees, Mediterranean Sea, Alps and the River Rhine. France is generally a lowland country, with most of its surface less than 200m above sea level. There are only three mountainous areas: the French Alps, the Pyrénées and the rather less mountainous Massif Central in central southern France.

Neighbouring countries

France shares a land border with five other EU countries – Spain, Italy, Luxembourg, Germany and Belgium – as well as with Switzerland. The Channel Tunnel is not only the first artificial link between England and France but an umbilical cord between the rest of Europe and Britain from which France is bound to benefit.

Internal organisation

FACT

■ The country's most important rivers are the Loire, the Rhône, the Seine and the Garonne.

France was divided into 22 official regions in the 1980s to provide a modern working framework for the economic development of the provinces and also to assist in the effective decentralization of industry. This move has served both to reintroduce several historic, provincial titles, such as Languedoc, Provence, etc., (lost after the 1789 Revolution) and to encourage a resurgence of local feeling within the regions. The 96 *départements* which make up the Metropolitan regions date from immediately after the Revolution in 1790. They were formed for administrative purposes after the old feudal domains had been swept away, along with the vestiges of the *ancien régime*. Each department has a directly elected *conseil général* (council). Finally, there are the smallest internal administrative divisions within France, the *communes*, of which there are some 37,500 each with a council and a mayor elected every six years. Mayors are influential figures in France, being both a servant of the local people and responsible to the state. In addition, the island of Corsica (annexed by revolutionary France in 1789) is officially an integrated part of France and forms two *départements*.

Population

The current population of France comprises approximately 60.1 million people. Over half this number are city dwellers. This includes one million immigrants from the former French colony of Algeria and 2.5 million immigrants from other EU and European countries, of which over half a million are from Portugal, and the remainder from Italy, Spain, former Yugoslavia, Poland and the other Accession Countries. The rest of the immigrant population is derived from the Mahgreb (Morocco and Tunisia) and more recently from Asia. It is not known how many illegal immigrants there are in France, but some estimates put it as high as three million.

The populations of the largest cities of France and their urban areas are:

- Bordeaux – 882,150
- Lille – 1,108,400
- Lyon – 1,597,660
- Marseille – 1,398,146
- Nice – 556,525
- Paris – 10,561,573
- Rouen – 448,000
- Toulouse – 917,300

Other territories

In addition to mainland France there are the overseas territories of French Polynesia (including Tahiti) and New Caledonia, the French Southern and Antarctic Territories and the Wallis and Futuna islands, and the overseas *départements* (*départements d'outre-mer*) of French Guiana, Guadeloupe, Martinique, Mayotte and Réunion. The latter have a greater degree of autonomy than internal regions, but are still *départements* of France. Thanks to world time zones the euro became legal currency in Réunion a few hours before it did in France.

Monaco has the status of a principality and is not a French *département*.

Climatic zones

As a very large country France experiences wide weather variations. These variations are not gradual but are very sharply defined in different parts of the country.

Continental zone

Continental weather affects the north-eastern quarter of France; this features warm summers, but with fairly high rainfall and consistently cold winters. Continental weather also characterises the Auvergne, Burgundy, and the Rhône Valley.

Mediterranean zone

Mediterranean weather affects the south and south-eastern corner of France: Roussillon, the Riviera and Provence. This climate is characterized by hot summers and warm winters; rainfall is low and erratic throughout the year.

Mountain zone

Mountain weather affects the Alps, Pyrenees and Massif Central, bringing with it cool summers with frequent rain and very cold winters with long periods of both sunny weather and rain or snow.

Oceanic zone

Ocean weather affects the western seaboard of France from the Loire to the Basque region and the central regions: warm summers and mild winters with very heavy rainfall are common to these areas.

Overall, France has no very extreme weather, whether hot, dry, cold or wet and exceptions to this are very occasional. The table below gives the average temperatures of the main regions of France in winter and in summer (in degrees Celsius).

Seasonal temperature averages		
	Winter average (°C)	Summer average (°C)
Paris	7°	25°
Alps	3°	25°
Alsace	5°	26°
Aquitaine	9°	25°
Brittany	9°	24°
Corsica	2°	28°
Languedoc	11°	28°
Loire	8°	24°
Pyrenees	10°	27°
Normandy	8°	22°
Provence	12°	28°

Regions and departments

Many foreigners feel that they know very little about most of the French regions even if they have visited France many times over several years. This is understandable in that although a large and diverse country, popular tourism for many years was mainly confined to Paris and certain fashionable coastal regions, notably in the north and south of France. In recent years, however, the regions have gained a degree of autonomy, and under the policy of decentralisation they have become much more self-promoting and accessible, and in addition, the majority have been transformed by economic development. Thus all the regions can be considered potential destinations for anyone wishing to settle and work in France: the choice will largely depend on the lifestyle desired, personal preference for a particular area, and/or regional employment opportunities.

The French sometimes refer to their country as *l'hexagone* and a quick glance at any map will show why. The country is very approximately six-sided with the Mediterranean, the Atlantic and the Channel on three 'sides' and the Alps, Pyrenees and the River Rhine on the other sides forming natural barriers between France and her neighbours. Internally, France is divided into 23 areas known as regions. The measure of autonomy of the French regions is nothing like as federally developed as it is for instance in Germany. In most cases the regional divisions correspond to the natural differences in geography between them.

Each region is sub-divided into *départements*. Each of the 96 *départements* has an administrative centre, which is either a major city or the counterpart of a county town. The *départements* used to be under the direct control of Paris. Now the regions have more influence the *départements* have rather subsided in importance although they are still crucial to the administration. The *départements* are sub-divided into communes which have their own authorities, very much like town or parish councils.

Welcome and information facilities

As one would expect of a country with a huge tourist industry, France has no shortage of welcome and information centres, about 3,600 of them. The better known and larger towns and cities each have an *Office du Tourisme* while tourist bureaux *Syndicats d'Initiative* can be found in the main square or near the town centre of many smaller towns. The latter usually operate from more modest premises and for shorter hours than an *Office de Tourisme*. There is also a *Comité Régional du Tourisme* (CRT) for each region, in the main regional town, where information for the entire region is centralised. In addition, each *département* has a *Comité Départemental du Tourisme* which is probably a better bet for local information than the CRTs .

Tourist offices in Paris

The central administration office of the *Office de Tourisme* (www.paris-info.com) in Paris is in the rue des Pyramides, but it does not have public access. The offices open to the public (*Bureaux d'Accueil*) are in key tourist places like l'Opera and the Eiffel Tower. In addition, there are welcome offices *Accueil de France* at the main Parisian rail stations: Gare du Nord and Gare de Lyon and also at the main provincial railway stations such as Marseille and Strasbourg and at the airport in Nice. All tourist offices provide multilingual assistance, maps and brochures and also lists of hotels, restaurants etc. The *Bureaux d'Accueil* also provide a useful hotel booking service at the point of arrival and you can also book accommodation online through the tourist office websites.

FACT

■ Administrative matters are usually handled on a departmental basis, but when talking about culture, scenery or even cuisine the variations are usually defined on a regional basis.

FACT

■ The excellent web directory (www.1001france.com.fr) compiled by the French Tourist office gives the addresses of the all tourist offices mentioned in the text.

■ POLITICS

Government and politics

The French republican system of government was set up in 1792, three years after the storming of the Bastille and the outbreak of the Revolution. As such, France was one of the earliest modern republics and over the years, this has been refined to an efficient and well-balanced form of government with its own peculiarities. The current republic is the fifth and was established in 1958. It has more in common with the USA, which also has a written constitution and a presidential system, than the UK, which has no written constitution and is a monarchy.

The President is Head of State and Head of the Government: he (there has as yet been no woman president) must abide by the rules of the constitution but has limited powers to amend it. Thus the President is an active politician, not merely an official figurehead; a constitutional council ensures that the constitution is followed properly. The President is elected by popular vote every five years (Jacques Chirac had it changed from seven) and the presidency can't be transferred to another person. The President appoints a Prime Minister, and through him or her, other ministers, to head the various ministries and government departments. Ministers and even the Prime Minister need not be elected officials. Thus Dominique de Villepin was Prime Minister under Chirac without ever being elected to public office. The current President is Nicolas Sarkozy, from the right-wing UMP party. He was elected in May 2007, with 53% of the vote and was given a further mandate for his policies of reform in the legislative elections shortly afterwards. At the time of going to print, he has proved a flamboyant and energetic President, courting media attention, as much in his private as his public life (very unusual until now for a French politician). He has been critical of

his predecessor, the Gaullist Jacques Chirac, who was tainted by corruption scandals, and has asserted his belief in transparency. Sarkozy has begun to ease the tax burden on the French people and attack the too-costly pensions privileges of certain vested interests. He has also been vocal in terms of his commitment to looking for a solution to the social problems of the *banlieues* but has yet to provide significant resources in this area.

Owing to the power vested in the Presidential office, the French Parliament has slightly less importance than in other countries. It introduces and reviews legislation, but much of this has been formulated beforehand and will be approved as a matter of course. The President is usually bound by the decisions of Parliament but can, in certain circumstances, overrule

Nicholas Sarkozy during the French presidential election

them. Parliament consists of two houses: the Assemblée Nationale with 577 Members of Parliament (*députés*) who must be elected every five years by the people; and the Sénat (also called as *Haute Assemblée*), consisting of 321 members elected every nine years (one third of the seats being contested every three years) by local town councillors (*conseillers généraux*).

The National Assembly (lower house) deputies are elected in districts of varying sizes, which works out roughly at one deputy per 100,000 inhabitants of France. The term of the legislature is five years but it can be abridged if the President of the Republic decides to dissolve the Assembly. Chirac did this in 1997 when he dissolved the Assembly nine months early in an attempt to give his Gaullist-led government a clear mandate for the move to a single European currency.

The long-term of office of the senators in the upper house promotes political stability, which is further strengthened by the fact that, unlike the National Assembly, the Senate cannot be dissolved. The Constitution also confers on the President of the Senate the job of taking over the Presidency of the Republic should the office suddenly be vacated as in a resignation or (as happened with President Pompidou), if the President dies in office. The Sénat reviews the legislation of the Assemblée Nationale but, in effect, cannot overrule it.

TIP

■ For up-to-date information about the French Government visit the French Prime Minister's website (www.premier-ministre.gouv.fr).

Women in politics

It used to be said that women governed France from the bedroom. Historically, there was no alternative as the Salic Law excluded women from succession to the French crown. This meant there was no tradition of leaders or role models after Jeanne d'Arc until Edith Cresson became the first woman Prime Minister in 1991–1992. French women didn't get the vote or the right to stand as political candidates until 1945 (compared with 1929 in the UK and 1893 in New Zealand). Although this appeared to change dramatically with the large number of woman ministers appointed to the Sarkozy government (see 'Women in France' above for more on this), France still has a smaller number of women in national government than any other EU nation and is 58th in the world league of female representation in politics, behind many developing countries. In 2002 a 'Parity' law was passed under which 50% of candidates in all French elections have to be female. Despite this legal underpinning of equality, in 2007 only 107 women out of a total of 577 deputies were elected to the lower chamber. Prominent French female politicians currently include Ségolène Royal (the socialist candidate in the Presidential elections), Christine Lagarde, the Finance Minister, Rachida Dati, the Justice Minister and Michèle Alliot-Marie, the Interior Minister.

Elections

All French elections have an unusual double-ballot system. The first election includes all nominees, the second only the two candidates who receive the two highest numbers of votes. In the case of governmental elections, the two ballots are held about a week apart. Proportional representation is used in some elections.

It is not unusual for the President to be of a different political persuasion to the government. This was the case during the last term of the late President Mitterrand. Such an anomaly (i.e. a president and a government of different political colours) can arise in France where the balance of power tends to be held by a coalition of parties and because the presidential and the parliamentary elections are out of sync.

Administration

Région

The other layers of political administration in France are the *Région*, The *Département* and the *Commune*. The *Région* is the newest administrative unit and was established in 1982. There are 26 regions in France, 22 of them are in Metropolitan France and the remaining four are overseas. Since the mid-1980s each region has had its own executive and elected assembly – the *Assemblée Régional*, whose members are elected for six years through a system of proportional representation.

Département

The *Département* was first instituted in 1789 and was the administrative district of the Republic. France comprises 100 *départements*, 96 of which are in Metropolitan France and four overseas (Martinique, Guadeloupe, Réunion and French Guiana), known as *Départements d'Outre-Mer et Territoires d'Outre-Mer* or *DOM-TOM*. From 1800 to 1982 the executive power of the *département* was invested in the Prefect. Since 1982 the Prefect has been replaced by a Chairman of the General Council who is elected from among the general council members for a period of three years. The General Councillors are elected for six years in a two-round majority voting election. Half the members of the general council come up for re-election every three years.

Commune

The *commune* or municipality is the smallest and oldest administrative unit instituted in 1789 and is the ground level administrative unit of France. There are almost 37,000 communes – a large number by European national standards. The reason for this is that the term applies to communities regardless of size: 80% of municipalities have fewer than 1,000 inhabitants. Because of this, the government brought in a new law in 2002 to encourage the very small communes to band together into communities or associations of several communities known as *intercommunalités* to develop their shared local interests and execute greater powers in the spheres of culture, tourism and economic matters. The Prefect is still the intermediary between the *département* and the seat of government in Paris. In addition to these political divisions there are over 200 *Pays de France* which are smaller regions usually used by locals to describe where they come from in France. The executive of the *commune* is the mayor. He or she is elected for six years by the municipal council and is chosen from its ranks. The mayor has a dual role as both an official of the

Party Websites

- www.parti-socialiste.fr (PS)
- www.u-m-p.org (UMP)
- www.les-verts.org (Greens)
- www.frontnational.com (FN)

municipality and the representative of the state in the municipality. In the latter function, he or she performs marriages, keeps the civil register of births, marriages and deaths and is an officer of the *police judiciare*. He or she is also responsible for administrative functions such as publishing laws and regulations, establishing the electoral role, and the draft roll of those eligible for national military service.

Each commune has an elected council, the number of its members being proportional to the population of the commune. Municipal councillors are elected for six years by direct universal suffrage and they shape local policies, define the administrative operations of the municipality, vote the budget and manage the property and facilities of the commune.

Political parties

The French political system hosts a wide range of political parties and the balance of power depends on coalition (known in France as 'cohabitation'). The main parties include the *Parti Socialiste* (PS) and *l'Union pour un Mouvement Populaire* (UMP) a composite right-wing party which currently dominates the government and is President Chirac's party. *The Front National* (FN), founded in 1972 manifests extreme Right tendencies mixed with Roman Catholic fundamentalism. Its splenetic founder, Jean-Marie Le Pen was jubilant that his support extended around the country and amounted to a sizeable percentage (17%) of the plebiscite in the Presidential elections of 2002. His percentage fell in 2007 because of the robust performance of Nicolas Sarkozy. The FN campaigns mainly on immigration, in particular, non-European immigration, which it would like not only to end but to reverse. Finally, like most European countries, France has its ecology parties: the Green Party (Les Verts) was founded in 1984 and is a confederation of several ecological groups including Génération Ecologie.

Europe

Issues such as the Maastricht treaty and the French decision to join the European single currency, which they did in January 1999, have historically given the French a reputation for being solid supporters of Europe. However, the success of Jean Marie Le Pen and the rejection by referendum of the European Constitution in 2005 showed the extent to which the French people have become disillusioned with the EU (if only momentarily). There is a perception, as elsewhere, that Europe is having a negative impact on people's daily lives and encroaching on their autonomy and freedom of action. The Constitution received across the board support from the political establishment and yet it was still rejected. As such, the referendum was a political slap on the wrists for governments all over the Union. Many of the items in the Constitution may be enacted through the EU Reform Treaty that is undergoing an uncertain ratification process at the time of going to print.

The European Parliament building, Strasbourg

The economy

Often the economic importance of France is underestimated when compared to other major world powers. In general, the economy has been successful since the end of the Second World War and at times in the 1960s France had a rate of growth comparable to that of the USA. France is the sixth largest economy in the world and the third largest in Europe after Germany and the UK. France introduced a 35-hour working week in 2002, to tackle unemployment which had escalated to 12.8% (nearly 4 million people), one of the highest totals in the EU. Unemployment is currently just under 10%. There is uncertainty however as to whether the 35-hour week will be retained or not. One of the first measures of the Sarkozy government in 2007 was to allow employees the choice of whether to take overtime payment for time worked above and beyond 35-hours, rather than having to take days off in lieu, which was the previous rule. This measure was partly a response to complaints by workers that it was impossible for them to increase their incomes by working harder. It also gives a measure of flexibility to employers in terms of being able to employ current staff for longer hours at busy times rather than having to take on the burden of extra social charges should they want to employ extra members of staff.

In recent years France has oscillated between deciding that it could no longer afford the high cost of social support and welfare and deciding after all, that the government's various belt-tightening tactics were insupportable. There has been a general trend nevertheless towards reducing spending on welfare, which included Lionel Jospin's government (1997–2002). The union lobby, although not strong throughout private sector, is well represented in the public sector and any attempt at serious economic reform has been fiercely opposed by public sector vested interests. The recent conservative governments have cut both income tax

FACT

■ France joined the Eurozone in 2002 thus achieving the Franco-German goal of European Monetary Union. Britain opted out of monetary union and didn't replace the pound with the euro currency, although British businesses are dealing in euros and have euro bank accounts.

and spending on social welfare and the Sarkozy government is likely to continue the programme of raising employment age, cutting unemployment and retirement benefits and reforming national health insurance regimens.

Traditionally, economic setbacks have been seen as temporary and France has remained optimistic about its future. In the 1970s when economic prospects were poor, both government and business seemed keen to invest money and effort in research and technology projects for the future – investments which paid off by putting France at the forefront in generating technological progress in everything from nuclear power to satellite launchers, not to mention the precursor of the internet, Minitel, which is now linked to the internet. Nevertheless, in recent years, fears about globalisation and the relocation of French companies outside France have created a certain amount of pessimism among the French themselves.

With the money supply under the control of the European Central Bank, inflation had remained low at under 2% and economic growth had been averaging over 3% between 1997 and 2004. In 2007 the gross domestic product (GDP) growth was a more modest 1.8%, with the economy affected by the sub-prime crisis that began in the US and high energy and food prices have caused inflation to rise. One factor significant in the generally reliable performance of the French economy has been the gradual evolution from state-controlled or state-partnership industries to private companies. The list of enterprises sold or being sold off in France is expected to help her maintain a strong economic position both by keeping abreast of new technology and international markets and through the government's continued support of French companies and products, especially in export markets. Such a situation obviously bodes well for those considering employment with French companies.

France is one of the leading countries within Europe to encourage regional development, with the state agency DIACT to oversee this. Consequently there is no stark north–south prosperity divide as there is in Italy and the UK. At one time France was centralised, with Paris like an octopus controlling the provinces with its tentacles. This is also much less the case than formerly as there is increasing emphasis on regional control.

There is no doubt that France sees the EU as being an excellent way of promoting its own interests. French business and industry were well prepared to take full advantage of the single market, being both competitive and technologically minded. The central position of the country within the EU is of great importance. The Channel Tunnel link with the UK is valuable to both countries, and unlike neighbouring Belgium or the Netherlands or the south of England, there is plenty of space in France for industrial development.

FACT

■ One area hit by cheap imports in recent years is the already shrinking textiles industry.

■ LOCAL GOVERNMENT

The préfecture and mairie

At this point it is as well to mention something about local government in France. The first radical reforms of the system, which had lasted, with a few non-integral reforms, since the Napoleonic era, took place under the Socialist government of 1981–86. Thus it can be seen that until quite recent times, a highly centralized

2

2

2

22

2

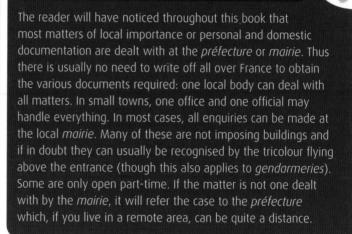

Where to go

The reader will have noticed throughout this book that most matters of local importance or personal and domestic documentation are dealt with at the *préfecture* or *mairie*. Thus there is usually no need to write off all over France to obtain the various documents required: one local body can deal with all matters. In small towns, one office and one official may handle everything. In most cases, all enquiries can be made at the local *mairie*. Many of these are not imposing buildings and if in doubt they can usually be recognised by the tricolour flying above the entrance (though this also applies to *gendarmeries*). Some are only open part-time. If the matter is not one dealt with by the *mairie*, it will refer the case to the *préfecture* which, if you live in a remote area, can be quite a distance.

system of government existed. Most decisions were made in Paris by the President and then handed down to and carried out by local officials in each *département* and region. Under this system *départements* enjoyed virtually no say in local affairs; they were subject to edicts which emanated from Paris. The chief official in each area (*le préfet*) operated from the *Préfecture* was merely the local political executor of central government. Each *département* had a *préfet*, *préfecture* and *sous-préfectures*, but the regions had no administrative, only a geographical significance. In the early 1980s however, the situation changed radically. Individual regions and *départements* were then given their own councils and assemblies, the prerogative to introduce certain laws and the freedom to raise funds and to spend these as they chose. As a result of these changes the *préfet* lost much of their authority and were rechristened *Commissionnaire de la République* while their powers devolved onto the locally elected councillors of the communes, departments and regions. However, in France such changes take a long time to work through and it is only in the last few years that the original préfectural system has diminished hugely.

The *mairie*, with the mayor (*le maire*) as head of the local *commune*, is equivalent to a town or parish council: this unit existed before the government reforms, although after them it gained a little more independence.

Despite this devolution, France is still a rather centralised country and by no means as federally organised as Germany or as locally devolved as Switzerland. Individual regions and *départements* do not have total independence and tend to present a unified national image in most cases.

Dealing with the mairie or préfecture

The reception you get at either a *mairie* or *préfecture* will vary greatly. Some officials are extremely helpful, while others are positively hostile, and it can take a good deal of effort and charm to squeeze the information needed from this latter group. French bureaucracy is not especially complicated, but a good deal more formal than in many other countries. A small charge is sometimes levied for some of the services which the *mairie* and *préfecture* offer.

One of the problems with dealing with local authorities, as an expatriate, is that you may not have the documents which every French national has as a matter of course. Nationals will always have an identity card and, when a couple marry, a *Livre de Famille* is issued which records various details about them, their marriage and family. For this reason it is essential to keep every official French document which you are given and a supply of photocopies too: never part with the originals unless absolutely essential. In the case of documents issued outside of France, keep an official French translation. On visits to the *mairie* or *préfecture* on some enquiry, it is as well to take the whole lot with you. It is also useful to keep contact with a friend in your own country who can track down any official documents you might need in your dealings with the authorities.

Local council websites

Larger towns and many others as well have websites. These offer information on tourism, sport, useful addresses, etc. Some offer free e-mail addresses and other services. The aim is to have a website for every town hall and to set up complete online forms for construction permits, birth certificates and all the other documents connected with bureaucratic procedures in France.

■ RELIGION

Catholicism

France is primarily a Roman Catholic country. Despite its influence throughout French history, the Church is now neither as strict or strong as in the past, and as in other highly developed Western European countries there has been a steady decline in the number of practitioners. About 67% (some estimates put the figure over 70%) of French people consider themselves Catholics (i.e. have been baptised). Although the Church now tends to keep its distance from French politics (the French state was officially secularised in 1905), this didn't stop its clerics dabbling in left-wing politics on social issues just after the Second World War. As a result there are many spiritual and charitable organisations that continue to be dynamic today. Some of the best known are *Le Secours Catholique* or *Caritas France*, created after the Second World War has an estimated 68,000 volunteers. Another, *Les Chiffoniers d'Emmaus* founded by Abbé Pierre, is an international

charity that helps the underprivileged and aims at the eradication of poverty.

The priesthood has suffered a dramatic decline in recruits. There are estimated to be barely 100 new recruits to the priesthood annually compared with about 650 per year in the 1960s and the total number has declined from 45,000 then to under 22,000 now. The priesthood is thus an ageing body of shepherds and their flock is meagre; it is estimated that about 14% of the population regularly attend Mass. To satisfy the need for some kind of religion, albeit more relevant than the established one, there are many unofficial religious groups that meet in private homes.

The Catholic Church continues to exercise its influence in education, with 95% of private schools in France being Catholic schools, including primary establishments, *collèges* (first stage of secondary education) and 1,100 *lycées* (second stage secondary schools). Between them Catholic schools have about 2 million pupils or 17% of the school-age population. And the church does not evince feebleness in upholding the right to state aid for Catholic schools, which are separate from the rest of the French education system. When the French government banned the wearing of the Muslim veil in state (secular) schools, the Catholic schools offered their services and tolerance of the veil to Muslims students; in Marseille 70% of female pupils in some Catholic schools are Muslims.

In France a civil wedding ceremony must be held to validate a marriage legally and this is performed at the *mairie* in front of the mayor who wears a tricolour sash. A church ceremony is optional and has no legal significance: some couples choose to have both, whereas others settle for a civil ceremony.

Other religions

Protestantism

A mere 1.64% of the French population (about 950,000) are Protestant. The three regions with the highest concentration of Protestants are Paris, Alsace-Lorraine and the south of the country. The predominant faction is the Calvinist Reformed Church (450,000 members). The only women priests in France are to be found in this church. Other Protestants include: Lutherans (270,000) most of whom are in Alsace-Lorraine, and the remainder are a mixture of Evangelicals, Adventists, Pentecostalists, etc.

Judaism

There are between 550,000 and 750,000 Jews in France representing a religion which has been present in France since the 1st century AD. The largest populations are to be found in Paris, Marseille and Alsace. About 60,000 French Jews have emigrated to Israel.

Islam

The second largest religion in France is Islam and the Muslim community of France numbers around 5 million. Many of them are French immigrants who arrived in bulk in the 1950s and 60s. They represent several factions of Islam including Sunnis of Maghreban, i.e. north African origin; Turkish Islam which incorporates both Sunnis and Shiites, and most recently, African Islam which has marabouts (religious leaders) for the various brotherhoods it tends to form.

English and American churches

Churches can be a good way of meeting people, especially for families. The Intercontinental Church Society (☎01926 430347; www.ics-uk/org) can supply maps and contact details of Anglican churches in France. The American Church in Paris is in the 7th arrondissement in Paris (☎01 45 56 09 50; www.acparis.org).

REGIONAL GUIDE

The following regional guide aims to introduce the different areas of France mentioning their salient points, general characteristics and advantages and disadvantages to be taken into consideration when choosing an area to live, work and or retire to.

Alsace

Main cities: Strasbourg, Mulhouse, Colmar

Départements: Bas-Rhin, Haut-Rhin

Office de tourisme: 17 Pl. de la Cathédrale, 67082 Strasbourg; ☎03 88 52 28 28; www.ot-strasbourg.fr

Alsace is located in the far east of France and borders Germany to which, along with part of Lorraine it has belonged at various historical junctures. Consequently the region has a Germanic feel, evident in its people, dialects, architecture and cuisine. It is very scenic, largely unspoiled and generally an attractive area in which to live. The history of the Alsatian wines predates even the Romans who are credited with having taken the vine to other parts of France. Beer is another local speciality as is the formidable *eau-de-vie*. The *truite au bleu* (blue trout) is a gastronomic speciality as are many other fish from the rivers of Alsace. You can apply for a fishing permit from any *mairie* in the area.

Mulhouse is an important industrial area, which enjoys a thriving economy. This has not always been the case however; Alsace was once very much a fringe region and somewhat underdeveloped. Its recent and rapid development is primarily due to its connections with Germany and its centrality within the EU, which is certain to become even more important in future. A new TGV (Train à Grande Vitesse) high-speed train link from Strasbourg to Paris takes two hours and twenty minutes.

The area has excellent road connections to Paris (500km approximately) and also to Frankfurt in Germany and Basel and Zurich in Switzerland; as such, it is very much a euro-centre with promising employment potential for British expatriates.

FACT

■ For information on the different regions and contact details for tourist offices see uk.franceguide.com. For information on the industries and employment potential in each region see the chapter Working in France.

REGIONSOFFRANCE

Marseille, Rhone & Les Alpes

Languedoc Roussillion

Loire Valley

Paris, Ile De France

Strasbourg Cathedral

Aquitaine

Main city: Bordeaux

Départements: Dordogne, Gironde, Landes, Lot-et-Garonne, Pyrénées-Atlantiques

Office de tourisme: 21, cours de l'intendance, 33000 Bordeaux Cedex; ☎05 56 52 61 40; www.tourisme-gironde.fr

Aquitaine is a large region of south-west France and is probably one of the best known areas in France among holiday-makers and wine buffs. The Lot and Dordogne are dotted with foreign holiday homes and the area is very scenic, with rolling hills, forests and the attractive River Garonne valley – there is also an extensive Atlantic coastline. Despite being very far south Aquitaine does not have a hot and dry climate, and is generally considered to have some of the most pleasant and temperate weather in France,

Essentially, the region is agricultural (containing some of France's most famous vineyards), and therefore largely quiet and unspoiled. Some areas can be very remote and inaccessible although the south of the region offers ready access to Spain and good TGV connections provide easy access to Paris in three hours. This combination of rural quietude and accessibility has resulted in the area gaining popularity and attracting new residents. Biarritz on the coast near the Spanish border has been a popular and fashionable summer resort since the 19th century. It comes

Strasbourg

The capital of Alsace, Strasbourg, has been for centuries a staging point on the east–west trade route and its location on the Rhine made it an important centre for commercial river traffic. Nowadays it is the seat of the European Parliament and the Council of Europe. Strasbourg is a fairly small and compact city, but important economically and administratively. It has largely shaken off its quaint image of the past and taken on the mantle of an important and dynamic Euro-city. It offers a high quality of life, with good housing and facilities. Taking into consideration Strasbourg's Euro-city status it may be particularly suited to executives and professionals.

alive over the summer months and survives during the winter on the extortionate rates it has charged visitors in the tourist season. Bayonne is the other well known resort and is near Biarritz.

Auvergne

Main city: Clermont-Ferrand

Départements: Allier, Cantal, Haute-Loire, Puy de Dôme

Office de tourisme: Place de la Victoire, 63000 Clermont-Ferrand. ☎04 73 90 04 11; www.ot-clermont-ferrand.fr

Auvergne is one of the lesser-known and more remote regions of France. It occupies much of the Massif Central – one of the three really mountainous areas in France apart from the Alps and the Pyrénées. In many ways the Auvergne is a vestige of the France of former times and has a rich architectural heritage of *châteaux* and churches in thinly populated landscapes and

Bordeaux

Bordeaux, situated on the River Garonne, 0 is a solid city built on the wealth of its mercantile classes and its former position as a great seaport. Following the loss of the French colonies and a decline in shipping requirements for various goods (including slaves), the city fell into decline after the Second World War, relying mainly on the wine trade with which is still strongly associated. Since the 1970s Bordeaux has become very much one of France's new techno-cities. Development has centred on electronics and a new container port on the nearby Médoc peninsula. The result is a very affluent and bustling city, despite its remoteness from the rest of France. However, it isn't considered one of the most attractive or historically interesting of French cities. Bordeaux is a good place to live for those who hope to work within the various technical industries. These pay good wages and there is good (although not especially cheap) housing and facilities for employees in those industries. The city itself is not especially to be recommended for those who are retiring or who are looking for a relaxed pace of life. Apart from its business interests Bordeaux is also a very busy (and congested, although much less so since the introduction of the tram network, *le tramway*) convention and exhibition city.

> **FACT**
>
> ■ The way of life is relaxed and property, apart from holiday homes, is modestly priced, though not cheap.

Clermont-Ferrand

Clermont-Ferrand is the lively political and economic centre for the whole Massif Central and the birthplace of the Michelin tyre company.

hence offers a rather slow and gentle pace of life. The region does contain a small number of rather unattractive industrial towns, such as St Etienne.

The A71 connects the Auvergne to Paris (300km approximately) so the region is not as cut off as it once was, and retains its useful proximity to the Alpine resorts and the south of France. The Auvergne does not offer the best employment potential for prospective residents, but it does offer an unhurried pace of life with the added advantage of some of the lowest property prices in the whole country.

Brittany

Main cities: Rennes, Brest, Nantes

Départements: Côtes d'Armor, Finistère, Ille-et-Vilaine, Morbihan

Office de tourisme: Chapelle Saint-Yves, 11, rue Saint-Yves, CS 26410, 35064 Rennes Cedex; ☎02 99 67 11 11; www.tourisme-rennes.com

Brittany is another French region that has some echoes in British ears. Apart from the name and certain Celtic traditions however, Brittany is very much a 'foreign' land. The ancient Breton language is one of a group of languages including Gaelic and Cornish, spoken by the pre-Roman tribes of Britain and Gaul. Breton like Welsh and Gaelic is still spoken, albeit by a dwindling number of Bretons, mainly the old.

Rennes

The ancient capital of Brittany, Rennes, has only recently been designated its major city. Previously, economic dominance was held by Nantes (62 miles/100km to the south) which is now capital of the Loire-West region. As a result of this, Rennes is now a city of importance in its own right. It has the Technopole Rennes-Atalante, a prestigious science park comprising the universities, research institutes and companies. Especially important are information technology, telecommunications, agro-industries, biotechnology and nutrition and the environment. The advantage of its location is that the pace of life tends to be slower and more relaxed and property prices lower than might be expected. Employment opportunities in Rennes are increasing.

However the language has experienced a revival (in much the same way as Welsh has) over recent years. Other British associations also exist, such as old trading links with Cornwall, Wales and Ireland, which can be traced back over hundreds of years. And there is an old district of Brittany still sometimes referred to as La Cornouaille, the French name for Cornwall.

Unfortunately the Atlantic-facing coastline also means that the weather, though fair in summer, can be very wild during the winter months and some areas are still remote with few facilities. However, the fact that most of Brittany is unspoiled and has a unique and inspiring culture with its own traditions and important literary figures including the novelist Henri Queffelec, more than makes up for these drawbacks. Towns such as Quimper and Brest are busy but remain attractive. The area as a whole is popular with tourists and holiday-home owners with the result that property prices have been climbing steadily.

Burgundy

Main city: Dijon

Départements: Côte d'Or, Nièvre, Saône-et-Loire, Yonne

Office de tourisme: 11 rue des Forges, BP 82296, 21022 Dijon Cedex; ☎0892 700 558; www.dijon-tourism.com

Burgundy starts near the small medieval town of Auxerre and reaches down to just north of the metropolis of Lyon. It is another area of France whose name is famous thanks to the wine that takes its name from the region. For 600 years Burgundy was an independent kingdom with its heyday in medieval times. Many of the great vineyards were run by religious orders whose expertise in cultivation and distillation was unrivalled in Europe.

Although prosperous, Burgundy's position in the hierarchy of the most economically important regions is not high; it is similar to the Auvergne in that respect. The area's countryside isn't industrialised, and not especially attractive by French standards. Some parts are very isolated. That said, there is excellent access to both Paris (65 miles/100km), Lyon and beyond, by TGV train and A6 autoroute. These factors are sure to enhance future development of the region. Property prices are higher than average in Burgundy but there is only minimal interest from holiday and retirement homeowners and the buyers are usually Parisians in search of a country bolthole. The region boasts no large cities except for Dijon (population 1.6 million), which is a lively university city with a vibrant cultural life. If you prefer to live and work in a small-scale city, you could do a lot worse than Dijon. Important towns in Burgundy include Mâcon, Chalon-sur-Saône and Beaune.

FACT

■ A map of the Burgundy area reads like a wine list from which Nuits St Georges, Mersault, Chassagne-Montrachet, Mercurey, Pouilly-Fuissé are just some of the possible selections.

Champagne-Ardenne

Main city: Reims

Départements: Ardennes, Aube, Haute-Marne, Marne

Office de tourisme: 2, rue Guillaume de Machault, 51100 Reims; ☎03 26 77 45 25; www.reims-tourism.com

Like burgundy, Champagne-Ardenne is a region that gives its name to one of France's most famous products, and is yet another example of French, near-religious celebration of food and drink. Ever since Dom Pérignon, a 17th century monk, discovered that stopping the bottles of fermenting wine in his abbey cellars with cork made them pop when drawn, and fizz when poured, – whereupon he is said to have exclaimed *'Je bois les étoiles!'* (I am drinking the stars) – the production of champagne has dominated most aspects of life in this area in one way or another.

Despite the chalky rolling landscape that imparts special properties to the wine, Champagne is not considered one of the most scenically attractive areas of France and has not traditionally been popular with foreign residents. However, the region is convenient for Paris, and the north (Ardennes) shares a border with Belgium (Brussels 270km). Apart from Reims there are no other major cities, important towns being the twin towns of Charleville-Mézières famous for puppetry and Medieval Troyes famous for its architecture.

FACT

■ Champagne production has been the main source of regional employment and left its mark upon the culture and architecture of the region.

Corsica

Main cities: Ajaccio and Bastia

Départements: Haute-Corse, Corse du Sud

Agence du Tourisme de la Corse: 17 Blvd. Du Roi-Jérôme, BP 19, 20181 Ajaccio cedex 01; ☎04 95 51 00 00; www.visit-corsica.com

Despite being an island in the Mediterranean with Italian associations of longer duration than French ones, Corsica (La Corse), is nevertheless a *bona fide* region of France, albeit with a greater measure of autonomy than the mainland regions and a strong antipathy to being under anybody at all. Before 1768 it was a disputed territory but in that year the French bought it outright from Genoa, then an independent maritime republic. Napoleon, who came from Ajaccio, is only Corsica's second most famous son (unless perhaps you are French), the first is Christopher Columbus, who was born in Calvi which was under Genoese domination at the time (which is why the Genoese claim Columbus as their son too).

The island is a mere 180km long and a maximum of 80 km wide, and is sparsely populated, very mountainous with deep gulleys and tree covered slopes. The *laricio* pine which grows there is traditionally prized for ships' masts. The interior is covered with *maquis* (a mixture of wild flowers, herbs and dense scrub). A view of Corsica from the sea suggests a mountain rising from it. The beaches of the 600 mile coastline, which bring the tourist hordes to the western side of the island in July and August, are magnificent. Apart from tourism and agriculture, Corsica is devoid of industry.

In recent years more holiday-home owners, particularly from Italy, have been buying up property and prices, once rock bottom, are rising. There are few developments of the apartment/villa complex variety and no high rise blocks. Corsica has little potential as a place to live and work but retirement for those fit enough to enjoy the magnificent walks, or a holiday home, are realistic options. The locals speak a blend of French and Italian. Slogans such as *I francesi fora!* (French get out), *Corsica Nazione* and others in support of the FLNC (Corsica's liberation movement) are daubed on any flat upright surface, but it's hard to see liberation from France as very practical. One indisputable advantage, however, would be that Corsica would get to keep the profits of tourism, most of which are swiped by the mainland; but there again, France has poured money into Corsica for development and wants some return on the investment.

Largely free from any expatriate influences, Corsica offers a mainly good climate and the lazy pace of life you would expect from a backwater. It is possible to get a good impression of the island from the train but don't look for a TGV: the railway was inaugurated in 1888 and has 230km of track, 12 bridges (including Gustav Eiffel's viaduct nearly 300ft high) and 38 tunnels.

Bastia, is the commercial capital, while the small town of Corte, in the centre of the island, is the site of the island's university, only reopened in the 1990s, after a very long vac of 220 years. A swathe of land through the centre is protected as the Park Natural Regional de la Corse and spectacular scenery can be found among the island's 20 or so peaks, which surge up 2000m or more into the ether. Starting a business in Corsica would probably involve paying protection money, popularly known as 'revolutionary taxes' to the FLNC. According to fairly recent accounts, this can costs thousands of euros per year.

Côte d'Azur

Main City: Nice

Département: Alpes-Maritimes

Office de tourisme des Congrès de Nice: 1 Esplanade Kennedy, Boite Postale 4079, 06000 Nice, Cedex 04; ☎0892 707 497;. For information on all the French Riviera: www.cote.azur.fr

The single *département* that makes up the Côte d'Azur must be one of the most exclusive of France. As such, a feeling exists among other French regions that it wishes to remain separate and considers itself superior to the rest of the country. The *département* runs along the coast from the Italian border, encompassing Monaco, and reaching just beyond Cannes. It continues inland for about 50km as far as the foothills of the Alps.

The Côte d'Azur is a *département* of the region referred to as PACA (Provence-Alpes-Côte d'Azur). That the Côte d'Azur is the most fashionable part of the south of France becomes evident from a run down of its resorts set among attractive and hilly scenery: Nice, Antibes, Cannes, Juan-les-Pins, St-Jean-Cap-Ferrat and Menton. Indeed, it is an area almost totally dedicated to up-market tourism, culture and showbiz. This region has the ideal facilities and climate for holiday and retirement homes. However, the property and general living costs in the area are probably the highest in France and so it is really only feasible for those with considerable means who aren't concerned with budgeting. Those seeking work would be ill advised to set up here without first having a prearranged well-paid job and having looked carefully at the costs of accommodation. The high crime rate that plagues the area is a further disadvantage to take into consideration before making any final decision.

Franche Comté

Main city: Besançon

Départements: Doubs, Jura, Haute-Saône, Territoire de Belfort

Office de tourisme: 2, Place de la Première Armée Française, Parc Micaud, 25000 Besançon; ☎03 81 80 92 55; www.besancon-tourisme.com

Franche Comté is an interesting but often overlooked region in the far east of the country. It shares a long border, and many other characteristics of culture, architecture and gastronomy with neighbouring Switzerland. The area is scenically outstanding mainly because of the long stretch of the Jura mountains which line the Franco-Swiss frontier and provide a landscape normally considered typically Swiss, rather than French. Much of the region is agricultural and unspoiled, Besançon being the only town of any size. Besançon has an historic Vauban fortress and is a popular location for trade fairs. Generally, the region is prosperous with good facilities; property prices tend to be higher than the French average.

One attraction of Franche Comté, which could prove a magnet to Euro-residents, is the close proximity of Switzerland. Lausanne is only 85km from Besançon along the N57, Geneva a little further. The possibility also exists of living in France (where living costs are much cheaper) but working in Switzerland (where wages are much higher). Switzerland issues a special permit for this purpose.

Languedoc-Roussillon

Main cities: Montpellier, Narbonne, Béziers

Départements: Aude, Gard, Hérault, Lozère, Pyrénées-Orientales

Office de tourisme: 30 allée Jean de Lattre de Tassingny, 34000 Montpellier; ☎04 67 60 60 60; www.ot-montpellier.fr

Languedoc-Roussillon, usually just called Languedoc, is undoubtedly one of the regions of France that have undergone the greatest transformation in the past two decades. It has become economically important and dynamic thanks to the administrations of the French government's regional development agency, DATAR. It offers many of the things that are best about France all in one place, and is also an area that has attracted a large number of new residents, both French and some foreign. Languedoc is bordered by the Pyrénées, the Spanish frontier, the Mediterranean and the River Rhône and extends into the Massif Central. The region therefore has a varied range of scenery and terrain from mountains to river deltas and coastal plains, to

Montpellier

Montpellier was a sleepy but cultural city that has risen to the challenge of being the hub of one of the most progressive regions of the country. It has a liveliness and ebullience and together with Perpignan, Béziers and Nîmes, offers good employment potential and a relaxed attitude to life. The good weather of the Midi is another plus point. Housing, facilities and wages are good while property and living costs are very far behind those to be found in the more fashionable and more expensive Riviera and Provence.

Fishing boats in the harbour off Gray du Roy, Languedoc-Roussillion

large cities and picturesque medieval villages. Much of the recent development and growth has been in the coastal strip and it is often not in the best taste. However, the traditional industry of the area is wine and the survival of this industry has resulted in the area remaining largely unspoiled. With all these different qualities Languedoc is potentially suitable for holiday homes, retirement or working.

Limousin

Main city: Limoges

Départements: Corrèze, Creuse, Haute-Vienne

Office de tourisme: 12 boulevard de Fleurus, 87000 Limoges; ☎05 55 34 46 87; www.tourismelimoges.com

Limousin is France at its most rural and remote. It is generally considered to be something of a gateway between the serious, industrious north and the relaxed, Mediterranean south of France. The region is very scenic and blends into the Auvergne region, which lies to the east: it is possible to travel kilometre after kilometre without finding a city or even a town of much consequence. The capital, Limoges, is the only large town and as such it offers a very quiet way of life. However it is not all serenity; new investment has given Limoges a 21st-century outlook. There is a science park, 12,000 companies, schools, university, research institutions and a lower rate of employment (6.2%) than the national one. Property and living costs are among the cheapest in France.

> **FACT**
>
> ■ Limoges has excellent properties (especially those suitable for renovation) at what seem to be bargain prices compared to the prices being asked for holiday villas in the Dordogne, just to the west.

The Loire Valley

Main city: Orléans

Départements: Cher, Eure-et-Loir, Indre, Indre-et-Loire, Loir-et-Cher, Loiret

Office de tourisme: 2 place Etape, 45000 Orléans; ☎02 38 24 05 05

Often called the centre – Val de Loire – this region is named from one of France's main rivers, the Loire. It winds its way from the Massif Central to the Atlantic Ocean beyond Nantes. The river gives its name to numerous *départements* and drains a vast area that is divided into two major regions also named from it. The Loire Valley is the inland Loire region and one of the most beautiful locations in all of France, mainly by virtue of its all-round picturesque, rather than stunning, scenery. The Valley also enjoys some of the most temperate weather in France, even though it is quite far north.

Apart from rural scenery the Loire Valley includes the famous *châteaux* of the Loire and consequently attracts convoys of tourists. The north-eastern part of the region (around the cathedral town of Chartres) is a popular roosting place for many Paris commuters, and the area as a whole attracts many native second home and retirement buyers, as well as foreigners. The region, while prosperous, has no great cities, although Paris is readily accessible on the A10, A11 and A71 autoroutes. Important towns in the area include Chartres, Orléans, Blois, Bourges, Châteauroux and Tours. Generally the level of facilities available in the Loire Valley is excellent and inhabitants can enjoy a pleasant, unhurried but modern way of life. Such quality of life is reflected in the prices, which are considerably above average, for houses of charm. Real bargains are definitely the exception. The popularity that this region enjoys, however, is a just reflection of its capacity to suit most requirements.

FACT

■ Reputedly, very clear French is spoken in the Loire Valley.

Lorraine

Main city: Nancy

Départements: Meurthe-et-Moselle, Meuse, Moselle, Vosges

Office de tourisme: Place Stanislas, BP 810 Nancy Cedex; ☎03 83 35 22 41; www.ot-nancy.fr

Lorraine occupies the far north-eastern corner of France and shares a lengthy border with Germany and shorter ones with Belgium and Luxembourg. The Vosges region's proximity to Germany has resulted in the area falling alternately into the clutches of France and Germany over the centuries and a strong Germanic influence, as in adjacent Alsace, remains.

Owing to its strategic importance, Lorraine is primarily known within France for its battlefields: Verdun, Metz, etc. The scenery is generally drab and dotted with

FACT

■ Living costs on Lorraine are generally low, as are property prices.

industrial towns and cities and to date the region has attracted few foreign residents, although its proximity to three other EU countries will no doubt prove advantageous for its future prospects. Access to the UK is good on the A26 and A4 autoroutes from Calais through Reims.

Nord-Pas-de-Calais

Main city: Lille

Départements: Nord and Pas de Calais

Office de tourisme: Palais Rihour, BP 205 Lille cedex; ☎08 9156 2004; www.lilletourism.com

Nord-Pas-de-Calais is one of France's smallest geographical regions with one of the most concentrated populations. It consists of several large towns and cities including Lille, Roubaix, Tourcoing, Arras and the major coastal ports of Calais and Dunkerque (Dunkirk). The urban sprawl also spreads across the border into Belgium. Lille is only 56 miles/90km away from Brussels and a new autoroute, the Belgian A8, will soon link them.

This area, known as *La Métropole du Nord*, is France's only major conurbation outside Paris – France doesn't otherwise have large metropolitan sprawls. The whole region is largely industrialized, including many declining industries, and is not the most scenically attractive of areas although some picturesque pockets still remain. On the other hand, local facilities are excellent. The region enjoys a closer proximity to the UK than does any other area in France (and endures a similar climate) and the Channel Tunnel entrance, to the west of Calais and linked to the A26 autoroute, provides potential for an economic boom in the area. The region also shares a border with Belgium, resulting in an inevitable Flemish influence. Overall, despite the current high rate of unemployment within the area, prospects should improve, and

Nancy

The capital of Lorraine, Nancy, is in many ways quite distinct from its own region: it is a reasonably attractive, uncongested city of 300,000 inhabitants and 55,000 students and is not as industrialized as its hinterland. There is much commercial and academic activity in Nancy, which is becoming something of an economic centre for Western Europe, not just France itself. The city enjoys a healthy prosperity, unlike some other parts of Lorraine and the facilities are excellent. In many ways the city of Metz, some 30 miles/50km away along the A31/N57, carries equal status with Nancy. The nearby German city of Saarbrucken is also an important commercial city.

Nord-Pas-de-Calais is most suitable for those intending to work in France or commute to the UK; those looking for holiday and retirement property will find more attractive spots further west.

Normandy

Main city: Rouen

Départements: Calvados, Eure, Manche, Orne, Seine-Maritime

Office de tourisme et des Congrès: Place de la Cathedrale, BP 666 76008 Rouen; ☎02 32 08 32 40; www.mairie-rouen.fr

Of all the regions of France, arguably Normandy is the best known to the British for both historical and recreational reasons. William the Conqueror set off from there to invade England, the D-Day landings on the beaches there evoke strong memories in those old enough to remember, and its other role as a social playground has attracted British clientele to le Touquet, Deauville, Trouville, etc., since the 19th century. Despite a continuing influx of *les Britanniques*, Normandy has a particularly strong local atmosphere. It is also one of the few places in France which does not produce wine – here the liquid products tend to be milk, cider and calvados (apple brandy). Normandy is unusual in that it is largely rural, but is also one of France's major and most important industrial areas; quiet, remote and scenic areas exist alongside heavily industrial and spoilt ones such as the nuclear waste reprocessing unit at La Hague on the coast. Employment prospects for unskilled labour in Normandy are among the poorest in France, but foreigners with technical skills can find opportunities in the high-tech industries which exist here. Normandy offers good access to the UK (via Dieppe, Le Havre and Cherbourg) which makes it popular with holiday and retirement-home buyers. Property prices tend to be low and bargains are readily available, with the exception of those areas which are popular with Paris commuters and weekenders. The culture, traditions and architecture of

Lille

One of France's largest cities, Lille is stylish and not as built-up or spoiled as might be expected. Many people with employment in this area settle in Lille, rather than in one of the duller, industrial towns surrounding it. Lille is developing as a modern and well-organised, but uncrowded, city which offers excellent facilities and good housing: it is particularly noted for its efficient public transport service. Paris is less than an hour away by TGV and London now less than an hour and a half away by Eurostar. Many of Europe's major cities can be reached quite easily by train and road.

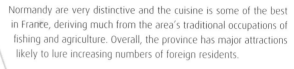

Normandy are very distinctive and the cuisine is some of the best in France, deriving much from the area's traditional occupations of fishing and agriculture. Overall, the province has major attractions likely to lure increasing numbers of foreign residents.

Paris and Ile de France

Main city: Paris

Départements: Essone, Hauts-de-Seine, Seine-et-Marne, Seine-Saint-Denis, Val-de-Marne, Val-de-Oise, Ville de Paris, Yvelines

Office de tourisme: numerous. Central Administrative Office (no access to public): 25 rue des Pyramides, 75001 Paris; ☎0892 681 3000 and there are welcome bureaux at key tourist points like the Eiffel Tower and Montmartre as well as the railway station Gare du Nord. More details on www.parisinfo.com

The Paris region, also known as Paris-Ile de France, is one of the smallest regions by area, but the one with the greatest population (nearly 11 million inhabitants). As in Greater London, the boundaries between the different *départements* and towns are not always clear and tend to merge into one another and to be known by various names. Until recently, Paris was the area in which most foreigners lived, mainly due to the fact that a largely centralised system of industry and commerce required that they work in the French capital. Property and other costs of living are very high. However, Paris is noted for its efficient and cheap system of public transport including the métro underground and the RER suburban train network, which makes many of the outlying areas more accessible for city commuters.

The Paris region is not unattractive, its geographical position provides surprisingly mild weather compared to the surrounding regions, and the general facilities available

---

Rouen

An industrial city, Rouen lies on the banks of the River Seine: many of its industries are in decline, although some high technology ones continue to prosper. Like Le Havre, few consider Rouen an attractive place to live. More attractive residential towns are to be found nearby and on the coast, north east of Le Havre. The residential suburbs that do exist in Rouen are on the right bank of the Seine. Rouen does not quite succeed in communicating the air of importance to which, as a cultural centre for museums, art, sculpture and public monuments of all kinds, it is rightly entitled.

Place de la Bastille

are the best to be found throughout France. Also, The Paris region is made up of many towns, some quite quaint, some modern. The surrounding towns, which inevitably fall under the influence of the capital, include Pontoise, St Denis, St Germain, Mantes, Versailles, Melun, Fontainebleau, Provins, Meaux, Bobigny, Nanterre, Creteil and Marne-la-Vallée.

Pays de la Loire

Main city: Nantes

Départements: Loire-Atlantique, Main-et-Loire, Mayenne, Sarthe, Vendée

Office de tourisme: 7 rue Valmy, BP 64106, 44041 Nantes Cedex 01; ☎0892 464 044; www.nantes-tourisme.com

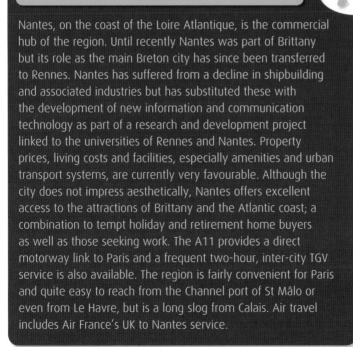

Nantes

Nantes, on the coast of the Loire Atlantique, is the commercial hub of the region. Until recently Nantes was part of Brittany but its role as the main Breton city has since been transferred to Rennes. Nantes has suffered from a decline in shipbuilding and associated industries but has substituted these with the development of new information and communication technology as part of a research and development project linked to the universities of Rennes and Nantes. Property prices, living costs and facilities, especially amenities and urban transport systems, are currently very favourable. Although the city does not impress aesthetically, Nantes offers excellent access to the attractions of Brittany and the Atlantic coast; a combination to tempt holiday and retirement home buyers as well as those seeking work. The A11 provides a direct motorway link to Paris and a frequent two-hour, inter-city TGV service is also available. The region is fairly convenient for Paris and quite easy to reach from the Channel port of St Mâlo or even from Le Havre, but is a long slog from Calais. Air travel includes Air France's UK to Nantes service.

The Pays de la Loire, is the second and the western region formed around the River Loire. Also called the Western Loire, it covers the lower reaches of the river as it winds its way to the Atlantic. The Vendée and the Loire Atlantique share a romantically wild Atlantic coastline stretching nearly 200 miles. One of the main resorts is La Baule with a long sandy beach, typical of the region. Further inland is the renowned motor-racing venue of Le Mans in the Sarthe department, named from the river running through it. There is also the Anjou region, based around the city of Angers, which is home to the National Riding School and the Cadre Noir crack cavalry regiment as well as the sparkling wines of Saumur.

Picardy

Main city: Amiens

Départements: Aisne, Oise, Somme

Office de tourisme: 6 bis, rue Dusevel, Boite Postale 1018, Cedex 1, 80010 Amiens; ☎03 22 71 60 50; www.amiens.fr

The Picardy region is one of the quieter and lesser explored French provinces. Historically it is probably chiefly known for its battlefields from both the Great War and the Second World War, which are scattered throughout the region. Also the Forest of Compiègne, where the 1918 armistice was signed and the 1000-room royal palace of the same name which provided a retreat for royalty from the 14th century and was also lived in by Napoleon Bonaparte. Picardy has some attractive areas and marvellous medieval ecclesiastical architecture in the towns and also the fortified churches and half-timbered houses of the Thiérache region in the south. No large cities exist, but important towns include Beauvais, Compiègne, Chantilly, Laon and St Quentin. For the property buyer Picardy is one of the easiest regions to reach from the UK with Eurostar and local trains from Calais and Boulogne. Amiens is just over an hour from Dieppe by road. Picardy has not suddenly been moved up a gear with its improved connections to the UK and its proximity and fast links to Paris; some suggest it may never do so. However, from the prospective resident's point of view, the main advantage is that property prices here are among the lowest to be found in France. This may prove to be a persuasive factor for those who either intend to farm in France, or who are looking forward to a quiet semi-retirement, specially British expats as it isn't too far away from the UK.

Poitou and Charentes

Main city: Poitiers

Départements: Charente, Charente-Maritime, Deux-Sèvres, Vienne

Office de tourisme: 45 Place Charles de Gaulle, Boite Postale 377, 86009 Poitiers Cedex; ☎05 49 41 21 24; www.ot-poitiers.fr

As the name suggests, Poitou Charentes comprises two small sub-regions, which form one region. The area of Poitou Maritime is very scenic, featuring a long coast on the Atlantic, and subsequently is popular with holiday makers. A tourist area, it is characterized by thronged summers and deserted winters and its popularity with holiday and retirement-home owners has forced property prices up. Quite a distinction exists between coast and countryside. La Rochelle and Rochefort are resort towns, while Poitiers (population 120,000) is something of a local commercial centre, offering a good, small-city, standard of living. Traditionally, Poitiers (formerly the duchy of Aquitaine's capital) forms the linguistic boundary between the *langue d'oie and the langue d'oc* (i.e. northern French where *oui* is yes and the southern dialects where *oc* is yes). Despite Poitiers's remoteness, La Rochelle is only 94 miles/150km away from Bordeaux.

Provence

Main city: Marseille

Départements: Alpes-de-Haute-Provence, Bouches-du-Rhône, Hautes-Alpes, Var, Vaucluse

Office de tourisme et des Congres: 4, La Canebière, 13001 Marseille; ☎04 91 13 89 00; www.marseille-tourisme.com

Provence is part of the region known as PACA (Provence-Alpes-Côtes d'Azur) which includes the departments of Hautes-Alpes and Alpes Maritimes. Publicity in Britain has resulted in this, one of the best known regions of France, becoming the one most in demand by potential British residents. However, Provence does retain its highly individual character. To the outsider it offers all that is typically 'south-of-France' by way of good weather, scenery, beaches and watersports, cuisine and fashion chic. However, Provence is more varied, both scenically and economically, than is usually assumed. The terrain is partly mountainous, partly hilly, and partly flat. Although famous for its tourist resorts and historic towns, Provence also has a great deal of industry, some of it heavy, in the Marseille-Toulon band of towns. The resorts of St Tropez and St Raphaël are in the east (note that the most fashionable part of the south of France, the Côte d'Azur, is not strictly part of Provence but a

FACT

■ Thanks to the interest in essential oils and herbal medicine the historic lavender industry of Provence is blooming again.

region in its own right) and major inland towns include Avignon, Orange, Digne-les-Bains and Aix-en-Provence.

Provence's vast number of holiday-home owners and retired people are not by any means solely British; many nationalities are attracted here by the good weather, the lifestyle and ambience. Over several years, such demand has inevitably put property prices beyond the means of many. Those who do manage to find something they can afford will also discover that the cost of living is generally very high and the main towns very crowded. Having said this, the sporting, social and cultural facilities are good and a Mediterranean atmosphere prevails, quite unlike anything to be found elsewhere. Considering the expense involved, those contemplating this area should either be comfortably off or have lucrative employment lined up. Seasonal work or house-sitting is also a possibility for those who wish to experience the idyll but are unable to afford to settle there.

Marseille

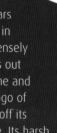

Once thought of as France's second city, in recent years Marseille has been overshadowed, economically and in population, by Lyon. Marseille is very compact and densely populated with an industrial hinterland which spreads out west and also east to Cassis, la Ciotat, Bandol, la Seyne and Toulon. Depicted in films since the 1930s as the Chicago of France, Marseille is a city that is trying hard to shake off its image of a tough and dirty city with a high crime rate. Its harsh reputation is mainly due to its own French mafia underworld called *Le Milieu*. However, Marseille has finally become a tourist destination rather than a place to pass through or go on business.

Marseille offers increasing numbers of high-paid jobs in the technological industries. It also has all the facilities of a big city (and all the congestion), and relatively moderate housing and living costs. Connections to Paris and London Waterloo are excellent; the TGV means it takes an incredible three hours to travel to Paris by rail. Marseille is also the French gateway to North Africa and Corsica and hence revels in a very cosmopolitan atmosphere. Despite the fact that Marseille has upped its visitor figures over recent years, there is some way to go before it is ranked as a top holiday destination, which for those who do choose to live there is a positive advantage. You could do worse than live and work in Marseille even though it is a million miles away from *La France Profond*.

Midi-Pyrénées

Main city: Toulouse

Départements: Ariège, Aveyron, Gers, Haute-Garonne, Hautes-Pyrénées, Lot, Tarn, Tarn-et-Garonne

Office de tourisme: Donjon du Capitole, BP 0801, 31080 Toulouse Cedex; ☎05 61 11 02 22; www.ot-toulouse.fr

The Midi-Pyrénées region is one of the largest in France and is wedged between Aquitaine to the north-east and Languedoc-Roussillon to the south-east. As its name suggests it includes some *départements* which take in the magnificent Pyrenean mountain landscapes, while others are just as remarkable, for instance the Aveyron with its high plateaus, the Tarn with its stunning gorges, while yet others are in the Midi region. Lot, and to a lesser extent Tarn-et-Garonne are some of the spots targeted for holiday and retirement homes, but the entire area attracts new residents of all nationalities. Consequently, prices tend to be very much above average.

Gers has been growing in popularity for some time. The British are often attracted to places with an English connection and Gers has plenty of them. Most of the 100 or so walled towns in the area were originally built by the English 600 years ago when the area of Gascony, of which Gers is a part, came under the English crown. The old town of Auch is the administrative centre of the Gers. The Spanish border is a two and a half-hour drive, and the coast at Biarritz two hours. Contrary to expectation, the region is suitable for those seeking work: generally very prosperous, good opportunities are available in the capital city of Toulouse. The Pyrénées region is quite easily accessible including the ski resorts of St Lary Soulan and the Vallée de Luchon, with Bordeaux, Lyon, Spain and the south coast all within fairly easy reach; the A61 and A62 link the Atlantic and Mediterranean and Paris is only five hours away by TGV.

FACT

With its scenic beauty and atmosphere, Midi-Pyrénées has a lot to offer and is largely quiet and unspoiled with a favourable climate.

Toulouse

The focal point of the region for those seeking employment, Toulouse is a fast-growing and forward-looking city offering many employment opportunities. Central Toulouse is an attractive and historic city with a great deal of character, a fine old university and several art museums. The extensive suburbs, however, are modern and unattractive and include large shopping centres and housing estates. This cohesion of the traditional and the modern makes for an excellent quality of city life, with the added advantage of easy access to the local countryside. The prevailing high-tech industries mean that Toulouse tends to be a very executive and professional city. The Airbus factory is the city's biggest employer. Wages are at the top of the French scale, but, correspondingly, property prices and costs of living are increasing.

Rhone valley

Main city: Lyon

Départements: Ain, Ardèche, Drôme, Loire, Rhône

Office de tourisme: place Bellecour, B. P. 2254, 69214 Lyon Cedex 2; ☎04 72 77 69 69; www.lyon-france.com

Rhône is one of the regions of France which follows broadly geographic lines, taking in the long valley and plain of the River Rhône between the Alps and the Massif Central. It is part of the Rhône-Alpes region which includes the Savoy Alpine region to the east. The Rhône is another of France's major rivers and a focal point for industrial activity and several nuclear power stations. Prices for property and costs of living tend to be quite high and although much of the region is agricultural it has become rather spoiled by development. However, the sheer employment potential and facilities available in the region do recommend it as a place to live. One other main attraction of the Rhône is its central location. Marseille, the south of France and Switzerland can be readily reached by autoroute and Paris is now only two hours from Lyon by TGV (quicker than by air shuttle). Thus, despite the industrial scenery within Rhône itself, it is now fairly easy to reach the surrounding, attractive countryside.

Savoie and Dauphiny

Main city: Grenoble

Départements: Isère, Haute-Savoie, Savoie

Office de tourisme: 14 rue de la République, B P 227, 38019 Grenoble Cedex; ☎04 76 42 41 41; www.grenoble-isere.info

Lyon

One of the first cities in France to push ahead with new technology, Lyon is now France's second commercial and industrial city and booming in economic terms. In 1998 Lyon's old town comprising Medieval and Renaissance buildings became a Unesco World Heritage Site. Major national and multi-national firms have bases there in preference to Paris and a frenetic international atmosphere is the norm. Although not structurally very attractive, Lyon is fast becoming a key European city. Pleasant, reasonably priced accommodation in Lyon itself is rare, and many people commute to the city from surrounding suburbs. Facilities for entertainment and culture are superb, and the city is said to be the gastronomic capital of France, thus offering an enviable style of life for those with an epicure's standards. Bourg-en-Bresse is another important centre within the region.

Historically, Savoy and Dauphiny are separate regions but the French administration regards them as a single entity. The region lies in the French Alps and shares extensive borders with Switzerland and Italy and shares certain characteristics with both of those countries. Savoy and Dauphiny is one of the country's most scenic regions and harbours some of the most breathtaking locations within a developed country that one could possibly find. Despite its Alpine situation the region is not remote, and its conservation is by design. It offers a good, modern standard of living with a high standard of facilities but, needless to say, the weather can be severe. It is an area that has attracted large numbers of new residents as well as those wanting holiday homes, and property prices are rising accordingly. The Alps are the home of France's skiing industry and many resorts of all classes are to be

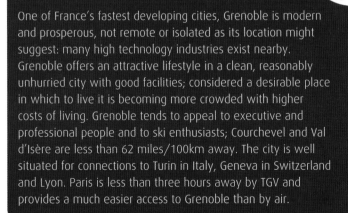

Grenoble

One of France's fastest developing cities, Grenoble is modern and prosperous, not remote or isolated as its location might suggest: many high technology industries exist nearby. Grenoble offers an attractive lifestyle in a clean, reasonably unhurried city with good facilities; considered a desirable place in which to live it is becoming more crowded with higher costs of living. Grenoble tends to appeal to executive and professional people and to ski enthusiasts; Courchevel and Val d'Isère are less than 62 miles/100km away. The city is well situated for connections to Turin in Italy, Geneva in Switzerland and Lyon. Paris is less than three hours away by TGV and provides a much easier access to Grenoble than by air.

found here. The area therefore has potential for those wishing to work in or run a business connected with skiing. The lakeside towns of Annecy and Evian have a milder microclimate, are only half an hour away from the main ski resorts and are expensive but popular places to retire to. In many ways, Savoy and Dauphiny are very untypical of France and do not offer the sort of lifestyle and character that are generally thought of as French. Important towns other than Grenoble include Mègeve, Annecy, Chambéry and Aix-les-Bains.

Appendices

■ USEFUL BOOKS

Guides

Antique & Flea Markets of London and Paris: by Rupert Thomas and Eglé Salvy (Thames and Hudson 1999 £12.95). Paris has a tradition of *marché aux puces* (flea markets) going back to medieval times. The contemporary versions attract millions of visitors annually.

A Little Tour in France: (Penguin) Henry James. A little out of date perhaps for the modern traveller, but gives an insight into sightseeing in a more elegant age.

Blue Guide Southwest France: by Delia Gray-Durant. Detailed information on cultural aspects of Southwest France including art, architecture and history.

Blue Guide Paris: by Delia Gray-Durant. New edition published in 2007.

Guide des Maison d'Hommes Célèbres: (Horay £12). Who lived where, and when (in French).

The Insider Guide to Working and Living in France: Rose Marie Burke (published by Western Web Works, LLC, PO Box 10168, Knoxville, Tennessee 37939; info@insiderparisguides.com).

The Homeowner's Guide to Living in France: by Richard Whiting.

Loire Valley (Eyewitness Travel Guides): DK Publishing. Detailed practical information.

Ouverts au Public: Caisse Nationale des Monuments Historiques. The official French-language guide to 1,200 sites open to the public.

The Robert Louis Stevenson Trail: *A Walking Tour in the Velay and Cevennes*: by Alan Castle. Robert Louis Stevenson's tale of his hike through the Massif Central has long captured the imagination of walkers. The 140 mile route is now known as Grande Randonée 70 (GR70).

The Rough Guide to France: (Rough Guids, 2007).

Three Rivers of France: (Pavilion £14.99). Freda White. Popular travel book covering the Lot, Tarn and Dordogne rivers of south-western France.

The Unofficial Guide to Paris: by David Applefield (2003).

General background and history

All You Need to Be Impossibly French: *A Witty Investigation into the Lives, Lusts, and Little Secrets of French Women*: by Helena Frith-Powell. An entertaining stereotypical take on French women from an outsider's point of view.

A Place of Greater Safety: (Penguin £7.99) The story of the French Revolution. New edition 2006.

Citizens: (Penguin £16). Simon Schama's acclaimed history of the French Revolution.

Fatal Avenue: *A Traveller's History of Northern France and Flanders 1346-1945* (2008): by Richard Holmes.

France 1848-1945: (Oxford University Press £17.99). Theodore Zeldin. An excellent take on the French psyche. Includes such chapter headings as 'How to charm a French grandmother'.

France and the French: by Rod Kedward. The ideology of Republicanism and an analysis of Frenchness.

The Last Great Frenchman: Charles Williams. A biography of General de Gaulle.

Mastering the Art of French Cooking: by Julia Child, Louisette Bertholle, Simone Beck and Sidonie Coryn.

Muslim Girls And the Other France: *Race, Identity Politics, & Social Exclusion*: by Tricia Danielle Keaton and Manthia Diawara.

The Price of Glory: Alistair Horne's account of one of history's grimest battles, Verdun in 1916.

Six Armies in Normandy: John Keegan. An account of the Allied invasion of France.

Tomorrow be Brave: The story of Susan Travers, the amazing history of the only woman ever to join the French Foreign Legion.

French literature and literature associated with France

A Year in the Merde: Steven Clarke's entertaining take on Paris in the noughties.

Atomised: by Michel Houellebecq. The novel that shook up the French left-wing intellectual postwar consensus (1998).

The Babel Guide to French Fiction in English Translation: Invaluable guide to French and Francophone literature available in English translation.

Birdsong: Sebastian Faulks's novel set in the First World War.

Black Dogs: Ian McEwan's version of the old French myth of ferocious dog/wolves.

Chocolat: by Joanne Harris (2000, Penguin). Beautifully written story of chocolatier versus church in a small French village. Other titles by the same author include *Blackberry Wine* and *Five Quarters of the Orange*.

Cross-Channel: (Cape £13.99). Julian Barnes's collection of short stories with an Anglo-French theme.

A Motor-Flight through France: (Picador). By the 19th/20th century American writer, Edith Wharton. An account of motoring through France with bygone stylishness.

A Moveable Feast: Hemingway in pre-war Paris.

The Earth (La Terre): Emile Zola's classic on French peasantry in the 19th century.

Le Grand Meaulnes: (Penguin). English title *The Lost Domain*. The only novel of Alain Fournier, who died young in the Great War. A classic, fantasy tale of childhood (the lost domain of the title) passing into adolescence, set in the Sologne countryside

The Horse of Pride: Pierre Jakez-Hélias. Life in rural Brittany in the early 20th century.

Paris, A Literary Companion: by Ian Littlewood.

Pig Tales: by Marie Darrieussecq. *Truisme* is the French title and is a play on words with the French word for female pig. This is a comic novel, a metaphorical tale of swine-like debauchery and perfume from one of France's foremost contemporary novelists.

Jean de Florette and sequel Manon des Sources: Familiar to many through the films of the same names, these Marcel Pagnol classics are almost obligatory reading, for anyone going to live in Provence.

The Time Out Book of Paris Short Stories: (Penguin) edited by Nicholas Royle. Stories by contemporary writers including Americans Erica Wagner and Maureen Freely.

Village in the Vaucluse: (Harvard). Laurence Wylie. French rural life through the ages.

Madame Bovary: Gustave Flaubert's classic of love, lust and betrayal, set in Normandy.

Montaillou: (Scolar Press £9.95). Emmanuel Le Roy Ladurie. The French historian's much lauded account of 14th-century village life following the suppression of the heretical Cathars.

Thérèse and The Frontenac Mystery: (Penguin). Novels set in the Landes (southwest) region of France.

Tender is the Night: (Penguin). Scott Fitzgerald's Riviera-based novel about capitalism, the film industry and psychotherapy.

Travels with a Donkey: (Oxford University Press and second hand bookshops). Robert Louis Stevenson's classic account of walking in the Cevennes with an obstreperous donkey.

◼ USEFUL WEBSITES

Learning French

- www.learndirect.co.uk. For details of the nearest French courses in your area
- www.souffle.asso.fr. An association of schools offering quality French language programmes
- www.loffice.org. Another organisation with its own quality label supported by the French government
- www.cesalanguages.com
- www.ef.com
- www.eurolingua.com
- www.learningfrench.co.uk
- www.bbc.co.uk/languages/french
- www.grantandcutler.com
- www.linguaphone.co.uk
- www.alliancefr.org
- www.berlitz.com
- www.paris-anglo.com: Comprehensive list of Paris language schools

Travel

By train

- www.eurostar.com
- www.raileurope.co.uk
- www.voyages-sncf.com
- www.sncf.fr
- www.thalys.com
- www.seat61.com/France.htm
- www.internationaltrainline.com

By car

- www.eurotunnel.com
- www.aferry.to (also does Euro Tunnel)
- www.directferries.com
- www.ferrybooker.com
- www.ferrycrossings-uk.co.uk
- www.brittany-ferries.com
- www.condorferries.co.uk
- www.norfolkline.com
- www.poferries.com
- www.seafrance.com
- www.speedferries.com
- www.transmancheferries.co.uk

- www.ldlines.co.uk
- www.autoroutes.fr
- www.securite-routiere.gouv.fr. French government road traffic information

By plane from the UK

- www.airfrance.co.uk
- www.british-airways.com
- www.flybmi.com
- www.easyjet.com
- www.euroexec.com. Flies from Brighton (Shoreham Airport) to Le Touquet. Fast check-in, avoid larger airport congestion
- www.flybe.com
- www.flyglobespan.com
- www.Jet2.com
- www.ryanair.com
- www.thomson.co.uk

By plane from North America

- www.aircanada.ca
- www.airfrance.com
- www.aa.com
- www.british-airways.com
- www.flycontinental.com
- www.delta-air.com
- www.ual.com
- www.usairways.com
- www.virgin-atlantic.com
- www.airbrokers.com
- www.nouvelles-frontieres.fr

By bus

- www.nationalexpress.com
- www.busabout.com
- www.eurolines.fr

Removals

UK

- www.bar.co.uk. The British Association of Removers
- www.alliedpickfords.co.uk
- www.anglofrench.co.uk
- www.bishopsmove.com
- www.edebros.co.uk
- www.farrerandfenwick.co.uk

- www.frenchmoves.co.uk
- www.kidds.co.uk
- www.amsmoving.co.uk
- www.robinsons-intl.com
- International Removers:
- www.alliedintl.com
- www.unitedvanlines.com
- www.vanpac.com

Pets

- www.airpets.com
- www.dogsaway.co.uk
- www.ipata.com
- www.parair.co.uk

Renting

- www.pap.fr. Particulier a Particulier; direct from the owner, site in English and French

Expat websites

Expat forums
- www.fusac.fr
- www.craigslist.org

Expat networks
- www.americansintoulouse.com
- www.americansinfrance.net
- www.britishinfrance.com
- www.angloinfo.com. Everyday life in France for those living in or moving to France
- www.craigslist.org
- www.frenchentree.com

Expat shopping
- www.xpatshop.co.uk
- www.expatdirect.co.uk
- www.expatshopping.com
- www.britishcornershop.co.uk
- www.expatshopping.com
- www.expatessentials.co.uk

Self-catering

- www.rentals.com
- www.locations-vacances-en-france.com
- www.appart-in-france.com
- www.toutpartout.com

Short lets

- www.only-apartments.com
- www.marie-a-tout-prix.com
- www.perfectplaces.com
- Agencies:
- www.athomeinfrance.com
- www.justfrance.com. Superior and luxury vacation and holiday rentals
- www.cheznous.com. Prospective tenants deal with owners direct
- www.cosmopolitanservices.com. Relocation assistance for both companies and their executives
- www.paris-apts.com. Short-term fully furnished Parisian flats
- www.quality-villas.co.uk
- www.apartrental.com. For Paris and the south of France

House sitting

- www.mindmyhouse.com
- www.sabaticalhomes.com

Home exchange

- www.dialanexchange.com
- www.gti-home-exchange.com
- www.homebase-hols.com
- www.homeexchange.com
- www.intervac.com
- www.invented-city.com

Utilities

- www.energie-info.fr: consumer information site set up to explain the deregulated market
- www.edf.fr
- www.comparatel.fr: information on major telephone/internet/mobile phone providers
- www.laposte.com

Banking

- www.transat.tm.fr. Banque Transatlantique
- www.banqueparibas.net
- www.barclays.fr
- www.banquepopulaire.fr
- www.credit-agricole.fr
- www.hsbc.fr. Crédit Commercial de France
- www.creditmutuel.com
- www.credit-du-nord.fr
- www.socgen.com
- www.girobank.net

Education

International Schools in Paris

- www.asparis.org. American School of Paris
- www.britishschool.fr. British School of Paris
- www.anglophonesectionfontainebleau.com. College International de Fontainebleau
- www.eabjm.com. Ecole International de Paris
- www.isbi.com. L'Ermitage-International School of France
- www.isparis.edu email. The International School of Paris
- www.marymount.fr. Marymount International

Outside Paris

- www.bordeaux-school.com. Bordeaux International School
- www.isbi.com. CIV International School of Sophia Antipolis (Nice)
- www.isn-nice.or. International School of Nice
- www.mougins-school.com. Mougins School (Mougins near Cannes)
- www.ecis.org. European Council of International Schools; for a list of schools abroad offering the British Curriculum
- www.afsuk.org. International Youth Development
- www.enfamille.com. Study exchanges for six months for younger children

Continuing education

- www.aup.fr. The American University in Paris
- www.elderhostel.org. Opportunities for the over 55s

French government

- www.education.gouv.fr. Ministère de l'éducation nationale, de l'enseignement supérieur; French Ministry of Education

- www.campusfrance.org: A resource for foreign students wishing to study in France
- www.cnous.fr: For all practical aspects of student life in France
- www.impots.gouv.fr. French government tax department
- www.cnav.fr. Caisse Nationale d'Assurance Vieillesse; information on French pensions
- www.insee.fr. National Institute for Statistics and Economic Studies
- www.diplomatie.fr. For visas and work permits
- www.legifrance.gouv.fr. For updated versions of all French legislation, some of which has been translated into English

EU resources

- www.erasmus.ac.uk
- www.eurochoice.org.uk. A guide to higher education in Europe

Internships

- www.cei-frenchcentre.com. Centre d'Echanges Internationaux; runs work placements in France
- www.ambafrance-us.org
- www.frenchamericancenter.com. French-American Center (Montpellier)
- French-American Chamber of Commerce. _212 867 0123; www.ccife.org/use/new_york has a similar scheme to AIPT (see above). FACC-NY has an international career development programme for Americans to work as trainees and interns in France
- www.aipt.org. Association for International Practical Training (AIPT)
- www.emploi-international.org. A reciprocal agreement with the ANPE
- www.internshipsinternational.org
- www.fulbright-france.org
- www.ciep.fr. For assistant posts in French secondary schools
- www.info-france-usa.org
- www.cei4vents.com. Scheme to allow university students to get a temporary work permit
- www.diplomatie-gouv.fr. Short- and long-term internships in the public sector and non-governmental organisations
- www.faccnyc.org. French-American Chamber of Commerce

UK government

- www.pensionservice.gov.uk
- www.inlandrevenue.gov.uk/cnr
- www.dwp.gov.uk. Department of Work and Pensions
- www.fco.gov.uk. Foreign and Commonwealth Office

- www.hmrc.gov.uk. HM Revenue and Customs
- www.defra.gov.uk. UK Department of Food, Environment and Rural Affairs (DEFRA)

Employment

Government and EU
- www.apec.asso.fr. Association pour l'Emploi des Cadres
- www.cadremploi.fr
- www.anpe.fr Agence nationale pour l'emploi
- www.emploi-international.org
- www.jobcentreplus.gov.uk
- www.europa.eu.int/eures
- www.urssaf.fr. Information on social security payments for employers and the self-employed

The press
- www.talents.fr. Joint job site from Le Monde and Télérama
- www.lefigaro.fr/emploie. Le Figaro
- www.lexpress.fr. L'Express
- www.intemployment.com. International Employment Gazette: American online subscription magazine with details of professional jobs worldwide
- www.fusac.fr
- www.tes.co.uk. Times Education Supplement
- www.elgazette.com. EL Gazette for EFL jobs

Some other current international and French job websites
- www.apr-job.com
- www.careerbuilder.com
- www.overseasjobs.com
- www.init-emploi.tm.fr
- www.jobware.net
- www.michaelpage.fr
- www.monster.fr
- www.phospore.com
- www.webcible.com

Miscellaneous
- www.wwoof.org

Chambers of Commerce

- www.ccfgb.co.uk. French Chamber of Commerce in Great Britain
- www.amchamfrance.org. American Chamber of Commerce in France
- www.francobritishchamber.com

Buying

- www.fnaim.fr. French federation of estate agents
- www.snpi.com. National estate agents organisation

Property websites

- www.123immo.fr
- www.abonim.com
- www.century21.fr
- www.immoneuf.com. New property
- www.lesiteimmobilier.com
- www.letuc.com
- www.logic-immo.com
- www.nexdom.com
- www.orpi.com
- www.partenaire-europeen.fr
- www.proprietesdefrance.com. Upmarket properties
- www.seloger.com
- www.alps-property-finder.com
- www.everythingFrance.co.uk
- www.findyourproperty.com
- www.frenchconnections.co.uk
- www.french-property.com
- www.frenchpropertylinks.com
- www.french-property-news.com
- www.frenchways.com
- www.green-acre.com
- www.homesoverseas.co.uk
- www.houseweb.com
- www.livingfrance.com
- www.skiproperty.com

Private advertisers

- www.appelimmo.fr
- www.entreparticuliers.fr
- www.explorimmo.com
- www.journaldesparticuliers.com
- www.kitrouve.com

- www.lacentrale.fr
- www.lesiteimmobilier.com
- www.pap.fr
- www.paruvendu.fr

House and car insurance

- www.ffsa.fr. French federation of insurance firms
- www.french-insurance.com
- www.ericblairnet.com
- www.sellier-insurance.com
- www.steenandersen.net
- www.charente-properties.com
- www.agf.fr
- www.axa.fr
- www.groupeazur.fr
- www.gmf.fr
- www.maaf.fr
- www.macif.fr

Financial and legal

- www.irs.gov. USA tax
- www.service-public.fr
- www.impots.gouv.fr. France tax
- www.oec-paris.fr. Chartered accountants professional organisation
- www.francobritishchambers.com

Financial and tax advisory

- www.jurimodel.com
- www.axis-strategy.com
- www.bentley-jennison.co.uk
- www.blackstonefranks.com
- www.blevinsfranks.com
- www.brewindolphin.co.uk
- www.dixonwilson.co.uk
- www.hansard.com
- www.jpainternational.com
- www.siddalls.net

Legal advisory

- www.ahomeinfrance.com
- www.bennett-and-co.com
- www.bllaw.co.uk

- www.foxhayes.co.uk
- www.french-lawyer.com
- www.hfw.com
- www.howard-kennedy.com
- www.internationalpropertylaw.com
- www.jeffreyshenry.com
- www.kingsfords-solicitors.com
- www.lawoverseas.com
- www.lpalaw.com.fr
- www.pannone.com
- www.prettys.co.uk
- www.russell-cooke.co.uk
- www.stephensmithfranceltd.com
- www.taylorssolicitors.co.uk
- www.french-property-news.com/turnerandco.htm
- www.templeton-france.com
- www.ttuk.com

Health

- www.dh.gov.uk. for European Health card (EHIC)
- www.cdc.gov. General travel health advice
- www.assurancemaladie.sante.gouv.fr. The French healthcare system
- www.ameli.fr. The French healthcare system

Health insurance.

- www.french-insurance.com
- www.amariz.co.uk
- www.axappphealthcare.co.uk
- www.bupa-int.com
- www.exclusivehealthcare.com
- www.exeterfriendly.co.uk
- www.expacare.net
- www.goodhealthworldwide.com
- www.healthcareinternational.com
- www.insurancewide.com
- www.ihi.com
- www.taurusinsuranceservices.com

Tourism

French government tourist offices abroad

- http://ca.franceguide.com. Maison de la France Canada
- http://ie.franceguide.com. Maison de la France Ireland

- http://uk.franceguide.com. Maison de la France Great Britain
- http://us.franceguide.com. Maison de la France USA

Regional tourist offices in France

- www.parisinfo.com
- www.tourisme-aquitaine.fr and www.bordeaux-tourisme.com
- www.sunfrance.com (héérault tourism)
- www.visitprovence.com
- www.poitou-charentes-vacances.com
- www.tourisme-atlantique.com
- www.tourisme-mayenne.com
- www.enpaysdeloire.com
- www.paysdelaloire.fr
- www.tourismebretagne.com
- www.normandy-tourism.org
- www.northernfrance-tourism.com
- www.tourisme-gironde.fr

Other tourist sites

- www.francetourisme.com
- www.francefestivales.com
- www.monuments-nationaux.fr

◼ WEIGHTS AND MEASURES: METRIC CONVERSION

France uses the metric system in all respects. The standards of measurement are of course recognisable and even, partly, mandatory in spite of resistance from market sellers such as The Metric Martyr. Temperature is always measured in Celsius. Metric conversion tables (including clothes and shoe size conversions) are given below. Measurements are quoted as a decimal and not a fraction; for example, on road signs, 'Toulon 12.7km'.

Conversion charts

Length (NB 12 inches = 1 foot, 10 mm = 1 cm, 100 cm = 1 metre)

inches	1	2	3	4	5	6	9	12		
cm	2.5	5	7.5	10	12.5	15.2	23	30		

cm	1	2	3	5	10	20	25	50	75	100
inches	0.4	0.8	1.2	2	4	8	10	20	30	39

Weight (NB 14lb = 1 stone, 2240lb = 1 ton, 1,000 kg = 1 metric tonne)

lb	1	2	3	5	10	14	44	100	2246
kg	0.45	0.9	1.4	2.3	4.5	6.4	20	45	1016

kg	1	2	3	5	10	25	50	100	1000
lb	2.2	4.4	6.6	11	22	55	110	220	2204

Distance

mile	1	5	10	20	30	40	50	75	100	150
km	1.6	8	16	32	48	64	80	120	161	241

km	1	5	10	20	30	40	50	100	150	200
mile	0.6	3.1	6.2	12	19	25	31	62	93	124

Volume

1 litre = 0.2 UK gallons

1 UK gallon = 4.5 litres

1 litre = 0.26 US gallons

1 US gallon = 3.8 litres

Clothes

UK	8	10	12	14	16	18	20
Europe	36	38	40	42	44	46	48
USA	6	8	10	12	14	18	

Shoes

UK	3	4	5	6	7	8	9	10	11
Europe	36	37	38	39	40	41/42	43	44	45
USA	2.5	3.3	4.5	5.5	6.5	7.5	8.5	9.5	10.5

■ EMBASSIES

French embassies abroad

Australia: 6 Perth Avenue, Yarralumla ACT 2600, Canberra; ☎+61 2 621 601 00; www.ambafrance-au.org

Bangladesh: Road 108, House 18, Gulshan, P.O. Box 22, Dacca 1212; ☎+880 2 882 33 20; www.ambafrance-bd.org

Canada: 42 Promenade Sussex, Ottawa, Ontario, (ON) K1M2C9; ☎+1 613 789 17 95; www.ambafrance-ca.org

Egypt: 29 avenue Charles de Gaulle, BP 1777, Guiza, Cairo; ☎+20 2 3 567 32 00; www.ambafrance-eg.org

India: 2/50-E Shantipath Chanakyapuri, New Delhi 110 021; ☎+91 11 2419 6100; www.france-in-india.org

Ireland: 36 Ailesbury Road, Ballsbridge, Dublin 4; ☎+353 1 277 5000; www.ambafrance-ie.org

Kenya: Barclays Plaza Building, 9th Floor, Loita Street, Nairobi; ☎+254 20 277 80 00; www.ambafrance-ke.org

New Zealand: Rural Bank Building, 13th floor 34-42 Manners Street, PO Box 11-343 Wellington; ☎+64 4 384 25 55; www.ambafrance-nz.org

Pakistan: Diplomatic Enclave G/5, GPO Box 1068, Islamabad; ☎+92 51 201 14 14; www.ambafra-pk.org

South Africa: 250 Melk Street, New Muckleneuk, Pretoria, 0181; ☎+27 12 42 51 600; www.ambafrance-rsa.org

Sri Lanka: 89 Rosmead Place, Colombo 7; ☎+94 11 269 88 15; www.ambafrance-lk.org

Uganda: Lumumba Avenue, 16, Nakasero, PO Box 7212, Kampala; ☎+256 414 342 120; www.ambafrance-ug.org

United States of America: 4101 Reservoir road, NW Washington -DC 20007; ☎+1 202 944 60 00; www.ambafrance-us.org

United Kingdom; 58 Knightsbridge, London SW1X 7JT; ☎+44 207 07 31 000; www.ambafrance-uk.org

Zimbabwe; 76 Samora Machel Avenue, 11th floor, Bank Chambers, P.O. Box 1378, Harare; ☎+263 4 703 216; www.ambafrance-zw.org

Embassies in France

Australia: 4, rue Jean Rey, 75724 Paris Cedex 15; ☎+33 (0)1 40 59 33 00; www.france.embassy.gov.au

Bangladesh: 39, rue Erlanger, 75016 Paris; ☎+33 (0)146 51 90 33

Canada: 35, avenue Montaigne, 75008 Paris; ☎+33 (0)1 44 43 29 00; www.international.gc.ca

Egypt: 56, avenue d'Iena, 75116 Paris; ☎+33 (0)1 47 20 97 70; www.ambassade-egypte.com

India: 15, rue Alfred Dehodencq, 75016 Paris; ☎+33 (0)1 40 50 70 70; www.amb-inde.fr

Ireland: 12, avenue Foch, 75116 Paris; ☎+33 (0)1 44 17 67 00; www.embassyofirelandparis.com

Kenya: 3, rue Freycinet, 75116 Paris; ☎+33 (0)1 56 62 25 25; www.kenyaembassyparis.org

New Zealand: 7ter, rue Léonard de Vinci, 75116 Paris; ☎+33 (0)1 45 01 43 43; www.nzembassy.com

Pakistan: 18, rue Lord Byron, 75008 Paris; ☎+33 (0)1 45 62 23 32

South Africa: 59, Quai d'Orsay, 75343 Paris; ☎+33 (0)1 53 59 23 23; www.afriquesud.net

Sri Lanka: 15, rue d'Astrog; 75008 Paris; ☎+33 (0)1 42 66 35 01

Uganda: 13, avenue Raymond Poincaré, 75116 Paris; ☎+33 (0)1 56 90 12 20; www.ugandaembassy.fr

United States of America: 2, avenue Gabriel; 75382 Paris Cedex 08; ☎+33 (0)1 43 12 22 22; www.amb-usa.fr

United Kingdom: 35, rue du Faubourg St Honoré, 75383 Paris Cedex 08; ☎+33 (0)1 44 51 31 00; www.britishembassy.gov.uk

Zimbabwe: 12, rue Lord Byron, 75008 Paris; ☎+33 (0)1 56 88 16 00; www.ambassade-zimbabwe.com

▌ PHOTO CREDITS

p5	2006 Football World Cup	Gisela Giardino (info@giselagiardino.com.ar) YES
p6	Sarlat	Ela 2007 (www.flickr.com/photos/6449867@N00/429469833)
p8	The Calanques, Marseilles	Globetrotter2000 (www.flickr.com/photos/20687176@N04/2236530231)
p10	The Eiffel Tower	Rebecca Woodworth (rebecca@midkid.freeserve.co.uk)
P24	Visit Paris	Denis (tidenis@gmail.com)
P28	Velib, the municipal bike service	Adam Alpern (adam.alpern@gmail.com)
P42	500 Euro note	L Javier Modino Martinez (Javier.modino@gmail.com)
P47	In search of the most expensive cup of coffee in Paris	Ben Pons (www.flickr.com/photos/beair/169679632)
P48	A glass of wine	Greg 50 (www.flickr.com/photos/pluribus/2334906062)
P50	Eurostar breakfast	Amy L Ross (www.lapetiteamericaine.wordpress.com)
P52	Tableau noir, poubelles et mile	Peter J. Sieger (http://creativecommons.org/licences/by/2.0deed.em)
p70	Butte au Calles	Alexandre Simoes (www.flickr.com/photos/alexsimoes/2130029062)
p71	A heron in the Bois de Boulogne	Etienne Portelance (etienne.portelance@gmail.com)
p73	Café in the 11th	Pete Sieger (www.flickr.com/photos/23944110@N00/2111355697)
p74	Canal St Martin, 10th Paris	Nicolas Mirguet (www.flickr.com/photos/scalino/1033011720)
p76	La Defense	Ashley Duffus (ash_ley20@msn.com)
P106	Bergerac en Dordogne	Beatrice Domejean (beatricedomejean@yahoo.fr)
p109	Nantes	Pascal Poggi (paspog@noos.fr)
p116	Bourges	Nicola Fredella (www.flickr.com/photos/mieru79/2244667707)
p126	Pont-en-Royans	Christian Selchow (s.selchow@googlemail.com)
p131	Saumur	Dale C Carr (d.c.carr@keyaccess.nl)
p145	Strasbourg	Fr Antunes (Antunesrodrigues@mail.telepac.pt)
p166	Crumbling House – Marseilles, France	John A Belcher (jablife@mac.com)
p172	Under construction	Michaek Van Fleet (www.flickr.com/photos/signalstation)
p175	Construction in Nantes	Pascal Poggi (paspog@noos.fr)
p177	Snow stops construction Saumur	Irene Kightley (hardworkinghippy@aol.com)
p179	Early spring garden	Irene Kightley (hardworkinghippy@aol.com)
p185	Great Hall Sarzay Chateau	Julie Webb-Reeman (juliereeman@yahoo.com)
p195	Fava beans	L & S (laitue@gmail.com)
p195	Charcuterie de Corse	Paul Niekel (www.flickr.com/photos/paaulniekel/506229693)
p196	Charcuterie	Elisabeth Kamp (Elisabethkamp@wanadoo.nl)
p196	Marche bio vin bio	Charles Patrigeon (charles.patrigeon@gmail.com)
p197	Paris, Sunday bio marche	Bob Laughton (www.flickr.com/photos/laughtonb/37551924)
p198	Women and wine	Jocelyn Durston (www.flickr.com/photos/jocelyndurston)
p198	Rue Tiqetonne shop	Guy Veale (gbveale@googlemail.com)
p199	Shop rue St Antoine, Paris 010506	Fanny (www.playlikeagirl.fr)
p205	On the phone	Germain Maurice (gmaurice@erralt.info)
p214	French medicine	Riana Lagarde (riana.lagarde@gmail.com)
p218	Hopital-Lariboisiere	Holopherne (www.flickr.com/photos/holopherne/515908558)
p219	Hospital Saint Jacques	Salena Semmens (www.flickr.com/photos/salenasemmens/1366739983)
p249	Gare TGV de Lyon Saint Exupery	Patrick Guyennon (www.flickr.com/photos/indeepdark/32266474)
p251	TGV Duplex	Francois Proulx (www.flickr.com/photos/francois/4308346)
p270, 336	La precision du geste	Daniel Guffanti (gufphoto@gmail.com)
p279	La Grand Arche de la Defense	Staffan Holersson (staffh@gmail.com)
p303	Restoration	Robert France (robert.france73@orange.fr)
p322	Closed factory in Boulogne	Marie C Cudraz (mariecudraz@yahoo.com)
p331	Vignes de la nuageuse Carcassone	Etienne Boucher (etienne@novat.qc.ca)
p340	Chickens	hardworkinghippy Irene Kightley (hardworkinghippy@aol.com)
p346	Vigneron, anciens futs	Julie Kertesz (www.flickr.com/photos/joyoflife/247280687)
p357	The colours of autumn	Catherine Merlen (CatMer@gmail.com)

p366	Alpine chalets	Julian Dow (j.a.t.dow@bio.gla.ac.uk)
p370	Secondhand shop in Verteillac	Marie E Bryan (doktora-blogger@usa.net)
p379	The Gite	Jo Hinde (www.flickr.com/photos/jojo79/1367154461)
p387	Lost Paradise (apples)	Mona Routier (snooty@noos.fr)
p395	Aubergines – permaculture	Irene Kightley (hardworkinghippy@aol.com)
p404,423	Femme rock	Juan Carlos Prieto (wwww.ochobits.cim.mx)
p407	Bal folk	Pascal Blachot (pascal.blanchot@orange.fr)
p432	Rachida Dati at the Place Vendôme	Benjamin Lemaire (www.Benjamin-Lemaire.info)
p442	Nicholas Sarkozy	Guillaume Paumier/Wikimedia Commons, http://commons.wikimpia.org/wiki/User:Gionnon
p450	Beau temps sur la cathedrale d'Amiens	David Tabary (www.flickr.com/photos/megathud/417793156)
p453	Flying buttresses of Strasbourg Cathedral	Allan Hise (allan@hise.org)
p454	Biarritz (Labourd)	Adrian Lagorse (lebasque78140@yahoo.fr)
p462	Chateau de Chambord	Eva Wilder (evenstar_9@yahoo.com)
p463	The river Indres, passing along the Sleeping Beauty castle	PierrickMouazan@gmail.com
p463	Harvest near Mont St Michel	Keith Havercroft (keithhavercroft@hotmail.co.uk)
p464	Mont St Michael	Keith Fulton (keith_fulton@yahoo.com)
p465	Place de la Bastille	Rita Crane (www.ritacranestudio.com)

Any additional images in the book were supplied from www.istock.com

▚ INDEX